Praise for *The Foresig*

"By far the best collection of vital information on foresight strategies and futures thinking. This outstanding resource links readers to thousands of ideas, approaches, organizations and people in the futures field. It is required reading for 21st century thinkers." - Janna Q. Anderson, Elon U/Pew; Director, Imagining the Internet Center

"A marvelous compendium. At a time when the future itself is in doubt, this Guide should prove a boon to policy-makers in business and government, teachers and students of all ages. Read this book because it is important, but also because it offers a wealth of fascinating ideas." - William E. Halal, Professor of Management, George Washington U; Bangkok U; Founder, TechCast Global

"What a work! It is all in here; this is the book to read to understand and overlook the entire field of Foresight." - Pero Micic, CEO, FutureManagement Group; Author, The Five Futures Glasses

"A magisterial compilation of concepts, models, and advice." - Christine Peterson, Chairman, Foresight Institute; Author, Unbounding the Future

"A wonderful resource for aspiring futurists as well as anybody just interested in learning about foresight. A comprehensive Foresight 101 book that both professionals and students will enjoy!" - Anne Boysen, Data Scientist, Google; Founder, After the Millennials

"A comprehensive directory of resources, a complete education on foresight models that can be applied to personal, organizational, social, and global change, and a gateway to the emerging discipline of Foresight." - James Lee, Founder, StratFI; Author, Foresight Investing

"John Smart and his team have compiled an encyclopedic resource for anticipating, creating and managing the future. This book addresses a complete range of readers interested in the foresight field, including students, educators, and organizational leaders. A remarkably complete source for our times." Pamela Douglas, Author, Future of Television

"Very inspiring and complete book for everybody who is interested in foresight. John writes with passion for our field." Kaat Exterbille, Managing Director, Strategic Foresight, Kate Thomas & Kleyn Future Management Consultancy

"This impressive book is nothing less than an Almanac on the Future, ranging from the smallest personal to the biggest universal scales. It is an indispensable resource to skim, read, and use, again and again." - Clement Vidal, Co-Founder, Evo-Devo Universe community; Author, The Beginning and the End

"One part encyclopedia, one part text, one part self-help, one part editorial, and one part call to action. The field of Foresight seems much bigger now than it did before reading this, and my professional reading list is now on a super-exponential curve!" - Carrie Ann Zapka, Microbiologist, GOJO Industries

"The Guide provides a vast amount of useful foresight information for students, researchers, and self-leaders." - Verne Wheelwright, Director, Personal Futures; Author, It's Your Future

"The insights in this book are profound, and well-selected. They are masterfully synthesized from evidence-based discoveries across a breathtaking range of disciplines. Read this book for a much better view of the future." - Miguel Aznar, Author, Technology Challenged

"John Smart is one of the most holistic and brilliant futurists around. He has had an impressive forecast accuracy since my first exposure to his output in 2003. This massive project will go down as one of the seminal pre-Singularity texts." - Kartik Gada, Investment Banker; Author, The Accelerating Technonomic Medium

Series:

The Foresight Guide

Book 1:

Introduction to Foresight, Executive Edition:

Personal, Team, and

Organizational Adaptiveness

Dear David,
Thank You for
your Vision and
your Humanity?
Your Friend

Lead Author:

John Smart

Foresight University Press is an imprint of the Acceleration Studies Foundation, a 501c3 nonprofit. EIN: 57-1157861

For bulk purchase discounts, contact the publisher:

Foresight University Press
Ann Arbor, MI
guide@foresightu.com
foresightu.com

ISBN: 978-1-7365585-0-8
Library of Congress Control Number: 2021911294

Set in Palatino. Cover art selection by Dan Sutera. Design by Kevin Russell.
Printed in the United States of America.

First Edition

Publisher's Cataloging-in-Publication Data

Names: Smart, John, author. | Fant, Susan, author.
Series title: The foresight guide
Title: Introduction to foresight, executive edition: personal, team, and organizational
    adaptiveness.
    / John Smart, Susan Fant [and eight others].
Description: Ann Arbor, MI : Foresight University Press, 2021. | Includes bibliographic
    references. | Illus. with photos and diagrams. | Summary: Introduces the
    psychology of future thinking and methods of personal, team, and organizational
    foresight practice.
Identifiers: LCCN 2021911294 | ISBN 978173655852 (hardback) | ISBN 97817365585081
    (pbk.) | ISBN 9781736558515 (ebook)
Subjects: LCSH: Decision making. | Forecasting. | Strategic planning. | BISAC:
    PSYCHOLOGY / Applied Psychology. | PSYCHOLOGY / Cognitive Psychology &
    Cognition. | PSYCHOLOGY / Industrial & Organizational Psychology.
Classification: LCC CB158 S63 2021 | DDC 303.49 S63--dc23
LC record available at https://lccn.loc.gov/2021911294

Dedication

This book is dedicated to all our children. They will surprise and exceed us.
Life, as a complex network, is amazing. May our collective futures be even more amazing.

Acknowledgments

This *Guide* demanded seven years (2015-2021) of love and sweat. John considers writing the first edition of these books his **PhD in foresight**, done in an **autodidactic process**. His greatest thanks and love go to his wife, **Iveta Brigis**, who encouraged and inspired him, and sacrificed much as it was written. He is deeply grateful to his parents, **Beatrice Smart** and **John Smart** senior, who first encouraged him to "play the game" of thinking hard about the future. He thanks his mother-in-law, **Janina Brigis**, for her selfless help with our children.

John thanks his many inspiring mentors, including, **Ken Bullin** (Chadwick High School), **George Guffey** (UCLA), **Michael Freeling** (UCB), **Leroy Hood** (Caltech), **Francis Crick** (Salk Inst.), **Jonas Salk** (Salk Inst.), **James Miller** (UCSD), **Paul Saltman** (UCSD), **Thomas Bond** (UCSD), **Francis Heylighen** (VUB), **John Katzman** (Princeton Review), **Christine Peterson** (Foresight Inst.), **Steve Jurvetson** (DFJ), **Tim O'Reilly** (O'Reilly Media), **Peter Bishop** (U Houston), **Wendy Schultz** (U Houston), **Alvin Toffler** (Toffler & Associates), **Paul Saffo** (Stanford), **Stewart Brand** (Long Now Foundation), **Clem Bezold** (Inst. for Alternative Futures), **Art Shostak** (Drexel U), **Graham Molitor** (Public Policy Forecasting), **Bill Halal** (Georgetown U), **Wendell Bell** (Yale U), **Joe Voros** (Swinburne U), **John Peterson** (Arlington Inst.), **Steve Harris** (21st Century Medicine), **Jason Pistillo** (UAT), **Rebecca Whitehead** (UAT), **Jay Gary** (APF), **Joe Coates** (Coates & Jarratt), **Glen Hiemstra** (Futurist.com), **Bob Harrison** (POST), **Winli McAnally** (NPS), **Bob Huddleston** (NPS), **Ann Gallenson** (NPS), **Kartik Gada** (ATOM Institute), **Elle Martin** (LA Futurists), and **Fred Wendt**. In their own ways, each has seen that not only will our long-term futures be **amazing**, we must cross **many valleys** on the way there.

At Foresight University, we give special thanks to FERN Executive Director **Susan Fant** at U. Alabama, who motivated this work, and ran our Peer Advice Survey of foresight professionals, in the online *Guide*. Special thanks to **Joshua Davis**, FERN Publications Director, for parts of Chapter 1, and to **Anna-Leena Pešić**, for our first lists of foresight organizations. Thanks to **Susan Fant** and **Emily Medley** for running FERN's *Foresight Careers* conference in 2013 in Washington, DC, where we first imagined the *Guide*. Thanks to **John Schroeter** of the Abundant World Institute, who published a **chapter-length version** of the *Guide* in his Alvin Toffler-honoring anthology, *After Shock*, 2020.

Special thanks to **Kevin Russell**, for his diligence with our online *Guide*, at ForesightGuide.com. Thanks to **Tyler Gothelf**, **Cody Marx Bailey**, **Kaleb Griepp**, **Quinn Baetz**, and **Andrae Browne** for their work on the digital version. Thanks to **Dan Sutera** for our *ITF* cover and to **Dinara Strikis** for the *Guide's* title. Thanks to **Peter Diamandis**, **Neil Jacobstein**, **Daniel Kraft**, **Paul Saffo**, **Ramez Naam**, and **Aaron Frank** at **Singularity University** for their insights in exponential foresight and to **Alvis Brigis**, **Scott Lemon**, **Kartik Gada**, **Sean Daken**, and **Miguel Aznar** for discussions on accelerating change. Thanks to **Alex Selkin**, **Zhan Li**, and **George Paap** for editing the alpha draft of the *Guide*. Thanks to **Tyler Mongan** (HA:KU Global) and **Nakul Gupta** (USC Computer Science) for editing the beta draft. Special thanks to Nakul for his extensive collaboration on Book 2 (*BPF*). It is a rare thing in life to find a **true thought partner**, someone who sees the world and its issues so similarly. John has found one in Nakul.

On the complex systems front, John thanks his **Evo-Devo Universe (EDU)** complexity research colleagues **Clement Vidal**, **Georgi Georgiev**, **Claudio Flores-Martinez**, **Michael Price**, **Stan Salthe**, **Jim Coffman**, **John Campbell**, **Domino Valdano**, **Joe Brisendine** and **Peter Corning** for their insights in evolutionary development, and the **100+ EDU-affiliated** scholars, for all they have taught him about complex systems on our listserve, **EDU-Talk**. Thanks to **Francis Heylighen** at VUB for Principia Cybernetica Web, the first online compendium of complex systems thinking, and to **Bela Nagy**, **Jessica Trancik** and **Doyne Farmer** at the Santa Fe Institute, **Norman Johnson** at LANL, and **Chris Magee** at MIT for their collegiality and their work on performance curves. Thanks to **Carlos Gershenson** at the Conference on Complex Systems and **Yaneer Bar-Yam** at NECSI for refereeing our EDU academic papers, posters, and satellite meetings.

A special thanks to **Carl Sagan**, whose **Cosmic Calendar** metaphor introduced all of us to the **profound phenomenon of accelerating change**, when viewed from a **universal perspective**. Thanks to **Joseph Schumpeter** and **Julian Simon** for their work as explorers of human innovation; to **Kevin Kelly**, **Stewart Brand**, and **Ray Kurzweil** for their works on the future of humanity and technology; to physicists **Eric Chaisson**, **Paul Davies**, **Seth Lloyd**, and **Lee Smolin**, whose work is congruent with evo-devo models; to **Richard Dawkins** for his concept of the **meme**; to paleontologist **Simon Conway Morris**, for his work on **convergent evolution** (aka, universal development); to **David Brin**, for his work on societal transparency and immunity; and to **Alvin and Heidi Toffler** for their foresight scholarship and leadership. John had two private interviews with Alvin Toffler in 2008. Along with a few others Alvin was one of the **20th century's greatest and most influential futurists** (we offer our "top twenty-five" for the last century in Chapter 2). Alvin passed away in 2016 at 87. His wife and co-author Heidi passed away in 2019. We planned to ask both to write a foreword to this first edition. We are deeply thankful to esteemed foresight leader **Jay Gary,** recent past Chair of APF, our leading practice community, who **wrote our forward**. The Toffler's deaths remind us of a universal life lesson: *Tempus Fugit, so Carpe Diem!*

Lastly, we wish to thank the many colleagues and contacts who have provided feedback and insights for the ideas in this book. Though none would endorse everything here, everyone listed here has influenced this work. In alpha order, thanks to **Anthony Aguirre, Maria Andersen, Simon Anderson, Michael Andregg, Amara Angelica, Robert Aunger,** Jesse **Ausubel, Azeem Azhar, Yaneer Bar-Yam, Lisa Betts-Lacroix, Cody Marx Bailey, Craig Belanger, Wendell Bell, Clem Bezold, Alisha Bhagat, Peter Bishop, Ray Blackwood, Howard Bloom, Phil Bowermaster, Rachel Botsman, Anne Boysen, Charles Brass, James Breaux, Alvis Brigis, David Brin, Joe Brisendine, Damien Broderick, Erik Brynjolfsson, Eric Chaisson, Michael Chorost, Milan Cirvovic, Andy Clark, Bill Cockayne, José Cordeiro, Edward Corning, Peter Corning, Mike Courtney, Sean Daken, Nikola Danaylov, Jim Dator, Paul Davies, John Davis, Joshua Davis, Ross Dawson, Terrence Deacon, Peter Diamandis, Steven Dick, Jake Dunagan, Tyler Emerson, Emily Empel, Kaat Exterbille, Charles Fadel, Susan Fant, Doyne Farmer, Grant Fjermedal, Aaron Frank, Cindy Frewen, Thomas Frey, Robert Freitas, Kartik Gada, Eric Garland, Jay Gary, Georgi Georgiev, Johann Gevers, Jennifer Gidley, George Gilder, Norman Gilmore, Adam Gitzes, Jerome Glenn, Garry Golden, Marc Goodman, Bernard Goossens, Tyler Gothelf, Eric Gradman, Jordan Greenhall, Matthew Griffin, Nakul Gupta, John Hagel, William Halal, Gary Hamel, Robin Hanson, Steve Harris, Ken Haworth, Willis Harman, Peter Hayward, Francis Heylighen, Glen Hiemstra, Andy Hines, Tony Hsieh, Sohail Inayatullah, Geoffrey Irving, Neil Jacobstein, Bob Johansen, Steve Jurvetson, Stuart Kauffman, Kevin Kelly, Parag Khanna, Tony Kim, Andrey Korotayev, Sandjar Kozubaev, Daniel Kraft, Ray Kurzweil, Marv Langston, Cadell Last, James Lee, Michael Lee, Zhan Li, Alex Lightman, Hal Linstone, Scott Lemon, Tom and Jeannie Lombardo, James Lovelock, Christopher Magee, Timothy Mack, John Mahaffie, Michael Marien, Max Marmer, Claudio Martinez, Raymond Matison, Lara Matossian, Graham May, Andrew McAfee, Alex McManus, Syd Mead, Emily Medley, Pero Micic, Venessa Miemis, Ian Miles, Zoe Miller, Anthony Mills, Graham Molitor, Tyler Mongan, Hans Moravec, Joe Murphy, Ramez Naam, Thomas Nagel, Bela Nagy, George Paap, Jerry Paffendorf, Regina Pancake, Lewis Perelman, Stefan Pernar, Christine Peterson, John Peterson, Rafael Popper, William Poundstone, Giulio Prisco, Kacy Qua, Joe Quirk, Kate Raworth, Byron Reese, Jean Rintoul, Maureen Rhemann, Wayne Radinsky, Noah Raford, Rohan Roberts, Rene Rohrbeck, Hans Rosling, Kevin Russell, Peter Russell, Paul Saffo, Anders Sandberg, Ziauddin Sardar, Wendy Schultz, Gray Scott, Art Shostak, Lee Shupp, David Sinclair, Richard Slaughter, Stephan Spencer, Tom Standage, David Stehlik, Eric Steinhart, Dan Sutera, Max Tegmark, Alex Selkin, Philip Tetlock, Tim Tyler, Luke van der Laan, Domino Valdana, Clement Vidal, Vernor Vinge, Joseph Voros, Peter Wagner, Cynthia Wagner, Nikki Walker, Verne Wheelwright, Wilson Wong, Robert Wright, Lina Yang, Richard Yonck, Carrie Zapka,** and **Andrew Zolli** for their insights and encouragement.

Table of Contents

Foreword

Antarctica, our world's last frontier, lay undiscovered throughout history until 1820. As the decades passed, explorers mapped the basic geography of its massive coastline. It was not until 1911 that a Norwegian expedition crossed this desolate icy landscape to reach the geographic South Pole. In 1914, the British, led by Sir Ernest Shackleton, launched the "Trans-Antarctic Expedition," aspiring to be the first to cross our earth's most Southern Continent. They sailed south, breaking through the ice, only to be trapped by fast-changing weather. As their ship broke up in the ice, Shackleton marched his 22 men and 70 dogs to Elephant Island, and then embarked on a rescue mission to South Georgia Island for 800 miles in open waters in a 20-foot lifeboat.

It would take Shackleton five months to return to rescue his men. Today we remember Shackleton as an exemplary leader, who, under extreme circumstances, kept his team together to pursue the last great quest on earth across unknown lands.

Similar to the last frontier of Antarctica, the nature of the future laid undiscovered until the mid- 20th century. Since then, a host of explorers have mapped the field through tools and methodologies. Various books have opened our eyes to the future, and how to navigate it, by uncovering its foundations and collecting its knowledge base.

Not until the release of *The Foresight Guide*, by John Smart and the 4U team, has our world had a handbook that enables us to broadly explore the terrain of personal, team, and organizational foresight. In the spirit of Shackleton, Smart takes us deep into adaptive foresight, foresight that enables us to anticipate, innovate, and lead across the 21st century.

Whether for personal, team, organizational, or professional use, you will not find a better guide to the future than the '*Guide*.' It will become the go-to handbook to equip students, consultants, and professionals with the skills they need to survive and thrive throughout the 2020s and beyond.

Jay Gary, Ph.D., APF
Chair, Association of Professional Futurists
Washington, DC
November 1, 2020

Who is this Book For?

This book, *Introduction to Foresight, Executive Edition*, was written primarily for **executives, leaders, and self-leaders**, in any industry, seeking a brief but foundational introduction to **professional foresight practice**, for **themselves**, their **teams**, and their **firms**. It introduces **key ways to think more adaptively about the future,** and a selection of **acceleration-aware, evidence-based worldviews, frameworks, trends, predictions, and stories** about the 21st century.

There is also a larger **Student Edition** of this book, for students and leaders seeking the most **in-depth treatment** of these topics. That edition includes **six additional chapters**, on the topics of **personal foresight** (self-leadership), **departmental foresight, foresight models, growth curves**, and **foresight biases and practice traps**.

With either edition, we believe you will find no better map to **anticipating, creating, and leading the future**—for yourself, your family, your teams, your organizations, and for humanity itself, viewed as a complex network. Foresight is our **greatest superpower**, and improving it for ourselves and others is **a lifelong journey**. We believe it is one of the most **satisfying journeys** each of us can take as we seek to live with greater meaning, purpose, and impact in the world.

What is *The Foresight Guide*?

The Foresight Guide (aka, the *Guide*) introduces the **models and methods of professional foresight**, and **key trends, hypotheses, predictions, and stories** of **twenty-first century futures,** in a world of **accelerating change**. The *Guide* is split into two books. Book 1, *Introduction to Foresight, ITF*, covers **personal, team, and organizational foresight practice**. Book 2, *Big Picture Foresight, BPF*, covers **general futures thinking**, from **societal, global, and universal** perspectives. The topics of Book 1 are traditionally called **"Foresight",** and those of Book 2 are typically called **"Futures"**. Each book is offered in an **Executive Edition** and a longer **Student Edition**, addressing our two main audiences: **leaders and students**. An abridged free online version of the *Guide* can also be found at <u>ForesightGuide.com</u>.

Together, both books cover what we call **comprehensive (or full-spectrum) foresight**. We'll see that foresight can be as **personal** as managing our **inner sentiments and thoughts**, and as **universal** as developing our views on the **meaning of life** and the **nature of the universe**. Foresight can help us with **today's** priorities, with the **next quarter's** plans, with **leading** a team, and with building a **vision** to guide us for a **lifetime**. As a result, our books range from the personal (self-leadership) to the universal, covering the foresight practices, skills, and methods we can use as individuals and organizations, and also the big picture visions, goals, and values that can help us to create better futures for humanity.

These books are written and produced by **Foresight University (Foresight U, 4U)**, a learning and development organization that teaches foresight practice to individuals and teams. 4U is a division of the **Acceleration Studies Foundation (ASF)**, a 501c3 nonprofit. ASF was started in 2003 to research and better understand both human and universal processes of accelerating change. The *Guide's* production has also been helped by volunteers in the **Foresight Education and Research Network (FERN)**, a free group that orients newcomers to the world of professional foresight. In 2022, both ASF and FERN are unifying under a new nonprofit, the **Futuremedia Foundation**. The focus of our new nonprofit will be building an **online Futurepedia**, a community-edited wiki covering both **foresight and futures**.

This is the **First Edition** of this book. Periodically, as changes merit it, we plan to publish **new editions of the *Guide* in perpetuity.** Our growing group of authors and editors pledge to **keep improving it** to **better serve you** in coming years. To make it **better for the next edition**, please tell us: **Who have we missed acknowledging? What have we left out, or gotten wrong?** We warmly welcome your feedback and critiques at <u>guide@foresightu.com</u>.

The *Guide* is also a **work in progress**. It is full of **tentative models and claims**. Far too many are **poorly evidenced** at present. Thus it is unintentionally **biased, incomplete, and incorrect** in parts. Thank you for letting us know what we're **doing right**, and where we need to **do better**. The *Guide* also has a **non-neutral point of view**, presently typically that of its lead author, the academically-trained futurist <u>John Smart</u>. Feel free to **disagree with authorial bias** where found, and to point out **maladaptive bias** (at guide@foresightu.com) where you find it, so we can improve future editions.

The *Guide* is written in a **conversational** tone. We also make **calls to action** in various places for projects or activities that aspiring foresight leaders might do, both to advance their own careers and our emerging profession. A **Glossary of Terms** is included at the end of Book 2. **Notes** and **References** sections are planned to be added in the second edition. The online *Guide*, at **foresightguide.com**, also includes some material not included here.

We have **bolded** various parts of the *Guide* to aid in **sprint-reading**. To start, we recommend skim-reading **only the parts that seem most relevant to you, right now**. We've used **text boxes** to demarcate a few of our more lengthy **futures stories,** to make it easier to **find or skip** them. There are no **case studies** in this edition, but many of our stories serve to illustrate a **foresight concept**, or offer **lessons in foresight practice**.

To make it easier to **find people** while skimming, we've bolded all **names of persons**, but **not of organizations**. The latter are usually better known. We've mostly kept individual's names to **first and last names** (e.g., **John Kennedy** vs. **John F. Kennedy**) for simplicity, but left in middle initials for a few lesser-known individuals with common last names, or when they seem to exclusively prefer them.

Except when referring to specific persons or gender-relevant issues, we strive to use "**they**" in singular form, rather than "he or she," and "humanity" and "humankind" rather than "mankind," etc., to reduce gender bias. We strive to use "**we**" rather than "**I**" to express views that I/we believe are particularly common to all of us. The "**royal we**" is an aspiration to find **common ground**, and build **community**. We all function best as a **team**, in a supportive network that protects and critiques our core values.

To the best of our knowledge, all the **images** in this work are either reproduced with author permission, found using Creative Commons search, Google image search with usage rights labeled for reuse, retrieved from free-use repositories (Pexels, Pixabay, etc.), or are **fair use** (book covers and logos, with review). In the ebook and online *Guide*, images typically link to their web sources. Let us know if you'd like an image removed or its citation improved.

Overview

Foresight is a vast and vital topic. In the pages that follow we will consider foresight from three main perspectives:

1. **Evidence-based thinking** (seeking the most predictive data, analogies, and models to explain the world),

2. **Acceleration-awareness** (recognizing that certain special scientific, technological, economic, and societal processes have been engaged in exponential growth, on average, throughout all of human history), and

3. **Evo-devo thinking** (exploring both unpredictable and predictable processes of change in **networks** of individuals, organizations, and societies, and the hypothesis that our **universe itself** is an evo-devo system).

All three perspectives are also **worldviews**. The first worldview is simply that of established **Science** and its methods. The second worldview we call **Exponential Foresight**. The third we call **Evo-Devo Foresight**. The last two are **working hypotheses** in systems theory (philosophy of natural systems) today. We expect they will be validated by future science.

Exponential foresight, introduced in this book, and explored in-depth in Book 2, helps leaders to understand, benefit from, guide, and defend against the downsides of planet-scale processes of **accelerating change**. In recent decades, **exponential scientific, technological, entrepreneurial, and empowerment changes** have become the greatest set of drivers of human futures. We will see why certain forms of change will **inevitably get even faster and more morally complex** going forward. The best thinkers now realize, even without us having all the **math and science** yet, that **special aspects of our network civilization** have been **on-average accelerating**, with increasingly brief and local pauses, throughout **all human history**. Understanding **which societal processes accelerate, and why,** allows us to better **guide them** to preferred ends, to **profit** from the value that they create, and to **protect** against their **disruptive downsides**.

To analyze exponentials, we will introduce **two global megatrends: densification** and **dematerialization** or "D&D". We propose them as key **causal drivers** of **entrepreneurial, societal, and technological acceleration**. Because of D&D, certain **societal processes** will likely **continue to get more densely associated, miniaturized, digital, intelligent, and powerful** in years ahead. Because of D&D, they become **ever more resource-efficient and resource-independent** as well, allowing their **further acceleration**. Many of these processes **stabilize and improve** our societies, at the **network level**; however, a select few become **more destabilizing and dangerous** the faster they go. The **use and misuse** of accelerating science and technologies is creating more new **advantages, disruptions, opportunities, and risks (ADOR)** today than ever.

Evo-Devo Foresight, introduced in this book and explored in-depth in *BPF*, is a **set of hypotheses in systems thinking** that come from **biology, complex systems, and network theory**. It is the least-known, yet the most beneficial worldview, as it offers us a **framework** for distinguishing between **predictable** and **unpredictable changes**, for **improving the values** that **guide our decisions,** and for being **more adaptive,** in any environment. Recognizing **adaptiveness**, in both evolutionary and developmental terms, helps us to create our best **long-term strategy**. Both **individuals** and **groups** are often winning or losing in adaptiveness, but **the best-built networks**, of people, firms, and societies, **always improve,** through good times and bad. **Natural selection** makes well-built networks stronger, more resilient, and more adaptive.

Evo-devo foresight helps leaders and their teams to better understand and guide the **productive tension** between the **individual** and the **collective** in any system, and to differentiate **realistic** from **unrealistic** future stories. It explores the coexistence of and tension between **evolutionary processes,** operating largely through **individual entities in a system,** and **developmental processes,** operating in **collectives of individuals** (the system on average), and the way they **integrate** (interdepend) to create **adaptive networks ("evo-devo" systems)**.

Life itself, in all its exuberance, intelligence, and power, is **most complex known example** of such a network. Complex adaptive networks exhibit both **local diversity** and **global commonality**. Evo-devo models in biology tell us that one fundamental purpose of **evolutionary change** is to grow **network diversity and specialization**. Such change is **protective of the network** as a whole, while simultaneously creating **new opportunities and threats** for **specific actors**. This **network-first worldview** has much to teach us. For example, a network-centric, evo-devo view of **technology as a complex system** predicts that the **future of artificial intelligence (AI)**, a topic much in discussion at present, will be far more **bottom-up, collective, stable, ethical,** and *personalized* than many who talk about this topic presently realize.

Yet perhaps the most useful benefit of this worldview is that it offers us a **normative (goals- and values-based) model** of **adaptiveness**. When we can visualize and manage **tradeoffs** between **adaptive goals and values**, we can better achieve such hard-to-define outcomes as **personal success, organizational excellence, and societal progress**. We can see which personal, organizational, and societal changes we should strive to **speed up** and **free up**, and which we should strive to **slow down** and better **regulate**, to arrive at more **empowering** and **sustainable** futures.

Throughout this *Guide* you will encounter **scores of book references**. We will mention the **best books we know** on a wide variety of **foresight-related topics**. We propose that earnest students and leaders should aspire to "**sprint-read**" **one new book a week**, spending a **couple of hours** with each. See **Sprint Reading** in Chapter 5 for tips on how to do that. We also recommend **sprint-reading this book** at first, giving it just an **hour or three of your precious time,** and coming back to it later only if it "calls to you" after that initial sprint. When we sprint-read we get to choose how **widely**

and deeply we go into any topic, giving us **deep control** of our **learning process**. Sprint-reading, listening to, discussing, and arguing **"great inputs"** with a cognitively and skills-diverse group of friends and colleagues is one of the **best ways we know to stay oriented** to all the relevant new advantages, insights, possibilities, tools, and opportunities, and the new disruptions, problems, and risks, that our **ever-accelerating world** offers us.

As it says in its subtitle, the *Guide* will help us get better at **Anticipating, Innovating**, and **Leading** the future. We will see that these words represent **three basic, yet uniquely different, goals of foresight thinking**. We will also learn how to **integrate foresight with action**, in a classic **feedback cycle**, one that depends on **four skills of effective foresight**, and **four skills of effective action**. Together, we call these the **Eight Skills of Adaptive Foresight**. We will see that the **Eight Skills** are used daily by all of us, in better and worse ways. We'll see why we **can't neglect** any of them, and we will learn how to become **reasonably competent** in all eight. We can use each **well or poorly**, every day of our lives.

A great **paradox of change** is that our civilization, when viewed as a **complex network**, is more **Innovative, Intelligent, Empathic, Ethical, Strong, and Sustainable** than it has ever been in its 10,000 year history. We will call these six the **"IES Goals"**, and together they comprise our **normative adaptive foresight** model. Yet at the same time, some conditions are more **volatile, uncertain, regressive, and disruptive** for various **individual** people, groups, firms, and societies than in our recent past. In **America today**, rising inequality, middle class erosion, technological unemployment, political polarization, failing schools, debt, addiction, fake news, cybercrime, great power competition, pandemic, and climate change are just a few of the **problems we have created for ourselves**, and must **rely on ourselves** to solve.

The faster change goes, the **more foresight is in demand**, and the **more future stories will be told**, many of them quite poor at first. The *Guide* will help you **see past** the ever-growing levels of **future fantasy, noise, and hype**, to find the real **evidence, trends and signals** you need to guide your strategy. The better we get at **foresight,** the better we can **manage the downsides** and **lead the upsides** of relentless **accelerating change**. Each of us, born in a time of **Great Transitions** (see Book 2), can see that **right here, right now, is an especially amazing and fortunate time to be alive.**

Let us end our **Overview** by introducing and explaining **4U's three mottos**. We use an exclamation point after each to remind us that **emotional energy**, when invested in our **top priorities**, can help us to **live them more consciously**. You may find one or more of these mottos worth remembering and repeating, as **personal mantras**, to help you with your daily foresight and actions. We will repeat each of these, in the pages to come, whenever we think they might help.

Motto 1: People First!

Our first motto reminds us that **people**, not our beliefs, plans, politics, companies, governments, or even the rest of our natural world, are the most miraculous and important entities in the known universe. Growing our **ethics and empathy** with respect to all life, but most particularly, for **other humans**, the most **complex and conscious entities** on Earth, should be our highest priority. We must consciously strive to help each other thrive, and to work toward **positive sum futures** for all of us, regardless of our disagreements. We believe the evidence so far shows an **arrow of universal progress**, as futurist **Teilhard de Chardin** said long ago (see *BPF*). There is at least one apparent **purpose** to our universe, and to our own lives, as we will discuss, and it involves **increasing complexity and consciousness**. Human beings are the most complex, conscious, and foresighted entities on Earth. Yet psychologists tell us we are each truly conscious for only **minutes** in a typical day. We believe we can have much higher quality, continual, and more **collective consciousness**, and far better **foresight and action,** when we put **protecting and respecting each other first**, even in our disagreements.

Motto 2: Quality of Vision!

Our second motto claims that the **quality of our vision**, for ourselves, our families, our teams, our organizations, our societies, and our planet is the most important and useful thing we can use our consciousness, intelligence, ethics, and empathy to develop. We are each capable of an **astronomical number** of possible thoughts and actions, every second of every day. But only some of those thoughts and actions are going to be both **adaptive and progressive**. The better our quality of vision, for the next few seconds, the next few hours, the next day, the next month, the next quarter, the next year, the next decade, for the rest of our lives, for our kids, and for future generations, the better our actions can be. If **people** deserve to be our top priority **entities**, improving our **quality of vision** deserves to be our top priority **process**, in our view. The clearer we all can see what **we will, could, and should do next**, the better our world becomes. We'll offer our best tips on how to improve our vision in this *Guide*. Let us know what you like, and where we've fallen short.

Motto 3: Foresight Matters!

We can shorten the phrase "quality of vision" into a single word: *Foresight*. Our final motto reminds us that we presently live in a world where **foresight is often discounted, blocked, or ignored**. Many of us don't realize **how much better we can see** when we **choose to care** about our quality of vision, and when we use **good foresight process**. The future is also **political**, and everyone has their own agendas. Many powerful entities are happy to serve us a version of the future that best serves their ends, but not necessarily our own ends, or the ends of people as a whole. One big step in personal growth is to recognize that our ability to generate better personal and group foresight **matters greatly**, both to our **own lives** and to the lives of our **fellow humans**. As **complex networks**, our teams, our groups, and our species are **only as smart and strong** as the **foresight, diversity, and empowerment** of **each individual in that network**. No entity in our physical universe, having finite complexity in a reality with astronomical possibilities, can ever be **omniscient or omnipotent**. No one will ever have a monopoly on the future. The **most adaptive entities** have always been, and will always continue to be, **complex networks**, composed of individuals who are each partly different, and partly similar, at the same time. We will always **need each other** to thrive. Simultaneously growing both our **individual and collective foresight, diversity, ethics, empathy, ability, and consciousness** all appear to be part of **"what the universe wants."**

What to Read First

Chapter 1 of this book is the **Executive's Overview**. If you can make time to skim just **one chapter**, over one to three hours (the length of a movie, a good benchmark for a timed sprint), we recommend this one. **Appendix 1** will also help you apply key models in this book to yourself and your teams, and can also be completed in roughly an hour. It should also be a priority as well, as it challenges you to self-assess, plan and act.

In Chapter 1, you'll learn how **strategic optimism** and **defensive pessimism**, when each are **used well**, and **initially in that order**, help us **"feel our way"** to better personal, team, organizational, and societal futures. You will learn the art of balancing **Past, Present**, and **Future** thinking, and of assessing **Probable, Possible, Preferable and Preventable ("Four Ps") futures**, and managing their conflicts on teams. You'll learn to see the future as a series of accelerating **Advantages, Disruptions, Opportunities, and Risks (ADOR)**. In a world of accelerating change, ADOR is significantly more useful set of strategic assessments than that old chestnut, **SWOT** (Strengths, Weaknesses, Opportunities, and Threats). Appendix 1 will help you diagnose your and your team's **foresight feeling and thinking styles**, and learn a few key **skills, frameworks, and methods** that **great teams and organizations** use to create **effective foresight and action**, both day-by-day and for the long-term.

In later chapters, you will learn other **frameworks, methods, and habits** to help you and your teams to create **effective and adaptive strategy**, to put that strategy into **action**, to evaluate its **impact**, and to navigate the wild and wooly world of **future stories**. As we will see, many popular stories about the future are both **entertaining and unrealistic**. All future stories are told to fulfill a **desire** or advance an **agenda**, conscious or unconscious, for good or ill. **Great leaders** must learn to **craft effective future stories**, for various ends, and to see past all the **noise, agendas, and hype** in other's future stories, and unearth the **evidence, trends, and signals** they need to guide **strategy**.

Finally, if time is short, you may find value in selectively skimming any of **Foresight University's (4U's) foresight models and frameworks** covered in this book, at the page numbers listed below. These are our unique contributions to foresight research and practice to date. We list them here in alpha order, and again at the start of our **Index**:

Foresight Matters!

Chapter 1: An Introduction to Foresight – Humanity's Greatest Gift

What is Foresight?

Foresight is the act of looking to and thinking about the future. This activity can be amateur or professional, untrained or trained. By approaching it deliberately, we can get much better at it over time. Foresight is a fundamental trait of all living systems, from the simplest to the most complex. Informing our every action, it is how we make a better world.

Humanity has been given a number of **great gifts** over our evolutionary history. We think the **greatest** of these is our **advanced capacity for foresight, relative to all other species**. We will see that in the **predictive processing model** of neuroscience, **human intelligence** is now being understood as a process of foresight production, application, and improvement. Human beings possess a **uniquely evolved and developed forebrain** that can **predict and imagine** ourselves and others far into the future. We devise **intricate strategies, plans and tools** to try to get what we want. Our special capacities to **predict, imagine, and preference** the future are at the heart of human **adaptiveness**.

Olduvai Gorge, Tanzania. Birthplace of Our Story of Human Emergence

Four million years ago, our one meter tall *Australopithecus* **ancestors** came down from **protection of the trees**. There they had learned **cooperativity**, **manual dexterity**, and **precise prediction** of movement and action. But as their environment got drier, they had to venture to the ground. Naked and exposed on the African savannah, surrounded by much faster and more powerful predators, they were forced to adapt. Their ability to imagine and grasp **tools**, beginning with rocks and clubs, to move in **groups** to defend themselves, and to **predict danger** were all essential to their survival.

The picture above is of Olduvai Gorge in Tanzania. That is the first site where archeologists found transitional forms of the first **human beings**. *Australopithecus*, our pre-human ancestor, appears to have been the first to use tools, over three million years ago. But once we gained enough **intelligence and foresight** to start *improving* those tools, roughly two million years ago, our **human story** began. In places like Olduvai Gorge across Africa, *Homo habilis* learned to mass fabricate, distribute, and use **Oldowan tools**. We learned that acting in a **foresighted network**, in **cooperative groups**, armed with **tools**, we could defend ourselves, and hunt. Secondarily to such cooperation, we also used our tools and groups **competitively**, to fight and hunt each other, in increasingly clever ways.

Our history has been one of **accelerating social and technical complexity** ever after. Since the dawn of civilization, 10,000 years ago, just <u>400 generations</u> have created the amazingly complex world we live in today. **Each generation** has used **foresight and action**, as best they could. Each was **unsatisfied** with the **status quo**. Our generation stands on the shoulders of these 400 generations, and is biologically no different. What is very different today is the **complexity** of our culture and tools, and the **pace of change.** In just the last few decades, we all see and feel the **quickening**. Meaningful human change used to take a lifetime. Now we see useful and disruptive **digital change** happening every month.

Our second great gift is our special ability to build **science and technology**. Our bilateralism, grasping limbs, opposable thumbs and vocal capacities have allowed us to **continually change** our environment to suit our needs, and to alter our very nature. Ever since our species first emerged, we have used **foresight, technology**, and later **science**, and **cooperativity** to become **more complex, capable, and accelerative** than **biology alone**. To paraphrase the famous futurist **Buckminster Fuller**, humans are not nouns. We are verbs. We're always changing, becoming **something else**.

Humanity's last great gift is our special capacity for **ethics and empathy** toward each other and all **sentient life**. Throughout our history, perhaps because of our **special capacity for foresight**, all our most successful groups have been driven **primarily to cooperate**, and only **secondarily to compete**. This **hierarchy of priorities** in **human networks, first** to look out for others, beginning with our **kin** and friends (cooperation), and **second** to devise **cooperative rules** within which we strive to win and create **unique contributions** (competition), is called *coopetition*. Coopetition is the **"infinite game"** that almost all of us most like to play. We have learned that coopetition leads us, **most reliably**, to better futures.

Said more simply, as **David Goodhart** does in his lovely book of social activism <u>*Head Hand Heart*</u>, 2020, **the gifts of Head** (foresight), **of Hand** (ability), and **of Heart** (prosociality) are each our foundational human gifts. They are the key aptitudes of **adaptive human networks.** All three must be valued and developed well in **thriving societies**.

We believe that our essential **human nature** is not unique to us, but rather, **universal**. **Astrobiologists** tell us that **billions** of other **Earthlike planets** may exist in our universe, and there are likely **millions** of other **intelligent advanced civilizations** in our Galaxy alone. In Book 2, we'll offer a speculative proposal for why we haven't yet heard from any of those civilizations. We'll argue that all our **most accelerative and adaptive complex networks**, at every level of emergent complexity, are constrained by the laws of physics to develop in **increasingly** *local* **(dense and miniaturized) zones of space, time, energy, and matter**. In what we'll call the <u>transcension hypothesis</u>, we speculate that all civilizations, everywhere, may be constrained to venture ever further into **inner space**, not **outer space**, as they grow up. It also posits that **black hole-like domains**, built by far future human civilizations, may be **a developmental destination for advanced intelligence,** if they let us **instantly connect with** all other similarly advanced civilizations. We shall see, as they say.

Of these three gifts, foresight, technology and science, and empathy and ethics, foresight may be the most fundamental. **Operating at many levels**—from our genes and cells to our higher mind and now our learning technologies—various foresight processes have been **our species most defining trait.** Neuroscientist <u>Daniel Schacter</u> describes this in his concept of the <u>prospective brain (PDF)</u>. All animals are wired, at various levels, to **imagine and predict the future**, but human beings do so with a **complexity and usefulness** that far exceeds all other species. In *Homo Prospectus*, 2016, psychologist <u>Martin Seligman</u> says: "Our species is misnamed. Though sapiens defines us as 'wise,' what humans do especially well is prospect the future. We are *Homo prospectus*." This book explores the **new psychology and neuroscience of foresight**. We are learning to analyze emotion, intuition, deliberation, creativity, and imagination as **foresight processes**. Our abilities to **predict, create, cooperate**, and **compete** as a members of **complex networks** are all key to our impressive adaptiveness.

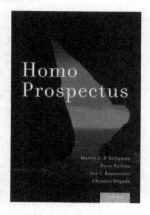

Seligman et al, 2016

More specifically, neuroscience and evolutionary biology tell us that we think incessantly about the future because we have been **adapted by natural selection** to do so. In a process called **active inference**, using <u>Bayesian probability</u> (a method of probabilistic prediction that is updated by learning), we continually **predict, imagine,** and **preference** the future, while trying to **minimize prediction error** (or, surprise). A leading model of how we do this, at present, is called the **Predictive Processing (PP) model.** After decades of guessing, neuroscience, computer science, cognitive science, and psychology are just now beginning to understanding animal minds in terms of **hierarchies of predictive (and creative) foresight-action cycles**, with our **top-down** (developmental) predictions and creative inferences emerging from **bottom-up** (evolutionary) information flow. This balancing of **top-down and bottom-up processes** is a key feature of **evo-devo systems. Andy Clark's** *Surfing Uncertainty: Prediction, Action and the Embodied Mind,* 2019, explores the science behind this new way of understanding the mind. It tells us that most of our future thinking is **unconscious**, and runs just **seconds to minutes ahead** of the present. But we also think, more briefly and irregularly, into **longer horizons.**

We particularly enjoy telling and listening to **stories about the future**, stories that give us a **bigger picture**, connecting us to each other and the world. When any of us **strongly believe** in the truthfulness of our future stories, we have historically called them **prophecies.** <u>Religious prophecy</u> is the best known example, but prophecies can also be ideological. <u>Self-fulfilling prophecies</u> are stories that we and others not only believe, but **act to make true.** Some of these are **self-improving prophecies** (no-Wikipedia page yet). They give us positive adaptive visions to aim for. There are also <u>self-preventing prophecies</u>, useful scare stories we tell, to spur changes that we think are necessary to avoid catastrophe. Other stories are <u>self-defeating prophecies</u>, causing harm to the believer. They may be based on false models, lack positive goals, or paralyze us with unjustified fear, pessimism, or doubt. We will learn how to approach future stories with a critical eye in this *Guide*, and how to keep our prophecies both self-improving and self-preventing.

Being a **foresight practitioner** today requires more than a little **courage** and some **dancing in the dark**. Our field is still emerging and poorly grounded, and foresight itself is not one single profession. It is instead an expanding and not always well-defined set of professions, ways of thinking, and practices that help individuals, organizations, and communities to better anticipate, create, and manage change. Yet, our field also has a **bright future ahead** of it, as we will see.

Foresight practices today can be as varied as the individuals who choose them — each unique and personal blends of **science, knowledge, and art**. A modern foresight professional may look like a <u>Futurist</u>, giving presentations to audiences; an <u>Advisor</u>, <u>Coach</u> or <u>Consultant</u>, offering guidance; a <u>Forecaster</u>, finding curves, trends and predicting; an <u>Intelligence</u> professional, doing sensemaking and pattern recognition; an <u>Analyst</u>, <u>Strategist</u>, <u>Planner</u>, or <u>Manager</u>, supporting decision-making, planning, policy, and action in an organization; a <u>Designer</u> or <u>Engineer</u>, creating products or services; an <u>Innovation Manager</u>, improving an organization's ideation and R&D processes; an <u>Entrepreneur</u>, starting new businesses; an <u>Investor</u> or <u>Venture Capitalist</u>, seeking new opportunities for capital; or an <u>Opinion Leader</u> or <u>Activist</u>, driving conversations and social change, to name some of the better-known choices on offer.

With this great breadth in mind, some basic questions must be raised at the beginning of this *Guide*. Why is it **valuable** to think about the future? Who **defines** the foresight field, and what is **professional**? How does one get **trained**? What are the important **domains, types, models,** and **methods** of foresight thinking and practice? What foreseeable changes, opportunities, and problems lie ahead for our **societies**, and how can foresight practice help us to better **manage** them? This chapter will **offer some preliminary answers** to these questions. Our answers won't be definitive, but hopefully they will be useful. They ought to **spur new questions** as well — and help you find new answers for yourself.

Foresight Professional – A Simple Definition

Pioneering futurist <u>Joe Coates</u> (1929-2014) one of John's mentors, offered our field a simple definition several decades ago that still seems hard to improve upon: a **foresight professional** is **anyone who takes money for looking to and analyzing the future, for a client**. Some aspect of that analysis must also look either **far enough ahead** (in the long-term), or in **enough detail** (in the short-term), that **uncertainty** becomes significant.

Joseph Coates

Most future thinkers do ***pro bono*** work. That means, we think, talk, or write about the future for free, usually out of our own interest. But, once our **income and job description** can be **tied to future thinking,** in any capacity, we belong in a different category. A future-thinker without a client is an <u>**amateur**</u>, a lover of the field—not yet a professional.

Usually, the first step toward professionalism is recognizing that **someone is already paying us** to look to and analyze the future in some capacity. **Stating our intention** to think ahead for others in some capacity, and eventually, formalizing it in our **job description**, are both small steps that will **start us** on our professional foresight journey. Coates told us that the intersection of **our skills and passions**, and **our clients' needs and wants** is where all good foresight work occurs. Futurist **Eric Garland,** who worked with Coates, wrote a <u>lovely elegy</u> for him. Joe was a **"fearless futurist"** willing to **criticize** as much as **praise**, and he lost clients occasionally as a result. Garland continues in Coates' tradition. We'll see it has much to teach us.

Any professional looking to get paid at least occasionally for foresight work, even if they do it only a few minutes or hours a week, should ask questions like the following:

- What kinds of foresight work am I particularly passionate about?
- What "universal" kinds should I pursue regardless of my passions?
- How much and what kinds of foresight should I practice at my job?
- Who are the right clients, inside or outside of my organization, for my foresight work?
- What kinds of foresight work do my clients expect? What kinds do they actually need?
- How will I know when my work is effective? How will I prove value?
- Who are my foresight colleagues, and how can they support my work?

We will offer some general answers to such questions in this *Guide*, but you will have to find your own personal answers, over a lifetime of foresight practice. We hope you celebrate your insights as they come, and enjoy the journey.

What is the Foresight Field?

<u>**Foresight**</u>, also known as **futurology**, **futures studies**, **futurism**, or **futuring**, is the art and practice of looking to the future. Our oldest written form of foresight thinking is <u>**political propaganda**</u>, like the *Prophecy of Neferti*, 1960 BCE, in Ancient Egypt. Our next oldest form is found in **religious prophecy**, like the <u>Delphic oracle</u> of Apollo in Ancient Greece (1400 BCE to 395 CE) and scores of prophets in later centuries in <u>Greek</u>, <u>Etruscan</u>, <u>Roman</u>, <u>Zoroastrian</u>, <u>Judaic</u>, <u>Christian</u>, <u>Islamic</u>, <u>Hindu</u>, <u>Confucian</u>, and more recent religions. Another ancient form of foresight is <u>**utopianism**</u>, idealistic political philosophy. We find utopian foresight in Plato's <u>*The Republic*</u>, 380 BCE, (Greece); in Europe in Thomas More's <u>*Utopia*</u>, 1516 (England); and in the philosophy of political authors like **Karl Marx** (Russia) and **Mao Zedong** (China).

But, while **political propaganda**, **religious prophecy**, and **utopian foresight** have all been central to human development and the formation of our modern societies, none of these are primary subjects of the *Guide*. We will focus mainly on **secular foresight**, a way of thinking that became popular in the **European Enlightenment (1650-1850)**. Secular foresight uses not only <u>visionary aspiration</u>, found in propaganda, prophecy and utopianism, but also <u>intuition</u>, <u>reason</u>, <u>evidence</u>, <u>discourse</u>, <u>critique</u>, and <u>experiment</u> in order to guide our individual and collective <u>values determination</u>, <u>analysis</u>, <u>strategy</u>, <u>goalsetting</u>, <u>planning</u>, and <u>action</u>.

In secular foresight, our first focus is <u>**strategic foresight**</u>, a set of practices and methods that emerged after World War II in the USA, Europe, and Asia. **Strategic foresight** is intended to improve **strategic management**. It uses practices like environmental scanning, intelligence, trends, forecasts, probabilistic predictions, argument mapping, scenarios, design thinking, visioning, analysis, and feedback to improve **personal, team or organizational strategy and action**.

More specifically, strategic foresight uses **foresight methods** and **future thinking** to **create, confirm, or alter strategies**, and often also **strategy's antecedents (goals, values, visions)** and **dependents (plans and actions)**. If our future thinking doesn't impact **strategy**, then it may be imagination, entertainment, or even education; but, it isn't strategic foresight. More specifically, strategic foresight seeks to tell us what to do to **be effective** at achieving the particular **goals or visions we have chosen**. Like strategy itself, strategic foresight is **prescriptive**, but not fully so. It tells us **what to do to get what we want**, but it does not tell us if our chosen goals and visions are **best** for us, others, and the planet over the **long term**.

Our second focus is **adaptive foresight**. Like biological adaptation, **adaptive foresight** is any strategy, plans, and actions that help us to **thrive (aka progress, improve, advance)** over the **long term**. It is prescriptive in a more powerful sense. **Adaptive foresight** seeks to answer the question: **what goals, values, and visions** should we, our teams, and our organizations have, to do the **best work we can**? As we will see, our goals should strive to be as **positive-sum**, and our values as **universal** as possible, to gain the greatest **long-term benefits** from our strategy.

Adaptive foresight is ultimately **normative**, meaning it **prioritizes** certain **goals, values**, and **values hierarchies**. Good normative foresight should be based on a **working theory of adaptiveness**, a theory that can be critiqued, tested, and improved over time. We will offer a draft of one such theory, **evolutionary development**, aka **evo-devo foresight**, in this *Guide*. We will use evo-devo thinking to construct simple models of **adaptive goals and values**, and relate those models to desirable states like **individual and organizational success** and **societal progress**. These are **challenging and speculative topics** for which science presently has only tentative and incomplete insights. Nevertheless, we will offer the best arguments and evidence we can marshal to date. Please let us know where we have fallen short.

To say this another way, **strategic thinking** is concerned with **instrumental values** (finding an effective **means to an end**, in the near term). **Adaptive thinking** is concerned with **intrinsic values**, or finding actions and ends that will provide the **greatest value over the long term**. The classic battle between **traditional corporate management**, which focuses primarily on **financial profit**, and **sustainable management**, which focuses the firm on competing sets of long-term benefits, including **social, governance, environmental**, and **profit** outcomes, highlights the difference between **strategic** and **adaptive foresight practice**. So also does conflict between **traditional investing** and **ESG (environmental, social, and governance) investing**. A manager, or investor, always has a **choice** to think either **strategically** (short-term effectiveness) or **adaptively** (long-term thriving). Sometimes we must think short-term simply to survive. But as soon as we can, we should also strive to see how we can improve the **bigger picture**. We will cover both views in this *Guide*.

So while foresight will often **start with effectiveness ("surviving")**, our greatest challenge is to **progress to adaptiveness ("thriving")**. We must also see **exactly who** is surviving and thriving, from a **network perspective**. In biological adaptation, there is a **perennial tradeoff** between **individual** and **group success**. Sometimes greater **group (network) adaptiveness** comes at a **cost to the individual**, as when we sacrifice for our children, overwork to meet a critical goal, or give our lives in war for a moral cause. Another tension is between **competing individuals and groups**. Over the **long-term**, and only **on average**, our **selective environment** will determine which strategies and actions are most adaptive.

We will see that foresight depends on **Four Skills** (the LAIS skills), that it can be done in **Five Steps** (the REOPS cycle), and that it can be practiced in any of **Six Domains** (Self, Teams, Organizations, Societies, Global, Universal), in any **industry**, using a wide variety of **practice specialties** and **methods**. Its forward view can be projected over **any time horizon**, from the next few seconds in <u>equity futures trading</u> to the next century in <u>urban planning</u> or <u>climate modeling</u>. It is both the **shared skills and domains** used across foresight problems and the **unique methods** developed within each industry and application that define and advance our field.

In coming decades, as our **digital platforms** and **AIs** continue to improve at predictably accelerating rates, and we run more experiments with our methods, more elements our practice, but never all, will be taught in our <u>social and economic sciences</u>. For a survey of our emerging field, and arguments and recommendations for professionalizing it, see **<u>Andy Hines'</u>** and **<u>Jeff Gold's</u>** article "<u>Professionalizing Foresight</u>," *J. Futures Studies*, 2013.

In a <u>prescient article on foresight</u> in 1999, at the close of the last millennium, the editor of *The Economist* observed "In every way that people, firms, or governments act and plan, they are making **implicit forecasts** about the future." A key challenge of this **new millennium** is to make our mostly **implicit and unconscious** forecasting, imagining, and goal-setting much more **explicit, collaborative, evidence-based, cognitively diverse, and conscious**. We must learn how to find the best foresight methods our various contexts. We must estimate how much useful **latent foresight** remains unclaimed. We must ask **how costly** it might be to acquire, and when the potential **return on investment** justifies further foresight work. We'll outline these and other worthy challenges in this *Guide*.

<u>Peter Bishop</u>, the past Director of the U. Houston Foresight MS program, uses a great email signature quotation: "change is hard, but stagnation is fatal." To **survive**, we all must engage in periodic change. Ideally, we will also learn how to **thrive**, how to use foresight to bring **lasting success** to our clients and ourselves, and **real progress** to the world. Using foresight for both purposes is a challenging, humbling, exciting, and rewarding lifelong journey.

The *Anna Karenina* Principle – A Basic Assumption of this *Guide*

Leo Tolstoy at Home, 1908

The Russian author **<u>Leo Tolstoy</u>** opens his novel *<u>Anna Karenina</u>*, 1878, which some consider the greatest work of fiction written to date, with a profound sentence: "Happy families are all alike, and unhappy ones are unhappy each in their own way." This insight in **social psychology** is now called the *<u>Anna Karenina</u>* **principle** (AK principle). It is a central idea in **evo-devo foresight**, and a basic assumption of this *Guide*.

We believe that in **foresight practice**, there are **many unique ways to fail**, and only a **few reliably effective ways to succeed**. We will explore this insight in the context of **Evolutionary-Developmental ("Evo-Devo") Foresight**, a practice model we derive from **evo-devo biology**. In our take on evo-devo models, the central purpose of **evolutionary processes**, whether viewed in organisms, in organizations, or in societies, is to *experiment*, in **unpredictable** ways, to **fail often**, and ideally, to **learn** from failures. The central purpose of **developmental processes** is to *protect* the system, to **predictably advance** a complex system through **stages** in a **life cycle**, stages that have **proven successful** in past environments, and to ensure that system **replicates,** so that the **network of systems** has the best chance to **survive**.

Developmental processes are conservative and predictable, but can only **protect** and **maintain** past states of adaptiveness, they *cannot improve* those states. **Evolutionary** processes, by contrast, are needed to respond to **change**, and under selection, they can deliver even **greater adaptiveness**. But because no complex system can ever be omniscient (have full knowledge of the future), no matter how complex it becomes, most evolutionary experiments will not improve adaptiveness. In the future, there will always be **vastly more ways to fail**, each one unique in its own kind of failure state, than to **succeed**.

Because we believe in the AK principle, we will spend most of the pages in this *Guide* seeking to describe **universal (developmental) models** for what successful ("happy") foresight is, and how we can do it well. When we talk about foresight failures, we will try to focus on the **predictable** kinds of failure (bias, problematic roles, misapplication of frameworks), rather than the vastly greater topic of unpredictable failure types. Our primary emphasis, in other words, is will not be on **evolutionary variety** in foresight practice, much of which will be **maladaptive**, but rather on **developmental optima**, on models and practices that seem the most useful in the most contexts.

The models that we introduce in this opening chapter all appear to us to have particularly **universal value**. Let us know if you disagree. We believe these models offer the reader **a strong foundation** for evolutionary experiments in foresight process and practice. Most foresight experiments will predictably fall far short of our goals for them, each in their own unique ways. But we must remember that it is only by having the **courage to experiment** that we will improve our lot.

The Six Domains of Foresight Practice

Foresight work can be done at six easily-distinguished levels of increasing **scale** and **complexity**. We call these the **Six Domains of Foresight.** We will address all six in this *Guide,* as we seek a truly **comprehensive look** at our field.

The **Six Domains of Foresight Practice (STOSGU Domains)** are:

- **S**elf (Personal) foresight, improving our self-awareness and self-leadership;

- **T**eam foresight, improving our relationships, families, and small group navigation of the future;

- **O**rganizational foresight, improving our companies and institutions abilities to create the futures they desire;

- **S**ocietal foresight, improving each society's economic, political, and cultural capacity to create the futures they desire;

- **G**lobal foresight, improving the ability of all our planet's societies to cooperate, to ethically compete, and to sustain our environment; and

- **U**niversal foresight, which includes science, systems philosophy, complexity studies, and our best models for universal change.

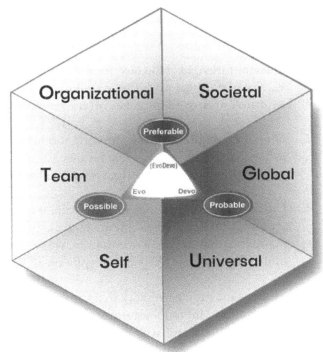

The Six Domains of Foresight Practice

We will see shortly that these domains map closely to the **Foresight Pyramid** (inset in the picture above), a **universal** way to understand how **intelligent systems** look to and navigate the future. In **evo-devo language**, we suspect that these six domains are not only **evolutionary creations**, found on Earth, but **developmental destinations**, meaning they are likely to exist on all planets with intelligent life in our universe. This makes the six domains a great simple way to describe the **scope and aims** of foresight work.

The first three of these six domains, **Self**, **Team**, and **Organizational foresight**, are the primary subjects of this book, *Introduction to Foresight*. The last three domains, **Societal**, **Global**, and **Universal foresight**, are the main subjects of Book 2, *Big Picture Foresight*. Let's say a bit more about each domain now.

1. **Self (Personal) foresight** is where good future thinking begins. To be effective, we must get better at anticipating, "*what-if*ing," and leading our own personal futures. **Better thinking and feeling**, as free from harmful cognitive and social biases and distortions as possible, is how we get to **better action**. We must learn to recognize **false or outdated thoughts and feelings**, and any **unconscious beliefs** that limit our potential to **see reality** and to be **responsible** to ourselves and others. The better we get at personal foresight, and at our own thinking and feeling, the better we can get at helping others to become their **best selves**.

2. **Team foresight** is the next important domain. It includes **relationships**, and all the various groups in which we participate, including **families, friends, and colleagues.** Our ethics and empathy, and our emotional intelligence really matter here. There is an emerging science of how to create and manage effective teams. Teams are often called humanity's top **"superpower"**. We would list teams second, after foresight itself. Working together, with trust and feedback, we can be much foresighted and impactful than we can alone.

3. **Organizational foresight** is the next important domain. To be adaptive, all organizations must build **effective teams** around an **organizational purpose**, use good **strategic foresight practices**, and ideally turn foresight into everyone's shared responsibility—building a **foresight culture**. We'll devote most of this book to this domain. In every context, on every timescale, organizations can be foresighted or not. Much depends on their past experience, priorities, processes, networks, and culture.

4. **Societal foresight** is the next important domain. Every society pursues its own preferred futures, with a rich variety of **political** priorities, **economic** models, and **cultural** values. As with organizations, societal diversity tends to improve adaptiveness of the network, but it may be positive or negative for individual societies.

5. **Global foresight** is the next important domain. It deals with transnational and planetary issues and trends. While it also includes possible futures, we will learn that it is weighted toward probable futures, toward processes and destinations that help us all to become **better stewards** of our planet.

6. **Universal foresight** is our final domain. It is about using **science** and **systems thinking** (aka, natural philosophy) to better see and manage the futures of complex systems at all scales. While it also includes possibility thinking, and uncertainty, we will see that the Universal domain is particularly helpful to understand what is likely to transpire on all Earthlike planets, due to the nature of physics and complexity.

While each of us may prefer to work in a subset of these domains, we should strive for **a basic competency in all six**, as all of them are important to long-term strategy. We call that **comprehensive, or "full-spectrum," foresight practice**. To lead ourselves and our teams well over the long term, we need good practice in all six domains.

The pioneering futurist **Bob Johansen**, in his latest book, *Full-Spectrum Thinking*, 2020, defines full-spectrum thinking as avoiding linear models and fixed categories. He says we need thinking that is sufficiently broad, diverse, and flexible to address our chaotic and unpredictable world. At the same time, Johansen also recognizes that some insights, values, and models are **so universal**, they have **value in every context**. The **Six Domains** are one such model. We can ground all of our future thinking in the analysis of these six categories of complex adaptive systems, in our view.

Gaining foresight in each of these domains requires taking increasingly complex, diverse, and expanded spatial and temporal perspectives on **change**. Considering the **Big Picture** consequences of our local and daily decisions has become more important in recent decades, as **societal complexity** and the **speed of change** have grown, and as the impacts of many forms of change (e.g., digitization, democratization, entrepreneurship, greenhouse gas pollution, pandemics) are increasingly **immediate** and **global** in scale.

Universal foresight is often the least appreciated of the six domains. Yet it is particularly useful for thinking about long-term processes in our environment, including **evolution**, **development**, **intelligence**, **adaptation**, and **accelerating change**. Starting with a better understanding of universal processes can often be the best way to ground our foresight work. We can frequently **"backcast"** from what we see at this largest scale of complexity and change, and ask what it implies for our societies, our organizations, our teams, and our personal lives. As we will propose, nowhere are the human implications of universal foresight more obvious and important than in the topic of **accelerating change.**

We are sometimes reminded by elders that life is not a spectator sport. We each only get **one life** to live, and if we want to live it well, we should think about the future in all the domains that matter to us. Each domain contributes to improving our **anticipation**, **creation**, and **leadership** of the future. Each makes a difference in our personal lives, in societies, and to humanity. Good foresight practice in each of these domains always relies on *some* experience and practice in each of the other remaining domains.

The best foresight practitioners discover which domains are their **weaker areas** then take **coaching from**, and **team up** with, others who are stronger in those domains. We can all use a team-oriented, **network-centric strategy** to deliver more comprehensive, balanced, and useful foresight than we can alone. Again, it is important to realize that people who are attracted to thinking in one or two of the six domains may not enjoy, or even be aware of, some of the others. If we have a **bias** or **weakness** in any of these domains, it makes sense to **take steps** to improve our abilities in them, and to build **partnerships** and **teams** that can strengthen our weaker areas. This *Guide* will do the best it can to help us all become more **comprehensive practitioners**, able to use and benefit from all six domains, as context demands.

Some questions to consider for yourself: Which of these **six domains** are your favorite? Do you appreciate the **value of each** in different contexts? Do you try to **improve** your weaker domains? How so? When do you notice yourself **mentally switching** from one domain to another in pursuit of greater foresight value? Do you **trust your intuition** about when to think **"big picture"** about a problem or issue and when to return to **personal, team, and organizational** thinking? How domain-comprehensive is your **network**? Do you have **mentors** or **advisors** in your weaker domains? How do you **help them** in return? How domain comprehensive is your **team**?

Futurists vs. Foresighters (Strategists): Which Are You?

There are two common types of foresight practitioners. The first is the **futurist**. Futurists are relatively well-known by the public, but a rarity in the workplace. The second is the **foresight professional**, or **foresighter**. Foresighter is a phrase coined in conversation by <u>Andy Hines</u> and <u>John Smart</u> in 2014. We were looking for a **single word** that describes not just those who **think and talk about the future**, but those who use **formal methods and frameworks** to do so. An alternative word for such folks is **strategist**, but it isn't quite right. Lots of folks do strategy, but most don't use formal methods of looking to the future **before** they create strategy. Less-known to the public, **foresighters are by far the main group of foresight practitioners**. The *Guide* seeks to help each of us become better futurists and foresighters alike. We all do a little of both in our lives, and both roles are needed, but the second is by far the most important to creating value.

A **futurist** is anyone who **speaks or writes publicly about the future of any topic**. We may only do this rarely, but if what we say has any impact, we may be called futurists by some, whether we want that label or not. The term futurist typically connotes a **qualitative, <u>story-driven</u> approach** to the future. It is commonly applied to people who are **generalists** in thinking and experience. Conversely, a minority of futurists are quantitative, evidence-based, and quite specialized in their storytelling.

To tell their stories well, futurists tend to rely on personal insights, intuition, narrative, and anecdotal experience. The better-known futurists usually spend a lot of time **consuming, producing, critiquing, and communicating future content**. As a rule, futurists tend to **enjoy** thinking about the future. That enjoyment is as useful a way to identify them as any other. Most futurists don't claim to **know the future**, but they do claim to **know many of the future stories being told** in their areas of specialization, and a **representative sample** of the data, trends, models, arguments, and issues referenced in those stories. The more successful futurists are also good at presenting those stories in an entertaining way.

A **foresight professional** (**foresighter**) is anyone who is **paid to do foresight work for others**, using a wide variety of specialty practices and methods we will discuss. Usually, this work is done in **specialized** industries, organizations, and contexts. We suggest that "**foresighter**" is the best single word for such individuals. We advocate its usage by all practitioners. By analogy, think of **officer, insurer, treasurer, manager, leader**, and other specialist and generalist words ending in **-er** that we use to describe any vital organizational function. Foresight is such a function.

The term **foresighter** connotes not only **specialty practice**, but a more balanced use of qualitative and quantitative approaches to foresight than the typical futurist. Foresighters tend to prefer **reason and evidence first** and **story and aspirational thinking second**, and they use **critique** and **formal methods** over argument or exposition. They are more apt to practice in just **one or a few industries**, and to have just one or a few clients, typically their **employer**. If their methods are academic and their forward view is longer-term, the foresighter might be called a "futurologist". If more quantitative and shorter-term, they might be called an "analyst". If more trend-based, a "forecaster". If more creative, a "designer." All of these and many other labels we will discuss are examples of foresight specialty practice.

Foresighters tend to **specialize** in **a small group of methods**, like scanning, risk analysis, scenarios, facilitation, forecasting, strategy, or planning. This can make them very effective for particular problems and contexts, but also makes it very important for them to work with **skills- and methods-diverse networks** and **teams**. Good teams can help them bring in outside expertise, and to take the wider view, prior to action, that they may personally discount or ignore.

Every one of us has occasionally inhabited the **futurist** role, often in discussions with friends and colleagues on some interesting topic. It is how many of us **first engage** with future thinking. Far more often however, we have all been **foresighters**, looking to and analyzing the future for others, in some specialized context or capacity. We would guess the **number of people formally engaged as foresighters** today is at least a **hundred thousand times larger** than the **number of futurists**. The financial value of foresighters work is surely greater by an even larger margin. **Professional foresight methods** are also far more diverse and specialized than **futures thinking methods**. Both roles are vital, and they overlap, but **professional foresight** serves a much more valuable and diverse set of societal needs than **futuring**.

In personality, most **futurists** are like <u>foxes</u>, broadly interested in and seeking to know a little about many different things. A few are like <u>hedgehogs</u>, knowing a lot about a few things. Most **foresighters**, by contrast, are **hedgehogs first**, and foxes secondarily, as their past experience and careers allow. For the original essay on these two personality types, see **Isaiah Berlin's** "<u>The Hedgehog and the Fox</u>" (1953). Whether we call ourselves futurists or foresighters, we

"**A fox knows many things...**

...but a hedgehog one important thing."

should strive to become "<u>T-shaped</u>" (aka "**shield-and-sword shaped**"), to use a term coined by <u>David Guest</u>. The **horizontal bar** of the T (our shield, or alternatively, the "hilt" of our sword) represents our "**foxlike**" qualities—that is, how broadly we **understand** relevant foresight methods and futures topics, and how well we **collaborate** in disciplines outside our own. The **vertical bar** of the T (the "blade" of our sword) represents our "**hedgehog-like**" qualities—namely, our **specialized abilities, credentials**, and **practice methods**. It is those hedgehog talents that we use to "cut" problems with, and typically create the greatest value for others.

Good leaders possess both kinds of qualities. They use shields and swords. After we've become T-shaped, with a serviceably broad, shield-like understanding of our organization and its environment, and one good cutting blade (a specialty we have mastered), we can strive to become "**star-shaped**," gaining additional expertise and credentials in **multiple specialties**. This can further improve our effectiveness, including in fertile **interdisciplinary areas** between specialties. One goal of long-term practice is to become <u>**polymaths**</u> (aka "Renaissance people"), gaining expertise in a large number of disciplines, industries, and foresight specialties. For anyone who is an <u>**autodidact**</u> (a person who enjoys self-directed learning), becoming a minor polymath is both an achievable and desirable goal.

In Chapter 2, we will introduce **Twenty Specialties** for foresight work in **strategic management.** Technically, these represent **forty specialties**, as **each is a pair of two specialties** that work well together in the organization. But, since each specialty pair is closely related, we call them **Twenty Specialties** for simplicity. Becoming skilled in **any one of these specialties** is a good entry to career foresight work on a team and in an organization. Gaining experience in several can further improve our value, credibility, and effectiveness as employees, managers and leaders.

As we learn our specialties, we must be careful not to **overspecialize**. As science fiction legend <u>**Robert Heinlein**</u> famously said, "[over]specialization is for insects." One lesson of humankind's astonishing progress is that *general* **intelligence affords us with** *general* **adaptiveness**. Humanity has developed a particularly general intelligence over time, one that helps us thrive in the widest range of environments, under diverse challenges. In our competitive world, we all must learn **specialties** to pay our bills. But both futurism and professional foresight also require **general knowledge across the six domains**, and a cognitively-, skills-, and experience-diverse

One view of a Star-Shaped Individual

network of clients and colleagues who can collaborate and compete with us to solve problems, and offer critical feedback to the foresight we produce.

Again, all of us inhabit these two roles at times, that of **futurist** (future thinker, visionary, storyteller, provocateur) and **foresighter** (specialist, researcher, strategist, consultant). Being effective in either role requires developing **insight** into client problems, practicing good **ethics** and **empathy**, learning their worldview and languages, gaining trust, and demonstrating value. But, the far larger numbers, the narrower and more evidence-based focus, and the typically less grandiose titles of **foresighters** tend to make them more trusted and successful than **futurists** in business environments.

Because the term futurist is used to describe **anyone** who tells stories about the future, it is often snickered over in boardrooms and organizations, where practicality dominates. Our futurist community includes <u>**imaginative futurists**</u>, whose future tales are entertaining but not always evidence-based, <u>**utopian**</u> and <u>**dystopian**</u> **futurists**, who offer visions that can inspire or scare us but have little or no probability of occurring, and <u>**preconventional futurists**</u>, dreamers and eccentrics who cheerfully pursue personal visions outside the norms and conventions of society. The last label comes from futurist **Peter Hayward**, director of the late Swinburne U. MS. in Strategic Foresight. As Hayward says, these folks will always be with us, and are socially important; but, they **limit the organizational impact** of the **futurist community**.

What's more, because leaders know it is one of their jobs to provide **vision** for the organization, futurists who discuss strategy, if their language is too **prescriptive or predictive**, can be seen as **competing with management** at the power and resource allocation game. Organizational futures are **political**. The most effective futurists and foresighters do not ignore these topics, but they learn how to discuss them with **empathy and tact**.

Future stories can have great value, particularly in influencing and entertaining, but they can also narrow and distract our thinking. They just **one tool** in the leader's toolkit. Sometimes, one clarifying bit of **critical data**, one good **model**, or one **causal inference** can be **worth a thousand stories** to a group that needs better **strategy**, or to a leader who needs a better **vision**. That is why, when we speak as futurists, we must strive to be **evidence-based**, both quantitative and qualitative, to tie our stories to **strategic implications**, **choices**, and **actions**, to offer examples of **SMART goals** (Specific, Measurable, Achievable, Relevant, Time-bound) suggested by our stories, and to refrain from being **too political**.

"Futurist" is a term best kept to a minimum in business environments.

So for **public speakers**, authors, or anyone else who enjoys telling future stories, the word "**futurist**" will be used by some to describe us, whether we like it or not. But in our organizational roles, as **foresight professionals,** it is usually far better to have a less controversial and more recognized job title than that of futurist. Titles like **strategist, forecaster, designer, analyst, trend researcher, technology scout, risk manager, planner, intelligence analyst, innovation manager, investment manager, evangelist, community manager**, and many others can work well. Thus most foresighters perform their foresight work without a self-description that makes their practice too obvious. Adopting a **lower profile** in foresight work can be a **career advantage**, especially in **personality-driven, change-averse, high-stakes, or troubled organizations**, where the **official future** is often a **highly contested** topic.

Those willing to raise their visibility, and help their organization, become more conscious in its foresight work, while sidestepping the issues with the word "futurist", should consider using the word "**foresight**" in their formal title. As the term is both multifaceted and less known, it can be **shaped** more easily to our interests than many others. For tips on the benefits of being in the **"white space"** (areas without competition) in the environment, see **Kim and Mauborgne**, *Blue Ocean Strategy*, 2015. The disadvantage of the foresight term, on the other hand, is that it requires **more education** of our audience to understand what it is that we do. Fortunately, books like this one can help with that education.

A general definition of a **foresight career** might be any **position, occupation, or role** that intentionally and methodically **engages and analyzes the future for a client** and that **impacts strategies, and often its antecedents and dependents,** as a part of its **function**. Ideally, this future analysis responsibility will be **explicitly stated** in our job description. Helping the world's **foresighters** to recognize who they are, and to learn how they can improve, is the primary goal of this *Guide*.

Analyzing Change: The Time Pyramid (Past, Future, Present)

Cognitive science tells us that all intelligent life uses **three time perspectives** to adapt to its environment:

- The **Past ("Before")**, aka <u>Hindsight</u>:
  History, experience, data, trends, practices, hypotheses, models

- The **Present ("Now")**, aka <u>Insight</u>:
  Introspection or self-awareness and understanding; and, extrospection or social- and situational-awareness and understanding

- The **Future ("Next")**, aka <u>Foresight</u>:
  Today's, short-term, medium-term, and long-term (we'll define these four time periods shortly) probabilities, possibilities, preferences, and preventable futures

The figure below is known as the **Foresight Hourglass**. It reminds us that the Past has **converged** on the Present, and that the Future is always **diverging out** in an expanding set of possibilities. Yet when we look deeper, we learn that the hourglass is an oversimplification. In reality, the Past has both **converged on the Present**, via developmental processes, and it has **diverged into many Presents**, via evolutionary processes. Similarly, evo-devo models tell us that the Future will always be a mix of **evolutionary divergence** and **developmental convergence.** In other words, both **"futures"** and **"future"** simultaneously coexist.

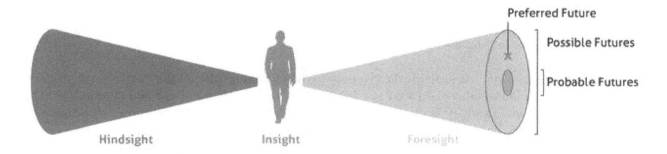

The Foresight Hourglass. (Foresight NZ, McGuiness Institute)

The hourglass reminds us we use three time orientations: our **hindsight** (knowledge of the past), **insight** (awareness of the present reality), and **foresight** (our ability to anticipate, create, and improve the future) to adapt. Note that the last of these three orientations, **foresight**, unlike the others, requires us to practice *both of the other two well*. That makes it the **hardest** of the three. But, foresight also offers us the greatest **reward**: a clearer and more adaptive **vision** of what may come, and **strategy** for what we may **do next** with our lives. Again, because foresight is so **potentially valuable**, our brains are **organized to constantly look ahead**, mostly at the unconscious and immediate level. Making our foresight more conscious and longer-term, and balancing it with past and present thinking, are keys to being more adaptive.

The graphic at right, from <u>MindTime.com</u>, gives **adjectives** that commonly associate with each of these time orientations. We **bounce rapidly** between all three orientations on this pyramid during the day, yet most of us tend to **favor** one or two orientations more, on average. When practiced well, our **preferred time orientations** can give us certain **advantages**:

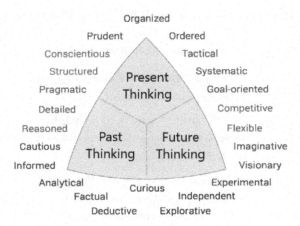

- **Past-oriented thinkers** can excel at seeing what has **worked so far**.

- **Present-oriented thinkers** can excel at **getting things done**.

- **Future-thinkers** can excel at seeing what **needs to get done**.

A free online <u>18-question test</u> at **MindTime** will assess our preferences for the orientations above. The **center of these graphics** is 33/33/33%. The "**You**" depicted in graphic at right (in this case, John) tends to be a **Future>Past>Present thinker** (roughly 40% Future, 35% Past, 25% Present in his **thinking frequency**, on average, estimated by deviation from the center). The **hierarchy** implicitly depicted in this graphic conveys a key insight. The **Present** is the *most socially important* of these three time orientations. It belongs where it is depicted, at the **top of our time pyramid.** In all adaptive systems (people, teams, firms, societies), our **Past** thinking (memory) and **Future** thinking (foresight) must be kept *in service* **to our Present thinking**, to be adaptive.

We can easily forget this insight. As individuals, it is easy to **dwell unhelpfully on the Past**, or to **daydream about the Future**. The pyramid reminds us that good **Past** and **Future** thinking is **both organized and kept useful** to the **Present**, the realm of **action**. As leaders and self-leaders, we must learn the **value and traps** of each arm of the Time Pyramid, and be able to help our teams **move between time orientations** as needed, just as we must help them move between **sentiments** (to be discussed). We must also see and manage **conflicts** between our **preferred time orientations** and **jobs**.

When we are not using our past, present, and future thinking preferences as well as we could, we may need to **change our thinking** (hard) or **change our job descriptions, teams, or routines** (easier) to be more adaptive. Think now about your own temporal thinking preferences: Where do **you** tend to live on this pyramid? What about your **team**? How would you **rank** your temporal preferences? Do you tend to think most about the **Past**? The **Present**? The **Future**? In what **contexts**? Recognizing your **temporal strengths and weaknesses** can help you realize what you need to do to become a more effective thinker and strategizer.

As one might expect, the three time orientations are implicit in several useful team and workplace assessments. One is **Deloitte's Business Chemistry** workplace styles assessment (picture below). Another is the **Keirsey Temperament Styles** (discussed later, in our section on The Four Ps). Both are based on psychology and neuroscience models. Deloitte independently discovered the time pyramid in its data. **Guardians, Drivers**, and **Pioneers** are their past-, present-, and future-oriented workplace styles. They also found a "**blended**" **style** of working, **Integrators**, folks who like to promote collaboration and interdependence among the three more **time-differentiated** working styles. Many individuals prefer just **one or two** of these working styles.

Given their particular value for increasing group performance, and their competitive nature, **Drivers** are often the **HIPPOs**, the **HIghest Paid Persons in the Organization.** We find them at the **top of the pyramid** in many corporate organization charts. Business Chemistry has been used with 200K individuals since 2010. Here is a free online 20-question test for self-diagnosing your and your team's use of these styles. **Christfort** and **Vickberg's** *Business Chemistry: Creating Powerful Work Relationships*, 2018, explores the styles, and offers advice for collaboration among them.

Which of these four workplace styles best describes **you**? In what contexts? Can you recognize **organizational contexts** where **relative strength** in any of these styles is critical to doing **good work**? Can you **delegate** problems to those who are better at a particular style than you? Can you **perform with average competence** with each of these styles, when needed?

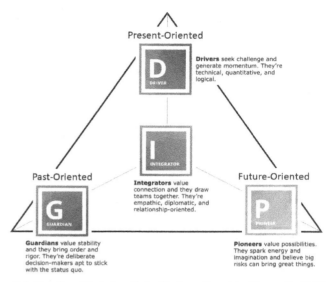

Deloitte's Four Workplace Styles (Business Chemistry Diagnostic, 2010)

What routines, recruitment strategies, or relationships will help your **team** be competent in all of these styles?

Integrating Foresight and Action: The Do Loop (LFAR Loop)

Cognitive science tells us that we adapt to our environment using a **"perception-action (PA)" cycle**. **Management theory** calls it a **decision cycle**. This cycle has **four discrete steps**: Perceive, Decide, Act, and get **Feedback** (PDAF). Saying these steps using **management terms**, the **key steps** we all take, to dynamically adapt, are **Learning, Foresight, Action,** and **Reviewing (LFAR)**. Thus we call this **foresight-action cycle** the **LFAR loop**, or the "**Do Loop**" for short.

The **Do loop** is the **most universal model we know** for how human beings integrate **foresight** and **action** to create **adaptive outcomes**. It is the foundational model of this *Guide*. As we will see, we all use this loop both **unconsciously and consciously** every day, in a great variety of activities. Every time we **complete** a Do loop with good **feedback** (the **Review** step), and begin again, we have a chance to grow our **competency** in a particular **activity**. Being an **adaptive manager and leader** depends on how well and frequently we and our teams use this loop.

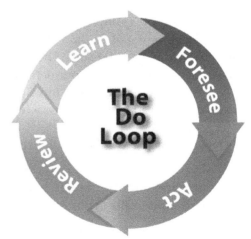

The Universal Foresight-Action Cycle (LFAR Loop, Do Loop) (Foresight University, 2015)

In Chapter 2, we will split the middle two of the LFAR steps, **Foresight** and **Action**, into three skills each. Using the **Foresight Pyramid** (to be discussed shortly), we will split **Foresight** into three key skills: **Anticipation, Innovation,** and **Strategy.** Using the work of Gallup, a management consultancy, we will also split **Action** into three key skills: **Execution, Influence,** and **Relating.** Together with **Learning** and **Reviewing,** this gives **Eight Skills** that we propose **all organizations must master** to continually integrate **foresight and action**, and successfully **adapt**.

Below are the **Four Steps** of the **LFAR loop** in graphic form:

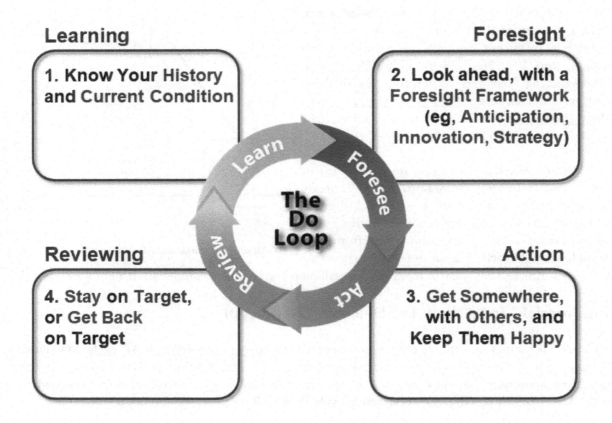

The **Four Steps** are a **simpler** foresight-action framework (by half) than the **Eight Skills**. Both describe the **Do loop**, in different levels of **detail**. In our experience, the **Four Steps** are the right level of detail for most foresight thinking done by **individuals** and **small teams. The LFAR steps** are easily remembered. By focusing on **cycling through the Four Steps** well, we can greatly improve our personal and team outcomes. The **Eight Skills**, by contrast, are an excellent model for **larger team and organizational foresight**. Which model you use should depend on the **results you get from each**, as measured in your **Review** step. Use a **level of complexity** that works best for your **context**.

Let's look now at each of the **LFAR steps,** and their associated **skills** (core competencies):

- **Learning** involves understanding the **past and the present**, to better see the future. Learning is technically **preparation for foresight**, but it is *so critical* to foresight production that we call learning one of **Four Essential Foresight Skills** in our model.

- **Foresight** involves the use of data, models, and a variety of **frameworks** to look ahead. The simplest foresight framework we find useful is the classic **Foresight Pyramid** (soon to be discussed). That pyramid gives us **three "core" foresight skills: Anticipation, Innovation,** and **Strategy**. Together with **Learning**, these are the four essential foresight skills.

- **Action** on teams requires three distinct skills, **Execution, Influence,** and **Relating** (keeping teams strong). Research by **Gallup** proposes that these are the three core **Action skills,** both in the **workplace** and in **life**.

- **Reviewing** (aka "after action review") involves collecting and interpreting the **results** of our actions. Technically, reviewing is not action, but it can greatly **improve our actions** in the next cycle. As with learning and foresight, reviewing is *so critical* to adaptive action that we group it with the three core action skills, giving **Four Essential Action Skills** in our model.

One key to using the **Do loop** well is to recognize that each of the four **LFAR steps** is best done to **improve the next step.** We **Learn** (past and present) to improve our **Foresight.** We foresee in order to better **Act.** We **Review** to find out what has improved, by how much, what hasn't, and what new **learning** might help us in the next turn of the loop. In practice, this isn't as easy as it sounds. Both we and our teams can **easily skip, reverse, or misuse any of these steps.**

Perhaps the most commonly skipped of the four steps is **Reviewing.** Gaining frequent, high-quality **feedback** is often key to improving. Good feedback includes **criticism** as well as **praise**, and many of us will postpone or avoid negative feedback. It helps to remember that the discomforts of **review** can **motivate us** to improve **learning, foresight**, and **action.** Both pleasure and pain, when they are learned from, are powerful aids to adaptiveness. Without good foresight and review, it is easy to confuse **effort** (action) with **effectiveness**. Many of us can point to **learning** we have recently done. But if our learning is not *in service* to better **foresight**, it is often simply entertainment, procrastination, or a waste of time.

To deepen our understanding of the **universality** of the **Four Steps of the Do Loop,** consider the following LFAR loops, selected from a great variety of behaviors, problem domains, and systems. In each of these examples, we can identify a universal **foresight-action loop**. The **step names** given below are different in each case, but the **loop itself** is universal. All of the loops below have been represented by us as four steps, though some original models may depict five or more steps. We will explore a number of these loops in greater depth in coming chapters:

- **Rao and Ballard's** <u>Predictive Processing Loop</u>.[1] (Update=Learn, Predict=Foresee, Sense=Act, Compare=Review). A very rapid (milliseconds) foresight-action cycle. This cycle determines how mammalian brains **see and think, mostly unconsciously.** It is also central to the design of **deep machine learning**.

- **John Boyd's** <u>OODA Loop</u> (Orient=Learn; Decide=Foresee; Act=Do; Observe=Review).[2] A rapid (seconds to minutes), **partly conscious** foresight-action cycle that is key to **competitive dominance** in a **threat environment**.

- **David Allen's** <u>Workflow Management Loop</u> (Collect & Process=Learn, Organize=Foresee, Act, Review) in **workflow** (information, task, time) **management**. Very helpful for **daily** task management.

- **David Kolb's** <u>Action (Experiential) Learning Loop</u> (Model=Learn, Plan an Experiment=Foresee, Experience=Act, Reflect=Review).[3] A very evidence-based model of how human **learning** actually occurs.

- **Clear and Duhigg's** <u>Habit Formation/Breaking Loop</u>[4,5] (Environmental Cue=Learn, Craving=Foresee, Response=Act, Reward=Review). A key model in habit formation and habit extinction in **behavior change**.

THE HABIT LOOP

(Clear, 2018)

- **Eric Ericsson's** <u>Deliberate Practice Loop</u> (Assess Weaknesses=Learn, Plan Targeted Practice=Foresee, Practice & Fail=Act, Review mistakes=Review).[2] An evidence-based model for how **peak performance** is achieved.

- **Eric Ries's** <u>Lean Startup Loop</u> (Learn, Envision, Build, Measure=Review) in **entrepreneurship**.[6] Also a key model for continual **business model innovation**.

- **Herbert Simon's** <u>Design Loop</u> (Define & Research=Learn; Ideate, Prototype & Choose=Foresee; Implement=Act, Learn=Review) in **innovation**.[7] Particularly useful for personal and team-based **design** and **prototyping**.

[1] Rao and Ballard, <u>Predictive coding in the visual cortex</u>, *Nature Neurosci* 2:79-87
[2] Daniel Ford, *A Vision So Noble: John Boyd, the OODA Loop, and America's War on Terror*, 2010.
[3] David Kolb, *Experiential Learning, 2nd Ed* (*1st Ed.* PDF), 2014.
[4] James Clear, *Atomic Habits: How to Build Good Habits and Break Bad Ones*, 2018.
[5] Charles Duhigg, *The Power of Habit*, 2014.
[6] Dennis Mathaisel, *Sustaining the Military Enterprise: Architecture for a Lean Transformation*, 2007.
[7] Liedtka et al., *Solving Problems with Design Thinking, Ten Stories of What Works*, 2013.

- **Kent Beck's** <u>Agile Development Loop</u> (Discover, Design, Develop, Test) in **engineering**, using processes like **scrum, Kanban, and lean production**.[8]

- **Edwards Deming's** <u>Quality Loop</u> (Observe=Learn; Plan=Foresee, Do=Act, Check & Adjust=Review) in **quality assurance**.[9] This loop helps us assess and manage the **quality** of products, services, and processes.

- The <u>**Scientific Method Loop**</u> (Observe=Learn, Hypothesis and Prediction=Foresee, Experiment=Act, Results=Review). This loop is how we get **closer to truth**.[10]

We'll say more about several of these loops in later chapters. For now, just consider the broad value of the LFAR steps, and notice that any of these loops can be run **faster** or **slower** depending on context. In some contexts, as with the **Predictive Processing loop** (unconscious thinking), the **OODA loop**, or the **Lean Startup loop**, we typically run our Do Loops very quickly. In an **Experiential Learning** loop, by contrast, we may want to run our loops more slowly at first, in a guided process of learning, practice, and review, to achieve **peak performance**. With **Quality loops**, when working in complex, expensive, or high-reliability contexts, we may run our Do Loops at the pace of days, weeks or even months for each step. But in all cases, as Boyd would say, we must keep our loops running **faster than relevant environmental change**, including our **competitors**, or we will become the **disrupted**, rather than being disruptors ourselves.

One key to professionalizing the foresight field is finding **better definitions** of what **foresight** work actually is, how it relates to action, and who engages in it. This is an exciting time for foresight practice, as our professional organizations are all searching for new and more inclusive definitions of our field. Our field must recognize all the parts of itself as it grows up, so we can better share and compare models and methods, and improve collaborative work on foresight problems. The **Do loop** is another model that **grounds our field**, in our view. We think the four steps of the Do loop are a **"minimum viable set"** of activities that improve **adaptiveness**. By assessing their use, we can immediately begin to diagnose **process deficiencies** in any team or organization, and get quick strategies for improvement.

Horizons of the Do Loop: The Power Law of Future Thinking

Do loops can be usefully divided into a minimum of **four time horizons**. As we'll see, the cycles of **learning, foresight, action, and review** that occur within each of these time horizons are often **qualitatively different** from the others.

4U's Four Horizons of Foresight are:

1. **Today's Foresight**   ("Present": **Now** to **End-of-Day**)
2. **Short-term Foresight**   (Next "T's": **Tomorrow** to **Three months**)
3. **Mid-term Foresight**   (Next "4's": Next **Quarter** to next **Four years**)
4. **Long-term Foresight**   (**>4 years,** decade, lifespan, future generations)

We have said that we are *Homo prospectus*, a **future-oriented** species. The **Predictive Processing model of mind** tells us we are constantly looking ahead. But as psychologist **Benjamin Libet** explains in *Mind Time*, 2005, the **catch** is that the **great majority** of our future thinking runs just **milliseconds to minutes** ahead of **now**, and is largely **unconscious**. In other words, all of us **mainly** think in **today's foresight**, mostly **unconsciously**. This first Do loop horizon is where we have the greatest number of **successes or failures** in foresight **practice**. This is a powerful insight. It tells us that improving our **quality of vision** over the next few minutes, hours, and days, in many turns of the Do loop, is typically our **best strategy** to generate **consistent and high-quality long-term vision**.

---

[8] Stellman and Greene, *Head First Agile: Principles, Ideas, and Real-World Practices*, 2017.
[9] W. Edwards Deming, *Out of the Crisis: The 14 Points for Future Management*, 1982.
[10] Henry Cowles, *The Scientific Method: An Evolution of Thinking from Darwin to Dewey*, 2020.

We call this insight the **Power Law of Future Thinking**. It is a key idea in the **psychology of foresight**. In most contexts,
for a variety of reasons, we are built to think **exponentially less frequently** (technically, *power law* less frequently) about events further ahead in time. One implication of the power law is that getting better at **today's foresight** is typically our best strategy for **general improvement** in foresight process. As we will learn, generally the most efficient way to improve the **short-term and mid-term foresight** that is **most valuable for our careers**, is to prioritize improving awareness, control, and ownership of **today's foresight**, which runs from **now** till our next **loss of consciousness**. This insight is often forgotten, especially by those who prefer looking to the **long-term**.

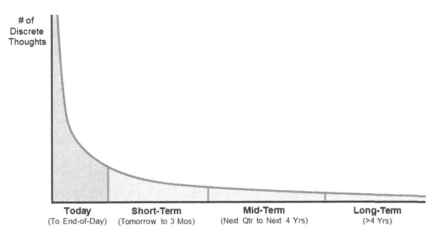

The Power Law of Future Thinking (55:25:15:5)

# of Discrete Thoughts

| Today (To End-of-Day) | Short-Term (Tomorrow to 3 Mos) | Mid-Term (Next Qtr to Next 4 Yrs) | Long-Term (>4 Yrs) |

Most future thinking is <24 hrs, and unconscious[1]

1. Benjamin Libet, *Mind Time: The Temporal Factor in Consciousness*, 2005.

People who excel at **today's foresight** are more **"Presentists"** than **"Futurists."** They practice being aware of and acting in their current surroundings, at thinking from **"now to next."** Whenever we use process tools like **daily reminders**, **priority lists, task lists, schedules, and plans**, we are *previsualizing* our day. When we make such tools **simple enough** to **use and review several times a day**, we are continually **"closing our loops"**, and getting helpful **feedback** on our actions. This lets us strengthen our **foresight habits** and build **key skills**.

As foresight professionals, the challenge that yields the **greatest benefits** for ourselves and our clients, is to become **conscious directors of our daily schedules and priorities**, and **detail-oriented managers of our emotions, thoughts, actions, time and energy** from **now to day's-end**. When we practice **today's foresight**, our hourly and daily **Do Loop** cycles are **far faster** than in the other horizons. We can **improve** accuracy, priorities, and capacity **far more quickly**, learning from **today's mistakes**. Most of the lessons and habits we learn in today's foresight are directly applicable to **tomorrow's** foresight as well. Practicing **short-term foresight** in turn will improve our medium and long-term foresight work. Stepping our way **down this curve**, stretching out our horizons **only as necessary**, is a key recipe for adaptiveness.

There is an adage that to get something done well and fast--the **Execution** skill—we should give it to a **busy person**. Likewise, if you want your mid-term and long-term foresight work done well and fast, give it to someone already good at **today's and short-term foresight and action**. If they aren't a long-term thinker themselves, such a person will **prioritize learning** who they need to bring in to help them **get it done**. A classic long-term thinker, unless aided by a good short-term thinker, may never get the job done. See Appendix 1, and the Student Edition of *ITF*, for more on these topics.

Managing Change: The Evo-Devo Pyramid

Cognitive science tells us the Do Loop is a fundamental way that we **manage change**, as a **cycle**. A philosophy of complexity called **evo-devo biology** gives us a second fundamental way that intelligent creatures **manage change**. That way is not a cycle, but a **pyramid**. **Both models seem equally fundamental**, in our view. Both should be understood by any leader or student seeking greater adaptiveness. The pyramid involves an interaction and conflict between **two fundamental processes** (the base of the pyramid) which together *create* a **third, emergent process**. We place that third process at the **top of the pyramid**, in a **complexity hierarchy**, and we tend to **value it the most in society**. Let's look now at three particularly useful applications of this evo-devo pyramid. We'll explore several more throughout this *Guide*.

1. Thinking Ahead: The Foresight Pyramid (Probable, Possible, Preferable)

Perhaps the first **universal model of foresight** was introduced by **Alvin Toffler** in 1970. Toffler is one of the best known and most influential futurists of the twentieth century. In his bestseller *Future Shock*, 1970, he helped us consider the psychological and societal effects of **accelerating change**. Technological, economic, and societal acceleration is a topic that a handful of authors have discussed since the late 1800s. Toffler's exposition was timely, coming after a decade of social turmoil and anxiety in America. He described the **curious acceleration of change** throughout human history, and highlighted the need for greater **foresight** to understand the nature and meaning of this acceleration, and to inform our **moral choices** in technology use.

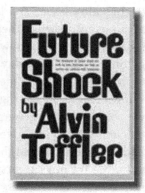

Toffler, 1970

In 2003, John started a small nonprofit, the <u>Acceleration Studies Foundation (ASF)</u>, to advocate for better study and management of global processes of accelerating change. We seek to understand accelerating change both from Toffler's view, looking back over human history, and from the astronomer **Carl Sagan's** perspective, as an apparently **universal process**, driven by still poorly understood physical and informational laws. Sagan popularized the phenomenon of universal accelerating change in his metaphor of the <u>Cosmic Calendar</u>, first in a prescient book, *Dragons of Eden*, 1977, and then in his acclaimed television series *Cosmos*, 1980. We'll return to the Cosmic Calendar at the end of this chapter. We argue it is a depiction of **complexity's** *evolutionary development*, in which the growth of adaptive physical and informational structure and function **occurs increasingly** *fast* **in increasingly** *local* **places in our universe**, ever since the emergence of the first galaxies. Later in this book, and at length in Book 2, we will propose **two key drivers of accelerating change** in human history, **densification** and **dematerialization ("D&D")**. We predict these D&D processes are universal, and thus constrain the nature of the future on all Earthlike planets in our universe.

Toward the end of *Future Shock*, Toffler proposed that foresight thinking can be divided into **three key types**. He also said that this division would help us to **professionalize** our field. Here is his original passage, with our bolding added:

> Every society faces not merely a succession of **probable** futures, but an array of **possible** futures, and a conflict over **preferable** futures. ... Determining the **probable** calls for a **science** of futurism. Delineating the **possible** calls for an **art** of futurism. Defining the **preferable** calls for a **politics** of futurism. The worldwide futurist movement today does not yet differentiate clearly among these functions. (p. 407, First Edition)

Toffler's proposal was seconded a decade later by **Roy Amara**, a leading foresight practitioner and president of the <u>Institute for the Future (IFTF)</u>, one of the first "think tanks" in the strategic foresight and futures studies field, established in 1968. In 1981, in an article in *The Futurist*, the magazine of the World Future Society, titled <u>"The futures field: searching for definitions and boundaries,"</u> Amara argued the primacy of these three approaches, the **probable**, the **possible**, and the **preferable**. Soon after, practitioners began calling this the **"Three Ps" Foresight Model**.

As we will now see, this model has very strong foundations. It represents both basic features of our **physical universe** and of **intelligence in living systems.** Science tells us that one set of universal laws and processes create **convergent, probable futures.** For example, think of **classical physics**, discovered by <u>Isaac Newton</u> in 1687. We know that another, separate set of laws and processes generate **divergent, possible futures**. Think of **quantum physics**, discovered in the 1930s. We also know that these **two opposing processes somehow worked together**, over universal history, to create **life,** a third and very special **complex adaptive system**, which alone has **sentiments** (positive and negative) and **preferences.** All life is **dependent** on these three universal processes. Even the simplest bacterium is kept alive by genes and evolved structures that generate **unpredictable** thoughts ("free will") and behavior, by genes and structures that **predict** (build a world model), and by genes and structures that express **elemental sentiments** (attraction and avoidance behaviors). A graphic representation of this **Classic Foresight Pyramid** is presented below:

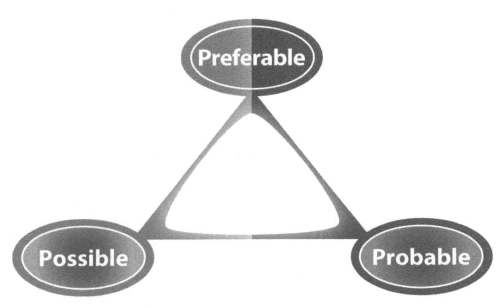

The Classic Foresight Pyramid

The **Classic Foresight Pyramid** tells us that although there are **three universal processes** relating to the future, **two of these are foundational**, and **the third (life, sentience)** is an **emergent and more valuable mix** of the first two. In universal history, the physics of the probable and of the possible, of the statistically **predictable** and the **unpredictable**, both operated **long before** life and its preferences arose. That gives us two reasons to understand preferences as the "top of the pyramid." First, life and its preferences emerged as a special mix of these two older and more fundamental physical processes. Second, **life, of all kinds,** is what we **care most** about. It is at the **top of our values hierarchy**, as it should be.

This pyramid is an application of **evo-devo foresight**, a prescientific model of **how complex systems adapt** that we use throughout this *Guide*. The pyramid reminds us that all living systems are driven by a **mix** of two truly fundamental types of change—the predictable and the unpredictable. It tells us that the three most important kinds of foresight thinking are to conceptualize **what will happen (the probable)**, **what can happen (the possible)**, and **what should happen (the preferable)**, in order to better adapt.

Here is the **Classic Foresight Pyramid** again in list form:

- **Probable Futures** (constraint-generating, uniformity-generating, predictable, secure, expected, familiar)
- **Possible Futures** (freedom-generating, variety-generating, unpredictable, creative, alternative, novel)
- **Preferable Futures** (individually or group-preferred values, goals and agendas for the future)

We will offer an improvement on this model, the **Modern Foresight Pyramid**, with a fourth kind of future, **negative sentiment,** a bit later. But first, let's look closer at each of these three kinds of futures, to better understand them:

The Probable. The first foresight type is the **probable**—this is the future that *will likely* happen tomorrow, whether we want it to or not. It can also be the **expected future,** but only when our expectations (and preferences) are good models of reality. Frequently they are not. If a future is going to happen independent of our desires, philosophers call this "**necessity**". The probable future is dominated by **convergent physical processes and convergent thinking**. Probability and predictive thinking is **striving** to find truth, and optima, and it **aspires** to eventually become a **computable science**, even though this kind of thinking does not always begin with good data or scientific rigor. Though it can be hard to do, this is the kind of foresight we recommend **starting with** when dealing with any problem, as it helps us to find potentially relevant **laws, limits, constraints, trends, and boundaries** acting to converge us toward a particular set of futures.

For examples of predictable, convergent, universality-generating processes, again think of <u>classical physics</u>, or the laws of <u>thermodynamics</u>. We can think also of <u>biological development</u>, <u>psychological development</u>, predicable aspects of <u>economic development</u>, <u>technological development</u>, and social and political development, including any values, goals, agendas, behaviors, and laws that appear to be <u>cultural universals</u>—like the statistically increasing preference for **democracy over autocracy** over the last several hundred years of <u>human development</u>. Any **historical curves, cycles, or trends** in **demographics, politics, economics, technology,** and any **probable future relationships** in an industry or firm's **cooperative and competitive environment** are all aspects of this fundamental foresight type.

The Possible. The second foresight type is the **possible**—also often called **alternative futures**. This is the set of things we think *could* happen tomorrow, or what philosophers call "**chance**." It is dominated by **divergent and locally unique physical processes and thinking.** <u>Quantum physics</u>, a process that is partly <u>indeterministic</u> and characterized by irreducible <u>uncertainty</u>, is one fundamental model of unpredictable, divergent, variety-generating universal processes. So is <u>chaos</u>, which applies to only **some** physical processes and systems, at **some** scales of space and time. The most complex example on Earth is the contingent, divergent and unpredictable branching we see in <u>biological evolution</u> and its "<u>tree of life</u>". A key example, in psychology, is the unpredictability of our individual **free will** and **imagination**. At the planetary level, imagine any of the vast number of environmental changes that we cannot predict in advance.

For organizational examples, think of any **choice** we might make, or **activity** we might do, that leads us into a future that is an **evolutionary experiment.** Exploring possible paths, or reacting to any local event, will always unpredictably change **some aspects** of our strategy, plans, or actions. Possible futures are the realm of **contingency, creativity, imagination, diversity, risk-taking**, and **experiment**. Artists, designers, experimenters, risk-takers, and entrepreneurs usually don't seek first to *know* **the future** (pursuing what we call a **developmental priority**). Instead, they strive to *create* **a future** (pursuing an **evolutionary priority**). Both, in our view, are equally fundamental and admirable goals.

The Preferable. The third foresight type is what we or our organizations **want**. We all generate preferences as **intelligent beings**. Activities like **visioning, goalsetting, strategy, and planning** are key aspects of **preference** foresight. In preferences, we seek to enlarge the **good** and minimize the **bad**. Even the simplest organisms are motivated by both **pleasure** and **pain**. Our *adaptive* **preferences** are a subset of our preferred visions, goals, values, and strategies. They are the ones that help us both to **survive and thrive**, in our cooperative and competitive environments.

As Toffler reminds us, all **preference** foresight is also **normative** (value-based) and **political**. Preferable futures are a subset of the probable and possible that we think will generate the **best outcomes** based on our particular **goals** and **values**. We'll offer a tentative model of some **universally adaptive goals and values** later. Figuring out how to **prioritize** and **balance** our goals, values, and visions via our strategies and actions is rarely obvious, however. There is always a tension between seeking what is **best for us, best for our group, or best for all** (<u>utilitarianism</u>).

Now for a little **preview**. In Chapter 3 we will consider the Three Ps as one version of a universal complexity model, the **Evo-Devo Pyramid**. We will see many different versions of this pyramid in Table 1 in that chapter. We propose that evo-devo models offer the most powerful way to understand adaptiveness in foresight work. We will see that each corner of this pyramid represents a different set of **universal actors, functions,** and **goals** that leaders must recognize and balance. These are summarized in the graphic below:

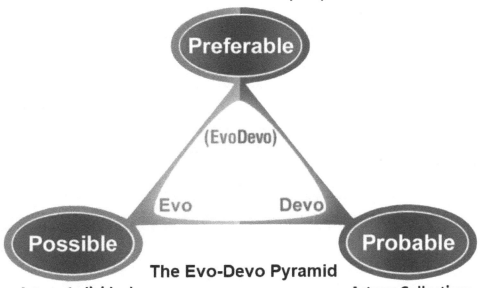

Actors: Adaptive Networks
Functions: Interdependence, Synchrony
Goals: Ethics and Empathy

Preferable

(EvoDevo)

Evo   Devo

Possible   Probable

The Evo-Devo Pyramid

Actors: Individuals
Functions: Diversification, Exploration
Goals: Innovation, Intelligence

Actors: Collectives
Functions: Optimality, Discovery
Goals: Strength, Sustainability

We call this the **Actor-Function-Goal version** of the **Evo-Devo Pyramid**. We propose that each of these **actor, function, and goal sets** are at the center of all **self-sustaining complex adaptive systems**. We will see that **individuals** (discreteness), **groups** (collectiveness), and **networks** (interdependence, integration) help complex systems to adapt at all scales. In Book 2, we'll also learn that *any* collection of physical systems capable of **Variation, Convergence, Replication, Inheritance, and Selection**, the VCRIS Evo-devo Model, whether it be replicating suns in a galaxy, replicating organisms in an ecology, replicating ideas ("memes") in human brains, replicating organizational systems in culture, or replicating technologies in society, can be understood as a **complex adaptive system**.

Again, this cartoon reminds us that **networks of complex systems** are particularly important. They belong at the "top of the pyramid" of adaptiveness. They contain a particularly general type of intelligence and adaptiveness. We'll learn later how to apply this pyramid to individuals, teams, organizations, societies, and our global civilization as complex systems. We claim that recognizing the **universality** of these three actors, understanding the **roles** that each plays in nature and in human life, and learning how they **interact**, can greatly improve our **foresight and action**.

Let us now briefly revisit the **Six Domains**, and **reconsider them** in terms of the Classic Foresight Pyramid. **Evo-devo thinking** allows us to say important things about these six domains. While actors in each of the six domains must navigate all corners of this pyramid, we can nevertheless propose three particularly important **evo-devo purposes** for three groups of the six domains, when considered as complex systems. Specifically, we can say:

- **Individuals** and **Teams**, as complex living systems, seem to have a **primary purpose** to explore and create **evolutionary possibilities** in thinking and action. More than any other, these systems generate a **great diversity of possible futures**, which are then selected on by the environment.

- **Global** and **Universal** systems, by contrast, appear to have a **primary purpose** to find and enforce **developmental probabilities**. More than any other, these systems act to **converge all actors** on a general set of **common futures**, futures that also **protect the complexity** of the whole.

- **Organizations** and **Societies**, sitting between these two more fundamental extremes of the Foresight Pyramid, appear to have a **primary purpose** to help **networks** select and manage **adaptive preferences**. More than any other systems, these two **manage the conflict** between possibility and probability (futures and future). They also **"bridge"** the small and the big actors in our environment.

The Six Domains of Foresight Practice

Whether or not you accept the value of evo-devo models, these **six domains** are easily distinguishable in human strategy, planning, and policy. All six are clearly important. They are a **good base** from which to define the **scope of our field**, and to conduct our work. We challenge skeptical readers to come up with a more useful alternative model.

Amazingly, even our **neural architecture** appears to be organized along the lines of the Classic Foresight Pyramid. A model of thinking called **active inference**, developed by neuroscientist <u>Karl Friston</u>, offers evidence for this hypothesis. This model is being used today in leading **AI development**. We will discuss it further in Book 2. In our interpretation of Friston's work, functional **neural networks**, whether biological or artificial, strive to improve at three things:

- **Predicting** in universally correct ways (seeing **Probable futures**)

- **Creating** a variety of competing inferences (recognizing **Possible futures**)

- **Selecting** and achieving positive visions, while **reducing prediction errors** (avoiding negative visions) (**Preferable futures**)

Technically, each of our brain's individual neural **networks** generates their own "bottom up" predictions, and we update those predictions in a "top down", global manner, using Bayesian methods—in an attempt to minimize predictive error—to see **probable** futures. At the same time, our diverse **networks** are constantly generating a variety of **possible** future models—for example, when we **argue with ourselves** as we consider a problem from several **viewpoints**.

Simultaneously, we **generate**, and try to **rank** and **synchronize**, our **preferred** visions, in a **primarily cooperative** and **secondarily competitive** manner—that special **network process** we call **"coopetition"** in this *Guide*. We engage in **self-selection** (culling, filtering) of those **visions**, both within our own brains and in our societies, using a **democratic voting processes** that is very similar to what we find in **beehives** and **animal herds**. Then, we work to **actualize** those visions.

Lastly, we **update** our predictions and visions in a self-selective **loop**, using **feedback**, again attempting to **minimize prediction error**. This **"Do loop"** of **learning, foresight, action**, and **feedback** is universal: it is how we adapt over time.

Given the **fundamental nature of future thinking**, as we've seen in both the Time Pyramid and the Foresight Pyramid, we might expect that it would be **deliberately taught in our schools** and **integrated into our organizational strategy**. Unfortunately, such a development remains to happen in modern societies. At present, far too many of us ignore the conscious practice of foresight, in our own lives, on our teams, and in our organizations. This may be partly because to practice future thinking well, we also must **deeply explore** both the **relevant past** and the **present**, and balance **probability, possibility, and preference** thinking. Foresight isn't easy, but when it is used in a Do loop, it offers by far the greatest reward—the ability to maintain and increase our adaptiveness.

As you consider your relationship to the **Classic Foresight Pyramid**, ask yourself: How would you **rank** each of these types of foresight thinking? Which do you prefer to do the **most**? Which the **least**? In what **contexts**? How do you **balance** these three in any context? How do you decide when it is most effective to **move** from one type of future thinking to another? When do you **overrely** on your preferred type? How can you best **improve** your least-preferred type? What about your **team**? We will wrestle with such vital questions throughout the *Guide*.

2. Normative Foresight: The Values Pyramid (True, Beautiful, Good)

Seeing the **probable** and the **possible** as the **two most fundamental ways of analyzing change** may have begun with the Greek philosopher <u>Democritus</u> (460-370 BCE), who said that, "Everything existing in the universe is the fruit of **necessity** and **chance**." Around then, a few Eastern and Western philosophers independently proposed the special importance of **three human goals, or sets of values,** the **True**, the **Good,** and the **Beautiful**. For simplicity, we will call these "**values**."

In the East, the <u>Bhagavad Gita</u>, 400 BCE, stressed the value of "words which are good and beautiful and true." In the West, <u>Plato</u> (390 BCE) and his student, <u>Aristotle</u> (350 BCE) both explored these three values as <u>transcendentals</u>, or universal properties of being. One of Aristotle's models divided human intellect into the **theoretical**, the **productive**, and the **practical**. In this model, our theoretical mind is concerned with knowledge and **truth**, our productive mind with the creation of unique and **beautiful** objects, and our practical mind with ethics, empathy, and the nature of the **good**.

Platonic Transcendentals (Universal Values)
The True, the Beautiful, and the Good

In this *Guide*, we will call these three special values sets **Plato's Pyramid**, and more simply, the **Values Pyramid**. Note that Plato's Pyramid is a **restatement** of the Foresight Pyramid, from a **values perspective**. **True** things are highly **probable**, **Beautiful** things explore the **possible**, and **Good** things are **preferable**. In truth, these two models are looking at the same things, **complexity and change**, from two closely related vantage points.

Consider how **Plato's Pyramid** associates with the **Classic Foresight Pyramid**:

- **Probability foresight** is motivated by **Truth- and Discovery-associated values**
- **Possibility foresight** is motivated by **Beauty-and Creativity-associated values**
- **Preference foresight** is motivated by **Goodness and Adaptiveness values**

Plato's Pyramid is thus the **simplest useful model of universal values**, and of **normative foresight**, that we know. We'll use it in several variations in this *Guide*. In Chapter 3, we'll see that this values pyramid is congruent with a set of three classic decision styles. These styles can be assessed with the **Kirton Adaption-Innovation (KAI) inventory**. The psychologist **Michael Kirton** has found that **most people (the "top of the pyramid", in population frequency) are preference thinkers.** He calls such folks **"bridgers"**, as one of their main societal roles is to **mediate the conflicts** between the two other, more basic and unique types. Those types either mildly or strongly prefer **possibility thinking ("innovators")** or **probability thinking** (he calls those folks **"adaptors"**, and we call them **"protectors"**). These two groups are often at odds with each other on teams, yet both are critical to adaptiveness. A good leader will ensure that **psychological safety** exists for **all three of these kinds of decisionmakers** on the team.

The slide below summarizes Kirton's model, with our **Protector** term substituted for Kirton's "Adaptor".

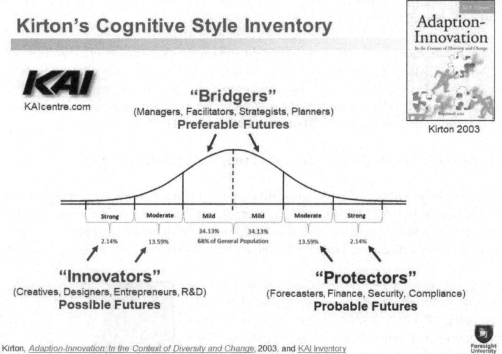

Kirton, *Adaption-Innovation: In the Context of Diversity and Change*, 2003. and KAI Inventory

Discerning readers will now recognize that the **Time Pyramid**, the **Foresight Pyramid**, and the **Values Pyramid, and this Cognitive Styles Pyramid** are all strongly correlated. Folks who think frequently and well about the **Past** can often be very good **Probability** thinkers: they are often motivated to **discover Truth**, and they tend to see causal **models, curves, and trends**. Those who think frequently and well about the **Future** can be very good **Possibility** thinkers: they are often motivated to **create Beauty**, and they tend see **options and uncertainties**. Those who think frequently and well about the **Present** can be very good **Preference** thinkers: they tend to see **shared visions and fears** held by stakeholders. They are often motivated to steer toward the **Good**, while avoiding the **Bad**, and to **measure their progress** in that regard.

In our view, these pyramids are congruent because they are each different perspectives on the same **universal evo-devo processes** used by **living systems.** We expect that all intelligent complex systems, on Earth and presumably elsewhere in our cosmos, will have to embody these **three relationships** to time, foresight, and values. All three corners of these pyramids seem to be fundamental to **how life manages complexity and change**.

Take a moment now to compare your reflections across each pyramid (Time, Foresight, and Values): Which pyramids, if any, were you less **aware of**? How can being more aware of each of these help your thinking? Do you tend to prefer the **same corners** of each pyramid? When is that not true? Do you have a good sense of when to use **each corner** of each pyramid, and when to switch perspectives? What about your **team**? When and where do you have difficulty switching from your preferred corners of any of these pyramids? In which are you most able to **delegate** tasks to others who are stronger in some corners of these than yourself? Least able? Why? We will discuss these challenges throughout the *Guide*.

3. Leading Others: The Leadership Pyramid (Hedgehog, Fox, Eagle)

We can now describe **three future modeling (worldview) styles** we all use, whether we are **leading ourselves** or **leading others**. These styles are also convergent with the pyramids that we have just discussed. We call those three the

Leadership Pyramid. We'll also discuss a fourth style, which occurs outside the pyramid, and is typically **maladaptive.** Psychologists and leadership scholars have given these styles descriptive animal names: The **Hedgehog**, the **Fox**, the **Eagle**, and the **Ostrich**. Again, their patterns seem universal, so we think they are well worth remembering and using.

We've previously introduced the **Fox** and the **Hedgehog**, identified by philosopher **Isaiah Berlin**. Recall that **Foxes** are **possibility oriented**, and skeptical of overarching theories. They like to **pick and choose** from a broad set of ideas and methods, gained from a wide variety of sources. They enjoy **"exploring uncertainty,"** and prize **creativity**. They can be **unpredictable** and **nonconformist**. We noted that the majority of **self-declared futurists** are foxes, but certainly not all.

Hedgehogs are more **probability oriented**. They prefer using models and frameworks. They are often motivated by a **single big idea, model, theory, belief, or authority structure**. They seek **certainty** and **truth-associated** values. In their areas of mastery, they can be **predictable** and **conformist**. They like working with **well-known** (if not well-evidenced) **processes, frameworks and steps** and **"solving the problem."** We noted that the majority of **foresighters (foresight professionals)**, people paid to look to and analyze the future for others, are hedgehogs. They have learned various **respected models, procedures and recipes** for foresight work, and they apply those in a great variety of contexts.

Notice that we have just described the **two fundamental corners,** or **"base"** of the **Time, Foresight, Values, and Cognitive Styles Pyramids**. Evo-devo thinking tells us a leadership style for the **"top" (and most frequent) corner** of this pyramid must also exist. As it strives to **integrate the** two more fundamental and conflicting types, it will tend to be the **most societally valued type**. That third leadership type is called the **Eagle**. This is the future thinker and leader who is more of a **presentist** than a futurist. The leader who particularly values searching for the **Good**, and recognizes it will always be some mix of both Truth (certainty, optimality) and Beauty (freedom, experimentation). The Eagle is a leader who seeks to **"bridge"** the two more basic types of future thinking, seeking **shared preferences and visions**, and the **most integrative strategy**.

Patricia Lustig

The Eagle type was first identified, to our knowledge, by futurist **Patricia Lustig** in her excellent brief book on our field, *Strategic Foresight*, 2015. As Lustig describes, the Eagle seeks to **blend** both Fox and Hedgehog perspectives. To do this well, this future thinker and leader must **fly high**, **bridging** different perspectives, and getting the **Big Picture, systems view**. They must range across all three corners of these pyramids. In **evo-devo terms**, the Eagle **balances** individual and community values, with a preference for improving the network. They know complex systems are **partly unpredictable ("evolving")**, and **partly predictable ("developing")**, and they seek to learn deeply from both views. As psychologist **Michael Kirton** (Chapter 3) has found, the **Eagle** ("bridger") is also the **most common** of the three types.

All three leadership types **create** strategic foresight, and **all three can be great leaders**. This diversity of styles is a strength of evo-devo systems, not a weakness. Nevertheless, the Eagle is potentially the best **integrator** of strategic foresight, and they can be the greatest of leaders. But just because we favor a particular style does not mean we do it well. Many Eagles undervalue or underexplore either the possible or the probable, or both, before they turn to their favorite (and most popular) **preference thinking**. Eagles cannot see anything well, or produce good strategy, without both Foxes and Hedgehogs also providing their own differentiated insights on the team. Another challenge for Eagles is that they don't fly high enough, at times. Their Big Picture is often still too small.

In a discerning study of leadership, *Time to Lead: Lessons for Today's Leaders*, 2020, business school professor **Jan-Benedict Steenkamp** offers sixteen examples of leaders, from seven different leadership styles (adaptive, persuasive, directive, disruptive, character, servant, and charismatic) who addressed problems based on whether they were **Hedgehogs, Foxes, Eagles**. He also introduces a **fourth** fundamental leadership type, **Ostriches**, folks who **avoid serious future thinking**, preferring to keep their "heads in the sand". In Chapter 5, we will introduce an important cousin of the Ostrich, the **Elephant**, someone who is primarily a **learner (past and present oriented)**, and like the Ostrich, is a reluctant leader.

Steenkamp calls Ostriches "hapless leaders". We all know such people, and we've all been ostriches at times. They are reactive, unforesighted, and tend to "go with the flow." Ostrich behavior is common, depending on the problem and context, but especially common in **large** and **bureaucratic** organizations. But we also find ostrich behavior under conditions of **stress** and **challenge**, and anywhere there is **low accountability or feedback**. Steenkamp's book offers a twenty-question "Hedgefox Assessment" to help you determine your preferences among these four personality types.

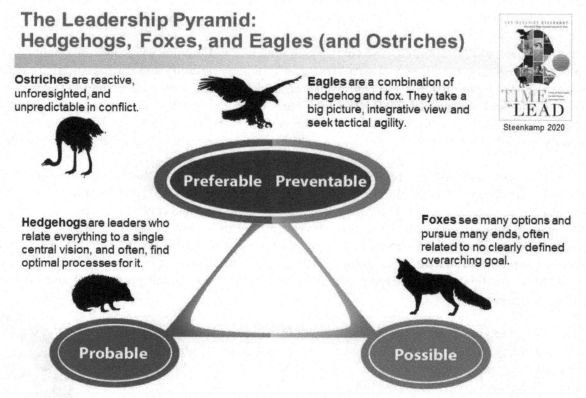

The Leadership Pyramid: Hedgehogs, Foxes, and Eagles (and Ostriches)

Ostriches are reactive, unforesighted, and unpredictable in conflict.

Eagles are a combination of hedgehog and fox. They take a big picture, integrative view and seek tactical agility.

Steenkamp 2020

Hedgehogs are leaders who relate everything to a single central vision, and often, find optimal processes for it.

Foxes see many options and pursue many ends, often related to no clearly defined overarching goal.

Preferable   Preventable

Probable

Possible

Q: What Is Your Type? In What Contexts? Can You Lead Other Types?

The **Leadership Pyramid** (picture above) reminds us that three of these leadership styles are particularly adaptive. This picture shows that the most effective leaders actually **split the preferable** into things we want (the **Preferable**) and plausible traps we want to avoid (the **Preventable**). In other words, there are actually **two types of Eagles**, those who prefer to think about **opportunity first**, and those who think **defensively first**, about pain and traps to prevent. This is called the **Modern Foresight Pyramid**, or the **Four Ps**. We'll introduce this improvement to the classic pyramid shortly.

To be their best, leaders in each style must know how to **work with** and **delegate to** others who have a different style. We all must think as Foxes, Hedgehogs, and Eagles at different times, with different levels of effort, to produce adaptive foresight and action. In other words, while we have preferences for one or more of these styles in different contexts, we all use each of these three future-thinking styles productively every day, and we must strive to get **better at all of them**. Even when we are particularly experienced with and effective at one of these types, we must always value, work well with, and delegate effectively to the other types on our teams, or we will soon be maladaptive.

We can even be successful **Ostriches** and **Elephants**, if we can **delegate** critical foresight processes and decisions to others, and **develop** them well. As the *Anna Karenina* **principle** reminds us, there are **many (evolutionary) ways to fail**, but only a **few (developmental) ways to succeed**. There are many ways to avoid foresight, and be an Ostrich. But there are only a few classic ways to succeed. **Hedgehogs, Foxes**, and **Eagles** describe those ways. When we are an Ostrich or an Elephant we must learn to **delegate** our team's foresight duties to **deputies** who are **strong** as one of the other types.

In Chapter 3 we will explore the **Korn Ferry Leadership Architect** model, covered in *FYI: For Your Improvement*, 2017, now in its sixth edition. Let us briefly preview it here. This evidence-based model includes **thirty-eight competencies** and a great variety of useful assessments.

The Korn Ferry model defines **Four Leadership Competencies:**

1. **Thought** Leadership (Being Strategic)   External Focus
2. **Results** Leadership (Being Outcome-Bound)   External Focus
3. **People** Leadership (Being a Developer)   Internal Focus
4. **Personal** Leadership (EQ, Ethics, Adaptability)   Internal Focus

Korn Ferry, 2017

Complex systems scholar and futurist **David Snowden,** creator of the <u>Cynefin</u> sensemaking framework, to be discussed later, observes that these four competencies are not equally important. Some leaders, if they can successfully **delegate and develop deputies**, can **specialize in the just last two** of these four. Snowden describes successful leaders that are good "**Coordinators**". They focus on People and Personal leadership, on developing and protecting their top people. Their deputies are the actual **Thought leaders** (strategy creators) and **Results leaders** (decision makers), in all or most organizational contexts. Such **specialization** can be particularly adaptive in **large** or **high complexity** organizations, where both strategy and operations can overwhelm the cognitive capacities of leaders.

In truth, all leaders are **Ostriches** in some areas of their organizations. We all face too much **complexity, diversity, and specialization** for our minds to grasp. How we deal with that reality determines whether our team is adaptive. Whether we tend to be a Hedgehog, Fox, Eagle, Ostrich, or some other animal, there are always ways we can lead well. The better we understand, respect and use all three corners of the Leadership Pyramid, the better our foresight will become.

The 80/20 and 95/5 Rules of Change

Have you heard of the **Pareto principle**, also called the **80/20 Rule**? It is fundamental **constraint of nature** that all practitioners should understand. Complexity scholars know it by a more arcane title, the **power law**. Power laws describe the distributions of variables in many natural complex systems. In systems subject to power laws, 80% of the most **contested** (competitive, selected) **effects** typically come from 20% of the **actors** (picture right).

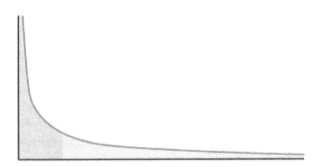

A power law distribution, a universal complexity curve. The "big head" is in green, and the "long tail" in yellow.

For example, consider that 20% of the citizens in capitalist economies typically have something like 80% of the wealth. For another example, even as levels of urbanization change and grow, 20% of "leading" cities typically contain 80% of a typical nation's urban population. In bookstores, 20% of the titles typically get 80% of the sales. When we are solving problems, 20% of the effort (ideally, our highest priority actions!) will often deliver 80% of the results we seek.

In each case, roughly **20% of the system actors or actions** are called the "**big head**" of the power law. Conversely, the remaining 80% of the citizens, cities, books, and problem solving activities, while they contribute only 20% of the **impact** on the most currently **contested** (competitive, selected) system variables, contain the **vast majority of diversity** among the full set of system variables. This 80% is called the "**long tail**" of the power law. The long tail's impressive and beautiful diversity **protects the network** when conditions **change**, or when status quo solutions are no longer adaptive. In that event, current leaders may lose power and trust, and one or more of the actors in the long tail may join the **new big head**. The long tail's superior capacity for **collective action** also occasionally returns the network to **power law form**, when it gets **too fat at the top** (plutocratic, restrictive, autocratic), as it often does. Unfortunately, America and many other advanced democracies have drifted into **plutocracy** since the mid-20th century, with the top 20% now owning much more than 80% of our national wealth. In *BPF*, we'll talk about long-tail activism that we predict will help us to reduce our dysfunctional level of plutocracy, returning America to a more universal, power law distribution of wealth and power.

In our view, the **80/20 Rule** describes a **universal relationship** between **processes of evolution and development**. From the perspective of **natural selection**, we can argue that the **"big head"** in any power law-dependent community of actors has **self-organized,** over prior cycles, to deliver most of the **impact** on all community variables presently under the greatest **selection pressure**. The **"long tail"**, by contrast, has self-organized to be a **reservoir** for the great majority of the community's **useful diversity**. Both **impact and diversity** are critical to being adaptive in a complex, unpredictable world. They are two ends of a continuum. **Both ends** of this power law curve are critical to see and to cultivate, to be adaptive.

This rule is obviously very important for foresight. It challenges us look for power law relationships, and for that small number of actions and strategies that are presently generating the most impact on the most contested variables. It also challenges us to be aware of, and to nurture, a wide range of more narrowly useful alternatives to our current actions and strategies, as any one of those could become the "big head" tomorrow, if our environment changes. Books like **Richard Koch's** *The 80/20 Principle*, 1999, *Living the 80/20 Way*, 2004 and *The 80/20 Manager*, 2013, offer great advice on using the **80/20 Rule** in life and management. Another good book on the use of power law strategy in business, focused on the market value of the 80%, is Chris Anderson's *The Long Tail*, 2006.

The **95/5 Rule**, we claim, is another **universal relationship** between **processes of evolution and development**. John developed it in a paper on the evo-devo nature of our universe in 2008. As a result, it is virtually unknown by comparison to the **80/20 Rule**, but we think it is no less important. The **95/5 Rule** describes the interaction between possible (unpredictable) and probable (predictable) processes in **living systems,** and many of the **organizational and social activities of humanity**. We also argue that it applies to our **most complex and intelligent technologies**, which are becoming increasingly based on the evo-devo processes used by living systems, as we will see.

John discovered this rule by recognizing that in biological organisms, roughly 95% of our genes engage in unpredictable recombination or mutation, over macroevolutionary time. Just like the long tail of the power law, these **"evolutionary genes"** enable chaotic, experimental exploration of the **possibility space** of form and function, and **enhanced innovation** under conditions of environmental stress. The remaining 5% of our genes (to a rough approximation in eukaryotes) are involved in predictable **developmental conservation**. They are **highly conserved** over their entire evolutionary history. Just like the big head of the power law, these **"developmental genes"** have self-organized for a special kind of predictable impact, that which makes the **hierarchical growth, maturity, and replication** of the organism a convergent, **high probability process**, even under great environmental **chaos, selection and change**.

We can observe this **95/5 Rule**, a 95% to 5% evo to devo, bottom-up to top-down, divergent to convergent, unpredictable to predictable ratio, in a **wide variety of complex systems** in nature. Let's look briefly at a few examples, to see the great breadth of operation of this apparently universal rule of change:

- **Genetic activity.** A very small subset of our genetic material, roughly 5%, is 'ultra-conserved' across complex organisms, like mice and humans, and is critical to the way those organisms **converge, top-down**, on a series of **future-predictable states** over their **life cycles**. For example, even though a majority of our genes are expressed in an organism to varying degrees *during* development, we can now make a case that everything that happens predictably the same to any set of "genetically identical" twins, over their lifetime, is due to a very small and special set of **conserved** and **top-down directive genes and processes**. Biologists call the most basic of these our 'developmental (or 'evo-devo') genetic toolkit.' By contrast, the vast majority of our genes, the other 95%, are constantly changing, especially over long timescales. In two identical twins, these "evolutionary genes" (in our definition) work in a bottom-up, chaotic, and competitive manner. They make the brain and tissue architectures, fingerprints, and personalities of each "identical" twin unpredictably different from each other. They also make each member of our species usefully different from each other, and from our parents. These evolutionary genes engage each organism in trillions of local, unpredictable experiments, and they make us greatly more **diverse** and **immune**, when we are viewed as a **complex network**. See John's paper *Evo-Devo Universe?*, 2008, for details.

- **Human thinking.** Physicist **Leonard Mlodinow** describes a 95/5 ratio in *Subliminal*, 2013, when he explains that the vast majority (perhaps 95%) of human thinking is bottom-up, creative, and unpredictable, driven by our unconscious synaptic networks. Only a critical subset (let's guess, 5%) of human thinking is top-down, optimization oriented, and conscious. Psychologists measure this "conscious" or "deliberate" time in minutes out of a typical day, versus hours we spend in largely unconscious, bottom-up, and locally-driven behaviors.

- **Organizational dynamics.** Futurist **Kevin Kelly** describes the **95/5 Rule** in *Out of Control*, 1994, when he explains that the vast majority of decisions made in organizations (again, let's argue, 95%), even in highly hierarchical ones like the military, happen in bottom-up, creative ways, based on the initiative and judgment of individual actors. Leaders seek to set up fair and useful top-down rules and directives (the 5%), but the time and energy people in most organizations spend paying attention to those directives, versus making their own bottom-up, local decisions, is likely as short as the conscious vs unconscious thinking we each do in a typical day.

- **Ideas for change. Robinson and Schroeder**, in *The Idea-Driven Organization*, 2014, show that the great majority of useful ideas for change also flow from the bottom-up, from employees, stakeholders, and customers to upper management, rather than vice versa. Whether those ideas are **listened to and acted on**, or not, is of course another matter. See our discussion of **innovation management** platforms in Chapter 4 for more on this vital process.

- **Social processes.** Many of these are subject to the **95/5 Rule** as well. If most social processes are 95% evolutionary and only 5% developmental to a first approximation, this helps us understand why it is **so easy to see** creative and unpredictable **"evolutionary noise"** around us, and **so hard to see** convergent and predictable **"developmental signal"**. Some scholars make the mistake of concluding that *all* social change is bottom-up, random and unpredictable. But as we will see throughout the *Guide*, the 5% of developmental processes in any complex system, few as they are, seem at least as important as the 95% of evolutionary processes in shaping the future, in living systems, social systems, technological systems, and the universe as a system. Even though they are in a small minority, developmental processes have a huge influence on the futures of biological organisms.

The **95/5 Rule** is the same as a **19:1 unpredictability to predictability ratio**, in analyzing change in any complex system. For simplicity, we round this to a **"20:1 ratio"** of typical evo to devo processes, in any complex system. In a nutshell, the **95/5 Rule** tells us that the vast majority of change in any **replicating complex system** is evolutionary, divergent and rapidly unpredictable, but a critical subset is just the opposite, developmental, convergent, and intrinsically predictable, both on average and over the long term. In living systems, **both processes** of change appear to be **equally important** to adaptation. In other words, **developmental processes**, though they are statistically much rarer and often much harder to see, model, and prove, are **just as important** as **evolutionary processes** to an organism's survival.

If our organizations, societies, and our most advanced technologies are also complex adaptive systems undergoing some form of natural selection, as we argue throughout the *Guide*, they too are driven by both unpredictable, bottom-up, and predictable, top-down processes of change. If we live in such an **"evo-devo universe"**, we will need to see and manage both processes better if we are to do good foresight work.

Consider a few of the **95/5 Rule's** implications for **organizations**. In adaptive organizations, only a critical subset, something like 5%, of organizational activities are driven by top-down commands and constraints, the initiatives and rulesets provided by leaders. The vast majority of change always happens instead in local, bottom-up contexts, subject to individual choice and initiative. This fact of nature is why **overcontrolling** an organization from the top quickly becomes a recipe for employee disengagement, inflexibility, and predatory power politics in top management. At the same time, a **lack of critical frameworks and rulesets** at the top is a recipe for anarchy and lack of direction.

Maintaining well-designed incentives, norms, processes and policy may be only 5% of the **job of management,** but getting that 5% right is key to preventing **organizational dysfunction**. There's a rule, Hanlon's razor, which says "Never attribute to malice that which can be explained by stupidity." The risk manager **Douglas Hubbard** offers Hanlon's corollary: "Never attribute to malice or stupidity that which can be explained by moderately rational individuals following misaligned incentives, norms, processes or policies in a complex system." **Organizational behavior** experts tell us that **systemic bias** in our top-down rulesets are a **root cause** of many social, organizational, and team problems.

Frederic Laloux's *Reinventing Organizations*, 2014 recognizes that **bottom-up** organizational structures work more like biological systems, and that these are usually more adaptive, in more environments, than are **top-heavy hierarchies**. The latter work best when **control and capacity for power**, not **innovative diversity**, are the overriding organizational needs. Unfortunately, Laloux then argues that bottom-up management, and "leaderless" organizations are now our ideal, in most contexts. The **95/5 Rule** tells us that this claim, and faddish notions like "holocracy" (fully decentralized organizations) are greatly overclaiming. With all complex networks, both **centralization** and **decentralization** are necessary. A top-down, bottom-up **power balance** always must be struck, and the devil is always in the details.

By contrast, **Brafman and Beckstrom**'s *The Starfish and the Spider*, 2008, compares **bottom-up, starfish-like organizational processes**, with top-down, **spider-like processes**. It recognizes that each process helps the other, and that a **blend of both** is typically best in organizations. **Laszlo Bock's** *Work Rules!*, 2016, also sees the value of **balancing** bottom-up and top-down control. It describes Google's experience with **objectives and key results (OKRs),** a bottom-up and empowering form of people management in which individual employees determine their own objectives (to some degree) and key results to be measured against in achieving those objectives (to a larger degree). Those OKRs then roll-up to their managers, rather than having performance standards set in a mostly top-down manner, as in traditional organizations.

In a topical example, the current efforts by visionaries to apply **decentralized blockchain technology** to everything online is a good example of the **excesses of bottom up thinking**. Humanity certainly needs **much more decentralization** of critical systems, to **limit the exploitations** of centralized systems in our current **plutocracy**. But it is easy to oversell what will **actually work**, against the efficiency, power, and scale of **critically (5%) centralized systems**. As **Kai Stinchcombe** persuasively argued in 2017, all blockchain platforms, by design, must be both much less efficient and less trust-building than centralized IT. As John argues in The Truth about Bitcoins and the Blockchain, 2017, the great majority of these bottom-up experiments will **fail**, and their successes will be **far more narrow in scope** than investors currently imagine.

In a slow-moving environment, a manager's top-down rules, policies, and control processes can grow easily grow past the 5% that will be most adaptive, most of the time. But as change management guru **John Kotter** argues in *Accelerate* (2014), as the **pace of change quickens**, the performance cost of maintaining **large top-down hierarchies** keeps growing, until that hierarchy threatens firm survival, and is shattered into more bottom-up networks, either by **internal reform**, or more commonly, by **competition, the marketplace, merger, downsizing, or bankruptcy** of the too-top-heavy firm.

As the **Classic Foresight Pyramid** tells us, anticipating the most-selected, highest impact 5% of predictable trends, processes, and destinations is one of the **two foundations** of good foresight. The other is exploring the unpredictable 95%, to really see what's possible. The more we have the luxury to do such thinking, prior to **creating strategy** and **taking action**, the more **adapted** we can become.

Knowing the **95/5 Rule**, and seeing it at work in human and other systems, will greatly aid the leader's foresight and strategy. Throughout the *Guide*, we will argue that just as important as seeing our evolutionary opportunities, risks, options, and alternative futures is understanding and taking advantage of our developmental futures, that small subset of social processes that are top-down, optimizing, convergent and highly probable. Both the **possible** and the **probable**, the **"evo"** and the **"devo"**, appear equally important to life, to society, and to our universe itself.

Intuition and Deliberation: Our Two Thinking Systems

The **neuroscience of foresight** has been advancing rapidly since new experimental tools and methods, like fMRI and optogenetics, were invented in the late 1990s and 2000's. The story of how our amazing minds emerged—and how and when they work well or fail—gets clearer every year. Let's look briefly at some of this science now.

Besides **active inference** (i.e., the Classic Foresight Pyramid), there is another evidence-based model in psychology that describes our mind as two feeling and thinking systems: <u>dual process theory</u>. This model will lead us to the Modern Foresight Pyramid shortly. It is a **helpful oversimplification** of another power law process that is particularly important in human brains. Dual process theory tells us that our minds **anticipate and make decisions** about the future in **two basic ways**. The first way is **very fast**—more **emotional** and **intuitive** than reasoned—and is **largely unconscious**. The second way is **slow**—more deliberative and reason-based than emotional—and significantly **more conscious**.

Nobel prize winner and behavioral economist <u>Daniel Kahneman</u> popularized these two decision-making systems in his bestseller, <u>*Thinking, Fast and Slow*</u>, 2012. Because we use emotion and reason to varying degrees in both of these systems, and because we don't have widely accepted models yet of what consciousness is as opposed to unconscious processes, Kahneman refers to them as simply **System 1** and **System 2**. In truth, these are two ends of a **continuum**. Empirically, the **difference in speed** between these two systems is the easiest way to tell them apart.

System 1 – Rapid, Unconscious, Emotional, "Intuitive" Thinking

Intuition is a term well-suited to designate **System 1.** It is our previously learned, and now **largely unconscious, primarily emotional and secondarily rational processes of thinking**. One major component of intuition is **instinct**, which is *genetic learning* in a previous life cycle, inherited via natural selection, and developmentally encoded into our neural structure (**"nature"**). Another component is our **prior learning** experiences in life (**"nurture"**). Many of the most powerful of these occur in our youth, during early development, and are quickly relegated to our **unconscious**.

All animals have at least the basic emotions of <u>pain and pleasure</u>, working in opposition with each other. In higher animals, emotions are tied to our **models of future pain or reward**, and they are usually unconsciously triggered, below our level of conscious awareness. The more complex our brains get, the more **thinking-dependent** and **context-dependent** our emotional and intuitive pleasure and pain combinations become. These dual drives to think ahead—first intuitively and **unconsciously**, and second, **deliberately** and **consciously**—are found in all higher animals.

We know that the phrase "higher animal" is offensive to some readers. We will endeavor to show that it is actually an evidence-based concept. There truly is an **arc of developmental complexity** to be found in life's evolutionary developmental history. Our leading species capacity for **foresight**, the **generality** of their **intelligence**, their capacity to **use technology** (aka "niche construction) and their degree and persistence of **consciousness** just some of the more obvious ways we can presently measure, if only roughly at present, higher levels of complexity emergence in humans and a few other species, and especially, in their **adaptive networks**.

Books like **Tor Norretrander's** *The User Illusion*, 1999, and **Leonard Mlodinow's** *Subliminal*, 2013, tell us that the various parts of our unconscious mind are endlessly **cooperating and competing** to try to better **anticipate** or make predictions about the world. EEG experiments—those that test electrical activity in the brain—have shown that **we are instantly surprised**, at the **unconscious level**, if the world behaves in a way contrary to any of our **unconscious predictions**.

In one famous experiment, when test subjects were shown a clip of a **dog quacking**, they became instantly yet unconsciously surprised; as recorded on EEG, then, about **half a second later**, they consciously recognized surprise. Unconsciously, we all have learned that **dogs generally bark** while moving their mouth. When we see that movement, our **intuition generates a prediction**. This prediction happens hundreds of milliseconds faster than our conscious awareness. Experiments like these tell us that human **consciousness** is an emergent **meta-process**, which always occurs **after**, and is often **subservient to**, all the **predictive, unconscious, Bayesian activities** of our brain. The latter, not our consciousness, make up the **vast majority** of our feeling and thinking processes.

Mlodinow, 2012

Our sense of **morality**, which we tend to think of as largely conscious and deliberative, **also** begins as an instinctual, intuitive, and unconscious process. For example, every species of monkey that has been tested exhibits an innate sense of **moral fairness**. They all have social **status hierarchies** based on **community judgments**. If they see another monkey of the same status get a better reward for the same task (say, getting a grape instead of a cucumber), they will typically get angry or hurt feelings and no longer participate in the experimenter's game. Their **prediction of fairness** has been violated, and their emotions guide them to an **adaptive response**.

Humans with lesions in their **amygdala**—a key relay station supporting **emotional** processing—will often **deliberate rationally** on possible actions, yet they **never come to a decision**. They get stuck in "**analysis paralysis**" because they either cannot access, or are not willing to rely on, their **gut**—the **intuitive processes** of System 1 that motivate us to make a **choice**. See **Antonio Damasio's** *Descartes' Error*, 2005, for more on how various forms of **emotional and unconscious prediction** are fundamental to thinking. It is these **intuitive processes** that allow us to make decisions **when rationality fails** to provide a clear answer, as it so often does in a complex world. In sum, **System 1, unconscious intuition, emotions**, and **empathy**, are at the core of **higher intelligence** in living systems. There are many implications of this insight.

For example, as we'll describe in Book 2, we predict **intuitive, unconscious, emotional processes** must be at the core of **all our higher machine intelligence** to come. Like us, their **artificial neural networks** will have to be **evo-devo systems, evolved, developed**, and continually **selected** for greater adaptiveness. Like us, they will be **finite** and computationally incomplete (having many questions without good answers). Like us, their futures will be full of uncertainty and "wicked problems". Because their still-finite rationality will frequently fail them, just as it fails us, they will also have to rely on their **gut intuition, emotions, and empathy** to guide their decisions. The futurist **Richard Yonck** explores this idea in *The Heart of the Machine: Our Future in a World of Artificial Emotional Intelligence*, 2017. Just as we seek to **educate our children** as best we can, we will have a **duty to train** our AI's intuitions and emotions as best we can. It will be an interesting time.

System 2 – Slower, Conscious, Rational, "Deliberative" Thinking

In animals with more complex brains, **self-consciousness** and **environmental awareness** incrementally emerges. Our self- and other awareness—the slower, deliberate thinking that we do in our conscious minds about ourselves and the world around us—occurs in classically "**top-down**" (**convergent, predictable, developmental**) manner. Consciousness **reliably emerges**, in a process of **neural synchronization** of large groups of unconscious processes, in all complex brains. In regulating ourselves, it is a "**top down**" system, but in the world, we use our **consciousness and its inventions** (language, logic, culture, technology) to act in a "**bottom-up**" (**divergent, unpredictable, evolutionary**) way. Our deliberative minds take us in all sorts of unique directions, creating an astonishing **diversity** of ideas and behaviors. This is the kind of thinking that Kahneman calls **System 2**. It is found in many **higher** (more generally adaptive) **animals** on Earth, not only among humans.

Modern neuroscience tells us that even our **awareness and consciousness**, as well as all our **deliberate thought-processes**, depend on many cooperating and competing **bottom-up predictions**, running **in parallel** in different regions of our brain. When we **consciously (deliberately) argue with ourselves** over what to do next, we do that using **spatially separate, "coopetitive" neural networks**. This process is presumably very similar to the way our **unconscious networks** cooperate and compete to **predict** what "should" happen next, as in the video of the dog quacking instead of barking.

In their article "Recognition by Top-Down and Bottom-Up Processing in Cortex: The Control of Selective Attention," **Graboi and Lisman**, 2003, provide evidence that our more conscious brain regions are constantly doing their own complex **top-down (global, emergent, convergent) predicting**, while acting as **bottom-up** sources of mental variety in the world. Our conscious output is greatly influenced by what is fed to it by **lower brain and sensory regions** in the neural hierarchy. Those regions are doing massively parallel **bottom-up prediction** activities, finding **patterns**, making **sense** of the world, and sorting **signals from noise**. **Prediction errors** occur at many levels of this hierarchy, whenever we find a **discrepancy** between what our **models predict**, and what our **senses** tell us about external and internal states. We use **error feedback** to try to minimize these prediction errors over time, so our models better reflect reality. We don't know all the details and levels of this predictive process yet, but the model seems roughly correct.

Neuroscientist and psychologist **Lisa Barrett** gives us a more nuanced understanding of Systems 1 and 2 in her exploration of the emerging **Predictive Processing framework** of mind. In her lay book, *Seven and Half Lessons About the Brain*, 2020, in her technical book, *How Emotions Are Made*, 2018, and in a journal article, Hutchinson and Barrett, "The Power of Predictions," *Curr. Dir. Psych. Sci.*, 2019, she explains that there is actually no clear distinction between these two systems of feeling and thinking. System 1 and 2 are simply **two ends of a continuum** of predictive thinking. One extreme is fast, unconscious, and emotional, and the other is slower, more conscious and more rational.

Recalling our **Power Law of Future Thinking**, we propose that **System 1** is strongly represented in the **"big head" of the power law**, the leftmost part of the curve in the picture at right. It dominates all the rapid and often unconscious **automatic predictions** that our brains do. **System 2**, by contrast, is more represented in the **"long tail" of future thinking**. It is most represented in all the slower, less frequent, more deliberative, and more diverse *types* of thinking that we do. Barrett theorizes that the **deliberative thinking occurs** primarily when we notice **prediction errors** ("surprise") between our intuitive models and our sense of reality. In that case, **error feedback** (the **Do loop**) makes us ask how to **update our models**. In both cases, making our predictive models **more conscious**, and looking for **data** to confirm or deny them, are key aims of good foresight.

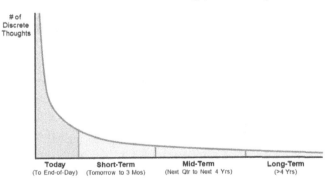

The Power Law of Future Thinking (55:25:15:5)

# of Discrete Thoughts

| Today (To End-of-Day) | Short-Term (Tomorrow to 3 Mos) | Mid-Term (Next Qtr to Next 4 Yrs) | Long-Term (>4 Yrs) |

Most future thinking is <24 hrs, and unconscious[1]

1. Benjamin Libet, *Mind Time: The Temporal Factor in Consciousness*, 2005.

Computational neuroscientists, like Rajesh Rao, model this predictive process in artificial neural networks. As we will see in *BPF*, **neuro-inspired ("brainlike") AI** has outperformed all our best **classical ("engineered") AI** since roughly 2010. This is early evidence, in our view, that **evo-devo methods**, not just mimicking the **design of the brain**, but mimicking **how our brain was built**, using **evo-devo genetics**, is the **necessary future of AI**. We've been using **biomimicry** since our first computers, designed by the polymath **John Von Neumann** in the 1940s. He learned that AND, OR, and NOT logic circuits were the leading biophysical model at the time for how biological neural networks worked, and he implemented that model in digital computers, as a first **"design for a brain."** Of course, our brains are far more complex than such simple models. In the **natural intelligence hypothesis** in *BPF*, we will predict that all our best future AI will be forced to increasingly become like **natural (biological) intelligence**. We believe there is **no other easily accessible design path** available to computer scientists to create what is now called **artificial general intelligence (AGI)**. **Evolution** got to both **general intelligence** and **collective empathy and ethics** first, and we predict that all our most useful and adaptive AIs will be forced, by the nature of our universe, to follow the same **evo-devo path**. We shall see.

Our most abstract System 2 networks reside in the <u>**executive function**</u> areas of our brain. In "<u>The Evolution of Foresight</u>," *Behavioral and Brain Sciences*, 2007, **Suddendorf and Corballis** outline **executive systems** in our <u>frontal ("foresight") lobe</u>—the **area in blue** in the picture at right. We all use these executive systems to model future actions in the world and engage in "**mental time travel**." **Humanity's** complex executive functions give us a unique advantage over all other animals in conducting **foresight**.

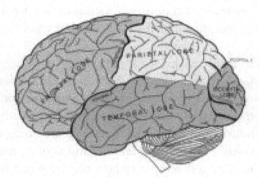

See Corballis' <u>*The Recursive Mind*</u>, 2014, for a tour of how we use this special feature of our intelligence, exploring different alternatives, times, and places in our past, present, and future. Based on **fMRI studies** of the thinking brain, neuroscientist <u>**Michael Gazzaniga**</u> has proposed a specific area of our frontal lobe, **Area 10** in our prefrontal cortex—an area twice as large in humans as in chimpanzees—as the primary place where our **most detailed deliberate simulations of our long-range future** take place. Conducting foresight is thus central not only to our subconscious, intuitive, emotional mind, it is central to our higher (System 2) thinking processes as well.

Such work supports the thesis that it is our species' **executive foresight**, our skill at **technology use**, and our **social empathy (connectedness) and ethics (interdependence)**, our heads, hands, and hearts, that are the three **most essential features** of higher intelligence and consciousness, not just in humans, but in any sufficiently complex life form. In Book 2, we will propose that our capacities in these three areas best explain why human civilization has been so **resilient under adversity**, and why it has **continually accelerated** in general adaptiveness, when viewed from a **network perspective**.

System 1 and 2 in Coopetition – Our Emotion-Cognition-Action Cycles

Terms like emotion and cognition, and Systems 1 and 2, are useful, but as **Lisa Barrett** reminds us, they are only rough models. Our brains are the **most complex systems in the known universe**. They have far more depth and nuance than we can describe with these binary categories. An excellent book that explores our continually improving metaphors and models for brain and mind is neuroscientist **Matt Cobb's** <u>*The Idea of the Brain: The Past and Future of Neuroscience*</u>, 2020. Nevertheless, even simple models, if grounded, can offer many helpful insights for foresight practice, as we will see.

In common parlance, the use of Systems 1 and 2 to generate action can be called an **ECA (Emotion-Cognition-Action) cycle**. Pop psychologists used to refer to emotion and cognition as "right brain" and "left brain" thinking. In reality, both systems operate on both sides of the brain, using highly interlaced neural pathways. The figure below depicts System 1 and 2 functions distributed **bilaterally**. <u>Lateralization of brain function</u> does occur, but in quite **specialized** and **complex** ways, secondary to **integration** as the brain's main theme. For example, there is some lateralization of consciousness. Our left parietal lobe is typically more active when we visualize ourselves in the **first person**, and our right when we visualize ourselves in the **third person**, taking a perspective **outside our bodies.** In what is called <u>Solomon's Paradox</u>, we are typically poor at taking our own advice. To combat this, we can use **self-distancing**, adopting a **third person perspective**, to give **advice to ourselves** from the outside, treating ourselves as someone else. That is advice that we will **actually take**.

The **ECA cycle** reminds us that we typically first **intuit our emotional states and signals** (and if we have emotional intelligence, others' as well) then we **intuit and deliberate our (and ideally, others) cognitive states and signals,** and then we **act**. Or we **short circuit** this cycle and jump right from personal emotion to action. Emotions are how we, as animals, navigated the world long before we had complex languages, sciences, and technologies. Our **mood** even determines the **quality** of our thinking. This **primacy of emotions** in our thinking is the reason **emotional intelligence** is more significant to career success than **analytical intelligence**. Fortunately, both our EQ and our IQ can be improved in practice, both via **professional therapy** and **self-therapy**.

Steven Pinker's *Rationality*, 2021, gives a masterful overview of the value and challenges of **evidence-based feelings and beliefs**. In the 1950's, psychologist **Albert Ellis** developed **Rational-Emotive Behavior Therapy (REBT)**, a very helpful set of practices. REBT posits that we have both **rational and irrational beliefs,** many of which are unconscious, and those beliefs

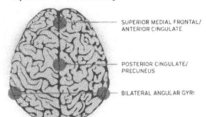
Areas of the Brain Affiliated with System 1 Processing

SUPERIOR MEDIAL FRONTAL/ ANTERIOR CINGULATE

POSTERIOR CINGULATE/ PRECUNEUS

BILATERAL ANGULAR GYRI

SYSTEM 1 CHARACTERISTICS
• Holistic
• Emotional; pleasure-pain oriented
• Behavior mediated by "vibes" from past experiences
• Encodes reality into concrete images, metaphors, and narratives
• More rapid processing; oriented toward immediate action
• Self-evidently valid; "experiencing is believing"

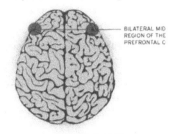
Areas of the Brain Affiliated with System 2 Processing

BILATERAL MID REGION OF THE PREFRONTAL C

SYSTEM 2 CHARACTERISTICS
• Analytical
• Logical; reason oriented
• Behavior mediated by conscious appraisal of events
• Encodes reality in abstract symbols, words, and numbers
• Slower processing; oriented toward delayed action
• Requires justification via logic and evidence

From Farrell, Goh, and Y

Our Intuitive (System 1) and Deliberative (System 2) Intelligences Each Operate On Both Sides of Our Brains

trigger our feelings and behaviors, both adaptive and maladaptive. When we **closely examine** our more **positive** and **negative feelings** (see next section) we can often uncover a **small set of irrational beliefs** that **consistently trigger** our **most maladaptive feelings, thoughts, and behaviors**. Common irrational beliefs Ellis found are 1) that we must always perform well and have the approval of significant others, 2) that we deserve to always be treated considerately and fairly, and 3) that we deserve to always live in a safe, easy, and hassle-free state of existence. REBT is a form of **Cognitive behavioral therapy (CBT)** helping us to **see and reprogram** harmful false beliefs. Ellis's many books, including *The Myth of Self-Esteem*, 2005, and *Overcoming Destructive Beliefs, Feelings, and Behaviors*, 2001, are great guides to this vital process. See Appendix 3 for more helpful books on CBT and REBT. These self-growth activities can be done as **self-therapy**, but they are the most powerful when they are also done in the context of an **accountability group (cohort)**.

Common **emotional mistakes** include: being ruled by our **fears** and **fantasies** instead of **practical visions**, not being open to the **signals of others**, not **communicating**, and being too quick and **emotionally safe** (rather than remaining vulnerable and uncertain) with our **judgments**. Common **cognition mistakes** include: not knowing our **intuitive biases**, and seeking to adjust for them via **deliberative processes**, not valuing **cognitive diversity**, not seeking **contrary evidence**, not developing **goals**, not **prioritizing** our actions, and not using **adaptive frameworks**, like the **Eight Skills** (Chapter 2).

Regarding **time orientations**, neuroscience has recently shown that we often use the **same neural areas** to **remember the past** as we do to **imagine the future**. In other words, how well and accurately we can **remember our past**, has a profound influence on what we can **foresee**. In a coming world of **lifelogs**, in which we have digital aids constantly recording our lives, we can imagine how **better digital memories**, and **artificial intelligence (AI)** that can learn from all that **historical data**—will profoundly enhance our ability to **understand ourselves** and **forecast our futures**, in all six domains.

There are many good psychological tips we can use today. In "Our Brains Are Terrible at Thinking About the Future," 2017, futurist **Jane McGonigal** tells us of fMRI studies suggesting that when most people imagine their far-future **selves**, they think of them as **strangers**. In such instances, we stop using our **prefrontal cortex** and its planning strengths. One way to re-involve prefrontal processes is to invest **positive and negative emotion** in images of our future selves. **Emotional investment** in our **visualizations of success and failure** will give our images of future selves greater **familiarity, detail and vividness**, and that can motivate us to make **painful but necessary change**.

As the pioneering futurist **Fred Polak** describes in his classic, *The Image of the Future* (PDF), 1973, a detailed **image of the future**—and the more **clearly, frequently, emotionally, and rationally** we envision both its **promise** and its **perils**—will tend to **pull us toward it, motivating us to actualize it**. We must also take care that ours is a **well-critiqued, moral, and evidence-based vision**, or else it may lead us to many undesirable outcomes. In our history many visions of the future, fervently believed, have led individuals, firms, and societies to very non-empathic and unethical destinations.

To revisit the three great gifts of humanity (foresight, science & technology, ethics & empathy), what we are learning about brains today is helping us not only to improve our **foresight** and **mental health**, it is already helping us build **much more capable** (and eventually, more **ethical** and **empathic**) **machine intelligences**. We do not think we can avoid that strange and scary future, but we can foresee and guide it much better and more consciously than we are today.

Emotional Foresight: Positive and Negative Future Sentiments

Let's say more now about **emotional foresight**, and consider how emotions shape our **preferences**, the top of our Foresight Pyramid. We've just seen that we tend to **feel first, fastest, and strongest**, and to **think second, slower, and more weakly**, about **promise and peril** ahead. The **most universal model for emotions** breaks them into **positive** and **negative sentiment**. Using primarily System 1, and secondarily System 2, there are **two** ways we **feel our way** into the future—**optimism** and **pessimism**. Each of us feels and thinks not only about **what we desire**, but about what we **desire to prevent**. Psychologists call the first sentiment **strategic optimism** and the second sentiment **defensive pessimism**.

Using and managing this **sentiment dyad** well is thus one key to better foresight work. Each **sentiment** is quite adaptive, in different contexts. As psychiatrist and neuroscientist **Dilip Jeste** describes in *Wiser*, 2020, some people have a natural inclination to **defensive pessimism**. As we'll see, such folks tend to be particularly good at seeing potential **Disruption and Risk**, both ahead of and more accurately than everyone else. By contrast, others have a natural inclination to **strategic optimism**. They are better at finding **Advantage and Opportunity**, ahead of and more accurately than everyone else.

Blending these two sentiments well, and **actively balancing** them, is a **third** sentiment state, **realism**. Realism is not cynicism or pessimism, as some mistakenly argue. It is also not "realpolitik", which is politics based on opportunism rather than moral considerations. We define realism as the ability to **simultaneously** see and analyze any problem or issue from **both sentiment states,** and to move easily and quickly between each as needed, not **remaining stuck** in either view. Realism is **ADOR balanced** thinking (we will discuss ADOR analysis shortly). It is the ability to analyze the **future implications** of a problem or issue using **both sentiment states**, gaining the benefits of each.

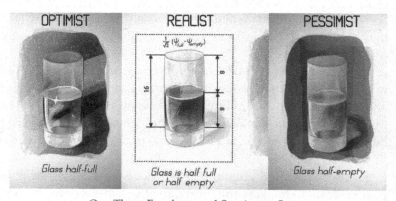

Our Three Fundamental Sentiment States

Our "**future feeling**" thus continually gives us **Two Fundamental Visions** for goals, strategy and plans, and an **Emergent Third Vision** that mixes the two. Effective leaders and self-leaders learn how and when to use **optimistic and pessimistic visions to guide strategy and action**. Some stakeholders will change when they "**See the Light**," or engage with **positive visions**. Others will change only when they "**Feel the Heat**," or experience **negative visions**. A third group will change only when they've **experienced both visions**. These are, as you might have guessed by now, a **Sentiment Pyramid**. Good optimistic visions tend to be **future** focused, good pessimistic visions are **past** focused (remembering past problems, limits, setbacks), and good realistic visions are **present** (action) focused. As we will see, starting first with optimism, then pessimism, then critiquing both and creating plans, is typically the best approach. We call this **sentiment contrasting**.

Both arms of this **sentiment dyad**—optimism and pessimism, praise and criticism, carrots and sticks, pleasure and pain, are critical to being adaptive. We claim they are universal in nature. The physicist futurist <u>David Brin</u> coined the term **"self-preventing prophecy"** in an article of the <u>same title</u> in 1999. Brin told us that **self-preventing prophecies** (**preventable** and avoidable **negative futures**) are a counterpart to **self-improving prophecies** (**preferable** and achievable positive futures). Both kinds of stories are deeply valuable. As we'll see, leaders and self-leaders must learn to **tell each story well**, in order to create good foresight and manage change. We'll say more about sentiment contrasting and sentiment ratios in Chapter 3. In our next section, we will now consider a few applications of this universal model in foresight practice.

David Brin

Emotional-Cognitive Growth: Climbing Developmental Pyramids

We've described several **triadic pyramids** (time, foresight, values, cognitive styles, leadership, and sentiment pyramids) that wise leaders and self-leaders can learn to manage. In **triadic pyramids**, we consider the value of **three processes**, and the way two fundamental, oppositional processes create a third, more complex and valued process. In Chapter 3, we'll see these as variations of the **Evo-Devo Pyramid,** a universal way to think about managing complexity and change.

We're now ready to talk about **developmental pyramids**. These are multi-stepped cousins of the single-step **triadic pyramids** we have been discussing so far. In developmental pyramids, we are asked to consider the way lower, and less valued levels (steps) of a **hierarchy** must be managed, to allow higher, more valued levels to emerge, in a **developmental process**. Both single-step and multi-step pyramids propose rough **hierarchies of adaptiveness**. Both argue that the best leaders are **students of human and social development**, and they strive to be **"developers" of others**. Let us look at a few developmental pyramids now, and consider some of their lessons for growing adaptive foresight on teams.

We've seen that we are **emotional-cognitive** creatures, evolved to **feel first** and **think second**. We've introduced the challenge of balancing **optimism and pessimism**, our universal **sentiment dyad,** and the proposition that **realism** is an appropriate balance of these two sentiment states. In Chapter 3, we'll discuss **sentiment leadership,** how we recognize which **sentiment ratios** are best for which contexts, and how we can **ethically nudge** ourselves and our teams into better ratios, when we get **off track**. These are key topics in **emotional intelligence**.

In his bestseller, *Emotional Intelligence,* 1995/2005, the psychologist **Dan Goleman** popularized the notion that EQ is more important than IQ in career success. We highly recommend everyone take a good EQ diagnostic, like **Bradberry and Greave's** *Emotional Intelligence 2.0,* 2009. It can help us with emotional management, empathy, and relationships in life. Goleman's lesser-known book, *Social Intelligence,* 2007, explores the balance between **emotion and cognition** (EQ and IQ), and the uses of **empathy, ethics, and cognition** in groups. Leading ourselves and our groups toward greater **social (network) intelligence** is our highest challenge and responsibility, in our view.

Both developmental and social psychology, and our **management literature**, have offered us various speculative but useful **developmental pyramids**. Let's briefly consider just three of these pyramids, and some lessons from each. The first, **Maslow's pyramid**, proposes conditions necessary for **psychological growth**. The second, **Lencioni's pyramid,** describes **emotional factors** in effective groups. The third, **Senge's pyramid**, describes **cognitive factors** in effective groups. Later in this chapter, we'll offer a fourth pyramid, a **Hierarchy of Adaptive Foresight Thinking**. In the Student Edition of *ITF*, we propose the **ASOFA pyramid**, five enablers and blocks to **personal foresight and action**.

Whenever we see a developmental pyramid, we can ask if it seems evidence-based, and if it offers actionable and testable strategies for **foresight development.** In our early state of social science, we shouldn't take any developmental pyramid too seriously. Nevertheless, there is great value in **thinking hierarchically** about our **leadership priorities** in fostering self- and group adaptiveness. This is how we can build the best **social intelligence** we can. In other words, good leadership requires us to **"manage the pyramids"** that we find valuable, as best we can., not only our single-step **triadic pyramids**, but multi-step **developmental pyramids** as well. The more relevant pyramids we can see and learn from, the better. As we'll see, the **Evo-Devo Pyramid** argues that we must climb any of these steps in both **evolutionary** (free, diverse, experimental) and **developmental** (constrained, convergent, progressive) ways, at the same time.

Perhaps the most famous developmental pyramid is **Abraham Maslow's** Hierarchy of Needs. It tells us what we must pay attention to, in order to get us to the "top step", **self-actualization**. One less-known lesson from this pyramid, as Maslow stated, is that satisfying the first four steps may **progressively decrease our motivation**. It is only when we get to **self-actualization**, and the **personal foresight** we generate once we feel safe, and most importantly, **unconditionally self-accepted (USA),** when our motivation becomes **inner-directed** (vs extrinsic) and we can become **consistently proactive**. Good leaders recognize

a **natural "lag"** between a group member feeling **accepted and respected**, and that person being **truly engaged** in the group's mission and goals. Read any of **Albert Ellis's** wise books (Appendix 3) for the **critical role of self-acceptance** in personal happiness, growth, and adaptiveness. We say more about his work in the Student Edition of this book.

To get to **self-actualization**, love, belonging, and esteem, of ourselves and others, should not be given conditional on performance. Only when they are given **unconditionally**, with no expectation of reciprocation, is the member on the path to actualization. This is why we love our **animals** so deeply. Their love is truly **unconditional**. Ideally, our **family and friends** love us in this way as well. Leaders can aspire to that kind of love. The classic book on **love, belonging, and esteem** is *The Ways and Power of Love*, 1954, written by the great sociologist, **Pitirim Sorokin**. For a modern update, we highly recommend **Rutger Bregman's** related book, *Humankind*, 2020. More simply, for all leaders who want to understand the power of **human empathy, ethics, and connectedness**, remember 4U's first motto: *People First!*

Another helpful developmental pyramid is found in **Patrick Lencioni's** bestselling "management fable", *The Five Dysfunctions of a Team*, 2002. This book proposes a hierarchy of five **emotion-dependent factors** that block teams from reaching their potential. Lencioni offers these as a **developmental hierarchy,** claiming the lower-level challenges must be conquered before higher-level ones can be addressed. Lencioni's pyramid looks at group adaptiveness from the **EQ side of the social equation,** and it uses the lens of **defensive pessimism,** telling us about **traps to avoid.** This pyramid emphasizes the **Seeing, Doing, and Reviewing** steps of the **Do loop**, and thus it shortchanges **Learning**. No developmental pyramid will be complete, but if they are reasonably evidence-based, relevant, and actionable insights, each can help teams to foster greater adaptiveness.

Five Dysfunctions of a Team (Lencioni, 2002)

One lesson from Lencioni's pyramid is that **trust** is often the first block to team performance. **Stephen Covey's** classic, *The Speed of Trust*, 2008, is a classic on that challenge. Today the psychology literature calls trust by another term, **psychological safety. Amy Edmondson** is a leading scholar of psychological safety. We highly recommend her book, *The Fearless Organization*, 2018. It is rich with practical tips for leaders in **protecting psychological safety**, so team members feel safe to discuss ideas, problems, and potential failures, without negative consequences, including discrimination, intimidation, sarcasm, and snark. In 2015 Google's people operations group surveyed 100,000 of their employees, seeking the top characteristics of **great managers**. They found that psychological safety was the **most necessary group norm** enabling team performance. They defined this norm as "Team members feel safe to take risks and be vulnerable in front of each other." They found four additional norms common to <u>Great Managers and Teams,</u> **Dependability** (of leaders and team members), **Structure and Clarity**, **Meaning of Work**, and **Impact of Work**. Like Lencioni, they offered these factors as a developmental progression (pyramid), with the first step (base) being psychological safety.

Another key lesson on **trust and teams** is found in **Tesedal Neeley's** excellent <u>Remote Work Revolution</u>, 2021. Neeley reminds us that in typical teaming, we begin by rapidly offering **cognitive trust**, and only slowly do we offer **emotional trust**. In other words, we communicate first in **System 1**, and we don't openly discuss **System 2**. This is of course **flipped** from how we actually think. Remote work makes the lag between cognitive and emotional trust establishment even longer, as nonverbal cues are less present. A good team leader will model empathy, create safe conditions for self-disclosure, and use a <u>variety of techniques</u> to overcome emotional limitations in remote work platforms. Over time, conversations can become much more **balanced** around both emotional and cognitive issues relevant to the team, and motivation and performance will grow.

Another lesson from Lencioni's pyramid is that the next most common block to team performance, after psychological safety, is a hidden **Fear of Conflict**. He tells us that a key duty of a good leader is to help the team recognize that a **trusted conflict, of a certain degree, is actually good for the team.** In our complex, uncertain world, it is very helpful to have both a **diversity of views**, and ethical, empathic, and **constructive conflict**s as we **craft strategy**. In 1994, **Goldberg and Ury** published the cartoon at right for the relationship between team **conflict and performance**. This insightful curve proposes there is an optimum frequency and amplitude of conflict (Point B), on teams, in groups, and in firms,, and that

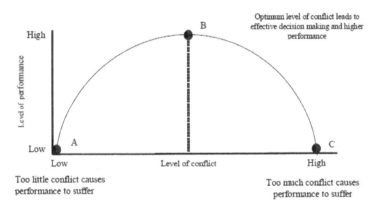

Conflict and Performance Curve (Goldberg & Ury, 1994)

performance drops on each side of that optimum. Too much, too little, or the wrong types of conflict will all hurt performance. In other words, because we are each unique and imperfect, facing complexities that far exceed us, **constructive conflicts** about what we don't know, or think we know, can **greatly improve** collective foresight and action.

The curve at right proposes that **better conflict management** allows both **higher rates of performance** and **higher rates of trusted, productive conflict**. It reminds us that the best team decisions often result from **strong battles between different, evidence-based views**, each working under conditions of **ambiguity and uncertainty**, and each running their own **LFAR loops,** under the loose guidance of leaders.

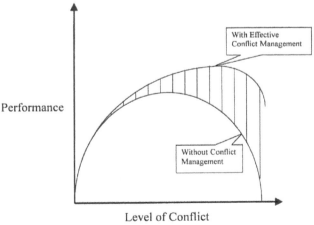

Conflict Improvement Potential (Goldberg & Ury, 1994)

As we'll see in the next section, the modern **Foresight Pyramid (Four Ps)** proposes that **predictive contrasting** and **sentiment contrasting** are the **two most important conflicts** that we must manage to produce great **strategic foresight**. It also reminds us that both individuals and teams will tend to **devalue and skip predictive contrasting**, the conflict at "bottom of the pyramid", even though **predictive contrasting sets the stage for sentiment contrasting,** and our normative conflicts over **strategy**. Effective leaders learn to adjust for these biases, and help their teams to recognize and overcome them.

A good textbook on constructive conflict leadership, focusing on social conflict, is **Kriesberg and Dayton's** *Constructive Conflicts*, 5th Ed., 2016. Like all texts (and our *Guide* itself) it can be studied by students, and skimmed by leaders. It offers case studies of functional and dysfunctional group conflict. All books on **constructive conflict** recognize the **value of ethical and empathic conflict**, in a culture of **psychological safety.** Leaders should strive to keep their more strategy- and mission-important conflict communications transparent to the team, and to shield the team from the more personal and strategically-peripheral conflicts. They should use both **democratic and autocratic processes** to resolve team conflicts, as needed. Per the **95/5 Rule**, we believe that 95% of the time, to a rough approximation, conflict resolutions should be as **democratic as possible**. The **5%** in any complex network (leaders, formal and informal) are only **rarely smarter** than the **95%** (all stakeholders, as a collective).

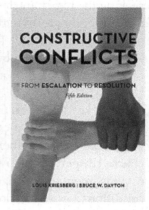

Kriesberg & Dayton 2016

In improving conflict management, it can also be very helpful to diagnose our **currently preferred style**. The **Thomas-Killman Instrument (TKI)** diagnoses **five predictable conflict management styles**. The TKI is a both an assessment and a developmental model. It asks the leader to recognize the value of **moving up and to the right** on two axes: **assertiveness and cooperativeness,** toward a **Collaborating** conflict management style.

From Ed Batista: Thomas-Kilmann Conflict Modes
www.edbatista.com/2007/01/conflict_modes_.html

Competing
- Zero-sum orientation
- Win/lose power struggle

Collaborating
- Expand range of possible options
- Achieve win/win outcomes

ASSERTIVENESS
Focus on my needs, desired outcomes and agenda

Compromising
- Minimally acceptable to all
- Relationships undamaged

Avoiding
- Withdraw from the situation
- Maintain neutrality

Accommodating
- Accede to the other party
- Maintain harmony

COOPERATIVENESS
Focus on others' needs and mutual relationships

Most of us have a "natural" conflict resolution style that corresponds with one of the five modes shown above. But all of these modes can be used effectively in the right situation. It's important to develop our ability to choose the right mode and increase our level of comfort with alternative styles.

The picture above summarizes these five common styles. We recommend the TKI assessment for all teams. We can all take this instrument to discover our **currently preferred conflict management style**. Which are you? Just like **Eagle** leaders, the **collaborating style** (upper right) can see the greatest **range of options**, and most easily **bridge differences** to find **positive-sum group outcomes**. When we know our personal style, we can better prevent it from negatively impacting team conflicts, and we can better see ways to nudge the team to a more **collaborative, positive-sum style**. In *BPF*, we'll discuss **positive-sum thinking and rulesets** as one foundation of all the most **adaptive human networks**.

A key role of the leader is to know not only their **conflict management style**, and the importance of a team that is thinking **positive-sum**, but **which conflicts to promote and manage,** and how to keep them **constructive**, not destructive. Shortly, we will describe the modern Foresight Pyramid, a model of foresight production that involves managing two separate conflicts within the group: the **intellectual ("cognitive") conflict** between **probable and possible futures (predictive contrasting)**, and the **emotional conflict** between **preferable and preventable futures (sentiment contrasting)**.

Recall that **dual process theory** argues that emotional-intuitive and cognitive-deliberative processes are the two key ways we think. Using dual process theory and the modern foresight pyramid, we propose that **predictive and sentiment contrasting** are the two most foundational **foresight conflicts** we must manage, in ourselves and on our teams. To help with the **sentiment contrasting challenge**, we have developed and student-tested a few frameworks of our own, including **GRASP thinking** and **ADOR analysis** (both discussed shortly). We hope you find them useful in your practice.

Our last developmental pyramid focuses on **Learning**, the first step of the Do loop. It also approaches learning from the **IQ** (much more than EQ) perspective, and it frames conflicts mainly from the **strategic optimism** perspective. Thus we find it a good complement to Lencioni's pyramid. This pyramid is found in **Peter Senge's** management classic *The Fifth Discipline: The Art and Practice of the Learning Organization,* 1999/2005. As we'll see in Chapter 4, Senge proposes that becoming a <u>learning organization</u> is the best way to stay competitive in a complex, uncertain, and accelerating business environment. We agree with his perspective, but only as a **first step**. More precisely, we propose that becoming a **Learning, Foresight, Action, and Reviewing (LFAR) organization** is actually the **most adaptive model**.

Senge offers us five organizational learning disciplines, in a **developmental progression**. **Mark Smith** depicts Senge's disciplines as a learning pyramid (picture right). At the base, in Senge's model, is <u>**systems thinking**</u>. Systems thinking occurs when the team seeks to identify relevant <u>actors</u>, <u>relationships</u>, and <u>constraints</u> on the organization. We list several good primers for **systems thinking** in Appendix 3. **Ackoff and Addison's** *Systems Thinking for Curious Managers,* 2010 is a current favorite. Most **strategic foresight programs** teach systems thinking as a **foundational course** in the development of our **rational faculties**. They have internalized Senge's insight, and you can as well.

Five Disciplines of a Learning Organization
Smith, 2001, based on Senge, 1999

Another point of this pyramid is that we use systems thinking to build **mental models** (collectively, a worldview) which guide our understanding, and the masteries we value. Another good book that helps managers become more data- and model-savvy is **Scott Page's** *The Model Thinker,* 2018. In the Student Edition of this book, Chapters 8 and 9 cover additional **models, curves, and cycles** helpful to organizational foresight. In Senge's view, we use **systems thinking, models,** and **implicit assumptions,** to find or make **frameworks (practice models)** and **methods** (across the LFAR steps). Then we seek to **gain mastery** in practicing those, in various contexts. **Teamwork** and developing **shared vision** are the highest-level developmental steps (disciplines) in his view. In Chapter 2, we'll propose **Twenty Specialties** that adaptive organizations can **master**. In the next section, we offer several useful **foresight frameworks**, and in Chapter 5, more frameworks, and 150 **methods**. We hope they help your foresight journey.

Senge's pyramid places **emotional challenges** as higher level ones. Lencioni reverses this order, which fits better with the reality that we **feel first**, and **think second**. Yet both pyramids are quite helpful. **Lencioni's** helps us to **manage and develop teams** from the perspective of **System 1** (intuition, emotion). **Senge's** helps us to manage and develop them via **System 2** (deliberation, cognition). We'll discuss Senge's pyramid again in Chapter 4. Both have much to teach us.

A Few Particularly Useful Foresight Frameworks

We are now ready to consider a handful of particularly general and valuable **foresight frameworks (procedures)** useful for ourselves, our teams, and our organizations. The first, the **Four Ps (Modern Foresight Pyramid)**, is a **foresight conflict management framework**. When we fuse it with the **Do loop**, we get **REOPS**, 4U's preferred **foresight production**

framework. In Chapter 2, we'll introduce the **Eight Skills**, 4U's team and organizational **adaptive foresight framework.** We will see other useful frameworks in Chapter 5.

We can think of frameworks like **recipes.** All good cooks **begin** their training with them, and will **often use them** as is, but they also **deviate creatively** in practice. Which frameworks you use, in any situation, and how you modify them, will be guided by your **intuition, preference, and results.** The more **experience** you gain analyzing the future for others, with feedback, the better you'll get at using frameworks, and integrating foresight and action for adaptive outcomes.

1. The Four Ps (Modern Foresight Pyramid): Mental Contrasting and Conflict Management

We've described the **Classic Foresight Pyramid** as a **universal** model of foresight, rooted in **physics,** in how nature works. But when we apply it to living systems, there is one big **shortcoming** to the model. It doesn't acknowledge **sentiment,** and the **duality of our emotions,** which is also the **duality of our outcomes** in terms of **values.** All living systems with complex brains regulate their behavior via **conflicts** between **pleasure seeking** and **pain avoidance.** In lower animals, much of this conflict is genetically regulated and instinctual. In higher animals, we engage in continual **conflict management** between **positive and negative internal and group sentiments,** guiding our **Do loops.**

The **Modern Foresight Pyramid,** which we will simply call the **foresight pyramid** in this *Guide*, splits **strategy** into these positive and negative elements. In this pyramid, **Four Assessments (Four Ps)** are central to foresight production:

1. **Probable** futures (trends, convergences, forecasting, prediction)
2. **Possible** futures (imagination, combinations, uncertainties, unknowns)
3. **Preferable** futures (optimism, opportunities, visions, goals, priorities)
4. **Preventable** futures (pessimism, threats, risks, disruptions, blocks)

Here is the **Modern Foresight Pyramid** in graphic form:

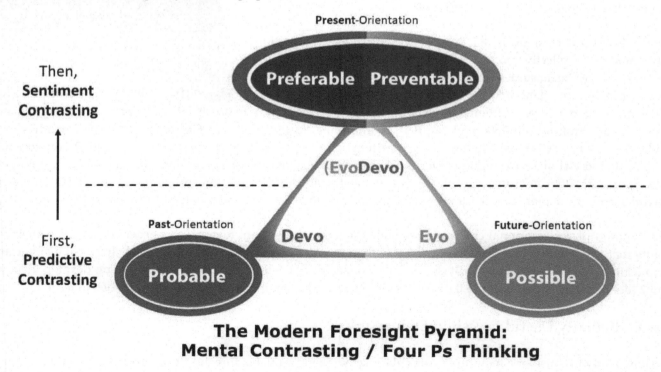

**The Modern Foresight Pyramid:
Mental Contrasting / Four Ps Thinking**

In this model, there are **two classic mental contrasts (conflicts)** we all engage in while doing foresight thinking. The first, which we call **predictive contrasting**, looks at relevant **probabilities** (predictable and expected processes), and contrasts them against relevant **possibilities** (unpredictable and unexpected processes) both in our **environment** and in **ourselves**. The second contrasts **positive and negative sentiment**, about our strategies and futures.

We can now state the **Four Ps** as two classic **mental contrasting** activities:

I. Predictive contrasting

- **Probable** futures (trends, convergences, forecasting, prediction)
- **Possible** futures (imagination, combinations, uncertainties, unknowns)

II. Sentiment contrasting

- **Preferable** futures (optimism, opportunities, visions, goals, priorities)
- **Preventable** futures (pessimism, threats, risks, disruptions, blocks)

Emeritus futurist <u>**Art Shostak**</u> gave us the **Four Ps model** in 2001. He recognized any discussion of the preferable, without the preventable, was **dangerously incomplete**. Our contribution is to offer Shostak's model as a **mental contrasting and conflict management framework**, using evo-devo thinking. The Modern Foresight Pyramid tells us that sentiment contrasting about **positive** and **negative** futures is typically our **highest value activity** ("top of the pyramid"). It also tells us such contrasting *depends* on doing good predictive contrasting (exploring **Probable** and **Possible** foresight) *before* we deeply engage **sentiment**. In other words, our most useful positive and negative visions emerge only *after* we have assessed both what is **most likely to happen** without our intervention, and the many kinds of **uncertainty** that could affect our strategy.

Art Shostak, 2020

Without formal studies to support this claim, but with evo-devo models to guide us, we propose that beginning our future thinking with **predictive contrasting**, first assessing relevant **probable futures**, and then relevant **possible futures**, is typically ideal preparation for **strategic thinking**. Likewise, we claim that the **most effective strategic plans** arise out of what psychologist **Gabrielle Oettingen** calls "**mental contrasting**," starting with **optimistic thinking**, followed by **pessimistic thinking**. Fortunately, this second claim has a great deal of evidence for it, as we will discuss.

In this *Guide*, we will use the term "**sentiment contrasting**" to refer to **Oettingen's first-optimism-then-pessimism thinking**. We redefine the term **mental contrasting** to include *both* types of contrasting—**predictive contrasting** *followed by* **sentiment contrasting**—in other words, using the **Four Ps**. In both processes of contrasting, we are maintaining a **productive conflict** between **two opposing ways of thinking**. Whether we do Four Ps thinking and feeling **quietly** in our minds, or **out loud**, on teams, we propose it is our most generally adaptive form of **foresight conflict management**.

Predictive contrasting is primarily **rationality guided** (System 2), but **emotion and intuition** (System 1) can also block us from using it effectively. Most people, including many foresight professionals, presently **don't care enough** about predictive contrasting, or its order. Fortuitously, by investing **emotion** into **how well** we do predictive contrasting, we can greatly improve it. **Sentiment contrasting**, by contrast, begins as a primarily **emotionally-guided** (System 1) process. We need to help it become more **deliberative** (System 2). To improve both, we can precede them with **learning**, and get **feedback** on their outputs. In other words, engage them in a **Do loop**.

In **sentiment contrasting**, we first prioritize **preferable futures** (what we want) and then explore **preventable futures** (plausible traps, risks, and setbacks) that could stop us from achieving our goals. As psychologist **Gabrielle Oettingen's** research (discussed under GRASP thinking) has shown, individuals and groups that do **sentiment contrasting**, beginning with optimism, will gain, depending on the task, **50-100% better predictive accuracy** with respect to their

plans, over any time horizon. They will also get **30%-150% more work done**! In the least quantitated (in Oettingen's studies) benefit, they are also more **motivated** to work through anticipated **difficulties**. In other words, improved predictive accuracy, productivity, and motivation are **three major adaptive benefits** to using this **sentiment contrasting** process. We think similar benefits could be quantified for using **predictive contrasting**. Those studies remain to be done.

Once we are using these two forms of mental contrasting, we are engaged in a powerful form of **strategic foresight**. **Strategy** can be defined both in **opportunistic** terms (to achieve preferable visions) and in **defensive** terms (to prevent traps and threats). As **Oettingen** and her husband, psychologist **Peter Gollwitzer** say, effective **strategic plans** include statements about getting and managing **Key Resources** (**positive** things that can help us) and using **If-Then statements in our plans** for preventing **setbacks or blocks** (plausible **negative** outcomes) based on anticipation or past experience. This **first positive**, **then negative** sentiment analysis, **prior** to creating our **plans**, is key to producing better foresight for ourselves, our teams, our firms, and society at large.

We will say more about what strategy is later. For now, consider that all good strategy must address the **Two Fundamental Goals or Purposes of Foresight**. It must **help us advance** and **prevent harm**. Good **strategy** is always about managing both **positive and negative outcomes**, and **positive and negative sentiments** in relation to those outcomes. Because this mental conflict management is how we actually think, the **Four Ps are simply a better set of assessments** than the Three Ps for looking to and analyzing the future.

Again, good professionals realize that **only the last two Ps** are of **significant interest** to the **typical stakeholder**, or the **typical client**. Most folks just don't care strongly about either the **Probable** or the **Possible** ("the bottom of the pyramid") or recognize the need to **contrast them**. Those who do have an interest will often care about **only one** of them. In modern Western culture, the **Possible** (imagination, design) is typically **much more popular** than the **Probable**. We call this state of mind **Freedom Bias (antiprediction bias)**, and will discuss it shortly, and throughout our *Guide*. Good leaders will help their teams to fight this bias, and become masters of probability thinking.

At the beginning of foresight work, we claim it is typically best to think and feel *first* of the **probable** and then the **probable (predictive contrasting)**, in that order, and *next* to think and feel about **both positive and negative futures (sentiment contrasting)**, again typically **in that order**. But as **dual process theory (System 1 and 2)** and **negativity bias** (to be discussed shortly) tell us, we commonly reverse this order. We often think first, longest, and strongest about **negative things** in general, before we think about positive things. Under **Negativity Bias** (introduced shortly), we don't spend enough time generating **Preferable futures**, and we don't think enough about **Preventable futures,** those specific disruptions, threats, traps, and setbacks that might block our goals. In other words, we often **diffuse** our negative thinking, focusing mainly on "safe" negatives, those that don't matter to strategy, rather than the relevant ones, those that cut close to the bone, and expose our real shortcomings and weaknesses. **Avoiding our most relevant negatives** (pain avoidance) is a common psychological motivator. But to be effective leaders and self-leaders, enduring some pain is always necessary to achieve the most desirable goals. We are truly self-directed when we can predict, accept, minimize, and guide the kinds of pain we must experience, to get to our goals.

The graphic below is a version of the **Modern Foresight Pyramid** that lists the **four main conflict groups in foresight work**. We have already seen the **Optimist and Pessimist** types. We have also discussed the **Anticipator and Innovator** types, and will explore them in depth in Chapter 2, in the context of the **Eight Skills**. Different people tend to stake out different positions among the Four Ps, often based on their **personalities**, as we will now discuss. Effective leaders must recognize these different positions, and manage their conflicts, to produce great foresight.

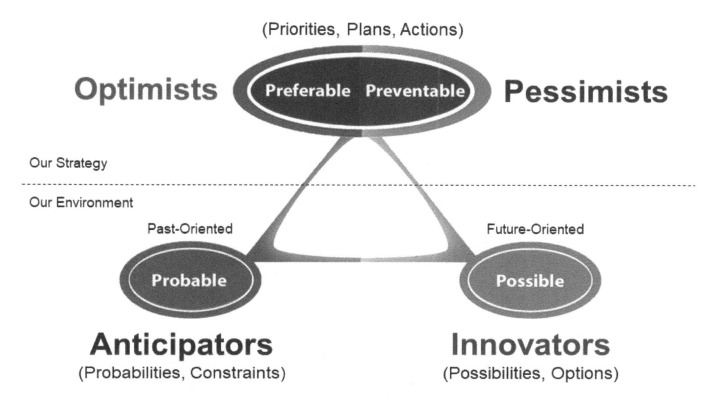

The Four Main Conflict Groups in Foresight Work

Fortunately, we can **easily identify** these **four types of productive conflict leaders**, and their affinity groups, by paying attention to their language and behaviors, and by using **formal assessments**. In the most Four Ps congruent assessment we know, different **personality types** are attracted to each of these four ways of thinking about the future. Psychologist **David Keirsey** has an excellent model, the **Four Temperaments,** a variation of the famous **Myers-Briggs Personality Types Inventory** (MBTI) test. We recommend taking both the Keirsey assessment and the MBTI for self-knowledge.

The MBTI was created in the mid-20th century by two autodidacts, **Isabel Myers** and her mother, **Katharine Briggs,** extending the work of analytical psychologist **Carl Jung**. Where the MBTI gives sixteen combinations of personality type, **Keirsey's Temperament Sorter** test identifies four classic types, and sixteen subtypes. In 4U 's assessment, Keirsey's four temperaments closely associate with the four kinds of foresight assessments, and thus also the **Evo-Devo Pyramid**. While no model is perfect, we think Keirsey has discovered **four particularly general (universal)** kinds of **personality type**. The **Four Temperaments** is thus simplest personality model we know that is very helpful for **leading group dynamics**.

In Keirsey's personality model, **Guardians** are the foundation of society. They seek to preserve the status quo, and what has worked in the past. They can be a bit serious. **Artisans** are creative, more spontaneous, and they like to enjoy themselves. **Idealists** are passionate about positive visions, growth, and personal development. **Rationals** are problem solvers, logical, and they value competence and ingenuity. Different **percentages** of these four types can be found in different populations, eras, cultures, organizations, and careers. In recent years, Keirsey has estimated the US population as 45% Guardian, 30% Artisan, 15% Idealist, and 10% Rational. The free 70-question <u>Keirsey Temperament Sorter</u> is an online self-assessment you can complete in 15 minutes. It will tell you your primary temperament type(s) and some "intelligence" subtypes related to the MBTI. You can also have your team and organization take this free test, or their for-pay variations at Keirsey.com. Keirsey's <u>Please Understand Me II</u>, 1998, is the classic text for exploring these four temperaments in society and on teams. Keirsey's <u>Portraits of Temperament</u>, 2nd Ed, 1988, offers a briefer introduction.

The picture below outlines Keirsey's temperaments, and their close relationship to the Four Ps. Knowing **who** on your team can be described by each of these temperaments, or combinations of temperaments, and ensuring that each temperament is adequately **represented** in discussions, can greatly help leaders with foresight conflict management.

Keirsey's Four Temperaments — Preferences for the Fours Ps
(Please Understand Me II, 1998)

There are many **mental contrasting lessons** to be found in the Keirsey model. For example, if we self-identify foremost as **Idealists**, as some (but certainly not all) futurists do, we must remind ourselves that the most **practical and valued form** of that idealism will be **strategic optimism**, mostly in the **now and near-term**, with only a small fraction of preference thinking, per the Power Law of Future Thinking, directed to the long-term future. As Idealists, we also need to think hard about what **traps** we must prevent, and work closely with our **Rational** colleagues to find more of those traps, and with our **Guardian** and **Artisan** colleagues to explore **probable** constraints and conditions, and the many hidden **possibilities and uncertainties** ahead. If we self-identify as **Rationals**, by contrast, we can cultivate our natural strength in **defensive pessimism**. We like to identify and fix **problems**, but we must remember that opportunity thinking, and working with **Idealist** colleagues, can help us find the **best problems to solve,** the ones with the greatest upside for us and our teams. If we are **Guardians**, or **Artisans**, we can again see our unique strengths, and recognize the value of the other types. **Guardians** can tell us what has **worked well so far**, and **Artisans** can show us what our, visions, logic and evidence **fails to see**. This model reminds us of the **value of all four assessments in foresight creation**.

Which of these four temperaments do you prefer to use in foresight? In which domains? Take the Keirsey test to get a sense of your typical preferences across all **Six Domains**. There is no Keirsey test yet that is **specific** to each domain. In evo-devo models, the **Personal and Team** domains are dominantly evolutionary, the **Global and Universal** domains are dominantly developmental, and the **Organizational and Societal** domains are a mix, or evo-devo. That means we may express a **somewhat different set of temperaments** in each of these three groups of foresight domains.

For a personal example, in the language of the **Six Domains**, John tends to be a **Guardian** in seeking to find and protect universal knowledge, an **Idealist** in the search for societal and global visions, and a **Rational** in analyzing organizational and societal problems. In novel situations on small teams, he is often an **Artisan**, and thus can easily overdo ideation and experiments, and must remind himself to get group buy-in prior to action. In truth, all of us range across this pyramid, *by context*. The better we see our and other's use of the four temperaments, the better our thinking and action can be.

For all their benefits, the Four Ps are not a *complete* model of **strategic foresight**. A full definition of **foresight work** requires adding a key step *ahead* of the Four Ps—**Learning**, and then placing all of these elements in a **Do loop**, in which our foresight product is **expressed** (action) and **critically reviewed** (review). Technically, learning is **preparation for foresight**, using the other two arms of the Time Pyramid, our relevant **past** and **present**. But in practice, it is essential foresight work. Most obviously, learning helps with the first P, assessing the **probable** future, by finding evidence-based historical **patterns, models and trends**. Slightly less obviously, we also use learning to improve our **possible, preferable**, and **preventable** futures assessments, by understanding their histories, successes, failures, and assumptions.

Learning and the Four Ps, embedded in a **Do loop** of **expression** and **review**, are thus our **basic model of strategic foresight**. We call this the **REOPS cycle** (discussed shortly), our framework for **five critical steps** in **strategic foresight production**. Of course, adaptive foresight requires not only foresight *production* but also effective **action**. We will discuss that challenge, the **foresight-action cycle**, and its **Eight Skills**, in Chapter 2.

2. GRASP Thinking: Personal Foresight Production

As we've said, **sentiment contrasting** is a specific type of **realism**, and **personal foresight,** in which we **contrast** our sentiment states back and forth between **strategic optimism** and **defensive pessimism**, to maximize their benefit to our forecasts, plans and actions. In studies over the last thirty years it has been compared to a wide variety of **non-sentiment planning** techniques, and to the use of various types of **both optimism and pessimism alone** prior to making **brief strategic plans and taking actions**.

Gabriele Oettingen

Most of these studies have been done by one of our leading foresight psychologists. **Gabriele Oettingen**. Her trade book, *Rethinking Positive Thinking*, 2014, and her contribution to the edited academic volume *The Psychology of the Thinking About the Future*, 2018, both outline her work. Oettingen began this personal foresight work testing **students** at the U. Hamburg and NYU, and has increasingly studied the **general populace** as well.

Oettingen learned that engaging **positive thinking alone** prior to planning **reduces motivation** for doing the actions that were visualized. If we dwell too long in an optimistic state, we can easily **feel like we've achieved the goal**, even though we haven't even started. **Negative thinking alone** prior to planning has different problems, including talking ourselves out of **goals**, the creation of **less ambitious and impactful plans**, and a **reduction in motivation** to begin actions. She has discovered that using a roughly **50:50 sentiment foresight ratio**, *first* of strategic optimism, *then* of defensive pessimism, then making plans, and then acting, is particularly effective.

In many randomized and controlled studies, by comparison various other personal foresight methods, sentiment contrasting has been shown to **significantly improve** three things: [11]

1. **Foresight accuracy** (50-100% **less error** in predicting what we'll get done, both **today** and in the **short-term**),

2. **Productivity** (30-150% **greater productivity** in a variety of timed tasks), and

3. **Motivation** to **persist** (not yet well-quantitated) is enhanced, even when faced with **difficult obstacles**.

---

[11] Gabriele Oettingen, *Rethinking Positive Thinking: Inside the New Science of Motivation*, 2014.

Oettingen also claims that sentiment contrasting also **reduces anxiety and regret**, regardless of outcome, creating a more **resilient** planner and actor. This effect seems to be more modest, and is presently less extensively supported. So for now, think about it as a way to improve our prediction, productivity, and persistence, especially in our *daily* plans and actions. Oettingen uses a four-step sentiment contrasting process, which she calls **WOOP**. It stands for **Wish** (aka Goal), **Outcome** (Positive Benefit), **Obstacles** (Potential Setbacks), and **Plan**. Using WOOP, the planner is urged to select an important, yet difficult Wish (Goal), then to think positively about the outcome, imagining its future benefits, then to think defensively about all the plausible ways the goal might not be achieved, and finally to create an **If-Then Plan** ("intention"). In the literature, WOOP is called Mental Contrasting with Implementation Intentions (MCII). As we've said, because we believe the **Four Ps** are a more fundamental model of foresight contrasting, we use the term **mental contrasting** to describe *both* **predictive contrasting** (probable then possible futures thinking) and **sentiment contrasting** (our term for Oettingen's work). Our GRASP thinking process, which we will introduce shortly, is based on the Four Ps.

In clinical trials, Oettingen found that **reverse contrasting**, or beginning with negative sentiment, then turning to positive sentiment, was **only** *half as effective*, on average, as doing the reverse, then planning. In other words, when we give in to **Negativity Bias** (discussed shortly), we get **roughly 50% less foresight accuracy and productivity** than if we started with a **positive vision**, then **contrasted** that vision with all the ways we might **fail**, and then made our **plans**. Unfortunately, **Negativity Bias is rampant** in many cultures and contexts today. Leaders who fight it have much to gain.

In a pioneering study in 1991, Oettingen found that obese women who contrasted **positive and negative images** (future expectations) of their weight loss outcomes **lost an average of 26 pounds more weight, one year later**, than women who had only a positive image of their future outcome. This was the first time she realized that sentiment contrasting prior to action created both a **more realistic forecast**, and **significantly more beneficial results**. In a later study, a **one-hour episode** of WOOP planning, done with students prior to taking **standardized tests** caused them to complete **40-60% more practice questions** over several weeks of self-study. They were also significantly more motivated and productive. WOOP interventions of greater length have also **increased academic grades** vs. control interventions over several years. Another **one-hour episode** of **sentiment contrasting** with **WOOP**, combined with **factual information** on the health benefits of eating more fruits and vegetables caused participants **to eat more fruits and vegetables for** *up to two years* after the intervention, by comparison to presenting factual information alone.

Consider that in a **one hour episode**, there is enough time for us to make our **visualizations particularly detailed and emotionally significant**. This is getting to the level of visualizations that many of the best **professional athletes** engage in prior to a competition. When was the last time you spent **15 minutes selecting a valuable near-term personal goal, 15 minutes visualizing yourself achieving it, 15 minutes visualizing the negatives** that might keep you from achieving it, and **15 minutes making an if-then plan?** If you gave any of your goals that kind of **emotional investment**, do you think it would increase your accuracy, productivity, and motivation to **check in on your plan** (run a Do loop) throughout the day? If you haven't done this yet for any of **Today's plans, now** may be a great time to start!

As **Fred Polak** said in *The Image of the Future* (PDF), 1973, our greatest task is to create a clear, plausible, and compelling **positive image of our future**—an image that will pull us toward it with its clarity and benefit. We need *Quality of Vision!* We need positive visions in every relevant time horizon: **today, tomorrow, next quarter, next year**, and the next decade, as well as for our **careers, children,** and **legacies**. Such visions are particularly important for our **self-image**. With all our **longer-term visions**, we also have to ensure **good values** are attached to them. Oettingen showed us there is a process, sentiment contrasting, that maximizes the power of visualizations. We believe that **GRASP thinking,** which fuses **sentiment contrasting** and the **Four Ps,** further maximizes that power, and can be used daily in our lives.

GRASP is 4U's fusion of WOOP, the Four Ps, and the GROW planning model (Goal, Reality, Obstacles/Options, Way Forward) from the 1970s. GROW was created by athletic coach **Tim Gallwey** in his classic, *The Inner Game of Tennis*, 1974, which described the **mental game** we all strive to **master internally first**, in order to excel at the **physical game.** GROW planning is also used in **John Whitmore's** *Coaching for Performance*, 1992, a classic on leadership and business coaching.

GRASP mental contrasting, or "**GRASP thinking,**" has five steps, as follows:

- **Goal**. First, among our current strategic options, we select a **goal**. We select this goal to be **important** and **difficult**, but **achievable**. We make an assessment of the **probability** that we can achieve it by a **specific time.** Emotionally, we should **feel optimistic and confident** about our selection.

- **Reality**. Then, we think about our current **reality**. We assess our present **distance** from the goal, in all the ways that **matter**. We imagine several of the **other possible outcomes** that don't involve achieving the goal. Emotionally, we should **feel insecure** about the many realistic outcomes that don't get us to our goal.

- **Advantages**. Then, we think **optimistically**, and **visualize in detail** some of the **advantages** we will get when we achieve the goal. We clearly imagine how our lives and future options will be both different and, in some ways, better. Emotionally, we should **feel excited** about the future benefits we may get.

- **Setbacks**. Then, we think **defensively**, and **visualize in detail** the most likely **setbacks** (obstacles),we will face on the way to the goal, given our history, habits, and current environment. This is a small subset of the possible outcomes. Emotionally, we should **feel alarmed** by the **most plausible** ways we might fail.

- **Plan**. Finally, we create our strategic **plan**, with both steps for acquiring or managing **key resources** that may help us execute the plan, and **if-then statements**, dealing with our reaction to possible **setbacks** on the way. Emotionally, when completed, we should allow ourselves to **feel confident** about the **quality of our plan**, and then quickly use that positive energy to **act**, before it subsides.

Here's a useful mnemonic (see picture right): How does one **climb a mountain**? "**One GRASP at a time.**"

Appendix 1 includes an exercise that prompts us to apply GRASP thinking to an important near term goal (today or tomorrow), and then evaluate the outcome. We hope you find it helpful. As the psychologist **Peter Gollwitzer** at NYU showed, beginning in the 1980s, **If/then anticipation of obstacles**, one of two key requirements in the **Plan** step in GRASP thinking, is a powerful way to increase motivation and productivity. If/then anticipation is especially helpful with people who usually have **difficulty with focusing attention**, being **patient**, or exercising **impulse control**. Since it is a method of **predicting likely distractions**, and how to

Alex Honnold, in Chin & Vasarhelyi's *Free Solo*, 2018

prevent them, **If/then anticipation** is extremely helpful for achieving **difficult long-term goals**. For more details on **If/then anticipation**, read **Gollwitzer and Oettingen**, *Implementation Intentions* (PDF), 2013.

In our view, when we make a quick **plan**, we must anticipate not only **obstacles** (negative) but first, **key resources** (positive) that might **help us**, and **strategies** for getting or managing them. A key resource might be something as simple as getting enough sleep the night before a planned action, or as complex as a framework or tool or a support network. When we find relationships, environments, habits, and processes that make us more effective, we need to try to get more of them. For example, if we know that getting up two hours before the rest of our family is presently our best way to get uninterrupted creative time every day, we must consciously recognize our need for that **key resource**, and make plans to get it (for example, strategies to get an afternoon nap, and/or get to bed earlier the night before). In other words, we must use **If/then anticipation** of both positive aids and negative obstacles in our **planning** step.

With regard to positive aids, many of us also do not look for **external help** to aid our growth. Today, coaches for any topic can be found on online platforms. A good coach teaches us how to push our own buttons. As our mastery grows, in any field, our **inner coach** can increasingly become the best guide to further progress. Others can a great help at the start of any new challenge, but they can never be as good at getting the best out of us, over the long term, as ourselves.

Some may like the simplicity of WOOP, others may prefer what we consider to be the additional rigor of GRASP. Use whichever **framework** feels useful and easy, for you. But please remember to contrast. We need **both predictive and sentiment contrasting** (internal conflict management) to make our **Do Loops as effective as possible**. While we don't have the data either way for **predictive contrasting**, in controlled studies, remember that **sentiment contrasting** greatly improves **foresight accuracy, productivity, and motivation**—versus optimism or pessimism alone[12]. Consider that the more **frequently** we do **GRASP thinking** throughout our day, beginning with **today's foresight** work, the **faster** we will get useful **feedback** between our plans and actions. We can use that feedback to improve our feelings, thoughts, forecasts, plans, and actions. This is essence of the **Do Loop**.

We challenge everyone to dedicate **one to two minutes** to each of the GRASP or WOOP steps in some of today's foresight challenges (**now till end-of-day**) that occur to us over the next week. We recommend that each of us spends **at least a minute per step** using GRASP thinking around our **most important goals for the day**—**before** we engage in action, and writing down at least a few words summarizing a near term action plan. **Five minutes sitting quietly**, writing tool in hand, is **not much to ask**, for the powerful benefits that will be gained by end-of-day, and again tomorrow. This is how better foresight begins, with each of us—it grows from the daily, continually repeated actions of our lives.

3. The REOPS Cycle: Organizational and Team Foresight Production

Combining **Learning** and the **Four Ps**, we can remember the core steps of strategic foresight production in an acronym, **REOPS,** helpful to **managers and teams**. The REOPS cycle covers foresight production, over any time horizon, *prior* to using it in **action**. The cycle has **five steps**, which are often best done **in sequential order**, as a **cycle**, ending with critically evaluated if-then plans. Paying **attention** to the **order and quality of each of these steps**, and **cycling through them for as long as we need to address criticism,** will reliably produce **more effective strategy**. If our foresight is followed by effective **action**, and guided by **good values**, it can then make us more **adaptive**. As a variation of the Do loop, consider the **iterative nature** of the **REOPS cycle. All foresight typically starts out poor.** It is only through **cycles of feedback,** with **diverse, tough, and honest critique,** that we get to better **strategy and plans**.

The **REOPS Cycle** tell us that foresight production requires five steps, done in a Do loop of sharing and critical review.:

1. **Research** (learning the **Past** and **Present** relevant to our scope of potential action)

2. **Expectations**, aka **Probable Futures** (probabilities, trends, constraints, convergences, forecasts— "developmental futures")

3. **Options**, aka **Possible Futures** (possibilities, ideas, potential actions, experiments, scenarios— "evolutionary futures")

4. **Priorities**, aka **Preferable Futures** (opportunities, visions, goals, basic plans—**strategic optimism**)

5. **Setbacks**, aka **Preventable Futures** (risks, blocks, traps, wildcards, uncertainties, if-then plans—**defensive pessimism**).

---

[12] Gabriele Oettingen, *Rethinking Positive Thinking: Inside the New Science of Motivation*, 2014.

Below is a cartoon of the cycle:

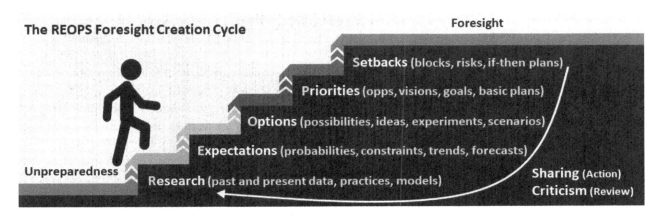

The REOPS Foresight Creation Cycle

Foresight

Setbacks (blocks, risks, if-then plans)
Priorities (opps, visions, goals, basic plans)
Options (possibilities, ideas, experiments, scenarios)
Expectations (probabilities, constraints, trends, forecasts)
Research (past and present data, practices, models)

Unpreparedness

Sharing (Action)
Criticism (Review)

REOPS is a progression (and in our graphic, a "staircase"), because these five steps of foresight production are typically best done **in this order**, ending in **if-then plans**. But, more fundamentally, **REOPS is a cycle**, as we evaluate our proposed strategy against potential **setbacks**, which typically starts us into new research, and we evaluate our **if-then plans** against a **critical community**, before we put them into action. Technically, **REOPSSR** is the full mnemonic for the basic strategic foresight production cycle. **REOPS assessments** are always followed by **Sharing** the foresight work (the Action of the foresight producer) then **Review** (critical feedback), leading to new Research. In practice, we drop the last **SR,** as these steps are **implicit** in understanding REOPS as a **cycle**.

We have just introduced a simpler version of the REOPS cycle, one particularly useful in **personal foresight**, called **GRASP thinking**. Whichever foresight framework we prefer to use, REOPS, GRASP, or another, the **Do loop** reminds us that we have to continually subject our foresight and action to critical **review**. A **sufficiently diverse and expert community** will invariably show us more potential **Setbacks** and negative visions (blocks, threats, risks, disruptions, wildcards, unknowns, and uncertainties) that we did not see in our first evaluation, and other potential **shortcomings** to our plans. That feedback will send us back into **Research**, which will modify our Expectations, Options, Priorities, and Setback analysis, resulting in **new and better plans**.

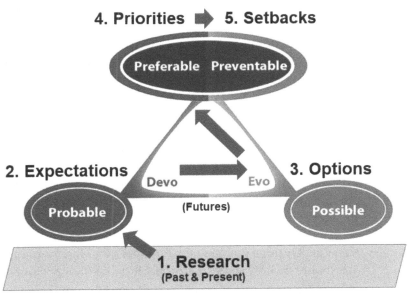

4. Priorities ➡ **5. Setbacks**

Preferable   Preventable

2. Expectations   **3. Options**

Devo   Evo

(Futures)

Probable   Possible

1. Research
(Past & Present)

REOPS: The Five Steps of Foresight Work

The graphic at right reminds us that the REOPS cycle is simply **Learning** the past and present relevant to our **scope of potential action**, followed by the **Four Ps**, and then by **expression** and **feedback** on the foresight we have produced. As **sentiment contrasting** tells us, good foresight work **ends with strategy** that takes account of both **strategic opportunities** and **defensive pessimism**, to maximize our chances of success.

In the **REOPS cycle**, our foresight production steps have been renamed from the **LAIS skills** (Chapter 2) plus **sentiment contrasting**, in an easy to remember acronym for **managers**. Just as GRASP is easy to remember and use, **REOPS** is an actual shorthand that is used to describe "<u>**Repeated Operations**</u>" in workflow. REOPS reminds us that good foresight requires **repeated cycles (operations)** of **foresight work, expression, and feedback**. In Chapter 2, we will pair **REOPS** with **Four Action Skills** to form the **Eight Skills of the Do Loop**, a **universal foresight-action cycle**. In Chapter 3, we will extend these **five steps** of foresight production to **seven tasks** of a foresight professional. The seven tasks are simply the five REOPS steps, followed by getting our work used (action), and evaluating (reviewing) its results.

Different people are better at some of the REOPS steps than others. Any one or more of these steps can be **devalued** by ourselves and our teams. We must fight that bias. **All five** are important. The best leaders know their and others **preferences**, and learn to work with **steps-balanced teams** when creating strategy. Similarly, if a professional is weak in **action** (expressing their work) or **review** (soliciting critique), their **Do loops** are at risk, and improvement may halt.

Shortly we will see that **negativity bias** (DROA bias) will often drive us to think of **negatives first** in a more diffuse and less useful way, and then positives, with what little time and energy we have left. We must consciously **reverse that order** if we are to be sufficiently **proactive**, not reactive. Also, **high-reliability organizations (HROs)** in defense, safety, government, health care, and other industries will sometimes **cut short the first three of the REOPS steps** to get quickly to the "familiar ground" of concrete goals, strategies, and actions. Alternatively, HROs may get stuck in **threat assessment** and **failure avoidance**, not seeing moderate-risk opportunities to grow.

To review the **REOPS Cycle**, good foresight creation will frequently:

1. Begin with **Research** (Learning), uncovering **Past** data, trends, models, and variables relevant to our foresight topic and estimating the **Present** conditions for those factors. Good research uses **First Principles Thinking**. It asks us to **investigate** a topic (issue, problem), and uncover the causal and correlative factors that most influence it. To do this well, we may have to consult the science, and look widely and far into the past to find evidence for our **models and hypotheses.** We may need to **run experiments** if we don't have the data to answer a question. As we do research, we discover strategies and solutions that already exist, in either the present or the past. Far too often, we shortchange this step and set out to "**reinvent the wheel**" in a slower, more expensive, and inferior process. When we've completed our initial **Research**, we can use it to:

2. Describe **Expected Futures** (forecast the **Probable**), including relevant **convergences, constraints, trends, predictions, bets, and investments** by competitors and stakeholders. This is not just the future that a **leader or an organization expects,** but the future that our foresight work indicates is **probable**, whether our clients consciously expect it or not. One challenge of this step is recognizing how much of the future we can actually **estimate well** today. The world, and our own futures, are far more predictable than many of us are willing to admit. Good anticipation thinking **anchors us** in the "framework of the probable." Sound **Research** and **Expectations** prepares us to:

3. Generate **Options** (imagine the **Possible**), looking for **plausible options, experiments, ideas,** and **innovations**. We should include some low-probability but high positive-impact possibilities (**wildcards/black swans**), which may help us generate even more ambitious visions. Together, Research (Learning) and Expectations (Anticipation) *usefully limit* the positive **possibility** thinking we should do. They **anchor** and **focus** our imagination. If we don't do these **two steps first**, we can **easily get lost** in unrealistic speculation, as far too much futurist work does today. These three steps prepare us to:

4. Converge on **Priorities** (select **Preferable** futures), to decide goals, visions, opportunities, strategies, and plans, among our all our **options**. Particularly helpful priorities are **shared and motivating visions** of states we want to reach, and **strategies and plans** that might get us there. Again, our chosen **priorities, opportunities, goals and visions**, will **anchor us** to particular set of desired outcomes. Strategic optimism drives this opportunity evaluation, prioritization, decisionmaking, and initial planning step. These four steps prepare us to:

5. Consider **Setbacks** (plausible **Preventable** futures) relevant to our goals and strategic plans. For this step, we put on our **defensive thinking-hat** and imagine likely **blocks**, **traps**, **threats**, **uncertainties**, and **negative outcomes**—including **negative wildcards** (low probability, high negative impact) that may derail us if we are unlucky or not careful enough. Better-imagined negative visions will scare and, subsequently, motivate us to go back to Step 1, to do more **Research** on evidence or models that might help us resolve uncertainties or on tools or strategies that might help us manage potential threats. When our imagined setbacks no longer cause us to restart the cycle, we are ready to **share** our foresight work, and **seek feedback** from our **critical community**. Once **their diverse and honest criticisms** of our tentative priorities, strategies, and plans no longer sends us back to Step 1, or once we decide we can **live with them**, we put our foresight into **action**.

There are many times when we will choose to **move nonsequentially** between the REOPS steps and the LAIS skills. But at the start of foresight work, the **order** of these steps will guide us well. Remember that many clients are less interested in the **first three** of the REOPS steps. They may be unmotivated to **learn** the relevant past and present, or think about **probable** futures. They may be only slightly more interested in exploring **possible** futures. Each can be **devalued** by clients who want to get quickly to **strategy** (opportunity and danger) and **action**. Among the first three REOPS steps, **probable foresight** (anticipation, the expected future) is typically the most undervalued assessment, both within the foresight profession and in most modern cultures. We will talk about that challenge, **Freedom Bias**, shortly.

4. ADOR Analysis (SWOT 2.0): Simple Task Analysis

ADOR analysis, developed by our team at 4U, is a sentiment-contrasting framework for quick and daily **task analysis** and **strategy production**. We **pronounce ADOR as "Aaay-door"**, to avoid confusing it with the word "adore".

ADOR analysis proposes **Two Fundamental Questions (Goals, Purposes) of Foresight** work, the first **opportunistic**, the second **defensive**. Each of these two fundamental questions can be usefully divided into **two assessments**. The first two assessments are more focused on our **external environment**, and we use environmental scanning primarily to do them. The second two assessments are more focused on **ourselves, our teams, and our organizations,** and we must use both external and internal analysis to answer them.

To summarize ADOR Analysis, the **First Question** that we all seek to use strategic foresight to answer is:

1. **How Do We Best Adapt and Advance?**
   This question can be managed with two assessments:

   <u>Advantage</u> **Assessment** and <u>Opportunity</u> **Assessment**

   - **Advantage** is concerned with **defining and measuring benefit, progress, or improvement** in our environment—both among our **competitors** and potential **collaborators**—and strategies to get more of it for ourselves and our partners.

   - **Opportunity** is recognizing **potentially good** strategies, innovations, experiments, and behaviors for **ourselves**. **Opportunities** can exist in both **benefit accumulation** and **risk reduction**, and they are often related to the **disruptions** presently occurring around us.

The **Second Question** we all must use strategic foresight to answer is:

2. **What Could Harm or Disrupt Us?**
   This question can also be managed with two assessments:

   <u>Disruption</u> **Assessment** and <u>Risk</u> **Assessment**.

- **Disruption** is concerned with **forced changes**, happening anywhere in our **environment**, that may be undesirable ("disruption") or unanticipated (also called "surprise"). Disruption is inevitably positive for some, and negative for others. Ideally, we will try to take **advantage** of the positives of disruption, while seeking to **mitigate** its negative effects at the same time.

- **Risk** is concerned with **bad things** that could happen—primarily to **ourselves**. We use the negative definition of risk here, which is also called "**Threats**." We must know their likelihood, their potential magnitude, and strategies to **manage** and **mitigate** them.

These **Two Questions** answer the broad "Why" of foresight work. They tell us **why foresight matters**, to individuals, teams, organizations, and societies. The **Four Assessments**, by extension, answer the "**What**" of foresight thinking and practice. They tell us **what assessments we must continually make**, as primary goals of our practice. We will refer to ADOR frequently throughout the *Guide*. **It is to ADOR in our environment that we must continually adapt**. As the slide below shows, **ADOR analysis (Advantages, Disruptions, Opportunities, and Risks)** focuses us on **strategic optimism first**, and on **defensive pessimism second**. ADOR reminds us to start our strategic foresight analysis with **environmental scanning**, then proceed to **internal assessment**.

ADOR Analysis:
Outside In + Mental Contrasting = A Better SWOT

Q1. How can we adapt and advance?
- Pain Point Solutions
- Best Case Scenarios
- Black Swans (Positive)

Q2. What could harm or disrupt us?
- Burning Platforms
- Worst Case Scenarios
- Black Swans (Negative)

External

- **Advantage**
- **Disruption**
- - - - - - - - - - - - - - - -
- **Opportunity**

Internal

- **Risk** ("Threat")

Balanced Foresight

ADOR analysis is an upgrade of SWOT analysis that assesses:
- **First External (Environmental), then Internal Perspectives**
- **First Positive, then Negative Potentials**

Foresight University

Observant readers will note that ADOR analysis is an update of an older double dyad analysis tool, **SWOT (Strengths, Weaknesses, Opportunities, and Threats) analysis**, created by <u>Albert Humphrey</u> at SRI in 1966. **SWOT analysis** also requires **four strategic assessments**: first of our **internal** Strengths & Weaknesses and second of **external** Opportunities & Threats. SWOT remains popular and relevant today.

In our view, SWOT is useful for occasional whole-organization assessments, but has many disadvantages for use with daily and weekly tasks. The **order of SWOT**, starting with internal and then external assessments, is **less effective** for evaluating relevant external change than ADOR. In ADOR analysis, foresight professionals are asked to first assess **external Advantages**, then **external Disruptions**, then **internal Opportunities**, and finally **internal Risks**, in that order.

Good foresight typically begins with **environmental assessments** relative to tasks, and then **moves inward**. SWOT's "Strengths" and "Weaknesses" terms for internal positives and negatives are also weak categories to use. Strengths and Weaknesses should be evaluated **in relation** to our current Opportunities and Risks (threats). We often need to **partner with others** to gain an opportunity, or mitigate a risk. In short, ADOR is a more useful strategic analysis framework.

Remember also that **Advantages** are new adaptive capacities being **gained by others**, but **not yet by us**. The word **advantage** reminds us that we have a **primary responsibility** in foresight to **scan** for **daily positive change, happening externally**. **Disruptions** are **forced changes or catastrophes** that are harming some while **creating new advantages** for others. Catastrophes are **almost always positive for some**, while being **negative for others**. The word **disruption** reminds us to find both the **positives and negatives** of all forced change.

We must continually be **"of two minds"** in ADOR analysis, acknowledging and rewarding both our **strategic optimists** and **defensive pessimists**. We must learn how to **integrate these opposing mindsets** to generate adaptive strategy and action. **Roger Martin's** *The Opposable Mind: How Successful Leaders Win through Integrative Thinking*, 2007, offers a great introduction to oppositional and integrative thinking styles.

With ADOR, we are asked to work **outside in**, first **scanning** for relevant **external changes** for others—both positive and negative. Then, we **translate those changes** into potential **Opportunities** and **Risks** for us, given our specific context. **Horizon scanning** (STEEPLES, DIMEFIL, etc.) and **emerging issues analysis** are thus the first two steps of ADOR analysis. **General threat identification** is previewed under **Disruptions**, but actual **risk assessment** is saved for the last of the four assessments, when we have the greatest context to allow us to determine both **action and inaction risk**. Very often we create future risk for ourselves by **refusing to act**, because we are being **overly cautious or conservative**.

Here's how **ADOR analysis** works in practice. Note first two are **Learning steps**, the second core **Foresight steps**.

1. **Scan for Advantages**
   Find <u>external</u> benchmarks, expertise, data, and advances, relevant to task– **Past & Present**

2. **Scan for Disruptions**
   Find forced changes, to <u>others</u>, relevant to task– **Past & Present**

3. **Evaluate Opportunities**
   For <u>you and your team</u>, in delivering the task – **Future**

4. **Evaluate Risks**
   For <u>you and your team</u>, in delivering the task - **Future**

ADOR analysis maximizes both **situational awareness** and **strategic options**. Alternating sequences, like sentiment contrasting and ADOR analysis, are also found in the **Four LAIS Foresight Skills** (Chapter 2). We will see that the LAIS skills are an alternating sequence of **divergent**, **convergent**, **divergent**, and **convergent** types of future thinking.

Curiously, **alternating sequences** between **two opposing processes**, and several other universal patterns we will encounter later (e.g., cycles, positive and negative feedback, thresholds, differentiation, integration) are found in **all living systems**. They are critical to keeping complex systems **balanced, responsive, and adaptive**. We believe the world needs more and better **biologically-based models** of foresight and action—grounded by evidence and science, especially by the science of **complex systems**—to improve foresight practice and make it more generally adaptive.

As we'll describe, ADOR analysis helps us to fight a **common bias** in our evolutionary psychology, in our media, and in our culture, the **DROA Bias**, in which we tend to feel and think first and strongest in **intuitive and defensive** ways about disruption and risk (System 1), and in which deliberative and aspirational feeling and thinking are much weaker and secondary responses (System 2). That bias can be quite dangerous, as we will discuss.

5. The Futures Cone (Seven Ps): Complex Future Judgments

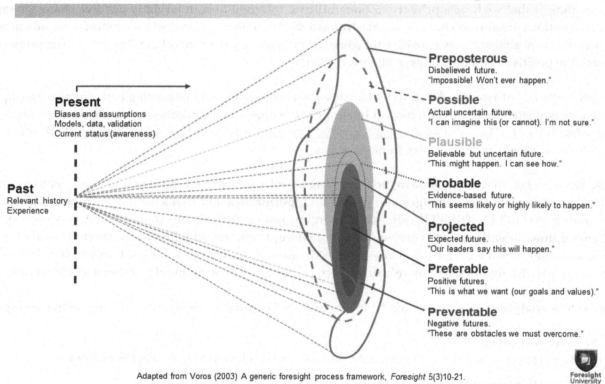

The Futures Cone: The Seven Ps of Future Judgments

Present
Biases and assumptions
Models, data, validation
Current status (awareness)

Past
Relevant history
Experience

Preposterous
Disbelieved future.
"Impossible! Won't ever happen."

Possible
Actual uncertain future.
"I can imagine this (or cannot). I'm not sure."

Plausible
Believable but uncertain future.
"This might happen. I can see how."

Probable
Evidence-based future.
"This seems likely or highly likely to happen."

Projected
Expected future.
"Our leaders say this will happen."

Preferable
Positive futures.
"This is what we want (our goals and values)."

Preventable
Negative futures.
"These are obstacles we must overcome."

Adapted from Voros (2003) A generic foresight process framework, *Foresight* 5(3)10-21.

Foresight University

One last framework and model, the **Futures Cone**, deserves inclusion in our opening chapter. It is an adaptation of the **Foresight Hourglass**, focusing on the most valuable types of **future judgments** we can make prior to strategy. Physicist and futurist **Joseph Voros** describes the history of this cone in "The Futures cone, use and history," 2017. In 1990, **Charles Taylor** depicted the **Foresight Hourglass** as a **futures "cone of plausibility,"** expanding in diameter as time horizons lengthen, and a **"back cone" of past possibilities**, collapsing down to the **present**. Futurists **Trevor Hancock** and **Clement Bezold** added several more kinds of futures to the cone in 1994. Voros created his version in 2000, reaching six judgments in 2017. We have added a seventh judgment (Preventable futures) in the model depicted above.

Due to Taylor's original coining, this diagram of **expanding futures** possibilities is widely called the "**Cone of Plausibility.**" This phrase is misnamed. Plausibility is only the third largest boundary in this diagram. Plausible futures are always a subset of possible futures. We think the **Cone of Future Judgments** and Voros' summary term—the **Futures Cone**—are the best descriptions for this diagram. The **Futures Cone** reminds us of **seven assessments** that can be very helpful when making high-stakes future decisions. Some benefits and challenges of making each of these assessments are summarized below:

1. **Preposterous Futures**. Sometimes, we **disbelieve** either the probable, possible, the preventable, or the preferable future. Disbelief can keep us from seeing trends and emergences, growing resilience to uncertainty, preventing threats, or seeing achievable positive futures. A **goal** of this judgement is to shrink or expand the **line of the preposterous** to the **line of the possible**.

2. **Possible futures**. Human knowledge and imagination are limited. As Shakespeare says in *Hamlet*, "There are more things in heaven and Earth, Horatio, than are dreamt of in your philosophy." A **goal** of this judgment is to **expand** knowledge and imagination to see a fuller set of these futures. In particular, we want to see **wildcards** (unlikely yet highly impactful futures, positive or negative).

3. **Plausible futures**. Too often, the future surprises us. We didn't have a sufficiently good model of what could happen. With sufficient work on the possible, work on our faulty assumptions and biases, and diversity of input, we can reduce surprise. A **goal** of this judgment is to **expand the plausible** to get closer to the edge of the possible, but not beyond it.

4. **Probable futures**. Knowing some of what is very likely to happen **centers us**. At best, it is a **stake in the ground**, usefully tethering our exploration, and a constraining framework for what can happen. A **goal** of this judgment is to make that probabilistic framework as **evidence-based** and **well-criticized** as possible.

5. **Projected futures**. Our **expected** futures are where most of investment and influence are **politically directed**. Opposing them can be risky, and often, **judo is required** to deflect them toward a better path. A **goal** of this judgment is move the **projected future** closer to most **preferable future**. We can help those with influence see more of the truly preferable, or if that is not possible, we can try to limit the damage from, and sometimes, take advantage of, the leader's poor foresight.

6. **Preferable futures**. What we want needs to be possible and plausible. One goal of this judgment is to find a personal vision that seems **likely to make us more adaptive**. A deeper goal is to find **shared vision**, one that seems likely to make **our entire network** more adaptive.

7. **Preventable futures**. What we want must avoid the most likely and obvious threats and risks, and some of the less obvious ones. A **goal** of this judgment is to see the "**cliffs**" of the **likely but less preferred outcomes** that exist around our most preferred future states, and a **representative sample** of the large group of less likely but more damaging outcomes. The better we see relevant negative futures, the better we can defend against them.

The **Futures Cone** is worth using for **high-profile, high-cost projects**, and when we are ready to think deeply about the **assumptions, judgment culture and biases** in any organization. But, for most applications, the **Four Ps**, or better yet, the **REOPS Cycle** are more than sufficient to deliver good foresight work. We think there is a declining utility with regard to the number of steps (and alliteration!) in any analytical framework. In most contexts, **Seven Ps** are "**three Ps too many**" for foresight practice. As an alternative to the Futures Cone, we find both the **Eight Skills** (Chapter 2), and **FTI's Strategic Foresight Framework** (Chapter 5) particularly helpful for teams and organizations.

Freedom Bias: Why Does Prediction Get Such a Bad Name?

A broad devaluing of our probable future occurs in many foresight practitioner communities today. This **bias against discovering the probable** greatly impairs our use of **predictive contrasting**, and the **Foresight Pyramid**. **Freedom bias** makes the **foundations of foresight work** dangerously **imbalanced and incomplete**. Consider a few examples.

Reddit Futurology, currently the largest online platform dedicated to the future, defines **"Future(s) Studies"** on its home page as follows: "practitioners realize there is no **single future**, only **alternative futures** ahead." The World Future Society 2014 conference brochure read: "The future is not a **destination**. It's the end result of the **actions** we take today." The home page of the new School for the Future of Innovation in Society at ASU proudly proclaims, an adaptation of Shakespeare's *Julius Caesar*: "It is not in the **stars** to hold our destiny, but in **ourselves**." Even the Association for Professional Futurists, our fields most developed professional organization, presently claims on their FAQ page, under their **definition of a Futurist**: "It is not the goal of a futurist to **predict** what will happen in the future." Even the great futurist **Amy Webb**, in her generally excellent book on foresight, *The Signals are Talking*, 2018 quotes the Heisenberg Uncertainty Principle in **quantum physics** as an example that "we must agree at the outset that there is no one, predetermined future." As we will continue to see in this *Guide*, each of these views are commonly held, each appeals to our natural **desire for agency** in the world, and yet each are also **dangerously imbalanced and incomplete**.

We've said that **predictive processing** and **active inference** are two basic ways our brains actually seem to work, at the unconscious and conscious levels. Ignoring anticipation, and its frequent forecasts and predictions, thus seeks to **"define away" a third of our field, probability foresight**. It ignores futurists like the late, great **Hans Rosling** of Gapminder, who have made many commendable **probabilistic predictions** of societal change in their work.

To see the danger of this bias in our collective thinking, ask yourself: which is more dangerous for the world: the belief that there are no universal principles behind the **ethics and empathy** we all show to each other, no **arc of developmental complexity** in extant life forms and their societies, **no science of developmental ethics and interactions** to be discovered, or the postmodernist belief that our morality and emotions are just **random products of evolution**, likely to be different on every planet, with no intrinsically "better" or "worse" rulesets, and no "higher" and "lower" forms of general adaptiveness? As we will discuss, there truly does appear to be an **arc of progress**, a **predictable direction,** to universal change. Surviving complex networks get **more regulated**, and use **more fine-grained judgments,** about everything. We must learn to see both evolution and development at work, even if we cannot model the latter well yet in our science.

When we **choose not to see developmental directionality** in our history and future, it is easy for **selfish individualism**, **situational ethics**, and various forms of **wishful thinking** and **evidence-poor ideology** to run our lives. In America today, too many on our political **Right** have an unjustified belief in the unregulated **"free market"**. Too many on our **Left** have an equally unjustified belief in **eliminating judgments** among different cultural beliefs, norms, laws, and actions, in the pursuit of **"deep egalitarianism."** As we'll argue in *BPF*, the real developmental future of adaptive societies seems likely to be much more **centrist, constrained, and nuanced** than either of these **creative choices of political belief**.

We call such thinking **Freedom Bias.** It has many other names, including **Antiprediction Bias, Evolutionary Bias, or Underdetermination Bias.** Freedom bias arises whenever a foresight practitioner imagines the relevant future as **more free, less constrained, and less predictable** than it actually is. In reality, there is one **set of physical laws**, including **quantum physics and chaos,** which create **divergent, unpredictable futures,** and another, *opposing set* of physical laws, including **classical mechanics, relativity and thermodynamics,** which converge the universe on **one predictable future**. Theorists in **quantum gravity** have been trying to get these **two sets** of physical laws to talk to each other, so far with **very limited results**. They both seem equally fundamental. In our **Evo-Devo Model**, we call unpredictable, divergent, **"futures" creating** processes **evolutionary**. We call predictable, convergent, **"future" creating** processes **developmental**.

Both realities, **futures and future,** appear to exist not only in physics, but in every other complex system, including chemistry, biology, psychology, society, and technology. On Earth, natural selection has created billions of breathtakingly **unique species**, and at the same time, many **universal systems, forms, and functions** that astrobiologists predict will be found on **all Earthlike planets** in our universe. Many astrobiologists now think there are more than a **billion Earthlike** planets in our galaxy alone. We recommend using the simpler and increasingly prevalent term, **Earthlike**, rather than the more common "Earth-like", as planets like ours appear to be a **predictable and ubiquitous developmental destination** in our universe. Whenever we find similar structures and functions in different species and biomes on Earth scientists call this process **"convergent evolution"**. We will argue that a good deal of this evolutionary convergence deserves a better, more accurate name, **"universal development"**.

Neural networks, for example, are very likely a universal way that cells give **higher mind** to multicellular systems. We now know they were **independently invented by communities of cells at least three times** on Earth! No wonder that we are finding them to be foundational structures for our best **learning machines**. Not only obvious things, like the **periodic table**, but less obvious ones, like the roughly **thirty-five body plans** that have been used by all life on Earth, are likely universal. So too are fats, proteins, nucleic acids, cells, eyes, muscles, skeletons, immune systems, emotions, empathy, morality, warfare, laws, levers, wheels, engines, and computers. Given the constraints of our universe's particular physical laws, both known and unknown, we can predict these and much more will **develop**, in complex life, on all Earthlike planets, which themselves appear to be **very special nurseries** for evo-devo molecular complexity. These and many other adaptive solutions will have some features that are **locally divergent** (futures) and others that are **globally convergent** (future), throughout our universe. We must do our best to try to **see both realities**, as best we can. This is not a paradox, it is how **nature** apparently works.

We can understand how freedom bias arises. The **great majority of change** in our environment does appear to **grow rapidly unpredictable**, the further ahead we look. Recall the **95/5 Rule,** which tells us that the great majority of change we observe in complex systems, something like 95%, appears to be **evolutionary**, and thus largely unpredictable.

We've said that **evolutionary processes** appear to be self-organized to explore, experiment, and create diversity, to increase the chance for selective success. But all our adaptive complex systems are **evo-devo** in nature. This means they also have **developmental processes** at their core. These latter processes converge, preserve, and stabilize a small subset of the physical and informational features of the system, presumably to maintain its complexity and allow it to survive and replicate. The **95/5 Rule** tells us that **a special subset of developmental drivers and outcomes** are always **statistically predictable,** if we have the **right math and models**, or have **seen a previous replication of the system.** They **use local and short-term chaos and contingency** to reliably converge on far-future structural and functional destinations.

Even **chaos theory**, which describes **deterministic chaotic systems**, a special subset of complex systems, demonstrates many predictable patterns, cycles, and trends, including feedback loops, self-similarity, fractals, and self-organization in its dynamics. Only a subset of physical systems, at some scales, are known to be chaotic. Many are not. All **complex adaptive systems**, whether physical, chemical, biological, social, or technological, can be demonstrated to have **memory** and **replication**, and are **networks under selection**. This gives them **even more** predictable features. If we ignore all these **statistically predictable elements,** we ignore all the "top-down" features of complex systems that constrain and guide them. **When we have freedom bias, we lose sight of the developmental forest, and get lost in the evolutionary trees.**

Many foresight practitioners will grant there are *parts* of the future that are predictable (demography, humanity's negative impact on the biosphere, information growth, accelerating technological change), but they misconstrue quantum physics, nonlinear science and chaos theory to argue there is often **no predictability "where it matters,"** in complex human social and organizational domains. That view is simply wrong, as we'll argue for societal change in Book 2.

We will also argue that in a wide variety of complex systems, including organisms, organizations, societies, technologies, the **predictable 5%** of processes **appear to be just as important** as the **unpredictable 95%** to our **adaptiveness**. So while we **see twenty times more** evolutionary, unpredictable change around us than we see developmental, predictable change, the 5% that we can in-principle predict is just as important as the other 95%, to our adaptiveness. For example, in all complex organisms, the roughly 5% of **highly conserved** (unchanging, core developmental) **genes and processes** appear to be **just as important** as the **non-conserved (evolutionary) genes and processes**, to life's adaptiveness. So too it appears to be with organizations and societies, if they are also **evo-devo complex systems under selection**.

So far, science has found **previously hidden predictability** at every scale and in every natural environment. For our **universe** as a system, such processes as thermodynamics, nuclear physics and classical mechanics, which we understand well, and processes like dark energy, accelerating change, and information and intelligence growth, which we don't yet understand well, all offer us **predictable trends and destinations** that we must learn to better see and manage.

In our **societal, global, organizational, team**, and **self domains**, there is also much that is predictable, as we'll discuss. Science already tells us that several processes and events in the **Six Domains** *are* convergent destinations, single, predictable outcomes that societies everywhere are funneling toward, regardless of our individual choices, or more curiously, as a result of the **average distribution** of those choices.

A wise (and anonymous) leader in the professional futurist community has told us that convincing our current professional foresight community that **developmental thinking is just as important** as evolutionary thinking may be a "Quixotic quest". That is how strong **antiprediction bias (freedom bias)** is in some of our foresight practice communities, at present. Many foresight educators mistakenly even tell their students that "prediction is poor practice." As we will discuss, practitioners who like to do forecasting, for example, created their own associations, like the International Institute of Forecasters (IIF), beginning in the 1980s, because too many **professional futurists did not embrace** their methods and worldview.

International Inst. Of Forecasters
One Good Forecasting Community

At a time when startups are launching blockchain-based and cryptocurrency-based **prediction markets** like Metaculus, Augur, and PredictIt, at least our younger foresight practitioners must grant that **probability, forecasting, and prediction** are all foresight fundamentals. As the Foresight Pyramid reminds us, understanding as many of **our most probable future destinations as we can, prior to exploring alternatives**, is critical to making wiser strategies, plans, and actions.

Negativity Bias: Why Future Feelings Often Lead with the Negative

Negativity Bias is one of the most important yet under-recognized biases of human thinking. Because of negativity bias, we often **register negative stimuli faster, stronger, and dwell on them for much longer** than equivalent positive stimuli. This is a very common bias, arising due to the reality of the **AK Principle**. At any time, in any environment, there are always **many more ways we could lose** some or all of what we have, and **regress**, than there are **ways we could win**, and **progress**. We have also been **evolutionarily selected** to **pay more attention to negative stimuli**, because they matter much more to our **short-term survival**. **Positive stimuli** matter more to our **long-term adaptiveness**, so they are more **weakly selected for** in the human psyche. This insight has pervasive implications for good foresight practice.

Just as Freedom bias impairs our use of **predictive contrasting**, Negativity bias impairs our use of **sentiment contrasting**. Just like positive-only thinking, it makes our visions dangerously imbalanced. In the Four Ps model, it disrupts our work at the **top of the Foresight Pyramid**, the domain we value the most. Oettingen showed that the most effective sentiment foresight starts by clearly visualizing potential **positives**, and then, **focusing negative thinking** on the **relevant negatives** that might block our positives. Negativity bias reverses this order, making our foresight only half as effective.

Tierney and Bauermeister's *The Power of Bad*, 2019, gives a great recent overview of this bias, and how to combat it. Negativity bias is closely related to **loss aversion bias**, and to **drama bias**, our tendency, in telling stories, to put characters into jeopardy or negative situations as soon as we get the audience to care about them. Negative events generate much more **drama** than positive events. **Dystopias** greatly outnumber **protopias** (plausible stories of better future worlds). We say more about drama bias, and other emotional-cognitive biases, in the Student Edition of this book.

Using our ADOR analysis categories, we can give Negativity Bias another, perhaps more useful name for foresight work. Negativity bias pushes most individuals, teams, firms, our media, and culture, in most environments, to **feel and think first, strongest, and longest** about **Disruption and Risk** (**Preventable futures**) and only secondarily, and more weakly and briefly, about **Opportunity and Advantage** (**Preferable futures**). Using ADOR terms, we call this the **DROA Bias**. When under a **DROA bias**, we tend to seek out **Disruption** stories first and strongest, and think of them in overly negative terms (as catastrophes) and with too much drama. We also think a lot about **Risks**, but **quite diffusely**, with too much attention to "**threats du jour**," not threats ranked by relevance and probability. Only then do we consider **Opportunities**, and just the ones that don't conflict with prior **negative judgments**. We spend the **least time** evaluating key new **Advantages** (tools, capacities, wealth, innovations), as that would **conflict with our negative worldview**.

In other words, we tend to think about *everything* in **DROA order**, when we should typically be thinking, unless we are in immediate **jeopardy, conflict, or crisis**, in **ADOR order**. Most of us no longer live on the savanna, with danger lurking behind every bush. Instead, **advantage and opportunity** are accelerating all around us. In reality, there are so many **positive changes happening globally** today, at an **accelerating rate**—and **primarily to others, not us**—that not assessing their potential opportunities (and when relevant to strategy, risks) seriously degrades our ability to see the new tools, platforms, policies, strategies, and partnerships that could help us to better adapt.

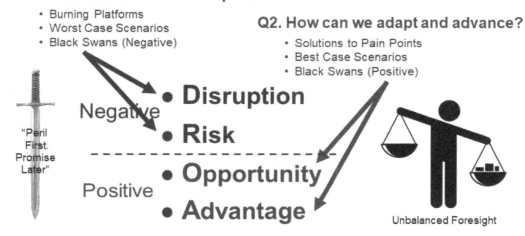

DROA Bias Reverses the Two Questions of Foresight

Q1. What could harm or disrupt us?
- Burning Platforms
- Worst Case Scenarios
- Black Swans (Negative)

Q2. How can we adapt and advance?
- Solutions to Pain Points
- Best Case Scenarios
- Black Swans (Positive)

"Peril First. Promise Later"

Negative
- **Disruption**
- **Risk**

Positive
- **Opportunity**
- **Advantage**

Unbalanced Foresight

This reversal degrades our foresight capacity by 50%![1]

1. Gabriele Oettingen, *Rethinking Positive Thinking: The New Science of Motivation*, 2014.

Foresight University

Again, Oettingen's studies show that our foresight can be **twice as effective, and our plans more than twice as productive,** when we **fight negativity bias** and instead **start positive**, then consider mainly the **negatives to those positives**. Using ADOR analysis can help greatly here. Recall that with ADOR analysis, first we scan for **positive progress** in our environment (Advantage, for others), then consider forced changes (Disruption), a **negative** for some, positive for others, then we create a **positive vision** for us (Opportunity), and only then do we assess potential **threats and blocks to that vision** (Risk). That's how to create focused strategy, and **rapid progress**. We don't get distracted by irrelevancies.

Negativity bias is why our **most popular news platforms** give the most attention to **disruptions and catastrophes**, often outliers, or in distant places unlikely to affect us. We never get coverage based on the real severity and frequency of our problems, or any **prioritized models** of those problems. We pay our next level of attention to **possible risks**, though we tend to miss the ones most relevant to us, and we weigh them poorly. We pay even less attention to **possible opportunities for ourselves**, and as a result, we **miss many of them**. We pay the least attention to **new advantages**, occurring for others, as that can generate envy, anger, and feelings of inferiority. Reporting **other's gains** is not a good way to keep an audience for long. **Tim Wu's** *The Attention Merchants: The Epic Battle to Get Inside Our Heads*, 2010, details the methods used to distract us from the most advantageous news, and entertained by manufactured drama. **Julian Simon's** classic, *Hoodwinking the Nation*, 1999, explains how media, experts, and politicians exploit our natural anxieties for personal gain. We also fall victim to this bias in our **parenting**, when we are **overcautious** with and **overprotective** of our children, focusing them on avoiding risk, rather than taking **calculated risks** in order to gain new advantages. We fall victim in our societies, when we retreat into **safetyism**, pursuing a **false illusion of security** by creating overly restrictive norms, regulations, and civil penalties that discourage **risk, experiment, failure, and innovation**.

Again, when we are in a DROA bias we are the poorest at **seeing advantages unfolding around us**. We ignore all the new tools, services, and all the ways life is **improving for others** in various contexts. When we do recognize advantage, we tend to fixate on **outlier success stories**, which often have little to teach us. Instead, we should be seeking to notice and learn from those doing many small things **incrementally better** than us, those who are **solving problems**, creating useful new **rules, capacities, specializations**, and **partnerships**, and **benchmarking** our practices against them. We need a **global perspective** to see these advantages. We often have to look well outside our **affinity groups** to see them.

Other negativity biases can coexist with and amplify DROA bias. Many **HROs (High-Reliability Orgs)**, including those in security, defense, and health care often have **mission bias** to see threat first, and advantage second. Some of us (but, thankfully, not all) will get more **pessimistic and dogmatic** with age or experience. **Social media** today, being first generation, without good **AI filters**, also feeds DROA bias, with negative drama, trolling, and clickbait. Since 2010, some social media users have learned that edge-of-plausibility **outrage statements** get the greatest **engagement ("viral outrage")** on many platforms. This has led us to the problem of **fake news**. It is not currently easy to sort such news out of our feeds. We will see in Book 2 how our coming **Personal AIs** will be a powerful (yet optional) tool for doing so. Fake news causes us to doubt **real news**, and its distraction and negative drama saps our energy to create **positive visions**.

Evidence-based negative visions, told at the right time, are very important. We've described **David Brin's** concept of **self-preventing prophecies** as a counterpart to **self-improving prophecies**. A well-meaning, plausible, yet shocking **scare-story**, like the notion of our planet plausibly being four to six degrees hotter in 2100, as is forecast by many **climate decarbonization groups** today, can jolt us out complacency to **action**.

Effective organizations must regularly use negative visions, especially when there is **complacency** around the current status quo, or **arrogance** and **groupthink**, often because of a firm's past success, in a different environment. In the 1930's organizational psychology pioneer <u>Kurt Lewin</u>, told us that **change management** often begins with leaders **"unfreezing"** a team or organization, by communicating **potential forthcoming crises**. The team can then use the **energy of the perceived crisis** to **"change"** to a new strategic direction, and then **"refreeze"** policies and norms around the new direction, to prevent backsliding into old ways. In the 1980's, management guru **John Kotter** developed Lewin's insights into a classic **eight step model** of change management, well-described in <u>*Leading Change*</u>, 2012.

Consider also that the entire **defense functions and industries**, in every country, and the **security functions and industries**, in every organization, dedicate the majority of their foresight and action to **managing the negative**, by seeking to **anticipate, prevent, and prepare for undesirable futures**. The **US Armed Services (Army, Navy, Marines, Air Force, Coast Guard)**, and our newer security and defense branches **(Public Health, Homeland Security, NOAA, Space Force)** all have been strong **champions and practitioners** of foresight work since our field's inception. Their missions make them particularly dependent on both building **adaptive capacity** and **preventing catastrophe**. They are continually comparing and **contrasting positive and negative future visions**. In our contention, this is typically best done in ADOR order.

Over the short term, **fear and crisis framing** can be very effective. But over the long term, people **discount the messenger** who is always bringing negative news. In organizational foresight, we ignore **ADOR priority order** at our own and others peril. Even in change management, prior to **crisis communication**, good leaders will **first assess** environmental **advantages** and organizational **opportunity**, to convince themselves that there are strategic solutions to be found, before sounding the alarm. If we don't see and learn to analyze real accelerating advantages and disruptions first, we will often miss seeing the best solutions. Our strategy becomes **weaker** and more **parochial** as a result.

Fortunately, many daily **routines** will reinforce a **balanced, positive-first, negative-second, outside-in ADOR analytical approach**. We have offered a **sentiment contrasting** framework—**GRASP thinking**—which individuals and teams can use to counter DROA bias. Many professional communities practice ADOR process. A subset of news sources report positive-first, evidence-based news. These provide a **vital balance** against typical **sensationalist** news sources. In our view, even platforms run by defense and intelligence communities that tend to focus on risk (threat) and disruption first, opportunity and advances second, are less effective than those that are ADOR-prioritized.

We'll discuss **DROA bias** further in Chapter 3, with **Sentiment Management** on teams. Fortunately, in a world of **accelerating AI,** we can predict that powerful tools will increasingly be available to help us **manage DROA bias** and shift us back into **ADOR priority**, for those seeking greater foresight accuracy and productivity. But our algorithms and human processes to fix this problem are only now being developed. Until our AI tools becomes significantly more **personalized** and **responsive** to our needs, what we call **Personal AI,** we must learn to manage DROA bias ourselves.

Foresight, Media and Social Progress

As we will describe in greater detail in *BPF,* our world is rapidly getting better, in myriad ways, when considered as a single **complex network**. This developmental arc is well-described in books like **Steven Pinker's** *Better Angels of Our Nature: Why Violence Has Declined,* 2011, which document sharply declining global trends in interpersonal violence over the last few thousand years, and statistician **Hans Rosling's** *Factfulness: Ten Reasons We're Wrong About the World—And Why Things are Better than You Think,* 2018, which documents many positive trends in global development. **Bailey and Tupy's** *Ten Global Trends Every Smart Person Should Know,* 2020, make the same case. Such books can convince discerning readers that our societies are not only evolving but developing, in many positive and measurable ways. Global development is making the average member of our civilization more adaptive, much faster than most of us realize.

Rosling, 2018

Unfortunately Americans, with our plutocratic network news, our first-generation social media, our individualist ideals, our eroded public education, and our ongoing loss of manufacturing jobs, are particularly susceptible to DROA bias at present. In a 2016 YouGov survey:

- 65% of Americans said the world is **getting worse**
- 29% it is **staying the same**
- 6% it is generally **getting better**.

As we will learn in this *Guide,* **only the 6%** are seeing the **real trendlines**. The rest are being **hoodwinked by the headlines**, as **Julian Simon** would say. This is not to say that all trends are positive. Many are not, even in societies with great affluence. The **great inequalities** that new affluence creates, at first, cause a great number of societal problems that must be corrected, with activism. Many have observed how affluence and abundance create **new freedoms and problems**, including obesity, diabetes, overconsumption, and alienation. But for every affluent country with a particular problem, there is another country, perhaps a Norway, a Finland, a Singapore, an Israel, or an Australia, showing how to better manage that problem. Not only America, but Europe, China, and Russia all offer particular clever solutions to learn from. The larger arc of history, and most global trends, show exponential progress for humanity as a whole.

Misaligned incentives and **insufficient transparency** in government can also give false perceptions of risk. Some "hawks" in our defense community have historically presented certain enemies as more dangerous than they are. This bias is exacerbated when **elites expect to benefit**—either in anticipated security, power, or profit—from such a depiction. In well-known examples, America's more hawkish leaders manipulated us into unnecessarily broad conflicts, as in the 1964 Gulf of Tonkin incident used to justify the Vietnam War (1965-1975), and the false intelligence created to justify America's Iraq War (2003-2011). The world is a **dangerous place,** but usually in ways we don't think enough about. **Infectious diseases**, for example, are a far greater threat to human life and progress than mass terrorism (with the exception of bioterrorism, which itself is a long-known and very real threat). We learned this with the Spanish Flu in 1917, and many famously warned us of it again in recent years, including **Larry Brilliant** and **Bill Gates**. But, we did not heed their and others warnings, and now the **COVID-19 pandemic** has taught this fact to us again.

We all have **limited stores of willpower** and limited ability to **respond to danger**. If we spend our waking hours scared of and talking about the **wrong things**, we won't have the energy or perspective to evaluate and respond to the truly dangerous things. We also won't be able to see or aid the world **as it is**, engaged **in uneven yet continual progress**.

This *Guide* will do its best to help the reader see the **daily advances** of civilization, when viewed as a **complex network**. It is those advances, properties of the **system as a whole**, which create opportunities for us, and give each of us greater **potential ability** to fix our problems. We can turn many **disruptions** and **"problems of progress"** into **opportunities**, when we are ADOR-prioritized. To do so, we must **look past the headlines** to see the **accelerating trendlines** at work.

Fortunately, the more effectively we use **hindsight, insight,** and **foresight**, the more we can see what is **actually happening and emerging**, rather than what people **want to talk about**. The better we learn to see the many forms of weekly and daily **progress**, the global Advantages and personal Opportunities in ADOR analysis, the better we can see the ways that societies, organizations, and individuals try to **block progress**, and maintain the **status quo**, in service to their own agendas for power and profit. As a result, the better we become at leading ourselves and others to better futures, and catalyzing **measurable positive change**.

The Wonderful and Challenging World of Foresight

We think the phrase "The Wonderful and Challenging World of Foresight" is a nice summary of the **nature of our field**. We're always balancing **promise and problems, visions and nightmares**. Foresight can help us see **wonderful new advantages and opportunities**, and **defend against disruptions and risks,** but it isn't easy. We have to **challenge ourselves continually** to uncover ADOR, to develop strategy for it, to act with ethics and empathy, and to better adapt.

Today is an exciting time for foresight work—never has our society been more complex and fast-paced, and never have we had as many tools and opportunities available to greatly improve our lives, our teams, our organizations, and our world. We have many problems and threats to manage as well, of course. Moreover, as our technical abilities have grown, the **age-old threats and hardships** of our natural environment have **receded in severity**. In their place, new problems and disruptions, ones we have **created for ourselves**, due to our accelerating capacity to manipulate our environment, have taken center stage. We call these new challenges **Problems of Progress**, and will explore many of them in *BPF*.

We've been a **fantastically successful species**. Some say too successful, as measured by our total numbers and by both our intended and unintended impacts on the world. We now live in a geological epoch of our own making—called the <u>**Anthropocene**</u>—an era of large scale intentional environmental alteration, including human-made climate change. The Anthropocene began roughly **8,000 years ago**. At that time only about ten million of us lived on Earth. Yet, even back then, large numbers of unsustainably-acting early humans apparently managed to <u>burn one-fifth of Earth's ice-free land</u> for forest clearing and hunting. Even earlier, we **hunted to extinction** most species of **megafauna** on Earth.

While there were some communities that lived in balance with the land, and while early communities were far more **egalitarian** and **democratic** than our later empires and states, most people in those earlier eras appear to have lived with **strikingly unsustainable habits** in relation to their environment. They were no better than us, just less powerful. It is our new power that has created new challenges to be overcome. Fortunately, when we zoom out to the Big Picture, we can see how our resource use, once accelerating, is now saturating, as we increasingly reach the limits of the ecosystem.

As we will see in Book 2, the more complex our societies become, the more we are **substituting bits for atoms**, in a **global megatrend** called **dematerialization**. Read **Andrew McAfee's** <u>*More from Less*</u>, 2019, for an introduction to the dematerialization story. We are also using another more dangerous megatrend, **densification**, to increasingly densify and miniaturize our species' critical support systems, greatly increasing both their power and efficiency per capita. We propose that these two trends, **densification and dematerialization ("D&D)**, are at the heart **of accelerating change**.

At present, there are many negative effects of our accelerating development. We are still gobbling up our rainforest, polluting and overfishing our oceans, and draining our aquifers. Climate change threatens to **desertify** large areas of land with hundreds of millions of inhabitants, like the American Southwest. Today we 7.6 billion human beings and our roughly 25 billion domesticated animals make up **97% of the carbon mass of all terrestrial mammals**. We're turning our ecosystems into a vast carbon monoculture. WWF's *Living Planet Report*, 2014, estimates that we've reduced vertebrate wildlife populations (mammals, birds, reptiles, amphibians, and fish) roughly **fifty percent in just the last 40 years** (1970-2010). Freshwater populations have declined even farther, an **80% loss**, as we've polluted, overfished, and introduced new species into all our easiest-to-access freshwater.

We're also still ignorant of the **biospheric diversity we are destroying**. We don't even know how many species we are killing. It is perhaps dozens a day, and 1,000 fold higher than the background rate that would go extinct without our impact. While we know nearly all phyla, classes and orders, and most families and genera on our precious planet, we've mapped just 14% of species on land and 9% of those in the oceans, if the estimate of 8.7 million species (excluding prokaryotes) on Earth is accurate. See **Vaclav Smil's** *Harvesting the Biosphere (PDF)*, *Pop. & Dev. Review*, 2011, and the Smithsonian's Mass Extinction, 2014, for good overviews of these deeply troubling issues.

Meanwhile, our global carbon emissions continue to grow, to planet-altering levels. They plateaued to just 0.4% growth in 2013-2016, but then returned to a saddening 2% growth in 2017. We haven't yet reached **Peak CO2**, though it's clear to evidence-based thinkers that we must. At the same time, as a **self-preventing prophecy**, our media have greatly oversold our **certainty** about the severity of the problem we'll face over the next few decades. In truth, we **simply don't know how bad it will get.** All we know is what we are presently doing to the planet, much of which is unsustainable.

Fortunately, we can see good ways out of these problems. This century, we will stop, then reverse our total population growth, greatly decarbonize our energy, food, transportation, and manufacturing industries, make cities far smarter and more sustainable, and rewild much of our natural world. Less obviously to some, we will also shift the large majority of our global food supply to plants and cultured meat. But all of this will take time, and require strategic foresight, smart activism, conflict, and crises. While we see the solutions, our current investment in them is shamefully small. So we will have to act a lot faster, and smarter, and invest far more in the right solutions.

Again, each of our greatest problems today are **problems of progress.** They are byproducts of our **tremendous successes in recent millennia.** Though there are plenty of **doomsayers** who make a business of telling us otherwise, including a number we'll meet and critique in this *Guide*. Yet our collective foresight and collective action are both far more advanced today than when we first set foot on the African savannah. They are also **accelerating**, driven by **universal tailwinds**, as we will see. Better foresight can guide us to the solutions we need, and help us find ways out of the traps we create when we are selfish, greedy and short-sighted. We'll explore many examples of better and worse paths ahead in this *Guide*.

History Matters! – Historical and Sentinel Foresight

Retrofuturism is the act of reviewing past images and writings about the future. We engage in this review for many purposes, including entertainment, art, and education. The blog Paleofuture offers many retrofuturist depictions, beginning in the 1870s. It is alternately hilarious, inspiring, sobering, and educational to look at historical visions of our future. See RetroFuture.com and r/RetroFuturism for a great set of such visions.

Historical foresight analysis (HFA) is retrofuturism done with the intention of **improving today's foresight practice**. It may review only at the past foresight work, but the personal history of the authors, their methods, their worldview, their culture, their hits and misses, and other contemporary future thinkers, in order to draw practice lessons from their work. HFA can tell us a lot about what kinds of change has been **predicted long in advance**, and what kinds of change have been **less predictable**, and yet were still **rapidly detected** and **rapidly reacted to** when necessary, using **intelligence systems** and ideally, **resources kept in reserve**. We can do HFA in all ten of the **STEEPLECOP** (Scientific, Technological,

Economic, Environmental, Political, Legal, Ethical, Cultural, Organizational, and Personal) **environmental scanning domains** (we will introduce STEEPLECOP in Chapter 5). HFA can also tell us about the worldviews, mindsets, and processes we need to be good **predictors** of developmental events, **and reactors** to evolutionary events, and the way our assumptions, motivations, and biases regulate our ability to foresee and respond.

In the foresight literature, being either a **good predictor** of developmental events, or a **good builder of intelligence systems** capable of rapid response and reserves for evolutionary events, is called being a **sentinel.** There are two obvious ways to be a sentinel. We can live in a **sentinel environment**, one where **prediction, detection and reaction** are prized, or we can be a **sentinel thinker**, or both. Learning the conditions that create sentinel thinkers and sentinel environments can tell us much about how to improve foresight process.

HFA teaches the value of **specialized experience**, of living in **innovation cultures**, or of living in **complex, disruptive, and risky environments**, of having a strong **understanding of history** and **current reality**, of having strong **intelligence, sensemaking, and response** capabilities, and of the special predictability of certain domains in **science and technology**.

Since we began taking foresight writings seriously at the end of the 19th century, we have published a rich trove of Four Ps foresight. We find many artfully **creative** and **imaginative** explorations of **possible futures** in this literature. We find much that is **aspirational (visionary), describing preferable futures and preventable calamities and dystopias.** Some of these preferable and preventable stories seem timeless, even today. Most foresight works are products of their **local environments**, appropriate then but **anachronisms** now, as society changes and progresses. But, some are the opposite, particularly **timeless and universal** in their scope and relevance. Understanding the backgrounds, processes, and contexts of the great predictors, creatives, and vision leaders can help us better anticipate change today as well.

HFA tells us that **history matters**. History is our starting point in foresight work. The better we learn and understand past trends, cycles, models, and causal factors, the better we can interpret our **present**, and see our probable and possible **futures**. A good HFA example in probable foresight is *Technological Forecasting: 1970-1993* (PDF), by **Coates et al.,** *Technological Forecasting & Social Change*, 1994. This study is one of many that observed that developments in **certain technology classes**, including our **information and communications technologies**, have been **significantly more predictable than others** in recent decades. We'll explore why this is so in Book 2, in our discussion of accelerating change.

Before we discuss the many predictable ways probable foresight can **fail**, let's look at a few historical examples of **predictive success** to get a better sense of what it typically takes to succeed ("happy families are all alike"), and to appreciate the value that better prediction can bring, to individuals, organizations, and societies.

Consider this image from a late-1930's German magazine, anticipating the **wireless videophone**. This anticipation was a natural mental leap for its author, as German engineers had recently exhibited the world's first public videophone in 1936, across 100 miles of coaxial cable between Berlin and Leipzig. Contemplating that demonstration, and shrinking the device into a purse-sized **wearable wireless**, the artist cleverly foresaw how **smartphone use** might lure us out of in-person and into virtual conversations, seventy years before the iPhone.

Wireless Videophone Concept, 1930s

In other words, Germany in 1936 had developed a **future-inevitable** technology, **digital telepresence**, which anyone could have recognized would one day be **ubiquitous**. They had also done this **far earlier** than the rest of the world. This happened because Germany, from 1800-1945, was a **sentinel innovation environment**. Only the **timing** of this development going global was unclear. Read **Todd Rider's** *Forgotten Creators* (free PDF), 2020 for a history of German science and technology innovation from 1800-1945. Germany was consistently leading the world in science, technology, and trade, until their **values failed them** in World Wars I and II. The lessons of their failure must never be forgotten.

Consider that in 1910, just prior to World War I, Germany's **trade GDP** was more than the next three European nations **added together**, and rivaled the USA's. At the time, they were **comprehensively winning** the global economic war, the **real war of the future**. But, their backward-looking political leadership did not recognize that that economic competition was the real battleground, the leading edge of civilization's progressive development. In **political foresight**, their leadership was stuck in the **domination and zero-sum mindset** of previous centuries. Their **flawed worldview** led them and other Axis nations into the inhumanity of WWI, and again later into the atrocities of WWII. *Foresight matters.*

On a more positive note, great predictions, especially of **highly probable futures**, can create **vivid images** that inspire people to work to make them true even many decades later. Consider the great **Vannevar Bush**, founder of the US's National Science Foundation, another **sentinel thinker**. In a famous *Atlantic* essay, "As We May Think," 1945, he gave the world an aspirational vision of the **world wide web**. This essay influenced many innovators for decades afterward. Bush's vision of a coming global public resource of **updatable pages and a network of links** was exciting and compelling. His proposed engineering approach of microfiche was impractical, but his vision of all the world's knowledge, organized and free to everyone, was deeply motivating nonetheless. As better technology emerged, step by step, it materialized just as Bush predicted. Bush was not a perfect predictor. No one is. He famously didn't think space flight would work. But, we don't need to be a perfect predictor to greatly improve the world with sentinel foresight.

Doug Englebart was an engineer deeply influenced by Bush's essay. In the 1960's he developed **electronic hypertext**, the **mouse**, **networked computers**, and a **graphical user interface**, all of which he first displayed in what is called the Mother of All Demos (see the amazing YouTube video) in 1968. In 1987, **Bill Atkinson** created HyperCard for the Apple Macintosh, a memex for individual computers. In 1991, **Tim Berners-Lee** made the first memex web-browser, and invented URLs. In 1994, **Ward Cunningham** made the first publicly editable web page. In 2001, **Jimmy Wales** and **Larry Sanger** launched Wikipedia. All of these were sentinel inventions of sentinel thinkers, each standing on the shoulders of Bush's vision, and taking another developmental step forward.

The futurist **Amy Webb** has a nice phrase, **"find the fringe"**. By this she means cultivating an **intelligence system**, including a **network** of sentinel thinkers and information sources. Learn from that network, appreciate its members, and you can see both what will come and what may come, and craft strategy to take advantage of that **sentinel foresight**.

Consider also Will Jenkins, another less-known sentinel thinker. His science-fiction short story, "A Logic Named Joe," 1946, written under his pen name, **Murray Leinster**, offers a great early description of **personal computers**, called "logics", as an electronic fusion of a typewriter and then-new television sets. More impressively, he also described **the internet**, as electronic networks of logics, linked via **servers** called "tanks" causing great changes in future society. Leinster foresaw **electronic logics in every home**, offering communications, entertainment, education, shopping, dating, and many other services.

Will Jenkins (aka Murray Leinster)
in his home study, 1930s.

While nearly everyone else at the time was writing about bigger mainframes and hierarchical, centralized computing, Leinster was writing about **decentralized networks**, **democratization**, and **miniaturization**, their beneficial and harmful impacts on society. This network changed behavior so much that one character notes "logics are civilization." He thus anticipated both PCs and the web. Leinster credited part of this insight to reading Bush's sentinel essay. **Sentinel foresight**, in other words, emerges from high-quality **sentinel learning**, in a **Do loop**. **Great inputs create great outputs**!

After **Microsoft** was blindsided by the rapid rise of the web in the 1990s, Bill Gates is reported to have joked to his strategy team, "find me the person who predicted the [rapid rise of the] web, and we'll make him CEO." HFA tells us that Jenkins did that, in 1946. A stream of visionaries after him did as well, from the 1950s to the 1990s, including <u>Doug Englebart</u>, <u>Ted Nelson</u>, and former Senator and Vice President <u>Al Gore</u> (disregard the jokes, he really did get it). They and many others all saw and described, with varying degrees of precision, how big the internet's effect would be.

There are many kinds of sentinel environments today. The **Nordic democracies** point to the future of policy and governance in social democratic capitalist societies. Cities like **Shenzhen** and **Silicon Valley** point to the future of entrepreneurial and technological innovation. Cities and regions like Singapore, Oslo, Amsterdam, Beijing, New York, Austin, Boston, Lagos, Buenos Aires, Sydney, Johannesburg, are just some of the better known sentinel environments for various urban and societal futures today. The good news is, unlike the past, we can use digital intelligence platforms to collect, teach, critique, and profit from the foresight of these environments and thinkers, far easier than ever before.

The problem with human culture is that our memory for the visionaries who **"got to the future first"** has been very poor. Because many of us don't like to **envision**, at least in predictive ways, the ones that really did get important things right are assumed to be flukes. But they very often are not. They were in the right place, with the right inputs, to make the right conclusions. We can study them and their environments and replicate their success. Fortunately, because of new digital and crowd foresight tools we will discuss, finding the visionaries, those who clearly saw what **will be**, what **could be**, what **should be**, and what we should **prevent**, gets better every year. We're digging the Bush's, Jenkins's and Nelson's out of our historical record, and telling their amazing stories increasingly well. Most auspiciously, in our view, our culture will dispose of the self-harming bias that "predicting the future doesn't work." Let's say it again: *History matters!*

Foresight Matters! – Seeing Lost Progress Opportunities (LPOs)

Counterfactuals in human affairs are also called <u>Alternate History</u>. They come in three types:

1. **Regressive** – Example: Hitler wins WWII, or other past events leading to an alternate **dystopian present**, like **Philip Dick's** *The Man in the High Castle*, 1962/2015.

2. **Alternative** – Examples: Many of the wars, decisions, and competitions in our history, leading to **different present**, but not a world that **most of us** would identify as **objectively better or worse**.

3. **Progressive** – Definition: Past plausible events that, had they occurred, would have likely led to a world that **most of us** would describe as an **objectively better present**.

We give **progressive counterfactuals** a second, more descriptive name: **lost progress opportunities (LPOs).** We'll use that name and its abbreviation, LPOs, in this *Guide*. Finding major LPOs is a worthy exercise. It requires us to use **hindsight** (learn what actually happened, and what might have happened differently), **insight** (knowledge of our present state) and **foresight** (the likelihood that past choices would have created a better world today). Wherever we find them, LPOs argue that **plausibly better foresight,** occurring in the past at the **right time**, to the **right individuals**, accompanied by **plausible action**, might have led to **major improvements** in our present world. LPOs challenge us to improve our **quality of vision**. They remind us how **better foresight today** could help us to achieve **much better tomorrows**.

Modern counterfactual collections, like **Niall Ferguson's** *Virtual History*, 2000, and **Robert Cowley's** *The Collected What If?*, 2006, typically offer only a handful of **LPOs**. Most counterfactuals are **alternative** (not obviously better, just interestingly different) or **regressive**. Both types are easier to write, and can be entertaining and dramatic, but are less helpful to understanding **societal progress**, one of the goals of this *Guide*. Telling dystopian stories tells us something about what **progress isn't**, but we really start to understand the concept of progress, and can more easily apply it to our present lives, when we find stories of **lost opportunities** that most of us would agree, had they occurred in the past, in a plausible fashion, would likely have led to a **significantly better modern world**.

Below are a few **LPO stories**. More can be found on each of these, and others, in our online *Guide*. We plan to eventually publish some of our collected LPO stories as a future book in our *Guide* series. (Our tentative title: *Lost Progress*). In the meantime, we encourage readers to **send us your candidate LPO stories**, at guide@foresightu.com. We may adapt and publish, with attribution, any submissions that we feel are particularly instructive or significant. As you read the following LPOs, ask yourself: How many do you **agree** with? What is the **probability** that we'd live in a **much better world today** if any of these had occurred? In what specific ways might our current lives have become **more adaptive**? What **adaptive valleys** (initial problems of progress) might we have faced, with **early versions** of these innovations, before they would have become **net progressive**? What **lessons** do they offer us today, in better foresight and action?

In 200 BCE, could the **Phoenicians**, **Ancient Greeks**, **Hebrews**, **Early Romans**, or another of the other literate and extensively trading Mediterranean civilizations have **invented the movable-type printing press, sixteen hundred years before Gutenberg?** It certainly seems so to us. They had both cheap ink and paper, broad literacy, extensive free trade, recently invented languages with a *simple* 23-character alphabet, metal and wood stamps (used to imprint clay and wax), and even olive and clothes presses. Had a small printing press been invented, copied, and used by pre-Roman Empire merchants to **trade papyrus,** stamped with printed maps, drawings, news, humor, stories, and practical advice, this would likely have led to a great **flourishing of knowledge and invention**. A regional printing industry, in turn, would likely have limited the power of the **monotheistic religions** (Christianity, Islam) that arose later, prevented the **thousand-year Dark Ages** that occurred in the West after the fall of the Roman Empire in 476 CE, and accelerated the emergence of **democracies**, which need an educated populace. See "**200 BCE: A Printing Press in Ancient Greece**" for this LPO story. If the tinkerers and entrepreneurs in these civilizations had developed just a bit more foresight in the right place and time, we would all be living in a **much more advanced world** today. *Education foresight matters!*

In 50 CE, could <u>Hero of Alexandria</u> have **invented the first practical steam engine for warship propulsion and water pumping, sixteen hundred years before impulse steam turbines** by **Giovanni Branca** (1629) and **John Wilkins** (1648)? It seems so. Hero invented a simple rotary steam engine, the <u>Aeolipile</u>, and even used it to open temple doors. He also perfected the **hand water pump** of the Greek inventor <u>Ctesibius</u>. The Romans used **Hero's metal pump** and a fire hose to put out fires. All Hero needed was to add a **small metal windmill rotating on an axle** inside the output jet from his boiler. That single improvement would have created both the first **practical steam ship engine (and propeller)**, and a powerful **steam-powered water pump**. A better way for Roman slaves to **pump water up into cisterns** would have greatly improved Roman water works and aqueducts. But, most obviously, faster <u>Roman triremes</u> were a **vital military interest**. Even a first generation **steam turbine Aeolipile**, driven by a slave-stoked fire using **Roman charcoal** (one of their many inventions) would have been **greatly faster than human rowers**. Many seafaring nations would have eventually copied this engine, and continually improved it. In reality, Charles Parsons invented the steam turbine in 1884. See our counterfactual, "**50 CE: A Steam Engine in Ancient Rome,**" for more on this story, and how the **steam age** could have arrived on Earth a millennia and a half earlier. *Engineering foresight matters!*

In 1000 CE, could <u>Norse Vikings</u> have permanently colonized Newfoundland, **bringing a <u>Norse democracy</u> to North America 700 years before the United States?** It seems so. Norse democracy began in Iceland in 930 CE, their <u>Greenland settlement</u> started in 980, lasted 500 years, and had at least 400 low-producing farms and 2,500 souls. Thorfinn Karlsefni's expedition from <u>Greenland to Newfoundland Island in 1009</u> had between 160 and 250 settlers, and was just one of several expeditions to North America from Greenland. If at any point over those 500 years the Norse had had the **foresight to run five or more smaller settlements in parallel**, each on different islands in different Indian territories, and to **continually be exploring** for new North American Indian **food and tool trading communities**, some of their settlements would have thrived, and the Greenland way station would not have been abandoned. Attacks on the settlements would have happened at different times in different places, as **each indigenous tribe was quite different in culture and beliefs,**

and lacked the **boats, infrastructure and trust** for continent wide communication. The Norse were not afraid to risk death in making first contact, and many tribes would have **traded with Europeans bearing useful gifts**. Some Indian nations would have become **allies, scouts, and defenders**, as happened hundreds of years later. Had the Norse recognized more of their **strategic mobility, trust, and trade advantages**, and used them heavily in the New World, we'd have had a **Western technological democracy in North America** seven hundred years earlier. And what might that have given us? See "1000 CE: A Norse Democracy in America" for more. *Exploration foresight matters!*

In 1912, could all the ship's passengers, and even the RMS *Titanic* itself, have been saved by **returning to the iceberg** that it hit, and using its cranes, steel cables, steel bars, and hammers, **lashing the front of the ship to the berg,** preventing the aft compartments from flooding? It certainly seems so. At the very least, the ship would have sank much more slowly, and hundreds of additional passengers could have been evacuated to the iceberg, lifeboats and rafts before the ship sank, and before rescue ships arrived the next morning. But, to find this solution in the **two hours** they had, the ship's leaders would likely have needed a more **open, collaborative, problem-solving process** than the closed, top-down, and information-denying processes the ship's captain actually used. See "**1912: A Saved Titanic (Collaborative Foresight)**," for more. *Foresight process matters!*

In 1938, could we have had a **US constitutional amendment**, led by President **Franklin Roosevelt**, requiring every sitting President to **justify any foreign war** in their **annual State of the Union** address, and a **national referendum every four years into any war,** on whether continuation of that war was **desired by the public paying for it** with their lives and dollars? This provision of a **democratic oversight mechanism for extended warfare** was actually plausible in that special time. In 1934, responding to two widely read books on the extensive **US and European war profiteering** that occurred during **World War I**, the US Senate's **Nye Committee** found evidence of price fixing and unjustified profits by the US arms industry during the war, and political pressure by US bank CEOs on President **Woodrow Wilson** to intervene in WW I to protect their foreign loans. In response, Senator **Louis Ludlow** introduced the Ludlow Amendment, a public war referendum, several times between 1935 and 1940. It was voted on by Congress in 1938, and its public popularity peaked at 75%. The amendment was aggressively resisted by President Roosevelt, who wanted freedom to go to war as he pleased. In our alternative history, Roosevelt could have had the vision to sit down with Ludlow, improve the language of his amendment a bit, and create a truly valuable mechanism for our democracy, allowing **American citizens** themselves the **authority to terminate perpetual wars of dubious value.** *Governance foresight matters!*

In 1965, could the US have **won the Vietnam War** by creating a defensible microstate of **New South Vietnam**, using the land below the Mekong River? If we had used the Mekong as a northern border, that would have allowed us to secure a far smaller and far more defensible area for Vietnam's noncommunist citizens. A New South Vietnam microstate would have been **an "island"** we could easily have defended for the **20% of South Vietnamese who actually wanted capitalism**, very much like Taiwan, the small Asian capitalist territory we were already defending. America's defense leaders just needed to realize that if we could not secure the **far larger South Vietnam**, an artificial state that had only recently been created, and which was in truth **80% nationalist**, this "island strategy" would be our natural **fallback solution**. What would Asia and America be like today if we had won that failed and deeply divisive war, empowering **eight million South Vietnamese capitalists and entrepreneurs**, and establishing a **US military base in the Mekong Delta** in the 1960s, as we did in Taiwan, South Korea and Japan? See "**1965: A Defended South Vietnam (Vietnam War)**," for this fascinating counterfactual. *Defense foresight matters!*

In 1970, could America and the world have had its **first permanent "Exhibition City,"** featuring the latest and the greatest in innovative and futuristic technologies, being tested and integrated into daily life? We nearly did. In October 1966, **Walt Disney** made a **visionary 25-minute film** (YouTube link here) introducing the Florida state legislature to his plans for EPCOT, the Experimental Prototype Community of Tomorrow. EPCOT was envisioned as a place where corporate R&D groups and entrepreneurs would live and work together, accelerating solutions to US and global problems, and a **showcase of innovation process to global visitors**. Two weeks later, Disney was diagnosed with metastatic lung cancer, and he died two months later. Imagine how much better society would be today, if Walt had lived, or if he had used his last weeks alive to appoint a successor with commitment to the vision. EPCOT would have become the **world's first permanent crowdsourced innovation showcase and city**, beginning in 1970, rather than the simple entertainment attraction his successors made. See "1970: A Fully-Realized EPCOT (Innovation Showcase)" for more. *Innovation foresight matters!*

In 1990, right after the fall of the Soviet Union, could the US have led a **new Marshall Plan for Russia and the former Soviet States?** It certainly seems so. At that special time, the West had the surplus wealth to engage in such a charitable undertaking. Western academics like **Jeffrey Sachs** were brought in to Poland, and then Russia and other former soviet states, to rewrite their constitutions and help them convert to capitalist economies. But, without **massive aid for small businesses, extensive support for families**, and **technical and higher education for the youth** who would be the skilled labor and entrepreneurs in the new economies, and *all* of that aid being made conditional on **stepwise democratic reforms**, Russia and other former Soviet states would predictably turn to theft of state riches by oligarchs, innovation-crushing oligopoly, organized crime, and corruption. With a **Post-Soviet Marshall Plan**, we would not have had a Russia that was as **integrated** with the US and West today as, say West Germany was by 1975, thirty years after the Marshall Plan. But, we may not have had a Russia working openly to subvert US elections, or to capture the Crimea or subvert US interests in the Middle East. We'd very likely have had a Ukraine and Baltic States that were far more integrated with Europe. All of the Soviet States would have **much less poverty and lack of opportunity**, and all would be farther on the path to **post-authoritarian** institutions, markets, and civil society than today. *Humanitarian foresight matters!*

In 2000, if US politicians had decided to start subsidizing the growth of the Information Superhighway, and made low-cost fiber and high-speed cellular access a **public right**, the way Finland did with internet access in 2010, what would our world be like today? How much farther along would the **web, mobile, the cloud, AI, the internet of things**, and all the useful new tech and business models we can build on top of this critical communication infrastructure be today? Telecom and cable oligopolies **naturally seek to slow down** the growth of wired and wireless bandwidth, as more bandwidth disrupts their scarcity-based business models. Many municipal and nonprofit broadband initiatives have been sued and killed by cable oligopolies, to prevent competition from emerging. Even Google Fiber gave up in the face of telco opposition. The same kind of blockage to commerce and movement occurred in the era of **private roads and turnpikes** in the US, before they were **nationalized**, and **highway access** was made both a **public-private partnership** and a **free public good**. If we'd had real political leadership on bandwidth, access, and affordability issues beginning in the early 1990s, during the **first internet boom**, how much more **digitally advanced** would the US and the world be today? See "2000: Subsidized American Broadband" for more on this LPO. *Digital foresight matters!*

In 2010, could we have continued to invest tens of millions a year in developing **DRACO**, a universal antiviral adjuvant developed by **Todd Rider** at MIT's Lincoln Lab, and in **CANARY**, a genetically engineered B-cell that can be grown on a chip to identify pathogens at very low concentrations, developed by another Lincoln Lab team? If we had seriously funded **antiviral defense and detection** over the last ten years, when **COVID-19** occurred in 2019 we would have had both **cheap mass testing** and a **universal antiviral adjuvant**, a therapeutic arguably even more valuable than **vaccines** in pandemics, as it is immediately deployable and effective. There are many such adjuvants available. **N-hydroxycitidine**, for example, is an apparently safe oral amino acid derivative that been proven to prevent Covid infection in human epithelial cells, and it prevents infection from all RNA viruses when taken within 12 hours of infection (in ferrets). It is on a **very slow track to human use**, due to unforesighted policy. For viral detection, Abbot's 13 minute **ID Now rapid Covid test** was proven to have high specificity and sensitivity in May 2020, and it is cheap to administer. It could have been immediately scaled up and made available in all US hospitals, schools, airports, and offices, greatly shortening our **mass quarantine**. If we had funded this antiviral, immunity, and viral testing work in earnest over the last decade, we could have **averted hundreds of thousands of deaths** and **trillions of dollars** in lost jobs and lost productivity. We would have done "smart" rather than "dumb" quarantining. See John's article, "Will COVID-19 Bring Serious Antiviral Defense Spending to the US?," 2020, for more on this tragic LPO. *Public health foresight matters!*

In 2015, could the US intelligence agencies, and Western journalists, have exposed the **depth of Russian manipulation of Western democratic opinion and elections** via **fake news**? All the information trails were there, waiting to be picked up. Russia's intelligence agency, the FSB, with extensive funding from Putin's oligarchs, founded the <u>Internet Research Agency</u> (IRA) in 2013. The IRA employed 1,000 people, many of whom used thousands of fake user accounts and bots to spread fake, emotionally charged, politically polarizing stories and opinions on social media. The IRA was used extensively on global news sites to influence opinion about Russia's invasion and annexation of Crimea from Ukraine in 2014, and to **steal the Ukraine elections** for their proxy, <u>**Petro Poroshenko**</u>, in 2014. US President **Barak Obama's** team was <u>warned several times by our national security agencies in 2014</u> about the scope of Russia's **disinformation arm**, and its strategy to push US and European elections to **far-right populists**. If President Obama's team had seen, and just as importantly, been willing to **publicly politicize** the scope of **Russian disinformation**, we could have taken measures to **limit the spread of fake news in our social**

Bryan, 2018

media prior to the 2016 US elections. A 2015 bill to **hold social media sites accountable for their stories** would have gone a long way. Given his economic dependence on Russia, Trump might not have won the Republican primary, or the 2016 election. See **Jack Bryan's** documentary *Active Measures*, 2018, for more on this LPO. *Media foresight matters!*

This last counterfactual makes clear that **learning** is often critical to improving our social and global foresight. Without an evidence-based press and an electorate willing to learn, we cannot have a **healthy democracy**. The most important foundation for learning, of course, is **science**. Without an **educated citizenry**, with strong critical thinking capabilities and a hunger for evidence, **democracies are weak and easily divided.** Astronomer and futurist **Carl Sagan's** classic, *The Demon-Haunted World*, 1997, described our foundational need for strong science, rationality, and critical thinking education. The end of this important book offers a **prescient warning** of the possibility of the **America we live in today**, in which education and media standards erosion, manufacturing and middle class loss, plutocracy, fake news, conspiracy theories, polarization, and populism abound. We will get out of the **holes we've dug for ourselves**, but it will take time.

Fortunately, the mid-21st century emergence of **Personal AIs (PAIs)** which we will explore in Book 2, will greatly improve personal and collective rates of learning. They will guide us, increasingly, to **evidence-based inputs**. When we choose not to follow evidence, others will know. We will come to view our PAIs as nothing less than our **digital self**, a self that experiences **accelerating intelligence and capabilities,** unlike our biological self. We propose that PAIs will even **live on**, if we or our children wish them to do so, **interacting** with our family and friends, and i**mproving their sentience and usefulness** every year, even after we die. The **late 21st century** will be **different**, in some quite profound ways, than today.

We hope this brief survey of a few historical **LPOs** has provided enough evidence that good foresight, coming to the right people at the right time, can fix many of our big problems, help us avoid disasters, and greatly improve our lives. In truth, there is always a vast amount of **latent foresight** around us, "**waiting patiently for our wits to grow sharper,**" to use **Eden Philpott's** lovely phrase.

These LPOs remind us that not only **foresight**, but being **rational**, and **deeply valuing scientific knowledge**, and the **ethical and empathic experimentation** with **technology**, with all its unknowns and controversies, are among the foundations of **societal progress**. Psychologist **Steven Pinker's** *Rationality: What it Is, Why it Seems Scarce, and Why it Matters*, 2021, continues Sagan's crusade for **strengthening rationality** in ourselves, our teams, and our societies. **Uncovering latent foresight**, evaluating it **rationally**, and **routing it** to those who need it most, are key responsibilities for all of us, as citizens of this amazing, accelerating planet. Our **Futurepedia project** (Chapter 6) is our own best strategy for helping the world in that regard. *Foresight matters!*

Adaptive Foresight: Models, Values, and Visons of Success and Progress

We've said that **adaptive foresight** is foresight that is based on our current **theory of adaptation**. It is concerned not only with surviving, but **thriving,** for the greatest number of us, in the widest range of environments. Such foresight necessarily generates **visions** of potential **personal success** and **societal progress**, and it promotes **goals and values** intended to make individuals, teams, and societies more adaptive.

We'd like now to offer our own **Hierarchy of Thinking in Adaptive Foresight**. This is both a simple mental model and a quick graphical way to explain our assumptions about how good foresight emerges, step-by-step, in both an evolutionary and a developmental process. Our hierarchy will be kept to five steps, for simplicity. The hierarchies and steps we find most valuable, for ourselves and our teams, says a good deal about how we view foresight production.

Below is a graphical summary of our proposed hierarchy. We hope you find it helpful.

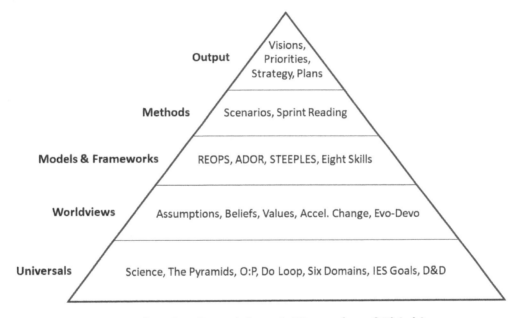

Adaptive Foresight – A Hierarchy of Thinking

In our view, the most fundamental step of good foresight work, is recognizing and applying **Universals,** or models, processes, and principles that we expect to be valid and constraining in every Earthlike environment in our universe. In our **Overview**, we said that **Science, Acceleration Awareness,** and **Evo-Devo Foresight** are three fundamental **Worldviews** we use in this *Guide*. To be more exact, these are three *belief systems* that we use to *uncover* universals.

Science is the most fundamental of these belief systems. The **ways** science is practiced by humans will always be imperfect, and unique to each culture. But science itself has been so successful in uncovering the hidden structure of reality, in every area of inquiry, we can call it a **Universal way of knowing.** By contrast, our models of both **accelerating change** and of **evo-devo processes** are **Worldviews** at present. They are partly-evidenced **philosophies**, based on certain assumptions and beliefs about the nature of complex systems. They need further study, definition, and validation. Nevertheless, we think some variant of both worldviews will become part of established science in the future.

In the graphic above we list some **products** of both worldviews, like the Evo-Devo Pyramids, the Optimism:Pessimism conflict, the Do Loop, the Six Domains, the IES Goals, and D&D, that *we propose are universals*, necessarily operating in all complex and intelligent life. Future science will either validate or invalidate our view.

A third level of thinking we use is our **Models** (causal and categorical), **and Frameworks** (recipes for practice methods). Models and frameworks we find useful include the Four Ps, REOPS, ADOR analysis, the Eight Skills, and STEEPLES scanning (Chapter 5). It can be difficult to **differentiate** between models and frameworks. Perhaps the most salient difference is that **frameworks** are models we use not just to define causes and categories, but in **practice**, in our work.

A fourth level of thinking all attend to, well or poorly, is **Methods**. Many methods can be misused unless they are part of a practice framework. For example, we contend that scenario methods are best used within a foresight production framework that includes an early step involving probable foresight assessment, to weed out implausible scenarios. We will introduce a few methods, like Sprint Reading, that are our own variations on the literature.

The last level we all attend to, and the most societally valued, is the **Output** we produce. Visions, Priorities, Strategies, and Plans are **particularly valuable products** of foresight. When they lead us into action, they are all key ways our foresight makes us adaptive, or not. They belong at the top of our pyramid of foresight thinking. Of all of these, our **shared visions** matter most to our long-term future. These visions feed back to shape our shared **worldviews**, the lowest level of our thinking hierarchy that is largely within our control. In other words, our shared visions, and their implicit models and values, belong at the **top** of this hierarchy, as our most important foresight output. Let us defend this claim with an example.

Thomas Sowell is one of America's leading scholars of economic and political development, personal responsibility, social opportunity, and the ways that **race and culture** can help or hinder **social progress.** He is both politically on the Right and Left, with complex, nuanced positions. For more on Sowell's contributions to society, we recommend this 2021 article by **Samuel Kronen.** Sowell has written more than fifty books over his 90 years of life to date. Of all of these, the one he considers the most important is *A Conflict of Visions*, 1987. *Conflict* describes the perennial political struggle between **two competing shared visions.** The first is the **constrained vision**, which sees **human nature** as primarily static, selfish, and engaged in zero-sum games. The second is the **unconstrained vision**, which sees human nature as malleable, learning, improvable, engaged in **positive-sum games**, and periodically upgrading our moral norms, laws, policies, and technologies, to advance both cooperation and competiveness. Each vision shapes our views of the responsibilities of the individual, organizations, institutions, and states.

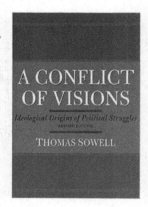

Sowell, 1987

Both visions have value. For most of our history, the constrained vision has dominated. But the faster the world goes, and the longer our horizons, the more the unconstrained vision should guide our thinking. **Robert Wright's** *Nonzero*, 2000, elegantly describes how we have increasingly learned how to find and play **positive-sum games** in all eras of our history. Ethics, democracy, and capitalism are all systems built on **positive sum rulesets**, discovered and improved by us over time. The **constrained vision** certainly applies to **particular** individuals, organizations, and societies at times. There are also **universal constraints** that we think will always apply to human nature itself. But the **unconstrained vision**, and the **rules, norms, priorities, strategies, and plans** we derive from it, best describes the **future of network humanity**, in our view. When we are thinking **positive-sum**, not just about ourselves, or our group, but about the **greatest good for the network**, we rise above traditional Right wing and Left wing political views. We are thinking **Upwing**, a term coined by the pioneering 20th century futurist **FM-2030 (aka F.M. Esfandiary).** A new term for this kind of thinking is **Forward**, popularized by political outsider (and now Independent) **Andrew Yang.** As Upwingers, as Forward thinkers we can best see and guide **accelerating progress.** We will explore this perspective further in *BPF*.

We can all benefit from regularly reviewing our **tentative models of success and progress.** Having models lets us boldly envision our own life, and combat the disempowering **cynicism, fear, and disengagement** we find in much of our media and in too many of our lovely fellow humans. Progress models are tricky, as they are by definition **normative**—or dependent on both our **values** and **models** of **adaptiveness.** Many readers may disagree with our models of progress and adaptiveness. But, hopefully they will at least challenge you to examine and refine your own. One of our **hidden foresight challenges** is to be aware of our and others **worldviews, goals, values, and visions**, and to make ours as **explicit**, **critiqued**, and **evidence-based** as we can.

As **Gerhard Vorster**, CSO at Deloitte Asia Pacific says, the most valuable **asset** of any firm is its **talent**, and specifically the **discretionary effort** (above and beyond the expected effort) that every firm's talent may apply. Such effort can vary greatly per person and per day, and *depends strongly* on the firm's **vision, rules, and leadership**.[13] Great firms today need a **higher purpose**: a set of **goals** that clearly strive to create a **better future**, and **values** that support that purpose. Organizations without **higher purpose**, a vision of how they contribute to **progress**, and **fair rules and good values**, simply won't attract the **talent they need to win** in a world of ever more rapid and disruptive industry change.

When we are guided by **adaptive goals and values**, we are on firm ground to do what the late management guru **Steven Covey** calls in *The 8th Habit*, 2005, **"Finding Our 'Voice,' and Helping Others to Find Theirs."** By this, he means both gaining the wisdom to see **higher goals and values**, and finding our own unique contributions, within those constraints. To aid in that process, Covey recommends creating our own **Personal Mission Statement**. Covey's audiobook, *How to Develop Your Personal Mission Statement*, 2012, can help with that. Futurist **Verne Wheelwright's** *It's Your Future … Make it a Good One!*, 2012 is another great guide to personal strategic foresight and planning. As we get more effective at living up to our values and visions, we can increasingly help others to do the same, practicing **personal development**.

A Vision of Global Foresight Culture

Great visions are **aspirational**, **motivating**, and above all, **adaptive**. Ever since futurist **Bertrand de Jouvenel's** *The Art of Conjecture*, 1967, and **Fred Polak's** *The Image of the Future*, 1973—two pioneering works on the **power of "future images"**—good foresight practitioners have realized that our greatest calling is to **help our clients find worthy positive images (visions)** to **steer toward**, and **plausible negative images** (shocks, blocks, traps, dystopias) to actively **prevent**.

A **positive vision** will pull a group toward a particular future, with a strength proportional to the group's belief in the **worthiness and credibility** of the vision and its leadership. Ensuring the **worthiness** of our visions, and the **morality** of our leaders is no small thing. Many leaders use visions, persuasion and propaganda to steer groups to futures that are **dehumanizing**, **unsustainable**, or **impractical**. One strategy to ensure worthy visions is to align them well with existing **group goals, values, ethics, feelings, and purpose**, and to ensure that goals and values are as **universal as possible**. Another strategy is to subject our visions to **feedback** and **criticism** from anyone who will be impacted by them. A third strategy is to search for the most **positive-sum** outcomes we think we can attain, over the time horizon of our vision. Sometimes we need to **stretch our horizon** to see a particularly compelling vision. At other times, we can usefully **shorten it,** and **focus** our team to reach goals they previously thought were unattainable within that time horizon.

Given the challenges of visioning, what visions can we offer of a better **foresight culture**? Most obviously, good **foresight culture begins** with **recognizing its great value.** The more of us who believe that **thinking, debating, and teaching about the future** is important, the more we will **integrate it into our lives**, and the more we will thrive. Foresight cultures, on teams, in organizations, and in societies, recognize there are many ways to manage the future, including **prediction, forecasting, intelligence, insurance, sensing, rapid reaction, planning, visioning, innovation, and strategy**. Such cultures know that while we are still early in understanding which methods are right for which contexts, by choosing to **prioritize foresight,** we invariably get better at it, and expand our tools and improve our data sets. Such cultures also know our future has become **too important** for us to leave it to **any other stewards than ourselves**.

Imagine if future thinking, debate, and visioning were common in our **educational system**, as **Peter Bishop** proposes in his *Teach the Future* initiative. Miraculously, even at the **age of two**, some children talk about what they might do in a

---

[13] Van der Laan and Yap, *Foresight & Strategy in the Asia Pacific Region*, 2016.

few moments or **even tomorrow**. This is how early our future thinking starts. We can grow this **superpower**, recognize its great value, and **deliberately nurture** its evolution and development. The great futurist **John McHale**, in *The Future of the Future*, 1969, told us that future thinking in childhood should be integrated throughout the K-12 curriculum. The earlier we start, the better we get at both our personal and collective efforts in foresight and action.

Imagine a future where both **mature organizations** and **startups** realize that refining, testing, and improving their **foresight process** will yield far more innovative, profitable, and sustainable products and services. Imagine our academics and analysts learning how to **quantify the value lost** when we don't use good foresight process. Those possibilities are emerging today, and they are being greatly accelerated by our new digital tools and platforms.

Today, we live in a world with **digital abundance**. By 2018, users of digital platforms like **Google, Facebook**, and **Android** had become the largest coherent groups on Earth. By 2020, the site **Reddit Futurology** had **15 million "futurists"** on their platform. There are more than **55 million software developers** using the open source software platform **GitHub**. There are scores of cloud services, platforms, AI, digital currencies, smart contracts, and other innovations emerging every month now. Looking ahead, we can see how we will create a world with **general abundance**, where all of us have our **basic needs met**, and we are free to climb our developmental pyramids, each in our own unique ways.

A key **big picture vision** that more of us must learn to see is that certain **accelerating trends and destinations** for humanity, perhaps most importantly including the **emergence of increasingly life-like thinking, acting, and feeling machines**, as extensions of our **heads, hands, and hearts**, are becoming **highly predictable**. As **John Kasson** states, we need many more people working to **"civilize the machine,"** because our accelerating machines, **science and technology** in all their forms, are uniquely able to **amplify** our actions today, for **good** or **ill**. They are uniquely able to **create or destroy value**. That is the human condition in the 21st century.

There are many ways accelerating change will create **pain, disruption, and regression** for some of us, but it will **continue** nonetheless. **Complexity acceleration**, in **increasingly local places** in our universe, appears to be just as **unrelenting a force as gravity**. We think future scientific theory will establish this. We see no way, short of a **species-ending event**, that accelerating change could stop. Ideas of technological relinquishment, stasis, or regression are naïve nostalgia. We are on for the ride. We biological humans **do not seem to be powerful enough to prevent this process**, even if we wanted to.

We are in a truly unique period in our 10,000 year history. We live at the singular time in which **technology itself** is showing it can **learn** and **improve** at rates that make biology look like it is **standing still**. Many **perils and pitfalls** lie ahead. Increasingly useful, efficient, intelligent, and individually flawed (just like us) AIs, machines, and their networks will continue to emerge, and increasingly shape our environment. Fortunately, history shows that **catastrophes**, when they have occurred, have almost always **catalyzed new complexity and antifragility in life's networks**. Networks, not individuals, are always winning the **universal game** of adaptation, progress, and acceleration. Our emerging **human-machine network**, too, will surely win, if we **pay close attention** to how life itself has done so well, so far.

As the astronomer **Carl Sagan** famously observed, our universe has been developing new complexity at an accelerating rate since our first Galaxies emerged via gravitational attraction. **D&D in complex adaptive systems**, in our view, is the central driver of this **universal exponential process**. **Life** on Earth, for its part, has accelerated its **network complexity and intelligence** for over 3.5 billion years. **Humans** are just the latest chapter in a very long book. It is not wrong, in our view, to say that the **universe** appears to be **using** the **laws of physics and information,** and as a later key development, **life and complex intelligence**, to **create accelerating change**. Sagan's Cosmic Calendar (picture below) is a famous graphical depiction of this acceleration. It depicts the **developmental acceleration** of increasingly local complexity and intelligence in special places in our universe. It also argues, implicitly, that some of the human story depicted in the last frame is developmental. What this image minimizes is the **vast evolutionary variety** that created this acceleration. It leaves out our **free individual choice**. We must learn to see and balance both visions. Both appear to be true.

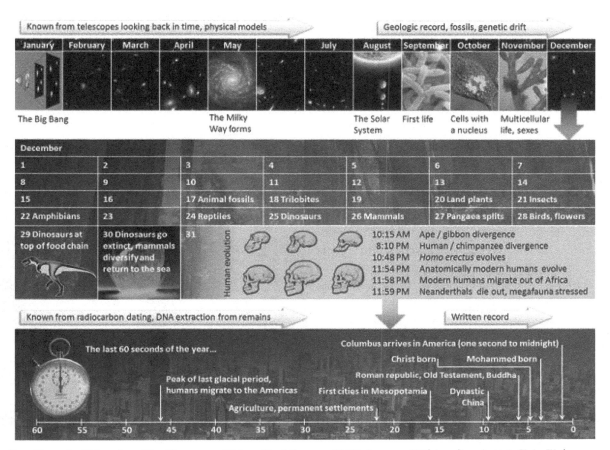

The Cosmic Calendar. *The Dragons of Eden*, Carl Sagan, 1977. Image: Wikipedia. Artist: Eric Fisk

If **intelligence and complexity are important** to our universe, the image above is arguably something we should expect. Accelerating change, massive parallelism, and network-centric development may be ways our universe "rigs the rules", to ensure that diverse forms of life, complexity, and consciousness emerge. If our **universe itself replicates**, as several cosmologists propose, it may have *self-organized*, over many past cycles, for **its evolved and developed intelligence to matter to its future**, the way life's intelligence has self-organized, via evo-devo processes, to matter to its own future. If network intelligence **develops** at an accelerating rate in **many parallel places** in our universe, if it grows, on average, more **empathic, ethical, capable, and stable**, and if it **eventually communicates** with all the other diverse and limited local intelligences, our own local intelligence may even **serve a higher purpose**, as we will argue in *BPF*. Our intelligence, in other words, may be **useful**, both to our **cosmic community**, and to our **universe itself**. We shall see, as they say.

The universe's **leading intelligence**, in our little corner, is **us**. We human beings are presently leading this accelerating development, on this amazing and special planet, but that is **no guarantee** that we will make **ethical** and **humanizing** choices, or even that we'll **survive** the coming changes. Each of us has a great deal of evolutionary bfreedom, and developmental failures do sometimes occur. We believe we have an ethical duty to understand, protect and advance Earth's complexity and consciousness, and to treat each other with the **fairness, love, courage, and honesty** we all deserve. More than ever, the world needs more **foresighted people** willing to contemplate and validate **developmental destinations**, and to help us move toward them in **more empathic, ethical, and humanizing ways**. We hope this vision inspires you to become a better **all-around foresight professional—better leaders of yourself first**, and of **others second**. We all can participate in the improvement of foresight culture, however best fits our path.

Welcome to the Field!

Chapter 2: The Foresight Profession – State of Our Field

A Very Brief History of Our Field

Strategic foresight originated in 17th century Europe during the <u>**Age of Enlightenment**</u>, which simultaneously birthed **modern science**, **reasoning**, and **foresight**. The **European Enlightenment**, with its free thinking, democratic ideals and evidence-seeking priorities, was a **great leap forward** for humanity. In the Enlightenment we see the first modern approaches to freedom of thought and action, individual rights, the scientific method, egalitarianism, democracy, and the separation of church and state. <u>**Baruch Spinoza**</u> was a key influence on the emergence of our **modern democratic state**. He popularized a mindset of **rational inquiry** and **skepticism** in which modern, evidence-based foresight could emerge and flourish. **Steven Nadler's** *Spinoza*, 2001, introduces this key Enlightenment thinker. His ideas remain foundational today.

European Enlightenment, 1650-1850

One key mental development that allowed science, reasoning, and evidence-based foresight to emerge was <u>**inductive reasoning**</u>. **Induction** requires observing **individual instances** of any process, then finding a **general rule** to describe them. In other words, it entails reasoning "upward"—from particulars to universals. Inductive thinking became legitimate only with <u>**probability theory**</u>, which began with a collaboration by <u>**Blaise Pascal**</u> and <u>**Pierre de Fermat**</u>, on how to <u>estimate the future</u> in games of chance in 1654. Their key insights led to Hugyens' *On Reasoning in Games of Chance*, 1657, **Cardano's** *Book on Games of Chance*, 1663, and particularly general, **Bernoulli's** *The Art of Conjecturing*, 1713. Though this type of reasoning was described by <u>**Aristotle**</u> in Ancient Greece, we needed two additional millennia, and the emergence of probability theory, to finally convince serious people that **inductive methods** deserved the same attention that <u>**deduction**</u> (logic) always enjoyed. These key advances paved the way for the birth of <u>**statistics**</u> in 1750.

From this era onward, the **shortcomings of our deductive logic and rationality** (top-down, **developmental thinking**) could finally be **balanced** by clever **observation, experiment, and induction** (bottom-up, **evolutionary thinking**). Neither set of mental processes alone creates an adaptive **intelligence**. Deduction alone makes us **prisoners of our mental models**. Observation alone leads to endless **unchecked beliefs and stories**. Induction, via the **scientific method**, gives us the means to **escape from our heads,** to **rise above our mental limits**—to alter, falsify and verify our models via experiments and collecting data. In the language of the Foresight Pyramid, **empiricism**, **theory**, and **utility** (**possible, probable, and preferable assessments**) are each fundamental **goals of science** as a method of knowing and adapting.

Another major foresight advance in this era came from **philosophers of** <u>**mechanics**</u>, later called **physicists**. Chief among them was <u>**Isaac Newton,**</u> who co-invented <u>**calculus**</u> (the mathematics of change) and who published the first comprehensive set of <u>**universal laws of motion**</u> in *Principia Mathematica* in 1687. After *Principia*, people knew that by building instruments, forming hypotheses, doing experiments, collecting data, and building models, they could develop <u>**probabilistic explanations**</u> of the past, present, and future of complex systems, even at the universal scale.

Enlightenment optimism also birthed our first popular **visionaries** in **qualitative foresight**, like <u>Louis Mercer</u> and his utopian novel <u>*The Year 2440*</u>, 1770, widely read across Europe in twenty-five print editions. The fertile era from roughly 1750 to 1850, called the <u>**First Industrial Revolution**</u>, is our candidate for our first modern **Foresight Spring**. In this time we made our first modern attempts to **model and understand humanity** as a complex system.

This era included Belgian statistician **Adolphe Quetelet**, and his <u>*Treatise on Man*</u>, 1835, which introduced the idea of **"social physics"** (later called <u>sociology</u>), the collection of data on crime and social events to build predictive models of the **"average [hu]man,"** and the recognition that we could find a great variety of <u>statistical laws</u> for social processes. This work led philosopher **August Comte**, another founder of modern **sociology**, to propose his <u>Law of Three Stages</u>, an early **developmental model** of social change. In Comte's model, societies typically begin **Theological**, then become **Metaphysical**, then become **Scientific** as social complexity grows. Encouraged by Newton's progress in the physical sciences, Comte extrapolated deductive thinking to its logical extreme in <u>*A General View of Positivism*</u>, 1844, proposing, quite incorrectly in our view, that all social knowledge must ultimately derive from logical and mathematical precepts and laws. In reality, humanity will never get smart enough to escape induction. Both **inductive uncertainty (evolutionary process)** and **deductive certainty (developmental process)** are central to the pursuit of knowledge. As one of the many benefits of the **95/5 Rule**, we can also infer that **induction will be more useful than deduction** in the **great majority** of contexts requiring **strategic analysis**. We must become **induction masters**, twenty times more than we **deduce**.

So while logic and rationality have their uses, Comte's **logical positivism** was a dangerously incomplete way to understand the world. <u>**Probability and statistics**</u>, and the **statistical laws and correlations** we find in many complex systems, have typically proven far better lenses to describe our environment than logic, rigorous causality, and equations. As dual process theory reminds us, in social systems, factors like **intuition, instinct, emotion, culture, custom, vision, and possibility** are typically far more important than **rationality** in ascertaining what humans may do next.

While they were born in the Enlightenment (1600-1800), deductive and inductive methods of foresight only began to see broad use in science, philosophy, government, and commerce during the great changes unleashed by the <u>**Second Industrial Revolution**</u> (1850-1900), during which **oil, steel, and electrification** emerged, as well as the **first giant industrial corporations** (Standard Oil, US Steel, General Electric, etc.). Then it took a further fifty years after this productivity and wealth revolution for **modern management, strategy, and foresight processes** to emerge.

The field of **strategic planning** was first taught at Harvard in the 1930s. The field of strategic foresight was born in the mid-1940's, immediately after World War II, with the funding of the world's first formal foresight think tanks, SRI and RAND. These initial foresight practitioner communities were dominated by **engineers and scientists**, and had a probability and forecasting focus. Their main customers were government and defense clients. By the 1960s, several leading management consultancies began to permanently do professional foresight work, primarily serving business clients. These included the Boston Consulting Group (BCG) and the Institute for the Future (IFTF). The 1960s also gave us our first university courses on foresight, and our first general and academic foresight communities, like the World Future Society (WFS) and World Futures Studies Federation (WFSF).

As an **academic field**, foresight is a **late bloomer** by comparison to related professions, such as economics, sociology, political science, and science and technology studies. Foresight is underdeveloped in relation to its specialty and related professions, such as forecasting, planning, risk management, and leadership. Nevertheless, the long-term future of our field is bright. We will discuss many paths ahead to its practice maturity. We offer a **longer history of foresight**, over Five Eras of Practice, in Appendix 2 in Book 2.

Twenty-Five Top Futurists and Foresighters of the Twentieth Century

To close our brief history, let us now offer some of our favorite **benchmark examples** of futures and/or foresight value and impact in the last century. We offer a list of Top Foresighters and Futurists of the Twentieth Century, based on either the **value or impact** of their published work across the **six futures domains,** or on our **foresight profession,** as we see it. There are many great past futurists and foresighters to learn from and to be inspired by, as we chart our own careers.

Modern professional foresight started, after WW II, as a **US-centric, gender-imbalanced, and ethnically-narrow** activity. We look forward to offering a far more international, ethnically diverse and gender-balanced Top Twenty-Five list for 2000-2025, in the next edition of the *Guide*. To that end, see futurist **Ross Dawson's** excellent global list of top female futurists. We are slowly gaining the gender, ethnic, cultural, and experience diversity our field needs and deserves.

The best **futures work**, in our view, is **uniquely creative** (evolutionary), but also seeks to describe **universals** (development), and the nature and future of our **civilization**. It says something in each of the Six Domains, tells stories across the Four Ps, and touches, at least briefly, all of the STEEPLES (Science, Technology, Economy, Environment, Politics, Law, Ethics, and Society) categories (Chapter 5). The best work has been lauded by some, and has also advanced future thinking. The author **Henry Adams** is a benchmark. He said much about the relationship between **technology and society**, and published the first simple model of **accelerating change as a universal process in 1909.** He expected this acceleration to occur on **all planets with intelligent life** (right). Adams is our first 20th century pick in our list below. Each of the individuals on this list has been both a **futurist** in some respects, and a **foresighter**, advancing practice in our vital and emerging field.

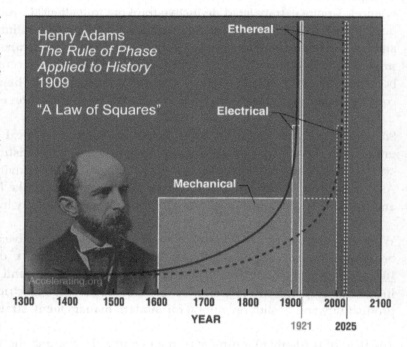

Here then is our current list of the **Top Twenty-Five Futurists and Foresighters** of the last century:

Henry Adams, **H.G. Wells**, **Herman Kahn**, **Buckminster Fuller**, **Harrison Brown**, **Daniel Bell**, **Arthur Clarke**, **Julian Simon**, **Alvin Toffler**, **Gerard Piel**, **Donella Meadows**, **Hazel Henderson**, **Stewart Brand**, **Gro Brundtland**, **Peter Drucker**, **Carl Sagan**, **Roy Amara**, **Olaf Helmer**, **Robert Theobald**, **Barbara Hubbard**, **Hans Moravec**, **Peter Schwartz**, **George Gilder**, **Ray Kurzweil**, and **Hans Rosling**.

A few lesser-known figures, like **Gerard Piel**, editor of *Scientific American*, who explored **accelerating change in a key book in 1972,** are included in the list above. As we say in *BPF*, we consider accelerating change to be a **still-neglected universal developmental process**, one that tells us a lot about the **nature of the future**. For one, predicts an **eventual end to Earth's multi-billion year history of acceleration**, once the **inner space limits** of physics are finally reached, perhaps just a **few centuries** from now. We believe we live in a **very special time** in cosmic history. We shall see.

Who would you add? Who would you demote? We'll explain our choices in a later edition of the *Guide*. In the meantime, look up these author's Wikipedia pages (linked) for more on their great work. Now there are *hundreds more* excellent futurists or foresighters we could have named. **Bertrand de Jouvenel**, **Johan Galtung**, **Kenneth Boulding**, **Isaac Asimov**, **Fred Polak**, **Peter Medawar**, **Eleonora Masini**, **E.F. Schumacher**, **Elise Boulding**, **Burnham Beckwith**, **Doug Englebart**,

__Willis Harman__, __Barry Hughes__, __Jerome Glenn__, __Ted Gordon__, __Joseph Coates__, __Vary Coates__, __Jim Dator__, __Peter Bishop__, __Michael Marien__, __Graham Molitor__, __Warren Wagar__, __Sohail Inayatullah__, __Richard Slaughter__, __Wendy Schultz__, __Clement Bezold__, __Kevin Kelly__, and many others belong in a __Top 50__ and an __Honorable Mentions__ list. Some of these and others, like __Philip Tetlock__, __Amy Webb__, __Shoshanna Zuboff__, __Cory Doctorow__, __Steven Pinker__, and __Rutger Bregman__ also belong in a __Top 25 or Top 50 for 2000-2025__ list. We plan to have those lists in the next edition of the *Guide*. Would you make different choices? Let us know!

The Current State of Our Field

In this chapter we offer an overview of the current state of **professional foresight** and the practice of **strategic foresight**—primarily as practiced on **small teams**. Our field is a global community of people driven to **anticipate, create, lead**, and **protect** the future, the **Four Ps of Future Thinking**. It is filled with many colorful and inspiring personalities, but it is also still nascent, lacking in evidence-based, consensus practices and models. It has much room for improvement and growth. In 2015 we started **Foresight University** to do our small part to help advance foresight models and practice.

We will turn now to a **popular myth**, then acknowledge an **open secret**, and then dive deeper into the **Do loop**, the universal way that intelligent beings **integrate foresight and action**. Most helpfully perhaps, we'll introduce the **Eight Skills of Adaptive Foresight**, our Do loop-derived model for practicing great foresight on teams and in organizations.

In Chapter 3, we'll offer a selection of **proof points (success stories)** in applying each of the **Four Foresight Skills (LAIS)**, with examples primarily in **organizational foresight**. In future editions, we plan to supplement the *Guide* with **case studies** as well. **Case-based learning** is a uniquely powerful and interactive way for students and leaders to internalize the value of foresight work.

Foresight's Great Myth

Foresight's **Great Myth** is that it is rarely worth doing, because it is so often wrong. Recall that foresight has four core practice types. The first, **probable futures**, is about forecasting and prediction. The second, **possible futures**, is about generating alternatives, scenarios, experiments, and uncovering wildcards. The third is about exploring **preferable futures** (strategies, policies, plans, surveys, visions, agendas). The fourth, **preventable futures**, is concerned with protection from plausible risks, via tools like defensive thinking, intelligence gathering, and risk assessment.

Each of us will be quite wrong at times when we explore the Four Ps. Great histories of **probable foresight failures** include **William Sherden's** *The Fortune Sellers*, 1997, **Steven Schnaars** *Megamistakes*, 1989, **Laura Lee's** *Bad Predictions*, 2000, **Nicholas Taleb's** *Fooled by Randomness*, 2005, **Bob Seidensticker's** *Future Hype*, 2006, **Adam Gordon's** *Future Savvy*, 2008, and **Doug Hubbard's** *The Failure of Risk Management*, 2008. For more on our poor record of exploring the scope of **possible futures**, see **Nicholas Taleb's** *The Black Swan*, 2010. Our weak ability to see and plan for **preferable and preventable futures** is well documented in books like **Henry Mintzberg's** *The Rise and Fall of Strategic Planning*, 2000, **Walter Kiechel's** *The Lords of Strategy*, 2010, and **Clay Christensen's** *The Innovators Dilemma*, 2013. Sherden's book is particularly great, outlining many 20th century **management fads in strategy, planning, and foresight.**

Sherden 1997

It is alternately amusing, enlightening, and sobering to read these books. It is amusing to see how wrong we can be, enlightening to realize how much we can improve, and sobering to learn how much suffering and ignorance our poor foresight has caused humanity over the centuries. We routinely ignore probability estimates, inadequately explore possibilities, fail to find shared visions, and arrogantly discount or miss threats. Given how poorly we often **think**, it is no wonder we **see so little**.

Our history of mistakes when thinking about the future has allowed a great myth, the "**Myth of Ineffectiveness**" to arise in foresight work. This myth is sometimes voiced as an explicit belief, but more often is implicitly held, both by many of our clients and by lay observers of our profession. Each of the Four Ps deserves a **strong defense** against this myth. Because human beings fail the most often and the most obviously at **probable foresight**, which requires us to describe falsifiably specific futures that we expect, this is the area of our practice that is most commonly and deeply devalued today. But, all four practice types are underused today due to this myth.

Recall the *Anna Karenina* **principle;** there are always many evolutionary ways to fail, and just a few developmental ways to succeed. Consider its application to **probability foresight practice**. We can fail in forecasting or predicting without good knowledge or proper models of the system in question. We can fail by straying into fields where we have inadequate expertise. We can fail by predicting from a position of known or unconscious bias. We can fail by neglecting to subject our forecasts and predictions to intense criticism from an appropriately skilled and cognitively diverse crowd. We can fail by forecasting or predicting only infrequently, thus never learning accuracy and conservatism.

Many common failure modes will be discussed in this *Guide*. Poor forecasters, failed experimenters, and unsuccessful strategists are unhappy each in their own way. Unintended consequences and combinatorial explosions of contingencies make evolutionary things, but not developmental things, more uncertain over time. Yet, even with the many ways we can fail, the modern foresight field has been paid to engage in over seventy years of such efforts; and, we're increasingly finding those developmental attractors—the universal processes that enhance our foresight—in each of the Four Ps.

Our profession has gotten steadily better at foresight, in every domain. Never have there been **more specialists** conducting such extensive modeling, forecasting, prediction, uncertainty exploring, visioning, preference mapping, facilitation, and strategizing in the world. Never has there been a **richer data environment** for exploring Four Ps futures, and never has there been **more economic value** created by those who have been generating good foresight and strategy. Now is a very exciting time for professionals doing foresight work. We can see a path ahead to its maturity.

Foresight's Open Secret

Foresight's **Open Secret** is that it is **only valuable to a point**. Any of its skills, models, and methods can quickly become a **waste** of our client's time and money. With respect to foresight **methods** and **products**, there may be **little strategic value** in the thinking process, method, or type of work being requested by our client. Alternatively, our client may be in **no position to act** on the foresight produced, which is the **real problem** that needs to be **named and fixed**. In such cases, the effort we would spend cannot be justified by a realistic **benefit-cost analysis**. Every skill, model, or method—whether in foresight or action—supplies a **declining value** the more it is pursued to the neglect of others.

For both individuals and teams, it is easy to spend too much time **ruminating on the past** or **contemplating the future**. We all know that planning, done too far in advance, or in too much detail, can easily be a waste of time. So too with other foresight methods. Ideally, we use past and future thinking to **improve our capacity** to act better in the **present**. Empowering and expanding our **sense of the Present**, and our **capacity to act well in it**, is the **Temporal Goal of Foresight Work**. All three time orientations must be actively managed, in pursuit of **present and future adaptiveness**.

Good practitioners remind their clients of this open secret: they help their clients **learn for themselves** when foresight work is **no longer valuable** and it's time to **switch gears**. Shortly, we will describe how our **foresight skills** must be continually balanced against **action skills** if we are to remain **adaptive**.

As we will see, sometimes we need:

1. A better understanding of the past or present (the **Learning** skill),

2. To forecast or predict what is likely to come next (the **Anticipation** skill)

3. To imagine or design new possibilities (the **Innovation** skill)

4. Better visions, policies, and plans (the **Strategy** skill),

5. To take action (the **Execution** skill)

6. Greater sway with stakeholders (the **Influence** skill),

7. Better care and renewal of our teams (the **Relating** skill),

8. More feedback on and analysis of recent activities (the **Reviewing** skill).

All of these **Eight Skills** are critical to success. For simplicity, we call the first four **Foresight Skills**, which we will discuss now, and the second four **Action Skills**, discussed next. As a group, these skills work together to make teams and firms more adaptive. Learning to **survive and thrive**, in any environment, is the top goal of foresight work and of life itself.

LAIS: The Four Skills of Strategic Foresight

Let's look closer now at the **Four Skills** of strategic foresight work. They are the **simplest** model that we recommend for thinking about **strategic foresight competencies**. No other foresight text that we know presently uses this model. We hope it gains wider adoption in management and leadership in coming years.

A great **elevator-pitch definition** of foresight, taught to John by emeritus U. Houston professor of foresight **Peter Bishop**, is that **"foresight is anything we do *prior* to strategy."** Bishop reminds us that this is not technically accurate, as foresight actually **ends with strategy**, but it is one good way to quickly introduce our **value**. Many graduate schools teach **strategy and planning**. Many big companies have a **strategy department**. But few schools teach, and very few organizations use, a **formal set of practices**, done as **inputs to strategy**, that will reliably make our strategy both more **future-aware** and **future-resilient**. Like the term **"strategic foresight,"** Bishop's snappy definition is a clever **one-sentence summary** of both the proper place of our field within **strategic management**, and of the value of our work.

Peter Bishop

Calling foresight the **"front end of strategy"** helps our clients to realize that if they **don't do anything before** they jump into **strategy work**—and most teams **typically do not**—they are **missing an entire set of practices** that can greatly improve their decision making and outcomes. These practices have been developed over the **last sixty years**, and they are what we call **strategic foresight**.

Technically, we can define **strategic foresight** as future thinking that has the **potential** (the capacity), **if acted upon (using action skills)**, to make an actor (individual, team, organization, society) more **adaptive** or **successful**. In a fusion of the Do loop and the Foresight Pyramid, this requires a minimum of **Four Foresight Skills**:

1. **Learning (the relevant Past and Present)**

2. **Anticipation (the relevant Probable)**

3. **Innovation (the relevant Possible)**

4. **Strategy (the relevant Preferable and Preventable)**

We use the acronym **LAIS**, for **Learning, Anticipation, Innovation**, and **Strategy**, for these four skills. Implicit in the LAIS model is splitting **Strategy** into **positive and negative sentiment**, and doing first **predictive contrasting**, then **sentiment contrasting** in initial strategy creation. The professional's responsibility for **foresight conflict management** is represented in the **Four Ps** and its various frameworks, including **ADOR analysis** and the **REOPS cycle**.

Again, **Learning** is technically not foresight, but **preparation** for foresight work. But directed learning is so critical how we perceive, formulate and research a problem that we include it as an **essential foresight skill**. No one can achieve adaptive foresight without **good models of both the relevant past (hindsight)** and **the present (insight)**. At the same time, no foresight is beneficial unless it causes **adaptive action**.

We've said that there are **Four Action Skills**:

5. **Execution (Product thinking)**

6. **Influence (Market thinking)**

7. **Relating (Team thinking)**

8. **Reviewing (Adjustment thinking)**

The Do loop reminds us that **strategic foresight** is a great start, but it isn't enough for adaptiveness. We must translate our foresight into **products or services**, serve a **market** with those actions, maintain a strong **team**, and continually **adjust** our results. The successful combination of **foresight** and **action** is called **adaptive foresight** in this *Guide*. For those who like acronyms, we can call the **Eight Skills of Adaptive Foresight**, the **LAIS Foresight Skills**, and the **EIRR Action Skills**, and both the **LAISEIRR (pronounced "laser") skills**. All eight are vitally important for teams and organizations.

We further claim that while these skills can keep us adaptive in the **short-term**, over the **long-term**, we must also have **adaptive goals and values**. If our **character and conduct** are out of line with **universal principles (truths, wisdom)** we will eventually fail. We will return to our vital **goals and values** (normative foresight) later in this chapter.

Let's look closer now at the **Four Skills of Strategic Foresight**:

1. **Learning**. First we must try to understand where we came from and where we are. We collect relevant history, trends, cycles, causal factors, and models. We look carefully and analytically at potentially relevant history, and far and wide (horizon scanning) at the present environment. This is largely **divergent** thinking.

2. **Anticipation**. Next, we identify and extrapolate (forecast) key trends, consider how they may interact to create more change, and make some probabilistic predictions. We look for constraints and likely outcomes of the past and current state, both obvious and hidden, and we try to estimate risks. This is largely **convergent** thinking.

3. **Innovation (aka, Imagination)**. Next, we try to imagine alternative possibilities that spring from our learning and anticipation. What are some of the first, second and third order implications of the changes we expect? What changes and wildcards are we missing? What experiments might we or others do, to either gather more foresight, create, or adapt? This is largely a return to **divergent** thinking.

4. **Strategy**. Finally, we arrive at the fourth foresight practice, the only one covered well in typical management and policy texts. With strategy, we analyze all the above data and try to come up with the most resilient and high value set of actions we can, based on our resources and goals. We stress test those strategies those against both the **future** we expect and the **futures** we can imagine, and come up with both tactical and strategic **plans**, for reaching our goals, avoiding traps, and monitoring progress. This again is ultimately **convergent** thinking.

Each of us is more attracted to some of these skills than others. Each skill is also more commonly associated with certain professional roles in our organizations and society. For example:

1. **Learning** is commonly practiced by **researchers, historians, intelligence gatherers, educators, quantifiers**, and **accountants**.

2. **Anticipation** is common in **convergence- and consistency-oriented** activities like **forecasting, engineering, security, sustainability, and theoretical science**.

3. **Innovation** is common in **exploration-oriented and diversity-oriented** activities like **design, art, entertainment, entrepreneurship, R&D,** and **experimental science**.

4. **Strategy** is common in bridging and decision-making activities like **visioning, strategy, planning, management, politics, facilitation, and leadership**.

A good foresight professional is **aware of all these roles, specializations, and communities**, and seeks to **engage** with each as appropriate. Let's say amore now about **Learning**, one skill that is **commonly shortchanged** in foresight practice. **Cognitive science** tells us that before we engage in foresight, we begin with some form of **learning**. We need knowledge of the **relevant Past** of a particular problem, including identifying relevant trends, cycles, and models that have operated in the past, and we need intelligence, environmental scanning, and data collection in the **Present** to understand where we are today, and the current values of those relevant trends, cycles, and causal factors, as we understand them.

Some people on a team will be naturally **more interested** and **better** than others at **learning from the Past** (historical research, data collection, trends, forecasts, models). A good learner of past history may care a lot about **data pedigrees**, referencing the source and quality of their data, and the assumptions behind it. They will also weigh the **tradeoffs** between using existing data and getting better data for their trends, forecasts, and models. Others are naturally better at **learning from the Present** (intelligence gathering, events monitoring, horizon scanning). They care a lot about **scanning** for, **sourcing** and **interpreting** data. If we don't have both priorities in our learning process, the quality of our work will suffer. Ideally, our learners will enjoy doing both, but if they don't, we need to do these as separate processes.

A well-known rule of forecasting is that we must **first look back at least twice as far as we wish to look forward**, to see the **relevant trends, cycles, causal factors, and most evidence-based models** applicable to any complex system. We must also adopt a **curious, critical, and evidence-based attitude** during our learning activities. We should also seek **critical input** from **diverse thinkers**, and from **SMEs (subject matter experts)** with **deep experience in the problem area**. Foresight practitioners who skimp on learning can jump into a problem with old and inferior models and outdated information, and they may ignore expert advice. Fortunately, what we neglect at first can often be remedied if we run our **Do Loops** fast and well. With experience-diverse **feedback** in the **Review** skill, we can correct many early errors.

Not sufficiently addressing any of the LAIS skills can be called the **Four Cardinal Errors (or "Sins") of Foresight Work**. The top mistakes we must avoid in strategic foresight work are:

1. Not sufficiently **uncovering** the relevant Past and Present **(Learning)**

2. Not sufficiently **discovering Probable** Futures **(Anticipation)**

3. Not sufficiently **exploring Possible** Futures **(Innovation)**

4. Not sufficiently **envisioning Preferable and Preventable** Futures **(Strategy)**

In addition, the **order** of LAIS practice seems to **matter often**, particularly at the **beginning** of foresight work. Just as sentiment contrasting has an empirically-discovered ideal order, so we believe does predictive contrasting, and learning prior to prediction. We can call **LAIS (or if you prefer, REOPS)** the **Initial Order of Operations in Strategic Foresight** practice. These are **sequences**, best used early and deliberately in foresight production. The graphic below illustrates the typical order, with Learning as the "base" of the Foresight Pyramid.

To summarize, in the **LAIS (aka the REOPS) model**, good strategic foresight work initially:

- Starts with **Learning (Research)** both **relevant history** and **current status**,

- Then it **Anticipates (Expectations) probable foresight** (relevant trends and constraints)

- Then it **Innovates (Options)** (explores, imagines, and prototypes) relevant **possible foresight**.

- Then it produces **Strategy,** involving both **Priorities** and **Setbacks** that might plausibly block those priorities.

- Strategies are then tested by **action** and **feedback**, via four **Action Skills**.

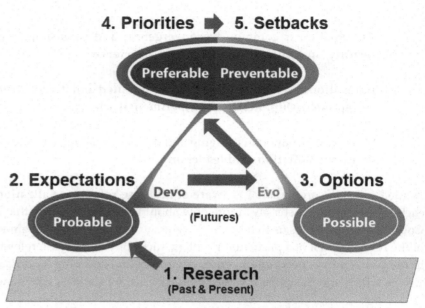

REOPS: The Five Steps of Foresight Work

In practice, we will jump back and forth across the LAIS skills (the REOPS cycle) as context demands. Yet this order of operations is often the most effective way to start our work. Because it is based on the **Do Loop**, our universal perception-decision-action-feedback cycle, this order will reliably deliver and improve results. The **more cycles we turn** on this loop, the better we get at producing, applying, and evaluating good work. Let's dig further into each of these LAIS skills now.

1. Flaring into the Past and Present (Learning)

Learning is, for the most part, mentally **divergent**. To use the evocative language of the Stanford design school (d.School), as we learn we are **"flaring"** into a variety of potentially relevant histories and current status accounts (intelligence reports), seeking useful data and trends. This learning **prepares us** to do good **anticipation**, to attempt to see and describe relevant aspects of the probable future. A good scan of the past will tell us the relevant trends, cycles, causal factors, and models that may influence or control the futures we care about. A good **scan** of the present will tell us the **current state** of those trends, cycles, and factors, and surface **emerging issues** we may need to take into account.

It is easy to **skip or skimp** on the **Learning** step. In our **personal** and **team foresight**, we often do this when we have a **bias for action**, especially, easy, pleasurable, **unprioritized** action (aka, **procrastination**). Unless we take the time to learn some of the history of the issue, the tools now available, and how experts currently do things, we will often waste precious time in **low-value foresight and action**, or **reinvent the wheel**, when it was waiting there for us to **use all along.**

Many **organizations** also skimp on learning, particularly when strategy teams feel **pressed for time**. If a strategy team does not create time for **research and intelligence**, and task specific people with **learning**, they won't find **good solutions** for their problems which **already exist today**, or existed in the **past**. Workers need to be trained in problem research, benchmarking, and best practice documentation. Even something as simple as an **organizational wiki**, if people are incentivized to maintain it, goes a long way to improving **organizational memory** of good strategies and practice.

We cannot express the number of **poor foresight studies** we've read that are **not credible**, simply because the authors **didn't take enough time to learn** about how the world actually works—and its past and current status—in the areas relevant to their problem domain. Unfortunately, many **foresight graduate programs** today don't require sufficient learning of relevant **history**, or intelligence gathering of **current events**, prior to foresight discussion and content production. As a result, their student and alumni work remains rudimentary by comparison to its potential.

2. Focusing on the Probable (Anticipation)

Anticipation, the first core (pyramid) foresight skill, is a **convergent** mental process. In d.School language, it is mental **"focusing,"** not flaring. The process of **Anticipation**, of trend collection, model exploration, forecasting, risk assessment, and probabilistic **prediction**, helps us to bound the landscape of possibilities. The more thinking we and our teams do about relevant high-probability trends, the more islands we can see in the sea of uncertainty. Those **anticipated, expected**, and **bettable** trends and outcomes will helpfully **constrain, guide**, and **empower** all our other foresight activities.

Fortunately, as data has grown rapidly since the advent of the internet, and as computer hardware, software, networks, and machine learning have grown exponentially cheaper, we have seen the rise of new forms of **machine, expert, and crowd anticipation**. We have new communities like <u>Kaggle</u> (acquired by Google in 2017), that do data science and machine learning competitions, and new crowd prediction markets, like <u>Metaculus</u>, that make it a collective game to improve anticipation. **Predictive analytics** are being usefully applied in all six domains. In fact, the **misuse** of these powerful tools in online platforms has created a number of new problems for our societies, as we'll see in Book 2.

As with learning, many practitioners will skimp on the anticipation step. Some of us like to jump right into the "**fun**" of imagining possibilities, telling stories, or making prototypes, without doing **grunt work** of discovering key trends, forces, convergences, and constraints that limit future possibilities. Such an approach gives us **no framework, map, or compass** for the probable future landscape. We can quickly get **lost in a wilderness** of low probability thinking and imagining.

If our organization doesn't collect, purchase, or create their own trends, forecasts, and convergences, and if we don't give time for anticipation—or better yet, task a person or team to do that work—we won't be able to **direct our innovation** in order to take advantage of the parts of the future that we **can roughly predict**. Just like planning too far ahead, without learning and anticipation our team will come up with **innovations and strategies for a future that may never arrive**.

Just like each of the other LAIS foresight skills, it is easy to do either **too little or too much** anticipation, and over-rely or under-rely on trends, expectations, historical bets, and models. Like much in life, we must find an **optimal balance**, and a balance learned with experience, experiment, self-honesty, humility, and transparency.

3. Reflaring into the Possible (Imagination and Innovation)

Once we've mentally prepared with learning and anticipation, we are well-equipped to **flare again**, to **imagine, explore**, and **create**, a wide variety of relevant **possible** options. We call this foresight skill **innovation** rather than imagination, because it is easy for human minds to imagine **implausible and irrelevant** possibilities. **Imagination**, which we use in **brainstorming, storytelling, what-ifing,** and *early* in **design thinking**, is where possibility thinking **starts**, but it is not where it should **end**.

An **innovation**, by contrast, is an idea, product, or service that is both **new** (an **imagination**, an **invention**) and that has **found a market, some group that *attests to its value***. Likewise, the best possible futures are not only imaginations (inventions), but innovations. An innovation, in this context, is **any future idea** that seems **relevant** to some **group of stakeholders**, after **surviving a plausibility critique**. It might be a **threat** we weren't previously thinking about, a **goal** we didn't realize we might achieve, or a potential **new policy, product, or service**. If some **group** (technically, three or more people) still likes it after critique, it is not just imagination, but something with greater value, innovation.

It is important not to be too critical of possibility thinking in its early, divergent stages. But, unless such thinking is eventually **critiqued** for plausibility and relevance, its value will be limited. Early on, we may brainstorm all we want, but only a small subset of this work will find an **audience**. The rest is often so **fanciful** that it would undermine the imaginer's credibility if it were printed and distributed publicly. Only the most relevant and plausible possibilities deserve to be communicated to the **strategy team**. This includes **wildcards**, low probability but high impact events, positive or negative, that we can adapt to better if we prepare **contingency plans** ahead of the possibility.

Many foresight graduate programs attract students who **enjoy and are very good at** both imagination and innovation. Some practitioners mistakenly consider it the **primary activity** of our field. In reality, this skill must be kept in balance with the other foresight skills. The easiest way to keep that balance is to remember our **LAIS order of operations**, and to run **Do Loops** with critical feedback on all possibility thinking, until a few really valuable innovations emerge.

4. Refocusing on the Preferred and Preventable (Goals, Visions, Priorities and Plans)

Ideally, prior to engaging in strategy, we will have **surveyed** the **political** landscape of **preferable** futures and **strategies** relevant to the future of an issue (**learning**), developed a model of probable futures, given our and others current expectations, investments, and strategies (**anticipation**), and imagined (**innovated**) plausible and relevant possibilities, good and bad, that might improve, alter, or disrupt us. Now we are ready for **strategy**, creating new **visions**, **guiding policy** and coordinated **action plans** to achieve positive results and avoid traps. Then we **act**, and if we are fortunate, we become more adaptive. Strategy returns us to "**focus**". We must **prioritize** our visions, policy, and action plans.

In the short-run, we do these things via the **Eight Skills**, but in the long-term successful **leadership** and **activism** also requires good values and ethics. Not only **competence**, but also **character** and **authority**. In the long-term, **adaptive foresight** becomes **normative**. As we gain wisdom, we learn see how we can **create value daily** for ourselves and others, and we try measure, however imperfectly, both **personal success** and **social progress**. We also learn to continually critique our visions and strategies in a critical and diverse community, using a Do loop framework like the REOPS cycle. We must make our foresight, as **transparent, accessible and understood** by stakeholders as possible, to get the best futures available. We will discuss these open, collective, and digital trends in our last chapter, The Future of Foresight.

As the philosopher **Seneca** said, "To **wish** to progress is the largest part of progress." Perhaps the most important mindset in foresight, is to develop enough passion, judgment, and perseverance to believe that we can be **of service to others** with our **quality of vision**, to believe that individually, we can **create value daily**, and to believe that collectively, we can **all improve the world**. These are each vitally important beliefs.

The Eight Skills of Adaptive Foresight (The LAISEIRR Skills)

The **Eight Skills** are the main organizational foresight practice model we use at 4U. It is a synthesis of the **perception-decision-action-feedback cycle** of cognitive science, the **foresight pyramid**, and the **three action skills** of Gallup, the management consultancy. It originated in discussions between **Joshua Davis** and **John Smart** in 2014. It has benefited from periodic feedback from foresight and industry experts.

For individuals, we believe that the **Four Steps of the Do loop, Learning, Foresight, Action, and Review**, are often sufficient complexity for many daily activities. Personally, we don't often don't need to think about kinds of foresight, or kinds of action we engage in. It is often sufficient to remember to **learn** a few things, **look ahead** a bit, **act**, and then **check** our results. But once we are operating in **relation to others**, on teams and in organizations, we benefit greatly when we **decompose** the two middle steps of the Do loop, **foresight** and **action**, into **three core skills** each. Doing so gives us **Eight Skills**, any one of which can help us in our loops, and any one of which can be underused, misused or overused.

The better we and our teams can **see and cycle through** these skills, the more effective and adaptive we can become. We've said that we can remember the **Eight Skills** as "**LAISEIRR**," a misspelling of "**laser**". We can also remember them with the phrase "**A LAISEIRR focus can bring success**". We may rarely cycle through them in strict **LAISEIRR order** but the more we see, talk about, and improve each, the better we can **apply each**, when the context demands.

The graphic below summarizes the Do loop, the Four Steps, and the Eight Skills, and some of the authors who have done work exploring the value of each, for individuals, teams, and organizations.

The Eight Skills of Adaptive Foresight

Below is a depiction of the **dominant** (but not exclusive) **thinking styles** used in each. The Eight Skills employ, by turns, **divergent**, **convergent**, **redivergent**, **reconvergent**, **translational**, **radiative**, **integrative**, and **cyclical** thinking.

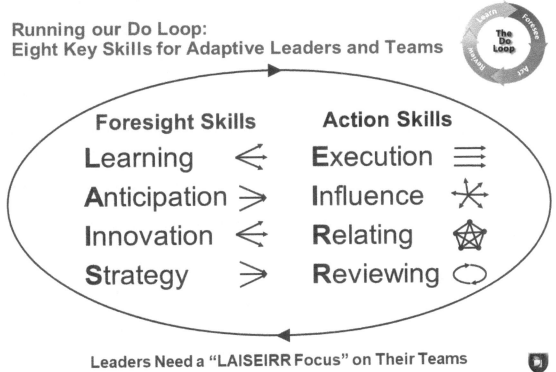

Few of us **naturally** excel at **all eight** of these skills. Fortunately, once we recognize their **critical value**, we can strive to become **reasonably competent** with each of them. Continually assessing our abilities in all eight of these skills, and **remedying** any deficiencies, is a key first step in building **adaptive foresight**. Of course, it is even easier for our **teams** to become competent at all of them. **Skills-based recruitment and teaming** is a great strategy to rapidly improve group adaptiveness. In our view, these eight are the **key skills to assess** in **organizational recruitment**. In addition to skills assessment, **normative foresight**—recognizing that the **values and character of ourselves and our teams matter more** than anything else over the long term, is another assessment priority, to be discussed shortly.

One challenge in our field is to help foresight practitioners realize that Skills 5, 6, and 7, the traditional **Product**, **Market**, and **Team** functions in an organization, are our responsibilities as well. Every foresight professional, whether we work with others or are a sole practitioner, must **Execute** good work (our Product or Service), must have **Influence** on our clients (Market), and must **Relate** to, motivate and treat ourselves and our colleagues well (Team). We must also continually **Review** our work. Both we and our clients need strong expertise in the **Four Action Skills** for our work to be effective and adaptive. Too many foresighters skimp on developing these last four skills, and their impact suffers.

The Three Gears of Enterprise: Product, Market, and Team

Do you value each of the Eight Skills? Are you weaker in some, and stronger in others? None can be neglected for long, in our view. We will explore examples (proof points) of the **first four** of these skills in Chapter 3, and **all eight** in Chapter 4.

Twenty Specialties of Organizational Foresight

Based on our analysis of the management and foresight literature, we propose that **Twenty Foresight Specialties** (actually, twenty *specialty pairs* that group well together) are particularly important in helping **organizations** to navigate the future. These are all specialties of **strategic management**.

The world is a complex place, and adaptive foresight in organizations of any size requires a diverse set of specialties. It is a common (and wrong) belief that most organizations "don't try to know the future." In reality, all management teams extrapolate from the past, and often assume too many things won't change. They can improve their foresight process, by reading and using books like this *Guide*, but we must also remember that management itself is just one, top-down component of the organization. All organizations have local pockets of foresight excellence, in various specialties.

As futurist **Kevin Kelly** says in his classic, _Out of Control_, 1994, **95% of organizational foresight occurs bottom-up**, across many people, teams, specialties, and departments. Everyone does foresight, both personally and on teams. The top foresight challenges for **management** include recognizing **all the ways** the firm already does foresight work, mostly bottom-up, and **developing and coordinating that foresight,** and getting it applied in rapid Do loops across the firm.

The **Twenty Foresight Specialties** listed below are **top practices in organizational foresight**. They are **what foresighters do**, in modern organizations, as they look to their **strategic horizons.** These specialties include **both top-down and bottom-up processes**, and are **balanced across the Eight Skills**. Note that **Management and Leadership** (#18) is just one of these. It is the most **global and top-down** specialty in this list. It makes up just 1/20th, or 5%, of the foresight done in a large organization, in this particular categorization. The remaining 95% can be considered **local and bottom-up** (deferential to management). We think these specialties are **diverse enough** to represent organizational foresight practice, in all its complexity and value. We will consider these specialties as components of the **Eight Skills** in Chapter 4.

The **Twenty Foresight Specialties**, in alphabetical order, are:

1. **Accounting & Intangibles**,
2. **Alternatives & Scenarios**,
3. **Analysis & Decision Support**,
4. **Auditing & Change Management**,
5. **Benchmarking & Quality**,
6. **Data Science & Machine Learning**,
7. **Entrepreneurship & Intrapreneurship**,
8. **Facilitation & Gaming**,
9. **Forecasting & Prediction**,
10. **Human Resources & Performance Management**,
11. **Ideation & Design**,
12. **Innovation & Research & Development**,
13. **Intelligence & Knowledge Management**,
14. **Investing & Finance**,
15. **Law & Security**,
16. **Learning & Development**,
17. **Management & Leadership**,
18. **Marketing & Sales**,
19. **Risk Management & Insurance**,
20. **Visioning/Goals/Strategy & Planning**.

Cloudy Horizon, California

Again, these **Twenty Specialties** are our **best current model** of the full scope of foresight work within **strategic management**. We should take a moment to consider how many of these practice specialties we are presently familiar with and how many we already use in our organizations and practice—at least in some basic form. While we could have chosen fewer specialties to address in this *Guide*, doing so would give a **biased and incomplete picture** of how diverse, effective, and necessary organizational foresight practice has become.

Fortunately, all of these specialties now have **formal practice communities**, and we'll introduce some leading ones below. Proficiency in any of these specialties can be critical to solving a foresight problem. If we are missing any of these specialties and they are relevant to our challenges, our plans and actions will suffer as a result. The twenty specialties **end with strategy** to remind us of what good strategy often requires. If we or our teams skip doing any of the **first nineteen** practice specialties listed above, and instead jump into the **twentieth** practice—**visioning, goalsetting, strategy and planning**—we are only doing a very small subset of strategic foresight work. Such a narrow view of how to manage the future will end up hurting us. We need to see and balance all the specialized ways we get to good strategy.

The first two graduate foresight programs in our field were originally called "Futures Studies," at the U. of Houston (M.S., established in 1974) and "Alternative Futures" at the U. of Hawaii (Ph.D., started in 1977). In the forty-plus years since, graduate **Strategic Foresight** programs have slowly expanded globally. There are today twenty-two M.S. or Ph.D. foresight programs, by our count, and a smaller number of foresight certificate programs. Most expose their students, at least briefly, to a **few** of the above specialties, but none yet teach the **basics of all twenty specialties**, to our knowledge. We think that presently limits foresight's ability to **integrate** into the **management and policy** professions.

We at **4U** will do our best to influence the existing academic and executive foresight programs to include essential thinking and methods from all **Twenty Specialties** in their curriculum. We also must teach not only strategic foresight, but a variety of **normative foresight** models. The better our students understand **all the values systems** in use, the better they can work with others, and develop their own. Once an appropriate variety of foresight is widely recognized by organizational leaders, and its adaptive value is well understood, our field will be on a path to its maturity.

In one vision for our field, we can imagine top practitioners of many of these **Twenty Specialties** having **C-level positions** in our more foresighted organizations. But, until something of that nature happens, and until more leaders in many of these organizational specialties recognize their role in **foresight production**, our field will remain underdeveloped. The leadership of top organizations will not recognize the foresight work they already do, as "**foresight by other names**," and the **case for foresight as a leadership priority** cannot be well made within the organization. Making strategic foresight, in all its diversity, a conscious leadership priority is thus among the greatest goals of our field.

None of us will ever be experts in all of these specialties, but each of us can seek out some specialty training in a few of these, to complement our general foresight knowledge. For each specialty we've named one **Foresight Specialty Association** below that is advancing professional practice. We've focused this list on associations primarily oriented to **corporate clients**, though many associations have internal communities and workgroups oriented to government, defense, nonprofits, education, individuals, and other clients as well.

Joining one or more of these **associations** at a time, taking their training, and attending their **conferences** will give us access to specialist foresight methods and knowledge that is typically covered only lightly in our primary foresight associations. This will also allow us to build new friendships and gain new practice opportunities. Of course, reading and publishing in a few of these **journals** will also further the field and could benefit our own professional distinctions. Furthermore, individually **shifting our memberships** among these specialty associations every few years, picking up new **certifications** whenever they may be helpful, is a great way for general foresight practitioners to engage in a specialty-diverse **continuing education**.

In alpha order, here are the **Twenty Specialty Groups of Strategic Foresight**, and a little info on some of the **leading practitioner communities for each specialty group**. Again, becoming competent in the basics of these **Twenty Specialties** is a wise approach to professional development. We will list these communities again in Appendix 3. Hopefully our emerging primary foresight practice organizations and graduate programs will develop closer relationships with these associations in coming years. **Joining at least one of these associations**, and becoming **proficient in their methods**, is the start of your **professional foresight** journey.

1. **Accounting & Intangibles** – Institute of Management Accountants **(IMA)**. Since 1919. The leading association for cost accounting, financial planning, and decision support, top metrics for any for-profit firm. Annual Conference, CMA certification. Strategic Finance; Assessing intangible assets and liabilities is done in specialties like management accounting, marketing, analysis, and strategy. Many intangibles are not easily measured, or even seen. We need surveys, focus groups, and other tools to track and analyze intangible variables, like morale, reputation, and customer satisfaction. The National Customer Service Association **(NCSA)** is a leading practice community for customer satisfaction. For intangibles, see **Douglas Hubbard's** *How to Measure Anything*, 2014.

2. **Alternatives & Scenarios** – Association of Professional Futurists **(APF)**. Since 2002. Presently our leading strategic foresight practitioner community. Good business focus. Regular Gatherings. This community is particularly oriented to both exploring possible futures (alternatives & scenarios) and envisioning preferable futures (facilitation, stakeholder analysis, etc.). They are less focused, at present, on forecasting, prediction markets, and other approaches to probable futures. For that specialty, see Forecasting & Prediction.

3. **Analysis & Decision Support** – Institute for Operations Research and the Mgmt Sciences **(INFORMS)**. Since 1995. Advancing operations research, management sciences, and data analytics. Annual Conference and Business Analytics Conference. Many Chapters. Publish thirteen journals; European Working Group on Decision Support Systems **(EWG-DSS)**. Annual international conference on Decision Support System Technology. Modeling, expert systems, data visualization, GIS, decision making and support.

4. **Auditing & Change Management –** Institute of Internal Auditors **(IIA)**. Since 1941. Certifications and conferences. Auditing is a critical skill that tells leaders if their accounting and metrics are accurate. Many firms neglect it; Association of Change Management Professionals **(ACMP)**. Since 2009. Standardizing and promoting the discipline of change management, which seeks to diagnose problems and turn around firms. Seven Chapters. Annual conference (900 attendees).

5. **Benchmarking & Quality –** Benchmarking, or determining best practices ("quality," at the firm level) by looking at the competitive environment, is a key step in organizational strategy. The Benchmarking Network **(BN)** lists a variety of industry benchmarking associations. A good starter is the Balanced Scorecard Institute **(BSI)**. Since 1997. Balanced scorecards are a well-respected benchmarking tool. Certifications. 5,000 practitioners; American Society for Quality **(ASQ)**. Since 1946. Promoting the practice of performance feedback and continual quality improvement (TQM, Lean Six Sigma, etc.). 80K members. Various certifications and conferences. Eight magazines and journals.

6. **Data Science & Machine Learning –** Open Data Science Community **(OSDC)**. 140K members. One of the largest conferences in data science, Open Data Science (Asia, Europe, and NA). Data science includes predictive analytics (PA), and the rapidly-improving field of machine learning (ML, aka "AI"). OSDC runs an Accelerate AI Summit, for business professionals, and an AI Learning Accelerator community, focused on predictive analytics and machine learning; Kaggle, the world's leading Data Science Problem Competition Platform and Kaggle Learning, which offers certificates in data science; Digital Analytics Association **(DAA)**. 20K members. Produce the eMetrics, Text Analytics, and Digital Analytics Summits. Predictive Analytics World (another group) is the leading cross-industry event for predictive analytics professionals.

7. **Entrepreneurship & Intrapreneurship –** Founder Institute **(FI)**. Since 2009. Teaching founders to do internal or external startups. Also Lean Startup Circles. Since 2009. Communities to implement Eric Ries' Lean Startup; Intrapreneurship is a specialty that facilitates disrupting one's current product and service mix from within, creating ideal environments for self-funded startups and spinouts. It gets harder the larger the firm, and is a specialty that deserves its own professional association. Intrapreneurship deserves its own association. The Intrapreneurship Conference is a step in that direction. See **Owens and Fernandez's** *The Lean Enterprise: How Corporations Can Innovate Like Startups*, 2014, for key intrapreneurship practice tips.

8. **Facilitation & Gaming –** International Association of Facilitators **(IAF)**. Since 1994. Group processes, consensus facilitation, conflict resolution, KM. Offer certified professional facilitator programs and IAF endorsed training programs. Members in 65 countries. IAFNAC is their annual North American conference; North American Simulation and Gaming Assn **(NASAGA)**. Game-based simulation and learning. Physical and digital "serious games," strategy games, wargames, gamestorming. Annual conference.

9. **Forecasting & Prediction –** International Institute of Forecasters **(IIF)**. Since 1981. Advancing forecasting, quantitative and judgmental, as a multidisciplinary field of research and practice. Annual International Symposium on Forecasting, training Workshops. Publishes *Foresight: The Journal of Applied Forecasting* and *International Journal of Forecasting*; Prediction Markets do not yet have a dedicated association. Data Science/PA is the closest community at present. The *Journal of Prediction Markets* is an open access journal covering this emerging field since 2007. See **Tetlock** and **Gardner's** *Superforecasting*, 2015, for emerging practices in collective probabilistic foresight.

10. **Human Resources & Performance Management –** Society for Human Resource Mgmt **(SHRM)**. Since 1948. Promotes HR (people operations, analytics, labor management) as a field, via education, certification, lobbying, and networking. 275K members. *HR Magazine*, others. Annual conference; Performance management is a

specialty of HR and organizational development that focuses on firm, team, and employee performance. The KPI Institute **(KPII)** is a leading practitioner community. They offer certifications in many management practices, including Benchmarking (best practices), Key Performance Indicators (KPIs), a subset of benchmarking focused on firm performance, and Objectives and Key Results (OKRs), which empower employees to set their own performance objectives, in a bottom-up manner, and help each other achieve them.

11. **Ideation & Design** – There is no professional association yet for Ideation Management, a vital process that is a critical precursor to innovation, involving articulating, sizing, and prioritizing customer and firm problems, incentivizing solutions (with prizes, bounties, tournaments, reputation, culture), and refining and prioritizing the best ideas. Fortunately there are now several good Idea Management/ Evaluation Platforms, and some large online technical solver communities like InnoCentive. See Terwiesch and Ulrich's *Innovation Tournaments*, 2009, for good practices. A partly-related community is the American Creativity Association **(ACA)**. Since 1990. Creativity, problem solving, ideation theory, tools, methods. They run an Annual Conference. Non-associated journals: *Creativity Research Journal* and *Journal of Creative Behavior*; *AIGA: The Professional Association for Design* **(AIGA)**. Since 1914. Product, service, and environmental design is another key foresight specialty, focused on creating better futures, typically in a hands on, iterative manner. Annual Design Competitions, Chapters, Student Groups, Professional Dev. Good magazine: *Wallpaper*.

12. **Innovation & Research & Development** – International Society of Professional Innovation Mgmt **(ISPIM)**. Since 1983. R&D leaders, industrialists, institutions, and consultants in innovation mgmt. Runs Regional ISPIM Conferences. Publishes *International Journal of Innovation Management*; *Research and Development Management Association* **(RADMA)**. Publishes the academic and business journal *R&D Management*.

13. **Intelligence & Knowledge Management** – Collective Intelligence Academic Community **(CIAC)**. Annual conference. Digital CI platforms, human computer interaction, crowdsourcing, crowd-solving, crowdfunding, and crowd-founding, group incentives and dynamics; Strategic and Competitive Intelligence Professionals **(SCIP)**. Since 1986. Helps professionals in competitive intelligence (legal and ethical information gathering and analysis). Runs an Annual Conference and Regional Summits. Bi-monthly *CI Magazine*; The Knowledge Management Professional Society **(KMPro)**. The largest knowledge management practice group. It offers certifications and training. KM is another field early in development. Most organizations don't even have good wikis or incentives to capture and refine their deep organizational knowledge.

14. **Investing & Finance** – CFA Institute **(CFAI)**. Since 1946. Global association of 110K investment professionals. Offers Chartered Financial Analyst (CFA) and other certifications. Conferences, webinars, and events. *Financial Analysts Journal*, *CFA Institute Magazine*. Alternative: American Association of Individual Investors **(AAII)**. 150K members. *AAII Journal*, Conference; There are many specialty finance practitioner communities. One for entrepreneurs is the National Venture Capital Association **(NVCA)**. Global events and platforms for entrepreneurs, angel investors, and venture capitalists.

15. **Law & Security** – American Bar Association **(ABA)**. Since 1878. For lawyers & non-lawyers. Improving legal profession, advancing the rule of law. 400K members. Advocacy groups. *ABA Journal*, >100 specialty periodicals, many specialty law conferences; Security Industry Association **(SIA)**. Since 1969. Covers both physical and info security (InfoSec, Cybersecurity). DEF CON is the best known "hacker" convention. There are a plethora of others. Find a security association focused on personal industry and clients, covering both physical and information security, and learn best practices.

16. **Learning & Development** – Association for Talent Development **(ATD)**. Since 1945. Leading professional association for workplace training, learning and development (L&D). Three annual conferences, L&D

<u>certifications</u>, local chapters. *T+D Magazine*. Workplace training is being greatly empowered today by EdTech startups and behavioral science.

17. **Management & Leadership** – <u>American Management Association</u> **(AMA)**. Since 1923. Full-spectrum training in firm, product, service, and project leadership, analysis, comm., IT, marketing, sales, PR, human resources, finance, project mgmt. <u>Books</u>, <u>papers</u>, <u>podcasts</u>, <u>webinars</u>, <u>webcasts</u>, etc.; <u>Project Management Institute</u> **(PMI)**, and <u>PMP Certification</u>. 270 chapters; <u>International Leadership Association</u> **(ILA)**. Since 1999. Advancing leadership practices. <u>ILA Global Conference</u>. Publishes <u>*Journal of Leadership Studies*</u>, <u>*Leadership Excellence*</u>. There are also many specialized leadership development programs, publications, and communities for almost every industry, and for most of the specialties listed above.

18. **Marketing & Sales** – <u>American Marketing Association</u> **(AMA)**. Since 1937. Advancing the practice and scholarship of marketing, including advertising, customer modeling and metrics. 30K members. <u>Certification</u> & training. <u>Marketing News</u>, seven journals. Many <u>conferences</u>; <u>National Association of Sales Professionals</u> **(NASP)**. Since 1991. <u>Certification</u> and training in effective sales trends, strategies, and customer acquisition techniques. For some texts for foresight professionals, see Hanan's <u>Consultative Selling, 8th Ed</u>, 2011, and Rackham's classic <u>SPIN Selling</u>, 1988.

19. **Risk Management & Insurance** – <u>Risk Management Society</u> **(RIMS)**. Since 2000. Global leader in risk mgmt. practices (insurance, finance, accounting, legal, IT, HR, etc.). Annual <u>RIMS Conference</u> and <u>Enterprise Risk Mgmt. Conf</u>. Global <u>Chapters</u>. *Risk Management*. There are many specialty insurance practitioner communities. <u>American Insurance Association</u> **(AIA)** is the leading trade association for big insurance providers. Since 1866. <u>NAIFA</u> represents insurance and financial advisors.

20. **Vision/Goals/Strategy & Planning** – <u>Association for Strategic Planning</u> **(ASP)**. Since 1999. Advancing visioning, goalsetting, strategy and planning development and deployment for business, nonprofits, and govt. <u>Annual Conference</u>, certificate programs. Sixteen <u>Chapters</u>. Strategic planning resources; <u>American Planning Association</u> **(APA)**. Since 1978. Advancing the art and science of urban and regional planning. Runs <u>American Institute of Certified Planners</u>. Publishes *Planning* magazine, <u>*Journal of the American Planning Association*</u>.

There are also **specialty industry organizations** that offer foresight knowledge and training that may be helpful for our clients. The <u>Institute of Management Consultants</u>, <u>Investment Management Consultants Association</u>, <u>National Speakers Association</u>, <u>National Venture Capital Association</u>, and the <u>Police Futurists International</u> are a few examples. See Appendix 2 for research tips on finding <u>industry foresight organizations</u> useful to your particular organization.

Some foresight practitioners, including academics, consider **specialty practices** like Learning & Development, Intelligence, Ideation, Innovation, Entrepreneurship, Design, Risk Management, Strategy, Planning, Benchmarking, Quality, and Change Management to be "outside the boundaries" of our profession. Again, that seems a major oversight to us, as these are all critical ways that organizations adapt the future. Ignoring them just puts us out of touch with the **real foresight functions** being used today, and less able to help our clients. Our field's historical narrowness of vision regarding the scope of foresight is understandable, given its youth and its current lack of strong theoretical grounding. But, the danger of such parochial perspectives is that they relegate foresight to an ineffectual corner of organizational practice, rather than recognizing it for the **universal set of processes** that it is.

Note that a few of the **Twenty Specialties**, particularly **Management and Leadership**, are also **meta-specialties, like foresight**. Good **management** requires short-term foresight, and many other skills, found in any text on <u>strategic management</u>. Effective **leadership** requires both medium-term and longer-term foresight, good values, and additional skills and personal qualities on top of management strengths.

Again, unlike the **Eight Skills**, which we all will depend on frequently in our careers, we don't need to be **competent** in all or even most of these specialties to be a great foresight professional. But, we should have a **basic knowledge** of all of them, and should be able to recognize when a specialist can help us solve a problem, and partner with or delegate to them. The better our teams are at navigating these specialties, the better we'll get at leading foresight in our organizations.

The Do Loop in Three Levels of Detail – Steps, Skills, and Specialties

We can now combine the **Four Steps**, **Eight Skills**, and **Twenty Specialties** to look at the **Do loop**, from an **organizational foresight perspective,** in three levels of detail. This is a quick way to summarize how organizations perform Do loop responsibilities, each team cycling at different speeds based on the task, using a wide range of **specialties** in strategic management. We've listed the twenty specialties in ***bold italics*** below:

I. LEARNING
1. **Learning – Investigative** thinking
    Accounting & Intangibles, Intelligence & Knowledge Management,
    Learning & Development

II. FORESIGHT
2. **Anticipation – Probability** thinking
    Data Science & Machine Learning, Forecasting & Prediction,
    Investing and Finance, Law & Security, Risk Management & Insurance

3. **Innovation – Possibility** thinking
    Alternatives & Scenarios, Entrepreneurship & Intrapreneurship,
    Facilitation & Gaming, Ideation & Design, Innovation & R&D)

4. **Strategy – Preference & Prevention** thinking
    Analysis & Decision Support, Strategy & Planning

III. ACTION
5. **Execution – Production** thinking
    Product/Service/Project Management & Leadership

6. **Influence – Market** thinking
    Sales & Marketing Management

7. **Relating – Team** thinking
    Human Resources & Performance Management

IV. REVIEWING
8. **Reviewing – Adjustment** thinking
    Auditing & Change Management, Benchmarking & Quality

The Do Loop of Adaptive Foresight
An Organizational Specialty Model

LEARN **FORESEE** **ACT** **REVIEW**

1. Learning – "Knowing Your History and Status" (Investigative thinking)
- Accounting & Intangibles
- Intelligence & Knowl. Mgmt
- Learning & Dev. (Training)

2. Anticipation – "Probability Foresight" (Convergent thinking)
- Data Science & Machine Learning
- Forecasting & Prediction
- Investing & Finance
- Law & Security
- Risk Management & Insurance

3. Innovation – "Possiblity Foresight" (Divergent thinking)
- Alternatives & Scenarios
- Entrepreneurship & Intrapreneurship
- Facilitation & Simulations
- Ideation & Design
- Innovation & R&D

4. Strategy – "Preferable and Preventable Futures" (Adaptive thinking)
- Analysis & Decision Support
- Strategy & Planning

5. Execution – "Getting Somewhere" (Production thinking)
- Management & Leadership

6. Influence – "Recruiting Others" (Market thinking)
- Marketing & Sales

7. Relating – "Keeping Others On Your Team" (Team thinking)
- HR & Performance Management

8. Reviewing – "Staying On Target" (Adjustment thinking)
- Auditing & Change Management
- Benchmarking & Quality

Twenty Specialties
Eight Skills
Four Steps

 Learn. Foresee. Act. Review.

From: *Introduction to Foresight: Anticipating, Creating, and Leading the Future*, 2021. by John Smart, with the Foresight U and FERN Communities. Free online at ForesightGuide.com.

Foresight Education and Research Network

The graphic above is **4U's "One Sheet"** outlining three levels of detail, **Steps**, **Skills**, and **Specialties**, in which **Adaptive Strategic Foresight** is practiced in organizations. **Individuals** need the steps, **teams** need the skills, and **organizations** need the specialties. This model neglects **values**, which are a separate topic.

The simplicity of the **Four Steps** makes them excellent for personal life management, and for introductory work with teams and organizations. The additional detail in the **Eight Skills** model is helpful for foresight and action on teams. The practice detail in the **Twenty Specialties** is useful for leaders and managers influencing an organization's entire foresight process, and for coordinating foresight work within and across departments. In practice, good managers may be content using the **Four Steps** constantly, the **Eight Skills** frequently, and understanding and delegating into all the **specialties**, and becoming proficient in a few of them over their careers. Let's look at one of these right now, to appreciate its value.

Specialty Focus: Financial and Investing Foresight

We won't delve into most of the **Twenty Specialties** of foresight in this edition of the *Guide*. Several of the books in Appendix 3 can help with that. Nevertheless, we'd like to briefly discuss one of them now: **Investing & Finance**, with a focus on **personal investing and saving**. Investing for wealth building is a key aspect of **Personal Foresight**, which we cover in a full chapter in the Student Edition of this book. Much of what we say also applies to organizational investing and cash flow management. Practicing medium-term and long-term personal investing will not only considerably strengthen our **anticipation**, it will improve our ability to affect positive change with our families, our favorite organizations, and the world—and ideally, even achieve <u>financial independence</u> during our careers. **Teaching our children** to invest is another classic way we can help them to develop **Four Ps foresight skills.**

The **anticipation** skill is underdeveloped in many current foresight practitioners, as we will discuss. Most people believe the myth that the small investor can't beat the market, over the long term, by making better choices than the market average in their investments. As we will discuss, passive investing communities like the Motley Fool have demonstrated that this is not true. Their **stock advisor picks** have earned returns of **greater than 15% per year over the last twenty five years,** well above the market average, simply by picking better run companies with greater growth potential than the average. To invest well in any industry, we must continually improve our **organizational and societal** anticipation skills. We learn to better assess **good management**, **strong teams**, and **value creation**. We can also build **discipline** with **personal finances**, tracking our **spending** and learning how to **save** so that we can **invest.**

A good starter book on **saving** is **Andrew Tobias's** *The Only Investment Guide You Will Ever Need*, 1978/2016. It explores the discipline of **saving**, and knowing the **future value of money**. **Robin** and **Dominguez's** *Your Money or Your Life*, 1992/2018, is also helpful for those who don't save enough, or those who save too much, and live too little. If we find ourselves **emotionally blocked** from saving, **Morgan Housel's** *The Psychology of Money*, 2020 is a good introduction to **our beliefs and habits around money**, and how easily they can help or hurt us. The <u>article</u> that birthed Housel's book begins with an engaging **life story of two investors** and their very different approaches to saving and investing. Our favorite starter book on **investing** is **Tom and David Gardner's** *The Motley Fool Investment Guide, 3rd Ed*, 2017. It explains how to invest passively, using little of our precious time, in a process that will secure **financial independence**, over thirty or more years, for *anyone* who saves just **$100 a week** ($5000 a year). This goal is entirely achievable for most Americans. They simply must **prioritize it**, and understand investing's value. Professional futurist and investment advisor **James Lee's** *Foresight Investing*, 2021, offers excellent tips on **financial foresight** and **growth industry** investing.

How hard is it to get **market-beating returns** over the years? Remember, as investing legends like **Warren Buffet** and **Charlie Munger** have long said, that the **efficient market hypothesis is a myth**. Even systems as **chaotic** as the **weather** and **investment markets** always exhibit several **regularly predictable patterns**. **Lo** and **MacKinlay's** *A Non-Random Walk Down Wall Street*, 2001, makes a good case for the market's **continual partial predictability**, like any complex system. Market movement is often random on average, to a first approximation but many **technological**, **economic** and **governance** changes are also partly predictable, and **human nature** itself is partly predictable. Looking at **big picture trends**, using **contrarian investing strategies**, and well-timed use of **market cycles**, we can regularly find and profit from predictable patterns in markets and other economic, social, political, and technological systems driven partly by human psychology.

Lo & McKinlay, 2001

Perhaps the greatest investment vehicle presently available to each of us in the US is the tax-free **Roth IRA** (Individual Retirement Account). We can **open Custodial Roth IRA for our children as early as age 8, when they earn allowance.** They convert to traditional Roth IRAs at the age of 18. Schwab and Fidelity both offer Custodial IRAs. We are each allowed to **save up to $6,000 a year** in our Roth IRAs ($7,000 when we are over 50). These savings go into the fund after taxes. Our Roth IRA thus **grows tax-free**. There are no taxes or penalties on early withdrawals of past contributions, only earnings. There is a 10% penalty and taxation on early withdrawal of most earnings, but *no penalties* on early withdrawal for first time home purchase, college tuition, and birth or adoption expenses. When we reach **59.5 years of age**, the money is fully ours, to leave in or take out as we wish. The Roth IRA is such a **great deal** for the average investor it is **amazing** that more of us don't maximize this opportunity for having our **investment earnings** rapidly outpace our **salaries**, and gaining **permanent financial independence.**

Let's look at some numbers. Investing **$100 a week ($5,000 a year)** in your Roth IRA, from the **age of 15 to 65** (50 years of investing) **compounding annually at 9% a year** (just a bit better than our last decade's market average return) **will give you $4.8M to spend on whatever you wish in the "wisdom phase" of your life.** That sounds great, but now consider what happens if you become a **serious passive investor**, following guidance like Motley Fool, and get a **12% a year average return**. What **retirement IRA asset value** would you predict for yourself and your family?

Amazingly, you will retire with $15M. If you achieve 15% a year, you will retire with **$47M**. Starting at **age 8** will increase your children's returns far above even these impressive numbers. This is the magic of **exponential compounding**. All of these returns would be *30-50% less* if we had saved in a **standard taxable account**. Try Nerdwallet's Roth IRA Calculator (picture right, with 15% a year compounded growth) to explore different Roth saving and interest futures.

Roth IRA Calculator

John often uses this example in his workshops on **exponential thinking**. In this example of **decent exponential growth**, annual returns appear to do **nothing** for the first twenty years, and then **"blow up"** in the next twenty (see curve at right). As **linear** thinkers, we *overpredict* **early performance with exponential processes, and** *greatly underpredict* **later performance**. If you are **willing to pick individual stocks**, we recommend investing your $6-7K of allowed annual Roth investments in just **one or two new stocks every year**, the ones you expect to be the **greatest gainers** over at least a decade. Let's discuss one such example stock pick now.

Air Taxis: A Potential Long-Term Investment in the Future of Cities

If you'd invested in Tesla at its IPO price of $17 in 2010, it was up **41X** by 2021, eleven years later. In 2010, few investors and car companies realized that almost all commercial transport will go electric before 2050. Now, **everyone** sees it. Electric air taxies are in a similar position today. John thinks the **air taxi market** will grow more valuable than Tesla and Uber combined, given electric air transport's many advantages over ground (**5x increased average speed**, **sustainability**, **quietness**, high **safety**), and its projected **very low costs at scale ($3/passenger mile)**. We live in amazing times.

John, who is *not* **a registered investment advisor**, invested all of his allowed $7,000 Roth contribution in 2021 in a single stock, an R&D phase **air taxi company,** Joby Aviation (NYSE: JOBY). He plans to do the same in 2022. He expects Joby will be a leader in a valuable new global transportation sector over the **next two decades. If this stock rises 50X over the next twenty years (a CAGR of 21.6% a year), this two-year investment will return $700,000** for John's retirement, or for his children. It is just one example of the **diverse exponential investment bets** we can make today, picking **new ones** every year or two, just like any venture capitalist, and **holding them for the long term**, regardless of **short-term volatility**.

At present, few investors realize the **multi-trillion dollar size** of this emerging market. Few recognize how many **companies, capital** and **talent** have entered this sector, or how safe, autonomous, fast, inexpensive, green, and valuable air taxis will be for cities. There will inevitably be a few highly publicized accidents, but they won't be stopped. In our view, **air taxi networks** are part of that **inevitable 5%** of societal changes that are **developmental**, not evolutionary. They will help **solve urban gridlock** (self-driving cars can't do that), **vastly accelerate travel** within and between cities, and give **urban residents easy access to nature**. If Joby doesn't win top share of the commercial **air taxi market**, it may win other multibillion dollar drone markets, like **military transport, air ambulance, firefighting, cropdusting**, and others.

Ironically, **Elon Musk**, founder of Tesla and SpaceX, has a bias against air taxis. No futurist has perfect foresight. Musk chose to invest instead in The Boring Company (still private, but IPO planned), an important but far slower developing and lower capacity solution for city mobility, **building tunnels underground**. In our view, solutions like the <u>Hyperloop</u> will remain tech demonstrators, and futurist oddities, like <u>monorails</u>. They are poor competition to <u>high speed rail</u>, a mature technology that has been highly automated by China and can scale to thousands of passengers per train. We expect **underground US high speed rail** only in the **second half of the 21ˢᵗ century**, once autonomous excavators and trucks emerge. **Commercial air taxis** will scale **soon**, and **exponentially**. They are the mobility solution that cities need most for the next fifty years. John's article, <u>Our Amazing Aerial Future</u>, 2018, is a good place to learn more. Of course, don't invest based on solely what you hear from any single source, including this *Guide*. **Do your own due diligence**.

As we gain wisdom in life, we can focus our saving and investing not just on **making returns**, but on **creating future value** (experiences, impact, ability). We seek **long-term purposes** for our capital, purposes deeply tied to our **values**. The field of **Impact Investing**, an outgrowth of the 20th century's <u>socially responsible investing</u>, recognizes that the deepest purpose of wealth management is **global value creation**. We'll say more about that topic in *BPF*. For now, we recommend books like **Ronald Cohen's** *Impact*, 2020, **Rodin and Brandenburg's** *The Power of Impact Investing*, 2014 and **Pamela Ryan's** *Impact Imperative*, 2019. Impact investors recognize that investments are not only a way **to build wealth**, but to **express our values**, and promote **innovation**, **good management,** and **global good**.

Chinese citizens save well, retaining **over 40% of their income**. Their big challenge is using those savings to create value, in a nation that restricts their economic and social freedoms. For decades, they left savings in banks, or focused only on second homes (real estate), rather than finding **well-run companies solving important problems**. **Americans** save **just 8% of their income** on average. We invest far too little, and many of us **retire poor**. But we have much greater **freedoms** to start companies and to invest in great companies, freedoms we often ignore. Yet we can easily change that, at any time.

From a risk perspective, there are **two types** of investing, <u>Conservative/ Value/ Long-term</u> and <u>Speculative/ Mid- and Short-term</u> (four years or less). One commonly recommended mix is **80% conservative** and **20% speculative** investing. Once we have enough savings and personal insurance to cover catastrophes, it is valuable be **engaged in both**, as **each will teach us different things.** If we do only one type of investing, we miss out on the foresight lessons we can gain.

For **conservative investing**, we want to decide on a good **passive investment strategy** (an approach that takes little time and energy to manage). One intro book here, to complement the Motley Fool, is **Rowland** and **Lawson's** *The Permanent Portfolio*, 2012, a strategy developed by the late investment analyst <u>Harry Browne</u>. The Permanent Portfolio's **four classic asset classes** are <u>Index Stocks</u>, <u>Long-Term Treasury Bonds</u>, <u>Gold</u>, and <u>Cash</u>. Brown recommended placing a **quarter** of one's conservative long-term investments in each of these four asset classes, and **rebalancing** them back to 25% per asset class annually, based on their performance.

Rowland & Lawson, 2012

Historically, a simple **asset-class diversified** approach like the **permanent portfolio,** with a good diversified exposure to index funds and companies in both **developed and emerging markets**, has been a good way to **capture our share** of humanity's accelerating <u>technical productivity</u> without being an active investor, and without the volatility of investing only in stocks. Another way to diversify is to use a **professional investment platform**, and let them make investment decisions. Platforms like <u>Wealthfront</u>, popular with Silicon Valley data geeks, have **modest fees**, which decrease depending on one's level of investment, and a good **track record**. Now, we could stay a passive strategy like the permanent portfolio or Wealthfront, but we learn the most about ourselves and the world by also engaging in active (speculative) investing, and using some minority fraction of our investing funds. If we can find time, we should learn about **active strategies and opportunities** by reading respected **investment newsletters**—like those of <u>Motley Fool</u> and <u>Seeking Alpha</u>—and participating in an **investing learning organization**—like the <u>CFA Institute</u> or the <u>American Association of Individual Investors</u>.

One way to potentially improve the Permanent Portfolio strategy would be to substitute potentially better versions of the above asset classes. For example, we could swap Technology Stocks for Index Stocks, our Favorite Country or Company's Bonds for Treasury Bonds, Commodities or Bitcoin for Gold, and the currencies of more fiscally conservative countries like Switzerland, Norway, or Singapore for US Dollars. Such changes would make our investments less diverse and more risky. To counter that, we can also **add new asset classes**, such as Real Estate, through REITS or some other passive vehicle. Yet certain asset classes also seem to have **intrinsic advantages** in a world of **accelerating change**.

In *BPF*, as the topic of **D&D investing**, we will explore the idea that **digital technology equities**, and **stocks of companies that leverage such technologies**, may continue to outperform all other asset classes until **the great majority of the world** is using these rapidly diffusing new platforms, decades from now. We'll describe two potentially universal megatrends, **densification** and **dematerialization ("D&D")**, which are at the center of accelerating technical productivity. Air taxi networks, self-driving cars, and subsidized and diversely constructed high-density housing, like we see in Singapore today, are all industries that will greatly **densify** our leading cities. As we'll see each of these industries will also be significantly more **dematerialized** (software- and simulation-based and autonomous) in coming years. The better we see D&D advances in leading societal systems, the better we understand accelerating change.

On top of exponential technical productivity, there are also many irregular cycles, including **waves of hype and gloom, and cheap or expensive capital**. America is now in an **equities boom since 2010.** It may now be in a **bubble**, with at least a near-term peak. But if a "stock crash" occurs in the early or mid-2020s, as some expect, it will only be **temporary**, as long as **technical productivity growth continues to accelerate in coming decades.** We will see that such accelerating change is predictable, as our leading technological platforms become increasingly **resource-efficient and intelligent**.

Even for most companies that lose 50 to 90% of their value in a crash, but survive, a **five to ten year hold** has historically recovered that value, and exceeded it greatly in the next boom market. As we'll discuss in *BPF*, the **faster and more complex** the world's **technological networks** get, the shorter these recovery periods have become. After the 1929 market crash, it took **twenty five years** for the market as a whole to reach its previous peak. In the crashes of 1999 and 2008, both **market recoveries** took under a decade. In Book 2 we will claim that the speed of general market recovery is accelerating the closer we approach the **technological singularity (the emergence of generally human-competitive AI).**

History also shows that **well-managed companies**, with lots of **optionality** (future prospects), always recover in a small fraction of the market's recovery time. The key here is to identify companies with good prospects and management, companies likely to survive a downturn. As **Tom and David Gardner** describe in *The Motley Fool Investment Guide, 3rd Ed*, 2017, their stock picking track record over the last twenty-five years, shared publicly with their community, picking just five stocks to invest in every month, and holding for the long term, has provided average annual returns of **15% for Tom Gardner,** and **20% for David Gardner,** host of their *Rule Breaker Investing* podcast, over the last twenty-five years, with each using slightly different **investment criteria.** Such returns are well above the American stock market's average returns of **8-9% since the 1920's**, and their portfolios have also had less volatility than the general market (at right) per decade.

The annual return of the US stock market in the 1990s has seen a few "lost decades" (picture right). Some doomsayers, often older folks who grew up in a world without digital platforms

US Stock annualized returns by decade

Decade	Total Return	Excess Return
1920s	14.3%	10.2%
1930s	-0.3%	-1.1%
1940s	8.3%	7.6%
1950s	18.8%	16.6%
1960s	5.2%	1.0%
1970s	4.6%	-1.9%
1980s	17.5%	7.8%
1990s	18.6%	13.0%
2000s	-1.0%	-4.3%
2010s	13.2%	12.7%
Average	9.6%	5.8%

Source: Convoy Investments

and their new dynamics, think we will enter one of those lost decades next. We disagree. Even if we experience a low growth decade like the 1960s (5% a year), which is plausible but unlikely, a good set of well-managed, well-capitalized, and growing companies will **continue to produce value faster than any other asset we can easily invest in.** Great companies deserve to be saved for, found and held **for the long term**, by as **many of the world's citizens as possible.** That's the surest route to **financial independence**, for all of us.

At present, during the **COVID-19 pandemic**, America is seeing a <u>K-shaped recovery</u>, a situation where the richest 1-10% of Americans, well invested in the stock market via options and retirement accounts, are rapidly growing their net worth, while the great majority of our citizens are seeing no gains or are in trouble, with new job insecurity, declining savings and wealth, and eroding salaries and benefits relative to their parents. Massive quantitative easing has temporarily improved the average American's financial picture. New startups are being created at rapid rates, and we may see a strong recovery, with higher wages for the working class. But economically, much remains uncertain in the short term.

But in the longer-term, a **new investing environment** appears to have emerged with the start of our **"Digital Supernova"** in 2008, with the rise of smartphones, the cloud, and AI. We explain in Book 2 why we expect certain high-growth **technology stocks** to continue to outperform all other asset classes up to and beyond the **technological singularity**, or the arrival of general artificial intelligence, perhaps later this century. **Cathie Wood** of Ark Invest is an example of D&D-centric investment thinking. Books like **Brynjolfsson and McAfee's** *Machine, Platform, Crowd*, 2018, are good intros to some of the new technological and human forces creating value. The podcast *Acquired*, by venture capitalists **Ben Gilbert** and **David Rosenthal**, is excellent for understanding technology companies and their initial public offerings (IPOs).

In coming decades, collective forecasting platforms (e.g. the <u>Good Judgment Project</u>), Bayesian polling platforms (see **Nate Silver's** *The Signal and the Noise*, 2012), predictive analytics platforms (see **Eric Siegel's** *Predictive Analytics*, 2012), and other **human-machine intelligence teaming platforms** will convince us all that **accelerating technical productivity is real**, and that since roughly 2010, it has become the **most important wealth-creation force** on the planet. We believe that keeping a good portion of our savings in **well-run companies that are constantly improving their technology and services, to create value** is the **single greatest financial decision** the average 21st century citizen can make.

D&D investing is surely a speculative investment strategy, so it should not be the **majority** of our investments. Furthermore, none of the authors of this *Guide* are registered investment advisors, so please **take this information to your professional advisors** to get counsel before making any investments. But, at the same time, realize that the classic balance of asset classes advocated in the Permanent Portfolio appears to have permanently changed, circa 2010, to **favor equities** for many decades to come, even with their **cyclic volatility** by decade. Today, a growing number of passive investors keep **50% of their portfolios in equities**, typically in exchange traded funds, 20% in bonds, 10% in cash, and 20% in other asset classes. You must find a mix that fits best with your view of the long-term future.

Whether or not our **medium-term** (next quarter to the next four years) bets pay off, doing a little speculative investing on a continual basis will motivate us to understand, learn, and potentially profit from **predictable business changes** going on in the world. Active investors, whether full-time ("traders") or part-time (most of us), profit by gaining superior **market intelligence** and **learning** (knowing what's going on) in their area of interest, better **strategic agility** (ability to execute faster than the average investor), good **risk management** (hedging strategies), and often, better-than-average anticipation skill and **forecasting** abilities. These are all useful skills for a foresight professional, in general.

Alice Schroeder's *The Snowball: Warren Buffett and the Business of Life*, 2009, is a great introduction to an investable holding company, <u>Berkshire Hathaway</u>, that has greatly beat average market returns for fifty years. They are now the **10th most valuable company in the world**. There are many such successes to study and emulate. When forecasting, most successful investors follow **Scott Armstrong's** maxim that a good forecast should be <u>conservative</u>. Many good investments are also <u>contrarian</u>—we learn when the **majority is acting foolishly** and when to **bet against them**. Many times we may not know the future, but we can more easily know when others are acting riskily and making unlikely bets. Many aspects of an industry or company are unpredictable, but many aspects of human psychology are broadly predictable.

As **James Lee,** futurist and registered investment advisor at StratFI reminds us, being among the early group to see convergence of key trends and developments is another way anticipation can help us. By understanding **relevant hard trends** and "starting with certainty" as futurist **Daniel Burrus** recommends, even the part-time active investor can intermittently find and take early advantage of major market changes, as when a relatively unknown firm becomes the early leader of an inevitable **new business category.** Historical examples include Wise.io innovating machine learning as a service, Netbase inventing social media marketing analytics, Piqora starting visual analytics, and many others.

Many independent and converging trends and developments came together to make Amazon the early leader in online shopping, Apple's iPhone the early leader in smartphones, Netflix the early leader in streaming video, and Bitcoin a useful (yet quite limited) crowd-owned digital store of value. Looking ahead, we see many more convergences coming (location based services, B2B rapid prototyping, miniaturized satellites, eVTOL air taxis, etc.). Being early to see any high-probability convergence, and finding the current momentum leaders, can be highly profitable.

Lee proposes four questions to guide us when investing:

1. **What?** What industry sectors, products, services, or asset classes are poised to create obvious value?
2. **How?** Which companies, assets, or instruments can best allow us to participate in this emerging value?
3. **When?** When should we enter and exit an investment, given market, media, and sentiment cycles?
4. **Why?** Why are we investing, and what is acceptable risk and financial success for us, on a personal level?

To be successful in speculative investing, as with most things in life, we don't need to be better than the best, just **better than most**—a condition worth striving for. If we make **lots of small bets**, and treat every speculation as a **learning experience**, we will gain foresight expertise, particularly the ability to **quickly sum up** a complex situation and **make a decision** ("take a position" in trader speak). With practice we will improve our ability to quickly see and profit from a subset of statistically predictable patterns, as long as we **stay in the game**. Good luck, and happy saving and investing.

Six Roles for Foresight Leaders: Some Essential Societal Functions

There are many ways we can look to the future. In some organizations, the foresight professional may be expected to be an **independent**, extroverted **generalist**, continually expanding the client's horizons, and consistently delivering new learning. For others, the foresight professional may be expected to be a **team player**, a **specialist**, or an employee happy to **work alone** on a particular foresight method, competency, or product. But while there are a great breadth of *ways of practice*, there are some **simplifying models** for **particularly essential and adaptive foresight roles and careers.**

Here is our favorite model, derived (no surprise!) from the **Foresight Pyramid**. Recall that the pyramid tells us that foresight thinking can be grouped into three basic types:

1. Discovering **Probable** futures (what is likely to happen), which we also call **developmental** futures.
2. Exploring **Possible** futures (what might happen), which we also call **evolutionary** futures.
3. Determining **Preferable and Preventable** futures (what we want to happen and to avoid), also called **evo-devo** or **adaptive** futures.

The figure below, **Six Evo-Devo Priorities Foresight Leaders,** offers 4U's model of **six essential societal foresight roles (functions)**, grouped into three word pairs, **Experimenting-Innovating, Discovering-Protecting,** and **Consulting-**

Managing. We derive this from the **Evo-Devo (Foresight) Pyramid**. In Chapter 3 (Many Faces of the Evo-Devo Pyramid), we will summarize some of the ways this apparently universal pyramid helps us to **see and improve** the most essential elements of **complex adaptive systems.**

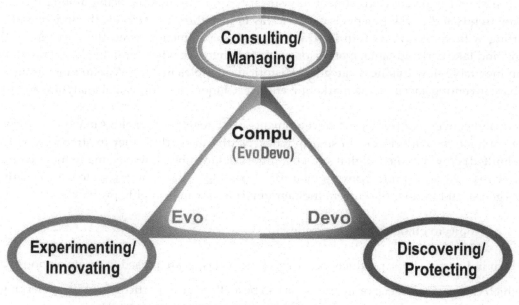

Six Evo-Devo Priorities for Foresight Leaders

When we consider foresight roles and careers that associate well with these function words, we can propose **six social functions** where foresight is particularly essential and adaptive for societies. We call these the **Six Roles**:

	Social Role	Goals and Values Priorities	Foresight Priorities
1.	**Creative Foresighter**	**Experimenting** (and Beauty)	**Possibility-first**
2.	**Entrepreneur Foresighter**	**Innovating** (and Disrupting)	**Possibility-first**
3.	**Consultant Foresighter**	**Consulting** (Externally)	**Prefer & Prevent first**
4.	**Manager Foresighter**	**Managing** (Internally)	**Prefer & Prevent-first**
5.	**Academic Foresighter**	**Discovering** (and Explaining)	**Probability-first**
6.	**Defense Foresighter**	**Protecting** (and Sustaining)	**Probability-first**

We propose that all six of these roles serve a **particularly essential and general societal purpose,** in an evo-devo sense. Regardless of how much or little they are **valued** in any particular society, all societies need Creatives (experimenters and artists), Entrepreneurs (innovators and disruptors), Consultants (external bridgers), Managers (internal bridgers), Academics (discoverers and explainers), and Defenders (protectors and sustainers). All six roles seem critical to **maintaining adaptive networks (collectives).**

There are of course many other societal roles we could list, but we would argue that all of them can be categorized as **variations of these six**. Realize that these **roles** do not necessarily define our **careers**. Instead, each role suggests a **set of careers** that depend particularly on that role. Any careers can be done using any of the six roles. When we are young, we may need to **experiment** with all of these roles before we can know which suit us best. Again, we think these roles are particularly basic, and possibly universal ways to think about our **potential social impact** in the world.

Of course, each role uses all of the **Four Ps**. Each uses **probability** and **possibility** foresight to generate **preferred** and **preventable** strategies and actions. Nevertheless, two of these roles (Academic and Defense) focus more on uncovering **probable** futures, two roles (Creative and Entrepreneur) focus more on exploring **possible** futures, and two (Consultant and Manager) are **bridging** roles, more focused on managing diverse foresight inputs **toward desired outcomes and away from avoidable outcomes**. This is helpful to understand, as we ask how our preferred roles fit into society.

Let's say a bit more now about the **foresight tendencies** in each group of social roles:

Group 1, Creative and **Entrepreneur** roles, are primarily about describing, creating, or trying out "**experimental and innovative**" futures, with developmental thinking as a secondary theme, in service to a creative drive to achieve a beautiful, novel, valuable, or disruptive thing. These roles are frequently in tension or conflict (ideally ethical and productive conflict) with the last two roles.

Group 2, Academic and **Defense** roles are primarily about discovering and explaining (academics) or protecting and sustaining (defense) "**environmentally optimal**" futures, with evolutionary thinking secondary, in service to better understanding, predicting, and securing what exists. These roles are often in tension and conflict (ideally ethical and productive) with the first two roles.

Group 3, Consultant and **Manager**, the two **bridging roles**, involve working toward "**collectively preferred and preventable**" futures, either as an **external** (Consultant) or internal (Manager) change leader. These two roles are where the great majority of **organizational foresight careers** are practiced, across the **twenty specialties**.

Let's look closer now at each of these **six societal foresight roles**:

1. **Creatives** (those whose primary role is to create new things, in the arts, design, R&D, or any other industry). **Rebecca Keegan's** *The Futurist: The Life and Films of James Cameron*, 2010, is a great biography of one such future thinker, film-maker **James Cameron**. **Thomas Edison** (inventor), **Grace Hopper** (computer programming pioneer), **Octavia Butler** (science-fiction author), are other examples of prominent future thinkers driven by more by creative, exploratory passions than any other motivation. They have a **passion for the possible.**

2. **Entrepreneurs** seek to translate their creative visions into **useful products and services**, with **teams**. They are also driven by the possible. Apple computer co-founder Steve Jobs is a well-known example. Note that the urge to create, explore, and invent (creatives) and the drive to innovate (create a successful product or service as an entrepreneur) are closely related. Nevertheless, there are real differences. As we'll describe in Book 2, **technology-enabled entrepreneurs** have become particularly powerful in recent decades. **Software platform startups** (Facebook, Google, Amazon, etc.) can now scale so fast, and create so many new personal freedoms and constraints, they are increasingly driving societal change. They need better oversight as a result.

3. **Academic foresighters** have been with us since at least the Greek Lyceum, founded by **Aristotle** in 334 BCE. They gained prominence with the birth of **statistics**. We find them used in government in America at least as early as the 1930s, in President **Herbert Hoover's** Committee on Recent Social Trends, tasked to do a statistical survey of twenty-four aspects of American life during the Great Depression, and to recommend federal actions on social and economic problems. Academics who run our **graduate foresight degree programs**, like **Andy Hines** at U. Houston, are prominent examples of this role. But anyone, in or out of universities, who is primarily motivated to **discover, understand, and explain** aspects of the world is an example of this role.

4. **Defense foresighters** are commonly found in our **intelligence communities**, which emerged in WWI and which professionalized after WW II. Intelligence, trend analysis and foresight think tanks like SRI, RAND, ONR, DARPA and others all emerged in US during the 1940s-1950s and beyond. **Herman Kahn** is a famous

example of such a foresight leader. There are many others today in our armed services and intelligence communities. Historically, defense included only **security and military** roles. But, since the rise of **environmentalism** in the 1970s, and **social justice movements** in the 21st century, this social role now also includes anyone that **fights for environmental protection**, the **rights of oppressed groups**, or any other **environmental or social protection role**. A certain type of person is drawn to the **mission of protection**, and they may engage in **occasional conflict** in that protection. Such an individual can come from any political persuasion.

5. **Consultant foresighters** have always been with us, but this group grew to prominence in our modern corporate environment in the 1950s. They have been the **most visible providers of organizational foresight**, but they are not the largest group of bridgers. Consultants are by definition **external partners to a team**. Many internal consultants are also inside organizations, offering advice to internal teams that they do not manage. They are often **informal leaders.** A key way to differentiate a consultant from a manager is whether they are focused on the **practice of external consulting** (offering decision analysis, strategic priorities, external support or advice), or whether they are more focused **managing** aspects of foresight and action in an organization.

6. **Manager foresighters** are the **largest and most diverse societal foresight role**. They **manage internal foresight and action** in the organization, across the **twenty specialties**. Some managers are **formal leaders** as well. As with entrepreneurs, managers are often **unrecognized and unrewarded** for the foresight they produce in their roles. Managers do not always supervise people. Product, process, or service managers may have no direct reports. But, they must manage some organizational process, and use foresight and action that role.

Like the other applications of the Evo-Devo Pyramid in this *Guide*, we can predict that in adaptive societies, we will have significantly greater numbers of Consultants and Managers in our population, than the other four types. But this may be the only way these two roles are "more important" to society. All three corners of this pyramid are needed to make an adaptive society. All six roles are vital, as are many other more specialized roles that we can relate to these six.

Again, while each of us may prefer to focus on one or a few of these six roles in many contexts, effective evo-devo foresight requires using and balancing **all three groups** of this **Societal Roles Triad**. We all engage at least a little in **each of these six roles** over our careers. Some of us **switch roles many times** over our careers. Nevertheless, most of us **focus** on **just a few** of these at a time. Our clients will typically also **mentally assign us to just one or two of these** at a time, based on our most public or client-facing activities, as a **mental shortcut** for who we are as professionals.

Now consider: Which of these six roles are **most attractive** to you? Which are least attractive? In the list above, put a **check** next to roles which come naturally, an **X** next to those that don't, and a **question mark** next to roles that may need more exploration. In the Career Options chapter of the online *Guide*, we offer a rough categorization of a few better-known foresight leaders into *one primary role apiece* for each of these six types. See that list if you'd like some examples of **practicing professionals** that appear to be particularly focused on **one** of these six societal roles over others. The earlier we find our **preferred roles**, and learn to value and collaborate with all of the other roles, the sooner we can find success. Finding our place in this social space—and our own unique specialties— are key steps in our professional journey.

Normative Foresight Pyramids: Finding Values and Visions of Success

Now it's time to discuss one last great foresight challenge, building the **values and visions** that will help us lead a **successful life**. This complex topic is called **normative foresight**. Using evo-devo models, we find it most helpful to approach this topic via **normative foresight pyramids**. With the **right values and visions** in place, we can use all the **foresight tools** in this book to thrive. Without good values and visions, we may still use the tools well in the short term, but we will have built our house on a poor **foundation**. Hence, we won't achieve lasting success.

Any book on foresight should discuss **character, values, meaning, and purpose**, with a **search for universality**, even as that search will always be tentative and incomplete. As we explore the models that follow, we can each ask ourselves where we agree and disagree. We should all take time to reflect on what success and progress mean to us, personally. Our thoughts and beliefs on adaptive visions, values, meaning, and the purpose our lives will always be incomplete, but they can become clearer with time, as we live, articulate our beliefs to others, acquire feedback, and learn. Running our **Do loops** in normative foresight work, analyzing our values and actions, will guide us to success.

1. Plato's Pyramid – Three Values of Life

In our search for a solid foundation for **adaptiveness** and **values**, let's revisit **Plato's Pyramid**. Recall that this is the **Evo-Devo Pyramid**, seen from a values perspective. Let's see again why these three special perspectives give us **three simple and universal ways** to understand **goals, meaning, and purpose in life**.

Plato's _Republic_, 380 BCE, is one of the most influential works of philosophy and political theory in history. Plato was especially concerned with, truth, and **the ideal world**, yet he also believed that pursuit of **Goodness** was the central goal for humanity. Speaking through the character of **Socrates**, in the "Form of the Good," Plato argued that all our other ideals derive from this pursuit. Over his long (eighty year) life, Plato also made a few statements concerning three ideals: **beauty, goodness, and truth**. Around the same time in the East, the Bhagavad Gita mentioned these three perspectives as a group, talking about the value of words and actions that are "**beautiful, good, and true**."

Plato's student, **Aristotle**, cared more about the **commonsense world**. Plato was more theoretical, Aristotle more practical. Aristotle proposed that there are five **Transcendentals**, or essential properties of value: Being, Something, Unity, Goodness, and Truth. The first three of these, Being, Something, and Unity, can be grouped together as Beingness, survival, existence, or the **Universe itself**. Beingness is an _inherently_ Beautiful thing, as we are each unique creations in the universe, but it is not necessarily a Good or True thing. A minimum model of essential human properties, then, in our view, are **Beingness (Beauty)**, **Goodness**, and **Truth**.

Plato and Aristotle, at the Academy in Athens (Raphael, 1511)

Those who have adopted this perspective, like the philosopher **Ken Wilber**, developer of integral theory, speak of a **Transcendental Triad** of dimensions of experience, and of three basic human goals, our perennial search for **Beauty, Goodness**, and **Truth**. In a bit more detail, the **Values Pyramid** can be understood as:

- Creativity, arts, innovation (**Beauty**) – **Possibilities**   (First Person View)
- Ethics, politics, business, religion (**Goodness**) – **Preferences**   (Second Person View)
- Logic, science, sustainability (**Truth**) – **Probabilities**   (Third Person View)

The purposes of life don't get any simpler than this, in our view. Like the **Four Ps**, if we drop any one of these out of our values, desires, and plans, we become dangerously imbalanced and incomplete. When we include all three, **Plato's Pyramid** gives us an excellent start at **personal life goals**. In our thoughts, words, and actions, we should all seek to appreciate and advance, at the very minimum, the goals of **Beauty**, **Goodness**, and **Truth**.

We should also recognize that these three goals are **sometimes in opposition** to each other, in our own minds and in society. Plato's pyramid tells us that **Beauty** and **Truth**, in particular, are often in conflict with each other. The minds of the **Artist-Creator** and the **Scientist-Defender** are two ends of a vital pair. Both Beauty and Truth are different kinds of Goodness, each particularly valuable in certain contexts. The pyramid also tells us that **Goodness** is the **most frequent and important**. It typically **deserves priority** in resolving conflicts with the other goals.

Again, Plato's Pyramid is a clear summary of the **goals of evolutionary development**. The production and pursuit of **beauty** is an **evolutionary process (exploring the possible).** Think of the astonishingly exuberant and beautiful diversity of life's species and adaptations. In contrast, the pursuit of **truth** is a **developmental process** (finding the probable). The search for **goodness** is a mixed, or evo-devo pursuit (expressing the preferable). It bridges the values of beauty and truth and results in a third, unique value.

We propose that the **pursuit of success, progress, and happiness** must always involve simultaneously pursuing **all three values and their dependent goals.** Our unique and beautiful evolutionary journeys, and how we choose to take them, are always as important as our developmental destinations. We never fully arrive anywhere, and yet, we are always improving, if we journey the right way.

In this view, the deepest **meanings of life** can be stated as three sometimes conflicting challenges:

1. **Enjoying** and enriching our experimental, creative, and **beautiful journeys (evolution),**

2. **Seeking** and protecting **truth** (predictability) and deriving **incrementally more optimal destinations** from our current truth **(development)**, and

3. **Striving** to be good—to **minimize** *unnecessary* **error, suffering, and coercion** and to maximize those **necessary kinds of error, suffering, and coercion** that are in service to **adapting**, for ourselves, our families, and life as a network **(evo-devo)**.

In each of these challenges, the devil is in the details. Adaptiveness always requires error, suffering, and coercion, and sometimes we sacrifice ourselves for greater good. As we will explore in *BPF*, considering ourselves as a **member of a complex network**, and asking how we can improve the adaptiveness of the network as a whole, is generally the best course. This philosophy might be called **Network Adaptiveness**. It is not simply **Utilitarianism** (seeking the greatest good for the greatest number), but something more complex, balancing both evolutionary and developmental goals.

If we wish to help ourselves and others to find deeper meaning in our personal lives, we can focus on goals like **beauty, creativity, and intelligence (evolutionary goals)**, on goals like **goodness, connectedness, ethics, and empathy (evo-devo goals)** or on goals like **truth, security, and sustainability (developmental goals)**, or on any combination of these. This is a **minimum viable set** of adaptive goals, in our view. As Plato said, the pursuit of **Goodness** is uniquely able to **bridge** all three. It belongs at the top of the pyramid, and in the **center of our lives.**

Any of these pursuits will create authentic meaning in our lives, but we will propose that the network state of **Interdependence (Connectedness)** is the central goal of adaptive collectives of living systems. Connectedness is built on the twin goals of **empathy** and **ethics**, and these two goals generate the most frequent and important kinds of meaning we can have in our lives. Expressing and receiving **Love** and practicing and pursuing the **Good** are the **most meaningful activities we can engage in**. When we shortchange either, we shortchange our own happiness and ability to thrive.

All self-leaders and team-leaders should keep some version of **Plato's Pyramid** in mind. We'll offer two other versions of this pyramid, the **Five E's** (Chapter 3) and the **Six IES Goals** (later in this chapter and in Chapter 3). Prioritizing and balancing some version of these goals is how we can best measure and guide **personal success** and **social progress**, and lead ourselves and others to better futures.

2. Kirton's Pyramid – Three Decision Styles

Another helpful application of Plato's Pyramid has been developed by the psychologist **Michael Kirton**. In the 1970s, Kirton recognized that people tend to approach problem solving and decision making in one of two fundamental styles, either as what he called **Innovators**, seeking to imagine, create, and experiment with new ways of doing things, or as what he calls **Adaptors**, or what we call **Protectors**, folks seeking to protect the status quo, and to better predict and defend against harm. These two groups often fight with each other in any organization and society. Kirton also discovered a **mix** of these styles in a third group he called **Bridgers**, as they "bridge" the two more fundamental decisionmaking styles.

In 1978, he developed an instrument, the **Kirton Adaption-Innovation** assessment, or **KAI**, to assess these three styles. His group has administered it to tens of thousands of people in the years since. As Kirton describes in *Adaption-Innovation*, 2003, **Innovators** are particularly focused on **Possible** futures, and **Future-first** thinking, **Protectors** on **Probable** futures, and **Past-first** thinking, and **Bridgers** are heavily focused on **Preferable** futures, and **Present-first** thinking. Bridgers, by far the **largest group** of the three, generally seek to **balance** and synthesize the possible and probable (innovation and protection) usually in some style that acknowledges the value of both. That strategy usually, but not always, produces the most generally (democratically) preferred futures for the group.

Kirton found a **normal distribution** of these three styles of problem solving and decision-making in the population. He discovered that the largest group of people, roughly **two-thirds** of humanity, are **Bridgers**, with a **third** of us at each of the other two extremes, as **Innovators** or **Adaptors**. This Bridger-dominant distribution may have a biological basis in population genetics. It seems a key aspect of the **sociobiology of adaptive networks**. All healthy groups are **coopetitive**. They are **cooperators first** and **competitors second**, within some shared **ethical and empathic framework**.

Social media today gives **illusion** that we are increasingly polarized with respect to **decision styles**, with **fewer Bridgers** among us. In reality, we have grown more polarized with respect to the **stories we choose to explain the world**, not our decision styles. These are two very different things. The latter has always cycled chaotically between **polarization and centrism**, and is much easier to change. Cognitively, the majority of us remain **Bridgers**, even in this era of **identity politics**. Most of us want to **find common ground,** as soon as **our toxic environment lets us**, as we will discuss in *BPF*.

We like Kirton's Innovator and Bridger terms, but are less thrilled with his Adaptor term. Kirton's "Adaptors" are motivated to **protect** the status quo and **predict** and avoid preventable harm. We refer to Kirton's Adaptors as "**Protectors**" and "**Anticipators**". Again, Kirton found that these **three decisionmaking styles** are **normally distributed** in the population (see the "normal curve" of these three decisionmaking styles in the graphic below). These three cognitive styles are deeply congruent with both the **Foresight Pyramid**, and with the three **time orientations**. As a result, they seem to be a particularly universally adaptive model.

We've summarized Kirton's model in the graphic below:

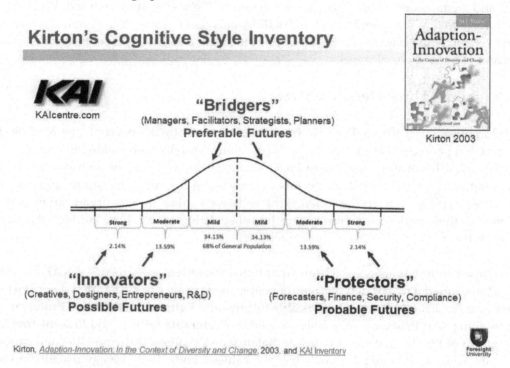

Both Kirton's research and the Foresight Pyramid argue that these three are **fundamental decisionmaking styles** that we all use on a regular basis. Each of us also has a general preference, in different contexts, for one or two of these styles over the others. Nevertheless, all three are necessary to adapt. As Kirton describes, different organizations attract different distributions of these three fundamental types, and if they get too many of one type, they can run into trouble. Strong **teams** require a healthy mix of each cognitive style, and all teams should **diagnose themselves** on these three variables, to understand their current mix.

An **innovation-centric organization**, like a startup, an R&D lab, or a creative agency, naturally attracts **Innovators**. It may need to value and support more **Protectors**. A **high-reliability organization (HRO)**, like a defense agency, a health care firm, or the government, with a low tolerance of failure, naturally attracts **Protectors**. It typically needs to value and support more **Innovators**. A political group, consultancy, managerial, or facilitator community naturally attracts **Bridgers**. It may need to value and support more of each of the two more fundamental types. Different jobs within the organization also attract higher percentages of each of the three types.

Which of these three thinking types do we think we tend to be, most of the time? Recall the **Six Classic Types of Foresight Leader** discussed in the previous chapter. They are rearranged here to fit Kirton's normal curve.

Our Labels	Social Role	Modified Kirton Labels
Experimenting (and Beauty)	**Creative**	**Strong Innovator**
Innovating (and Disrupting)	**Entrepreneur**	**Innovator**
Prioritizing (and Changing)	**Consultant**	**Bridger-Innovator**
Managing (and Bridging)	**Manager**	**Bridger-Protector**
Discovering (and Explaining)	**Academic**	**Protectors**
Protecting (and Sustaining)	**Defense**	**Strong Protectors**

Kirton's test may help us better identify which roles are best suited for us. We may already know the answer. But, if not, we can take the **Kirton Cognitive Styles** assessment at <u>KAIcentre.com</u> to find out. The KAI has 32 questions, takes 15 minutes to complete, and costs $15/person. Unfortunately, Kirton still requires a KAI-certified trainer to administer and debrief the results, so it's not yet online. For anyone who'd like to take it, email one of the KAI Centre's registered practitioners at the Kirton website.

3. Keirsey's Pyramid – Four Personality Types

In Chapter 1 we introduced **David Keirsey**'s personality model, the **Four Temperaments,** a variation of the **Myers-Briggs Personality Types Inventory** (MBTI) that we find particularly insightful. **Keirsey's Temperament Sorter** simplifies the MTBI into **four classic types,** and four subtypes (the classic Myers-Briggs combinations) within each major type. We've seen that Keirsey's model associates closely with the **Modern Foresight Pyramid (the Four Ps).** For this reason, we consider these four personality types as particularly universal. They all contribute to adaptiveness, in basic ways.

These models stem from work in psychological types by the founder of analytical psychology, **Carl Jung**. Some of his work has **evo-devo structure**. Jung proposed that healthy personal development is a perennial conflict between the **needs of individuation** (an evolutionary value) and the **expectations of the collective** (a developmental value). He famously called the shared mental models of the collective, both instinctual and cultural, our species' "collective unconscious." Again, for those wishing to learn more, Keirsey's *Please Understand Me II*, 1998, is a good book exploring the universality of these four temperaments. It also offers insights on related intelligence types.

The picture below outlines **Keirsey's Four Temperaments, mapped to the Four Ps**.

Keirsey's Four Temperaments — Preferences for the Fours Ps
(Please Understand Me II, 1998)

Which of these temperaments most often describes you? The free 70-question <u>Keirsey Temperament Sorter</u> is an **online self-assessment** you can complete in 15 minutes. We recommend everyone take this test. It will force you to make 70 (sometimes difficult) choices between two responses. On average, **half the population** chooses each of the two responses.

Consider **retaking it** in different life contexts, and see if and how your answers **change**. You may find you predictably **bounce,** based on context, between **at least two** of Keirsey's temperament types.

As Keirsey says, each of these personality types are so basic and useful, that **we all actually express all four of them**, in **different degrees** in different **societal and problem contexts**. We all can adopt each of these "mindsets" at times within our own mind. Yet all of us will have at least a mild **preference** for one of these types more often than others, **on average**. Knowing your most preferred temperament, and others temperaments, can be very helpful, in relationships, for work, for leadership, and for general social intelligence.

Consider that each of these temperaments prioritizes a **different set of values**, and that **each** approach may be particularly universal. Can you see the adaptiveness of **all** of these values? Can you relate well to others who prioritize different sets of these values than you do?

Keirsey's model reminds us we can all have different values, and yet each of us can be **"right"**. It is only when we have sufficient **diversity of values**, in our own (often arguing) mindsets, on our teams, in our firms, and in our societies, that we can be adaptive. There is no benefit to trying to change others to value what we most value. We are each going prefer slightly different values, and our differences, properly managed, will make us more adaptive. There is great **strength in values diversity**, and we can have **productive values conflicts**, as long as we are not neglecting **universal values**.

Consider also that each of these temperaments may be particularly attracted to **different foresight assessments (Four Ps)**, and to **different foresight methods and frameworks**. Getting them all to agree on team process can sometimes be difficult. Our Four Ps mapping of Keirsey's types reminds us that **two of these conflicts**, between **Guardian and Artisan** thinking, and between **Idealist and Rational** thinking, are particularly fundamental and useful to foresight creation.

This mapping also reminds us of the **REOPS cycle** and **GRASP thinking**. To lead ourselves well, we want to value **Learning** the relevant past and present about our problem or task, then some degree of **Guardian** thinking (understanding expectations, the status quo), then **Artisan** thinking (understanding all the ways people might approach a problem or task) then **Idealist** thinking (asking ourselves what outcome would be most ideal) then **Rational** thinking (asking what procedures and tools will most help, and the ways we might fail). This model tells us that when we **consciously** use a REOPS or GRASP process, we are implicitly taking a **"multi-valued" approach to foresight creation**. Not values in terms of culture, but values in terms of universal processes, independent of culture.

4. The IES Goals – Six Goals of Life as a Network (an Evo-Devo Model)

In Chapter 1 we saw that **Plato's Values Pyramid** is congruent with both the **Time and Foresight Pyramids**. In our view, these are each different perspectives on the **Evo-Devo Pyramid,** our proposed **universal model for adaptive processes in complex systems**. We'll explore some of the many faces of that pyramid in Chapter 3. As we'll now briefly describe, we can expand this Values Pyramid into **Six Goals** that must be managed well by *intelligent* complex adaptive systems.

All **adaptive organisms, groups, and societies** seek to advance and balance at least the following six goals:

1. More **Innovation** (freedom, creativity, experimentation, beauty, inspiration, re-creation, play, fun)
2. More **Intelligence** (information, knowledge, insight, simulated options, individuality, diversity)
3. More **Empathy** (self-esteem, love, emotion, synchronization, consciousness, connectedness)
4. More **Ethics** (conscience, judgment, equity, merit, rulesets, interdependence)
5. More **Strength** (ability, power, wealth, security, resilience, antifragility)
6. More **Sustainability** (truth, order, belief, responsibility, science, rationality, optimality)

We call these the **IES Goals**, as the first two start with **I**, the middle two with **E**, and the last two with **S**. In *BPF*, will see that the two "**I**" goals, **Innovation and Intelligence**, are primarily goals of **evolutionary processes**, the two "**S**" goals, **Strength and Sustainability**, are primarily goals of **developmental processes**, and the "**E**" goals, Empathy and Ethics, keep complex systems **interdependent**. They regulate their operation as a **cooperative and competitive network**.

The core purpose of **evolution**, we propose, is to **experiment** and to **create** diverse and novel forms and intelligence that may protect the system (species) as a whole from future disruptions. The core purpose of **development**, we propose, is to **protect** and **cycle** the systemic capabilities, resilience, and sustainability that have ensured our past survival. These two goal sets are in **tension with each other**, often pulling the system (organism, group, organization) in different directions, toward different ends. The core purpose of the middle goals, **Empathy and Ethics**, is to keep every intelligent network **interdependent**, to keep the network more adaptive than separate individuals, or groups. The middle goals use the tension between the often opposing evolutionary and developmental goals to "**compute the good**" **for the network**. The **centrality** of the two "E" goals reminds us that *people issues* **deserve top priority**. *People first!* is 4U's first motto.

The figure below proposes that adaptive thinking about the IES Goals can be represented as a **normal (Gaussian) distribution**, a **hierarchy of goals**, with **Connectedness** (Empathy and Ethics) as the **most frequently pursued goal** at the center of living systems. In Chapter 3, we'll discuss least **two values** that closely each of these **six goals**. That gives us a minimum of **twelve values** that human networks must manage well, in pursuit of adaptiveness.

Here are the **IES Goals** in cartoon form:

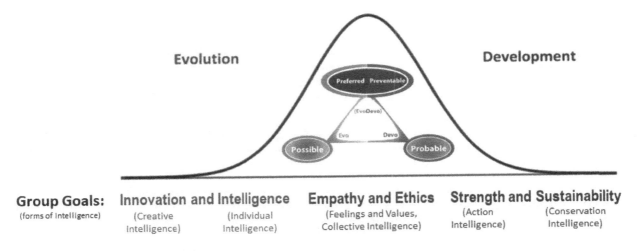

The IES Goals (Six Goals of Complex Systems) – An Evo-Devo Model

We can now make some observations about this simple normative model:

- Consider the **usefulness of each of these goals** to all **living systems, and to humanity as a complex network**. We can't ignore any of them if we are seeking long-term success and progress, for any **adaptive network,** whether it is a network of **mindsets** (arguing in our own minds), or any **team**, **organization**, or **society**.

- Note the way the **evolutionary goals** relate to the **developmental goals**. Innovation goals are often **at odds** with sustainability goals, for example. Each set pulls us toward different ends. They create competitions and conflicts that must be managed by "**bridging**" **interactions**, in our own minds, on teams, in firms, and in society.

- Consider that **empathy and ethics (aka connectedness and interdependence)** are how all intelligent collectives manage the conflicts between these goals, and come to an adaptive preference, most often in a **democratic, bottom-up, and coopetitive manner.** For example, an adaptive preference emerges in our own minds, when we argue with ourselves over any topic. A similar kind of empathic, and ethical coopetition happens in adaptive groups and societies, when leaders sustain a culture and processes that are **primarily democratic**, with trusted competition and conflict, yet also **sometimes autocratic**, as when rapid reaction, mass coordination, and simplicity of response are required.

- Consider that the **vast majority of conversations and conflicts** people have, in their families, organizations and society, are around **collective feelings (empathy) and ethics (fairness)**, and **managing the perennial conflict** between **innovation (newness)** and **sustainability (the status quo)**. For example, the great majority of communications that children express during development, are either **emotional-cognitive ones**, **centered around empathy or its absence**, or **cognitive-emotional ones**, **centered around fairness and ethics**. In this evo-devo model, the **state and nature of our connectedness (empathy and ethics)**, the feelings and rules we negotiate to "bridge" differences with others, is **our central goal**, both as individuals and as a species.

Again, the **Gaussian curve** that Kirton found helps us recognize both the **evo-devo (blended, contrasted) nature** of the IES goals, and the **unique centrality and importance** of **empathy and ethics** in our lives, firms, and societies. This model of **normative foresight** thus includes a simple but very useful **values hierarchy**. In **tradeoffs** between **conflicting values**, **empathy and ethics** should be our prime consideration. More generally, as we described in Chapter 1, our great capacity for **foresight**, the use of **technology** to solve problems, and **ethical and empathic coopetition**—*head, hand, and heart*, are the **three greatest gifts** we have been given. They all deserve to be top priorities in our personal and professional lives.

One insight that comes from exploration of our **current human values,** and our aspiration to find **universal values,** is that **transformation in our mindsets** will be necessary to develop significantly better organizations, politics, economies, and societies. While we will always have **unique** temperaments and cultures, we must all **increasingly share** any universal values and priorities. Individual leaders and cultures can be sentinels, but unless deep appreciation for our shared values has **diffused into all our cultures**, humanity as a system will remain fragile to chaos and change.

Few have said this better than the late, great futurist <u>**Willis Harman**</u>. Harman started his career as an engineer, doing **organizational foresight** at SRI in the 1960s, working on easily measured variables and models in **"outer space"**, or tech and societal change. He ended his career in psychology and sociology, focusing on the far less tangible and measurable variables and models of **"inner space"**, of **unconscious and conscious mindset change**. He moved to the Institute of Noetic Sciences (IONS) to do this work. IONS is a "New Age" institute, which means it gives too much credence to **evidence-poor topics** like parapsychology, quantum consciousness, etc. But it also does some **good humanistic work**.

Harman's last book, <u>*Global Mind Change: The Promise of the 21st Century,*</u> 1998, is recommended reading. It has much to say on humanity's great need for achieving **a more universal mindset and values**. The great consciousness futurist **Barbara Hubbard**, the integral philosopher **Ken Wilber**, and a handful of others also stress these themes. In our STEEPLECOP scanning categories (Science, Tech, Economy, Environment, Politics, Law, Culture, Organizations, People, see Chapter 5), the works of each of these authors **span the categories of outer and inner space** particularly well, in our view. All of these works predict a coming **Great Transition** (paradigm shift), in our current **individual and global mindsets**.

Harman, for example, reminds us of the illogic and unforesighted priorities of a society where:

> Nuclear weapons are made [, in massive quantities,] for national security,
> Economic logic [, missing intangible factors and their value,] is used to make social decisions,
> Knowledge is based on a science which ignores [higher purpose, duty,] courage and virtue.

Harman describes a number of previous **paradigm shifts** in both **science** and **mind** (worldview), and wisely reminds us that **neither Science nor Religion will ever disappear,** as each serves **universal functions for our species**. He also reminds us that one of our **greatest societal challenges** is to further mature these two perennial and different ways of knowing, so that they better **support and value each other,** rather than fostering **unproductive conflict** at our most basic levels of **belief and ethics**. We'll say more about these vital topics in *BPF*.

How Large is the Professional Foresight Community?

If asked, how many people around the world would **self-describe as foresight professionals** today?

The website <u>Inside Jobs</u> reports that "<u>futurist</u>" is one of several little-known job classifications with "awesome or unusual perks," whatever that means. They don't yet list "foresight specialist" "forecaster" or other foresight-related terms. They also estimate 75% of futurists hold bachelors, 21% masters, and 4% doctoral degrees, and that our salaries range from $33K to $111K. A 2009 BLS article on the <u>futurist occupation</u> estimated that there were roughly 750 income-generating self-declared futurists in the US. That number seems too low, and is surely much larger today. As futurist **Amy Webb** has <u>observed</u>, the demand for futurism has always grown greatly when societal and technological disruptions occur. The disruptions of the last decade, including the 2008 Financial Crisis, the rise of the tech giants, and the COVID-19 pandemic of 2020, have all driven a **great recent increase** in futurism and self-declared futurists.

Based on our search for the futurist term on personal profiles on <u>LinkedIn</u>, the leading global business social network, we'd guess there are now on the order of **20,000 income-generating, self-declared futurists** practicing globally today. That's a reasonably large number, but as we've seen, the label **futurist** is simply the most visible and public of the titles used in our profession. It is far too narrow and simplistic a way to understand the **foresight profession**. Economists, investment professionals, policy and strategy professionals, forecasters, marketers, just about everyone does some foresight work, in some context. We'd define a **foresight professional** as anyone **who regularly evaluates aspects of the future** for their clients or organizations, using any of the **Twenty Specialties**.

LinkedIn: A Global Business Social Network

LinkedIn had 750 million global users in 2020. They now presumably have the majority of the 600 million or so people with a college degree globally, and we'd guess roughly half of the world's 800 million postsecondary-educated knowledge workers. These 800 million are our pool of current potential foresight practitioners, a pool that should grow greatly in coming decades, as they represent only 25% of our current global workforce of roughly 3 billion. Given current global penetration rates, we guess that LinkedIn's current user base represents **roughly a third** of those who might self-identify as foresight professionals today. In other words, our online pool of **self-identifying foresight practitioners** still has a lot of room for growth as it becomes more globally representative and diverse.

Out of 280M global LinkedIn users at the time of our initial search below (2014), there were **just 5,000 people** in which the word "**futurist**" could be found on a member profile. That number is now **7,900**. We simply tripled this current number and rounded down for a back-of-the-envelope estimate of **20,000** self-identifying professional futurists. By contrast, searching a more varied set of words for various foresight specialties, returned following profile counts:

5,000 "futurist"	166K "innovation and future"
6,000 "strategic foresight"	169K "vision and future"
7K "actuarial and future"	185K "predictive"
8K "Delphi and future"	293K "scenarios"
10K "probability and future"	415K "create and future"
12K "uncertainty and future"	500K "strategist"
24K "foresight"	513K "intelligence and future"
28K "scanning and future"	610K "analytics and future"
29K "alternatives and future"	690K "strategy and future"
48K "scenarios and future"	1.0M "planning and future"
60K "trend and future"	1.5M "innovation"
79K "prediction"	2.1M "future"
80K "statistical and future"	2.3M "forecasting"
82K "forecast and future"	7.6M "strategic planning"
138K "risk management and future"	23.2M "strategy"

[Note: Since the word **"futures"** is a **dual-use term**, describing both a diversity of outcomes, and <u>financial derivatives trading</u> (a type of investment foresight), we avoided using that term in our searches.]

So how big does our **foresight community** become once we include **a broadly representative set** of organizational foresight work? Taking the half-million **"strategists"** above, doubling it for global representation, then multiplying by ten to represent the other (less popular) specialties, we'd guess there are **roughly 10 million** people who could be prompted to self-identify as **full-time foresight professionals globally**. We'd also guess there are at least four times the number who use the word "strategy", or roughly **100 million part-time foresight professionals**, who would self-identify as doing some type of formal foresight work for less than fifty percent of their annual work hours. This is a **very big community**! It is waiting to be better networked and trained.

What Do We Call Ourselves?

Google's <u>Ngram Viewer</u> is a tool that shows word frequencies as a proportion of all books published between 1500 and 2008 that have been digitized for public access. In the 30 million digitized books as of 2015 (already representing 23% of an estimated 130 million extant books), we found the following trends with respect to future-related terms:

- **"futurology"** peaked in the late 1970s and this word has lost 80% of its relative use since. It holds out today in a few places in Europe.

- **"futures studies"** peaked in the early 1980s and is roughly half as popular (a 50% drop) today.

- **"futurist"** grew rapidly from the early 1900s to 2000, saw a 20% drop since, and is now rising again.

- **"foresight"** peaked in the late 1500s, again in 1650 and the early 1800s, became half as popular since, and grew 23% in popularity from 2000 to 2008, and has grown further since.

- **"future"** is the only word that has shown steady, but very slow growth since the 1550s. Today it is roughly **twice as popular** in social discourse as it was in 1650, at the start of the European Enlightenment.

The data seem to support our advice that, unless we are **public speakers** and others designate us as **"futurists"** in that role, it will be more effective for most of us to use terms like **"strategist"**, **"foresight analyst," "long-term analyst," "forecaster," "intelligence analyst," "strategic planner," "risk manager," "trend researcher"** and **other** specialty phrases to self-describe our organizational work. Consider that **"strategist"** is roughly **100X as popular** as **"futurist"** on LinkedIn member profiles, both in 2014 and today.

For those willing to innovate, "**foresighter**" is our most recommended single word for general professional self-description, though it will surely remain little-known for years to come. For now, we recommend just claiming it, and forging ahead. When folks ask us its meaning, we can explain it as: "**any professional tasked to look to and analyze aspects of the future, for a client.**"

Strategic foresight is a hybrid field. It combines the strengths of psychology, anthropology, statistics, philosophy, sociology, and several other disciplines to achieve its own distinct objectives. The value of **hybrid thinking** (combining multiple fields of knowledge) to professional culture is now becoming clear. Foresight can embrace our hybridity while still remaining our own vital and definitive field. As described in Chapter 1 (Futurists and Foresighters), we all can begin **T-shaped**, able to hybridize insights from many bodies of knowledge, while also gaining deep expertise in a few areas. Over time, we can strive to become **Star-shaped**, picking up new specialty knowledge over our careers, and building a network of specialist collaborators whom we trust. T-shaped and Star-shaped individuals, working together in **diverse networks**, is where **hybridization** shines.

Where we "Foresight Professionals" hang our shingles, apparently.

In sum, while our **self-title** can be important, recognizing the **full variety** of practitioners who work today to improve organizational foresight is significantly more important. Learning from and being able to work with all the specialty practitioners will maximize our effectiveness and professional development.

Comprehensive Foresight Practice Communities – A Select List

Included below is a select list of **comprehensive (six domain) foresight practice** communities in our emerging field. This list is repeated in Appendix 3. We repeat the list because we think communities like these **especially deserve our participation and support.** Further, involving ourselves in their development can, in turn, help **develop our field** and **expand its ability to benefit us in every domain.**

A few of these, like **APF**, are also **professional associations**, but most are not at present. Each community tends to focus on different aspects of the **six domains**, but each also seeks to be **comprehensive**. All also profess certain particularly **high-quality worldviews**, in our view. Participating in any of these can expose us to a **great variety of methods and options** in foresight practice. Each community has advantages and shortcomings, but all are doing good work in our field. Each has free publications, podcasts, discussion groups, or other output, which can help us decide if we want to get more involved with them. **Volunteering positions** are also available with all of them.

1. Association of Professional Futurists **(APF)**. Since 2002. Presently led by futurist **Shermon Cruz**, APF is an online organization of roughly 500 members dedicated to development and support of professional consulting or organizational futurists. They run an Annual Conference an annual Professional Development Workshop co-located with the WFS conference, and more frequent Virtual Gatherings. They have a great discussion list and a thriving practice support community. Their main focus is **organizational foresight**. They have a task force, led by **Andy Hines**, engaged in better defining and professionalizing foresight practice. APF is the first organization that we recommend joining, to meet other colleagues working to improve **organizational foresight** practice.

2. <u>Foresight University</u> **(4U)**. Led by futurist **John Smart**, we are the training and development group behind *The Foresight Guide*. We offer books, online courses, and consulting in foresight development. 4U is the education and training division of the <u>Acceleration Studies Foundation (ASF)</u> a 501c3 nonprofit, founded in 2003 to promote better understanding and management of global processes of accelerating change. In 2021, ASF is changing its name to the Futuremedia Foundation, and launching Futurepedia, a Wikipedia for futures topics and ideas. In addition to 4U, ASF presently supports the <u>Foresight Education and Research Network</u> (<u>FERN</u>), a free foresight onramp for those new to our field, the <u>GlobalForesight.org</u> foresight links site, the 5,000 member <u>Global Foresight discussion group</u> on LinkedIn, and the <u>Evo-Devo Universe</u> complex systems research, conferencing, and publishing community, founded in 2008.

3. <u>The Millennium Project</u> **(TMP)**. Since 1996. A non-profit think tank of more than 3,500 scholars, business, and policy futurists. Led by eminent futurist **Jerry Glenn**, TMP collects research and feedback from its <u>60 Nodes</u> globally for its regular <u>State of the Future</u> report. TMP also publishes the excellent *Futures Research Methodology* book, and special studies, most recently *Work 2050: Three Scenarios* (<u>PDF</u>). They're also developing an online <u>Global Futures Intelligence System (GFIS)</u>. TMP is not yet an association, but it functions as one for **policy and governance foresight**. We particularly recommend this community for **societal and global foresight**. Their worldview is close to the authors of this *Guide*.

4. <u>Long Now Foundation</u>. Long Now is an SF-based nonprofit founded by the eminent ecological and community futurist **Stewart Brand**, author of the *Whole Earth Catalog*. It provides a counterpoint to the "faster/cheaper" modern mindset by promoting "slower/better" thinking. It runs the excellent monthly <u>Seminars on Long-Term Thinking</u> (audio and video archives available). Some particularly excellent **societal and global foresight** talks can be found at their website. They are light on action and activism (personal, team, and organizational foresight), but strong on big picture thinking. Their worldview is close to the authors of this *Guide*.

5. <u>Singularity University</u>. SU, founded by eminent futurists **Peter Diamandis** and **Ray Kurzweil**, aims to promote **organizational**, **societal and global foresight**, with a focus on using **entrepreneurship**, **science** and **technology** to solve humanity's grand challenges. They run <u>Executive Education</u> programs in exponential thinking, and maintain a <u>Global Network of SU Chapters</u>. Their flagship annual conference, <u>SU Global Summit</u>, explores exponential change and entrepreneurship activities in many areas. They also run industry conference series, an annual <u>Exponential Medicine</u> conference, and occasional conferences in <u>Exponential Manufacturing</u> and <u>Exponential Finance</u>, a startup accelerator, <u>SU Ventures</u>, and <u>Singularity Hub</u>, a media website reporting on exponential advances. Their worldview is close to the authors of this *Guide*.

6. <u>Open ExO</u>. Co-founded and led by futurist **Salim Ismail**, formerly at SU, Open ExO has the same **exponential worldview** as SU, but is more focused on **personal, team, and organizational foresight**. It operates a global network of **coaches** who are certified in "transformation" of individuals, teams, and organizations to help them leverage exponential thinking and tools. In organizational change, it is particularly focused on helping **startups**. They run many ExO webinars and a biannual online <u>ExO World Small Business Summit</u>. Their foundational books are *Exponential Organizations: Why New Organizations are 10X Faster*, 2014, and *Exponential Transformation: Evolve Your Organization with a 10 Week Sprint*, 2019. As with SU, we recommend this community for those looking to take **exponential thinking seriously** in their own lives, and to **act like an entrepreneur** in their organizations.

7. <u>Good Judgment Open</u>. Co-founded and led by political science and forecasting academic **Philip Tetlock** at U. Pennsylvania. A community of <u>Good Judgment</u>, a forecasting services firm. Good Judgment helps corporate and government clients improve forecasting. Good Judgment Open allows anyone to sponsor forecasting challenges, to anticipate major political, economic, and technological events of the coming year. *The Economist* and others have sponsored challenges there. Their foundational book is *Superforecasting: The Art and Science of*

Prediction, 2015. They are one of the leading open prediction markets. We also recommend Metaculus, a community run by physicist **Anthony Aguirre**, which started as a science and technology prediction platform but has become a general prediction platform. The future of prediction markets is bright, and for those of us who like to predict, our participation in these crowd platforms is both helpful and rewarding.

8. World Future Society **(WFS)**. Since 1966. Led by futurist **Julie Friedman Steele** since 2015. In their heyday, WFS covered **all six domains of foresight**. They published *The Futurist* magazine from 1967-2015, and the academic foresight journal *World Future Review*. Until 2015, they ran an annual conference, World Future, which attracted 1,000 attendees. In 2013, WFS had ~15 full-time staff in Washington, DC. Unfortunately, they ran into financial difficulties circa 2015, sadly having never built an endowment, and were forced to let go all their full-time staff. A new management group purchased their assets in 2015, and they now operate out of Chicago. Since 2015, they have focused more on **societal and global foresight**, fostering collaborative discussions around the grand challenges facing humanity.

9. World Futures Studies Federation **(WFSF)**. Since 1973. Presently directed by academic and policy futurist **Erik Øverland**, WFSF is a professional association for roughly 300 academic futurists seeking to advance the field of futures studies (futurology). They run an Annual International Conference and an Online Centre for Pedagogical Resources in Futures Studies in partnership with UNESCO. They take an academic approach to foresight, and cover **all six domains**, with a particular emphasis on **societal and global foresight**. Originally heavy with Marxist thinkers, postmodernists, cultural relativists, and idealistic "revolutionaries" of various types, they have fortunately been returning to pragmatic, evidence-based, and Western liberal social democratic thinking. We recommend that foresight graduate students and educators join them.

10. International Futures Forum **(IFF)**. Since 2001. Directed by futurist **Graham Leicester**, they are a learning community that does consulting, workshops, and publications. IFF is a charity based in Scotland, with practice groups globally. They have worked with a wide variety of partners and clients addressing complex problems and the challenges and opportunities of the 21st century. They are strong in **whole systems thinking**, building a **learning organization**, and methods like the **Three Horizons Framework** (Chapter 5). Their Five Principles explain their philosophical approach. **Systems thinkers** will value their holistic approach to problems.

To all of our foresight students and leaders: Do you know of other **leading communities** improving **comprehensive foresight** around the world? Let us know, we'd love to publish **Top Twenty-Five** and **Top Fifty** lists. Learning-related organizations like TED, whose short videos offer engaging future insights in all six domains, and invite each of us to become public speakers via their TEDx network, would surely qualify for a larger list.

There are also many **professional associations** offering training in the **Twenty Specialties of Strategic Management**. While foresight specialty communities by definition do not aspire to do comprehensive foresight, there are always individuals and practice groups within them that take a particularly comprehensive approach.

In the US, depending upon our practice, we ought to consider joining groups like AIGA: The Professional Association for Design, the American Management Association, the American Planning Association, the American Society for Training and Development, the Association for Strategic Planning, the Association of Change Management Professionals, the Digital Analytics Association, the International Institute of Forecasters, the National Speakers Association, the Risk Management Society, the Society of Actuaries, the Strategic and Competitive Intelligence Professionals, or any of the other industry organizations listed in our online *Guide*.

By joining groups that most interest us—and volunteering, donating, attending their conferences, posting on their blogs, or engaging in whatever kind of participation best fits our needs and abilities—we can make a lasting impact on our field. In short: **Participate, don't spectate**. Foresight is an emerging field, and it can greatly use our help.

Foresight Training Options

The vast majority of foresight professionals are trained **informally**, both on-the-job and via conferences, workshops, and in self-study. Our field attracts individuals with undergraduate or graduate degrees in business, engineering, statistics, economics, the social sciences, journalism, the humanities, and just about every other discipline on offer. Such diversity is central to foresight. No matter the field, there are folks in it who are paid look to and analyze the future. For many practitioners, there eventually comes a time when they seek **formal training**.

There are three main training options in our field. They are:

1. Getting a **multi-day foresight certification**
2. Taking a **multi-week strategic foresight course**
3. Getting an **M.S. or a Ph.D.** in primary or specialty foresight

Each of these options requires an increasingly large commitment of time, energy, and resources. On average, higher levels of commitment, if accompanied by higher levels of personal effort, will result in deeper and more valuable professional connections. Not all of us need a broad network of foresight practitioner connections however. Often a narrow and specialized network, built within our practice specialties and industries, is more valuable for our careers and impact. We must ask ourselves which level of foresight training best suits our current needs. Starting with light initial training, but in a high quality program, is often the wisest choice.

1. Multi-Day Foresight Certifications

There are a small number (at least twelve, by our count) of formal foresight certificate programs, ranging from five days to ten weeks in length. These, and standalone foresight courses, are good entry points for foresight training.

The University of Houston's foresight graduate program offers a popular five-day certificate in strategic foresight. The European Business School, University of Manchester, and University of Oxford also offer five-day programs. Singularity University offers a variety of programs for managers and entrepreneurs. Draper University is an entrepreneurship training program, started in 2013 by venture capitalist Tim Draper, with a ten-week residential and shorter executive and startup programs, which introduce futures research, ideation methods, and predictive analytics to entrepreneurs.

Six European foresight consultancies, led by Kairos Future in Sweden, offer an International Certified Future Strategist certificate program where students work on foresight consultancy projects as part of their training. The Turku School of Economics in Finland offers a nine day Certified Foresight Professional course. The World Future Society offers master courses during two days prior to their annual conference. The Association of Professional Futurists offers online and traditional professional development seminars. These are all great training options for incoming foresight professionals.

In addition to certification, those interested in strategic foresight consulting should **read widely** in their industry of practice, including **books on strategic foresight practice** (see Appendix 3). If they do organizational foresight, they should work through **case studies** in courses, books, and online libraries at top business schools, that describe organizational foresight challenges, strategic responses, and outcomes. If they are a consultant, they should consider engaging in case interviewing, which means analyzing **case studies under time pressure**, like a test, and with immediate feedback from an **evaluator-teacher**. At the beginning, such **rapid Do loops**, can be the fastest way to improve.

In case interviews, a student is given a question, problem, or challenge and asked to improve or resolve the situation, typically an organizational challenge that has occurred in real life. Good case studies assess general world and business knowledge, ethics, estimation, numerical and verbal reasoning skills, research, communication, empathy, and presentation skills. In short, they uncover our current capability to produce practical and influential business strategies and rough plans under time constraints—all key competencies of organizational foresight.

Cheng, 2012

Top business schools at Harvard, Chicago, MIT, and elsewhere have online **case study libraries**—many of which have strategic foresight components. We should read and analyze case studies in our industry of practice. **Victor Cheng's** *Case Interview Secrets*, 2012, and Caseinterview.com are great resources for case interview self-practice.

2. Multi-Week Foresight Courses

A few hundred foresight courses, on domain topics and on foresight methods and practice, are available from universities and other organizations globally. They are offered in both online and traditional formats. A number of small lists of foresight courses exist, but our field is presently in need of an **online global list of foresight courses** that fully represents our field's diversity of skills and methods.

One innovative new foresight course was **Singularity University's** Graduate Study Program (now called the Global Startup Program) started in 2009. It began as a ten-week program, and challenged 80 students from around the world to develop projects that could improve the lives of millions of people over ten years, by leveraging exponentially advancing technologies. They now offer a range of multi-week and multi-day executive programs, in person and online.

Singularity
University

Startup courses, like Plug & Play's Startup Camp, and startup MOOCs (massive open online courses) like Udacity's The Lean Launchpad and Coursera's Startup Engineering also offer multi-week training, but foresight is presently a minor component to these programs.

3. Foresight Academic Degrees

For those who want a formal academic degree in our field, there are presently twenty-three full-time graduate programs in general foresight topics and methods (M.S. and Ph.D. programs) available globally.

Our first two graduate programs in foresight emerged at the University of Houston, (M.S. only, since 1974, M.T. since 2014) and the University of Hawaii—Manoa (M.A. and Ph.D., since 1977). In the forty years since, close to thirty additional M.S. and Ph.D. programs in foresight have emerged globally, and the majority of these survive today. The strongest growth in foresight education, especially in certificate programs, has been in the last ten years.

U. Houston Foresight M.T.

Thirteen of these M.S. and Ph.D. programs teach in English, and ten in other languages. English-language graduate foresight programs now exist in **Canada** (Ontario College of Art and Design), **Denmark** (Aarhus U.), **Malta** (U. of Malta),

Finland (Turku School of Economics), **Germany** (European Business School), **Hungary** (Corvinus U.), **South Africa** (U. of Stellenbosch), **Taiwan** (Tamkang U.), and the **United States** (CA College of the Arts, U. of Houston, U. of Hawaii).

There are also non-English-language residency programs available in **Colombia** (EU Colombia) **France** (CNAM), **Germany** (Free U of Berlin), **India** (U Kerala), **Iran** (U Tehran), **Italy** (Leonardo Da Vinci U), **Mexico** (Monterrey IT), **Portugal** (U Lisbon), and **Taiwan** (Fo Guang). See FERN's list of **23 primary** (foresight-specialized) residency graduate programs, roughly **100 secondary** (foresight-related) foresight graduate programs, and a smaller number of **online**, **part-time** secondary foresight grad programs in 4U's wiki of foresight resources, **GlobalForesight.org**.

U. Hawaii Foresight
M.A. & Ph.D.

As we can see in the picture below, Asia, Africa, the Middle East, and Latin America all need more formal graduate and certificate training programs. This is a challenge for our students and leaders today. Humanity's emerging **global foresight culture** has to be built, location by location. We are building a **cathedral**, something beautiful but unfinished in our own lifetime. It may take another century to get our field to its maturity.

World Map of Primary Foresight Graduate and Certificate Programs

For the near-term future, our field would benefit greatly from **more low cost, high-quality online foresight degree and certificate programs**, both democratizing and demonetizing good foresight education. We might see online foresight degrees emerging from **innovative traditional institutions**, similar to the $7,000 Master's degree in Computer Science now available from Georgia Tech via Udacity. **Startups** might also produce a great **strategic foresight MS**, similar to the $10,000 MBA offered by Edtech startup Quantic. This is a great opportunity for a social entrepreneur. 4U would be happy to launch an MS program with the appropriate philanthropic funding, though it isn't our priority at present.

Foresight Impact Assessment and Competency Levels

How can we best **assess impact** in our foresight practice?

Public health futurist **Annette Gardner** has developed a helpful **foresight practice competency scale**. This scale is variation of the Knowledge, Attitude, and Practice (KAP) survey model for assessing professional competency, via quantitated surveys, based on the way the professional **enables behavior change** in their clients. The KAP model originated in public health, and is now being applied to other professional fields. It is client-centric, iterative, quantitative, and feedback-dependent, all great Do loop qualities for an impact assessment.

Below is **4U's adaptation** of Gardner's foresight impact competency scale language:

0 = No foresight – practitioner is fine with the status quo.

1 = Awareness of time, change, environment, the future, and basic aspects of complex systems, including **accelerating change** and **evolutionary development (evo-devo).**

2 = Interested in **learning foresight techniques**, and **connecting and learning with** other future-thinking practitioners, within our own industry, at least.

3 = Knowledgeable in some foresight models, methods, and frameworks, and **experienced** in applying some to ourselves or others, but not yet regularly applying **all** of the **Four Ps** or **Eight Skills**, in a **Do loop**.

4 = Individual change agent – experienced iteratively applying the **Four Ps** and **Eight Skills** to personal futures, and individually within the organization. A "developer" of individuals on teams.

5 = Group change agent – experienced engaging **teams and groups** to produce anticipatory (probable), creative (possible), aspirational (preferable), and defensive (preventable) foresight and change.

6 = Master teacher – able to **teach others to teach** foresight techniques, and to **help organizations** with leadership and policies that will grow and maintain good **foresight process** and **foresight culture**.

Not only should foresight professionals create positive, progressive, and adaptive change with their clients, ideally they will produce conditions that perpetuate such change. A master teacher, on the competency scale above, has made themselves particularly **redundant**, as an individual, in the system in which they practice. The client's processes and culture can now take care of themselves.

Now try a self-evaluation: Where would you presently **self-rate** on this impact competency scale? Where might your colleagues rank you? Your well-respected critics? Are you creating the conditions for a healthy set of **foresight processes** and **foresight culture** that is stronger than any individual? Is that the highest goal of your interactions with your clients?

Foresight Education: Opportunities and Challenges

How can we **make foresight education more relevant**, not only in **business** and **politics**, but in every field of human endeavor? How can we improve the **teaching of foresight**, in our organizations and schools, so that more people know its skills, domains, strengths, weaknesses, and where it fits in relation to **strategy and action**? Such questions have motivated us to write this *Guide*. For those considering a **formal education** in our field, or **training others** in their organizations or schools, this section may be of particular value.

With respect to university training, the value of most graduate foresight programs today is less in the skills learned, which are often **incomplete**. What is more valuable is the **self-commitment** and **reputation** we gain for taking the time to earn the credential or degree, and the lifelong **connections** we can make to a **community** of other talented folks who are **particularly motivated** to think about and improve the future, in all six domains.

Today, most foresight education programs are presently imbalanced with respect to the **Four Ps**. They typically neglect too many of the **anticipation skills** relevant to foresight (**probable futures**). Students don't learn to **predict, forecast, or think statistically and probabilistically** in some of the graduate foresight programs listed above. Some programs emphasize the **art of foresight (possible futures)**. Others emphasize its **politics (preferable and preventable futures)**. It is fine to have a focus, but all students should be able use and contrast **each of the Four Ps** to better navigate the future.

As foresight is such a nascent field today, typical academic programs work best for students who are **self-starters**, who are internally driven to better understand and guide change, and who enjoy working with a cognitively and skills-diverse community of visionary, critical and evidence-based colleagues. Individually, each of us can only see a small piece of what must and may lie ahead. Collectively we can see a much bigger picture. As student practitioners, in any program, we should be **introverted** enough to enjoy **producing** our own work, and **extroverted** enough to **share it regularly** for critique. By testing our methods, models, and insights against our colleagues, we can greatly improve them.

Most graduate foresight programs presently don't require **basic scientific literacy** of their students, or **strong verbal and analytical skills** as prerequisites, with remediation requirements, for entrants. Other serious academic disciplines have such prerequisites, and academic foresight education needs them too. Not only do our foresight programs need **higher entrance standards**, they must encompass more **diversity** of life and practice experience and cognitive traits. Based on what we know from **experiential (action) learning**, as advocated by futurist **Jose Ramos**, our programs should require students to do **several internships** during their training, for both internal and external clients.

With respect to the **Eight Skills**, most foresight training programs don't include much on **Learning** (research, intelligence), and they skimp on **Anticipation** (forecasting, risk assessment, investing, prediction). They are traditionally strongest in **Innovation** (scenarios, alternatives, uncertainties, design) and **Strategy** (visioning, preferencing, facilitation). Many don't do enough **Executing** (foresight production), **Influencing** (marketing their services), **Relating** (fitting in with other professional associations) and **Reviewing** (rigorous critique) of foresight products.

Because **every skill** of the Do loop reinforces the others, too many skill deficiencies creates a **vicious circle**. Too many of our graduate programs aren't regularly asking business, policy, defense, and other clients for **feedback** (review), allowing them to **prove their worth**. Their graduates don't know enough about **strategic management** to find their place in the **value chain**. This state of affairs has kept our graduate foresight programs small in number and slow to expand.

Most foresight programs today teach only a small subset of the domains, skills, specialties, models, and methods described in this *Guide*. Few seek to validate their preferred methods. Many foresight faculty have an **antiprediction bias**, stating that it is "not the job of foresight" to predict the future, when in reality, anticipation is a third (or fourth) of our job, and regular prediction is part of anticipation. All good programs must include some work on **prediction platforms**.

Many foresight programs are still more **top-down lecture** than they are **bottom-up elicitation** of the **student's foresight**, subjecting it to **peer and expert critique**. Leading MBA programs are always more **student elicitation and case work** than they are lecture, and academic foresight education must follow this example. Foresight programs, in those few universities where they exist, are typically both underfunded and poorly integrated with other disciplines within the university, including psychology, sociology, business administration, political science, public policy, engineering, etc. They are often poorly marketed to prospective students, and their enrollment numbers are quite small.

Part of the problem with academic foresight lies with **university leadership**, in our view. Leaders in most universities don't recognize how **fundamental** a topic foresight is to society, and the role that **academia**, even over business, must play to **ground and advance our field**, as with **other social sciences** (psychology, sociology, economics, etc.). **Psychology**, in fact, is an **ideal department** to host a good foresight program and foresight center, as **practical empirical research** can be done in how individuals and teams look to and analyze the future. See **Oettingen**, et al. (eds.), *The Psychology of Thinking About the Future*, 2019, for research on how we can we think well, or very poorly, about the future. None of this vital research is being conducted inside any **foresight degree program** at any university at present, to our knowledge.

University leaders who recognize the **value of foresight** to personal success and societal progress should integrate **basic foresight methods and content** into **all university courses**. They should use frameworks to **evaluate the quality of curricular foresight** and **of student-produced foresight** as well. There are a few benchmark models, like **Tamkang**

University in Taiwan, which requires all its undergraduates to take **three courses** on foresight methods or futures studies. But most universities do not require their students to learn the basics of even a third of the topics in this *Guide*.

In our view, every course that a student takes in the modern university should have some content and exercises asking the student to assess the **probable, possible, preferable and preventable futures** of that topic. Many textbooks have a **few pages** on "the future of x" at the end, and some professors charitably offer **one or two classes** on the future of their topic at the end of a ten- or fifteen-week college course. But treating foresight only as a **capstone**, not as a vital practice to be engaged in **throughout the course**, predictably yields **limited and low-quality** future thinking, discussion, and action. The future is **one third** of psychology's **Temporal Triad**. It deserves to be **integrated** throughout the **university curriculum**, and into every **learning and development** program in the organization as well.

We must also remember the **Open Secret of Foresight**. It is only useful to a point. Too much time spent thinking about or making strategy for the future in any course will have sharply **declining returns**. A good course will continually shift the student across the Eight Skills, balancing foresight and action. As for the foresight graduate programs themselves, they must all be **outcome-evaluated**. Faculty must continually ask: How did the learning, activities, resources, and communities of the program contribute, or not contribute, to the **future success** of the student and her organization?

Educator **Donald Kirkpatrick's** *Four Levels of Learning Evaluation* offers a good starter model for evaluating the value of **foresight education**, either in an organization or in a degree-granting school. Kirkpatrick was past president of the American Society for Training and Development (ASTD). He recommends that all learning programs cyclically evaluate themselves, and get externally evaluated, in four quantifiable ways:

1. **Reaction**. How did the student **feel and think** about the training? This should be quantified by pre-training and post-training surveys.

2. **Learning**. What **knowledge, skills, and attitude changes** occurred? This should also be quantified by pre- and post-training tests. For attitudes, assessments can be quantified using short-response questions.

3. **Behavior**. How did the student's **behavior change** as a result of training? This evaluation should be done "on the job," three to six months after training, to describe and quantify observable enduring change.

4. **ROI (Return on Investment)**. What were the useful **outcomes**, as a function of effort and money invested? What changes in job performance (ability), reward (pay, reputation), or adaptiveness (success) occurred? How could the program improve its ROI in any of its specific results? Does any other program offer a better ROI, specifically or generally, as a benchmark example for change?

Kirkpatrick tells us that levels three and four (Behavior and ROI) are best evaluated by **those impacted** by the training, as by a 360º performance evaluation, not by the trainers or even the students. If our foresight education programs do not provide such evaluations, we can **self-evaluate** by asking ourselves, our managers, and our direct reports these questions. If we don't like the answers, it's time to make changes until we do.

The longer we live, and the faster change goes, the more the most successful learners will be **autodidacts**, directing their own learning, and cultivating their curiosity, prioritization, and grit. A great starter book on self-learning is **Peter Hollins'** *The Science of Self-Learning*, 2018. We also recommend *Long Life Learning*, 2020, by entrepreneur **Michelle Weiss,** and *Academia Next*, 2020, by futurist **Bryan Alexander**. Weiss describes the need for corporate learning and development (L&D) programs to offer a **broad mix** of just-in-time microlearning, certificates, and formal programs, and to prioritize the **nonconsumers**, those who don't presently realize they need education, in their context. Alexander explores colleges and L&D programs as **complex adaptive systems**, and implications for education of **accelerating technological change**.

In *BPF*, we predict that the emergence of **Personal AI**, the first crude versions of which we expect in the 2030's, will be the greatest single learning development in human history. PAIs will enables each of us to **learn continuously**, and to increasingly **assess** education relevance, so we can **stay adaptive** in a world of accelerating change. We will increasingly come to see our "higher selves" as both biological and technological, and we'll use our digital selves to continue to learn, as adults, as rapidly as we learned when we were young children. This **network-centric, largely bottom-up AI future** seems implausible until you look at the **D&D trends** that are driving it forward.

In short, we must not overly rely on our universities, which are often well behind the curve, or our corporate L&D departments, which sometimes fear of losing workers to competition if they become too skilled, to be the lead architects of our learning journey. To learn the best we can, we must discover how to **direct our own learning**. For all of us, **most learning** throughout our careers occurs **informally** and **continually**, once we have the **right attitude and approach**.

At the same time, for the foresight field to fulfill its **great potential**, we will need more **M.S. and Ph.D. graduates** from our existing foresight graduate programs and from other disciplines, including psychology and self-learning, working in and starting **new degree-granting foresight programs**. We will also need a lot more **entrepreneurs** and **corporate L&D leaders** creating many more **foresight modules, courses, and certifications.** The more affordable and high-quality **foresight education programs** the world has, the more **powerful and impactful** our field becomes. For all its growing pains, we predict that our vital field will flower in coming decades. **Its future is bright.**

Our New Foresight Spring

Human civilization has had many peaks of interest in the future over the centuries. Some of these have been self-inflicted **positive manias or negative hysterias,** as in the apocalyptic visions as we neared our first millennium (read Lacey and Danziger's *The Year 1000*, 2002), and the very similar Y2K panic a millennium later. Other peaks have coincided with real impending threats. Most have been due to **rapid and disorienting technological or societal change**. When the public and organizational interest in the future is sustained and rational, we call it a **Foresight Spring**.

We argue that the period from **1960 to 1980** was America's most recent major foresight spring. This period started with President **John Kennedy's** New Frontier, a wave of idealism and big visioning. The politics and culture of this era responded to fear-inducing crises of the 1950s (nuclear escalation, duck and cover, Sputnik, the Korean War, the Cold War, HUAC) with aspirational ideas, movements and agendas. It experienced computerization, the Apollo space race, the Peace Corps, civil rights activism, the counterculture, women's rights, environmentalism, and other new thinking and experiments. In this context of disruptive change, **foresight practices** and **foresight communities** flourished.

Many of our modern think tanks, academic programs, and professional organizations emerged in this era. The World Future Society (WFS), the first large public futures association, was founded in 1966. Their WFS conference peaked in attendance around 5,000 in the early 1970s. As futurist Glen Hiemstra describes, at WFS 1980, the futurist **Buckminster Fuller** ran a massive World Game workshop, asking participants to envision how to shift the world's political systems **"from weaponry to livingry."** Such activities marked the **end of an era of bold visioning** by futurist associations. The rise of **neoconservatism** and a return to **materialism** in the 1980s made foresight more suspect, narrow and political. By the 1990s, WFS conferences had fallen to 800 increasingly elderly attendees, and the field was well into its latest Winter.

But since the advent of the smartphone in 2008 and the Great Financial Crisis in 2009, and particularly since the emergence of technology unicorns in 2011 and deep learning AI in 2012, we have entered a new **Foresight Spring**, a time of both rapid technological and societal change and rapidly rising public and professional interest in futures thinking and in foresight practice. We would average these disruptive events to call the year **2010** the start date of this latest spring. Perhaps it too will run for twenty years. The COVID-19 pandemic since 2020 has only heightened our foresight interest, as some of the most densified and dematerialized sectors of our economy have been greatly accelerated and enriched because of this catastrophe, while others have been hit hard and tragically, creating more societal inequality than ever. In response to all this new ADOR, there is a great deal of new work happening in organizational foresight specialties like forecasting, analytics, risk management, innovation management, planning, entrepreneurship, design, and intelligence.

Among the foresighted responses to the pandemic have been **new entrepreneurship,** aided by time at home and government subsidies, **new habits in remote work, learning, and telepresence, new flexibility of work and learning, new standards for work/life balance,** and **new capacities for biosurveillance and mass immunity** against future pathogens. The great majority of today's youth, growing up as **digital natives,** all expect exponential technical and entrepreneurship progress to continue. Many promising developments are minimally reported by our DROA-biased media, for example, when Sections III and IV of the JOBS Act became law in 2015, Equity Crowdfunding (Crowdfounding) became a **new source of funding for startups,** and a **new investing modality** for everyone. For the first time, average, non-accredited investors were able to invest in small companies via online platforms. As platforms for evaluating and recommending such small businesses to the average investor improve in coming years, small business entrepreneurship funding, and founder visions to create useful personal and local futures, will surely improve.

Online foresight communities are also flourishing. **Reddit's r/Futurology,** the largest online community for posting and commenting on societal and global foresight material, has grown to **15 million subscribers** as of 2020, with millions of monthly active users. The **frequency and pervasiveness of general futures thinking** in the US, among the public, may now be greater than it was in our last **Apollo-era heyday.** Unfortunately, given the rise of **plutocracy,** the distractions of **affluence,** the **dumbing-down of our media,** and the **erosion of our schooling standards,** the **average quality** of future thinking—but not the **top quality**—has also arguably declined since that era. The distribution of quality has widened.

Nevertheless, just as the European Renaissance (literally, "rebirth") gave birth to our modern sciences, every **Foresight Renaissance** (aka, Foresight Spring) **has acted to establish parts of our field more firmly in science.** Today this progress is happening in fields like psychology, neuroscience, economics, and our models of prediction, collective intelligence, machine intelligence, and prediction platforms. The scientific method isn't one method, but a **collection** of methods and models, the first of which emerged in the 17th century, and which matured into the set of enterprises we now call science. Likewise, foresight isn't one method, but a **collection** of useful methods and models, many of which will mature, with the help of AI, perhaps mid-21st century, into a set of grounded qualitative and quantitative **social and technical sciences,** disciplines that can be creative, anticipatory, and managerial as appropriate.

Society can be analyzed from a wide range of disciplines, anthropology, biology, chemistry, cognitive science, development, economics, engineering, evolution, complexity, computation, cybernetics, information theory, linguistics, physical sciences, psychology, semantics, statistics, and systems theory, to name just a few. These and other sciences are improving their methods and models, inevitably leading us to better understanding and anticipation of **societal systems.**

Many developments are taking analysis in a more scientific and quantitative direction. Most obvious are the **accelerating changes in information technology** since the mid-1990s, including the rise of the web, simulations, maps, sensors, mobile and wearable tech, social networks, enterprise software, cloud computing, and many other developments. These **permanent changes** in our computational and collaboration abilities, explored in Book 2, mean that ever more of the world is quantified, visualized, evidence-based, and statistically predictable. We are even seeing promising developments in economics, a social science that is finally becoming **usefully predictive** as it begins to understand and model technical productivity. See **Brynjolfsson** and **McAfee's** *The Second Machine Age,* 2014, for more on that story.

As our models and evidence gathering proceed, foresight practice will continue to evolve and develop. **Evolutionarily,** it will continue to split into **competing schools,** each with their own conflicting views of the future. Such disagreements are healthy, and they generate pressure for each school to clarify its assumptions and theory. As we seek experiments and evidence that will resolve our disagreements, we also get better **developmental foresight.** Not only do we learn to see and respect the uncertainty of many **evolutionary possibilities,** we learn to see and respect the high statistical probability of certain **developmental destinations,** waiting to emerge. We see more of both **our futures** and **our future.**

What Will Our Contribution Be?

The 21st century is a very exciting time to be a foresight professional. If <u>accelerating change</u> continues, humanity will experience more scientific and technological change before the end of this century than has occurred in all human history to date. How our new scientific knowledge and technical capabilities will affect business and social domains in the next generation is difficult to guess, though we'll make a few attempts throughout this *Guide*.

So far, we've seen that every year more scientific, technical, business, and social processes, trends, and events are becoming either **intuitively or statistically predictable**, and there are more tools, techniques, and people managing **uncertainty and risk**, and doing foresight work for **profit and benefit** ever before. All these folks must increasingly communicate, share knowledge, teach each other, and professionalize.

Professional foresight is today a lightly connected, and often misunderstood field. Yet as our Web gets smarter, as the <u>internet of things</u> emerges, as our <u>robots</u> proliferate, as we hit <u>Peak Oil Demand</u>, <u>Peak Population</u>, and <u>Peak Pollution</u>, as emerging nations move rapidly to lifestyles of the industrialized nations, as digital governance, digitally-aided activism, and climate change continue, as science decodes the mysteries of biological intelligence, morality, and empathy, and as we increasingly create <u>learning machines</u> that can both **evolve and develop**, we can confidently foresee a continued flux of major disruptions ahead. People need help **navigating all this change** more today than ever before.

This book's lead contributing author, **Susan Fant**, directs the <u>Foresight Education and Research Network (FERN)</u>, a free onramp to foresight education, practice, and research. We created FERN to help more people engage with and appreciate foresight's value. FERN launched <u>GlobalForesight.org</u>, the first online wiki for foresight students, grads, professionals, and advocates, it runs the 5,600 member <u>Global Foresight discussion community</u> on LinkedIn, and it produced a *Foresight Careers* conference in 2013, at which we decided to do this *Guide*. We are now folding FERN into Foresight University as we enter the next phase of our own foresight journey. What will you contribute to our vital and still underserved field?

Some say foresight work is no better than <u>gambling</u> on random events. But, even random individual events can frequently (pun intended!) be described as probabilities when viewed from a collective perspective. Games of chance taught us this in the 1600's, and **Earnest Rutherford's** models of <u>nuclear decay</u> in 1907 did so again with natural systems. We must get beyond our **antiprediction bias**. Many individually random natural, social, economic, and technological events happen inside a **framework of probabilities and other constraints** on their **collective and network behavior**.

Increasingly, foresight professionals are finding those probabilities and constraints, discovering possible alternatives within known constraints, and learning more of the **forecasting rules** helpful in various **societal games**. All of this will slowly but steadily improve our odds of predictive success. Better forecasting and prediction are key skills of not only of great gamblers, statisticians, and scientists, but of great investors, planners, innovators, managers, and leaders. Those who fail to realize this fact will increasingly be at a disadvantage to those who do not have an antiprediction bias.

Academics, technologists, businesses, institutions, and the general public are slowly warming to the idea that with a little effort and <u>evidence-based practice</u>, much better **marginal foresight**, in each of the **Four Ps**, is often achievable at moderate cost, foresight that can provide great personal, team, and organizational advantage. For the future-focused self-starter and active learner, foresight practice opportunities are everywhere, once we know how to look for them.

The going won't always be easy. Most organizations still don't understand the **breadth** of foresight practice already occurring today, or its **promise** once we make it more conscious and deliberate. It may be a decade or two yet, and more powerful digital foresight tools and platforms, before our field becomes more w idely known, and foresight jobs and training explode. In the meantime, **success** in a foresight career requires sound **ethics**, good **empathy**, an ability to unearth and frame the hidden **foresight problems** of our clients, **humility** in the value and limits of our methods, and yet a **strong belief** that our content and methods can help our clients achieve better strategy, planning, and action.

Foresight practitioners must remember they are <u>pioneers</u>, explorers, trailblazers in a **new** and sometimes **hostile** frontier. The **vistas** can be breathtaking, but we must be cautious. If we stray too far afield in our work, we risk getting shot down by critics and ending up with our face in the dirt and arrows in our backs. Many organizational leaders are legitimately skeptical of our still-developing methods and value. We are sometimes called impractical <u>idealists</u>, <u>quacks</u>, self-appointed <u>gurus</u>, <u>shamans</u>, or <u>con artists</u>. A few **rogue futurists** do fit these descriptions (see the Student Edition for a sample of dysfunctional futurist types), and we need to challenge shoddy thinking and behavior from our colleagues, especially when it has influence. But, by and large, we are a practical, curious, courageous, humble, evidence-seeking and ethical community.

Albert Bierstadt, *The Oregon Trail*, 1869

As good pioneers, we must learn to **support and rely on each other** and to effectively <u>circle our wagons</u> and fight for our causes when conflict comes. By helping each other to continually improve our practice, and being vigilant and responsive to criticism and challenges, we will assuredly settle the foresight frontier. We will turn our field into a mature and vital set of professional and academic disciplines, and be successful at navigating ever more complex and interesting futures. We can each **do our small part** today to grow our field, to learn from and support each other, to help our clients cope with the now and the next, and very importantly, make time to **enjoy the journey** together.

Welcome to the Profession!

Chapter 3: Adaptive Foresight – Essential Tasks and Skills

This chapter takes us deeper into essential **personal and team** tasks and skills of **adaptive strategic foresight,** for working professionals in any industry. It sets us up for discussing **organizational foresight** in the next two chapters.

The Many Faces of the Evo-Devo Pyramid: The Four Ps in Universal Context

The most universal model we have proposed for foresight practice and process, besides the **Do Loop,** is the **Four Ps,** and the **Evo-Devo Pyramid** from which they derive. Let us return to that pyramid now, and see the most foundational ways can view the **essential tasks of foresight work.** We have claimed that good practitioners strive to see and use these **four future thinking types.** We must rise above any **personal bias** we may have to **oversimplify our foresight,** by preferring to spend more time with just one, two, or three of these types. We must do our best to **see and master all four,** using each type with a depth and power appropriate to our particular **foresight context.** In their simplest form, here they are again, as the **Classic Foresight Pyramid,** presented in our recommended **initial order of operations**:

1. **Probable Futures** (constraint- and uniformity-generating, predictable, secure, expected, familiar)
2. **Possible Futures** (freedom- and variety-generating, unpredictable, creative, alternative, novel)
3. **Preferable and Preventable Futures** (individually or group-preferred values, goals, and agendas; avoidable mistakes, blocks and setbacks)

The Four Universal Future Thinking Types (the Four Ps)

Many future thinkers will **take sides,** when discussing a topic or system, on the question of whether "**one future**" or "**many futures**" lie ahead. They assume that **only one** of these **states of reality** can be true. **Evo-devo thinking** tells us that **both perspectives are always true,** for every complex system and environment. A much more useful question is to ask how we can **better determine** what is **predictable** and what is **unpredictable** in the variables of any process, event, or system relevant to our **strategy.** We must learn to simultaneously see the constraints of the **probable** and the freedoms of the **possible,** and then derive those **preferable and preventable futures** that seem particularly **adaptive.** Well-balanced strategic foresight frameworks like the **Four Ps (REOPS cycle),** and **ADOR analysis,** when combined with normative foresight models like the **IES Goals,** can help us greatly in that regard.

Let's now revisit the **Modern Foresight Pyramid,** which tells us that to produce good foresight, we must make **four complementary future assessments.** Working left to right, bottom to top, the pyramid tells us it is typically best to begin with **probable** foresight, then explore the **possible,** then the **preferable,** and finally the **preventable.** We've said that futurist **Alvin Toffler** described the Classic (Three Ps) Foresight Pyramid in *Future Shock* in 1970, that **Roy Amara** developed it further in the 1980s, and that **Art Shostak** gave us the modern (Four Ps) pyramid in 2001. Here it is again:

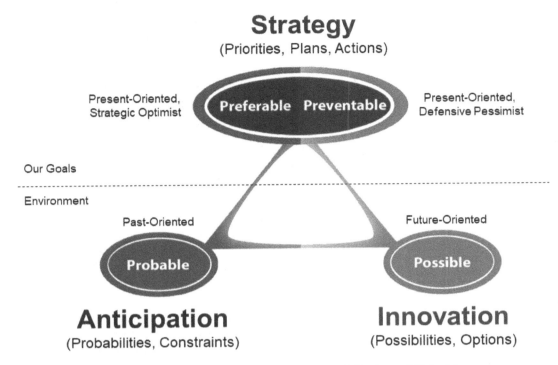

Strategy
(Priorities, Plans, Actions)

Present-Oriented,
Strategic Optimist

Preferable   Preventable

Present-Oriented,
Defensive Pessimist

Our Goals
- -
Environment

Past-Oriented

Probable

Future-Oriented

Possible

Anticipation
(Probabilities, Constraints)

Innovation
(Possibilities, Options)

The Four Ps (Three Skills) of Future Thinking

Whether we prefer to think of this pyramid in terms of the **Four Ps**, or more simply, as the core **AIS skills**, we should recognize their **relationships**, and that the **first two** are both **more fundamental** and will be **less valued** by our clients.

Many others have seen this pyramid as well. The eminent technology forecaster **Hal Linstone** offered a triadic perspective in *Multiple Perspectives for Decisionmaking*, 1984. Editor of the journal *Technological Forecasting & Social Change*, Linstone **saw forecastable technological change** as the top driver of **probable futures**, **personal change** as the top driver of exploratory, unpredictable, **possible futures**, and **organizational change** as the leading system driving **preferable futures**. Futurists **Gross and Singh**, in "Adventures in Learning," 1987, also describe **small-group leadership** with this triad. They observed that leaders in small groups tend to be Laissez-faire (Possibility oriented), Authoritarian (Probability oriented), or Democratic (Preference oriented). In our view, these and other scholars are all describing **different versions of the Evo-Devo Pyramid**, the three most fundamental processes complex systems use to adapt to change.

The **Evo-Devo Pyramid** tells us that life and its **preferences** have **emerged, over universal history,** from a special fusion of the laws of **possibility** and **probability**. What intelligent beings think should and should not happen is always a **mix, and special subset,** of two more **fundamental** processes: what **could happen** and what **will happen**, based on the physical and informational laws of complex systems. The **Evo-Devo Pyramid** is our interpretation of the science and philosophy of **evo-devo biology.**

Note that the Evo-Devo Pyramid (below) has its **base reversed** from the Modern Foresight Pyramid. That is because **evo-devo theory**, as its name implies, begins with thinking about evolutionary process, and then developmental process. This is understandable, since, on average, **95% of observed change** is going to **look evolutionary** (unpredictable) for any complex system, and only 5% **will look developmental** (predictable). This 95/5 ratio can also cause us to think of the world as purely **evolutionary** (unpredictable, contingent), missing developmental processes entirely. But while the **order of thinking about these processes influences what we see**, and while we think **Devo-Evo biology** would be a better name both for this field and the pyramid, we will stick with conventional names. What matters most is **seeing the**

pyramid in reality, in all its dimensions, including **normative dimensions.** Learning to balance and regulate this pyramid is the **essence of adaptiveness**, and of **adaptive leadership**, in our view.

The pyramid below depicts three sets of **complex actors, functions, and goals** that are central to human collectives:

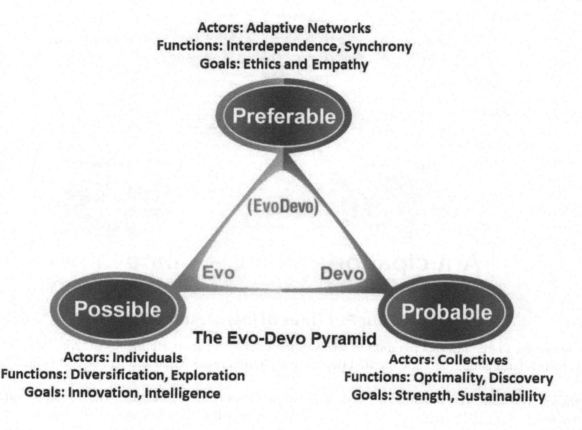

This **Actor-Function-Goal version** of the **Evo-Devo Pyramid** is easily derived from the writings of the theoretical biologists, ecologists and philosophers publishing in this new field of **evo-devo biology.** Several scholars in this field including **Stan Salthe, Eva Jablonka, Richard Reid,** and **Denis Noble** have observed that **all living systems** have two competing sets of **genes, phenotypes, and environmental factors**, managing **two opposing processes**, to create a third, emergent process. Let's briefly discuss each process now.

The first set of biology's most fundamental processes, which we can call the **evolutionary processes,** help life to **explore possibility.** These processes create diversity, experiments, and innovation, in contingent and unpredictable ways. Both the arrangements and the composition of an organism's genes, phenotypes, and environmental factors vary greatly over generations. The second set of fundamental processes, the **developmental processes**, help life to express **probability,** the predictable emergence of protective future complexity. Our developmental genes, phenotypes, and stable environmental factors—including the physical and informational laws of our universe—are **highly conserved, constraining and additive** over generations. They reliably converge organismic and societal complexity on a hierarchy of (in principle) future-predictable forms and functions.

These two processes **work together** to produce a third thing, a **self-maintaining, self-reproducing "evo-devo" network**, a system engaged in continual **life cycle.** Only **evo-devo systems** are capable of generating **preferences, positive and negative.** That makes this pyramid a **basic model of life,** and we expect, of every other **replicating complex adaptive system** in our universe.

Table 1 below summarizes some of the many ways we can see the **operation of evo-devo processes in nature and society.** It may be the **most important set of convergent insights** in this *Guide*. The more of these sets of evo-devo relationships that we can **see, use, improve, and balance**, in ourselves and on our teams, the more adaptive we can become.

The Evo-Devo Pyramid	Evolution	Development	Evo-Devo
Physical Laws & Processes	Quantum Physics, Chaos	General Relativity, Thermodynamics	Natural Selection, Complex Adaptiveness
The Foresight Pyramid	Possibility	Probability	Preference & Prevention
Foresight Terms	Futures	Future	Complexity
Foresight Skills (Core)	Innovation	Anticipation	Strategy
The Time Pyramid	Future	Past	Present
The Sentiment Pyramid	Optimism	Pessimism	Realism
Decision Styles (Kirton)	Innovator	Protector	Bridger
Temperaments (Keirsey)	Artisan	Guardian	Idealist, Rational
Business Styles (Deloitte)	Pioneer	Guardian	Driver, Integrator
The Values Pyramid	Beauty	Truth	Goodness
The Leadership Pyramid	Fox	Hedgehog	Eagle
Leadership Tendencies	Laissez-Faire	Authoritarian	Democratic
Reasoning Method	Induction	Deduction	Abduction
Scientific Approach	Empiricism	Theory	Utility
Dynamic	Divergent	Convergent	Integrated
Functions	Diversification, Exploration	Discovery, Optimality	Interdependence, Synchrony
IES Goals	Innovation Intelligence	Strength Sustainability	Ethics Empathy
Social Values	Freedom, Creativity, Insight, Diversity	Power, Security, Order, Truth	Esteem, Love, Conscience, Judgment
Social Goals	Experimenting Innovating	Discovering Protecting	Prioritizing Coordinating
Societal Roles	Entrepreneur Creative	Academic Defense	Consultant Manager
Drivers (Linstone)	Personal	Tech & Environment	Organizations
Leading Actors	**Individuals**	**Collective (Envir.)**	**Networks**

Table 1: The Many Faces of the Evo-Devo Pyramid

To recap, evo-devo theory tells us that:

1. **Growing diversity, innovation,** and **individual intelligence (people, groups, societies)** are key goals of **Evolutionary processes** in nature and society. These **divergent** processes explore **Possible** futures.

2. Growing **collective strength, security** and **truth (predictability)** are key goals of **Developmental process** in nature and society. These **convergent** processes find and maintain **Probable** futures.

3. The **95/5 Rule** (aka the 19:1 Ratio, which we round to the **"20:1 Ratio"**) tells us that while **evolutionary** and **developmental** processes seem **equally important to adaptation, evolutionary processes** can be *observed operating*, in complex systems, roughly **twenty times more often**. This is of course only a gross estimate.

4. These two processes, when used in **intelligent networks**, compute a set of **shared preferred visions, ethics, empathy, and values**, and shared **preventable futures** that adaptive systems seek to avoid.

As we'll discuss in *BPF*, **evo-devo models** can be given a single name, **networkism**. **Networkism** is a **worldview** that asks us to take a **network-first, evo-devo perspective** on both systems thinking and adaptiveness. It is a term that posits that all the most adaptive complex systems on Earth are **evolving, self-reproducing and self-maintaining complex networks,** under **selection**. Such networks regulate their intelligence via both evolutionary and developmental processes. **Ecologies** are evo-devo networks, the **human body** is a complex network of cell types and organ systems, our **brain** is a network of neural modules and ensembles, our **societies and economies** are complex networks of communication, ideas, behaviors and technologies, and now, our **leading AIs** are evolving and developing into such networks themselves. The **logic** that our AIs can deploy within their neural networks will have sharp limits by comparison to the complexity of the future, just as our own biological logic is limited. When logic fails, their neural networks will have also have to use **intuition** and **emotion** to guide them, just like us. Our coming AIs will **learn how to feel** complex forms of **strategic optimism** and **defensive pessimism**, about everything, just like us. They will have to **manage Four Ps conflicts** in their own minds and on their teams, just like us. They will be **bound by evo-devo processes** in nature, just like us.

In our view, both the **future of network science**, and the **future of AI** will require recognizing the **evo-devo nature of adaptive networks** in complex systems at **all scales**, from complex molecules to complex societies. For one example of this research frontier, **Cesar Hidalgo** at MIT, has developed measures of **economic complexity** that **accurately predict** the way dense, specialized, and diverse **networks of people**, both physical (cities and supply chains) and virtual (online networks) are growing out of originally sparse networks as they learn to innovate and produce economic value. His lay book, *Why Information Grows: The Evolution of Order from Atoms to Economies*, 2017, and his technical book, *The Atlas of Economic Complexity: Mapping Paths to Prosperity*, 2014, both describe his findings.

Hidalgo's team predicts the **economic value** produced by cities using two primary measures. An **evolutionary and "individual" measure**, that quantifies the **diversity** of knowledge contained in a physical or virtual network, and a **developmental and "collective" measure**, that assesses the **density of informational complexity (specialized** and **hierarchical knowledge)** contained in the network. Each measure is related to the other. One cannot get **highly specialized individuals, organizations, or societies,** producing the highest per capita economic value, without **great density and diversity of individuals and knowledge types (relative to each specialization)** within the network.

Restating this work in our own **hypothetical universal model**, we'd say **Densification** (the ever-growing Spatial, Temporal, Energetic and Material (STEM) density and efficiency of leading network interactions), always promotes **Dematerialization** (an ever-growing STEM-substitutability of network information, communication, and computation). We call the two together **"D&D"**. In *BPF*, we will explore how **D&D megatrends drive accelerating change**. We don't think we can **escape these megatrends**, or **prevent the emergence** of human-surpassing and lifelike AI. We can only **guide** these processes along **better or worse paths**. Said simply, we control their **evolution**, but not their **development**.

Work in **network science**, led by places like the Santa Fe Institute and MIT, makes clear that the **better our virtual telecommunications get**, the denser, more dematerialized, and more diverse interactions will win out over sparse and physical interactions. We've seen the acceleration of these D&D processes during our recent global pandemic. One clear D&D megatrend is the further exponential concentration of economic power in our **largest and densest urban areas** over our rural areas. Less obvious to some is that **middle-sized cities** with particular **industry specializations**, when connected well to other such cities with those same specializations, will greatly outcompete generalist large cities, as all cities run up against rising costs and limits to growth. **Usefully specialized small cities, towns, firms, teams, groups, and people** will do very well in the far more digitally connected, diverse, network environment of the 21st century.

Fully virtual networks will also be economic leaders, when they **densely link** diverse and complex practitioners around any persistent product, service, or problem. That of course is what our better-run **multinational corporations** try to do today. They become **network specialists**, not simply conglomerates. It is the useful **diversity, density, and complexity** of our knowledge, labor, technical, economic and political networks, and the **empathy and rulesets** that maintain that complexity, that are at the heart of adaptiveness. Such factors can be defined, measured and improved, with appropriate systems thinking. While they are speculative today, we hope you find evo-devo models helpful in your foresight journey. Knowing **what variables matter most** is one key to becoming a more effective and adaptive foresight professional.

The Seven Tasks of Professional Foresight

Journeying to Better Futures, Using the Seven Tasks (REOPS, Action, and Review)

The **simplest practice framework** that we recommend for foresight professionals combines the **REOPS cycle** (Learning and the Four Ps) and the **Do loop**, two **universal** models of **integrated foresight and action**. As the Four Ps tasks derive from the Evo-Devo Pyramid, it includes management of **sentiment, goals and values** as well. We call it the **Seven Tasks of Professional Foresight**. The tasks are simply the five REOPS steps of foresight production with two final steps, facilitating **client Action and Review**. These tasks remind us of our **top professional responsibilities**, to ourselves and our clients. We use the term **"client"** here to refer to whoever is asking for foresight work, in any context.

According to the **Seven Tasks**, an effective foresight professional must become good at:

1. **Learning (Research).** The first task of any good foresight professional is to help their client **acquire relevant learning** about their past and present environment that may be particularly useful to their problem and future. It begins with learning what problem their client thinks they need solved, or what service they have requested. It also includes research, horizon scanning and intelligence, and may involve reassessment of the problem or service as a result of what is learned. It may also include helping their client improve learning motivation and capacity, and building good learning habits, and a learning culture.

2. **Anticipation (Expectations).** The professional's second task is to help their client uncover aspects of the **probable future** that may be relevant to the problem, service, strategy or action. This includes helping their client to recognizing trends and constraints, critiquing and discounting unlikely futures ("reducing uncertainty"), making forecasts, advising on bets, finding convergences, and when probabilities seem high, making predictions.

3. **Innovation (Options).** The professional's third task is to help their client to better imagine and create aspects of the **possible future** relevant to the problem, service, strategy, or action. This may include helping the client with creative and design thinking, prototyping, brainstorming, scenarios, wildcards, and other kinds of alternative futures generation.

4. **Preference Strategy (Priorities).** The professional's fourth task is to use a mindset of **prioritization** and **strategic optimism**, to help their client to better see and plan their most **preferable futures**. This may include helping the client, formally or informally, with visioning, goalsetting, decision analysis, stakeholder input, problem diagnosis, strategy creation, and the production of well-critiqued, actionable plans. Getting the space and mindset to see the most worthy opportunities may require client retreats, workshops, or other guidance.

5. **Prevention Strategy (Setbacks)** The professional's fifth task is to characterize plausible setbacks, shortcomings, and traps that might threaten their priorities and plans. Analytical frameworks like **ADOR (Advantage, Disruption, Opportunity, and Risk),** and **predictive and sentiment contrasting (the Four Ps)** can help greatly with **defensive strategy** creation. Getting the space and mindset to see the most plausible blocks and threats may again require client retreats, workshops, feedback, premortems, or other guidance.

6. **Facilitating Action**. After getting client buy-in to the foresight produced (via REOPS cycles, with quality review), the professional should **offer to help** the client or a designated partner **to act on foresight output**. This might include **conflict management** (the future is political), and assessing client capacities in **Execution, Influence, and Relating** (Gallup's core **action skills**). The professional must also become reasonably **competent** in these action skills themselves, to produce and distribute their own work. If they are working with top leadership, the professional might help the client **diagnose** needs and capacities across the **twenty foresight specialties,** or **coach** the client in important elements of **strategic management** (see Chapters 5-9 in the Student Edition of this book).

7. **Facilitating Review**. The foresight professional's final task is to help their client to **"close the loop"** after action has occurred. They must **review the results** of their efforts with these tasks, after an appropriate **interval**. In this last task, the professional must **solicit client feedback** on both the **quality of the foresight** and the **action** that did or did not result. Was the foresight **effective** in the **short-term**? Was it **adaptive** over the **long-term**?

Some foresight professionals think the last two tasks, and especially formal engagement with the **Four Action Skills** (Execution, Influence, Relating, and Reviewing), are not part of our job. But, they are. The best foresight work doesn't end with **inputs to strategy**, with offensive and defensive **strategy creation**, or even with well-built, **actionable plans**. It always ends with **action and review**. Even if those producing foresight have little **influence** on action, we still have some influence, and we can always do **after-action review**. Doing this review for our own learning, and with limited client participation, is one level of professionalism. Getting clients to do it themselves, and checking up on their review, is an even better result. Review the **quality of action** that resulted allows us to **contextualize our work** in the context of the organization. We discover how we may do better the next time, and how our clients can do the same. By "closing our loops" with every engagement, not only our obvious loop of **foresight production** (the REOPS cycle) but by helping to close the loop of **client action and review**, we become far more valuable to those we serve.

It is often said that **ideas** (foresight products) are cheap, and **action** is dear. In truth, **both ideas and action can be priceless**, when they are **suited for the problem**, and are routed to and done by the **right people**, at the **right time**. Both **foresight and action** become their best only when they **work together**, in a continual **cycle**. We need all four steps of the Do loop to **"reduce uncertainty,"** as some foresight professionals like to say is their primary task.

As client trust grows in our work, some of our greatest value can come not just via our **foresight products**, but by **diagnosing** our client's strengths across the **Eight Skills,** and helping our clients to get better at **running their own Do loops, on every foresight horizon.** Our Eight Skills assessment (Appendix 1), can help with that. In Chapter 4, we'll delve deeper into each of the **Eight Skills of Adaptive Foresight**. They are key competencies that we think every **manager** and **leader** must have on their team, and the main **organizational foresight practice model** in our *Guide*.

Let us reflect for a moment on these seven tasks: Which are we currently best at? Do we presently work with others who are stronger in our weaker tasks? Do we have a good **"if-then plan"** to develop competency in our **weaker tasks**?

Knowing Our Place in the Value Chain: Strategic Specialization and Teaming

Recall our discussion of the **Twenty Specialty Practices of Strategic Management** in Chapter 1. These describe the many different foresight practices commonly found in larger or more complex organizations. Most professionals can only be competent in a few of these specialties. If we are asked to help with an organizational foresight problem, we must not only use good **strategic foresight process**, like the **LAIS skills (REOPS cycle)**, we must also be able to assess **foresight methods** and **practice specialties** which may be helpful to our client, but that we don't presently or cannot provide.

Consulting futurist **Luke van der Laan** says that one of the reasons the field of **strategic foresight** remains so **poorly integrated** into the rest of **management consulting** is that many "strategic foresight" practitioners **promise strategy production** for their client, but then they don't **deliver** actual strategy, or even **work with** their client's **strategy teams**. As a result, their engagements often fall short of client expectations.

As foresight professionals we must recognize that "strategic foresight" requires, at a minimum, the use and integration of **all four LAIS foresight skills**. For example, if we only prefer to do **trends and forecasting** (or more generally, **probable futures**), that is certainly **foresight work**, but we should not call this work *strategic* foresight. It is **anticipation**, one of four key skills that our client needs. If we only like to do **scenarios and alternatives**, we can again call that **foresight work**, but it is not *strategic* foresight. It is **innovation**, a form of structured creativity that finds an appreciative audience (a market of some size). It is fine for each of us to **specialize** in what we think we do best, but when we do, we have an **obligation to our clients** to help them see that they also need the **rest of the LAIS foresight skills**. Our clients need to understand and use **Do Loops**, and ideally, the **Eight Skills**. We in turn must pay attention to our **Seven Tasks**.

It is misleading, and a **disservice to our field**, for foresight professionals to offer a service that has "**strategic**" in its name if we don't actually **do strategy, or at least ensure that it gets done**. Remember our **definition of strategic foresight** from Chapter 1. If our work doesn't **create, confirm, or alter strategy**, it is not **strategic foresight**. Someone in the management value chain needs to ensure our work has this impact. Furthermore, to be minimally **adaptive foresight**, it *also* must **lead to action and review**—via the Do loop or the Eight Skills.

As **Richard Rumelt** says in his classic **Three-Step Model of Strategy**, all good strategy contains these critical elements:

1. a **diagnosis** of the status, opportunities and obstacles facing a system,
2. a **guiding policy** for the main goals and general direction, informing daily decisions,
3. a **coordinated set of actions** (subgoals, resource commitments, plans, incentives, measurements, consequences) to manage the guiding policy.

Rumelt, 2011

For more, see *Good Strategy / Bad Strategy*, 2011. As Rumelt says, if **a large majority of decision makers in an organization** can't describe the essence of their **guiding policy**, there really isn't yet a **true (collective) strategy** for the organization. Achieving all three elements requires a strong understanding of the **competitive environment** and the skillful use of the tools of **strategic management**. If a foresight professional is effective at **diagnosis**, but doesn't engage in the **remaining phases of strategy**, they should find and interface with colleagues or clients who can do this vital work.

Again, while every foresight professional should feel free to **specialize as they see fit**, ideally, every consultant will also be comfortable doing work on and facilitating conversations about **the Four Ps**. Predictive contrasting, followed by sentiment contrasting, and **positive and negative visioning**, should typically be done carefully in Rumelt's first and second steps of strategy creation. If the foresight professional precedes this with deliberate **learning** about past and present relevant to the diagnosis, they are doing the basics of **strategic foresight**.

If the foresight professional does not have the experience or training to produce good strategy, and is not familiar with the basics of **strategic management**, they must strive to **work with professionals who can do this work**, so that they can **ensure their foresight gets translated into real strategy, actions, and results**. In other words, knowing where we fit in the organization, both within the **Eight Skills** and the **Management Value Chain**, and working with the **best specialists**

we can within that value chain, is our key to having a **real impact with our clients**, and being treated with **respect** by our colleagues in management and leadership.

Some foresight professionals can produce good strategy, but many cannot. Many practitioners in our field prefer to focus on the production of **foresight documents**, **workshops**, **or facilitated events** where elements of the future are explored. Often, a few new initiatives, policies, and actions are recommended as a result of this work. Ideally, these outputs are well recorded, summarized, shared, and critiqued. Yet **none of this is a strategy**. It is simply a closing of one **Do loop**.

Many foresight professionals are quite **specialized**, both within the **Eight Skills** and within our core **four LAIS skills**. Specialization makes us particularly **competent**. But, we must also see the **bigger picture**, and understand how foresight translates to action. We must assess if our client's **Do Loops** are being run well, if any of the **Eight Skills** are being neglected, and which organizational foresight **practice specialties** are helpful, yet currently missing, in any engagement. In some aspects of our work, we must also **discuss values**, to help the organization to thrive.

Each skill itself may be best served by methods or practices that we ourselves are not good at. It is our job to identify what is needed, and help our clients get those solutions. Let's consider a few examples:

- For **Learning**, a foresight professional may specialize in practices like **horizon scanning** or **emerging issues analysis**, but not in useful others, such as **historical research**, **benchmarking** or **competitive intelligence**.

- For **Anticipation**, a foresight professional may do **Delphi**, **trend discovery**, **convergence mapping**, or **trait assessment**, but may not do **predictive analytics**, **forecasting**, **modeling**, **risk analysis**, or **prediction markets**.

- For **Innovation**, a foresight professional may like to do **creative visualization**, **scenarios**, **cross-impact analysis**, and **ideation**, but may not prefer to do **design thinking**, **opportunity assessment**, **morphological analysis**, **prototyping**, **ideation management platforms**, or **open innovation**.

- For **Strategy**, a foresight professional may be good at **facilitating preferable** and **preventable visions**, **prioritization**, **planning**, and **strategy gaming**, but not at Rumelt's three key elements of strategy (**diagnosis**, **guiding policy**, **coordinated actions**). Remember that many firms do not have a true strategy, but instead a loose set of **goals**, **plans**, **and slogans**. They may need a **strategy consultant** who can diagnose and fix this shortcoming, even more than they need other aspects of LAIS foresight.

There is also the matter of **client preferences** to negotiate. In practice, **any or all of the first three** of the **four LAIS skills**, while each are **critical precursors** to good strategy, may not **even interest** our clients. Clients usually care most about **strategy and planning**, or **what to do next**, and **how**. Some clients may not even care about the **process of strategy production itself**. They may instead favor open-ended or directed **strategy discussions**, creating **visions of positive (or negative) futures,** or any other activity that **alone** doesn't get us to **strategy itself**.

As **strategic foresight professionals**, we have to make sure our work doesn't end with **thought-provoking but soon forgotten or ignored foresight products, workshops, and events**, but take the necessary steps to help our clients **get to effective strategy, plans, action**, and **review**. To do this well, we must learn where we fit within the **Management Value Chain**, be able to diagnose where a team is weak on that chain, and be able to help our clients to recognize and get the critical **specialists and processes they need**. That is our **best recipe** for professional success.

Foresight Proof Points: Mastering the Four Foresight Skills

Let's now consider some **success examples**, aka "**proof points**", for **strategic foresight** done well, to help us better recognize good foresight work, in others, in ourselves and on our teams. These examples will focus on the **LAIS Foresight Skills**. Some will also give examples of **Action Skills**, as foresight must lead to effective action and review to be adaptive. We will explore organizational action in more depth in Chapters 4 and 5. But, keep in mind that such skills will be best covered in a **strategic management text**, not in this personal, team, and organizational **foresight text**. See Appendix 3 for several good books on strategic management.

For an **alternative formulation** of our LAIS strategic foresight model, we recommend the Future Today Institute's six-step **strategic foresight framework** (Chapter 5). It is implicitly LAIS-based, and it recognizes the centrality of **emotions in strategy production**, making it close to a **REOPS model** as well. In our view, these factors make it particularly deserving of your attention, as a complementary approach.

Our success examples in this chapter will span the **Self**, **Team**, **Organizational**, and **Societal (STOS)** practice domains. For simplicity, each example is typically considered with respect to just one, or a few, of the **Twenty Specialties**. Yet, just as adaptive foresight may require the use of many or all of the **Eight Skills**, many of these examples may require use the use of several of the **Twenty Specialties**, especially in large or complex organizations.

With these caveats, let's look at a few success examples, to see what can be accomplished with good foresight leadership, process and ideally, foresight culture on the team.

1. Learning Skill – Intelligence & Knowledge Management Specialty Focus

Examples: CompStat, Palantir, Intellipedia, Evidence-Based Management

Learning in the organization is most aided by three **foresight specialty practice pairs** in our model, **Accounting & Intangibles**, **Intelligence & Knowledge Management (KM)**, and **Learning & Development ("Training")**. Let's look now at a few generally recognized foresight successes in the organizational domain, focused mostly on the learning specialty of **Intelligence & KM**. We'll consider foresight examples from the other learning specialties in context throughout the *Guide*.

One 20th century **learning** proof point (Skill 1) in organizational **Intelligence & KM** which is also, secondarily, an **anticipatory** (data science, forecasting, security) proof point (Skill 2) can be found in CompStat, a platform originating in 1994 in New York City's Transit Police Unit for sharing crime statistics, resource management, tactical options, and feedback among law enforcement professionals in the unit. CompStat was originally called Charts of the Future, as it continuously tracked historical crime data and extrapolated future trends, initially via pins stuck on maps. It was the start in the US of what is now called **predictive policing**, or more generally, **intelligence-led policing**.

Under Chief **William Bratton**, CompStat was soon professionalized, and initially adopted in 77 precincts and 12 transit districts across New York City. It introduced statistical and predictive policing, crime mapping, weekly crime reports, and accountability of unit commanders for crime outcomes. It is also notable for incorporating broken windows theory, an evidence- and psychology-based criminology theory that focuses security professionals first on the most visible and easily fixable examples of crime, disorder, and anti-social behavior. Broken windows has occasionally been criticized as distracting our law enforcement from paying attention to more important community needs. This is incorrect. It is simply recognizing how environment shapes behavior, and that prioritizing visible and easy fixes to our environment, policing some of the more obvious effects of criminal behavior first, and giving the community voice and opportunity to help with such fixes, are good ways to quickly and measurably change the public perception of police competence, and to build trust that more complex problems can also be improved. An excellent (though self-congratulatory) account of CompStat's value in foresight, and some of the politics of its establishment, can be found in **Bratton and Knobler's** <u>Turnaround</u>, 1998. Their most recent book, <u>The Profession</u>, 2021 is also a candid and commendable account of US law enforcement's complex and checkered history in minority and race relations and community engagement.

Another powerful 21C Intelligence & KM platform, also primarily a learning and secondarily an anticipatory platform, is <u>Palantir</u>, founded in 2003. Palantir has developed an intelligence platform that they offer to military, intelligence, law enforcement, and civilian clients. It is a descendent of CompStat, though Palantir's platform does not yet have the same crime-reduction philosophy and management accountability features of its predecessor. Palantir built its first system <u>predicting and managing insurgencies in Iraq</u>, based on neural network fraud prediction software initially used at PayPal. It had demonstrable success in those applications. The company next applied their platform to law enforcement. It has not yet had the same level of success there, primarily due to ethical lapses. In that market, Palantir's leaders have exhibited insufficient transparency, including <u>not fully disclosing and getting prior public consent for its operation in New Orleans (2012-2018)</u>. The greater risk of **civil liberties infringement** for civil law enforcement use of such learning-predictive systems, makes it clear they need both greater **transparency** and **democratic oversight** to be successful.

Another 21C proof point for Intelligence & KM foresight is <u>Intellipedia</u>, the collaborative learning platform (wiki) established in late 2005 by **Chris Rasmussen** and other young analysts in the US intelligence community. Intellipedia was the first online KM system to get 16 different and compartmentalized intelligence agencies within the US to share their relevant classified knowledge with each other, on an ever-growing number of topics. It includes three classification levels, Sensitive, Secret, and Top Secret (specifically, just the lowest and largest rung of Top Secret). When first established, most senior officers expected it to fail, and some actively resisted it. Senior officers often prevented junior analysts from using it or citing it as a source, the way some teachers discourage the use of Wikipedia as a source, even today. But, within three years, Intellipedia had become a vital tool in intelligence knowledge management. Today every analyst, whether junior or senior, typically has a shortcut to it in their classified browser. It has vastly improved analyst knowledge of relevant history and current status of many of the most challenging topics in US intelligence. It has also become a "water cooler" for the many silos within the US intelligence community, as it offers a new way for professionals to share useful information and chat across the community, regardless of rank.

The ROI on launching a project like Intellipedia is clearly very large, were we to assess it based on community use, satisfaction, and learning. We might hope that its success would spur investment in the kind of <u>collaborative brief production and prediction platform</u> that was also originally envisioned as a feature of Intellipedia by Rasmussen, but never funded. In reality, the ordinary **politics and bureaucracy** of the defense establishment have caused it to move into any kind of anticipation function significantly slower than it might. Nevertheless, one can predict that a more Four Ps balanced platform will eventually emerge and be of great value in enhancing US security.

These learning proof points are focused on government, and the intelligence and security industries, as these are among John's clients, and they are often overlooked topics in civilian foresight work. But, there are many great examples of learning-driven corporate processes and cultures as well. **Evidence-based management** is one term scholars use to describe learning-driven organizations. **Marr and Davenport's** <u>The Intelligent Company</u>, 2010, introduces management tools (performance dashboards, balanced scorecards, KPIs, KPQs, intangibles surveys) that help leaders use **learning and facts** to guide their decisions. It gives examples of over a dozen companies, large and small, that use these tools well.

Google offers a particularly strong example of a learning-oriented, evidence-based corporate culture. They are constantly collecting data, and seeking to use the most evidence-based practices throughout the organization, in HR, R&D,

engineering, sales, and just about every other department. **Lazlo Bock's** *Work Rules!*, 2015, is a good overview of the **evidence-driven people management practices** Google uses to hire, manage, and retain talent.

IBM was once a strongly evidence-driven and R&D-based company, but it has begun to lose its way in recent decades, as **Robert Cringely** outlines in *The Decline and Fall of IBM*, 2014. IBM may be following a path that HP, GE and other industrial giants followed as they eroded their R&D-, evidence-, and learning-first cultures. It may yet turn around, but its window for doing so is closing. Microsoft, by contrast, has more successfully reorganized and renewed itself as a learning and innovation organization, and recognized that it must put value creation and customer and employee satisfaction at the center of its processes. Microsoft CEO **Satya Nadella's** *Hit Refresh*, 2017, offers an excellent (and self-congratulatory) account of their **learning-driven turnaround** in recent years.

2. Anticipation Skill – Forecasting & Prediction Specialty Focus

Examples: Verne, Clarke, Kahn, Kurzweil, Wells, Good Judgment Project, Predictive Analytics, Insurance

Anticipation is the classic skill by which foresight practitioners are **measured by the public**, after the fact. When we anticipate well, we can better explore possibilities and craft strategy to take advantage of what is likely to occur, often due to **processes far larger and more powerful than ourselves**, processes we can often only influence, not control. In our model, **organizational anticipation** is represented by five specialty practices, **Data Science & Machine Learning**, **Forecasting & Prediction**, **Investing & Finance**, **Law & Security**, and **Risk Management & Insurance**. Let's begin this section with a few anticipation successes, focusing on the most recognized practice specialty of **Forecasting & Prediction**. Let's also begin in a class of better known examples, anticipations published by **individual authors** of **foresight literature**. Then we'll discuss anticipation in organizations in each of the above specialties.

One 19th century example of commendable anticipation at the individual level is *Paris in the Twentieth Century*, 1863, by the then-young futurist **Jules Verne.** It was not published when it was finished, as the publisher who commissioned it deemed it **too far-fetched** for public consumption. It was eventually rediscovered in the 1990s in a family safe by Verne's great-grandson. *Paris* accurately portrayed large metropolitan cities, automobile culture, elevators, fax machines, a primitive internet, new weapons that would make World War unthinkable, suburbs, plutocracy, electronic music, homelessness, feminism, and mass entertainment culture, among several other insights.

Another great early 20th century publication on anticipation has the same title as the skill itself. *Anticipations: Of the Reaction of Mechanical and Scientific Progress Upon Human Life and Thought*, 1901, by another then-young futurist, **H.G. Wells**, was read widely at the time. Like *Paris*, *Anticipations* offers a broad set of accurate predictions and a much smaller set of culturally biased and flawed predictions, in various facets of **technology and society**. An academic biographer has described both the extent and accuracy of Wells predictions in this volume as "phenomenal."

Another lesser-known impressive and early 20th century work of **scientific anticipation** is *The Next Hundred Years: The Unfinished Business of Science*, 1936, by chemical engineer **Clifford Furnas**. It is a proof point for many brilliant predictions in **basic science foresight.** Science is not harder to predict than the other domains, as some foresight scholars have claimed. Like every field of human inquiry and action, science goes through **phases of greater and lesser predictability**, depending on whether **evolutionary** or **developmental factors** are more prevalent in its **growth dynamics** at the time. This work falls down on **social foresight**, due to its unrecognized cultural biases. Understanding **societal developmental megatrends**, discussed in Book 2, is a good way to adjust for the biases of one's particular time and culture. Until the late 20th century, a good case can be made that many major **political, legal, ethical, and societal megatrends** were harder to see than those in other STEEPLES domains. With the insights we gain from D&D, that is no longer true, in our view.

Another great set of anticipations is found in the work of the legendary science and science fiction author **Arthur C. Clarke.** We discuss Clarke's **three laws of prediction** in Book 2. Clarke had an aptitude and passion for learning about, popularizing and extrapolating science and technology, and a special interest in space futures. He also had a fearless imagination, and a humble, self-critical, open, and curious attitude. His aptitudes and passions, his personal qualities, and his twin professions as a science popularizer and science fiction author all likely contributed to his many successes as an anticipator of science and technology. His *Profiles of the Future*, 1958/84 is one of his best known anticipatory works.

As a young man, Clarke predicted the **geosynchronous satellite** in a technical article in *Wireless World* magazine in 1945. In *Profiles*, he brilliantly foresees an **electronic "global library"** (the web) arriving circa 2000 (he was just a few years off on its timing), **self-driving cars** that we interact with via **voice commands**, a proliferation of **passenger drones** ("VTOL passenger traffic"), and many other great calls. Perhaps his most important anticipation in this book is his discussion of the **imminent (eg, within a century) arrival of advanced artificial intelligence (AI)**, a topic he also explores in his novel and screenplay, *2001: A Space Odyssey*, 1968, one of the most influential science-fiction films of all time.

These are good examples of **sentinel foresight**, the common pattern that some thinkers—usually wide-reading and moderately polymathic in aspiration—will see aspects of the future well ahead of the rest of humanity. This is sometimes called **"genius foresight,"** but that is a less accurate and elitist term. History shows that **anyone is capable of sentinel foresight**. Having an outstanding IQ matters much less than being in the right place, at the right time, being receptive to insight, and trusting ones and others intuitions, over current cultural attitudes and biases.

We find **sentinel anticipatory technology foresight** in the writings of the cybernetics pioneer **Norbert Wiener** in the 1940s and 1950s, and economist and early computer scientist **Herbert Simon** in the 1950s and 1960s. Both of these individuals wrote about things like artificial intelligence, technological unemployment, and human-machine partnerships, far earlier and in many ways, **better and clearer** than most authors do today. When we take the time to revisit **original sentinel insights**, in any field, we can often see further and make better strategy today.

We define **fearless foresight** as future thinking that deals with **controversial but important topics**, and that makes **unpopular but potentially helpful predictions and value judgments** about the future. The professional futurist **Joe Coates,** who was not afraid to both **predict** and to **critique** his **clients and society**, exemplified this kind of thinking. Coates perhaps could have been nicer and more nuanced with some folks in his delivery, but his critiques were often just what was needed, at the right time, to expose the **hidden flaws or faulty assumptions** behind visions, arguments, strategies, or plans. All sentinel thinkers engage in fearless foresight at times, whether they intend to do so or not. Being **too far ahead of the curve** can frequently be controversial or unpopular. We want to learn to deliver fearless foresight, when we feel we must, with as much **empathy**, good **timing**, and **tact** as we can.

Perhaps Clarke's most **fearless prediction** in *Profiles* occurs in Chapter 18, **The Obsolescence of Man**. In that chapter, Clarke observes that technology, and particularly information technology, has already shown **vastly superior advantages in speed of "thinking", learning and capability improvement, and durability over biology**. He fearlessly states his view that intelligent, self-repairing, self-reproducing machines are inevitable. He recognized that a machine that can "think", and learn at the speed of electricity, **seven million times faster** than action potentials in our biological brains, and **simulate possible actions** at that astounding speed, must **increasingly drive** many aspects of our global future.

Once one realizes the **vast foresight and action differential**, between biology and technology, one **Big Question** becomes whether humanity will increasingly **merge with our machines,** so deeply that **"they" become "us."** This is called the **Humanoid hypothesis.** It posits the eventual **merger of humans and androids (humanlike technology).** That future seems **most desirable**, as it is the only one where (technologically augmented) **humans are still in charge.** Yet this hypothesis immediately begs a corollary **Big Question:** *how extensive* must this merger ultimately be? Must **humanity** become progressively **less biological and more technological** over time? Must this merger eventually birth a new, and **far more adaptive**, form of biologically-derived, but now purely **technological "life"**? That is the **Postbiological hypothesis**. We can find many insights in both hypotheses, and will consider them both in *BPF*.

Clarke also noted the great economic incentive to continue to improve **information technologies in particular**, over other technologies. It was clear even in 1960, though Clarke did not dwell on this scientific fact, that the laws of our particular universe, including quantum mechanics, make it curiously easy to create rapidly exponentially improving and increasingly miniaturized, information technology advances, and that this exponentiation will **dwarf all other technology progress dynamics** in its scope, power, and value creation. We'll explore that insight further in Book 2.

Clarke's anticipation is not perfect. No one's is. He did not **prioritize** the futures he imagined, based on their differential improvement rates. He says he was typically more interested in exploring possibilities (Skill 3, **Innovation**) than in anticipation. But if he *had prioritized*, he would have had to admit that **information technologies**, not the space technologies he so loved, would **increasingly drive our future**, unless **fundamental new sciences** were discovered.

Like all of us, Clarke's foresight was influenced by his **personal history**. He grew up just after the so-called '**Miraculous Years' of Science,** 1895-1930, a thirty-five year period when humanity discovered **many** astonishing and unexpected things in the **realm of the small**, including subatomic processes and their practical applications (X-rays, Roentgen 1985), nuclear reactions, and quantum physics, and a **much smaller number** of astonishing and unexpected things in the realm of the very large, including Special and General Relativity. See **Abraham Pais's** *Inward Bound*, 1988, for a great summary of how much weirder and more powerful our **"inner space" exploration** has proven, from a **physics perspective**.

Clarke can be forgiven for imagining that world-changing scientific discoveries might continue in coming decades. He imagines some of those futures in fanciful chapters on topics like antigravity, time travel, teleportation, and invisibility. Today, with decades of hindsight, we can argue those are very low probability developments, for biohuman-driven science. **John Horgan's** courageous book, *The End of Science*, 1997/2015, makes the unpopular but evidence-based case that *Homo sapiens* capacity to discover fundamental new science has been **saturating for more than seventy years**. We've reached **near-term limits** in what **biological humanity** can easily discover, at all scales of observation and experiment, from the quantum to the cosmological realms. In his later decades, **Werner Heisenberg**, one of the founders of quantum theory, also presciently observed this **saturation** in the magnitude and value of our physical discoveries. We expect it will take powerful new, and **non-biological intelligence** to get beyond our **biological conceptual limits**.

Clarke is also overly optimistic about both **biotechnology** and **medical advances**, in our view. Because humanity does not have a predictive **science of the cell**, and very unlikely to get such a science **in the near term**, without advanced quantum computing and AI, because **biology is a far less dematerialized system** than information technology, and because it is constrained by physics and ethics to evolve and develop at **far slower rates,** we find it easy to predict that humanity's **biotech innovation efforts, as a class**, will continue to **greatly underperform** our **infotech innovation** for the foreseeable future. See John's online essay, the *Limits of Biology*, 2001, for more on that (also unpopular) prediction.

In our view, the **space frontier** that Clarke loved so much will only have value in **further advancing Earth complexity**. Often our **passions** can bias us to see a less constrained future than actually exists. As we'll explore in *BPF*, while the accelerating history of complexity emergence has always included **short evolutionary forays "outward"** into **"next adjacent" space,** these have always been in service to the next, *increasingly more local*, developmental emergence of complexity, intelligence, and consciousness. Think of humanity's "Age of Exploration" prior to modern civilization. The **developmental trend**, for the most adaptive systems, has always been to venture further into **inner space**, not outer space. In what we call the **natural intelligence hypothesis**, we will argue that our future **self-aware AI**, if it must be **biologically imitative** and **evo-devo based**, will be forced by physical and informational laws, including **network ethics and empathy,** to **value most of the same things that we do,** as well as a few new things that we do not. We shall see.

Clarke also had an overly simple anticipatory view of **politics, economics, and culture.** He expected that all three would **recede in importance** as science advanced. He did not see the predictable rise of **plutocracy** to accompany tech-created wealth, and why plutocracy must be **regulated**, and wealth naturally (power law) **distributed**, to improve adaptiveness. In *BPF*, we will describe a **Law of Accelerating Sustainability** one way that the **future of culture** is quite predictable, in our view. Our "law" predicts an increasing **political and social focus on human safety and security, on social justice, and on environmental sustainability**, in direct proportion to our economic and technological development.

Anticipating a few more **cultural sustainability development trends** would have reined in some of Clarke's misses on topics like **supersonic transport** (too noise-disruptive and fuel-wasteful to be anything other than niche) or **land-based hovercraft** (they were identified by critics as environmentally unsound, even then). Yet, it is only because of Clarke's **many successes** as an anticipator that we can draw important lessons from his wins and failures for our own work. He was one of the 20th century's greatest futurists, and our long-term foresight owes him a tremendous debt.

Another famous 20th century anticipation proof point is found in the work of futurist <u>Herman Kahn</u> (1922-1983), and his team at the <u>Hudson Institute</u>. **Kahn** and **Anthony Weiner's** <u>*The Year 2000: A Framework for Speculation on the Next Thirty-Three Years*</u>, 1967, is perhaps their most famous long-term foresight work. Kahn was a foresight practitioner who recognized the value of **starting with the probable** future, then developing possible and preferable futures within the confines of the probable. A retrospective review of this book by **Richard Albright**, <u>*What Can Past Technology Forecasts Tell Us about the Future?*</u>, *Tech Forecasting & Social Change*, Jan 2002, found that 50% of the one hundred "very likely" technical innovation anticipations listed at the end of *The Year 2000* had been "good and timely" forecasts by 2000, and that forecasts in the subfield of **computers and communications** had enjoyed the highest success, at 80% correct.

The Year 2000 is insightful in both science and technology forecasting and in many economic and social forecasting areas as well. It misses some aspects of the probable S&T future. It assumed continued **centralization** of computing rather than seeing its **evo-devo phases** of **decentralization** (PCs, mobile era), followed by **recentralization** (cloud, platforms), and later, a **decentralization wave** again (edge computing, IoT), and so on. It did not recognize that information technology, like all other complex systems, is in a perpetual **evo-devo tension** between **bottom-up and top-down control**.

But even in 1967, Kahn and Weiner offered us the **exponential perspective**, citing the "bewildering speed of technological doubling" (<u>Moore's law</u> was then just two years old). In many ways, *The Year 2000* anticipated **Alvin Toffler's** discussion of socio-technical acceleration in <u>*Future Shock*</u>, 1970. Kahn popularized and accurately predicted various "<u>Long Booms</u>" in market- and technology-enabled **wealth creation**, punctuated by brief recessionary corrections, as the main signature of economic change in the 20th century. Kahn also gave us the very helpful term, "**multifold trend.**" Liberalization, democratization, improving ethics and empathy, and accelerating information, computation, and wealth creation are some of the better-known examples of such trends, but there are many others. We can call a trend **multifold** when it is particularly **general in nature**, operating in many environments, and measurable in **many (multifold) ways**. Some multifold trends are progressively or exponentially developmental. Others, like **plutocracy** and **pollution**, are **adaptation curves**. They predictably get worse initially, and then get better, in a **U-shaped cycle**, over longer timescales.

Another of Kahn's works of foresight, <u>*The Next 200 Years: A Scenario for America and the World*</u> (1976), is also quite prescient. He gets many technological and societal trends spot on, for example, accurately predicting a **roughly 500-fold drop** in the production price of **solar photovoltaic panels by the 2020s**. His big picture view of multifold trends was even better and more evidence-based than Toffler's in many ways. For good recent overviews of some of the drivers and implications of **accelerating change**, we recommend **Diamandis and Kotler's** <u>*Abundance*</u>, 2014, **McAfee and Brynjolfsson's** <u>*Machine, Platform, Crowd*</u>, 2017, **Steven Pinker's** <u>*The Better Angels of Our Nature*</u>, 2012, **Hans Rosling's** <u>*Factfulness*</u>, 2018, and other books in our book lists in Appendix 3.

Kahn makes mistakes of course. He oversimplifies environmental issues and pollution, and the political challenges of economic development. One of his major anticipatory mistakes in the economic domain was his assumption, and the curve he drew for it in *The Next 200 Years*, that **global economic growth must eventually saturate**, simply because **global human population growth must saturate, then decline, as economies develop**. Many other forecasters, assuming that **population drives and constrains economics,** still make this mistake today. His team rightly anticipated **global population saturation** quite early. Like most economists today, he mistakenly assumed that **only people create economic**

wealth, rather than recognizing the deeper, more universal dynamics of **accelerating value creation in complex networks, whether human or machine.** Specifically, Kahn did not see the multifold trends of **densification and dematerialization (D&D),** even though there was evidence for them by the early 1960s. These trends tell us that **economic growth** becomes increasingly based on *knowledge and bits, not things and atoms,* and thus increasingly **escapes local resource limits to growth.** If there will be a coming tapering of economic growth, it will be surprisingly short, before it accelerates even faster than before, in our coming **AI-driven,** and increasingly **postbiological, economy.**

Said another way, ever since the Information Revolution, humanity's fastest growing **marginal economic value creation** has been increasingly driven by our improvements to **machine capabilities and learning, and machine-to-machine communication, needs, and desires,** not by our biological human needs and desires. Because of D&D, the leading edge of civilization must increasingly enter **"inner space",** ever smaller scales of space, time, energy, and material complexity, to **create new value.** As strange as it seems, **economic growth,** just like **information, computational capacity,** and **intelligence growth,** will remain not only exponential, but actually *superexponential,* for the foreseeable future.

We can now see that our next great intelligence and action frontiers, like **quantum computing** and **nanotechnology,** require **virtually no physical resources to emerge and continue their acceleration.** What they *do* require is a well-built **network intelligence** to guide their evolutionary development, increasingly in **simulations. Our great challenge** is to better see, develop, and guide the **network ethics and empathy** needed to **humanize this accelerating future.**

Individually, none of us can be perfect anticipators. We are all fallible. For example, with **Ray Kurzweil,** the deservedly-famous technology futurist, we advise **deeply discounting most of his nanotechnological, biological, medical, and social change predictions.** We also advise pushing out most of his **AI and augmented reality predictions** by a minimum of twenty to thirty years. In the former areas he is writing outside of his expertise. The **predictive science** needed for strong nano, bio, and medical tech does not yet exist, and the **engineering** is still in its infancy. **IT and AI are far more exponential,** but even here, we think he seriously **underestimates the complexity** of the challenge, the necessity of **evo-devo approaches,** and the **societal regulation and pushback** that will slow **disturbing and disruptive change.**

We expect biomedical and biotech advances in particular will remain **quite minor, relative to infotech,** for at least the next couple of decades, as we'll discuss in *BPF.* Nevertheless, Kurzweil is to be greatly commended for telling us, beginning with his prescient book, *The Age of Intelligent Machines,* 1990, just how **powerful AI will be in coming decades,** and why it seems to emerge not only due to our **evolutionary choice,** but as a process of universal **development.**

Organizational anticipation is done in at least **five specialty practices,** as we have described. Let's look at those now. Some companies develop strong teams and processes in **Data Science & Machine Learning.** In many cases they are uncovering the near-term probable future, as with **predictive analytics,** but some are seeing the long term future very clearly as well. For example, both Google and Nvidia are **AI leaders** at present, and their long-term visions, market positions, cultures, and investments are presently quite helpful in maintaining their current leadership position.

Some of the best work in **machine learning** today uses both **AI and human teams** (either small teams or large crowds) to train the machine learning algorithms. For example, in 2017, the Cornell University Ornithology Lab launched Merlin, a smartphone app in which users build a global database of **bird pictures,** eBird. So far, tens of thousands of citizen scientists, and a small set of ornithology experts, have helped the deep learning AI behind Merlin to classify user images into **species.** In 2021, they added **bird sounds** as well. This free app is now amazingly good at **bird identification,** either by image or by sound. This **network-centric approach** is being used for many other AI/ML applications as well.

A 2017 Quartz article by **Alexandra Ossola,** delivered as their Weekly Obsession email (which we recommend subscribing to) focused on **Prediction.** It describes just how far **data science** has moved into prediction for organizations, as our machine learning algorithms, hardware, sensors, and datasets have advanced.

The graphic at right is a survey of Kaggle users from Ossola's article, showing their favorite machine prediction methods. Note that **standard logistic regression** remains the most popular method in this survey, as it has for decades. But notice also the diversity of alternative algorithms now in play, and the new value of bio-inspired methods like neural neteworks and Bayesian techniques. In *BPF*, we'll say why we predict that brain- and bio-inspired prediction methods, and eventually, an **evo-devo informed computer science**, will increasingly outcompete the more top-down and engineered approaches to machine prediction that are still dominant today.

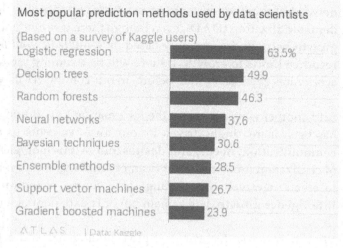

Most popular prediction methods used by data scientists

(Based on a survey of Kaggle users)

Method	%
Logistic regression	63.5%
Decision trees	49.9
Random forests	46.3
Neural networks	37.6
Bayesian techniques	30.6
Ensemble methods	28.5
Support vector machines	26.7
Gradient boosted machines	23.9

ATLAS | Data: Kaggle

Paul Saffo offers great general advice for **business forecasting teams** in *Six Rules for Effective Forecasting*, HBR, 2007. For team prediction, we also recommend **Michael Gilliland's** *The Business Forecasting Deal*, 2010, for some great examples of Intel, AstraZeneca, and Cisco using organizational forecasting well. Every good forecasting textbook offers success examples.

Every so often, leading futurists have called for **platforms and processes** to improve our **collective anticipation**. **H.G. Well's** BBC radio address, Wanted - Professors of Foresight!, 1932, was particularly influential in the last century. Wells challenge happened simultaneous with the rise of **statistical surveys** and **trendspotting** to inform policy, beginning in the **Hoover Administration** in the 1930s. Wells argued for greatly improved academic and government efforts in foresight, especially to anticipate and respond to **predictable unintended consequences (PUCs) of their innovations**.

Yes, "predictable unintended consequences" are really a thing. To see PUCs, we may have to get a diverse group to look critically and deeply at the worldviews, assumptions, and biases of those who are driving a change. A careful critique can often expose persistent flaws and biases in group models, and some obvious (on careful analysis) **unintended disruptions and downsides** that are likely to result from any group's expected strategies and plans.

America got a few **professors of foresight** in the 1970s, soon after another influential 20th century futurist, **Alvin Toffler,** in *Future Shock*, 1970, said the same thing Wells had said, forty years earlier. Remember that 1970 was the **zenith** (high point) of America's last great **Foresight Spring (1960-1980)**. In 1972, future-thinkers in the US Government established the bipartisan Office of Technology Assessment to advice our congress, which sadly has **virtually no scientific or technological prerequisites for admission**, on science and technology topics. The OTA produced 750 excellent studies, but they were sadly dismantled by neoconservatives in a political move in 1995. More fortuitously, our intelligence community and our defense think tanks and FFRDCs (federally funded research and development centers) continued to use anticipation methods, but one problem with their process is that much of their work is not openly published, or subject to external critique. Organizational politics will always limit what internal analysts can say about the future.

Fortunately, since 2011, **Philip Tetlock's** Good Judgment Project has demonstrated that the **best amateur forecasters consistently beat experts in the intelligence community** in estimating probabilities of societal events. They consistently beat experts by about 30%, even when those experts have **access to classified information**. This is a huge signal for the value of government anticipation and forecasting platforms. We are fortunately seeing small moves in that direction at present. **Tetlock's** *Superforecasting*, 2015, is a benchmark proof point for group forecasting and prediction processes that greatly outcompete other approaches. When America finally gets **another OTA**, and a gaggle of **prediction markets** with mobile-first design, we may again be in another **Governance Foresight Spring**. Until then, **keep your coat on.**

In 2021, **Michael Horowitz** et al. at the U. Penn's Perry World House, a global studies center, published Keeping Score: A New Approach to Geopolitical Forecasting (34 pp PDF). This visionary report outlines new research showing the value for the US Government of using prediction markets and forecasting aggregation platforms to understand probabilities of various events, and continually improve our world models. They note how many scenarios are written with vague weasel words, but forecasts are precise. Learning who is forecasting well can help us see where our assumptions and models are wrong. **Julia Ciocca** et al. at the Perry World House wrote a followup, How the US Government Can Learn to See the Future, Lawfareblog.com, 2021. The authors note the lack of rigor in most foresight assessments, and how easily we **misinterpret language** when **confidence intervals** and **probabilities** are not attached.

For example, US President **John Kennedy** launched the ill-fated Bay of Pigs Invasion in Cuba in 1961 because his analysts told him there was a **"fair" chance of success**. Kennedy did not know that **"fair"** meant a **30% chance** to those analysts. If he had, his personality was such that he would likely have commissioned more **fact-finding studies** (a favorite response of his) before agreeing to an invasion. That additional intelligence, if it was reasonably unbiased, might have uncovered his team's **flawed assumptions**. Whether we agree with this **alternative history** or not, we can at least agree that often, **probabilities matter**. We hope studies like Horowitz's are translated into real budgets for improved government foresight process. Don't hold your breath for it however. Government anticipation in a plutocracy typically serves the interest of the **elites**, more than seeking the **truth**. Until we return to a more **democratic state of governance**, one representing all our interests, we should not expect our best foresight to arise from most public institutions.

Consider two examples of **successful team anticipation** in for-profit organizations. Famously, Apple's product development teams anticipated the mass consumer demand for the **iPod, smartphone, and iPad**. They used anticipation to revolutionize those three product categories, recognizing that the key unlocks would be simple yet powerful user interfaces, backed by markets (iTunes, the App Store) with curated choice. These three products all obviously had to eventually exist, and each were **long anticipated** in science fiction. The iPad (tablet), for example, appeared in **Kubrick and Clarke's** film, *2001: A Space Odyssey*, 1968. Nevertheless, someone had to anticipate when the technology was right to launch the product, and the critical feature sets and marketing that would enable mass adoption. The 1990s and 2000s were filled with commercially failed or insignificant digital music players, early smartphones, and digital tablets.

Google's Artificial Intelligence group offers another corporate anticipation example. In 2015, Google famously released their core AI tools and libraries for public use, under an **open source license**. They realized the (then) **15 million coders on GitHub** were **a far more diverse network** than their 30,000 software engineers. Getting that coding community to **use their tools first** gave Google access to a key **development and hiring pool and market**. They realized that whoever took an **open strategy first**, supplying the easiest to use tools and development environment, would likely be able to marshal the **most AI talent**. Google did this **roughly a year before** Amazon, Facebook, Microsoft, and others did the same with their AI tools and libraries, with predictably less powerful results. This kind of team and corporate anticipation isn't as well-known as that of individual authors, but it happens all the time, and it is collectively much more important.

In another anticipation specialty, some companies build strong teams in **Investing & Finance**. This may include **internal investing teams** that appropriately manage a firm's investable assets, **creative financing** strategy, and even **algorithmic trading**. For accounts of the still-poorly-regulated and inequality-promoting Wild West world of machine trading, read **Scott Patterson's** *The Quants*, 2011, and *Dark Pools*, 2013. **Cryptocurrrencies** and **blockchain ICOs**, most of which we predict will not produce value, but rather separate many speculative and naïve investors from their savings, are a more recent example of the powerful, always evolving and volatile **investing and finance frontier**.

Some companies develop superior anticipation in **Law & Security**. The positive side of this is seen in corporate social responsibility initiatives and triple bottom line accounting. The negative is seen in new forms of tax sheltering and income and governance hiding, and those obfuscating new types of financial instruments and debt that helped create our 2008 Global Financial Crisis, and the corporate bailouts and K-shaped economic recovery that ensued.

For organizational leaders in **Risk Management & Insurance**, think of all the large reinsurers like **SwissRe**, who have the **most detailed risk models in the world today**. Think also of InsurTech startups like <u>Root</u>, whose leaders realized that an **app on our phone** that tracks our driving, and allows the insurer to give us custom rates based on both how often and how poorly we drive, would be even cheaper than requiring a $100 tracking dongle for the car. The latter is made by companies like <u>Octo</u>, and used by InsurTech startups like <u>Metromile</u>. Companies like Root and Metromile are gaining from implementing a useful new feature of car insurance (usage-based and driving-based rate determination). With luck, such value-creating companies are likely to gain success against incumbents. Root's strategy is the most dematerialized, giving it the potential to grow the fastest, all else equal. Getting better data is one of the foundations of **risk assessment**, a first step to better **risk management**. A classic tool for risk assessment is the **risk matrix**, seen in the picture at right. Such tools invite us to discover and categorize varieties of potential risk events. They are often used to surface **preventable futures**, prior to taking critical actions, particularly with **defense and security** teams.

Likelihood \ Impact	Negligible	Minor	Moderate	Significant	Severe
Very Likely	Low Med	Medium	Med Hi	High	High
Likely	Low	Low Med	Medium	Med Hi	High
Possible	Low	Low Med	Medium	Med Hi	Med Hi
Unlikely	Low	Low Med	Low Med	Medium	Med Hi
Very Unlikely	Low	Low	Low Med	Medium	Medium

Anticipation studies is a new academic field. <u>*The Handbook of Anticipation*</u>, **Robert Poli** (Ed.), 2019, explores a variety of anticipation models and frameworks, with papers of varying quality. Springer, the academic publisher of this volume, often sets astronomical prices for their academic works. This handbook is priced at **$599**, which is indefensible, in our view. In cases of **exploitative pricing like this**, some find it ethical to download books free from Lib Gen, the intellectual property violating platform, hosted on servers throughout the world. Its editors scan and distribute technical books globally, for free. Sci-Hub does the same for academic papers. In truth, much of the academic work locked up in high-priced academic texts and journals has been fully or partly **publicly funded**. Students in many countries are currently banned from sanctioned access to this vital knowledge. We at 4U believe the public needs **affordable access to scientific and technical knowledge**, with **sliding scales based on our ability to pay**. Until that future arrives, you may occasionally find it **ethically justifiable**, and an **act of social activism**, to use unsanctioned platforms that democratize vital knowledge. **As always, let your conscience be your guide.**

Again, our modern Western, freedom-oriented culture biases us against thinking, both frequently and carefully, about **probable futures**. We may not like believing that we are both **constrained** *and* **enabled** by the future, but the more we use **LAIS** skills, in a diverse and critical group, the more environmental constraint and probability we can see.

3. Innovation Skill – Alternatives & Scenarios Specialty Focus

Examples: Shell, Mont Fleur Scenarios, Scenario Learning, and Wargaming.

Innovation, or **possibility thinking**, is aided by five specialty practices in our model. These are **Alternatives & Scenarios**, **Entrepreneurship & Intrapreneurship**, **Facilitation & Gaming**, **Ideation & Design**, and **Innovation & R&D**. Let's now see a few 20C and 21C foresight successes, primarily focusing on the practice specialty of **Alternatives & Scenarios**, and a few examples in **organizational foresight** and **global-societal foresight** (the latter in governmental foresight) domains. We'll also mention a few innovation-oriented firms in each of these specialties at the end of this section.

One of the best-known 20th century proof points in the practice specialty of **Alternatives & Scenarios**, is Royal Dutch/Shell's **scenario planning** process. It was described by **Peter Schwartz** in *The Art of the Long View*, 1991, the first widely-read publication on scenario planning. Schwartz was head of Shell's London scenario planning department from 1982-86. Scenario planning was initiated at Shell in the early 1970s, under **Pierre Wack**. As **Art Kleiner** says in *The Man Who Saw the Future*, in *Strategy+Business* (Spring 2003), Wack's team, and his scenario planning successors at Shell, have been credited with helping the company anticipate, among other major change, "the 1973 energy crisis, the oil price shock of 1979, the collapse of the oil market in 1986, the (1991) fall of the Soviet Union, the (2000's) rise of Muslim radicalism, and the increasing pressure on companies to address environmental and social problems." If even just a few of these claims are true, it's a stunning example of **the value of "what-ifing" the future** on a regular basis.

Unfortunately, getting the details on the nature of these anticipations is difficult at present. Some of these claims may be myth, others are inflated. **Angela Wilkinson**, former member of the Shell scenario team, and former faculty in the Oxford Scenarios Programme takes a critical tone. She says, in a 2013 *HBR* article co-written with **Roland Kupers**, that "We have no solid examples of Shell's having anticipated future developments better than other companies." But, to take Shell's defense, we must remember that unlike the scenario work of futurists like **Herman Kahn**, which was often highly effective in its focus on **probable futures**, or of normative futurists like **Gaston Berger** and **Bertrand de Jouvenel**, which focused scenarios on **preferable futures**, Shell focused their scenarios on **possible** (and at the same time, **plausible**) **futures**. Thus it makes sense, given the primarily **exploratory aim** of Shell's scenarios, that Wilkinson and Kupers find little specific anticipatory value in them.

In their article, Wilkinson and Kupers **assume** scenarios are used mainly to describe possible futures, which may be preferable or dystopian. In their view, scenarios are *not intended* to explore probable futures, in any way. This assumption about scenario work was **not true** in the early days of scenario use, as Kahn and others amply demonstrated. But it has become **so widespread** in foresight practice today, that we will restrict the use of the word scenario to this **modern definition**. In this *Guide*, a **scenario** is a story of a **plausibly possible future**. Just remember that in the early years of our field, scenarios were often used in a far more **Four Ps balanced** way. Some practitioners even evaluated their various elements, and their assumptions, for **probability**, not just plausibility.

We think **Four Ps future stories** are much more important and adaptive than simply constructing **possible futures stories (scenarios)**. Stories of **probable futures** we'll call things like **forecasts**, **probabilities**, and **predictions**. Stories of preferable futures we'll call things like **goals**, **visions**, **aspirations**, **strategies**, and **progress stories** (widely-held preferable future visions), among other names. We also recommend that the elements and assumptions of all scenarios be evaluated for both **plausibility** and **probability** by an experience-diverse crowd, prior to using them to create **strategy**.

Wilkinson and Kupers argue that scenarios make leaders comfortable with an ambiguous, open future, that they can counter hubris, expose assumptions, create shared and systemic sensemaking, and foster quicker adaptation in times of crisis. Again, anticipation isn't the goal of modern scenarios; but, if we do enough of them, besides uncovering more possibilities and options, they will end up anticipating some futures, and help us respond ahead of our competitors. The authors quote historian **Keetie Sluyterman**, who characterizes Shell as "perhaps faster than other companies in catching on to changes in market or culture, by virtue of its sensitivity to emerging topics such as climate change, the rise of China, and the controversial boom in the development of extensive unconventional gas resources in the United States."

Clearly, regular scenario work should make any strategy team more aware of possible futures, more able to identify early indicators and trends that might suggest alternative futures they've already considered, and more able to put **potential experiments, strategies, and plans** on the shelf, ready for use as needed. All of this may allow a company to profit faster and better than competitors if such change emerges.

In 1970, when they began their scenario work, Shell was already number two in the world in oil and gas company revenues, at \$10.8B, but still a good way behind Exxon, which had **60% greater** revenues (16.6B). By 2004, Shell had overtaken Exxon, which it has been well established did not have a similar commitment to foresight. If they had, they might have avoided the negligent Exxon Valdez oil spill in 1989. Shell was arguably then the leading oil and gas company in the world. BP was barely ahead of Shell in revenues ($285B vs $265B) in 2004, but only due to a supermerger between British Petroleum and Amoco in 1998. Yet Shell's 20th century scenario success was no guarantee of success in the 21st, especially as the entire industry has become disrupted by various **predictable trends**. Perhaps they should have done **more anticipation**. By 2017, Shell had fallen to sixth place, behind newly global Saudi and Chinese oil companies. BP, in turn, has fallen to eighth place after its Deepwater Horizon disaster (another lack of foresight and oversight) in 2010.

One can only imagine how much better Shell's foresight work might have been if they had prioritized the search for **probable futures**, to balance **possibility-oriented** scenario work. They might have recognized **global electrification, various sustainability trends, the rise of China, and supermergers**. Wack's team did start Shell down the anticipation road. They began a list of **apparently inevitable multifold trends** that they called **TINA Trends**. TINA stands for "There Is No Alternative" to the trend. Their list began with **liberalization** and **globalization**, two good examples of **societal development**. Unfortunately, they did not try to quantify, openly forecast, and crowd critique those trends. It is often **politically safer** to minimize anticipation, and such work does not seem to have extended past Wack's tenure.

For more on Shell, see the *Shell Global Scenarios to 2025*, 2005, a compendium of their global scenario work. See also Kupers and Wilkinson's *The Essence of Scenarios: Learning from the Shell Experience*, 2014, for an in-depth analysis of the value of scenario work to Shell and to other organizations for corporate innovation, strategy, and planning. Shell's scenarios are written as possibilities, but each has many **nuggets of anticipation** in them as well. For example, Shell's 2005 book above includes **a key D&D (densification and dematerialization) curve**. This curve shows *energy intensity saturation* **(declining use of energy per citizen)**, the **richer** (and more dense, efficient, and dematerialized) **every country becomes**.

If they had prioritized anticipation, Shell's team could have built and tested a **multifactor model** for why and how this curious energy use saturation occurs, and exploited the many business opportunities of this **global D&D process**. Until recently, such **curves** were **almost never seen in environmentalist's reports** about our future. Instead, our political Left typically prefers to tell **self-preventing prophecies** of **potential ecodisaster ahead**, based on false models of population growth and unrestrained energy use, while our Right shamefully **discounts or ignores** our still-growing environmental problems. Both are **lazy approaches** to the understanding the future. When we don't try to model and understand how society is actually evolving and developing, it can greatly skew our view of *what* to change. The **Left can overreact**, and **ban useful societal experiment, risk, and change**, and the **Right can underreact**, preventing needed legislation and keeping our science, technology, companies and the market from addressing necessary change.

The big picture story we tell in Book 2 is that **we will use powerful exponential processes, evidence-based policy, population reduction, and mindset change** to keep reducing our total and per capita impact on the natural world.. **Weizsacker et al's** *Factor Four: Doubling Wealth, Halving Resource Use*, 1998, and **Andrew McAfee's** *More from Less*, 2019, and are two good books on **exponential dematerialization** processes. Various anticipators have seen aspects of **societal D&D trends** for decades. The faster change goes, the more all of us can see and guide their necessary development.

In our read of history, the **great majority of human networks** are **naturally self-correcting systems**. Using exponentials better gives us **great strategic leverage,** for just about every human problem. We will **innovate** our way out of the environmental problems we have created. In the process, our civilization will inevitably get more **densified, digital, dematerialized, and complex.** We won't consume less, we'll consume **differently**, and **far less materially**, as our **values change**, and as our **Personal AIs advance**. Leaders and citizens need to understand how this self-correction is already occurring. As **ADOR analysis** reminds us, it is usually happening much better, at present, with **someone else**, not us.

Let's turn now to a commendable **government** example of **alternatives & scenario** use. In 1991, the **Mont Fleur scenarios for South Africa**, were developed by stakeholders (also an example of **facilitation & gaming**), by **Adam Kahane's** group at Generon Consulting. Kahane's team developed four scenarios, which were widely publicized (rare for political scenario work). They were used to stimulate both expert and public debate about what South Africa might be like in 2012, twenty years after its transition from an all-white government.

The four scenarios were given evocative names: **Ostrich, Lame Duck, Icarus, and Flight. Ostrich** (a non-representative government), served to highlight the risk and futility of the white government trying to avoid a negotiated settlement with the black majority. **Lame Duck** (incapacitated government and economy) imagined a long transition of power, with a constitutionally weak government, and low international investment due to prolonged political and economic uncertainty. **Icarus** (fly now, crash later) imagined a new black government coming to power on a wave of public support, and rapidly crashing the economy by (predictably, due to inexperience) embarking on large, unsustainable public spending programs. **Flight** (inclusive democracy and economic growth) imagined a rapid political settlement, with adoption of sound social and economic policies, inclusive democratic policies, and slower economic growth than Icarus at first, but **more prosperity in the long term**, as there would be no crash. See this PDF summary of the four scenarios.

Clearly these scenarios were **directive** and **prescriptive**, and they included a number of **probable outcomes**, given various assumptions. They are thus a strong blend of the **Four Ps,** as we believe all good scenarios should be. The **process of creating scenarios**, however, should be heavily weighted to **possibility exploration, inclusiveness**, and **unpredictability**, at least **at first**. In this sense, scenario creation is primarily an innovation skill, and only secondarily an anticipation and strategy skill. The scenario team for Mont Fleur included twenty-two diverse stakeholders who met three times, for a three day workshop each time, to generate scenarios in small and large group activities. After much initially divergent and creative work, the Generon facilitators consolidated them into this particularly **Four P's instructive** set of four. Note that they cleverly split the scenarios into **two preferable** outcomes, and **two preventable** outcomes, each with different degrees of positive and negative outcome. The scenarios were provocative and widely discussed, and they helped the country's politicians and the public avoid the more obvious pitfalls of the coming transition. Referring to them, **F. W. de Klerk**, the last white prime minister of South Africa, famously said "I am not an ostrich" at a press conference before the transition. This was a nice win for **scenario impact** validation.

As of 2001, Generon had run what they call **civic scenarios** for seven other countries, and could then point to the existence of at least six other such projects globally, run by other foresight teams inspired by their work. For methods, see Kahane's *Civic Scenarios as a Tool for Making History*, 2001. Kahane argues that civic scenarios offer four important outcomes. 1. Reframed mental models, 2. Shared commitment to change, developed through dialog, 3. Regenerated energy and optimism, and 4. Renewed action and momentum. These are testable claims, and it would be excellent to see more of the developed world's leaders employ civic scenarios to engage their citizens in public debate. In our next swing back from our current plutocracy toward a more representative democracy, we can be hopeful that this will occur.

For a good introduction to scenario planning teams and firms, see **Tom Chermack's** *Scenario Planning in Organizations*, 2011. One of our favorite advanced scenario planning books is Fahey and Randall's *Learning from the Future: Competitive Foresight Scenarios*, 1997. Now nearly twenty-five years old, it is as valuable as when it was written. In this edited volume, twenty-five highly experienced scenario developers share their insights regarding scenario use, in a range of corporate, nonprofit, and government environments, to explore the possible, generate competing visions, create tensions between them, and spur resolution of those tensions with better strategy. Fahey and Randall popularize the term **scenario learning,** as way to understand how scenarios fit into the organization. They note that foresight leaders don't primarily use scenarios for better planning: they use them as a **learning tool**, with the ultimate aim of improving organizational decision-making. Scenario learning may thus be a more general and useful term than scenario planning. It also reminds us that the best scenario production process must integrate well with **LAIS**, the **Four Foresight Skills**. We recommend facilitators review Fahey and Randall's classic book when developing scenarios within teams.

Let's look, more briefly now, at the other four **innovation practice specialties** in organizational foresight. Some companies are leaders in **Entrepreneurship & Intrapreneurship**. While entrepreneurship on its face might seem like it is the creation of a preferable future, in reality, **every venture** starts as a creative, experimental act. The vast majority of ventures **fail** on contact with reality. Only the strategy, analysis, and planning that precedes or accompanies a venture is clearly preference foresight. The entrepreneurship itself is both a preference of the leaders and a social experiment.

Thus **entrepreneurship** is, in its essence, an **experimental, exploratory activity**. It is truly different from both **strategy** and from **current business operations**. Leaders who understand this will keep their venture incubators and teams **insulated** from the rest of the firm, so they aren't held back by the larger organization's conservative and defensive politics and culture. They also develop the **respect for failure** of a good venture capitalist, expecting their entrepreneurs to fail fast, fail lightly, fail often, and to learn from their failures. Experiments usually must fail their way to success.

Owen and Fernandez's *The Lean Enterprise: How Corporations Can Innovate Like Startups*, 2014, and **Mui and Carroll's** *The New Killer Apps: How Large Companies Can Out-Innovate Start-Ups*, 2013, each offer good advice and examples of large firms doing both **internal and external venturing** successfully. **Chris William's** *Venturing in International Firms*, 2018, explores eight insightful examples of corporate entrepreneurship and intrapreneurship in a **multinational** context.

A counterintuitive **intrapreneurship success story** is offered in *The New Killer Apps*. It involves Xerox and their famous R&D lab, Xerox PARC. Students of business history know that Xerox famously failed to capitalize on their invention of the **desktop graphical computer**, which they developed in both hardware and software in the 1970s at PARC. They never found a mass market with these innovations, and just as surprisingly, they **never even licensed** this incredible innovation to others, like Apple, Microsoft, or IBM, who could scale it. But, as Mui and Carroll point out, Xerox spent just $43 million in today's dollars on PARC up to the 1980s. Their intrapreneurs *were* able to use that R&D to successfully launch the **laser printer**, which has generated $100B of revenues for Xerox to date. That outcome alone is a **fantastic rate of return**.

This is a great lesson in intrapreneurship and R&D. When a suite of amazing new tools and opportunities emerge all at once, as the **personal computer revolution** did at PARC in the 1970s, and as **cloud, AI, automation, and IoT platforms** are doing today, it is easy for a firm's foresight and strategy to be temporarily **overwhelmed**. Xerox clearly overfocused, leaving vast sums of "money on the table", but it did not threaten their survival. It takes just **one big commercial win, and an intellectual property and operational moat around that win**, to justify an R&D commitment. Firms don't need to get all the fruits of an R&D commitment—just a **defensible new product or service line** and **superior rate of return**. Xerox got big wins in both **printing** and **copying** due to their **long-term R&D commitment** with PARC. As a direct result, the company had an exponential growth phase that ran over two decades, to the mid-2000's. Sadly, by the mid-1990s, they were steadily reducing their basic R&D and venturing, just as did HP, GE and other giants. The challenges of global competition were too much for them. Nevertheless, they are a great historical success story in innovation practice.

Other innovation success stories are found in **Facilitation & Gaming**. **Wargaming** has long been used in military environments to **find opportunity** and **expose weakness** in strategy and tactics. **Mark Herman et al.'s** Wargaming for Leaders, 2009, describes the consulting giant Booz Allen Hamilton's (BAH's) work in this area for corporate and defense clients. Their games are typically done over three days, simulating the next three years of company operations, with the staged submission of strategic moves and plans by a company's product and marketing teams, and by competitor teams. Game facilitators then model or assign teams to play out responses by regulators, customers, and the general public.

A good **simulation game** may only lightly use computers (for financials and numeric dashboards). It will explore how an organization's competitive position and operating environment may change, based on moves the company's strategy teams employ. Herman et al. explore how Florida Power & Light used these games to reject a risky expansion idea, and change their approaches to safety policy and public outreach. Construction machinery manufacturer Caterpillar used the results of their game to evaluate merger scenarios, and change their R&D plans. The **industry modeling** required to develop a good game, and the creation of internal teams that are forced to **think like competitors** (or other threats), can be just as valuable to the organization, long term, as the strategy insights gained by simulations in each game.

There are many well-known success stories in another innovation specialty practice, **Ideation & Design**. **Design thinking** is a growing set of practices, championed by firms like IDEO, for imagining and prototyping new products and services, and reimagining and improving existing products and services. Such thinking starts from the customer's perspective and seeks unexpected solutions. **Tim Brown's** *Change by Design*, 2009, is a well-regarded primer on the topic. Brown is the CEO of IDEO. We also recommend The Accidental Design Thinker's "40 Design Thinking Success Stories," 2017, for some great proof points for this specialty practice.

A less-known design success story comes from AirBnB. Early in their startup phase they were not getting website traction. Since one of their founders, **Joe Gebbia**, had design thinking experience, they decided to **reimagine their website** from a customer-centric perspective. In a **brainstorming** session, they hypothesized that their bookings were poor mainly because the **photos** were **too amateurish**. Their creative solution was to rent a camera, go to client's homes, and take better photos themselves. Taking photos was **not a scalable strategy** as their strategy team said, but when Gebbia **ran this experiment**, it soon showed double the bookings at the homes with better pictures. This made it clear from the outset that **great photos** would be **central to their service**. This experiment may have even saved their company at its most vulnerable stage. **Continuous design thinking** can be critical for **startups**, many of which must **pivot often at first**, until they find the right pain points, solutions, customers, and business models. But everyone can use it.

Many organizations, from small startups to giants like AT&T's Bell Labs, Boeing and DARPA, excel in the most obvious innovation specialty practice, **Innovation & R&D**. A classic cautionary tale is found in the film photography giant Kodak. They **invented digital photography** in 1975. Their strategy teams even periodically commissioned **good internal foresight studies** on the future of this technology. But despite this, they could not turn this foresight into action. Their top leaders were too focused on their **cash cow**, **film**, to change. Even those that saw the danger were unable to battle the **tough internal politics** of change. They became **increasingly inflexible** as their **size and bureaucracy** grew.

Beginning in the 1970's, Kodak could have easily found **early adopter clients for digital photos**, for example, in the **intelligence and defense communities**. Those customers would have been quite happy with the grainy and expensive digital images at that time, due to the many benefits that **distributed databases** of such photographs offered. For example, the National Crime Information Center (NCIC) was created in 1967, twenty years before the web. As Kodak **climbed the experience curve** with digital photo production, manipulation, and storage, many cheaper commercial applications would have emerged. But **Kodak could not disrupt themselves**. Their past success with their existing technology prevented them from seeing and acting appropriately with the new, soon-to-be-better technology. This is the classic **"Innovator's Dilemma"**, well-described in Clay Christensen's *The Innovator's Dilemma: When New Technologies Cause Great Firms to Fail*, 1997/2013. They needed an **intrapreneurship capability**, which is rare in large companies.

As a result, much nimbler, smaller, and more innovative competitors like Fuji, who also started in film, progressively ate Kodaks lunch. From the beginning, Fuji had an extremely strong R&D focus, they paid handsomely for talent, and they adopted a **foresight culture** anchored by the **continuous improvement philosophy of Kaizen**. Kodak finally imploded in 2012. Fuji is highly innovative to this day, even as they have grown to become a multibillion dollar company.

The many **lost progress opportunities** for Kodak with digital photography are a good lesson in the challenges of **innovation**. In digital photography, Kodak had a great **invention** (design, prototype) could not turn it into an **innovation** (a new product or service that finds enough customers for commercial success). They had the **anticipatory foresight** to see its future, but not the **organizational culture or strategy** to allow **cannibalization** of their dominant film business. We'll revisit the innovator's dilemma at several points in the *Guide*. We need all Eight Skills to get a firm past **good strategic foresight** (which Kodak had) into **adaptive foresight**, which includes **successful action** and **review**.

For a few practical tips for innovation success, we recommend **Kelly and Littman's** *The Ten Faces of Innovation*, 2006, also by IDEO authors. These authors explore the human and process resources that help leaders **overcome internal resistance** to creative solutions. They profile particular types of people, including the *Anthropologist* (presenting data on consumer behavior and interests), the *Cross-Pollinator* (combining ideas and processes across silos), and the *Hurdler* (looking for creative ways around current blocks and constraints) who are vital to **successful internal innovation teams**. They also explore successful innovation examples from Kraft, Procter and Gamble, Safeway, and the Mayo Clinic.

Neal Thornberry's *Innovation Judo*, 2014, also addresses the challenges of internal innovation. It explores the many ways internal and external actors **("blockers")** try to **shoot down experiments** that could **threaten their power or process**, and the various **"judo skills"** innovators need to succeed. The team at Chrysler that created the Jeep Wrangler Rubicon in 2003 is a case study of innovation success tactics in this book. Even **government agencies** can lead such work. For example, on the **future of AI**, the US defense R&D agency DARPA is doing commendable work exploring our growing need for explainable, secure, and statistically trustable AI. We'll say more on that vital topic in *BPF*.

4. Strategy Skill – Strategy & Planning Specialty Focus.

Examples: Amazon, Apple, Google, and Rick Rescorla.

Strategy, or **preference and prevention thinking**, is aided by two specialty practices in our model, **Analysis & Decision Support** and **Strategy & Planning**. In other words, strategy development requires analysis, prioritizing, decision-making, visioning, and planning, around both desirable and avoidable futures. Great strategic foresight always builds on **Learning** (understanding relevant past and present), **Anticipation** (uncovering probable futures), and **Innovation** (imagining possible futures). We use it to craft **preferred and preventable futures**, and it gives us some **tools and guidelines** (problem diagnoses, coordinating policies, action plans) for how to get there.

Nineteenth-century Prussian commander **Helmuth von Moltke** famously said (in paraphrase): "No plan survives first contact with the enemy." Some have generalized this observation as: "**No strategic plan survives first contact with reality.**" Continual iteration of strategy and action, via the **Do Loop**, is the only way we adapt. Improving strategy requires repeated application of all **Eight Skills**. It is only when a strategy is **Executed**, and leaders attempt to use it to **Influence** their teams and stakeholders, **Relate** to them in the process, and **Review** its impact (the **Four Action Skills**), that we get to **test** any strategy against the world in a process of **natural selection**. With these caveats, let's survey a few obviously excellent strategies (in hindsight) by some of our more well-known business leaders in recent decades.

Consider Amazon's foray into Web Services in 2006. With revenues of $17B a year then, it created a platform to rival Google for cloud computing, with its AI products and services. This move made perfect strategic sense for Amazon, yet wasn't inevitable. They could easily have viewed their new cloud platform as a private defensive asset, to be kept as a trade secret. That top-down view is common in many companies. Instead, they anticipated (predicted) that they had fortuitously innovated an **inevitable new kind of global business infrastructure**, and that they could be **platform leaders** and the **first to scale it**. That was a much more top-down and bottom-up balanced (evo-devo) worldview.

Consider Apple's revitalization under **Steve Jobs**, with the iMacs, the iPod, the iPad, and the iPhone. Note that with least two of these categories, the iPod and the iPad, Apple was a fast follower (aka, second-mover), not a first mover. Being a fast follower is sometimes a superior launch strategy. It is often forgotten that Amazon was a second mover in online bookstores. Book Stacks Unlimited was started three years earlier, in 1992, and grew to 500K titles and 35 employees. They innovated the category, but didn't turn their early advantage into a dominant share. Amazon, under a more focused CEO **Jeff Bezos**, had **superior execution, marketing (influence), and scaling strategies**, and a **better name** as well. They rapidly overtook Book Stacks—which was sold to Barnes & Noble (who also failed to scale online) in the late 1990s.

Think also of Google's decision to open up and give away the mobile operating system Android, a great **counterstrategy** against Apple's iOS. As **Gerald Nanninga** notes, this decision also saved Google's primary search engine business, as global web traffic moved predictably from desktops to phones. Think also of Dell's Assembled to Order strategy, which allowed Dell to beat the majors in personal computing at the time (IBM, Compact, HP) without carrying finished inventory. As **Vivek Singh** notes on Quora, this was a great strategic move, and an example of **process dematerialization**.

Think also of Toyota's strategy to create a culture of **continuous business process innovation**, aka **kaizen**. This allowed them to beat the US car majors on quality in the 1970s. Then, after protective tariffs were introduced by the US, Toyota imported that strategy and culture to their US manufacturing plants, beginning in 1986, disproving the many naysayers who said "it won't work in America." Toyota's Kentucky plant is presently their largest manufacturing facility in the world. See **Jeff Liker's** *The Toyota Way*, 2004, for this inspiring business lesson, and a nice overview of kaizen.

We also recommend **Scott Galloway's** book, *The Four: The Hidden DNA of Amazon, Apple, Facebook, and Google,* 2017, for examples of smart strategic management by teams at four of America's current tech titans. Our leading tech firms are now so successful they need to be much more strongly regulated, and several need antitrust action. We also recommend **McAfee and Brynjolfsson's** *Machine, Platform, Crowd,* 2017, on **three tech-enabled trends** (data-driven software, applications as platforms, and crowd creation and feedback) that have become critical drivers of change. They are major new **developmental trends** (anticipations) that we can use well or poorly, again depending on our **strategy**.

For our last strategy proof point in this section, consider the story of Rick Rescorla. It offers a heroic example of a leader integrating all **Eight Skills**, and devising a **powerful strategy** that was successfully **implemented**, in the process saving thousands of lives. It is an indication of **how little foresight is valued in modern American culture** that Rescorla's actions remain so unknown by the populace in relation to the seminal event, the **9/11 terrorist attacks**, in which they occurred. Like any good **case history**, this story offers us plenty of lessons in how we can each see and prepare for both the probability and possibility of **catastrophes**, whether large or small, for ourselves, our teams, our organizations and our societies.

Rick Rescorla
(1939-2001)

Rescorla was a decorated officer in the UK, Rhodesian, and US military, the latter as a Colonel in Vietnam. After returning to the US from the Vietnam War, he wrote a textbook on criminal justice, then left teaching for the higher pay and responsibility of corporate security. He began his corporate career as a non-supervising member of the security team with Dean Witter Reynolds at their World Trade Center offices in New York City in 1985. After the 1988 terrorist bombing of Pan Am Flight 103 over Lockerbie, Scotland, he anticipated a plausible terrorist attack on the World Trade Center. He asked a colleague trained in counterterrorism, **Daniel Hill**, to **review the WTC's security for threats and vulnerabilities**. In wargames, this is called a **Red Team exercise**. Hill noted the easy accessibility of load-bearing columns in the WTC basement and said "I'd drive a truck full of explosives in here, walk out, and light it off." Rescorla and Hill then wrote a joint letter to the Port Authority of NY and New Jersey, insisting on the need for more WTC security, specifically including the basement. Sadly, Rescorla and Hill's recommendations were ignored, and no security changes occurred.

After the 1993 **WTC truck bombing**, which targeted the basement exactly as his team had anticipated, Rescorla was promoted to **head of security** at Dean Witter. He then hired Hill and another expert, **Fred McBee**, as consultants, and built an experience-diverse **advisory team** of security professionals and stakeholders, informally dubbed "**Team Rescorla**." Hill next predicted that the first WTC attack was likely planned by a radical imam at a mosque in NY or New Jersey. Later that year, followers of Imam **Omar Rahman** of Brooklyn were arrested for the bombing.

Then, as **James Stewart** notes in a 2002 New Yorker article, based on a **flight simulator exercise** done by McBee, his team created a chilling scenario for Dean Witter management of what the next WTC attack might look like. They imagined an air-cargo plane loaded with explosives, chemical, radiological or biological weapons, which could easily be used by terrorists to crash into the towers. Their report said "the ground is secure, but the next attack may come from the air."

When Dean Witter merged with Morgan Stanley in 1997, Rescorla recommended to his superiors that Morgan Stanley leave the towers for New Jersey, to lower their security risk. But, their lease ran to 2006, and a move then was financially out of the question, so Rescorla secured authority to devise an **emergency evacuation plan** for all the firm's employees, who occupied twenty-two floors in the South Tower, and four floors in a neighboring building. Crucially, he also got **smoke extractors** and **more powerful emergency lights** installed in the WTC **stairwells**. Finally, he instituted a series of **security drills** to train all the firm's employees in rapid evacuation procedures. As employees recall, these drills were done frequently enough, every three to six months, to be an **annoyance** to top management.

On the morning of **September 11, 2001**, Rescorla heard the explosion in the North Tower of the WTC, and began immediately ordering all Morgan Stanley employees to head down the stairwells in pairs, per the security plan. Crucially, he chose to **ignore** the Port Authority's announcement in the South Tower, over the P.A. system, urging people to stay at their desks, so as to not "interfere" with the North Tower evacuation. That order was a typical **reactive "do nothing" response** to crisis, common with **unforesighted leadership**. He **saw through it**, and continued executing his strategy.

As a result of Rescorla's commendable **foresight and action**, both **beforehand** and **in the moment**, Rescorla is credited with successfully evacuating **all but five of the firm's 2,687 employees** from the towers and nearby buildings prior to their collapse. He was last seen on the 10th floor of the South Tower, heading upstairs with his bullhorn, walkie-talkie, and phone. He chose to stay until the last person under his care was safely out of the building, as he told his wife on his cellphone shortly before the tower's collapse. Watch the History Channel's excellent *The Man Who Predicted 9/11*, 2005, for an overview of this inspiring story, and the skills, habits, and attitudes a leader needs to generate adaptive foresight.

Rescorla's story offers us a powerful example of use of each of the **Eight Skills**. He was effective in **learning** (bringing in diverse experts to deepen understanding of the threats), in **anticipation** (successful prediction of major risks, more than once), **innovation** (taking responsibility to devise and implement creative solutions) and **strategy** (devising, drilling, and executing effective security responses, within the limits set by his superiors). He also used **Execution**, **Influencing**, **Relating** and **Reviewing** to get his safety protocols in place, to secure top cover from leadership, to get employees familiar with them, and improve the protocols based on periodic feedback. Finally, Rescorla also demonstrates the **exemplary ethics and empathy** of a great leader as well.

There is also a **government-level security counterfactual** that we can add to this story. Imagine if one of Rescorla associates, or someone in US domestic counterterrorism, had been privy to Team Rescorla's plane scenario. Imagine that they had also recognized that a **large plane full of both passengers and jet fuel** would be an **even simpler and more cost-effective weapon** than one laden with explosives or radiological weapons. Someone could have then **deduced** that this threat could be reduced by greater security on commercial planes, and greater oversight of US flight schools. El Al, the Israeli airline, has long been recognized as a physical and process security leader, having had only one actual hijacking since its inception in 1948, despite countless attempts. In 2001, US airlines and airports used few of El Al's innovations. Finally, imagine that someone had raised the **public heat** regarding this threat, by **publishing this scenario**, in journals or lay print media, with **recommended solutions**, or better yet, including the plot in a **dramatic film**.

There's a great saying about **change**, attributed to 40th US President <u>Ronald Reagan</u>: "When you can't make them see the light, make them feel the heat." This can be paraphrased as: "**Sometimes strategic optimism motivates best, other times defensive pessimism**." Said another way, sometimes we are convinced by what **Dan Kahneman** in *Thinking, Fast and Slow*, 2013, calls **System 2** thinking (logic, rational argument, evidence), while at other times we need **System 1** appeals (intuition and emotion, including **fear**) to motivate change. Sometimes it takes **recognition of a threat in a mass medium**, such as a widely seen article or film, to create the **heat** that will cause large, change-averse organizations, like **airlines, airports,** and the **US government**, to execute the strategies that we **anticipate** will lead us to better futures.

As an example this last claim, consider the **public pressure to make progress in nuclear disarmament talks** that followed the <u>ABC television</u> debut of the nuclear holocaust film, *The Day After*, 1983. This film garnered 100 million viewers on its first showing. It was credited by policymakers, and then-President Reagan, with generating pressure on the US administration make progress on nuclear disarmament during the Cold War. The film was also shown on Soviet television in 1987, where it had a similar effect. *Reagan's Secret War*, 2009, gives a declassified account of this president's dual desire to reduce America's reliance on expensive and unusable nuclear weapons, and to end the global influence of the Soviet Union, and the tradeoffs his team made in managing those two, sometimes conflicting, strategic goals.

As **Taylor Downing's** excellent book, *1983*, 2018, describes, Reagan's anticommunist policies actually led us to a **second peak of Cold War tensions,** and **near-launches of nuclear missiles, in 1983**. This was nearly as dangerous a time as the Cuban Missile Crisis of 1962, though the events of the second peak are far less widely known. It appears in hindsight that the stressful secret events of that year, and the public reaction to this effectively visionary and dystopian film were both important influences on Reagan's commitment to making progress on nuclear disarmament, culminating in the Intermediate-Range Nuclear Forces Treaty of 1987, a major step forward at the time. *Global foresight matters!*

Surfacing Our Implicit Assumptions and Models

As the late great professional futurist **Joe Coates** used to say, one of the most important values of foresight work is to **expose our hidden assumptions** about the world, and to then allow us to **improve them**. To explore this insight, consider the following **educational foresight** example.

Perelman.1992

School's Out, 1992, by the policy analyst **Lewis Perelman**, is a mostly-prescient work of 20th century **sentinel foresight**. See Perelman's 1993 *Wired* article, also called "School's Out," for a synopsis of the book. In both the article and the book, Perelman offers us a powerful vision for **lifelong digital and AI-enhanced education**, **competency certifications**, and **competency-based hiring**. Though it was written at the **dawn of the web**, this book broadly anticipated the continued advance of technological unemployment, the rise of the gig economy, and the great promise of educational software, including, MOOCs, micro-certifications, adaptive learning, and other features of our current **EdTech startup landscape**. In both normative and structural terms, it offers an **aspirational vision** for the future of the **education industry** over the next fifty years.

But, even with all its merits, Perelman makes **assumptions**, many of them implicit, that make him anticipate that his vision will materialize much **faster**, and with far greater **scope**, than reality will allow, in our view.

In one mistaken assumption, Perelman assumes that companies will want to move to **competency-based testing and hiring** a lot more rapidly than they have. We would argue that such a movement, as it involves expensive and controversial **behavior change** on the part of companies, will require much more evidence for its value, and data mining, models, and AI to help us determine which competencies actually matter to firms, and adaptive testing platforms to assess and improve them. Companies like **Indeed** have recently dipped their toes into **competency assessment**, but only in very modest ways to date. Perelman also assumed EdTech companies would be a lot more focused on building measurable, predictive, prioritized, and **learning optimized platforms** than they have been to date. His **end vision** in these cases seems correct, but his **timing** for each was far too premature.

In actuality, improving educational software and solutions is **technically a lot harder and more expensive** than Perelman imagined. There has also been far less **motivation** than he assumed would exist to **build efficient learning systems**, and get them past the **political and labor gatekeepers** at schools. As a result, his vision of digital education has been far slower to emerge than all who care about performance, personal responsibility, and competitiveness would have liked.

Yet Perelman's most significant mistaken assumptions, in our view, are **political**. Perelman is a **libertarian**, an evidence-poor political worldview, and this worldview is implicit, not explicit, in much of his writing. His libertarian worldview leads him to predict that entrepreneurs will increasingly both **disrupt and replace our public educational system** as digital technologies mature. Nothing of the kind will happen in the foreseeable future, in our view.

To his credit, Perelman highlights just how **expensive, change-averse, ineffective, and nonadaptive** our current public educational systems are in America. But, showing how bad a system is does not tell us what comes next. **Democracy** is just as flawed, in many ways, as our **public education systems**. As **Winston Churchill** famously quipped, "Democracy is the worst form of government, except for all the others." So too, we predict that America's **commitment to public education** is now and will continue to be a choice the voting public makes as the lesser of various evils.

America's liberal democracy will struggle to slowly reform public education, at an **often-maddening pace**, but we will never replace it with the **free market**, as far ahead as we can see today, even with the disruptive advances in EdTech and Personal AIs that we can see coming. To its great detriment, Libertarian thinking ignores our responsibility to create a strong and efficient **democratic state**, and to use that state to **enforce** the **free market** and **support** a strong **civil society**.

As Harvard business professor **Rebecca Henderson** describes in her excellent *Reimagining Capitalism*, 2020, the **free market**, the **state**, and **civil society** are the **three great pillars** of all democratic civilizations. As we argue in *BPF*, the neoconservatives and their plutocratic funders have **withered and weakened** the state and civil society since the 1970s. We believe it is one of our highest personal and collective responsibilities to **restore the strength and effectiveness of all three of these pillars.** We predict that democracies will use emerging powers like **Personal AIs** to do so.

Let us now offer a different model than Perelman's for the **future of public education**. It relies on what we would characterize as a set of **techno-liberal**, rather than libertarian, **political assumptions**. We've listed some of those assumptions below, as an exercise in **assumption mapping**, so they can be more easily critiqued by our readers as well. We will offer trends and arguments to support several of these assumptions in Book 2. Some **assumptions we make**, relevant to the future of public education, are the following:

1. Science and technology will continue to **accelerate**, assuming no extinction-level events for our civilization. This in turn will cause **accelerating wealth production** in all our industrial democracies.

2. Libertarian values (specifically, shrinking the state) will **never be a voting majority** in any **democracy with accelerating wealth,** due to the **obviously growing wealth** created in such societies.

3. We get more **plutocratic** and **neoconservative** values in **corporations** and **government** on average as wealth and tech grows. Plutocratic values naturally seek to **consolidate power and privilege**, and **limit competition** and freedom that might disrupt such power and privilege.

4. We also get more **liberal and egalitarian values** in our **citizens** and **communities** as wealth and tech grows. Issues of **social justice, fairness, and inequality** grow ever more important among the electorate. Eventually they get **voting power** to get their voices heard, periodically causing **democratic reforms**.

5. Issues of **personal productivity and competition** (important issues, championed by the political Right) grow **less important for the average voter, as economic wealth and technological capabilities accelerate**. What we care about instead are **fairer rules** and **technological wealth redistribution**, both to the middle class and to the less advantaged. We call this megatrend the **Law of Accelerating Sustainability** in Book 2.

6. **Public education** will continue to get **most of our education budget** in this political environment. There will be more **charter schools** (promoting educational freedom) and **private schools** (especially for the rich), but as minority trends. The total **size and power of the state**, and secondarily, of **public education budgets**, will **continue to grow**, even as various actors seek to limit governmental size and effectiveness.

Note that other than **Assumption 1**, on which we are sure Perelman would also agree, the rest of our assumptions are likely to differ from his, either by a little or a lot. Our assumptions also rely on a different set of **hypotheses** (causal models) than his about **STEEPLES trends** in modern democracies.

Assumption 5, what we call the **Law of Accelerating Sustainability,** is particularly important to explain and defend. It argues that **what voters want most** in liberal democracies, as societal wealth grows, is more **social justice, egalitarianism, and sustainability,** *not* more personal productivity. It argues that not only do we want to be **more accomplished than our parents in things we value,** we also **value different things,** and want to **do less work than they did, in more flexible ways,** and we want **more meaningful work.** We will **reshape our government, markets, and civil society** to create a reality that **increasingly offers us all of these things,** as that's the future we want, as voters.

In years before we get powerful **personal AIs** and can use them to educate ourselves in real-time (see Book 2), we expect to see many **commendable but incremental initiatives** in public school reform. **Diane Tavenner's** great and predictably controversial book *Prepared: What Kids Need for a Fulfilled Life,* 2019, is an inspiring example of how to blend **rigorous academics** with **personal growth** in today's public schools. It is a model we could employ much more widely, wherever we can reform our **unions** and our **educational governance**.

Tavenner. 2019

Demonstrating what is possible with vision and resolve, a few **sentinel countries** have **redesigned their entire high school public education systems in recent decades.** Finland is one of the best-known examples. They **eliminated half of their curriculum** and **replaced it with freedom,** in a **modified Montessori schooling model,** a move Perelman would surely champion. They also supported that change with **extensive human, financial, and infrastructure resources,** a move he would surely (and incorrectly) oppose. See **Sean Faust's** *The Finland Phenomenon,* 2016, for that inspiring story. But **this change took two decades,** and **great leadership,** from politicians, unions, and citizens.

Something similar *could* happen widely in America over the next two decades, but Finland's freedom- and innovation-maximizing approach seems far more likely to continue to arrive piecemeal, in a handful of US states, and in a few creative or wealthy enclaves. We should look instead to **accelerating tech** and **consumer and voter activism** to eventually **force** major educational change. A good overview of EdTech today can be found in the free EdSurge newsletter. In our view, the most positive long-term EdTech trend in the 21st century may be emergence of **Personal AIs.** They will be part of **"teacherless general education" platforms** that may be quite powerful and customizable by the 2040s. Once Personal AIs are in mass use, we predict that our leading EdTech platforms will be able to correct for the many enduring deficits of public school networks. In the meantime, the great majority of our schools seem likely to improve much more slowly than many of us would like, for a host of cultural, political and organizational reasons.

In sum, **our predictions** are always based on **our assumptions and models.** We need to expose, critique, and test those assumptions, models, and predictions as best we can. Let's conclude this section with a few questions for yourself and your teams: How **explicit** are you in your assumptions and models? In your communication? Do you try to find **quantitative data and trends** to support or contradict them? How often do you and your team use a roughly **scientific approach** in your foresight work? How often do you generate hypotheses (models), predictions, and confidence intervals? Have you asked what types of experiments or results might **change your predictions**?

Telling Better Future Stories, Using the Four Ps

Stories are very seductive and powerful. As future thinkers, we tell many types. A good story, in film, print, or spoken, can quickly transport us a different world, both emotionally and rationally, faster and deeper than perhaps than any other device. Given how easy it is for us to **lose ourselves** in our stories, we should take extra care that they make sense, and are adaptive. **Jonathan Gottschall's** *The Storytelling Animal: How Stories Make Us Human,* 2013, explores our universal craving for stories, and offers a useful theory of why they can be so compelling. A good story **simulates reality** with a **memorable and greatly reduced set of causal factors,** giving us a **simple narrative** that still creates mental models that help us prepare for and adapt to a much more complex and less comprehensible world.

Unfortunately, it is much easier to **hook people into a story** than it is to make that story **reflect reality**. As storytellers, foresight professionals have a **duty** not to take the easy path. Books like **Lisa Cron's** *Wired for Story*, 2012, and **Carmine Gallo's** *Talk Like TED*, 2015, give us helpful tips for meeting our evolved cognitive desires for simple, dramatic, comprehensible stories. Such books offer good advice, as long as our manipulation remains **ethical and evidence-based**. If we don't tell stories that are **evidence-based**—while this storytelling advice may help make us **successful with others**—our stories themselves won't foster better models and foresight. If we want to really help people prepare for and adapt better to the future, we have to go beyond simply being **entertaining** to **creating adaptive value** for our clients. Let's discuss that challenge now.

Gotschall and many others would argue that we all live much of our lives **depending on pleasurable fictions** that we have constructed in our heads. We use those fictions to **rationalize** our lives and the state of the world. We also like to learn about **reality**, but often only as a **second level priority**. Entertainment is often our first priority, for better or worse. **Consider that just over half the books** in a typical large bookstore (in John's past estimations) are in the **nonfiction** genre, with hundreds of subgenres. The other half of the books in a large bookstore are typically **fiction**, with a large but slightly reduced number of subgenres. There are almost **twice as many nonfiction titles** in the top 100 sellers on Amazon than fiction. Yet **fiction blockbusters**, as individual titles, persistently **outsell** nonfiction blockbusters by a great margin. We humans do like to learn how the world **actually works**, but we like to be **entertained** at least as much, and we want to **share** the best entertainment we find, the "big head" of the power law of fiction stories, as a **common experience**. We have to recognize this reality, be on guard against all the entertaining but faulty stories we generate.

All humans, including our audiences and clients, are **experience seekers** as much as we are **meaning makers.** We love a good story with both likeable and odious characters, with mystery and unpredictability, with a compelling set of narratives, dramatic tension, and complex emotion. Whether the story and its models are **probable** is often of very secondary importance. It need only be **true to our emotions and values** for us to love it and be strongly influenced by it.

This is why we love science fiction franchises like *Star Trek* or *Star Wars* so much. On a rational level, we know these stories could not happen as written, but as long as their **values and emotions seem authentic,** and the **plot holes** aren't so large that they trigger our **disbelief**, we are both entertained and influenced. We can recognize that these **morality tales** are an **effort at nonfiction**, in emotions and values. We like imagining how we would react, in a **similar scenario**.

Makers of propaganda, a special kind of **faulty story** (see next section) used to influence others, have long known that the **truer we make a story emotionally**, the easier it is to **slip in rational falsehoods**. In Book 2, we will argue that the **wealthier** our societies get, the more the average citizen prefers **entertainment first**, and **reality second**. This increasing preference for **entertainment over reality** seems a predictable macrotrend of societal development. It is a trend all professionals must understand, to improve foresight culture in any organization. Identifying propaganda, hidden agendas, and the faulty parts of any popular story becomes particularly important the more complex society becomes.

Future fiction is a subgenre of science-fiction. Science fiction itself seeks to entertain first, and doesn't necessarily strive for realism. It is related to but different from another sci-fi subgenre, **hard science fiction**, which has story elements that are both **scientifically plausible and technically presented**. Hard sci-fi can teach us a lot about science and technology, but it isn't necessarily intended to be a socially or politically probable future.

Future fiction, as we define it, is a future story that is not only **STEEPLES plausible**, it is a story that a **majority of critics** would **rate as probable**, in most of its **primary plot structure**. Good future fiction comes with **notes that reference nonfiction literature** to support some of its claims, and it does not have to be technical in its descriptions. It often describes significant **positives *and* negatives** ahead, bringing **ADOR** to its structure. It also typically occurs within the **next few decades**, since beyond that, it is hard to get a **critical majority** to agree on much.

Peter Singer and **August Cole's** *Burn-In: A Novel of the Real Robotic Revolution*, 2020, about humans and AI-equipped robots **teaming** to solve crimes in a mid-21st century Washington DC is a great recent example of future fiction. Singer and Cole call this **"useful fiction"**, but that is a slight misnomer. **All fiction is useful**, to someone. *Burn-In* is actually **future fiction**, of very high caliber. In their notes, the authors reference supporting sources for many of the events depicted in the story. **When it is Four P's balanced, future fiction is particularly valuable for foresight work**, and the best is entertaining as well. We hope that **future fiction** becomes its own recognized genre by booksellers in coming years. We should all regularly read and share such work, as a way to both **entertain and inform ourselves**, and to learn how to **tell better future stories**.

Cole & Singer, 2020

There is also a large category of future stories, which we call **Faulty stories** (discussed in our next section), that must be identified, so we can find the fiction that helps us most with future thinking. Faulty stories are often **quite engaging**, but they are **implausible as written**, in one or more critical plot elements. Faulty stories can be entertainment, propaganda or sales jobs. They can promote both obvious and hidden agendas. If we don't discover their flaws, we and others can be unduly influenced by them, and our foresight will suffer.

For foresight practitioners, the most important story elements are **the Four Ps**. Within any story, we can identify four future story elements: **Probable**, **Possible**, **Preferable**, and **Preventable stories**. What we want to do with each of these **future story elements** is to find **"weebles,"** important, well-critiqued, partly-evidenced, and still plausible stories. We will discuss some examples of **weeble stories** shortly. We also want to reliably identify **faulty stories**, and be strategic with them. If others (competitors, clients, the public) believe a story, and we think it is faulty, we may be able to use that knowledge to our advantage.

The slide below summarizes some of the foresighter's top storytelling challenges. Let briefly discuss faulty stories now, and after that, weeble stories.

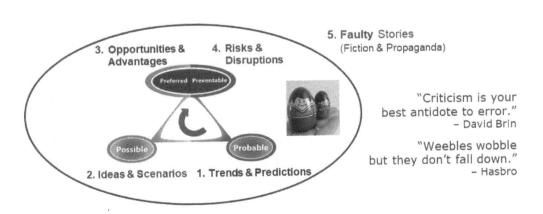

Find Weebles in the Four Future Story Genres.
Find and Be Strategic with Faulty Stories.

3. Opportunities & Advantages   4. Risks & Disruptions

5. **Faulty** Stories (Fiction & Propaganda)

Preferred   Preventable

Possible   Probable

2. Ideas & Scenarios   1. Trends & Predictions

"Criticism is your best antidote to error."
– David Brin

"Weebles wobble but they don't fall down."
– Hasbro

Your team needs **cognitively diverse SMEs** who **enjoy critiquing** future stories.
The **Four P's** stories that **survive criticism** are **weebles**. Collect and use them well.

Most future stories are **faulty**, or wrong in critical or relevant aspects.
Faulty stories may be **default views** of competitors or clients.
Be **strategic** with them. Sometimes it is best not to try to expose their faults.

Foresight University

Critiquing Faulty Stories (Finding Faulty Parts in Futures Stories)

Learning to identify faulty stories, being strategic with them, and never telling them as truth ourselves, is one of the ways we **build credibility** in our profession. Recognizing that certain parts of a future story sound more like fiction than reality allows us to be entertained by that story, while keeping it from influencing our or our client's strategy. Unfortunately, many elements of faulty stories are not recognized as such—by the teller, the audience, or both. We often aren't **sufficiently critical** in evaluating a future story's **Four Ps plot elements**; instead, we suspend disbelief, and we let it entertain us. That's fine for the general public, but it isn't our role, as foresight professionals.

It's not easy to do **controlled experiments** in the foresight field. We can assess our foresight later for accuracy, but often the best we can do before the fact is to ensure that our forecasts, predictions, opinions, and speculations are **well-critiqued**, and prune away the most implausible ones. Criticism is also central to <u>peer review</u>—a prerequisite of good science. As automated semantic understanding and analysis tools improve in coming years, the level of critical and peer review for any future story will become more visible for more of the stories we find on the web. In the meantime, we must do our own investigation and criticism solicitation, using our best professional networks.

Recall our **LAIS Order of Operations** in Strategic Foresight. Following this order can be very helpful when we wish to generate stories that are not faulty. But among the Eight Skills, iterated **Review** of our stories is particularly important. There is a type of peer review called <u>**open peer commentary**</u>, where reviewers from a variety of specialties are solicited to **publicly comment** on a paper, and the author is allowed a **brief public response** to each commentary, and both are posted as **addenda** to every published paper. Open peer commentary is a particularly good way to **show and measure the level and quality of criticism that exists for controversial, abstract, or speculative claims.** Unfortunately, it is rarely done in foresight journals and scholarship today. We hope more foresight journals engage in **open peer commentary** in coming years. They need it, as the **papers and models in our field are often particularly speculative,** by nature.

Unfortunately, many future stories we find in print, including many <u>scenarios</u> (stories of possible futures), even in our journals, contain many story elements that are **highly implausible** as written. In fact, many scenarios offered as future possibilities seem **so implausible that practical-minded folks will judge them a waste of time to finish reading**. In just a few sentences, a poorly written scenario can demonstrate an author's **ignorance of key trends or preventable futures**, and signal to the reader we are reading **future fantasy**, not plausible reality.

Scenarios should be developed only **after** a foresight professional has explored the varieties of **probable foresight** that may be relevant to the story. They also should intelligently explore plausible but different **possible futures**, and the **competing and cooperating preference landscape** in relation to the future being contemplated. If they don't begin with **learning** (research), they are unlikely to be realistic. It is a disservice to proffer such stories as plausible, when an evidence-based audience could quickly refute faulty elements in our stories.

One way to identify **faulty futures stories** is to ask if they are appropriately balancing evolutionary and developmental process. There are both **divergent futures** and a **convergent future** always lying ahead of us. In Chapter 7, we will discuss **Dator's Four Futures** framework. Each of of Dator's futures are always occurring, to various actors. All four stories deserve to be told. Another way is to examine the **motives** of the storyteller. If they are **financially invested in** or **emotionally enamored** by a certain future, they may be tempted to tell a story without regard to evidence against it. The most effective way to identify faulty stories is to subject them to careful, open, and cognitively diverse critique. Faulty stories will very quickly be flagged as such by many experts in any good crowd. Only true believers, those benefiting financially or reputationally, and those seeking entertainment or conflict ("trolls") will continue to tell them at that point.

Of course, merely because a story is faulty doesn't mean it won't have deep or lasting **influence** on the future—or that we could easily end its telling by exposing its faults. We all get value from telling a few stories that are **obviously faulty** in part, and they may serve **deep moral or emotional needs**. This is true with many of our **political, religious, and**

motivational stories. We believe in many stories not for their **literal truthfulness** (which we may feel we cannot evaluate), but for their **societal, community, and personal benefits**. Nevertheless, the **IES goals** argue that we progress as our stories become both more evidence-based and more expressive of **all of our universal values**. Pointing out a story's true and beneficial parts, while exposing its apparent faults and harms, is a great way to reform it for the better. A few examples of what we believe to be faulty stories may help here.

Identifying Faulty Story Elements Example: Human Bioimmortality.

Consider human longevity stories. **Biological immortality** is a popular but faulty story, promulgated by longevity futurists like **Aubrey de Grey**, his SENS (Strategies for Engineered "Negligible Senescence") nonprofit, and others today. But ask any **molecular biologist** about the imperfect error correction and progressive trash accumulation that inevitably occurs in every differentiated biological cell over its lifetime, and it is easy to see that this goal is **impossible for humans** to accomplish. We are still decades away from a good predictive science of the cell.

Yes, we are learning to **partly rejuvenate** cells and tissues today, and **anti-aging, longevity and rejuvenation medicine** are vital and expanding fields. But experts know just how **limited** our therapies will remain, in all complex organisms, which have **evolved to recycle themselves** on a cyclic basis. We can surely gain several more decades of healthy lifespan. We are now learning how to measure epigenetic aging at the cellular level, and partly reverse it, restoring more youthful vitality to cells. We may be able to entirely rejuvenate our blood and immune systems, by stem cell reprogramming. But we won't be able to use these processes to significantly rejuvenate complex, **postmitotic structures** like the **human brain**. Over time, all differentiated cells accumulate molecular entropy and eventually die, by current evolutionary design.

Yes, some **future machine intelligence**, with advanced quantum computing capacity, including the ability to broadly simulate molecular dynamics, and the ability redesign our DNA, may in the **far future** reverse this unfortunate reality. But, we humans do not have any chance of doing this in the foreseeable future. We can't even make synthetic biology work at the level of single cells. Many people wish we could be **bioimmortal**, but wishing doesn't make it plausible.

There are several progress stories in human longevity that are not faulty. But, they require us to recalibrate our expectations. Many gerontologists expect that we could easily get **twenty or thirty more years of vital**, **healthy longevity over the next twenty or thirty years,** if we get a much better understanding of processes like aging (senescence), autophagy, apoptosis, rejuvenation, and immune and brain function at the molecular, cellular, organ, and physiological levels. We've already been able to do rejuvenation, to some degree, in many animals and humans, with such regimens as **intermittent fasting** and **caloric-restriction**. Over the last decade, we have begun investigating powerful new therapies that may eliminate **senescent cells (senolytics),** and drugs like **rapamycin** that can put our cells into a lower aging, protective mode, and may give us a decade or two of additional high functioning healthspan and lifespan. Stem cell reprogramming and bone marrow regrafting might allow us to significantly rejuvenate our blood and immune functions in old age. We should probably all be storing **cord blood (rich with stem cells)** when we have children today. But none of this is *anything close* to bioimmortality. None of it will ever give us more than another **thirty years of vitality**.

Computational biologist **Andrew Steele's** *Ageless: The New Science of Getting Older Without Getting Old,* 2021 gives a good summary of the valuable but quite limited longevity and vitality gains we might see in the next few decades. Societies with many more **vital 100 year olds** are probable in the 2030's and beyond. Even now we can take senolytics and effective aging-reducing therapies. For this kind of *very limited* vitality and longevity progress, groups like de Grey's SENS are well worth investing in. Due to the advocacy work of such groups, and of a handful of leading universities, the US National Institutes of Health is finally (but still reluctantly) investing in **longevity research**. Shame on them.

But at the same time, we must recognize the impossibility of the "bioimmortality" stories being told by many SENS cheerleaders. There is no way we could have **"negligible senescence" at the cellular level**, for any complex organism, until we have AIs smart enough to **redesign eukaryotic cells**. Such advanced AIs, not us, will be the only entities that

---

could deliver that future state. Just as importantly, it is not at all obvious today how many of us will **want bioimmortality** in that **future, AI-centric world.** Whether we will want to even stay biological at that point will depend on the **nature and quality of technological versus biological mind.** If you could be **more conscious, empathic, emotional, intelligent, and connected to all other life as a digital being,** and **think and feel millions of times faster than your biological counterpart,** would you even want **to remain indefinitely in biological form?** We think not, as we'll discuss in *BPF*.

Identifying Faulty Story Elements Example: Mars Colonization Stories

Consider next the stories of **biological humans colonizing Mars,** a hostile, airless, and far-too-small planet, with only 38% of Earth's gravity, to be hospitable to human life. Space medicine is already advanced enough that we can predict that anyone who chooses to live on Mars for any length of time will do permanent major damage to their bodies due to its very low gravity. Like bioimmortality, the Mars colonization story inspires innovation and investment in space technology. The story is exciting, and it has value, but its many grave faults also must be exposed.

A good online prediction market today, polling subject matter experts, would argue that humanity will send just a **handful of explorers** to Mars over the next fifty years, mostly for **very short durations.** Only a **few individualists, libertarians, and iconoclasts** will live on Mars for long periods, and they will **sacrifice much** for that choice. **Robots and AI** are the ideal way we presently explore our solar system. We don't even need the raw materials of the asteroids, unlike what space boosters claim. There are vast raw materials here on Earth. Our ocean floors are rich with <u>polymetallic nodules</u> that our undersea robots have barely sampled. Only one nation, Japan, has started any <u>undersea mining</u>.

Every planet in our solar system, other than our amazing, precious Earth, is a **desolate wasteland.** The Moon and Mars are like Mount Everest. We'll go there for the adventure, and to do a little new science (which will be much overhyped), but they are horribly expensive places to go, and sterile and uninteresting to inhabit. The main value of space is anything we put up there that **looks back at Earth,** so we can better improve this, our **one and only habitable planet.**

Humanity's true future, as we will argue in *BPF*, is to **continue heading to inner space,** further into the domain of the very small, very dense, very virtual, and very conscious. Almost none of us will leave Earth for the vast, slow, dangerous, and simple frontier of **outer space.** The main values of space for humanity are as a **perfect heat dump** for creating **accelerating complexity on Earth,** and a place to build useful structures in **near-earth orbit,** to improve our **life on Earth,** or to improve our understanding of the **universe,** and its many other **Earthlike planets.** We expect future science to discover that all of the intelligences on those planets are also **accelerating into inner space.** We think the destiny of all advanced intelligence is to **escape our universe,** rather than to expand across its vast and desolate landscape.

Yes, human exploration of our solar system (not interstellar space) has value. It will be inspiring to watch handfuls of human adventurers explore Mars, Europa, and other not-quite-habitable environments. But we'll never go there for any more fundamental purpose. We will build a limited number of structures on the Moon, and better ones in near-earth orbit, but other than for **adventure tourism,** putting humans in space is a very low-value pursuit. In our view, all our greatest advances will continue to happen **right here on Earth,** in the increasingly **dense, dematerialized, and valuable frontiers of inner space.** Science doesn't know what happens **inside black holes,** and we don't know what's **outside our universe.** But we can predict that members of all advanced intelligences will want to **connect** with all the other advanced civilizations in our universe, because many of us want that ourselves. If **inner space allows that connectivity,** as several physicists have speculated, and if we are accelerating to that destination as a **developmental process,** that sounds a lot more interesting to us than anything else we might do in our cosmic future, as we'll argue in *BPF*. We shall see.

Generalist futurists who like to learn and write in many areas, and **creative futurists** who like to imagine alternative worlds, are two types of practitioners who are particularly in need of **strong criticism** of their future fiction prior to publication. Both our generalist and creative tendencies can easily lead us to opinions, predictions, and stories that may sound great at first blush, at least from some perspectives, but which can be flagged as implausible, impossible, illogical, impractical, or ridiculous to many in a cognitively and experience diverse **crowd**.

All foresight professionals must **speculate** at times, and creative thinking will often lead us to new insights, but our speculation needs to be kept subject to our professional and organizational objectives. Speculation also should be compartmentalized, or confined to the proper times and places, or it becomes confused with reality. We all know a few people who can't do this compartmentalization well, and they live largely in fantasies of their own creation. **Paul and Elder's** *Critical Thinking, 2nd Edition*, 2013, is an excellent text that tells us our **creativity** must be continually grounded both in **reality** and **utility**, if it is to be adaptive. We need to use all three corners of the Classic Foresight Pyramid. In our next generation of **open online foresight platforms** and processes, we can hope that the global community of future thinkers will better critique our future stories, expose more of their faulty aspects, and make better future thinking accessible to all of us. We'll discuss our own small effort in that regard, **Futurepedia**, at the end of this book.

Collecting Weeble Stories (Important, Well-Criticized and Plausible Futures)

All serious foresight professionals, no matter what they do in their private lives and minds, will strive to **publicly** tell and write **Four Ps-balanced stories** that have **survived** a great deal of expert and lay **criticism**. Running a Do loop of research, creation (foresight), telling (action) and criticism (review) will give our stories the best **plausibility** and **probability** of coming true, at least in part. We call any important, well-critiqued, and still plausible stories **weeble stories**. Because of all the **criticism they have received, wobbled through, and survived,** such stories are particularly valuable to collect, understand and employ.

The Weeble is a small egg-shaped toy, first sold by Hasbro in 1971, and still sold today. Almost all of a weeble's weight is in the bottom of the egg, so **when anyone knocks it over, it wobbles right back up**. The same is true for any good future story. As the commercials used to say, "**Weebles wobble, but they don't fall down**." John keeps a Weeble on his desk, to remind him of the key qualities that all good future stories need, in order for us to have reasonable confidence that they truly are of value.

Weeble, 1971
(Author's collection)

A **weeble story** is a relevant trend, prediction, risk, scenario, opportunity, strategy, progress vision, or other judgment about the past, present, or future that has **seen a lot of past criticism (attempts to knock it down),** yet so far, it has "kept getting back up." Implicit trends or conditions seem to support it, so the story remains **plausible**. A good weeble story will be both **meaningful** (the future will change in important ways if it is true), and will have a **history of withstanding criticism in its essential claims,** even as it has been **changed and improved by criticism in many of its story elements.**

The best weeble stories **are continually attracting evidence and argument for them,** because the current explicit and implicit trends or conditions increasingly appear to support them. By continuing to wobble along, they have earned the right to be taken seriously. Some weeble stories naturally attract criticism when they make **specific or strong future claims**. Others when they **go against current conventions or assumptions**. Others when they are **alluring but counterintuitive**. Others are criticized if they are **inconvenient** (think of climate change), and if someone will **lose money, power or status** or if many will have to **modify their behavior** if the story turns out to be true (again, think of climate change). Still other weeble stories **do not attract a lot criticism,** either because are missing any of these factors, are technical, complex, or abstract, or for some other reason. In that case, the author or user of the story will need to make an **extra effort** to get that story **sufficiently critiqued**, and it must also **survive** that critique, if it is to qualify as a weeble.

As foresight practitioners, we want to find as many weeble stories that seem relevant to our clients as we can, and attempt to write new ones ourselves. These are the stories we want to tell clients when we think they will do the most good. Try to tell your more speculative "pre-weeble" stories initially in **private conversations** with critical, but supportive colleagues, and make sure they survive their criticism before sharing them more widely. If we must discuss **speculations in public**, we should make sure they are clearly acknowledged as **speculations** and always **ask for critique**. If criticism is the best antidote to error, private criticism and qualifiers are the best protectors of our **reputation**.

Some weebles stories are **wildcards**, futures that we consider to be **low probability events**, yet if they occurred, they would have a **high probability** of either positive or negative ADOR impact. Besides the general class of relevant, high probability future events, we want to find relevant wildcards whenever we can. We also want to build **scanning systems** and **early warning signals analysis** for the occurrence of relevant negative events, and work out strategies for keeping negative events low probability, and reacting rapidly and efficiently to them when they do occur.

These are all examples of good **risk management**, a key foresight specialty practice. **John Petersen's** classic, _Out of the Blue: Wildcards and Other Big Future Surprises_, 1997, and **Nicholas Taleb's** _The Black Swan: The Impact of the Highly Improbable_, 2010, are two good introductions to **wildcard identification and management**. Taleb's book also considers how wildcards impact a system's robustness and its **antifragility**, or ability to learn and get stronger after any error or catastrophe. We'll talk more about antifragility, and analyze it as a form of **immunity**, in Book 2. All complex adaptive systems, whether biological, societal, or technological, have network-based **immune systems** that secure their critical processes. If we are **blind to the operation** of those immune systems, we don't understand how **security** (one of the IES values) works, and can be improved, for the system in question (organism, society, AI).

Just as life advances by **trial and lots of error,** human foresight advances only by telling lots of **imaginable stories**, subjecting them to careful critique, and separating out the majority of partly or greatly **faulty stories** from the much smaller set of **weebles.** Let us now ask: What kind of factors contribute to the **creation** of faulty stories? What kind of activities can our teams engage in, to **convert** some of our faulty stories into weebles? Let's look at one example.

Turning Faulty Stories into Weeble Stories: Flying Firefighters vs. Firefighting Drones

The image below was produced for a series on **pop futurism** titled _In the Year 2000_. It is one of 87 far-future visions published in that series over the first decade of the 20th century, 1899-1910. Like all pop futurism, _In the Year 2000_ mixes both **entertainment** (storytelling) with a few serious attempts at **foresight**. Anyone with engineering experience in the 1900s would have recognized this **human wing contraption** as an aspirational yet improbable future.

Firefighting in the Year 2000, Jean-Marc Côté, 1900 World Exhibition, Paris.

We'd all **love to fly** like this, but even then a **good engineer** could estimate the energy density, miniaturization, and power-to-weight ratios needed for such machines, and call it unlikely. It is an attractive story, with **humans as heroes**. It is even plausible, eventually. But a **more valuable exercise** is to ask **what will outcompete this story**, long before it is possible. What can be **delivered well ahead** of this vision, on the **trend lines of firefighting technology development**?

If asked, most of us today would agree that some form of **firefighting robot** would be safer, more efficient and more probable than employing humans in this risky way. But even the artist who drew this, **circa 1899**, if they'd had access to a **critical engineering crowd**, could have known this as well. There were already large collections of **mechanical automatons** in the 19th century. Engineers knew the superior abilities of **machines** to **leverage power** and operate in **dangerous circumstances**. Many engineers had made helicopter designs. The French inventor **Gustave d'Amecourt**, coined the word helicopter in 1861. **Thomas Edison** built a **helicopter prototype** with an internal combustion engine in 1885. Though it did not fly, he even used it to predict the **power-to-weight ratio** it would need in order for it to fly.

Drawing **humans sitting inside helicopters, spraying water and rescuing people with mechanical arms,** would have been **less entertaining** but far more **prescient and useful work of foresight**. When the future thinker seeks to entertain as well as educate, it is easy to produce faulty visions. Of course, until we had **drones** as a **reference point**, those attracted to the vision of the **human firefighting hero** could still imagine some kind of **winged backpack** being built that would allow people to fly up the outside of a building, rescue someone, and even carry a hose and spray it into a building. Still pursuing this **faulty vision**, we've even seen <u>firefighting jetpacks</u> developed in a few countries, notably Dubai. This is happening, in our view, because the developers of those jetpacks are **conflating their desire to fly like a bird**, which will increasingly happen, with the **use of such contraptions for fighting fires**, which will never happen at scale. In our view, **futurists and engineers should know better by now**.

Why does this foresight **matter**? Why should we **weed out faulty stories like this** as early as we can? Because **the stakes are high** around many of our stories. The earlier we can see the optimal **developmental solutions** ahead of us, the earlier we can invest in delivering them. With firefighting, **people are still dying** because we don't have the **quality of vision** and the **policy, R&D, and entrepreneurial commitments** that we should. **Wildfires are a deadly, multi-billion dollar annual problem,** all over the world, growing because of **climate change**. Humanity needs **better wilderness management,** with many more **controlled, robotically-managed burns,** and we need much **better defenses against wildfires.** We can already see many of the **coming developmental solutions to fight wildfires.** We just need the **courage, investment, and strategies** to make them happen **now**, not **decades from now**.

Firefighting drone swarms are an **obvious next-gen solution** for defending people and property near wilderness. Such drones, and an **infrared sensor network** around our buildings, can **inexpensively monitor** and **rapidly extinguish embers** that make it across any **firebreak** and land on **structures.** They will also be able to **pick up water** from preexisting water tanks, installed near those buildings, in fire-prone areas, dual-use tanks that also supply water to homes year round. Think of Los Angeles County's <u>69 Bravo</u> (3 mins, Vimeo, 2016), for helicopter water resupply, but instead for drones. Unmanned, **heat-resistant drones** can deliver **much less water, much more precisely,** closely, and economically. Fire departments also need to be able to **rapidly create backburns and firebreaks** to protect people and property. **Fire line explosives**, experimented with and then sadly discontinued due to overcaution, can rapidly and safely create **large and precise firebreaks.** Drones can do **rapid backburns near buildings** to **remove fire stock.** All of these strategies work even in **high winds**. These powerful technologies belong in the **firefighter's arsenal**.

This vision, in various guises, has been around for several decades now. Fire line explosives were used in the 1970's. Robotics competitions, to use **wheeled robots to extinguish fires**, have been running in the US since the 1990s. We just need to make it happen. We think firefighting departments will eventually deploy **drone swarms** and **unmanned bulldozers,** and homeowners near wilderness will depend on them. They will use drones and unmanned vehicles for many other useful purposes (deliveries, security) as well.

Of course, *diffusion* **of this coming development, against various forms of social and organizational blocks**, is another matter entirely. These predictable developments must navigate **political (risk, safety) and labor (job security) hurdles.** **Entrepreneurs** will need to rely on all of the **Eight Skills** to build these solutions, demonstrate their efficacy, get **fire departments** to see their value, and get **political and public cover** to deploy them. But this development will come, in our view. So let's tell and critique this **useful weeble story** as **fearlessly** and **impatiently** as we can.

So what **lessons** can we draw from this weeble story, and from the faulty story of flying firefighters that long predates it? One lesson is that in telling any future story, we should recognize our **emotional attachments and biases, and avoid conflating our goals**. A second lesson is that we should seek to find **developmental trends**. A third lesson is that we should pay attention to all the **blocking factors** that will delay a developmental future from arriving as early as it otherwise might, and ask what **strategies** we can use to overcome those factors, and catalyze positive developments.

Many faulty futures stories are circulating today. Scientific and technological stories that we think are **mostly hype** today are any kind of genetic engineering for human enhancement, nootropics, space elevators, molecular assemblers, desktop additive manufacturing, and many other entertaining and often discussed things. Even standard tropes like artificial intelligence, the internet of things, robotics, and virtual and augmented reality are always **vastly oversold in the short term,** both by the **opportunistic press** and by our **amateur futurist community**. The more knowledge we have of the **STEEPLES constraints and drivers** behind any story being told, and the **level of expert criticism** that has been levied against it already, the better we can determine if it is a probable, possible, progress, preventable, or faulty story. As we find and tell weeble stories in each of the Four Ps, we **build a map** we can use to **create better strategy**, in every domain.

Creating Shared Visions (Motivating and Adaptive Progress Stories)

To create a good **map of the future**, we must collect weebles across the Four Ps. What's more, the more well-critiqued stories we have of all four types, the better we can adapt. But as we have said before, the stories at the **"top of the pyramid,"** our **preferable and preventable futures**, are the ones we and our clients naturally care about most. More than anything else, we seek to find ethical and adaptive **positive visions** that inspire us, and plausible **negative visions** that scare us into making necessary changes. Leadership involves learning how to **create such stories** for ourselves and our teams, and **tell them** in a way that will **recruit and motivate others** to help us make our positive visions real.

Preferred futures that are **widely agreed upon** and **motivating** for the stakeholders can be called **progress stories**. But we must remember that it is easier to craft useful **preventable futures** than **progress stories**. The **DROA bias** reminds us that humanity has an evolutionary bias against telling too many stories about **progress**. It has been far more adaptive for us, up until very recently in our history, to point out the **risks, dangers, and problems of the future**.

As a result, we tend to **tell progress stories only to ourselves, quietly**. Since they typically receive less exposure and critique, these stories are often **simplistic and vague**. But, when we tell them **aloud** and **solicit critique** from others, we can adapt them to be much more **practical, nuanced, and motivating**. Collecting and sharing our more important and complex progress stories is an outcome that we hope to inspire among all who are reading this *Guide*.

Particularly important to find and tell, in our view, are **exponential progress stories**, because all our best visions contain both anticipation of **exponential scientific and technological change**, and explicit ideas of personal, team, organizational, global, or universal **progress** that we might make, given the predictable reality of **accelerating change**.

<u>**Peter Diamandis**</u> of Singularity University encourages finding your **MTP**, or **Massive Transformative Purpose**, a modern variation of the BHAG (Big, Hairy, Audacious Goal) proposed by **Jim Collins and Jerry Porras** in <u>*Built to Last*</u>, 1994. Since 2009, companies like MITRE and Google have talked about **Moonshot** and **10X Thinking** in search of ways that our teams, companies, industry, or society can use **exponential trends** in order to create a greatly better future—and solve one or more of our current biggest problems or constraints.

Progress stories require intellectual effort, courage, and collective foresight. The "**p-word**" isn't popular with some in our culture. Some intellectuals, journalists, pessimists, and others still believe the fiction that our world is not improving at an accelerating rate in numerous way. They instead maintain that it is "stagnant," "getting steadily worse," now at "critical point" or even "falling apart". As a result, their big picture visions are faulty. Not seeing accelerating progress can be **emotionally satisfying**. It allows the storyteller to play the hero, truthteller, or rescuer role. But that story simply doesn't fit with how complexity evolution and development apparently work in our universe, at the network level.

As we've covered in our discussion of **DROA bias**, we argue that such views are incorrect. While many *individual* (evolutionary) actors, organizations and nations are always facing crises and critical points, civilization as a whole—as a complex network—is always developing its intelligence, complexity, abilities, and immunity. Our civilization as a whole has never been more resilient, capable, intelligent, or rapidly learning, as it is right now.

When we encounter cynical and pessimistic people, we can challenge them to look at websites like <u>HumanProgress.org</u>, which documents just a few of our continual advances, and to take **Gapminder's** most recent (and annually changing) brief <u>"State of the World" test</u>. Of the 12,000 people who took this brief test in 2017 in 14 countries, the **average correct score is only 41%**. At present **eighty percent** of all respondents score *worse* than random (50%). **Americans**, misled by our **DROA-based** and **plutocratic media**, do **particularly poorly** on these tests relative to other advanced democracies. Only 10% do better than random on Rosling's test, and none of the 12,000 people he surveyed got all twelve questions right. This *Guide's* primary author (John) got only 9 of the 12 questions right, and he prides himself on researching and seeing the **positive trends** in the world. We should all take the test and see how well we do!

The lesson here is that old information, evolutionary biases and the media can skew us to see civilization's problems as much worse than they actually are. Read *Factfulness*, 2018, for more on our many positive global trends, and read **Bailey and Tupy's** *Ten Global Trends Every Smart Person Should Know*, 2020, for more on accelerating **human progress**, and for more how **Americans**, among all the economically prosperous countries, are presently **particularly poor** at seeing it. We believe that versions of books like these should be **required reading** in every **middle school and high school** in America. Those years are a special time when many of us will develop our first sophisticated **worldviews**.

Bailey & Tupy, 2020

But, as we'll describe in *BPF*, all of the problems we face today, including the host of problems created by our recent decades of **accelerating tech-created wealth and plutocracy**, are **problems of progress.** They are either **problems we've created for ourselves**, due to less adaptive **ethical and empathic choices**, or they are **initial side effects** of our scientific, technical, and economic successes. In what is called the **adaptation curve**, many societal changes bring both new benefits and new problems, especially in the **first generation**. Problems often **stay bad in the second generation**. Finally, in the **third generation**, we begin to institute new regulations, innovations, and behaviors, and other **solutions** that get us out of our new problems. The more seriously we discuss and critique those solutions in advance, the sooner we can get the progress we seek.

We don't yet have a **science of progress**, but rather a useful collection of beliefs and philosophies in that regard. Nevertheless, good philosophers are always looking to a future where science can validate and improve our imperfect models. So, even though the "p-word" (progress) has many different meanings for each of us, we each already have some concept of what progress word means, and what directions will lead us to a better place than where we are today.

The pioneering futurist **Fred Polak** in his classic, *The Image of the Future*, 1955, famously claimed that our personal and cultural **images of how the world works**—and the **images of the futures that we believe we can have as a result,** are key determinants of our behavior. Futurist **Elise Boulding** published an abridged English version of Polak's *The Image of the Future* in 1973. The <u>PDF can be found here</u>. Economist and sociologist **Kenneth Boulding's** brief book *The Image*, 1956, offers his own version of the benefits of a **positive vision-driven view** of the future. In Polak and the Boulding's views, finding and sharing the **most useful and motivating visions we can find** is one of our top responsibilities, both as foresight professionals and as individuals. Aside from universal forces we don't control, the futures we build for ourselves flow directly from our *imaginations*. So, let's conduct **best visioning that we can** on a regular basis and choose to believe that we and humanity deserve great futures—because we do.

Polak and Boulding also remind us that all our science, technology, economics, politics, and social beliefs are, at root, **experimental mental constructions** (evolutionary paths). Only a small fraction of these "memes" will end up being **universal truths** (developmental processes and destinations). We often can't determine in advance which of our memes will survive the test of time. Therefore, to have the greatest positive impact on our futures, we must recognize that the **quality of our positive visions** can often be the greatest lever for personal and social change. Other scholars in cognitive science, psychology, sociology, and philosophy have since said these things, but the clarity and scope of Polak and Boulding on this point have not yet been surpassed, to our knowledge.

Our visions may start out poor, but the more we evolve and develop them, the more effective we become. We mustn't skimp on daily visioning, both for ourselves and for our clients. We should also have regular social contact with others who can hear them, and offer feedback. Moreover, we should continue to develop the kinds of talent, experiences, and intelligences that will support and grow our ability to imagine the future. A nice intro to personal visioning and daily journaling is **Lucia Cappachioni's** *Visioning*, 2000.

We are all on a **vision quest** (We think *Vision Quest*, 1985, is a great movie, BTW), whether we recognize it or not. Every futurist and foresighter who thinks they see a little bit more of the future than others, can use that **gift** to help others to craft better progress stories. The late leadership author **Stephen Covey** calls this the opportunity to "Find your Voice, and Inspire Others to Find Theirs." He explores it in *The Eighth Habit*, 2005, a sequel to his bestseller *The 7 Habits of Highly Effective People*, 1989/2013. As Covey says, finding our **voice and vision**, and helping others to **find theirs** (these are technically two habits, to be accurate) can move us from effectiveness to **greatness** in our leadership journey.

As committed future thinkers, we can ask: How might our present reality be significantly better? What is the quality of our personal, team, organizational, and societal visions? Have we carefully anticipated what **must** come next? Have we carefully imagined what **may** come? What each of us truly **wants**? What we should most want to **prevent**? Once we have what we believe are motivating yet practical visions, do we have the courage to share them, and get them constructively critiqued? Such questions can help us with our personal, team, and organizational vision quests.

Sentiment Leadership I: Valuable Optimism to Pessimism (O:P) Ratios

We've said that **emotional foresight** requires being **aware of** and able to **ethically influence** our and others' emotions toward more accurate and adaptive states of mind. Let's discuss it now, in **team and organizational context**.

Books like **Bradberry and Greaves'** *Emotional Intelligence 2.0*, 2009, offer good diagnostics and tips for improving our emotional intelligence—or EI. **Dan Goleman's** *Social Intelligence*, 2007, reminds us that being aware of and responsive to others emotional states is also a key habit of **strong teams.** Social intelligence (SI) requires a foundation of EI, and more. To build both, we must learn to balance **introspection** (watching ourselves) with **extrospection** (watching and having empathy with and ethics for others). We must be both **"in our heads"** and **"in the world"** in the right ratio.

Once one has good **emotional awareness, emotional self-control,** and **emotional ownership** (ASO of the ASOFA challenges, described in the Student Edition), including managing our **strategic optimism** and **defensive pessimism**, perhaps the next most important challenge in EI and SI is to seek to ethically influence the **optimism and pessimism of others**, toward more adaptive responses. In that journey, we move from **sentiment foresight** to sentiment *leadership*.

Just as the **mindfulness hypothesis** tells us that most of the time we want to stay in the **Present**, not the Past or Future, we can offer an **emotional effectiveness hypothesis**, proposing that most of the time we want to be sitting in **realism**, which we define as **balancing optimistic and pessimistic feeling and thinking** in the *right ratios for each context*. Even as we acknowledge our own **natural set points** as optimists or pessimists, we must see the value of **maintaining a great variety of optimism and pessimism ratios** in our future feeling and thinking. Let us look closer now at this hypothesis.

Consider how our personal **Optimism:Pessimism feeling and thinking ratios** can either **support** or **work against** our tasks. Clearly, a **50:50 balance** between both sentiments is only sometimes going to be the most adaptive. We have proposed that it makes sense for **GRASP thinking**, in **task planning**, but even there we will find it valuable, in certain contexts, to spend more time on the optimistic or pessimistic aspects of GRASP. So where should our balance point be, in different contexts, and how can we become more aware of our current balance when **feeling, thinking and planning**? Which **O:P ratios** may be most adaptive, on teams and in organizations, in various contexts?

To begin to address this important question, let's look briefly at **sentiment ratios**, and make some initial observations. Many biological properties are **exponentials**, measured in doublings. For example, every **ten decibels** is a perceived (sensed) **doubling in loudness**. A threshold is crossed with each doubling, changing its nature. We will use this same convention to classify a set of seven different O:P ratios, and say a little about each of them, with the aim of advancing our insight and foresight in sentiment leadership.

The table below summarizes the main ratios we will discuss:

O:P Ratio	Common Life Contexts
1:1	Sentiment Contrasting, GRASP Thinking; "Realism"
2:1	Advantage & Opportunity Assessment; Strategic Optimism
1:2	Disruption & Risk Assessment; Defensive Pessimism
4:1	Relationship Management and Novel Environments
1:4	Criticism Production and Crisis Environments
8:1	Visioning & Selling (productive) and Manias (counterproductive)
1:8	Conflict States (productive) and Panics (counterproductive)

Let's first review the value of a **1:1** optimism: pessimism ratio for quick strategic planning (sentiment contrasting). Then we'll talk about the apparent value of **three successive doublings** of these ratios, both in **optimism ratios (2:1, 4:1 and 8:1)** and in **pessimism ratios (1:2, 1:4 and 1:8)** in our foresight thinking. Like every ten decibels, each of these doublings creates a **noticeably different emotional environment** than the previous. Each new threshold can be adaptive or not, depending on appropriateness for the task at hand.

1. 1:1 O:P Ratio: Sentiment Contrasting for Accuracy, Ability, and Persistence

As we have said, one of the most exciting foresight findings of recent years is a process of sentiment-balancing that we call **sentiment contrasting**. It involves a targeted use, and a **roughly 1:1 balancing** of optimism and pessimism, in that order, to gain the optimum levels of performance in our lives and on our teams. The psychologist **Gabrielle Oettingen** has done scores of randomized controlled trials (RCTs) on the effects of future thought on cognition, emotion, and behavior. She has done the hard experimental work exploring variations of optimistic and pessimistic thinking.

Oettingen explores these results in *Rethinking Positive Thinking*, 2015. She addresses the traps of being too optimistic, of being too pessimistic, of being neither (apathy), and the ideal order of our feeling and thinking in approaching any task.

In Oettingen's view, an ideal **average O:P ratio prior to much of our task planning** is roughly **1:1**. She discovered that if her subjects are asked to first be **optimistic**, imagining themselves having achieved a worthy, complex task, envisioning how good they will feel, and then to be **pessimistic**, spending a roughly equal amount of time imagining **predictable ways they might fail**, and **obstacles** they will have to overcome, those subjects consistently do three things better than every other experimental group:

1. They are more **foresighted**. They can **predict**, much more **accurately** (with 50-100% less prediction error), how much of the task they will complete, in the next few hours, days, or months. There is a plausible argument (but not much evidence yet) that they are also more **prioritized**.

2. They have greater **ability (productivity)**. They will get more done (30-150% more) in the same amount of time.

3. They have more **persistence (motivation)**, to continue a task even when setbacks occur. Because they **believe** more strongly in their predictions, they act with greater **determination** to make them real.

Consider **how valuable this finding is** for our lives. Subjects asked to be pessimistic before a task, to be optimistic, to be neither, or to be both, but starting with pessimism, are all **significantly worse both at predicting their behavior**, and at **getting things done**. If we **pay close attention** to our feelings, before contemplating any task, and spend a small amount of time first in a state of **strategic optimism**, imagining the benefits of achieving our plans, then roughly the same amount of time in **defensive pessimism**, imagining all the ways we might fail, we will invariably make **much better plans**, and achieve more **planned actions**. We will also be more **motivated to persist**, regardless of obstacles.

2. 2:1 and 1:2 O:P Ratios: Opportunity vs. Risk Orientation

In contrast to Oettingen, the psychologist **Dilip Jeste** tells us that a **2:1 Optimism:Pessimism ratio** may be so adaptive, that it might be an ideal **Internal Set Point** for **self-talk**, in most life contexts. We also interpret Jeste as saying a **2:1 O:P set point** represents the self-talk of a **Strategic Optimist**, in most contexts. In other words, in the modern world, with all its opportunities, most of us should be strategic optimists, most of the time.

With respect to ADOR, a 2:1 set point orients us to the **Advantages** and **Opportunities** around us. We would agree wit Jeste that something like a **2:1 O:P ratio** is where we typically want to be when we aren't yet doing planning (sentiment contrasting, 1:1), assessing an uncertainty (potential risk), starting something new, responding to a crisis, or any of a number of other **special contexts** we will discuss in the next few pages.

As Jeste observes, there are so many things we can **control** in our lives, and so many **opportunities** for **improving** our state of existence, no matter how challenged we are, that if we *don't* typically have two strategically optimistic thoughts for every one defensively pessimistic thought, with thoughts and actions within our **span of control**, we will **continually miss key ways to better our lives**. There are just so many ways we can use **small-scale, today's, and near-term foresight** to **make progress** on the things we care about.

This **2:1 Internal Set Point ratio** can also create what psychologist **Shelly Taylor**, in her book *Positive Illusions*, 1991, calls "healthy self-deceptions." We can usefully imagine ourselves as **smarter and better off** than we actually are, and if we do not overdo it, this kind of **mild self-deception** is empowering. We just have to be careful not to overuse it, or we may become arrogant, passive, and self-deluding.

By contrast, an **adaptive 1:2 Optimism:Pessimism ratio**, in ADOR terms, can be defined as the set point of a typical **Defensive Pessimist**. Such a ratio orients us twice as much, in mental time and priorities, to the **Risks and Disruptions** around us. In older individuals, studies have shown that defensive pessimists live, on average, <u>10% longer than optimists</u>. They take more precautions, and they live less chaotic lives. Organizational psychologists also tell us that having some defensive pessimists on our teams is deeply effective for previsualizing and avoiding problems.

On a regular basis, we will encounter places where we aren't sure what the risks are, or where disruptions need to be evaluated. In that state, it makes great sense to be **temporarily** twice as defensively pessimistic as we are optimistic, until we have made some **assessment** of the potential risks, and disruptions, and have responded by improving thinking, our preparation state, or our environment.

When we are not thinking defensively, it can be maladaptive to stay in a 1:2 O:P ratio. If we are **indiscriminately** pessimistic, we can get stuck in a **negative mental prison of our own making**. We may become "explanatory pessimists," seeing the negative of everything, as our first response. We stop seeing all the positive paths all around us. In other words, even those who are by nature defensive pessimists need to be able to **shift to other ratios**, as context demands.

3. 4:1 and 1:4 O:P Ratios: Relating and Novelty vs. Criticism and Crises

The next optimistic doubling in sentiment ratios (4:1) is greatly useful in at least two contexts. First, we need it for **relationship management** (relating with others, and leading or managing others) and for **novelty points** (when we are faced with novel tools, rules, or conditions). The next doubling on the pessimistic side (1:4) seems very helpful in **crises** (actual damage and disruption) and for evaluating **criticism** (an ego threat), in the review step of our **Do loops**.

The **4:1 O:P ratio hypothesis** for relationships is found in the work of psychologist **John Gottman**. He proposed an ideal ratio of positive and negative communications to create a predictably stable marriage. His empirical work found a **5:1** to be the ideal ratio, close enough to our 4:1 that we lump his work in with this category. In Gottman's view, our **partner** should be a **source of optimism**, in thinking and communication, roughly five times more than they are of pessimism.

We would predict a model of an **adaptive marriage**, versus a **stable marriage** (what Gottman may be measuring), would give us something closer to a **4:1 O:P ratio**. Many marriages are kept stable for the **purpose of stability**, not for the adaptive benefit of the partners. In our view, we should all seek out as much **criticism**, delivered with as much **empathy and ethics** as possible, as we can tolerate, to be adaptive. We'd suggest that is probably something closer to 4:1 than 5:1. In support of our view, **Tierney and Bauermeister's** *The Power of Bad: How the Negativity Effect Rules Us and How We Can Rule It*, 2019, offers the 4:1 O:P ratio as a general Rule of Thumb, "It takes four good things to overcome one bad thing."

Thus, even if we are naturally **strategic optimists**, maintaining an **emotionally adaptive relationship**, with **our spouses, our children, our teammates, and our neighbors**, will require us to **self-censor our internal negative thoughts at least twice as often as we communicate them**. Over time, we may even be able to **think** in this 4:1 ratio, when thinking of others, even as we think 2:1 with ourselves (typical self-talk). It may become automatic for us, in this context, and thus prevent us from saying unnecessarily critical or hurtful things.

Conversely, if we are naturally **realists**, we should probably strive to be **four times as optimistic with others** as we tend to be with ourselves. If we are **defensive pessimists**, we should strive to be **eight times as optimistic**, when thinking of and communicating with others. Tierney and Bauermeister offer tips for improving our O:P communication ratio without becoming unrealistic. **Cognitive behavioral therapy (CBT)**, **Rational-Emotive Behavior Therapy (REBT)**, and even today's simple **CBT Personal AIs**, like Woebot, can also help us in that regard.

Others have replicated this research. Again, we think a **4:1 Optimism:Pessimism relationship communication ratio** seems particularly adaptive both in **relationships** and in **managing others**, as a rough average. To keep our fears at bay and our hopes strong, we all need to be encouraged and complimented significantly more often than criticized. But, if we get too much positive feedback, relative to criticism, we may not perform the difficult work of change.

We'd also predict this 4:1 ratio also applies to the kind of communications our **firms** should make with their **employees**, and that our **governments and politicians** should make with their **citizens**. If our firms and leaders aren't talking about

opportunity and benefit four times more than they are about **danger, compliance, and penalties** for misbehaving, something is seriously wrong. They are **leading with sticks, not carrots.** When we communicate in **perpetual crisis mode**, hope and innovation are degraded, and the relationship suffers. If we call to mind how far many firms and politicians are from this kind of **4:1 relationship-building communication** today, we can see how much opportunity for greater **social trust** we are throwing away—and how much collective opportunity we are losing—every day.

At the same time, every so often we are going to have to do, or contemplate doing, something **largely new**—laden with both opportunity and risk. We can call that a **novelty point.** In such contexts, we may have to learn new things about our environment, try out new tasks and new behaviors, start a new venture, or otherwise enter into "startup" mode. In that state, a **4:1 Startup/Novelty Optimism:Pessimism ratio** may again be ideal, because positive change is hard—and because novelty (a new tool, a new emergence, a new rule) often brings the **cognitive overhead** of a great number of new possibilities to strategically explore. We will need strong strategic optimism to get us through the valleys and challenges ahead and to surface the opportunities and strategies that may otherwise be hidden from us.

Ask any **entrepreneur**—a person who is continually forced to learn and try new things in order to keep their business afloat—and they will explain they often use **extreme strategic optimism** to keep them going. Novelty isn't a state we stay in forever (and staying there too long is not adaptive, we also need predictable structure); but, when we are in it, we need lots of strategic optimism to guide us through.

Conversely, an **adaptive 1:4 O:P ratio** can occur at any **crisis point.** In a crisis, we face not only risks and disruptions that must be assessed, but a **danger or catastrophe** to which we must respond. We may have suffered some **loss or damage**, either anticipated or not. We may have received a bad performance evaluation, been diagnosed with a serious illness, had our property stolen, hurt someone else (intentionally or not), or otherwise became involved in a crisis.

A 1:4 O:P ratio may also be adaptive when we are receiving **criticism**, a **verbal disruption** to both our equilibrium and our ego. In that context, it is adaptive for us to review (pay attention to) that criticism, to embrace its pain where it seems warranted, and to think about what we can do to prevent such negative feedback in the future. We will need that defensive pessimism to produce the new strategies and plans that will help us to adapt to the damage or disruption.

Again, crisis and criticism aren't states we stay in forever. Experiencing either for too long is stressful. But leaders, teams, organizations, and governments may find it valuable to consciously use this 1:4 ratio whenever they are in a **crisis**, or are responding to some implicit **critique** (as when a firm gets negative press, or is boycotted by some of its customers). Admitting the negative, and taking immediate steps to respond to it, can be a powerful way to rebuild trust.

At the same time, we should be careful not to **overuse** either the 4:1 or 1:4 sentiment states. It's easy for an individual, a team, or an organization to overuse positive communication, and ignore problems. It is also easy for us to overuse negative or danger or compliance-focused communications, and to overfocus on crises. We must recognize **declining returns** for each of these sentiment states.

4. 8:1 and 1:8 O:P Ratios: Selling and Manias vs. Conflicts and Panics

The last sentiment ratio set we will discuss, 8:1 and 1:8 is so extreme that it seems adaptive only in special contexts, for short periods. Unfortunately, the 1:8 ratio is common in our modern mass media environment, as we will see.

Adaptive **8:1 Optimism:Pessimism ratios** are found frequently in sales. When one is **selling** something, it makes sense to deeply accentuate the positive until the sale "closes." The seller is spinning a strongly positive illusion that is greatly oversimplified but effective. All great sellers and influencers know the value of this ratio. **Effective sales people** will mention a few **innocuous negatives**, to defuse the buyer's suspicions that they are being manipulated. But, they are also being deceptive, and that doesn't build lasting trust. A **great salesperson** will mention some **real negatives**, educating the buyer, and **building trust**, and then counter it with so many positives that again, the sale remains compelling.

A **nonadaptive 8:1 O:P ratio** occurs when we are engaged in a **mania** of some type. **Charles Mackay's** classic, <u>*Extraordinary Popular Delusions and the Madness of Crowds*</u>, 1841, is a classic book on this ratio. It shows how perennial episodes of **manic and panic thinking** have occurred throughout history. Investment manias emerge when **greed** outcompetes **common sense**—as in the **dot com mania**, various **real estate manias**, and recent **bitcoin and ICO investment manias**. Such thinking also happens in **utopianism**, where we become obsessed with imagining **unrealistically perfect, harmonious, or ideal** future realities. We rightly call a utopian thinker a **Pollyanna**, someone so focused on the positive potential of things that they fail to anticipate or prepare for **disaster**. In manias, we are obsessed with fantasies. We never see the risk and danger, or defend ourselves from preventable futures.

An **adaptive 1:8 Optimism:Pessimism ratio** occurs when we are engaged in **conflict**. In a fight for a **moral cause**, it helps, on occasion, to focus our attention on all the **negative or objectionable aspects** of our opponent, to motivate us to the painful, risky activities, including personal sacrifice, as in a <u>just war</u>, that a resolution of that conflict may demand. More commonly, an **expose**, a detailed **critique** of some deeply flawed system, is another kind of conflict where this extreme ratio can be very helpful. We use it in **investigative journalism**, when we report on a **crisis, crime or corruption**, and its complex causes. Extensive negative criticism and communication seems warranted in such contexts, for **short periods**. Sometimes an expose is needed to jar an audience out of complacency into recognizing the seriousness of a problem.

This is also what we do in our minds when we are watching **dystopia stories** as entertainment. In our rough guess, we'd estimate that most of us choose to watch protopias and dystopias in a **1:8 ratio**. We may do this because we enjoy the **drama of conflict**, and its **resolution**. Note however, that almost all of the dramas we prefer will end up with some **positive ending**, so while they may be in 1:8 in O:P ratio in their plot and general experience, in their key character development arcs they are far less pessimistic. Even in **dystopic settings**, we look for a **positive character development** and **satisfying resolutions** of conflict. A **search for conflict**, and its **resolution**, are how we all generate **drama**.

Consider also how fleeting is **human happiness**. We quickly grow **dissatisfied** with our current state, no matter how **privileged** it may be in objective terms. Subjectively, we serially focus on various flaws in our experiences, however minor. Just like **positive illusions**, more temporary **negative illusions** can get us to fix those flaws, and progress.

A **maladaptive 1:8 O:P ratio** occurs in **panics**, where we fall into **unjustified fear**, often in **herds**, as in a **stock market panic**. It also happens when a **propagandist** manufactures **false panic** and **fake threats**. A short seller may try to create and profit from such panic. Autocratic leaders find this useful when seeking to scare their citizens into obedience. Panic engages our fear centers (limbic system), creating a <u>fight-or-flight response</u> (now also called the acute stress response). It activates our sympathetic nervous system, preparing us to **flight or flee**. This activation is adaptive for the **short-term**, when we need to **prepare for conflict** or **conflict resolution or avoidance**, but **chronic activation** of this stress response is emotionally unhealthy for any person, group or society.

A **1:8 O:P ratio** is thus a **terrible prescription for non-fiction news and media**. Nevertheless, much of our **network news** and much **social media** has gravitated to this sentiment ratio in recent years, as this ratio grabs our attention, creating **false panic**. Persistent **1:2, 1:4 or 1:8 ratios** are each increasingly extreme versions of the **DROA bias**. When we use them chronically, these ratios are a major threat to humanity's ability to see **advantage** and **opportunity** around us.

As **Barry Glassner's** <u>*The Culture of Fear: Why Americans Are Afraid of the Wrong Things*</u>, 1999/2018, reminds us, this wasn't true of most network news sixty years ago. Some of our more popular news sources have been negativity biased since the rise of <u>yellow journalism</u> in the late 1800s. But only recently has this come to describe the **great majority** of mass media. These negative O:P ratios grew as our media channels became more commercially driven, and became 24-hour in the 1980s. Since then, leading platforms no longer seek to inspire, envision, and debate, but rather, to peddle dramatic stories of disruption, risk or threat. At the same time, as plutocracy has grown, regulations for fair and balanced content have been dismantled.

Today's mass media presents the world around us as a series of **manufactured crises and dramas**. Such news transforms the world into a **never-ending car crash**, and turns those willing to consume it into **perpetual rubberneckers**. Futurist and politician **Al Gore's** *The Assault on Reason*, 2008/2017 nicely summarizes our current **mass media dystopia**, and it presciently predicted our current epidemic of **fake news**. **Rutger Bregman's** *Humankind: A Hopeful History*, 2020, cites recent studies showing how damaging the continual consumption of such news is to our mental and physical health.

Dan Goleman calls this this kind of communication "**amygdala hijacking**." It uses System 1, our emotional brain, to keep us focused on catastrophes and crises, both real and imagined. Enduring such news or entertainment is emotionally exhausting. It drains our willpower, and makes us less confident and innovative. We need to recognize when we are being manipulated, spending too much time in a **"takedown"** of the world around us, and break away from this **toxic sentiment ratio**. All our major networks, on both the political Right and Left, now do this perpetually. Perhaps a more descriptive name for **Fox News** would be "**Foxhole News/**" They report constant **dramatized conflict**, encouraging us to **retreat to our "foxholes" and gated communities**, rather than engage with others who think differently from us, to find shared positive visions for the future. **CNN's** better name, as **Peter Diamandis** says, might be "**Constantly Negative News**." **Facebook**, for its part, has become "**Fakebook**" in recent years. It is only now beginning to develop the tools to identify fake news, after being forced to do so after the election of 2016. It also has **no interest** in putting any of those tools in **our own hands**, as that would disrupt its **microtargeting and push-based advertising** model.

To protect our **personal agency**, we should minimize our exposure to **fake crisis media**. One way to avoid media DROA bias is to get most of our news from **online newsletters** which focus their content on productive news and tips (see Appendix 3 for a starter list), from **weeklies**—like, *The Economist*, and *Businessweek*—and from **biweeklies** and **monthlies**—like, *Science News*. We recommend judicious use of platforms like RealClear World, Medium, Quora, LinkedIn, and Reddit. Reading most of our news **a week behind** lets us put it in **proper context**, and it helps us **avoid the daily drama**. **Creating value every day**, not seeking drama, should be our top adaptive priority.

Fortunately, we can now see a world ahead where our **Personal AIs (PAIs)** will help ensure we don't get our personal agency and attention hijacked. In a world of PAIs, which we predict will emerge beginning in the 2030's, increasing numbers of us will be able to choose to get the **media and advertising we need**, not the media and advertising that pays **top dollar for our eyeballs**, delivered in the **ideal sentiment ratios** for each context. We'll explore this vision in Book 2.

A good leader and self-leader recognizes these **O:P Ratios**, and knows how to ethically influence themselves and others toward a better ratio for each context. Before concluding, let us reflect: Do we have trouble using any of these sentiment ratios in our sentiment foresight work? Do we, or our teams, tend to overuse any? If so, how can we adjust for that bias? Let us recognize the adaptive value of each ratio, and learn to switch between them as needed.

Sentiment Leadership II: Success Visions, Failure Scenarios, Reality Checks

Every organization has its own culture, influenced by its particular context. Many so-called <u>high-reliability organizations (HROs)</u> are defensively pessimistic by mission. Many organizations that have often or recently been in crisis may also become defensively pessimistic. By contrast, organizations that are constantly prospecting or growing may be strategically optimistic. But, just because an organization has a particular **sentiment culture**, we shouldn't use that culture as an excuse to avoid leading our teams into different sentiment ratios as needed.

It is true, as <u>Peter Drucker</u> says, that "culture eats strategy for breakfast." But, it is also true, as **Katzenbach and Harshak** say in "<u>Stop Blaming Your Culture</u>," *Strategy+Business*, 2011, that a manager can do a lot to **lead their sentiment ratios** for their **teams**, day by day, **regardless of organizational culture**. Good leaders begin that process by taking **personal**

responsibility for their own sentiment (self-leadership), by not letting others determine their own attitudes for them, and by helping their **direct reports** to learn to do the same.

Let's look now at **three basic strategies** for managing team sentiment, and tipping it into greater optimism, pessimism, or realism, as the leader or their teammates believe is most appropriate for each context.

1. **Success Visioning**. To empower the **strategic optimists** on their teams, and defeat parochialism and fear, leaders can do **Success Visioning** (aka **Stretch Goalsetting**), asking or telling the group: "Imagine we've achieved this (desirable future). How did we get here?" This strategy is well known to every good leader. The trick is knowing when to do it, and how far out to look. As the **Do loop** tells us, we want to set up a **success cycle**, rewarding **incremental progress**. In some cases, when momentum or trust are weak, we may be visioning just a **few hours or a day ahead**. Whatever our horizon, make the success vision **challenging yet achievable**, and **celebrate incremental success**.

2. **Failure Visioning.** To empower the **defensive pessimists** on our teams, and defeat groupthink and ego, leaders can do **Failure Visioning** (aka, **Premortems**), asking or telling the group: "Imagine this (high-profile project) has failed. How did it happen?" This lesser-known strategy is critical if our defensive pessimists are fearful of speaking their minds (optimistic groupthink), or if the team has experienced past success and is beginning to feel invincible. If we don't want to "out" the defensive pessimists to their teammates on a key project, we can ask everyone to **confidentially** submit one reason—on a 3 x 5 card, perhaps—why the project might fail or be delayed. Then, we can discuss some of these in group, without revealing the sources. See **Gary Klein**, "Performing a Project Premortem," *HBR* 2007 for tips on using this great strategy. The team software company Atlassian offers a nice **premortem framework** in their commendable Team Playbook.

3. **Reality (Status) Checks**. To empower the **realists** on our teams, and prepare us for a new round of **mental contrasting**, which will **reprioritize us**, and hopefully, help us accomplish more of the **next top things**, leaders can find the right time and context to bring the team **back into the Present**, with **Reality/ Status/ Progress Checks**. They can ask the group: "What is our status on priorities? How much still to do? What are our blocks? Do we need to update strategy? Revise plan?" Typically, this process involves both reviewing current strategy and the metrics and feedback the group is using (or neglecting) to measure status against plan. Sometimes, **intelligence** will be needed to be collected to answer the status question. Then, **GRASP thinking**, a **REOPS cycle**, or a brief **foresight retreat** may be needed to update strategy and/or plan.

When leaders use these tools, they can **ethically nudge** their teams into sentiment ratios that are much more adaptive for the context, and greatly improve **sentiment foresight. Failure visioning** is the **most underused** by leaders today. All three should be **practiced consciously by the leader and their team,** until everyone can use each of them automatically, intuitively, and rapidly, shifting between each as context demands. All three tools should also be used as **transparently** as possible. The **leader can often ask the team** whether its sentiment ratio seems to be out of balance, or inappropriate to the context. The **team can often recognize** that it is out of balance, and any team member can learn to use success visioning, failure visioning, or reality checks to get the team back on track.

Leadership and Values Models

Our last section in this chapter, and perhaps the most important, involves leadership and values models that take us **beyond sentiment.** In a complex world, with accelerating ADOR, countless opportunities for cooperation, and continual competition between ideas, priorities, and strategies, our **leadership and normative models** can help us make the **best choices we can**. These models are not perfect, but none are. We hope at least that you find them **helpful** in your journey.

Introduction to Adaptive Leadership: Domains, Competencies and Values

Harvard business professor **John Kotter** says the fundamental purpose of **management** is to keep the **current system functioning**, while the fundamental purpose of **leadership** is to produce **useful change**. Leadership thus incorporates management, yet is also something more. That more is **longer-term foresight**: the ability to see the best route (top-down leaders) or to enable the team to see it (bottom-up leaders), and **longer-term action**: the ability to help the team achieve its ends. Thus, both motiving **strategic foresight** and nurturing **group action** are imperative for leaders' success.

Korn Ferry (via their subsidiary, PDI Ninth House) models leadership as dependent on **Four Leadership Factors:**

Thought Leadership (Being Strategic)	External Focus
Results Leadership (Being Outcome-Bound)	External Focus
People Leadership (Being a Developer)	Internal Focus
Personal Leadership (EQ, Ethics, Adaptability)	Internal Focus

We recommend Korn Ferry's leadership workbook, *FYI: For Your Improvement*, 2017, 6th Edition. They usefully divide these **Four Critical Leadership Factors** into **12 Clusters** and **38 Competencies** (PDF). Improving **foresight** and **360° feedback** for these factors is a great general model for organizational leadership. These four factors can be remembered as **TRPP** ("Leadership is a TRPP", or "**Teddy Roosevelt** was a Pioneering President"). The first two domains are about **External** (e.g., Organizational) **Change**. The second two are about **Internal Change**, building interpersonal and personal competencies, so teams and individuals can adapt and thrive. Below are some competencies in each domain:

Korn Ferry, 2017

External Domains	Competencies
1. **Thought** Leadership.	Vision, Strategy, Finance Discipline, Strategic Judgment, Innovation
2. **Results** Leadership	Motivate Results, Ensure Execution, Fiscal Strength, Lead Courageously, Focus on Customer

Internal Domains	Competencies
3. **People** Leadership	Engage, Inspire, Promote Collaboration, Build Talent, Relate, Ensure Psychological Safety
4. **Personal** Leadership	Integrity, Credibility, Inspire Trust, Personal Judgment, Learn, **Adapt**

This is a powerful model. The last competency in bold, **Adaptiveness**, is a great one-word summary of what a good leader needs to do for themselves in particular. In 2016, **Sunnie Giles** surveyed 195 leaders in 30 global organizations in 15 countries around the world, and had them identify a **Top Ten** of leadership competencies, picked from a supplied list of seventy-four competency prompts. As reported in her *HBR* article, here were the Top Ten Competencies by CEO vote. The appropriate TRPP domain is listed at right of each:

1.	Has high ethical and moral standards	(Personal)
2.	Gives goals and objectives with loose guidelines/direction	(Thought)
3.	Clearly communicates expectations	(People)
4.	Has the flexibility to change opinions	(Personal)
5.	Is committed to my ongoing training	(People)
6.	Communicates often and openly	(People)
7.	Is open to new ideas and approaches	(Thought)

8. Creates a feeling of succeeding and failing together   (People)
9. Helps me grow into a next-generation leader   (People)
10. Provides safety for trial and error   (People)

Note that **Results leadership** didn't even make the Top Ten in Giles's survey. Some management scholars say that Results and even Thought leadership can be a **result** of good people and self-leadership. As we have said earlier, complexity and strategy thought leader **David Snowden** has a model of leadership that classifies some top leaders as **Coordinators** and **Decision makers**. Such leaders focus mainly on **two** of the four Korn Ferry factors, **People** and **Personal** leadership. They emphasize selecting, developing, protecting, and setting an example for their top people, who are themselves accountable for Thought and Results leadership. Such specialization can be ideal for leaders in **large**, **rapidly changing**, or **complex** organizations. Note also the **number one competency** on this list. To become better leaders over the long term, we must prioritize **normative foresight**, holding the right **goals and values**, and **balancing** them well in ourselves, to model them on our teams. Having the **right values** will prevent us from ethical and empathic lapses which may **derail our careers** and greatly **limit our influence** over a lifetime.

Let us turn to the subject of **values models** now. What follows is our favorite model, derived from the **Classic Foresight Pyramid**, for what **universal goals and values** must entail. We will offer it in two versions. The first, the **Five E's**, may be the easiest to remember and use. The second, the **Six IES Goals**, is more complex, as it associates with **twelve values** that are commonly seen in discussions around any issue, conflict, or project. Hopefully one or more of these versions may be of value to you and your teams.

Five E's of Adaptive Systems (Individuals, Organizations, and Societies)

We have said how much wisdom we find in in the *Anna Karenina* **principle**, summed up by **Leo Tolstoy**'s opening line in that novel, "Happy families are all alike, unhappy families are unhappy each in their own way." There are many ways for people, teams, firms, and societies to fail or fall off the mark, but only a few universal ways to be adaptive, regardless of context. In all adaptive intelligent systems, whether individuals, organizations, or societies, we believe we can identify **universal goals and values**—recurrent among each, regardless of culture, time, or context.

Recall **Plato's Pyramid**, our simplest model of adaptive values. We can build any number of useful and more complex values models as expansions of that universal triad. We call one useful expansion the **Five E's**. Plato said that **goodness** was the most important of the transcendental values. It deserves **central (top) priority** in our thinking. In books like *Timaeus*, Plato examines **many different forms of the Good**. We have summarized his views on the most important **goals for a good life** in the following simple model.

In **Plato's Five E's**, healthy people, teams, societies care about and manage **five values and goals:**

1. **Empathy** (Good feelings, connectedness)

2. **Ethics** (Good thoughts, rulesets)

3. **Empowerment** (Good strategies, plans, actions, abilities)

4. **Evidence-seeking** (Science, truth)

5. **Expression** (Freedom, beauty)

This model **privileges goodness**, with three of the five categories (60%) being about the Good. It also offers more specific guidance than Plato's Pyramid, while remaining easy to remember. We find it more useful in organizational contexts, and recommend it leaders and teams. These five categories are organized in a rough rank order. In our version of the Five E's model, empathy and love come first, and are the strongest factors in network cohesion, per dual process theory.

Next, come our deliberate ethical thoughts and rulesets. Together, empathy and ethics are our "conscience". Then comes our strategies, plans, actions, and abilities to do good, then the pursuit of knowledge, then freedom and creativity. All are important, but the Five E's propose a rough **priority of goals** that can be used to resolve conflicts and dilemmas.

When we are using the Five E's model, we try to consciously think of and prioritize **Empathy** and **Ethics** first, and typically **in that order,** to honor the insights of **dual process theory** in human psychology. Then we should think of **Empowerment**, then **Evidence-Seeking,** and lastly, **Expression.** We also may reverse any of these steps, or take them out of order, depending on our preference and context. In our view, keeping your organizations **mission** and **vison** centered on the **Five Es**, using variations of them in your **internal and external communications** and **measuring your impact** in each of these critical intangibles, via **feedback**, is a great simple formula for **long-term success.**

We are now ready to offer a second expansion of Plato's Pyramid, the **Six IES Goals**. This one focuses us more consciously on **evolutionary** and **developmental** drivers, and on managing their conflicts via **empathy and ethics** (interdependence). Whether you prefer to use **Plato's Pyramid**, the **Five Es** or the **IES Goals**, each model will serve you well in normative judgments and strategies to grow adaptiveness.

Six Goals and Twelve Values of Adaptive Systems: The Evo-Devo Values Pyramid

In Chapter 1, we said that the Foresight Pyramid has another more accurate name, the **Evo-Devo Pyramid**. Each corner of the pyramid describes a **different set of actors**, **functions**, and **goals** that can be identified in self-sustaining **complex adaptive systems**. Again, these **three interacting sets** are summarized in the graphic below:

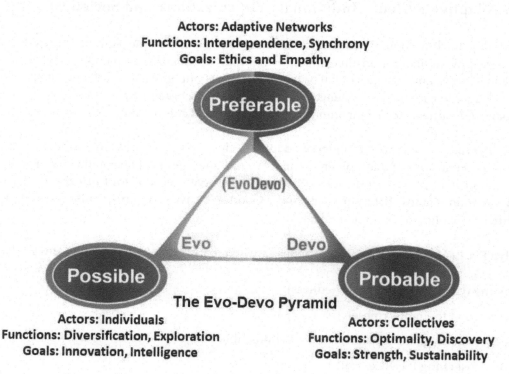

Actors: Adaptive Networks
Functions: Interdependence, Synchrony
Goals: Ethics and Empathy

Preferable

(EvoDevo)

Evo   Devo

Possible   Probable

The Evo-Devo Pyramid

Actors: Individuals
Functions: Diversification, Exploration
Goals: Innovation, Intelligence

Actors: Collectives
Functions: Optimality, Discovery
Goals: Strength, Sustainability

In Book 2 we will apply this pyramid to several complex systems, including **intelligent technology**, which may soon become self-sustaining. With evo-devo thinking, we can analyze any complex system from an **individual, collective,** and **network** perspective. When we value and integrate **all three perspectives**, we can greatly improve foresight and action.

We've just seen the **Five Es** as a simple expansion of Plato's Pyramid, emphasizing the Good. When we consider the nature and purpose of **evolutionary and developmental processes** in living systems, we can offer a second expansion that we call the **IES Goals**. In our analysis, as explained in **our evo-devo foresight** model, our most adaptive complex systems are continually advancing and balancing **two opposing sets of evolutionary and developmental goals, via cooperative and competitive networks**, which in turn express their own **evo-devo goals**. We can express these three sets of goals as follows:

1. <u>Evolutionary Goals</u>: **Innovation and Intelligence**

2. <u>Developmental Goals</u>: **Strength and Sustainability**

3. <u>Evo-Devo Goals</u>: **Empathy and Ethics** (aka, Connectedness and Interdependence)

We can also associate **Twelve Values** with these **Six Goals**, by attaching two culturally universal personal, organizational, and societal values to each goal, in **evo-devo pairs**, as follows:

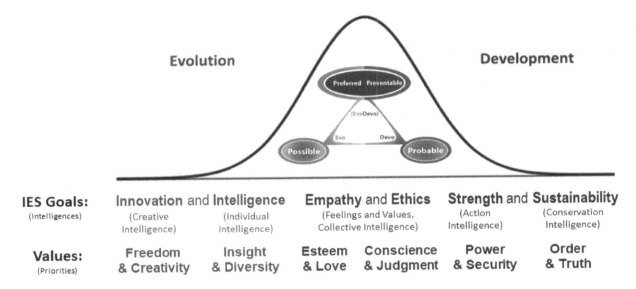

IES Goals:	**Innovation** and **Intelligence**		**Empathy** and **Ethics**		**Strength** and **Sustainability**	
(Intelligences)	(Creative Intelligence)	(Individual Intelligence)	(Feelings and Values, Collective Intelligence)		(Action Intelligence)	(Conservation Intelligence)
Values:	**Freedom & Creativity**	**Insight & Diversity**	**Esteem & Love**	**Conscience & Judgment**	**Power & Security**	**Order & Truth**
(Priorities)						

Goals and Values of Adaptive Leadership – An Evo-Devo Model

We can call these the **IES Goals**—due to their names, **Innovation, Intelligence, Empathy, Ethics, Strength, and Stability**. Below are a few words that expand a bit on the qualities of each of the twelve values:

1. **Empathy** (Connectedness) values:

    Esteem (esteem, worthiness, identity, acceptance, value)
    Love (compassion, forgiveness, understanding, synchronization, consciousness)

2. **Ethics** (Interdependence) values:

    Conscience (virtue, self-discipline, responsibility, norms, ideals)
    Judgment (fairness, merit, critique, positive-sumness, rulesets_

3. **Intelligence** values:

    Insight (**dematerialization**, virtualization, modeling, consciousness, intelligence)
    Diversity (information, individuation, specialization, difference, independence)

4. **Strength** values:

   Power (**densification**, wealth, speed, STEM compression, production efficiency and density)
   Security (awareness, protection, safety, risk management, immunity)

5. **Innovation** values:

   Freedom (bottom-upness, indeterminacy, options, uncertainty)
   Creativity (unpredictability, novelty, imagination, fiction, experiment, innovation)

6. **Sustainability** values:

   Order (top-downness, structure, regulation, constraint)
   Truth (predictability, optimization, accuracy, inertia, sustainability)

We've listed them here in a **rough hierarchy of values**, from the **center to the edges** of a normal (Gaussian) distribution. In other words, **empathy and ethics** discussions should be primary, **intelligence and strength** secondary, and **innovation and sustainability** tertiary, in a typical **normative strategic analysis**, for individuals, teams, and firms. We believe pursuing and balancing these goals and values for ourselves is <u>Adaptive Self-Leadership</u>, and pursuing them on teams is essential to **Adaptive Leadership**. We'll discuss our arguments for this hierarchy and distribution in *BPF*.

Several of these values pairs are **mildly polarized** to represent both **individual** and **network-centric** values. For example, for the **Empathy goal (values set)**, we can think of **Esteem** as dominantly an **individual** value, and **Love** as dominantly a **relational (network)** value. For the **Ethics goal**, **Conscience** is first an individual value, while **Judgment** is first a relational value, and so on. This mild polarization represents the perennial tension between **individual** and **group fitness** in all adaptive networks. We can also use **Plato's Pyramid** to classify these twelve values into **Three Values Sets of Adaptive Leadership**, as pictured below:

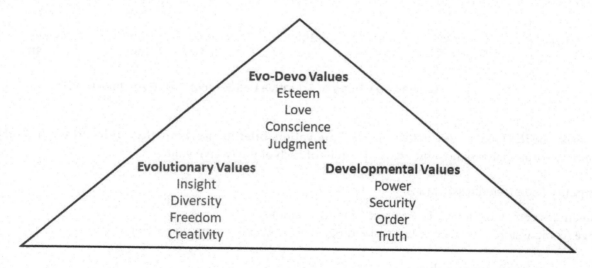

Three Values Sets of Adaptive Leadership – An Evo-Devo Model

Note that these three values groups are congruent with **Kirton's three decision styles**. We might call Kirton's three organizational types **Innovator-Experimenter-Creators**, **Defender-Investigator-Anticipators**, and **Strategist-Planner-Managers**. These are the values sets that motivate each of these kinds of people and groups, in an idealization.

Leaders who learn about, measure, and develop their teams with respect to **all three of these values sets**, and who consciously balance them against each other, will make **more adaptive organizations**, in our view. Of these three values types, the mixed (evo-devo) values at the **top of the pyramid** should be our top priority. They are the most frequent and important values that adaptive teams, firms, and societies must use to guide foresight and action.

We call these **adaptive goals and values** because in our view, **growing adaptiveness** is the top goal of human foresight and action. In evo-devo theoretical biology, neither evolutionary nor developmental processes are dominant in life. They are each fundamental processes, and we need each, in the right balance, to thrive, but our top priority is their *intersection*, or **adaptiveness itself**. Many of the worst decisions made by leaders have arisen when they give too much privilege to one of these two processes—or sets of goals and values—over the other. For example, we may mistakenly decide that a good end (future development) justifies a bad means (evolutionary action). We may decide that our means (evolutionary choices) are intrinsically good, and ignore the bad ends they are likely to create. We can avoid making values mistakes, and slipping into poor choices, by careful considerations of **network ethics and empathy**. They are always at the center of adaptiveness in human groups.

There are many good books on **management and leadership**. One classic we like is **Hamel and Pralahad's** *Competing for the Future*, 1996. It portrays both management and leadership as a **competition** to continually **envision more preferred and adaptive futures,** both for ourselves and our organizations. It thus takes a particularly foresight-oriented approach to leadership, and its normative discussions are well-balanced across the IES goals.

It is not this *Guide*'s intent to teach moral philosophy, management or leadership. However, in all of our books we will take the opportunity to say what we consider particularly fundamental and useful things about morality, management and leadership when considered from an evo-devo perspective. This model is speculative, but, it seems a good start, so we offer it for consideration and critique. We hope these thoughts serve helpful in everyone's journey.

We can summarize everything we've said so far by returning to our mottos:

> *People First!*
> *Quality of Vision!*
> *Adaptive Foresight Matters!*

Chapter 4: Organizational Foresight II – The Eight Skills

The Student Edition of *ITF* introduces **twelve classic departments of the firm:** Top Management, Metrics & Planning, Security & Risk Management, R&D, Operations, Human Resources, Sourcing, IT, Sales & Business Development, Marketing & Market Research, Customer Service, and Community Relations. Knowing how organizational departments typically operate is what we'd call a **basic level of organizational foresight.** Executives can read *Chapter 5: Org Foresight I* in that book if they'd like departmental refresher. Applying our **Do Loops on Teams, via the Eight Skills, in any department,** is the subject of this chapter. We consider this an **intermediate level of organizational foresight.**

LAISEIRR: The Eight Skills of Adaptive Foresight

In our review of the management literature, when we think about effective teams and organizations, we can identify eight key skills of **foresight** and **action.** These are **workplace skills,** and they make teams and organizations particularly effective in **short-term and mid-term foresight** activities, where one can often think less about **goals and values,** and instead measure success by **results,** or more specifically, by **effectiveness against plan.** Recall that the **Eight Skills** are:

Foresight Skills:

1. **Learning (investigative thinking)**
2. **Anticipation (probability foresight)**
3. **Innovation (possibility foresight)**
4. **Strategy (preference and prevention foresight)**

Action Skills:

5. **Execution (production thinking)**
6. **Influence (market thinking)**
7. **Relating (team thinking)**
8. **Reviewing (adjustment thinking)**

We've said, we can remember the **Eight Skills** as "**LAISEIRR**"—an acronym that misspells "**laser**"—and by the phrase: "**A LAISEIRR focus often brings success.**" These mnemonics are helpful, if these are the team and organizational skills that **matter most.**

The **Eight Skills** are our **<u>minimum viable model</u>** for workplace foresight and leadership. In our view, including fewer skill categories would **ignore** some key features of the organizational foresight process, while having more categories than eight would make our model **unnecessarily complex.** Note again that with a little inaccuracy, we can call first four of these **Foresight Skills** (key skills of **strategic foresight**), and the second four **Action Skills.**

In terms of their provenance, we've said that the **Eight Skills** are a synthesis of the following models:

- The **Learn-Foresee-Act-Review** (LFAR) loop of **cognitive science,**
- A great variety of **Do-loop models** of **strategic management,**

- Toffler-Amara's classic **Foresight Pyramid** (three **"Foresight skills"** of the Do Loop),
- Gallup's Three **Core Action** Skills (the "**Action**" **skills of the Do Loop**).

Each of us, as individuals and as teams, will **ignore, underuse, overuse, or misuse** some or all of these **steps and skills** at times. Nevertheless, we are all continually looping through parallel versions of this **universal cycle**, at various speeds and in many contexts. The more conscious we are of this process, the better we can **improve and adapt**.

Boyd's OODA Model of Competitive Dominance

Let's look briefly at **Boyd's OODA model** now, to see one particularly helpful application of the loop. John Boyd (1927-1997) was a brilliant, iconoclastic US Air Force colonel and military strategist. Among other contributions, he applied the LFAR loop to military strategy, aircraft design, and combat operations in rapidly changing environments, beginning with work during the **Vietnam War**. Boyd's term for the LFAR loop was the **OODA loop**.

Boyd's OODA loop involved four stages, as follows:

Colonel John Boyd

1. **Observe** (Perceive the results, and current state) → **Reviewing & Learning**
2. **Orient** (See probabilities and possibilities ahead) → **Foresight I**
3. **Decide** (Pick a strategy) → **Foresight II**
4. **Act** (Get something done) → **Action**

Boyd said our **speed of cycling** through this cognitive behavioral OODA loop determines both our **speed of learning** and our **speed of adapting** in competitive environments. The faster we can run our loop, the faster we can correct our mistakes, and respond to the actions—both helpful and aggressive—of others. In many kinds of conflicts, being able to "penetrate the loops" of our opponents can give us decisive advantages in **competitions and conflicts.** Saying "inside the loop" of those we are **cooperating with** can also help us to lead in initiating cooperative goals and behaviors. Technology, communications, and decentralized decision-making are just a few of the tools and strategies that can help teams run their loops quicker than larger adversaries and collaborators, and learn, foresee, act, and review more efficiently—becoming more adaptive as a result.

Boyd explored the OODA loop in military contexts. Others have generalized it to business strategy, law enforcement, litigation, and many other spheres. For more on Boyd, read **Robert Coram's** great biography, *Boyd: The Fighter Pilot Who Changed the Art of War*, 2004. For an overview of how Boyd has broadly influenced US security thinking, read **Grant Hammond's** *The Mind of War: John Boyd and American Security*, 2004. For a thoughtful application of Boyd's OODA loop to business coopetition, read **Chet Richards'** *Certain to Win: The Strategy of John Boyd, Applied to Business*, 2004.

We call our LFAR version of this loop a **Do Loop** because **successful Doing (Action)** is the **essence of adaptation**, and because **"Do"** is even shorter and easier to say than **"LFAR."** We think Boyd would approve of our shortening. Do loops are at the heart of effective foresight, management, and leadership.

The Eight Skills of Adaptive Foresight: A Deeper Look

The **Eight Skills** remind us that adaptive foresight is a never-ending, cyclical process, involving continual **reviewing** post-action, and **learning** prior to generating new foresight. To help our clients adapt, we need to talk about **all Eight Skills**—and the cyclic and iterative relationship between **foresight** and **action**.

Let's look briefly at some of the science that grounds the Eight Skills. We have mentioned that a basic model of cognitive science is the perception-action cycle in cognitive psychology and in ecological psychology. One technical name for this cycle is the <u>perception-decision-action-feedback (PDAF) cycle</u>. For more on PDAF cycles, see **Pecher and Zwaan's** classic *Grounding Cognition*, 2010. For an introduction to cycling, competing and cooperating neural circuits in our own brains, see neuroscientist **Gyorgy Buzsaki's** technical work, *The Brain from Inside Out*, 2020. Calling these universal cycles **LFAR loops**, rather than PDAF cycles, lets us use names with greater usefulness in **strategic management**.

LFAR is our simplest model for how we integrate **foresight** and **action**. First, we assess **current state** of our local environment (**learn**), then we **foresee**, then we **act**, and finally, we interpret the results of our actions (**review**). We must ask: Are our teams strong in all four of these steps? Do any need more attention or improvement?

Let us return to the **Eight Skills cartoon** from Chapter 2. The **names in grey** in the figure below refer to our initial **research influences** in building the model:

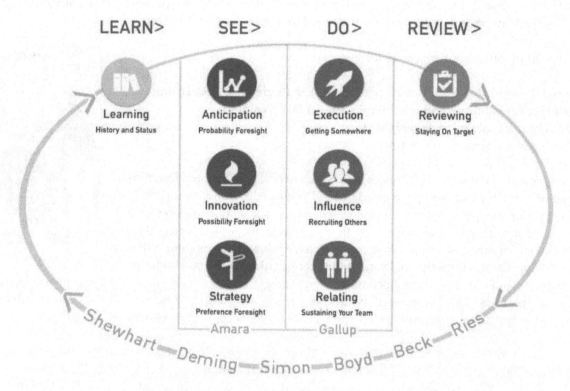

The Eight Skills of Adaptive Foresight

We've said the **Do Loop** has been used by many **management and decision theorists**, usually without recognizing its universality in **cognitive psychology**. For example, the Do Loop is central to **David Kolb's** model of <u>Experiential Learning</u>, <u>Erik Eriksson's</u> model of **Peak Performance**, James Clear's model of **Habit Formation**, **Walter Shewhart's** model of <u>Strategic Planning</u>, <u>Edwards Deming's</u> model of **Quality Management**, <u>Herbert Simon's</u> model of **Design Thinking**, <u>John Boyd's</u> model of **Military and Competitive Dominance**, <u>Kent Beck's</u> model of **Agile Development**, Eric **Ries's** model of the <u>Lean Startup</u>, and many others. These authors all use different terms and significations for the steps of their cycle—and sometimes more than four steps—but they all talk about this universal cycle and its steps, in our view.

Let's also revisit our graphical depiction of the **primary thinking style** used in each skill. Do you **notice yourself** using each? How often, and in what contexts? Recall that the **Four Foresight Skills** involve alternating **divergent (evolutionary), convergent (developmental), divergent,** and **convergent** thinking. The **Four Action Skills**, by contrast, depend on a mix of **translational, radiative, integrative,** and **cyclical** thinking. All of these are also **key biological processes**, used by **living networks** to act and adapt.

Running our Do Loop:
Eight Key Skills for Adaptive Leaders and Teams

Foresight Skills

Learning ⇐

Anticipation ⇒

Innovation ⇐

Strategy ⇒

Action Skills

Execution ⇛

Influence ✳

Relating ⬠

Reviewing ↻

Leaders Need a "LAISEIRR Focus" on Their Teams

John Smart, *The Foresight Guide*, 2021

Again, we propose that all eight skills are **central to good teams**. We can't neglect any of them. If we are **weak** in one or more, we should prioritize their improvement, build **routines** around them, and develop our teams to be at least of average strength in all eight processes. We must also guard against overusing and misusing our strongest skills. See Appendix 1 for questions to help your team think through personal strengths and weaknesses with these skills.

In organizations, there is a lot of **great strategic foresight** produced every year, but much of it **sits on shelves** after it is produced—**unread and unused**, because all Eight Skills aren't prioritized by leaders and managers. Much organizational foresight work does not **evaluated (reviewed) later** for its accuracy or its return on investment. The **strategy** skill may not result in coordinated **policies and plans**, those may not translate into the **three core action skills** (Rumelt's "coordinated actions") or the **review skill** may be neglected, often because leaders don't want **bad news**.

One **critique** of the **Eight Skills** model is that the **order of innovation and strategy** seem wrong. Some critics think we **first** generate strategy, **then** we innovate. But this **misdefines the concept of innovation**, focusing it only on physical products. **Innovation is first mental,** and **only later physical.** As the Foresight Pyramid says, innovation is the **exploration of possibility space.** We do this first and easiest mentally, and later, more slowly and expensively, physically. Innovation depends obviously on **learning** and **imagination,** to find **new ideas**, and on good process, like **design thinking**. But it actually depends on all of the LAISEIRR skills. **Strategy** (and planning) spans all eight skills, but its most important role is after we've done some mental innovation, and before physical prototyping or taking some new actions (Execution). Then **Influence** (learning if anyone wants our innovation), **Relating**, and **Review** come next.

Repetitively using our LAISEIRR skills, running our Do loops, is how we translate ideas (mental innovation) into products or services people want (physical innovation). This order is supported by **Action learning** theory, which tells us **we explore first**—in **mental innovation**—and **later act, producing prototypes,** and even later, **marketable products.** For more, see **David Kolb's**, *Experiential Learning, 2nd. Ed.,* 2014, a classic text on learning and doing.

As Boyd would argue, besides discovering all the **Do loops that matter**, foresight practitioners should ensure they have the right **Frequency, Strength, and Quality (do an "FSQ assessment")** with each loop that is relevant to a clients' problem, and for their own self-monitoring. Quality analysts (**Edward Deming**) are particularly aware of the value of identifying and monitoring all the relevant "quality loops." On top of this **Do loop focus**, we also recommend foresight practitioners focus on growing their understanding and use of *each* of the **Eight Skills**, discovering their skill deficiencies, and deciding which strategies and methods can best help them improve each skill. Let's revisit the **Eight Skills** and review how they associate with the **Twenty Specialties,** summarized in the list below:

I. <u>Learning (aka "Insight")</u>

   1. **Learning – "Knowing Your History and Status" (Investigative thinking)**
       Specialties: *Accounting & Intangibles, Intelligence & Knowledge Management, Learning & Development*

II. <u>Foresight</u>

   2. **Anticipation – "Probability Foresight" (Convergent thinking)**
       Specialties: *Data Science & Machine Learning, Forecasting & Prediction, Investing & Finance, Law & Security, Risk Mgmt & Insurance*

       Innovation – "Possibility Foresight" (Divergent thinking)
       Specialties: *Alternatives & Scenarios, Entrepreneurship & Intrapreneurship, Facilitation & Gaming, Ideation & Design, Innovation & R&D*

       Strategy – "Preference & Prevention Foresight" (Decisive thinking)
       Specialties: *Analysis & Decision Support, Strategy & Planning*

III. <u>Action</u>

   3. **Execution – "Getting Somewhere" (Production thinking)**
       Specialty: *Management & Leadership*

       Influence – "Recruiting Others" (Market thinking)
       Specialty: *Marketing & Sales*

       Relating – "Sustaining Your Team" (Team thinking)
       Specialty: *Human Resources & Performance Management*

IV. <u>Reviewing</u> (aka "Aftsight")

   4. **Reviewing – "Staying On Target" (Adjustment thinking)**
       Specialties: *Auditing & Change Management, Benchmarking & Quality*

In our mapping above, notice that five of twenty specialties associate with **Anticipation**, and five with **Innovation**, giving **ten** of the twenty specialties serving just these **two skills out of eight**. This makes sense, from an evo-devo perspective. These two skills, and **predictive contrasting,** form the **base of the Foresight Pyramid.** Our mental conflict between the probable and the possible is the most extensive, and the toughest to get right. The pyramid tells us that **Anticipation** and **Innovation** are the **two most foundational types** of foresight work. Nevertheless, one or more of these foundations are **commonly neglected** by organizations, which are often **biased to strategy**. Yet our model argues that **Strategy**, which has just two of the twenty specialties, is **entirely dependent** on these two types of thinking (**predictive contrasting**), and also on good **sentiment contrasting,** after predictability and unpredictability have been assessed.

Strategy is also dependent on Learning (foresight preparation) and Review (feedback). Notice that after **Anticipation** and **Innovation,** the largest set of the twenty specialties is found under **Learning** (three specialties) and **Review** (two specialties). **Action skills** get just one specialty each, in our **Adaptive Foresight** model. **Learning and the Four Ps**, the **LAIS strategic foresight skills**, comprise **fifteen of the twenty specialties**. These ratios make clear that this is a model of **adaptive foresight**, not of strategic management. Recall our One Sheet on Adaptive Foresight (without values):

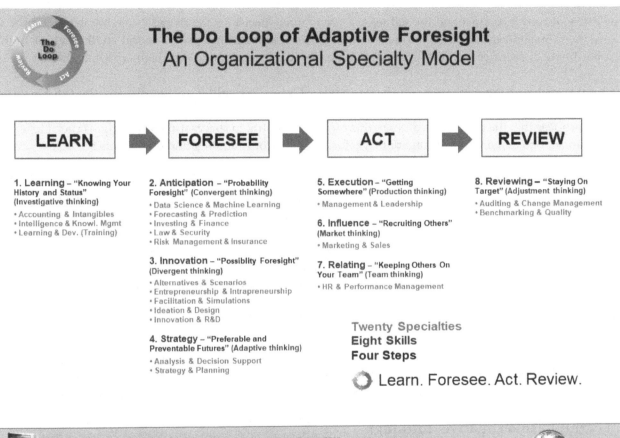

The Do Loop of Adaptive Foresight
An Organizational Specialty Model

LEARN → **FORESEE** → **ACT** → **REVIEW**

1. Learning – "Knowing Your History and Status" (Investigative thinking)
- Accounting & Intangibles
- Intelligence & Knowl. Mgmt
- Learning & Dev. (Training)

2. Anticipation – "Probability Foresight" (Convergent thinking)
- Data Science & Machine Learning
- Forecasting & Prediction
- Investing & Finance
- Law & Security
- Risk Management & Insurance

3. Innovation – "Possiblity Foresight" (Divergent thinking)
- Alternatives & Scenarios
- Entrepreneurship & Intrapreneurship
- Facilitation & Simulations
- Ideation & Design
- Innovation & R&D

4. Strategy – "Preferable and Preventable Futures" (Adaptive thinking)
- Analysis & Decision Support
- Strategy & Planning

5. Execution – "Getting Somewhere" (Production thinking)
- Management & Leadership

6. Influence – "Recruiting Others" (Market thinking)
- Marketing & Sales

7. Relating – "Keeping Others On Your Team" (Team thinking)
- HR & Performance Management

8. Reviewing – "Staying On Target" (Adjustment thinking)
- Auditing & Change Management
- Benchmarking & Quality

Twenty Specialties
Eight Skills
Four Steps

○ Learn. Foresee. Act. Review.

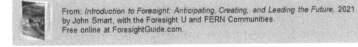

From: *Introduction to Foresight: Anticipating, Creating, and Leading the Future*, 2021. by John Smart, with the Foresight U and FERN Communities. Free online at ForesightGuide.com.

Foresight Education and Research Network

This One Sheet tells us that all firms practice foresight, but they often **fail to recognize it**. One of our jobs as foresight professionals is to help our clients see the foresight they are **already doing**, and to do more of it in the **right balance**. Models like these can help us assess our **priorities**. They also raise questions: Is our firm reasonably proficient in all eight skills? Which specialties might be most helpful to our **current strategy**? Which of those are presently weak on our team?

Normative Adaptive Foresight: Incorporating Values

In our view, **Adaptive Foresight** can be viewed from two lenses:

1. **Near-Term.** With today's foresight to much of the mid-term, **Adaptive Foresight** can be relatively **Non-Normative**. It stresses **effectiveness of the strategy in producing outcomes**, not whether it is the best strategy or outcome for the network. This near-term lens can focus mainly on good practice of our **Do loop**, the **Four Ps**, and the **Eight Skills** in a management environment.

2. **Long-term**. Over quarters and years, **Adaptive Foresight** must also be **Normative**. It will depend on the nature of our **goals, values, values hierarchies,** and our **values tradeoffs. Shared visions, ethics, and empathy** are critical to helping individuals see their role in achieving larger, long-term goals. We must have a view of the **"good of the network."** There will often be **individual risks and costs** of **collective success and progress.**

While the **Eight Skills** are very effective for near-term survival, they say little about the **higher goals** (aka "purposes") that we measure ourselves against and the **values** we use to make decisions. To discuss such important topics, we will need a normative foresight model. Such models help us make **tradeoffs** and resolve **moral challenges**, as in deciding when to subordinate or sacrifice our own goals and values for the greater good of the team, organization, or society.

So far we have introduced three evo-devo-derived models—**Plato's Pyramid**, the **Five E's,** and the **IES Goals**—as first draft for thinking about universally adaptive, **network goals.** All three are versions of our **normative model of adaptive foresight.** We propose that the goals and values in this model are central to **successful leadership**—crucial to recognizing and partaking in actions that are **long-term adaptive**, for ourselves, our families, and our societies.

We may find that any or all of these normative models integrate well with our own **personal, traditional** or **faith-based models.** At 4U, our model privileges the **values of empathy and ethics ("love and fairness") as the highest network priorities.** We will argue that each of these goals are **forms of intelligence** that are critical to **network adaptiveness.**

Whatever our own normative models may be, we recommend regularly evaluating whether we are personally **measuring up to our values** in our **current foresight and actions** and, moreover, we encourage running **Do Loops** on individual values, value hierarchies, and value tradeoffs, and critiquing and reevaluating them in light of their outcomes.

Running our Do Loops: The Eight Skills of Adaptive Foresight

Let's look one last time at each of the **Eight Skills,** and consider some of the ways that each is used to generate foresight in organizations. We will also consider how foresight practitioners can better **master and use each skill** with their clients. Running our relevant **Do Loops,** with appropriate FSQ, using each skill well, is key to successful (adaptive) foresight.

Skill 1. <u>Learning</u> (Investigative thinking)

Learning—including collective intelligence and empirical research (investigative thinking)—is foresight's foundational skill. Learning is the critical **preparation** we need to prepare for core (AIS) foresight thinking and analysis. Many firms don't have a name or formal department (like, Research, Intelligence, L&D, Metrics) for most of their learning/investigation skills. But, all successful firms employ people who are talented at this skill. Ideally, adaptive firms have individuals explicitly tasked with learning functions. Those that don't start decision-making with this skill are often **surprised and outpaced by the future**, rather than continually learning how to take best advantage of change.

In alpha order, the first specialty we will talk about in the learning skill is **Accounting & Intangibles**. The better we, our teams, and our firms can measure the significant processes in our internal and external environment, the better we can grasp our current conditions—which are at the foundation of foresight. The firm's relevant <u>indicators stem</u> from its strategic objectives; but, determining what to measure and how to best measure what we and our companies want is a constant learning process. **Ben Waber's** *People Analytics*, 2013 is a good book introducing evidence-based (learning-oriented) Human Resources practices. **Jack Stack's** *The Great Game of Business*, 2013, gives a great and inspiring intro to <u>open-book management</u>, which is also built on learning and metrics-based goals and team performance rewards. **Bob Eccle's** *One Report*, 2010, introduces simplified sustainability metrics and reporting, allowing the firm to continually learn and review its real state with respect to its profitability, governance, social impact, and environment.

Douglas Hubbard's *How to Measure Anything*, 2014, is a great guide to measuring and learning the status of **intangibles** that our teams and models indicate are important to our work. Many of the most relevant processes, opportunities, and problems around us aren't currently acknowledged, and thus are not even measured. However, doing continual surveys, polls, focus groups, and other means of feedback (**reviewing**) is the fundamental way to end our Do Loop by giving us useful information, which we can then **investigate** (via new learning) for hidden causes, histories, and relationships.

Good future-thinkers like to **measure phenomena** and to interpret **trends, data, and facts**, to find **evidence** to create, confirm, or alter their **strategies** and **worldview**. For a few examples of view-changing facts, see **Jessica William's** *50 Facts that Should Change the World*, 2007, and **Stephen Fender's** *50 Facts that Should Change the USA*, 2008. For one example, consider the following data from a 2013 *Lancet* series on <u>Maternal and Child Nutrition</u>: roughly **3 million children** (5 years and younger) **die every year**, **8,000 a day**, as a result of **lack of adequate food for the mother or child**. Just over half of these deaths occur in **one geographical location** of greatest need: <u>Sub-Saharan Africa</u>. Globally, **malnutrition** still accounts for 45% of child deaths! 165 million children are today <u>stunted</u> and <u>immunocompromised</u> because of **lack of sufficient nutrition** during their childhood. Such **"impactful facts"** cry out for humanitarian foresight and action.

Intelligence & Knowledge Management, which includes scanning and research, is the oldest term of art for how organizations learn about the environment. Collecting all the **facts relevant to our responsibilities** into a **dashboard**, and updating that dashboard regularly in our **news feed**, is a powerful aid to better foresight and action. Strictly speaking, intelligence is about better understanding the relevant past (hindsight) and present (insight)—both preconditions to superior anticipation, innovation, and strategy. This function is what a typical foresight practitioner starts with when researching a client's problem, or doing general scanning ("continuing education") for useful novelty. Focusing more narrowly on sociopolitical and defense futures, the new foresight field of **intelligence studies** has developed a number of useful methods and a graduate training community that serves many client types (politics, defense, law enforcement, business, NGOs). The field of **business intelligence** uses business and organizational data to study and benchmark organizational performance and processes, generating methods, tools, and platforms to improve organizational awareness and performance.

Many firms buy **intelligence**, as **industry foresight research**, from consultancies like McKinsey, Gartner, and IDG. Clients include C-level executives, technical innovators, strategists, planners, risk managers, leaders, journalists, and others. **Market research** is a lucrative business. A typical Gartner research subscription service covering the current conditions and future trends in a specialized industry with a reasonable market capitalization (for example, <u>call center technology</u>) might cost small to mid-sized firms $25K-50K annually. A good **industry research brief** covers the present (intelligence) and gives data and ideas on **probable**, **possible**, **preferable**, and **preventable** futures. A good **strategic foresight brief** has all of this, *plus* **strategic recommendations and options**, tailored to client need.

When John began his foresight career in 2000, many **industry research briefs** were kept behind paywalls. As global complexity, speed of change, and wealth have accelerated since, ever more of these previously expensive, proprietary briefs have been released as **open foresight**. They have become "table stakes", serving as **statements of competency** for the confidential strategy consulting offered by many consultancies. It is easier than ever for a team to learn a great deal about the past, present, and future of any industry by **comparing research briefs** found on the open web. Even competitive intelligence has become much easier for teams using all the new **open source intelligence**.

Another powerful learning and anticipation tool is **group polling**, or the gauging of group opinion, as practiced for society by leading firms like Pew, Gallup, and Zogby, by marketing firms and by consultants. Whenever the organization is faced with abstract, intangible complex, or unconventional variables and problems, polling can often help a team find where they are in an adaptive landscape, relative to potential collaborators, competitors, and threats.

Surveys, focus groups, and other interactive studies are a classic form of <u>**collective intelligence and consensus production**</u>. **James Surowiecki**, in *The Wisdom of Crowds*, 2005, introduces this idea more thoroughly with the "Jelly Bean

Estimation Challenge" (how many jelly beans are in this jar?) to remind us of value of <u>group intelligence</u>. A procedure that has been replicated continually over the last two centuries, polling a **knowledge-diverse crowd** and **averaging their guesses** usually greatly improves estimation accuracy. See the picture below for one example.

What's Your Guess?

Participants were asked to estimate the number of jelly beans in a jar.

The average estimate of all participants was very close to the actual count.

Together, we know more than we do alone.

Range: 409–5,365
Average: 1,653
Actual: 1,670

For illustrative purposes only. Illustration based on voluntary participation at adviser event in August 2013. Results audited by advisor.

"Wisdom of Crowds" Estimation Game (Vestory.com)

As **Don McDonald** notes, <u>markets work the same way, in theory</u>: integrating group knowledge into stock prices with presumably more accurate means than individual guesses by investors. That's why it's hard for individual investors and fund managers to consistently beat the market. They need both superior intelligence that is ethically obtained, and a faster decision-making ability (OODA loop) to outshine group learning and discern a more accurate future price. This is the theory behind **prediction markets**, anticipation tools that crowd-guess aspects of the future.

As coined by **Henry Jenkins**, conditions where participants make mostly independent decisions, with the right rules and aggregation methods, can also be called the "Wisdom of Crowds" (there is also a "Foolishness of Crowds). Prediction markets, group learning and intelligence tasks, like **knowledge management**, and forecasting methods, like **Delphi**, are forms of **collective intelligence**. Leaders often underestimate the power and usefulness of **collective intelligence,** which tells us that groups, under the right rules and connectivity, **consistently beat leaders and experts** in such skills as learning, sensemaking, and prediction. See MIT's <u>Center for Collective Intelligence</u> for more on this abstract but vital emerging topic. **Network science** will greatly improve our understanding of collective intelligence in coming years.

There are a large number of <u>intelligence gathering disciplines</u> that can be applied to firms. **George and Bruce's** <u>Analyzing Intelligence</u>, 2008, is a nice intro to the breath of modern intelligence work. Most leaders know about **environmental scanning**—an intelligence function in which investigators monitor events that might signal ongoing or upcoming change, catalog and evaluate this info, and distribute it to others. But, many are unaware of other specialties, such as **technical intelligence**, which can be used to determine if a technology actually works, or is mostly hype. Most leaders know about **competitive intelligence** (see <u>SCIP.org</u> for a professional association), but they often underuse it. Futurist **Seena Sharp's** <u>Competitive Intelligence Advantage</u>, 2009 is a helpful intro to competitive intelligence.

Knowledge management is another basic intelligence function. In addition to SCIP, there are a variety of professional associations (KMA, KMPro, IKMS, KMBA, KIPA) focused on advancing the collection and sharing of firm knowledge. KM pioneer **Ikujiro Nonaka** at UC Berkeley has a valuable four-category model (see picture at right) for different types of firm knowledge that a strong KM system should try to cultivate, improve, and preserve.

A third key learning specialty is **Learning and Development**, a term that can include both employee learning and organizational learning and development methods. As **Eric Hoffer** says, in a world of **constant change**, the **learners** inherit the future. Being a **lifelong learner**, taking regular training courses, and gaining new credentials every 5-10 years is a good strategy for staying adaptive. As learning platforms like MOOCs, wikis, computer adaptive testing, neuroscience-based training and others improve, we can get stronger skills and more "just-in-time learning" to help our foresight and action.

Experiential Knowledge assets

Tacit knowledge shared through common experiences

- Skills and know-how of individuals
- Care, love, trust, and security
- Energy, passion and tension

Conceptual Knowledge Assets

Explicit knowledge articulated through images, symbols, and language

- Product concepts
- Design
- Brand equity

Routine Knowledge Assets

Tacit knowledge routinized and embedded in actions and practices

- Know-how in daily operation
- Organizational routines
- Organizational culture

Systematic Knowledge Assets

Systemised and packed explicit knowledge

- Documents, specifications, manuals
- Database
- Patent and licenses

Four Categories of Knowledge Assets (Nonaka et al, 2000)

Online educational platforms like Udacity, Coursera, and 2U, with their micro-certifications, video learning companies like Lynda, and global online tutoring like TutorVista (which offers 24/7 tutoring from India, in any subject, at a disruptive price of $12-20/hour), are beginning to lower the cost of good individual and employee education. **Peter Brown et al**. have written a great new book on the cognitive science of successful learning, Make it Stick, 2014. **Tiago Forte** has a brilliant post (The Future of Education is Community, 2021) on **cohort learning** (sticking with your group for a long time, and having group accountability) as the **future of online learning**. To know more about the future of educational tech—as well as new tools to track and improve learning ROI—check out EdSurge's great free newsletter.

Peter Senge's *The Fifth Discipline: The Art and Practice of the Learning Organization*, 1999/2005, proposed that becoming a learning organization is the best way to stay competitive in a complex, accelerating economy. He also proposed that systems thinking is the foundational area, the "fifth discipline," that integrates four other key organizational learning disciplines: mental models, personal mastery, teamwork, and shared vision.

As we saw in Chapter 1, **Mark Smith** depicts Senge's five disciplines as a developmental pyramid (picture below). At the base of organizational learning, in Senge's view, is **systems thinking**. Systems thinking occurs when the team seeks to identify relevant actors, relationships, and constraints on the organization. Then we use our systems experience to find or build **mental models**, practice frameworks, and methods for our personal and organizational environments.

Then, we use these models, frameworks and methods to seek **individual mastery** in various specialties. At the same time, the organization's employees and stakeholders, interact with their individual mental models and masteries to do **teamwork**. Finally, with strong leadership and facilitation, team learning and foresight leads us to **shared visions** for our teams, and our learning cohort.

Consultants and leaders benefit greatly when they learn to become systems thinkers, as there can be great strategic value in having a good map of relevant actors, relationships, and constraints. Reliable starter books for systems thinking are **Ackoff and Addison's** masterful *Systems Thinking for Curious Managers*, 2010, **Eliyahu Goldratt's** *The Goal*, 2012 and *Theory of Constraints*, 1999, and **Donella Meadow's** *Thinking in Systems*, 2008.

Five Disciplines of a Learning Organization
Smith, 2001, based on Senge, 1999

We don't share Senge's premise that learning is the central skill of successful firms, but propose instead that it is the first of eight key skills. If we spend too much time or money learning, training, or generating models, our firm will quickly be overtaken in a competitive environment. Educational activities are always in an evolving tradeoff with the other seven skills. There's no single most important skill, in our view. If we had to pick favorites, a mixture of Skill **4**, Skill **5**, and **Skill 8 — Executing Good Strategy, with Review** — would be our picks for the **three "most central" skills** of the **Do Loop**.

Senge's model is appealing to learning-oriented managers, but it and other organizational learning models are not yet very evidence-based, as Senge's critics point out. One of the top learning priorities for any firm should be evidence-based management, a mixture of learning and review that seeks to find the best evidence available to guide our current policies and processes. See **Pfeffer and Sutton's** *Hard Facts, Dangerous Half-Truths, and Total Nonsense*, 2006, for one good take on how that works in practice.

Pfeffer&Sutton,2006

Good learning questions we can ask ourselves include: Can our teams provide hard evidence for the policies we are using, or are they the just opinions of the **HIPPOs** (HIghest-Paid Persons in our Organization)? Do we research the evidence for our critical policies? Or base our policies on our leader's force of personality, opinion, tradition, or other weakly-grounded alternatives? If so, our firm's foundation may be sand — and a storm could come any day now.

We should also recognize that in an environment of accelerating change, the faster competitive events occur, the less value there may be in long-term planning, and the more in just-in-time learning and just-in-time production and execution (learning, strategy, and execution). In fast-changing environments, we may need only just enough learning, anticipation, and contingency planning to capitalize on opportunities and avoid dangers quicker and more efficiently than our competition. It is a certainty that anyone who tries to see, plan and execute **too far in advance**, both in their personal life and in their organizations, will soon find out how much time and energy has been wasted and just how quickly their plans become unfit relative to reality.

It is often better to learn in small batches of work, continually improving with customer feedback, than it is to invest in large chunks — which require long-term strategy, and which commit us to big risks in search of economies of scale. Sometimes the first movers gain great competitive advantage; but, more often than not, being a fast follower — letting others do the costly experiments and jumping in quickly to replicate those who are successful — can be a much better strategy. See **George et al.'s** *Fast Innovation*, 2005, **Doz and Kosonen's** *Fast Strategy*, 2008, and **John Kotter's** *Accelerate*, 2014 for more on the subtleties of these topics.

In a lifetime of diligent **learning,** we will encounter many of our own **enlightening, impactful, or disturbing** facts. Some of these can help us make changes in ourselves, our companies, our industries, and our world. What we do with these facts—whether we share them with others, or integrate them into our **Do Loops**—is up to us.

Skill 2. <u>Anticipation</u> (Probability thinking)

In the **Evo-Devo** model of complex systems, the only foresight thinking and action skill that is as fundamental as **possibility** exploration and generation is **probability** exploration and generation—which should typically come first, as it improves efficiency and effectiveness. Even though we may only be able to usefully predict 5% or so of our future at any given time in various environments, as the **95/5 Rule** proposes, finding that special set of predictable elements—including which things are presently accelerating, converging, and emerging—and placing uncertainty boundaries around the less-predictable elements, gives us a **framework of constraints** on the future and a critical advantage in **strategy** and **action**. For one example of good open-access investing anticipation, read **Thomas Hainlin's** *From Headlines to Trendlines: Long-Term Investing for Wealth Expansion (PDF)*, 2013. The more high quality info is accessible via the web and the more evidence-based our models, the more key aspects of our near-term future become both predictable and profitable to understand.

Former US President **Bill Clinton**, Chair of the Clinton Global Initiative, likes to say that anticipators must learn to look **beyond the** *headlines*, which are often inflammatory and emotion-oriented, **to the** *trendlines*, which are often going the opposite direction to what the media is portraying, for their own self-serving reasons. Many editors know the maxim, "If it bleeds, it leads." Good foresighters recognize that most aspects of our modern world have grown **safer, stabler, richer, and cleaner**, on average. But, trendlines don't sell papers, so the headlines continue to drive most political and economic activity. As a result, we end up **obsessing over ever smaller risks and dangers**. One **silver lining** in this obsession is that the headlines—even as they distort our perception—do tend to encourage a **safer and better world**.

Data Science & Machine Learning are the first specialty (in alpha order) we'd like to direct attention to in Anticipation. Since the rise of the internet in the 1990s, big data in the 2000's, and cloud computing and **machine learning** in the 2010s, this has become the fastest-improving and most in-demand of all the anticipation specialties. The growth of open data, and the ability of our increasingly bio-inspired machine intelligences to use unstructured data, are also major new developments. See *BPF* for speculations on the big picture future of these technologies.

Deep machine learning leaders, like Google's DeepMind, machine learning as a service firm, like Wise.io, text analytics and intelligence companies, like Factual and Quid, predictive marketing companies, like Netbase and Leadspace, and human-machine intelligence and threat assessment platforms, like Palantir and Recorded Future, are just a few of the pioneers in this domain—which is seeing exponential investment and expansion.

A great community to get involved with is the <u>Open Data Science Community</u> **(OSDC)**. Consider attending their <u>Open Data Science</u> conference. Data science also includes <u>predictive analytics</u> **(PA)**. <u>Predictive Analytics World</u> is the leading cross-industry event for predictive analytics professionals, run by **Eric Siegel**. We recommend his non-specialist introduction to the field, *Predictive Analytics*, 2016.

Forecasting & Prediction are the best-known anticipation functions—though the former gets much better traction in organizations as so many people are still unaware how well crowd prediction works—as we discussed under collective intelligence. The <u>International Institute of Forecasters (IIF)</u> and **Scott Armstrong's** <u>ForecastingPrinciples.com</u> are two great practice communities. A great book on power of collective prediction is **Tetlock and Gardner's** *Superforecasting: The Art and Science of Prediction*, 2016.

As futurist <u>**Paul Saffo**</u> says, to master forecasting and prediction we must do it often, adhere to subjects we can model well (mentally or formally), understand and attempt to counter our biases, and follow up with post-forecast review and analysis. See Saffo's "Six Rules for Effective Forecasting," *Harvard Business Review*, 2007, (PDF) which offers a wise introduction to anticipation practice. Saffo's Six Rules are: 1) Define a Cone of Uncertainty, 2) Look for the S-Curve, 3) Embrace the Things that Don't Fit, 4) Hold Strong Opinions Weakly, 5) Look Back Twice as Far as We Look Forward (better yet, look back as far as our time and resources allow), and 6) Know When Not to Make a Forecast (Know When We Are Most Ignorant). This is all excellent anticipation advice.

Saffo genuflects to the popular (and incorrect) perspective that "forecasting is not about prediction," but per the **95/5 Rule**, this view is only **95% correct**. We agree entirely that forecasting is not about prediction for **evolutionary** processes and events, which are 95% of what we see in the world, but forecasting is *definitely* about prediction when we are seeking to find that **critical, constraining 5% of developmental processes** and events that are emerging all around us. The kicker is that those **5% of developmental processes** are **as important** in guiding change as the **95% of evolutionary processes**.

In other words, a review of the history of living systems argues that both evolutionary and developmental change appear to have **roughly equal impact** on the future. That's just how **evo-devo dynamics** works, in all complex adaptive systems, whether they are living systems, organizations, technologies, or societies. The **developmental genes in our body**— especially the ones **highly conserved** through millennia, though they are only about 5% of our genome—are **as critical in defining and maintaining who we are** as all the rest (the 95% evolutionary component) of our genome.

Developmental processes and events (think of globalization, information growth, Moore's law, mobile, cloud services), though they may be few in number, are often so powerful as causal agents and environmental factors, drivers, and constraints that they rival the much more common evolutionary processes and events in their influence on our future options and strategy. Remember, **finding relevant developmental (probable, predictable) processes and events** is the central goal of the **anticipation** skill.

Qualitative forecasting is also called **judgmental forecasting**, or **visioning**, if it is aspirational. Making qualitative forecasts is usually an excellent start, but turning some of those into **quantitative forecasts** and **predictions** can often be the most important for strategy. Once they become **specific**, their **after-the-fact error** can then be easily **reviewed** (Skill 8) and **adjustments** made for future anticipations. A great forecast or prediction necessarily has probability attached to it and is shared in a critical internal or external community, which can analyze results to better calibrate future forecasts.

Particularly specific forecasts are called **predictions**. Their specificity makes them both particularly valuable as well as risky. As a result, most of the professional foresight community performs them rarely. But, that is their loss, as there are a host of both obvious and latent details which we could pinpoint about any system's future state; and, as a matter of fact, it is the unapparent predictions, which stem from latent details, missed by others, that can often be most helpful in our client's strategy, plans, and actions.

Some foresight professionals, sadly, even try to convince their colleagues that "prediction is not something we do." That is simply incorrect. Any futurist who offers a **wildcard** is saying that particular future is a **low-probability, high-impact event**. That's a **prediction**. If we are to improve at forecasting and prediction, we need to be honest about how much we already execute, and try to assign probabilities to our anticipation work. If all we can presently see ahead are **low-probability predictions**, it's much better to communicate those than to do **no prediction at all**.

Reference class forecasting, developed by psychologists and economists **Daniel Kahneman and Amos Tversky**, is a clever strategy of measuring, predicting, and eliminating certain systemic biases in long-range forecasts. It starts by researching actual past outcomes in a reference class of similar actions to the one being forecast. Program management expert **Bent Flyvbjerg** developed methods for its use in large projects and contracts, common in construction, development, and defense. The basics of his method can be found in *Megaprojects and Risk*, 2003.

Flyvbjerg, 2003

As with all academics, his <u>papers</u> offer more subtleties of theory and practice. Flyvbjerg's research shows, for example, that **large public construction projects** are usually underbid by a certain typical percentage, and **defense contracts** underbid by another percentage, with adjustments for specific bidders, industries and countries. If we can find a good **reference class** for past forecasts in a particular country, industrial sector, and with a particular supplier, we can eliminate this predictable bias and significantly improve decisionmaking, procurement, forecasting and planning.

Information and communications technologies (ICT) will greatly impact anticipation in coming years. For one survey of what is coming, see **Keller and von der Gracht's** "<u>ICT Tools in Foresight</u>," *Technological Forecasting & Social Change*, June 2014. The authors proposed that in the 2020s, typical ICT-aided foresight exercises will shift from ICT's current use in scanning and data retrieval (Skill 1), to ICT for anticipation (Skill 2), strategy and decision-making (Skill 4), and execution (Skill 5). We can also foresee how 2020's ICT will improve the rest of the Eight Skills as well. Having **strong ICT competency** will help this decade's foresight consultants like never before. Let's look briefly at a few examples.

<u>**Predictive analytics**</u> is an exciting new field that analyzes current and historical data to make quantitative predictions. One of its key features is simple <u>mathematical modeling (correlational and causal models)</u>. It is a subset of **<u>data analytics</u>,** a term that has become popular with the rise of the modern web and **big data**. We recommend **Eric Siegel's** *Predictive Analytics*, 2013, for an excellent beginner's introduction to this rapidly emerging new field.

Siegel, 2013

To consider how **predictive analysis** can help with **strategy**, let's look at one example. In 2014, a **data science team** at Google conducted a study, "<u>Women Who Choose Computer Science—What Really Matters</u>", to learn how to improve the number of US women majoring in <u>computer science</u>. Their initial research surfaced **over twenty potentially important intervention variables**, and there was conflicting research on each variable's relative importance. Their team built a simple <u>logistic regression model</u> and used <u>conjoint analysis</u>, with good pre- and post-survey data, collected from a large group of women who had completed such majors, to help determine which variables were the most influential on each woman's decision. Such a model ranks the variables in importance, without indicating causal relationships. Their study found that **four variables** were particularly important , and especially two: **parental or peer encouragement**, regardless of the parent's or peer's profession or social status, and **positive exposure to <u>coding or puzzle solving</u> in high school**, regardless of whether it was an advanced AP computer science class or a much easier summer coding experience. This **great reduction in uncertainty**, from over twenty to two variables, allowed them to design interventions targeted to these two factors, and to measure their impact (ROI) versus other approaches. By **publishing their research**, they also invited others to use it, and independently verify or falsify their findings. All of this is **good science and analysis**. Today, it is still rarely done by corporate strategy groups.

The number of organizations doing strategy and policy interventions informed by this kind of predictive analytics work today is fewer than we might expect. Such work is often not expensive; it just requires an anticipative mindset and analytical approach. But, unless we have **science and evidence-based champions in the leadership suite**, organizations will often find it easier to resort to traditional **seat-of-the-pants heuristics**, or maintain the **do-nothing view** that the system must be **"too complex to predict."** We should not be surprised when such an approach gives us mediocre results. <u>SAS</u> and <u>SPSS</u> are two powerful, general-purpose **statistical software platforms** that make this kind of predictive work easier. Either are worth learning, especially by **entry-level foresighters** who want to differentiate themselves and add value to the organization. There are also a host of excellent <u>open source data analytics tools</u> available. Fortunately, as **big data and AI-backed analytics platforms** make anticipation **easier**—and as more leaders understand the **great performance gains available**—predictive modeling and analytics will increasingly be used in **business strategy**.

Two very promising and presently **underdeveloped** group anticipation methods are **<u>real-time Delphi</u>** (online group estimation and forecasting), and **<u>prediction markets</u>** (group forecasting offering financial reward or other incentives to find the best predictors by subject area). Prediction market can be thought of as either r **collective intelligence**, a learning specialty, or as **prediction**, an anticipation specialty, depending on our perspective. Both views are helpful to foresighted managers and leaders.

Huunu and Zocalo are two early efforts in the prediction market space. See **Cass Sunstein's** *Infotopia*, 2008, and **Don Thompson's** *Oracles: How Prediction Markets turn Employees into Visionaries*, 2012, for two good sources on real world experience with prediction markets today. As with group estimation (recall the Jelly Bean Estimation Challenge), studies have shown these platforms can provide more accurate forecasts and richer sets of alternative futures than those offered by individual experts. Even though it makes management more challenging, the data also show that leaders need measurable cognitive diversity on their anticipation teams if they want the best results on complex, poorly structured anticipation problems. See **Scott Page**, *The Difference*, 2005, for evidence for this claim. There's also strong evidence that we need to mix predictive analytic methods (data and algorithms) with methods that rely on collective human judgment (Delphi and prediction markets) when assessing more abstract variables. **Nate Silver's** impressive analytics techniques for predicting **US presidential primaries** in 2008 and 2012 were much less impressive when applied to **World Cup predictions** in 2014. Prediction markets need more research and development, to discover where and when they are most useful.

Thompson, 2012

A few foresight consultants offer **real-time Delphi platforms** today, but their software and interfaces are primitive at present. Many firms have **started and then abandoned internal prediction markets**, as implementation requires careful participant training and facilitation. Unfortunately, there are not many successful commercial offerings today in this space. One non-commercial research platform of note is **Philip Tetlock's** *Good Judgment Project* at the University of Pennsylvania and U.C. Berkeley. It is presently pioneering leading methods for social and political prediction and publishing its findings, which are impressive. But, today, public and private funding for collective forecasting research remains quite small. We may need both an improved semantic web, and better-validated methods, before we see real-time Delphi and prediction platforms flourish in corporate environments.

Investing & Finance (asset management) is an organizational specialty where predictive quantitative models have made major advances. We have discussed **investing as foresight practice** in Chapter 2. When it is done well, investing is both a financially and professionally rewarding anticipation skill. **Investment finance**, and specifically the **due diligence** prior to internal organizational investment and external venture capital—is another important economic anticipation function. These topics are treated extensively in the business literature, see Appendix 3 for several good books.

Law & Security are two related anticipation specialties that both seek to protect the firm's assets and guard against loss. Note that **protection**-oriented anticipations (law and security) are as important to the firm as **prediction**-oriented anticipations (predicting opportunities, as in investing, and predicting issues, threats, and risks as in risk management). Different personalities tend to be attracted each of these core functions of anticipation. Both of these functions help the firm survive, but perhaps the greatest goal of group anticipation, in a time of accelerating change, is to be able to occasionally see highly worthy opportunities continually opening up ahead.

Risk Management & Insurance is a newer specialist practice with its own literature and methods, but insurance is, of course, one of the oldest forms of organizational anticipation. As we've said, some of the most validated predictive models in the world are built by the reinsurers, like Munich Re, Swiss Re, and many others. This is to be expected, since they have so much money riding on their bets, and since they realize, from quality research, that anticipation works.

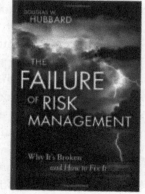

Many smart risk management strategies are available now, even to small firms. **Tom Kendrick's** *Identifying and Managing Project Risk*, 2009 and **Doug Hubbard's** *The Failure of Risk Management*, 2009/2020 are two good primers. Risk Management is now big and well-funded enough that it's

Hubbard, 2009

been misapplied by many firms, just as strategic planning was poorly applied in the 1960s-1980s. When a field has grown up enough to be critiqued—and when those critiques are acted upon by business leaders, we have progress of a sort.

Anticipation is concerned with foreseeing where things seem to be headed regardless of our individual creative acts, uncovering probable future opportunities and dangers, and protecting and preserving what we value. The skills of anticipation come largely from the rational and logical side of cognition (forecasting), and with managing negative emotions (fears, vulnerabilities) related to risks and uncertainties (security). We can oversimplify slightly and say anticipation is managed primarily "**from the head**." It is a conservative process, and it requires good data and models, and intellectual honesty.

One desirable anticipation practice is identifying environmental developments that are both increasingly inevitable *and* highly positive sum for everyone concerned, then getting on the right side of history with those expected developments in our missions, goals, and strategies, rather than an obstacle hindering those emerging realities.

Anticipation Example: Global Human Population

Let's look at a topic that most of us care deeply about: world population. It's easy to get scared about the future impacts of human population growth. Until just the last "day" of human history, it was a classic example of exponential growth. It took 200,000 years for us to reach our first 1 billion people, but just another 200 to go from there to 7 billion, more than a thousand fold increase in the rate of growth. That **looks scary**, on a precious planet with finite carrying capacity.

Yet good anticipators have known for **over fifty years** that our marginal rate of human population growth, the **second derivative of the growth curve**, has been decreasing ever faster since the mid-1960's. As our societies continue to **develop**, the population growth curve first flattens ("saturates"), then peaks, then reverses. Developed world parents almost always choose to have **fewer children than their parents**, and typically later in life, as their children gain **more options** for **personal development and achievement**. This is a universal trend, found in all cultures. We also know that **access to information**, exposure to other ways of living via our **digital culture**, greatly accelerates the **speed** of the transition. When we factor out immigration, populations are now stable or declining in the great majority of countries. The United States population continues to grow **only** because of immigration from the South. Meanwhile, Mexico, Central American and South American nations are all rapidly approaching their peak populations.

Academics call this process the **demographic transition.** But, even though the transition has been known for years, it did not become part of accepted social science until the **mid-2000's**. Like any information that doesn't fit with our preferred narratives, we been **collectively ignoring** the deceleration, and its many implications, until only very recently. The **transition's at least partially causal link to accelerating information technologies** was also covered decades ago, by demographers like **Ron Inglehart**, in courageous books like *The Silent Revolution*, 1977. It has also been ignored. For more on how we deal with true things that don't fit with our current worldview, see the IDABDAC stages (Ignoring, Denying, Anger, Bargaining, Depression, Acceptance, Commitment) in the Student Edition of this book.

Until quite recently it has been **more politically safe**, as well as **self-benefiting**, for most planners and authors to tell a **self-preventing prophecy** about how many more billions of humans we might see by century's end. But such prophecies, when they are not evidence-based, can make us blind to all the ways population growth is collapsing. We do not learn how we can best **aid** the transition. If we **ignore or discount** the demographic transition, it may occur, in each country, in far less desirable and humanizing ways that it otherwise might develop.

As the late, great statistician **Hans Rosling** of Gapminder said in *Don't Panic: The Truth About Population*, 2013, humanity hit Peak Child in 2000, stabilizing our global birthrate at roughly 130 million a year, due to a complex set of factors including growing economic opportunities, women's education, access to birth control, the rising cost of raising a child in modern societies (children become liabilities, not assets once a certain level of technology and public health exists) and mass electronic media showing people other ways to live. Other forces reducing population include expanding rights for women, urbanization, access to jobs, and sustainability culture and politics. We think access to online information (lifelong digital education) and digital entertainment and news that demonstrates the benefits of smaller families may be particularly cost effective ways to accelerate the transition, and spur societal change. At present, however, we **don't have good predictive models** of what works best, to aid the transition, both in general and in each country's unique context.

Since 2000, John has been arguing in his public talks that **the red curve in the UN projection at right is future fantasy.** Even the **orange curve**, which shows a possible **10 billion by 2100**, is not evidence-based. Charitably, one could argue these curves are offered as **self-preventing prophecies,** intended to scare us into getting more aggressive about resource conservation, environmental impact reduction, and population control. But, they are also a **systemic and self-serving bias**. They discount the **accelerating forces** that have been bending the population curve down since the 1970's, and keep **us from prioritizing and using those forces** more effectively today.

In 2004, **Ben Wattenberg's** *Fewer* described the new "demography of depopulation" for the planet. More recently, **Bricker and Ibbitson's** *Empty Planet*, 2020, has continued to make the case. Even today, most global thinkers are **still ignoring this predictable future**, and they are thus **missing its many lessons**. In *BPF*, we describe an **Age of Peaks** with respect to our species impact on our planet. In just the last decade, our civilization has passed Peak Child, Peak Steel Production, Peak Farmland, and Peak Oil Demand. Many other peaks, like Peak Car, Peak Cow, Peak

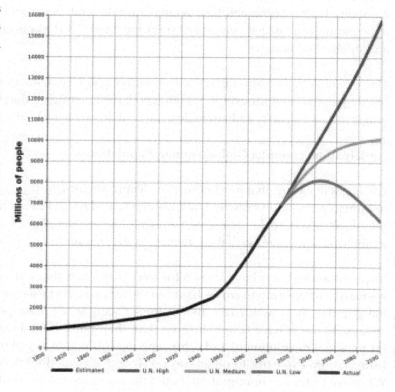

World Population Forecasts, 2010-2100
Three UN Projections (Wikipedia, 2010)

Species Loss, Peak CO2, and Peak People, are now looming just ahead. Very importantly, **these peaks only apply to** *biological* **humans and their consumption needs**, *not* to the numbers and needs of our **increasingly intelligent, miniaturized, dematerialized, and life-like machines**. We must **learn to see the difference**.

A few developed societies, worried about who will support the growing elderly, have paid families to have children, in the form of direct payments (Australia) or ramped up benefits (Germany, Japan, China), but such interventions have **not stabilized their shrinking population numbers**. Even when we look ahead to a **universal basic income**, a world in which it will be easier for families to choose to have more children, it seems clear to us that our societies will never again reach the 2.1 kids per couple that would be necessary for global population to keep growing. **That is because permanent values shifts** have occurred, as a function of our **ethical and empathic complexity**. **Self-actualization,** and providing the **best opportunities we can for our children** are our new top values in all developed and most developing countries. That is why societies are falling far below replacement rate in biological reproduction.

It is obvious to us **who will support our aging, shrinking population of peopl**e. It's will be our **increasingly self-improving AIs**, which will also continue to **reduce their critical resource needs** as D&D trends have demonstrated for decades. We predict the **ratio of machine to biological minds** will continue to **grow exponentially**, due to the dramatic advantages in speed, durability, efficiency, and complexity in machine evolutionary development. A century hence, the fraction of purely biological minds on Earth may be quite small. Privately, many experts see the logic of this weeble story, and so far, they haven't been able to defeat it, though many have tried. But publicly, as a society, we just don't want to admit this yet. So we keep generating and believing wildly inaccurate estimates of future biological population growth.

So how far ahead will **Peak (Biological) People** be? And what can we do to reduce it today? Rosling tells us the "pin code" for global human population today is **1114**. He means there are 1 billion humans in the Americas, 1 billion in Europe, 1 billion in Africa, and 4 billion in Asia. By 2100, **median UN projections** (which we argue are far too high) now expect our global population pin code to be **1145**. The Americas and Europe have stopped growing, other than immigration. At most one billion more of us will be added in Asia, but more likely half of that. In Bangladesh, for example, there are now 2.2 births per two adults, down from 6 in the 1970s. In a worst case scenario, if **present trends continue**, three billion more of us could emerge Africa, taking us to a **peak of 11 billion people in 2100**. But they won't. Exponentials and societal learning are always bending this growth curve downward. In today's best estimates, we will end up with a "pin code" close to **1124**, with **a peak around 8.3 billion people circa 2060**, then **global population decline**, at faster rates every decade afterward. Curiously, between **2060 and 2100** we also expect **general AI to arrive**. In *BPF*, we argue that the **rise of AI this century** will strongly drive societal values to **sustainability**.

Rosling's analysis tells us it is the **birth rate in underdeveloped countries in Africa**, and in a **few of the remaining underdeveloped countries in Asia**, that we should be **focusing on today**. In other words, all of us who care about sustainable human development, and providing the maximum resources to all the world's children as they increasingly seek developed world lifestyles should be looking at **helping most of Africa and parts of Asia today with significantly greater women's rights and education**, **paid jobs**, **access to birth control**, and **a range of targeted technological development activities**. That's where our last big population problem exists today. In Sub-Saharan Arica, which has the greatest population growth and societal needs, many countries still have corrupt and ineffective public schooling. Private schools in Kenya, Nigeria, and other countries are stepping in to educate neglected children for as little as $150 a year. These countries need development policies and opportunities that **empower families** and **accelerate the transition**.

Read **Irene Sun's** excellent book, *The Next Factory of the World: How Chinese Investment is Reshaping Africa*, 2017, for a good example of economic development that is working to change societal options and create local wealth much faster than most of us realize. As **China's labor population continues to inevitably shrink** (by 5M/year in 2018) and gets ever more expensive, enterprising Chinese manufacturers have moved their factories to other Asian countries, and now, to Africa. There are now more than 1500 Chinese firms manufacturing in China. Chinese entrepreneurs look at Africa and see opportunity, as they saw it in their own rural labor force a generation ago.

Sun, 2017

Americans and the West have a **bias about Africa.** We often assume it can't rapidly develop, for reasons including political corruption, traditions and culture. But, as Sun documents, that bias is incorrect. Chinese entrepreneurs are developing parts of Africa at a **vastly faster pace** than historical US and Western aid programs, most of which have underperformed for generations. Read **Bill Easterly's** *The White Man's Burden*, 2007, and *The Tyranny of Experts*, 2015, for that story. In 2020, as it struggles with mounting debt, China the nation has cut back on aid through its One Belt One Road initiative. But the development of Africa and Asia via China's global entrepreneurs continues to accelerate. **China the nation** may falter as it develops, but **Chinese entrepreneurship** is unlikely to do so. We must see the difference.

Much more Western help of African and Asian entrepreneurship could occur. Teaching people how to **build things, and sell them**, as well as how to do **service and knowledge work**, is fundamental to economic and social development. Strong societies need **engineers and builders** as much as they need **knowledge workers**. As AI starts to **empower entrepreneurs**, and give them more opportunities in manufacturing, software, platforms, and crowds, a **business-led African development strategy** will be increasingly prioritized, in our view. **Western development efforts** still do not take this **entrepreneurship-first perspective**. That seems to us to be one key reason they have **accomplished so little**.

For **anticipation in general**, whenever we've been lucky enough to discover something **important and developmental** coming our way, we have two major choices: we can **get in front of the parade early and help others see its** arrival, or get we can ignore it and get **shamed or forced into it later**. How we respond to emerging inevitabilities is our choice, but we are **more effective as leaders** when we can identify (learn and anticipate) and then align our strategy, execution, and influence behind the worthiest **developmental destinations** we can foresee. We'll say a lot more about developmental processes and forces in Book 2.

Skill 3. <u>Innovation</u> (Possibility thinking)

As individuals with finite intelligence in a complex world, our best survival strategy is to take a very creative, contingent, and experimental, <u>trial and error</u> approach to both our thinking, and our next actions. Only rarely, perhaps about five percent of the time, per the **95/5 Rule**, can foresight professionals or their clients see "one right future" ahead.

It is easy to imagine many divergent options and outcomes, and many roads can seem attractive. In such circumstances, we may follow the advice of President **Abraham Lincoln** when he said "<u>The best way to predict your future is to create it</u>." Or technologist **Alan Kay**, who said "The best way to predict the future is to invent it."

As the **95/5 Rule** proposes, perhaps **95% of the time**, **innovation**, a process of **unpredictable experimentation** is going to be the **most useful** of the two most basic foresight strategies, **innovation (evolution)** and **anticipation (development)**. Futurist **Brian Solis** offers a helpful overview of twelve key innovation processes (picture right). **Schlesinger et al.'s** <u>*Just Start*</u>, 2012, describes the need for **organizational and personal creativity** whenever we are faced with **VUCA (Volatility, Uncertainty, Complexity, and Ambiguity) in our environment**. We discuss VUCA in *BPF*. There we will also offer our own version of this classic acronym (**Volatility, Uncertainty, Complexity, and Acceleration**), to better describe the world that all organizational strategists face.

Twelve Pillars of Innovation, Solis, 2014
(See Solis, *What's the Future of Business?*, 2013)

Innovators are driven to **generate difference**, to create something **new**, and to **make a bet** on their chosen future. This **trail-and-error approach** to foresight is often the best solution, especially when the right strategy isn't obvious, as it usually isn't, due to **VUCA** and our **limited intelligence**. As always, the interaction of the innovator's creativity and the social and physical environment will decide if, where, and for how long each innovation will be **adaptive**.

Alternatives & Scenarios are the first specialty we will discuss under the innovation skill. One of the key roles of foresight professionals is to collect and imagine a wide range of possible futures, and then to subject those to evaluation and critique. Our profession calls these "<u>**alternative futures**</u>", and we use methods like <u>brainstorming</u>, <u>cross impact analysis</u>, <u>scenario analysis</u>, and <u>wild card imagination</u> to better anticipate <u>uncertainty</u>, explore the possibility space, and test possible visions, goals and strategies against many potential outcomes. We have also discussed a genre of foresight literature called <u>counterfactual history</u> that imagines alternatives to past historical events. But, while alternatives ideation may be the easiest and most enjoyable type of foresight work, its quality and impact varies widely. As we know, the value of any good idea can only be monetized by successful execution.

When the organization is in a resource-plentiful environment, when it is early in a decision process, or where a dominant strategy isn't clear, it is often best to run many small and often simultaneous innovation experiments, and carefully compare them before narrowing strategic options. **Running parallel experiments** is what an executive does when she assigns the same task to more than one team or individual, followed by a comparative evaluation. Often criticized as wasteful, this can be a very effective strategy for tough problems. Giving parallel, short-deadline assignments of the same task to independent teams, to maximize insights and options both at the beginning of projects and again at critical decision points, is commonly used in **leading management consultancies**, like <u>Boston Consulting Group</u> and <u>Bain & Company</u>. A **parallelization and selection** strategy was also famously used by US President **John Kennedy** with his advisors. It has been employed by several of our more innovative Presidents since. Parallelization and selection is also at the heart of many crowd innovation platforms, like <u>99 Designs</u> for graphic design, and <u>Open Ideo</u> for ideas for global development and social good.

Scenarios are possible futures that we should consider as inputs to strategy. A great book on them is **Fahey & Randall**, Eds., <u>*Learning from the Future: Competitive Foresight Scenarios*</u>, 1998. **Scenario learning** is the term Fahey and Randall use to describe the best way to use scenarios in organizations. It is an even better term in our view than **scenario planning**, the currently most popular term for this specialty practice. Scenario learning puts the focus on the way scenarios help us in our Do Loop, beginning with Skills 1 (learning), 2 (anticipation) and 3 (innovation), as inputs to strategy (Skill 4), rather than putting the focus on planning, which is the last output of Skill 4 prior to execution (action). Ideally, we generate scenarios as the third step of the LAIS skills (innovation), and then we use them on our teams to stimulate new investigation and discussion (learning). Done well, that process ends with better strategies and plans.

As we've said, Royal Dutch Shell (hereafter, "Shell") is arguably the most famous corporate user of scenarios. Since the 1970s, they've used them as inputs to their strategy. The great 20th century business futurist **Peter Schwartz**, in <u>*The Art of the Long View: Planning for Future in an Uncertain World*</u>, 1996, tells us that Shell anticipated, via scenario innovation, the OPEC Oil Crises of the 1970s. In <u>*Inevitable Surprises*</u>, 2004, he says that Shell also anticipated the fall of the Soviet Union in the late 1990s. Shell was able to capitalize on each of these events, and grow larger and more profitable relative to their competitors, not because they predicted them, but because they had *creatively pre-imagined them*, and then created good strategy, and *put it on the shelf* in case those events actually happened. That foresight allowed Shell to beat other large oil companies to execution, and the benefits of that execution. With regard to the fall of the Soviet Union, Shell foresighters realized that a major change in Russia's political status, if it eventually happened, might allow them to gain very favorable long term (20-year) gas and oil contracts, if they were **first movers**. They then positioned themselves strategically to be the first company able to make those (zero-sum game) contracts, and executed first and best when those conditions emerged, in the post-Cold War world.

Schwartz's pioneering foresight consultancy, <u>Global Business Network,</u> developed the most popular scenario construction technique circa 1987. In the **GBN scenario method**, two "important but uncertain" variables or trends are identified, and then extremes of both are

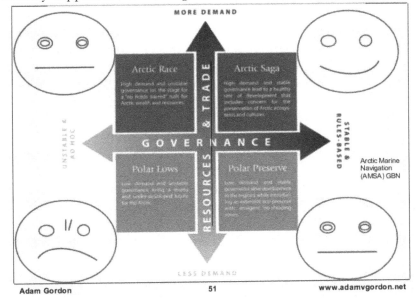

GBN Scenario Construction Method, Gordon, 2008.

205

imagined and given descriptive labels, as **future environmental states**, in a **two-by-two matrix**. The slide at right, by futurist **Adam Gordon**, author of the excellent *Future Savvy*, 2008, gives an example of this method, in an exercise exploring the futures of arctic marine navigation.

GBN scenarios are a good base method, but there are often many **more than two variables or trends that matter**, so a variety of scenario construction methods should be considered. In *Learning from the Future*, Fahey and Randall recommend building **at least five scenarios**. Having an **odd number above three** increases the chances of not missing anything important. It can also be a very good exercise to begin with an **"expected scenario"**, asking the **team** to look at history, current data, trends and forecasts, and then to build a rich narrative around a **"most likely" future world,** before veering off into important but uncertain scenarios. This advice is **anathema** to possibility-oriented foresighters, but it **enables predictive contrasting**. We believe it produces much better **sentiment contrasting** and **strategy** as a result.

As we'll describe in Chapter 5, <u>Dator's Four Futures</u> are classic change stories that offer four generic futures, Continuation, Transformation, Limits and Discipline, and Decline and Collapse. These changes are experienced by various subgroups, on various variables, at various times, in all collectives. In our view, **these four growth modes are so universal** they deserve to be **evaluated as four separate scenarios**, in addition to any other scenario-generation method we use. Alternatively, **every scenario** can include **elements from all four** of these growth modes. At any point in time, certain people, groups, organizations, and cultures will be in each of these classic **growth or change states**.

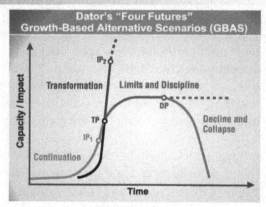

There are Four Key Stories and Expectation Sets with respect to change. Different groups experience each of these stories at the same time. The same people experience each of these stories at different times. Leaders must envision, and explore scenarios for, all four at different times.

Dator, Jim. 1979. *Perspectives in Cross-Cultural Psychology*, Academic Press.

Entrepreneurship & Intrapreneurship are another key set of business specialties that approach the future from the lens of innovation. They are focused on new processes, products, and projects that can become profitable enterprises. As <u>creative destruction</u> and <u>technological unemployment</u> are constantly eliminating both tasks and jobs, **entrepreneurship** seems a particularly necessary and rewarding foresight function. Foresight professionals that make their client firms more innovative, entrepreneurial or <u>intrapreneurial</u> (able to generate new business ventures from within established firms) provide them with a lasting ability to **survive ongoing uncertainty**—a foundational foresight skill.

As long as a firm can stay either as or more creative than its competitors, it can have several strategies in play that are gaining traction in the marketplace at any time. Its creative drive can continually keep it alive, even if it stumbles or moves backward for a time. **Eric Ries's** *The Lean Startup*, 2011, explains why startups are so much better at innovation than anyone else. **Owens and Fernandez's** *The Lean Enterprise*, 2014, shows how even large, mature firms can aggressively innovate if they are willing to pay the internal and external political costs. All good leaders learn to cultivate, at least in certain domains, a perennial **startup mindset** and **team culture**.

Darren Hardy's *The Entrepreneur Roller Coaster*, 2015, offers a motivating tour of the **emotional factors** blocking or aiding entrepreneurship, risk, and innovation, and how to manage them. Recall our discussion of <u>emotional intelligence</u> and the dual process model in Chapter 1.

Hardy, 2015

Risktakers and innovators will often think "automatic responses" and "emotions first," (**Dan Kahneman's** System 1). To retrain our subconscious emotional-cognitive systems to be more comfortable with risk and innovation, Hardy recommends reading one good book on each of these topics (entrepreneurship, risk, and innovation) **over and over** until its lessons are internalized, and recognized both **consciously and unconsciously** around us. For guiding teams through intimidating circumstances, he also notes that its far better to **"pull" them**, challenging them to emulate their leaders' examples, than to "push" them (command them)—which expresses much less empathy and demonstrates a "do as I say, not as I do" approach. Great innovators take personal responsibility for **leading by example**.

Successful innovation is still such a scarce skill that a past track record of entrepreneurial innovation has significant momentum attached to it. **John Kao's** *Innovation Nation*, 2007, argues this is one of the reasons our international investment community retains such faith in US innovation capacities, even as we have stumbled in recent years. Apple Computer's survival through its decade of creative crisis, from the mid-1980s to the mid-1990s might also be explained, in part, by how deep consumer loyalties to innovative companies can run.

Recalling military strategist **John Boyd**, the fastest and most resource efficient form of innovation is **Idea Generation**. Idea generation is predominantly divergent, "What-if"-style thinking. Any foresight professional who tries to imagine one or a range of possible futures, in a way that will achieve any degree of market success, for example, getting an idea accepted by clients as **plausible**, is using this function. But, the value of creative ideation can be poor if it is not based on good learning, subject to careful convergent selection (anticipation), and refined by critical feedback and review.

Facilitation & Gaming are another key foresight specialty. **Facilitators** can be thought of as a **catalyst** that helps people collaborate, and engage in collective intelligence (learning), anticipation, innovation, and the arrival at consensus strategy. All the best foresight leaders have a lot of experience with facilitation, which includes everything from designing good meetings to conflict management and mediation. The International Association of Facilitators (IAF) is a great practitioner community, and they offer certification and training programs—and a great conference.

Gaming has been used in foresight work since it first emerged, first as wargames in the 19th century and later as business strategy games in the 20th century. The Cold War theory of mutually assured destruction (MAD) emerged directly from political and defense simulation games at RAND, which were themselves based, in part, on the mathematics of game theory. The leading 20th century foresighter **Herman Kahn**—working first at RAND and then at his Hudson Institute— is perhaps best known for this kind of math and engineering-driven gaming work.

In reality, our predictive physical and informational theory, and its math and engineering, are still of only very limited use relative to the complexity of the world we model. That means the **empirical use of games**—to experiment with them and see what they show us—and the crafting of varied and potentially relevant game rules and gaming environments, is most often a much more useful way to anticipate and innovate important futures. Practitioners can use those game experiences as inputs to strategy. **Herman and Frost's** *Wargaming for Leaders*, 2008, offers excellent advice, from two BoozAllen consultants with extensive experience in gaming, on how to conduct useful simulation games, over an evening or a weekend, in corporate strategy meetings or in military foresight exercises. In most organizational applications, fancy computers are not needed. **Gray and Brown's** *Gamestorming*, 2010, includes over eighty games that teams can use to generate ideas, break down barriers, communicate better, and co-create better strategy. For those who want to use computers in their gaming foresight, the North American Simulation and Gaming Association (NASAGA) is a good practitioner community for both computer-based and non-digital simulation and learning. As computing power, big data, connectivity, VR/AR, GIS and the internet of things all continue to accelerate, **digital simulation games** have a very bright future ahead. We'll see them get increasingly important in all aspects of corporate, government, and defense work.

Ideation & Design is another critical specialty driving modern innovation. There is no professional association yet for **Ideation Management,** a critical precursor process to innovation, involving articulating, sizing, and prioritizing customer and firm problems, incentivizing solutions (with prizes, bounties, tournaments, reputation, culture), and **refining and**

prioritizing the best ideas. Fortunately there are now several good <u>Idea Management/Evaluation Platforms</u>, offered by companies like <u>BrightIdea</u>, <u>Datastation</u>, <u>CogniStreamer</u>, <u>Hype</u>, <u>IdeaScale</u>, <u>Imaginatik</u>, <u>Planview Spigit</u>, and others.

There are also large technical problem solver communities such as <u>InnoCentive</u>, which now has over 300,000 "solvers" in its community, most with advanced degrees or specialist skills. Recently, IM platforms have crossed the chasm of early adopter use. The IM "industry" now has tens of millions in annual sales. With leadership buy-in, adequate user training, and real rewards for innovators, IM platforms can unleash new creative capacity from our employees and customers, and draw forth a steady stream of next-step innovation proposals for management to evaluate.

As futurist **<u>Carrie Zapka</u>** reminds us, there are at least two schools of thought for facilitating and using employee ideas. The newer enterprise innovation school, also called **open innovation**, is platform-oriented. In this view, getting more diverse participants, customers, stakeholders, and the public, is the best way to find the best ideas, while also attracting many that won't be ready or relevant. Books like **Henry Chesbrough's** *Open Innovation*, 2005, **Stefan Lindegaard's** *Making Open Innovation Work*, 2011, and **Paul Sloane's** *A Guide to Open Innovation and Crowdsourcing*, 2011, advocate this open approach. **Terwiesch and Ulrich's** *Innovation Tournaments*, 2009, also discusses innovation tournaments (prizes, bounties), which harness collective intelligence and collaboration power to generate potentially successful ideas.

The traditional innovation school, also called **internal innovation**, is focused on inducing internal company talent to share their ideas for improvement, giving them resources to innovate, and to find learn from external innovation. We find this in the practice of **<u>Kaizen</u>** (continuous improvement) and related practices, including **<u>Lean enterprise</u>** and **<u>Six Sigma</u>**. We'll consider this school further under **Benchmarking & Quality** (the Reviewing skill) later in the chapter. Internal processes tend to generate small ideas, and are easier to build **intellectual property (IP)** around. Open processes are more variable, more often "swing for the fences", and are harder to build IP with. **Both are vital** to leading innovation.

Culture and policies that holds managers accountable to innovation, and empower employees to share small ideas and notice problems, are one key to the future of ideation management. **Robinson and Schroder's** *Ideas Are Free*, 2006, and their followup, *The Idea-Driven Organization: Unlocking the Power in Bottom-Up Ideas*, 2014, are quite helpful here. They tell us that teams don't need big budgets, fancy software, or crowds for world-class innovation, just good process and culture on their team, even if the larger organization is hostile to innovation.

<u>**Design thinking**</u>, with its user-centered mental and hands-on problem solving activities, offers another set of powerful conceptual and empirical tools to envision and create interesting products and services, and which entrepreneurs can then test out in the environment. <u>AIGA: The Professional Association for Design</u> (AIGA) is a great resource for this foresight specialty, and they conduct regular <u>Design Competitions</u>.

The last innovation specialty we must discuss is perhaps the most obvious, **Innovation Management & R&D**. Innovation is of course separate from ideation, as it is not just the generation of an idea that others recognize as potentially valuable, but the successful adoption of that idea as a product, service, or project in the marketplace.

Innovation management seeks to lead and maximize the value of **R&D**, design, and general innovation processes. The field of <u>innovation studies and management</u> is young and still poorly validated, but it offers helpful methods for maximizing the creative capacity and future-orientation of an organization. <u>International Society of Professional Innovation Mgmt</u> (ISPIM) is a leading practitioner community, serving R&D leaders, industrialists, institutions, and consultants in innovation mgmt. <u>Research and Development Management Association</u> (RADMA) is another smaller community, serving R&D leaders.

The late **Clay Christensen's** *The Innovator's DNA*, 2011, offers a well-considered recipe for business processes to maximize innovation, in firms of any size. **Jan Verloop's** *Insight in Innovation*, 2004, explores innovation as a business process, using historical Shell examples. **Tony Wagner's** *Creating Innovators*, 2012, has great insights on **K-12 innovation education**.

In the **Evo-Devo Foresight** model, a good practice guideline for the skill of **Innovation**, also called **evolutionary process** in this *Guide*, is to *love the journey* **(of exploration and creation)**. In biological life, the process of **evolution** displays a fundamental love, a pleasure-seeking drive, to explore an incredible variety of ways of living, and to create a breathtaking variety of forms. Innovation in the organization is concerned with imagining the possible and with creating what does not exist, in the hope of making something that will be adopted by others (social replication and "success").

Innovation uses rationality and logic to create this variety, but as any creative knows, the <u>creative process</u> is driven largely by **positive emotions** (freedom of expression, courage, optimism, excitement, the love of creation). It thrives best in a **psychologically safe environment** (though there may be deadlines, competition, or other urgencies or constraints), and benefits from self-confidence and personal willingness to risk. We can oversimplify a bit and say that due to the central role of emotion and positive visions in creativity, **innovation is managed primarily "from the heart."** The classic short film, *Why Man Creates*, 1968, offers a great overview of this critical foresight skill.

Great idea generators, innovators, and entrepreneurs are explorers who love the creative, risk-taking act. They may love it primarily in themselves, and simply demand it from others, even attempting to publicly humiliate them when they fall short of expectations, as **Steve Jobs** often did. See **Walter Isaacson's** *Steve Jobs*, 2011, for many such accounts. Alternatively, leaders may love and encourage ideation and innovation in all of their employees and stakeholders, as we saw with futurists **Larry Page** and **Sergey Brin's** tenure as CEOs at Google, where a culture of team innovation and a safe culture for innovation failure scaled well to a 50,000 person company, a rarity at that size. There is a good argument that Google's innovation focus has substantially slowed in its latest doubling, to 100,000+ employees, and under its switch to a new, transactional CEO, **Sundar Pichai**. Innovation always gets culturally harder as company **profits and size** grow.

The best innovation leaders not only pay attention to **ethics**, they maintain a climate of **positive, empathetic emotion** on their team. Do you **love the innovation process**? Are you willing to chuckle at and learn from failure, as many a great artist does? As a leader, we must be one of the more reserved displayers of positive emotion. But, being emotionally available, accepting our teams for who they are, encouraging their efforts at useful creativity, tolerating and learning from failure, and supplying them regular honest feedback are all keys to **peak creativity**.

Those working in strategy and innovation in big companies, and consultants, would do well to remember that most useful innovation comes first from the **small to mid-sized players in a market,** with the biggest players usually being **counterinnovative** (seeking to patent, slow down, and sit on innovation for as long as possible). We can call this classic economic dynamic the **Innovation 80/20 Rule**. Fortunately, once a really useful new innovation emerges from **one of the smaller players in the long tail**, and that firm **starts gaining market share** with it, the players in the **big head** have to respond by copying or acquiring it, or by rolling out the internal innovation their own engineers and innovators have long wanted to do but have been prevented from doing by conservative, profit-maximizing executive priorities.

Many top execs in big companies are far too short-term and shareholder oriented, but they just doing what they think is smartest for their firm. Their natural incentives, once they are big, is to more frequently **act in counterinnovative way**s themselves, and be on the lookout for small firms they can acquire to protect their market share. As long as **industry concentration** exists (a big head or oligopoly at the top), big company incentives will typically be aligned to try to **control and slow down innovation, maximizing current shareholder return**. Apple, Google, and others show us there are big company exceptions to this rule (company culture can be more powerful than this market pattern), and society needs big companies to do big R&D and to scale many innovations, but leaders should always **fund and patronize a good fraction of small firms** and their early stage R&D and innovation, as they are **aligned to innovate and to grow (rather than protect) their tiny market share**. Robust support of small-firms keeps our large firms accountable to the customer. A great book that explains this dynamic in the defense industry, where small contractors have long been *much* more innovative than large ones, is **James Hasik's** excellent *Arms and Innovation*, 2008.

Innovators also love divergence and freedom. The best way to incentivize innovation in any group of students, or of employees, is to **give people greater freedom the better they perform**. Such **freedom-for-merit** is problematic to those on the Left who think everyone needs to be treated the same, but it really works. See **Bob Compton's** *Finland Phenomenon*, 2011, for the power of incentivizing students with freedom when they are meeting standards in educational performance. Rewarding employees who are "meeting expectations" or above with **Free Fridays** or Google's 20% Time, or whatever other freedoms we can give, signals that we are serious about supporting innovation and personal growth.

Several things can block our love of the creative journey. The most common blocks to innovation are <u>distrust</u> and <u>fear</u>. After the **lack of freedom**, these are the greatest creativity-killers. Managing these negative emotions requires greater understanding (learning), seeing the value of freedom (innovation), and getting good at empathy and learning to trust (relating). Good books that will help you and your clients overcome distrust and fear are **Stephen Covey's** (the son) *The Speed of Trust*, 2008, **Ryan and Oestreich's** *Driving Fear Out of the Workplace*, 1998, and **Tom Rieger's** *Breaking the Fear Barrier*, 2011. **Amy Edmondson's** *The Fearless Organization*, 2018, is the leading work on why **psychological safety**, provide by leadership and organizational **norms, rules, and culture**, is a foundational factor for learning, innovation, and growth.

Covey, 2008

Having faith in our teams and valuing their creative journeys will motivate them to surprise us with beautiful new creations. As with the learning skill, managers must set limits on creative time and effort. Innovation must be balanced with the other skills. But, if we don't provide ourselves space and freedom to create, and if we don't have faith and trust in our creative capacity, and master our negative emotions, we will be out-innovated by those who really do love the innovation journey.

Skill 4. <u>Strategy</u> (Preference and Prevention thinking)

In our view, **executing adaptive strategy, with review** (Skills 4, 5, and 8) are the **heart of the Do Loop**. Doing these three skills well is most centrally what we want foresight to help us do. But, in a complex and evo-devo world, it takes a lot to stay adaptive. We've discussed thirteen **specialty practices** so far, activities that get us to the point of making good strategy. Now we'll look at two more, for creating strategy itself.

The first specialty we will address in the strategy skill is **Analysis & Decision Support**. This set of specialties helps us to generate and compare a variety of **future action options** for the organization, using some explicit criteria. One of the more technical versions of this, used commonly by big companies like Boeing and GE, is **real options analysis**, which they use prior to making big financial commitments.

Strategic analysis is used to make assumptions about how a system works, break the system into conceptual parts, and do <u>thinking about</u> and sometimes model how those parts interact, and their relevance to organizational objectives. There are a vast range of methods and communities applicable to strategy, including those from business, economics, engineering, computing, politics, intelligence, and others.

The <u>Institute for Operations Research and the Mgmt Sciences</u> (INFORMS) is a leading practitioner community for **operations research**, a technical and quantitative approach to process optimization. This specialty is called operations research in engineering, and is known in business as **management science**, and thus **OR/MS** is its combined label. For problems that can be well defined, which are only a subset of real-world problems, OR/MS and other <u>optimization</u> methods can get us to the "right" strategy, at least for the chosen objectives of the firm. But, whether those objectives are the best ones for a particular firm in a particular context is always an intuitive bet on the part of the leaders, and will ultimately be determined by the selective environment.

A word of caution is in order here: the concept of **"management science"**, which emerged in the 1970s, in the middle of our last **Foresight Spring (1960-1980)** is often a misnomer. Except in special ideal, low-complexity circumstances, **"management analysis"** is a more accurate title for the models, methods, and frameworks used in OR/MS. While this field can give us precise and technical answers, the effectiveness of those answers is another question entirely. We must be careful not to extrapolate away the full complexity of a situation in order to use our favorite analytical methods, and not to use qualitative approaches to the exclusion of qualitative ones, in any strategic decision.

Decision support is another general term for methods and technologies that help the firm make choices among known options. It is very similar to strategic analysis, but more focused on how strategy and other processes help us do better decision-making. This foresight specialty is smaller and less developed than analysis. The <u>European Working Group on Decision Support Systems</u> (EWG-DSS), and their conference, <u>Decision Support System Technology</u>, are a useful place to get help with decision modeling and the use of technology for better decision-making.

Again, the ultimate goal for any firm is to have a continually adaptive strategy and execution, even as environmental conditions periodically change. Most business problems, being primarily evolutionary and unpredictable in nature, have no obvious "right" answer. It is with those problems where experience, cognitive diversity, good use of the **Eight Skills**, and good values and character can really help the firm adapt.

The **Visioning, Goals, Strategy & Planning** specialty begins with activities like **Values** determination and **Visioning**, preference-driven, aspirational thinking that results in envisioned future states, with leadership buy-in to a subset of those visions). Some foresight consultancies have become well known for aspirational (vision- and values-driven) work.

A particularly evo-devo goalsetting process is called **<u>Objectives and Key Results (OKRs)</u>**. It is a largely bottom-up, transparent, employee-engaged goalsetting and results measuring method, pioneered by Intel in the 1970s, and refined by Google and in the 1990s and 2000s. For details on how to use OKRs in companies of any size, see <u>Google's tutorials on OKRs</u>, and **John Doerr's** excellent *Measure What Matters*, 2018. OKRs are a combination of top-down and bottom-up visioning, goalsetting, and strategy development, with the "what" (objectives, goals) often being management-led, and the "how" (key results to be measured) often being employee-led. OKRs should be revised regularly, and when the culture takes them seriously, as Intel and Google do, we can often get very large companies to change rapidly, as strategies are tied to measurable results, with quarterly, monthly, weekly, or daily feedback, depending on the result.

When comparing visions to scenarios, the futurist **<u>Clement Bezold</u>** likes to say "Visions are futures for the heart; scenarios are futures for the head." Finding the shared, motivating vision can be incredibly energizing for the team, as we've seen in many a startup and independent business unit. Think of the <u>Bandley III</u>, the Macintosh unit, under **Steve Jobs** at Apple in 1983. Scenarios, by contrast, immerse the client in options. One or two scenarios may be preferred, and it can be motivating to experience such a scenario. But, **strategic visions** are much more concise and specific than preferred scenarios, and they are intended to lead **directly** to action enablers like SMART goals and OKRs.

Strategy also includes **Framing** (determining the scope, depth, and methods of strategy and foresight work), a key activity discussed in **Hines and Bishop's** *Thinking About the Future*, 2013. Strategy work also involves **Prioritization** and **Goalsetting** (for example, using <u>SMART goal criteria</u>). Again, determining everyone's OKRs (measurable goals) is one of the most difficult yet empowering activities in <u>strategic management</u>. **Annika Steiber's** *The Google Model*, 2014, provides useful details on their management processes.

Steiber, 2014

For a great article describing how **executives** learn strategic thinking over their career, in a process of psychological development, or fail to learn it, see **Ellen Goldman's** "<u>Strategic Thinking at the Top</u>" (free), *MIT Sloan Mgmt Review*, Summer 2007. For a great history of strategy consulting, and how strategy is used, well and poorly, in modern firms, read **Walter Kiechel's** *Lords of Strategy*, 2010.

The **Planning** specialty in **Strategy & Planning** is often thought of as the last step before action, and the culmination of strategy and analysis. Whether simple or detailed, formal or informal, good plans help us to **coordinate** our resources and energies toward desired outcomes. **Strategic planning** has been used since the 1960s by larger firms, but as **Lou Gerstner** says in his classic "Can strategic planning pay off?", *McKinsey Quarterly*, 1973, and **Henry Mintzberg** explains in *The Rise and Fall of Strategic Planning*, 2000, it is very easy for a firm to over-plan, to use plans as a poor excuse for action, and especially to create plans that are not widely internalized or executed as written, even in the early steps. **Bradford and Duncan's** *Simplified Strategic Planning*, 2000, gives advice on how to avoid these traps with brief, fast, and continuous high-utility planning. Just like actions, plans must be **simple enough** to be continually **reviewed**.

A firm's plans may or may not involve broad foresight. Sometimes anticipation isn't possible, and one instead needs **strategic agility**, moving as quickly as possible from strategy to action. At other times, when facing big bets and costly decision points, and when a little reflection time can be found prior to the decision, the level of ideation (alternative futures generation), anticipation and strategy in the plan can be critical. Did the team explore the most relevant **probable** and **possible** futures related to objectives as part of strategic planning? If not, the plan will be blind to the environment, and may have little survival value.

In complex systems-based approach, **management** can **mentally or graphically map the rough fitness landscapes** of the relevant stakeholders. Actors are always on an **adaptive landscape** of **shifting peaks and valleys** in relevant **cooperative and competitive variables** (e.g. efficiency, performance, preference, product features, growth, margins, profit, assets, resources, partnerships, reputation, brand, etc.), as in the picture below. Figuring out which variables matter the most to one's strategy is of course an art. As **Fleming and Sorenson** note in "Navigating the Technology Landscape of Innovation," *MIT Sloan Management Review*, 2003, **leaders** can often **see only a little way out** on their firm's fitness landscapes from their current location. Their **teams**, and the **crowd**, can often see farther. Such analytical work can be very clarifying, **prior to strategy creation**. It can also be done **prior to scenario generation**, to understand the coopetitive environment.

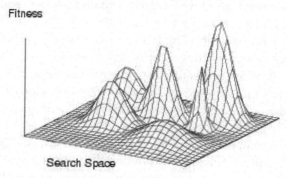

Even when quantitative analyses aren't available to us, the **adaptive fitness landscape** can still help us to mentally visualize our strategy. Such landscapes can be built out of any two variables, tangible or intangible, using estimates and online survey software. Some individuals, firms, and groups will always be adapting **better than others** (climbing adaptive

Fitness Landscape (A fitness variable (e.g. preference, growth, profit) and a search space (strategic options)

peaks, on various landscapes), and some will be **losing out** (falling into valleys). The **lay of the relevant landscapes** at any time can *always* be used to guide our strategies.

Leaders need to know what customers think of their products and policies relative to competitors (customer preference landscape), where they are in cash flow and sales momentum (financial landscape), which of their competitors are doing well and doing poorly (competitiveness landscape), and who their best potential allies are (strategic alliance landscape). For more on that, see **Doz and Hamel's** *Alliance Advantage*, 1998.

If learning is foresight's first skill, and strategy is the heart of foresight, then learning the relevant landscapes is the heart of strategy. Every manager's central goal is to **adapt enough to survive**, to keep successfully riding the tiger of change. Key to that survival is knowing where the peaks and valleys are on all the relevant landscapes, then developing strong **cooperative and competitive analysis, strategy, and plans** to capitalize on what our teams can see around us.

Skill 5. <u>Execution</u> (Production thinking)

The most obvious action skill is **Execution**. **Bossidy and Charan's** *Execution: The Discipline of Getting Things Done*, 2011, can help with improving this core skill. As we've said, **execution** shares the podium with **strategy** and **review** as the three most critical foresight skills. As the saying goes, "**Without execution, strategy is lame, and without strategy, execution is blind.**"

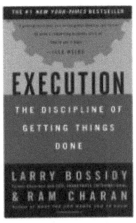

Bossidy&Charan,2011

We have assigned the **Management & Leadership** specialties to the execution skill, as managing execution is their central duty. All foresight students need to understand good practice in both of these, and use them in their work. But, as we've said these two are also **meta-specialties**, like foresight itself, and we'll address them as such throughout this guide.

For organizations, key execution specialties are **Product, Service, and Project Management**, a broad set of activities that can include operations, engineering, sourcing, logistics, IT platforms, knowledge management, and anything else necessary to production. A great management professional association is the <u>American Management Association</u> **(AMA)**, which addresses all of these subjects, and offers training and support in execution skills.

But, there are also specialty practitioner communities for product, service and project management that a good foresight practitioner should be aware of and consider joining as appropriate. For **Product Management**, the <u>Product Development and Management Association</u> has 3,500 members and offers a <u>New Product Development Professional certification</u>. For **Service Management** there are a few similar emerging professional associations. IBM has proposed a curriculum in IT-aided <u>service science, management, and engineering (SSME)</u>, but the field barely exists today.

PMI's PMP Certificate

Project Management is by far the best developed of these three execution-oriented functions. A leading text is **Harold Kerzner's** *Project Management: A Systems Approach*, 2013, now in its 11th edition. It is aligned with the <u>Project Management Professional (PMP) Certification Exam</u>, offered by the <u>Project Management Institute</u>. The institute also produces the *Product Management Body of Knowledge*, a dryer read than Kerzner's text. The PMP exam costs $400 (paper version). Roughly 600,000 people have gained a PMP certification to date. Assessing knowledge, not action, certification won't necessarily improve our execution thinking and behaviors, but if its lessons are internalized it has a potential to do so. If it also raises our credibility, it may be a good personal development strategy.

For foresight consultants, execution may involve producing **foresight products or services** (research, modeling, workshops, training, publications, etc.) for the client, or it may involve diagnosing and fixing **execution problems** with the client's team. When we situate **execution** within the employee's **Do loop**, the team's use of the **Eight Skills**, and the firm's use of the **Twenty Specialties**, in a culture aware of its **values**, we can truly help our clients be adaptive.

Another management specialty, <u>workflow management</u> is critical to empowering and motivating the team to **get things done**. **Jeff Sutherland's** *Scrum*, 2014, is a highly recommended set of simple workflow management habits for maximizing **adaptive execution** for small teams. In scrum, teams should be small enough (typically five to nine individuals) to engage in one or more daily fifteen minute "standup" meetings, maximizing learning, seeing, doing, and reviewing. **Scrum** has a cyclic structure that follows the **Do Loop**. We recommend that foresighters, managers, and leaders all use their own **scrum-like workflow systems** as core practice skills with their teams and clients.

For execution in general, **Stephen Covey's** *First Things First*, 1996, as not only a good guide to strategic **prioritization,** but also to fighting procrastination and **getting started**, which for many is the hardest step with execution. It reminds us that doing more of the *right* things first, and doing them *now* rather than later, is key to doing the best we can.

Endurance and focus are also key attributes of great executors. To build personal endurance, we recommend **Tony Schwartz's** *Be Excellent at Anything*, 2011. Cycling rapidly between execution and-recovery phases (high-intensity interval training) is an *excellent* way to build endurance for execution, both in our physical and mental work. For more on the psychology of focus, and many workflow tips, we recommend **Nir Eyal's** *Indistractable*, 2019.

Another key to successful execution, covered in Bossidy and Charan's work, is being able to reach out to experts when we run into trouble. There's almost always someone with **specialty talent** who can help us when we get stuck. Finding such talent and resources has never been easier with the modern web. We can start improving our execution today; by adopting helpful new **conscious routines,** which over time, will become powerful, **unconscious habits**.

Skill 6. Influence (Market thinking)

The next action (and thinking) skill is **Influence**. Foresight professionals use it to communicates the value of their work, and motivate the client to execute strategy and plans. Personal influence starts with **understanding the mindset** (worldview, assumptions, emotional state) of the **client and their culture**, which is often less future-oriented, and more change and risk averse, than the foresight professional's own mindset. Learning **self-restraint**, and knowing when **saying less** will yield **more results**, is a major part of the learning curve of many foresight practitioners.

Influence flows both **down from the top**, and **up from above**. We normally think of the first category, due to our evolutionary inclination to prosociality, but the second category is more prevalent and powerful, per the 95/5 Rule. **Doug Miller's** brilliant *Can the World Be Wrong? Where Global Public Opinion Says We're Headed*, 2015, charts all the ways the opinion of citizens, in every country, increasingly **constrains and directs** both corporate and government behavior. We'll explore his **demographic foresight** work in *BPF*. **Evo-devo thinking** tells us that **public opinion trends**, while often overlooked, represent the **vast majority** of long-term global influence. As Chairman of a global polling company, GlobeScan, Miller has documented rapid values shifts, towards **sustainability** and **ethical consumerism**, emerging across the world. Many of these values shifts are happening much faster in rapidly emerging nations, like China and India, than in Europe (the traditional societal values shift leader), and much more rapidly than in the lagging United States, except among our youth. Firms ignore these values shifts to their own detriment.

More obviously, influence is a key skill our clients need to succeed in the **market**. Today, media and markets are our greatest way to quickly influence mass behavior. Thus for modern organizations, the key influencing specialties are **Marketing & Sales Management**. Advertising, Business Development, Lead Generation, Market Research, Customer Service, and Customer Relationship Management (CRM) are all applications of this skill. The American Marketing Association **(AMA)** is a key marketing practitioner community, and the National Association of Sales Professionals **(NASP)** a leading sales practitioner community.

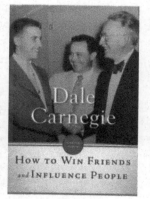

Dale Carnegie's *How to Win Friends and Influence People*, 1937/1998, is a classic primer on **personal influence**. **Warren Buffett** called this "the most successful self-help book of all time." Like other classics, it is worth reading a few times, until its advice is emotionally and cognitively automatic. But, as reviewer **Andrew Parodi** reminds us on Amazon, this book is incomplete. According to **Kemp and Claflin's** biography, *Dale Carnegie: The Man Who Influenced Millions*, 1989, Carnegie intended to include a final chapter, about the need to establish rules regarding, and regulate contact with, those **problematic people** who are consistently degrading productive collaboration.

Carnegie, 1937

Carnegie apparently left this unfinished chapter out of his manuscript when offered a trip to Europe. It also allowed the book to end on a positive note. That gave us a great book on influence, but one with few lessons on identifying and treating differently that **subset of people whom we can't positively influence** after many good efforts on our parts—due to their arrogant, inflexible, dogmatic, dominant, egotistical, unethical, borderline, or sociopathic personalities.

This is actually **Relating** advice (Skill 7), but it deserves discussing here, in the context of **mutual failure of influence**. In such circumstances, it will be our occasional responsibility to seek to remove such individuals from our teams, or at least from important management positions. If such an individual is our relationship or business partner or our client—and if either of us has been unable to influence the other to be more adaptive, despite our best efforts—a **relationship quarantine, holiday, or divorce** may be best for both of us. If limiting or eliminating contact isn't enough, **legal action or a direct competitive challenge** may be necessary as well. We must **stand up to bullies** where we find them.

Sales specialty classics that every <u>CMO</u> or CSO should own and use in their organizations are **Miller and Heiman's** *The New Strategic Selling*, 1985/2005, for general sales development, and the *New Conceptual Selling*, 1987/2005, the latter for face-to-face interactions. **Mack Hanan's** <u>*Consultative Selling, 8th Ed.*</u>, 1970/2011 is also a classic that focuses the sales effort on delivering measurable value to the client, and improving their margin, revenue or profit in a measurable way. See also **Neil Rackham's** inspirational classic <u>SPIN Selling</u>, 1988. Among more recent books, **Daniel Pink's** *To Sell is Human*, 2013, and **Robert Cialdini's** *Influence*, 2006, are both good primers on the way we use reciprocity, social proof, consistency, commitment, liking, authority, scarcity and other factors to shape our influence over others.

As with all of the **Eight Skills**, our psychological traits (e.g., extroversion vs. introversion, woo vs command) will greatly influence our baseline influence abilities. As personal traits are slow to change, the best strategy to rapidly grow organizational influence is to recruit team members who are naturally excellent at this professional skill and to give them leadership positions, freedom, incentives, and resources to address key marketing and influence challenges.

Richard H. Thaler
Cass R. Sunstein

Nudge

Improving Decisions
About Health, Wealth,
and Happiness

Thaler & Sunstein,
2009

In recent years, behavioral and social psychologists and economists are discovering just how strongly and predictably we are influenced by our **environment and social networks**. Books like **Thaler and Sunstein's** *Nudge*, 2009, **Dan Ariely's** *Predictably Irrational*, 2010, and **Sandy Pentland's** *Social Physics*, 2014, all make clear that environmental design and our choice of peers have major impacts on our thoughts and behaviors. We take most of our cues from our associates and environment. For example, organ donation rates, savings contribution rates, and many other **personal decisions** have shown 15-90% increases in participation based simply on switching environmental conditions from **default opt-out to default opt-in** (presumed consent). The UK government now its own "nudge unit" (<u>Behavioral Insights Team</u>). US President **Barak Obama** employed nudge pioneer **Cass Sunstein** in his first administration (2008-2012). See Sunstein's *Why Nudge?*, 2014, for more on how **issues of societal adaptiveness**, like obesity, smoking, distracted driving, crime, corrections, education, safety, and many others can be greatly affected by nudging influences. Nudging is a form of "<u>libertarian paternalism</u>" that will grow in our increasingly data rich and digitally-enhanced societies in coming years.

The human resources consulting firm <u>Humu</u>, founded in 2017 by **Laszlo Bock**, former VP of People Operations at Google, has built a "nudge engine," an AI that uses people analytics to offer 1500 (as of 2020) customized email templates to improve manager effectiveness, and help executives to better manage the "tails" (superstars and low performers) in the workplace. Bock argues that HR should prioritize getting help and feedback to those who are performing much worse than others, and supporting superstars who are performing well above average, and need to be appropriately recognized, resourced and challenged. They also empower companies to conduct experiments to measure the effectiveness of their nudges. This kind of evidence-based and AI-infused nudging is surely a key part of the **future of HR**.

Foresight consultants use influence in all stages of their work, including the initial client proposal, workshop facilitation, product development, service delivery, and review of their work. To have influence with clients, foresight work needs both <u>relevance</u> and <u>credibility</u>. The message must be tailored to the client's abilities and needs, but it must also be truthful and effective at altering or confirming strategy, or the foresight will have little adaptive value.

Skill 7. <u>Relating</u> (Team thinking)

The third action (and thinking) skill involves understanding and acting to serve the needs of the team. This may be our foresight production team, our organization, or the client team. Good relating begins with <u>emotional intelligence</u> among leaders and managers. Managing distrust and fear—the two creativity-killers mentioned under innovation—are key to good relating. Stress management is also important. Every team needs good management of both <u>sprints</u> and recoveries, as **Tony Schwartz** explains in *<u>Be Excellent at Anything</u>*, 2011. In its highest form, the relating skill can become what **Robert Greenleaf** calls *<u>Servant Leadership</u>*, 2012, an empowering and ethical approach to management that gives our people the freedom to innovate and to fail, yet also requires that they learn from their mistakes via good reviewing (Skill 8).

For organizations, the main relating specialties are **Human Resources & Performance Management**, and related HR topics including Compensation, Incentives, Ethics, Culture, and Employee Engagement. The relating skill also includes the firm's non-marketing relationships with its external stakeholders, what we might call issue or image performance management, including Communications, Public Relations, and Corporate Social Responsibility. The <u>Issue Management Council</u> is a professional association for **issue management**, where issues are defined as the gap between organizational actions and stakeholder expectations. Some might argue that Performance Management fits better under the **Execution** skill, but such a treatment seems insufficiently respectful of the role of **nurturing and sustaining relationships** in organizations. Performance management is at heart a **Relating** skill.

In human life, **relationships** have always been top priority, whether leaders recognize this fact or not. The quality of relationships not only is central to team performance, it largely determines how the team and company are perceived externally. Relationship-building and maintaining is thus the top human performance skill. Leaders can forget this, and HR has traditionally been one of the **least-valued departments** in the firm. But remember our motto: *People first!*

The <u>Society for Human Resource Management</u> (**SHRM**) is the leading US practitioner community in this specialty. It offers certifications including <u>Professional in Human Resources</u>, which can help any foresight professional working to maximize their impact with this skill. Reed and Bogardus' *<u>PHR/SPHR</u>*, 2012, is a study guide for those certifications. SHRM also offers <u>their own prep</u>.

In all **relationships**, it can also be valuable to think in simple terms, about <u>game theory</u>, a topic that is also relevant to strategy. The best relationships strive to create **positive sum (win-win)** and minimize **zero-sum (win-lose, adversarial)** interactions among all those in the group. **Robert Wright's** *<u>Nonzero</u>*, 2000 offers the classic big picture introduction to positive sum games across human history. Wright points out that all enduring social "games" like **personal and group ethics, capitalism, and democracy**, seek to structure cooperation and competition in ways that create **growing and measurable positive outcomes** for the group.

Fair competition with incentives can be greatly energizing to any group. But, nothing will kill a team's performance faster than **rules, policies or mandates** that are widely perceived as **arbitrary or unfair**. Leaders must continually adjust their policies and incentives for perceived fairness, be transparent and inclusive with process, and keep the **manager-employee relationship central**. We must act **People First**, even above the rules, which deserve to be continually revised, and periodically bent or broken. **Jack Stack's** *<u>The Great Game of Business</u>*, 2013, also stresses this perspective. It is an excellent primer both on **open book management** and the process of constant **open reviewing** (Skill 8).

Performance management is a specialty of HR and organizational development that focuses on firm, team, and employee performance. The KPI Institute (KPII) is a leading practitioner community. They offer certifications in many management practices, including Benchmarking (best practices), Key Performance Indicators (KPIs), a subset of benchmarking focused on firm performance, and Objectives and Key Results (OKRs), which empower employees to set their own performance objectives, in a bottom-up manner, and to help each other achieve them. We've already recommended a good book on Google's People Operations practices, **Laszlo Bock's** *Work Rules!*, 2015, which describes Benchmarking, KPIs and internally transparent OKRs for each employee. Knowing everyone's goals can help us to be more helpful to them.

As we've said, **Stephen Covey's** books are also some of the most timeless and accessible that we know in general professional development. They are particularly strong in relationship building. Nearly half (four) of the nine key workplace habits Covey describes in *The Seven Habits of Highly Effective People*, 1989/2013, and *The Eighth Habit*, 2005, are concerned with **relating better** to the needs of others and the team. These are: Thinking Win-Win (Positive Sumness), Seeking First to Understand (Empathize), Sharpening the Saw (Promoting Work-Life Balance and Renewal), and Helping Others Find their Voice (Professional Development).

In the language of the **Eight Skills**, Covey's other five habits involve **learning** (Synergize), **anticipation** (Be Proactive), **strategic vision** (Begin With the End in Mind), and **strategic prioritization** (Put First Things First. Find Your Voice). Using the **Eight Skills** model, we can propose that **innovating, influencing,** and **reviewing** are adaptive **foresight and success habits** that we must follow. Covey addresses **influence** in *The Speed of Trust*, 2008, recommended earlier. That leaves only **innovating** and **reviewing** as core foresight skills that are underrepresented in Covey's works on core habits.

The Franklin Covey Leadership Center is a great place for leadership training. No doubt the center has addressed these other critical skills in separate publications as well. But keep in mind what they, or any other consultancy, may miss or underrepresent. Teams need reasonable competency with **all Eight Skills** if they are to thrive.

Like influence, foresight consultants rely personally on the relating skill in all stages of their work. Consultants must relate well to their colleagues, on whom they depend for referrals and **social intelligence**. They need to understand the needs of their team, offer trust, personal freedoms, a development path, a good mission, adequate benefits, create demanding execution sprints, and provide healthy recovery time. They also need good mental models for how their production and client teams emotionally and intellectually perceive the world and their work. These relating skills build team strength and trust, and bring it to a place where it will accept, rather than resist, our regularly-needed changes in direction, small and large. We will now discuss that challenge under **reviewing** (Skill 8) the last skill in the **Do Loop**.

Skill 8. Reviewing (Adjustment thinking)

The last critical type of action and thinking requires looking at the recent past in order to improve our future. Nothing is perfect; and, everything can be improved. How do we know when we are **missing the mark**? And when we fall short, how do we generate the momentum to change? That is the reviewing skill, i.e., adjustment thinking. In our view, along with execution and strategy, it is one of the **three most critical skills** of the Do loop. Like the other seven skills, reviewing is very helpful to a point, but it can also be overdone and must be balanced with the other seven skills.

The first reviewing specialty we will discuss is **Auditing & Change Management**. **Auditing** is a subspecialty of both accounting and intelligence work that seeks to find out the real state of things, which may be very different from the state we think, or the state represented in the books. The Institute of Internal Auditors (IIA) offers certifications and conferences in this critical, and often-neglected specialty. Being constantly on the lookout for numbers that don't seem right, and learning how to interrogate them, is a critical reviewing skill. If we are the bearer of bad news, we may not find a receptive audience, either. Sometimes we will need to get particularly creative in communicating bad news and getting the protection and political impact necessary to be a successful whistleblower.

Harry Markopolous's fascinating book, *No One Would Listen: A True Financial Thriller*, 2010, details how his models and forensic accounting evidence predicted, with accumulating evidence, that **Bernie Madoff** was running a massive **Ponzi scheme**. Markopoulos alerted the SEC to this suspected fraud three times with supporting documents, in 2000, 2001, and 2005, and two additional times without documents. Each time they **ignored him** and failed to follow up, a common pattern with many whistleblowers. **Ignoring** is almost always the first of **seven common stages of adapting** to forced and **undesired change** (Ignoring, Denying, Arguing, Bargaining, Depression, Acceptance, Commitment). For more, see the **IDABDAC Stages of Adaptation to Forced Change** in the Student Edition of this book.

The Madoff fraud collapsed in 2008, losing $64 billion for investors, making it the largest **known** financial fraud in US history to date (it will be exceeded). It is a classic failure of financial foresight to convert to successful strategy and action. We should ask ourselves what we might have done differently if we, like Markopoulous, were one of the only reviewers publicly telling the truth at the time. Whistleblower protection laws are still weak, and whistleblowers must be willing to engage in a certain amount of legal, career, and family-risk if they wish to bring powerful actors to account.

As auditors of intangibles as well as tangible things, good foresighters also want to be constantly on the lookout for any expressed or implicit **group emotions, thoughts, values, assumptions, forecasts, and expectations** that don't seem reasonable in a particular context. In *Seeing What Others Don't*, 2013, cognitive psychologist and decision-making expert **Gary Klein** discusses the **project premortem** as a very powerful method to immediately audit for and eliminate overly optimistic groupthink with any high profile, critical, or complex project. The premortem can be used by any group facilitator to help make inflated expectations more realistic. We can think of the premortem as a way to quickly audit the opinion of **pessimists in the group who want to speak out**, but are being cowed by group bias to believe in some obviously unlikely futures. A reverse form, **success visions**, can be used if we think the group is being unreasonably pessimistic and we want to eliminate fatalistic thinking and get the group back on track to positive action. We discussed both of these in Chapter 3 and will see them again in Appendix 1 (Brief Foresight Skills Assessment.

Change management is leadership and management intended to diagnose and fix an **organizational problem**. It includes the set of practices we use to diagnose and turn around business processes and organizational strategy, often against political inertia. When firms get into trouble, they will often bring in a **turnaround team**, one with good experience in instituting the drastic reforms that may be necessary when the organization's structure or process have become seriously out of alignment with the competitive environment. The Association of Change Management Professionals (ACMP) is a newer practitioner community seeking to standardize and promote this leadership and management subspecialty.

Like foresight and leadership, change management requires all the **Eight Skills**, but we classify it as primarily a **reviewing** skill because it first requires adequately **diagnosing** organizational opportunities and problems (Rumelt's first step in strategy), recognizing what is and isn't working, then devising good strategy to seize opportunities and fix key problems, using influence to get people on board with the change plan, executing reforms, and continually reviewing whether strategy and action are successful, and further adjusting as necessary.

To prevent the need for a turnaround team in future years, some corporate boards of directors will even formalize some change management positions and processes in their organization during good times. As **Murray Lincoln**, one of the 20th century leaders of the **cooperative movement** liked to say, every company should have a "vice president in charge of revolution," someone who's primary task is to critique, challenge, and engender ferment among the more conventional colleagues. Periodically questioning their foundations is how all good firms stay strong.

Like all the specialties we've described, change management occurs in a **Do Loop.** The faster, more efficiently, and more strongly members of our organizations can run that loop, the more adaptive we become. This is described well in **John Kotter's** classic eight-step loop model in *Leading Change,* 2012. Another great resource on group behavior change, using both **influence and change management** skills, is **Grenny et al.'s** *Influencer: The Science of Leading Change,* 2013.

These and other change management works stress strategies that include focusing on **small behaviors** that signal the **new direction** to the group, publicly empowering the **early adopters** who model the changes we seek, and **structuring** the peer, physical, and digital environments to encourage change. **Stephen Guise's** *Mini Habits,* 2013, is a nice summary of the power of the "small good habit" strategy, both personally and for teams. Defining, asking for, and publicly rewarding small and very achievable "vital behaviors" that signal the new direction will help the organization instigate change more rapidly and confidently.

Grenny et al, 2013

Unlearning is another key life and organizational challenge that begins with the Reviewing skill. We must use **feedback** to figure out what we need to **unlearn**, so we can do better in the next cycle of the Do Loop. As **Will Rogers** and **Mark Twain** both said (in different variations): "**It isn't what we don't know that gives us the most trouble, it's what we know that is no longer so.**" The more we learn, the more some of what we've learned will have to be **unlearned**, in order for us to continue to develop. Unlearning is **often overlooked by both individuals and firms**, for strong psychological reasons. We all benefit from **positive illusions**. We like to believe we are **better than we actually are**. That illusion is adaptive, but only to a point. In addition to having a **positive self-image** and a **growth mindset**, we all must honestly ask ourselves and others **where we are failing**, and what **habits and beliefs** may be contributing to that failure. Then we must figure out how to set **new habits** and reinforce new **beliefs**. That is a Learning challenge, restarting our **Do Loop.**

Barry O'Reilly's *Unlearn,* 2018, is a helpful guide to this key challenge. Unlearning can be particularly difficult if we need to change things that were **learned early in life**, making them largely unconscious. In that case, we have to work particularly carefully in **today's foresight**, using tools like **mindfulness, accountability**, and **repetition**, to be aware of and change the habit. We must also learn to **forgive ourselves** for our past mistakes, and be ready to let things go. Psychologist **William Bridges** self-help classic, *Transitions,* 1980/2019, says that in any **transition**, to college graduate, to marriage, to parenthood, to business owner, to professional, parts of our former selves must **die**, in order for our new selves to fully **flourish. Wisdom** comes in recognizing what must be unlearned, and what must be protected and grown. If an **organization needs to unlearn, resistance** will always arise, and must be dealt with caringly but firmly. Those who cannot adopt the new behaviors must be given extra help until they can, or are managed off the team or out of the firm.

O'Reilly, 2018

Unlearning can be particularly hard when we believe that our old habits and beliefs **caused our past success. Caroll and Mui's** *Billion Dollar Lessons,* 2008, covers major business failures brought on by executive teams that became **mentally limited by their past successes**. Both individuals and teams must recognize when **conditions have changed**, and why what worked in the past will no longer work today. We must also ask ourselves if we were operating from **false beliefs**, ask how much of our success was due to **external factors**, including **luck**. As the **95/5 Rule** tells us, the great majority of what happens to us in life will be due to **contingent, unpredictable factors**, like being in the right place at the right time. But we also can **control** a small subset of things, and sometimes, those things make all the difference. As the saying goes, fortune favors the **prepared mind**. We all can benefit from better foresight, with continual **learning, predictive and sentiment contrasting, strategy**, in order to **recognize and capitalize** on luck.

For those leaders seeking motivating examples of how much organizational change can be accomplished when an organization faces **real crisis**, read **Bill Bratton's** *Turnaround*, 1998, on the NYPD, **Lou Gerstner's** *Who Says Elephants Can't Dance?*, 2003, on IBM's turnaround (before it's more recent fall), **Carlos Ghosn's** *Shift*, 2006, on Nissan's turnaround (before his personal fall), or General **Stanley McChrystal's** *Team of Teams*, 2015. These turnarounds are all captured well in these books, even as their leaders take credit for more than they should. **Turnarounds** always require some burying of old grievances and willingness to abandon old ways (forgiveness and unlearning, Skill 8), some time for the (usually new) leader to learn the lay of the land (learning, Skill 1) and try new things (innovation, Skill 2) before **employee judgment** is rendered. In other words, employees need **freedom and trust** to mentally fire up their Do Loops again.

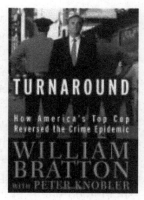

Bratton. 1998

Benchmarking & Quality are our last set of reviewing specialties to be discussed in this guide. Benchmarking determines best practices ("quality," at the firm level) by looking widely and carefully at the competitive environment, to see how others do things that we do, whether anyone is doing them **better**, and how we can institute **measurements** around **best practices**—which we can continually review to guide us to where we want to go.

The Benchmarking Network (BN) is a resource (not a community) that lists a variety of industry benchmarking associations. One good benchmarking community is the Balanced Scorecard Institute (BSI). Balanced scorecards are a respected performance management tool, developed by **Robert Kaplan and David Norton** in 1992, which focus the team on a small, mentally memorable set of financial and non-financial performance items, giving them target values, and generating corrective interventions when performance falls short of targets. The most popular scorecard system uses four organizational measures: Customer-Stakeholder, Financial, Internal Processes, and Organizational Capacity (People and Technology) performance. **Paul Niven's** *Balanced Scorecard Step-by-Step*, 2006, and **Kaplan and Norton's**, *The Strategy-Focused Organization*, 2001, and *Alignment*, 2006, are both helpful balanced scorecard primers.

Scorecards can be linked to a strategy map, to leading indicators (early signs of change), to various outcome measures ("lagging indicators"), and to strategic initiatives to achieve desired targets. Scorecards must be aligned to current management strategies, and redesigned when that strategy has outlived its usefulness. Proactive leaders can use them to signal when a crisis is emerging, and to initiate politically painful change.

The Balanced Scorecard Institute offers a BS Professional and BS Master Professional certificate. Results-based management is another scorecard style management approach that gets all the actors to plan, measure, and review the results of their interventions. It is gaining popularity in nonprofit sectors, and for dealing with any abstract projects where predefining ideal outcomes and impact are important to keep the organization accountable.

BSI's BSP and BSMP Certificates

The International Red Cross provides a nice overview of their use of results-based scorecards, to track both tangible and intangible variables and outcomes.

The last reviewing subspecialty we will discuss is **Quality**. We've previously discussed the Shewhart-Deming OPDCA quality cycle, a low-speed, high accuracy variation of the **Learn-See-Do-Review cycle (Do Loop)**. From quality pioneer **Edward Deming's** perspective, **reviewing** encompasses the last two steps in his OPDCA cycle (both "Checking" and then "Adjusting" after inspection). When we view these steps as two fifths of the Shewhart-Deming cycle, we can see that reviewing is a critical skill for all adaptive organizations.

In business contexts, __quality__ is defined as either the perceived "non-inferiority or superiority" of a product or service, or its "fitness for purpose." Both measures have merit. As we pursue quality, we should always ask when **satisficing**, and using the **80/20 Rule**, is good enough for what we need. We should recall __Voltaire's__ adage to __perfectionists__ that "the best is the enemy of good." We need only achieve quality that is **sufficient for the purpose and the strategy**. Many business competitions have been won by more rapid development and better promotion of **technically inferior but still useful products or standard**s. All the __technical standards wars__ we have seen in technology systems and products (AC vs. DC, VHS vs Betamax, CDMA vs. GSM, etc.) have taught us that quality is just **one element** of adaptiveness. Lower quality standards can often win, if they are the first to get strong network effects, or have other scaling advantages.

Learning from customers the **quality that they need**, by quickly running several Do Loops, and then hitting that target consistently, is more important than being the best. **Nancy Tague's** *Quality Toolbox*, 2005, is a good primer for useful quality management methods. The __American Society for Quality__ (ASQ) is the leading US quality practitioner community. There we can learn about such subspecialties and methods as TQM, Lean Six Sigma, and many others. They also offer eight __magazines and journals, as well as__ many __certifications and__ __conferences__.

Expert foresight consultants continually review, adjust, and critique their own work in order to keep improving professionally. Those that build __critical feedback__ into their production activities, including anonymous feedback when politics or friendships might otherwise weaken its feedback quality, and who subject each step in their process to __after-action evaluation__, will rapidly improve. But, critiquing isn't enough. After we find fault we must seek a practical way to fix what we don't like. And, if we can't fix it, we must learn to live with and continue to value what exists. After all, to be human is to continually make mistakes, and to continually hope to better ourselves, by trial and error.

We hope this overview of our **Adaptive Foresight** model is helpful to you and your teams. To deepen its value, the **Eight Skills** would benefit from **online diagnostics** for self-assessing and 360-feedback assessing each skill in individual, team, and organizational contexts. It would also be helped by **training curricula** to help those weak in any skill to build it up, and create skills-complementary teams. All of this should be done in a **quantitative manner**, to help validate the model. 4U may or may not be the ideal organization to develop such diagnostics and training, going forward. At present, with Futurepedia (Chapter 6), we have other top priorities. Our **Eight Skills model** is __Creative Commons BY-SA licensed__, so **any reader or consultancy** is encouraged to adapt and revise this model themselves, with attribution.

We Can Improve Each of the Eight Skills.
Balanced Foresight and Action Matter!

Chapter 5: Organizational Foresight III – Frameworks and Methods

We discussed some benefits and challenges of using the **Eight Skills on teams** in our last chapter. Now, we're ready to introduce several other helpful **Practice Frameworks** used by teams to produce foresight. Many of these are variations on the **Do loop**, the universal foresight-action cycle. We will then provide an **overview** of some of the leading foresight methods teams can use in the four **LAIS Strategic Foresight Skills**. Finally, we'll offer a list of **150+ Practice Methods**, classified across the **Eight Skills**. We consider the topics of this chapter an **advanced level of organizational foresight**.

Leaders must remember that **worldviews** we hold, the **models** we use, and the **values** we favor, each bias us to see certain **causal dynamics** in our **environment**, and to like **particular frameworks and methods** over others. We should be aware of that influence, and get regular critical feedback on whether it is evidence-based and adaptive.

Furthermore, knowing *when and how long* to apply any particular framework or method—and how to *customize it* to our needs—will always be **more of an art than a science**. Good executives will seek experience with a **variety** of frameworks and methods, **compete** them against each other, and continually **test and refine** them. **Experience diversity** as well as **cognitive diversity** with the use of these tools, can help protect us from overreliance on any of them.

I. Foresight Practice Frameworks

Frameworks—also termed <u>SOPs</u> (standard operating procedures) in industry, <u>rubrics</u> in academia, and <u>recipes</u> in the culinary field—are **practice guidelines** for professional work. Any model can be turned into framework when it is used as a set of **guidelines to produce outcomes** (research, education, publications, forecasts, models, advice) and when the outcomes of that work are **measured and evaluated**—with part of the evaluation being the consistency and correctness of application of the framework.

We've seen several frameworks for **foresight production** so far. Recall that Chapter 1 introduced GRASP thinking, ADOR analysis, the Four Ps, the REOPS cycle, and the Futures Cone. Two, the Do loop and the Eight Skills, are our preferred frameworks for integrating **foresight and action**. As with models, there are no perfect frameworks; but, knowing several good ones will make our work more consistent, our goals more conscious, and our processes easier to formally evaluate and review. Let's look now at a few more good foresight frameworks. We hope they inspire you to discover, adapt, or build some of your own.

1. FTI's Strategic Foresight ("Future Forecasting") Framework

The futurist **Amy Webb** is one of our field's emerging stars. Her consultancy, Future Today Institute (FTI), produces a great free annual <u>Tech Trends Report</u> (we offer starter lists for annual foresight reports in Book 2). Her **societal foresight** book, *The Big Nine*, 2020, is a trenchant analysis of the tech titans, and our need to better regulate them in our current era of **plutocratic capitalism**. We'll consider such topics in *BPF*.

Amy Webb, 2020

Webb's **organizational foresight** book, *The Signals are Talking*, 2018, offers a powerful **strategic foresight framework.** It involves six steps. Webb calls it a "future forecasting" framework, but to be accurate, forecasting is only one of the five steps. It is actually a great **strategic foresight framework**, as strategy is key to its structure. It is focused on identifying and doing **robust strategy around emerging trends.** We consider it **LAIS-centric**, and it is **well-balanced** across the LAIS skills. We especially like that it involves **two rounds of predictive contrasting, prior to strategy production.** Below are our interpretation of FTI's six steps, with some of their language adapted to our own terms:

1. **Find the Fringe.** First, cast a **wide Learning net**, emphasizing diverse and unusual sources. We have discussed this as cultivating a **network of sentinel thinkers and environments.** This step may be the most important. You are only as smart as your network. Appreciate and help its members. Map relationships between emerging issues and players, rounding up "unusual suspects."

2. **Identify Hidden Trends. Anticipate** hidden probable patterns, curves, and correlations in all this emerging data. Their acronym, **CIPHER** (Contradictions, Inflections, Practices, Hacks, Extremes, and Rarities) offers some helpful investigative practices.

3. **Stress-Test Your Trend. Innovate** (imagine) **possibilities** (alternatives, unknowns, uncertainties, wildcards) around your identified trend. Ask what you are missing. Categorize and challenge assumptions. Create counterarguments. Ask what evidence will scope, confirm or deny the trend.

4. **Calculate the ETA.** Return to **Anticipation, forecasting** the timing of the trend. Ask what **factors** may **accelerate** or **delay** its development. Assess both **internal developments** in tech companies, and **external developments** by competitors, regulators, and society. Define **threshold capacities** for early and mass adoption. Ask what data will help forecast the ETA for those capacities.

5. **Create Scenarios and Preliminary Strategies.** Return to **Innovation** (possibility) thinking. Build scenarios. Each should cover **probable, possible, preferable, and preventable (Four Ps) story elements.** Vary them around **important but uncertain** factors that may influence the future. Consider your and others **emotional reaction** to the story elements. Then give each **scenario a score**, rating them for criteria like plausibility and importance. Then create a **preliminary strategy** for each, assuming it occurs.

6. **Stress-Test Your Strategies.** Next, focus on your **strategies**, and the **plans** and **investments** you might make around them. What if you act on one scenario and another occurs? How well positioned will you be to pivot? Ask and answer a series of questions about your proposed trend-response strategies. Their **FUTURE** acronym (Foundation, Uniqueness, Trackability, Urgency, Recalibration, Extensibility) offers several very helpful **strategy-assessment questions.** Now, **Act!**

Fortuitously, FTI's framework recognizes that **emotions** are central to strategy production. All of us are **emotional first** and cognitive second in our priorities. Less fortuitously, this framework does not require **sentiment contrasting**, so we would advise you to **add sentiment conflict** (between Steps 5 and 6), first considering preferable scenarios, visions, and preliminary opportunity strategies, then plausible negative scenarios, traps, and threats, and how to prevent them. No framework is perfect. Use the ones that most appeal to you and your team. Be sure to apply all of your frameworks as a **cycle**, in a **Do loop.** Solicit feedback (Review) from a cognitively- and experience-diverse group, across all of the **STEEPLES scanning categories.** We'll revisit STEEPLES again in this chapter, this time as an **issue analysis framework.**

2. U. Houston's Foresight Research ("Forecasting") Framework

During his thirty-year tenure as professor of foresight at the University of Houston, **Peter Bishop**, a leading figure in our professional foresight community, developed an excellent **research framework** for producing briefing papers on foresight topics. (See "<u>Framework foresight</u>," **Peter Bishop**, *Futures*, 2013, for a detailed version). Students of the Houston strategic foresight master's program learn to apply the framework and are assessed on their application of it.

Here are U. Houston Foresight Research framework's five main sections and subsections (titles adapted):

1. **Introduction** (Problem Definition, Executive Summary)

2. **Current Assessment** (Current Conditions, Stakeholders, History, Constants)

3. **Forecast** (Cycles, Trends, Plans, Investments, Basic Forecast)

4. **Alternate Futures** (Potential Events, Issues, Ideas, Proposals, Uncertainties, Scenarios, Indicators)

5. **Information Sources** (Experts, Texts, Periodicals, Articles, Organizations, Websites)

Bishop sometimes calls this framework by another, **more anticipatory** name: **"Framework Forecasting."** In a workshop on foresight methodologies in Prague (<u>17 page PDF here</u>), he noted that the **forecasting process** always results in two types of forecasts, **baseline** and **alternative**. He thus describes Steps 3 and 4 of the Houston Foresight Research Framework as **two varieties of forecasting** and Step 5 can be considered to be documentation of these two types.

This name makes clear that **forecasting is fundamental** to what foresight professionals do, and that **anticipation is a key goal** (one of four, in the Four P's model) of all foresight research. In our view, this framework also invites the researcher to do engage in **quantitative probabilistic assessments** and where those **probabilities are high**, to make **specific predictions**, with **confidence intervals**, for any of these forecasts. In our language, the Houston Foresight Research framework begins with **Learning** (Current assessment), then proceeds to **Anticipation** (probable foresight), and then to **Innovation** (possible alternative futures). It is thus also a **LAIS-centric framework** that we strongly recommend.

This framework is intended as an *input* to Strategy, one classic definition of foresight work. To make this a **strategic foresight** framework, our LAIS model would add three additional steps, the consideration of **positive and negative strategic implications** (**preferable and preventable futures**, via **ADOR analysis** or any other method), then first-pass **strategic recommendations** (problem diagnosis, guiding policies, coordinated action plans). The Current Assessment (Step 2) would also include charting the landscape of other **current strategic bets and investments**. Alternatively, this model can be used with any other **strategic analysis framework**, in a **Do loop**, to offer a **robust foresight methodology**.

Foresight Research Framework Example: Underground Automated Highway Networks

In his Foresight MS at Houston in 2005, John applied this research framework to a long-term forecasting problem—namely, the question of whether and when **underground automated highway networks** might come to our leading cities (<u>PDF here</u>). He used the framework to argue that beginning in the 2030s, our wealthiest cities would likely find it affordable and valuable to use automated excavation and construction systems to start building underground freeway networks and parking garages. He proposed that they could do this by using advanced <u>tunnel boring machines</u> (TBMs) and <u>urban robo-trucks</u> to remove the <u>excavation tailings</u>, particularly at night when freeways are underused. Such growing underground networks would allow cities to increase density, increase the tax base, speed commuting, better fight gridlock, and reclaim some of their expensive surface real estate for higher-value uses, including living, walking, biking, and green space. As background trends, he noted the rise of zero emission vehicles (necessary for tunnels), and that the global operating number of TBMs was on a **three year doubling curve** at the time.

Tunnel Boring Machine

> Interestingly, this prediction was received as highly implausible by a few of John's foresight colleagues at the time, as well as by some of the experts he consulted. Yet there were also advocates for it in each group as well. As this book goes to press in 2021, **Elon Musk's Boring Company** is engaging in what was predicted as the **Basic Forecast**.

Employing a process like the Houston Foresight Research framework is a great way to **check our assumptions**, to gauge our own **levels of confidence** in our future views, and to have them **critiqued** by appropriately diverse communities of both **colleagues** and **subject matter experts**. Just don't expect your good calls to convince everyone at first.

3. 4U's Eight Skills as Competencies Framework

Throughout the last chapter, we explored the **Eight Skills** as a **foresight practice framework**. They are 4U's preferred recipe for producing, enacting and improving foresight on teams. We encourage all leaders and students to use these skills more **consciously and deliberately**, and to develop their own frameworks and methods for **monitoring their use**. To help with that, let us **reconsider the Eight Skills** one last time, as a set of **managerial competencies**. This may deepen our understanding of why each skill is central to **organizational adaptiveness**. Once we add **values** (adaptive leadership) to these skills, we think that gets us to a minimum viable model for long-term **success** and **progress**.

As a competency framework for our field (a defined set of **abilities and behaviors** necessary for effectiveness), the **Eight Skills** have the advantage of being terms already in common use by the global management community. Discussing adaptive foresight in **practice competency language** can also be helpful, to present it not as something privileged or specialized, but as abilities that all of us have, at least in modest amounts, as self-managers and relationship managers—skills that all managers, teams, and organizations can further develop as they gain experience.

Compared to typical managers and consultants, good **foresighters** are particularly focused on discovering, creating, and managing futures, per se. Their practices include: scoping, retrospecting, scanning, sensemaking, predicting, forecasting, baseline futuring, de-biasing, alternative futuring, visioning, facilitating, designing, goalsetting, and assessing foresight progress, capacity and performance. Our field is rich and rapidly changing, and we will develop many new competencies as new predictive analytics, machine learning, and crowd foresight tools and platforms emerge.

Specialty practices are recognized as important functions of strategic management, and have professional associations developing them. We've discussed the **Twenty Specialties** already. **Competencies** are less recognized as management functions, and may not be sponsored by any professional association. Of course these two overlap. We have described each of the twenty specialties below, this time using competency words commonly used in **managerial circles**.

As an exercise in running your **Do loops**, we suggest your team **build your own set** of the **most useful competencies and specialties** for each of the Eight Skills. An *incomplete*, demonstration set of **Eight Skills competencies**, written for the benefit of foresight consultants (not for typical organizations) is offered below.

1. **Learning** is scoping the client's needs, gaining the skills, and doing the research to allow foresight. Measurable competencies include:

   Scoping (aka Framing): defining and bounding the foresight topic, extent, and timeframe
   Mapping: building a map of the topic and categories for research
   Metrics and Data: determining and analyzing key data and indicators to know current status
   Hindsight: understanding historical context and the most recent discontinuities
   Learning and Development: engaging a team in training and skill building to improve foresight
   Scanning: finding emerging issues, indicators, and signals of change, aka "scanning hits"
   Intelligence/Sensemaking: analyzing and evaluating to gain insight into system patterns

2. Anticipating is identifying a set of convergent, baseline, expected futures. Measurable competencies include:

Predicting: making specific predictions of an expected future, using some model, with a probability attached
Forecasting: using trend analysis to estimate a variable of interest over a range of future dates
Baseline futuring: forecasting a baseline future, along with its assumptions and associated risk
Risk management: determining the risk environment and major uncertainties
Investing: determining the most viable current opportunities for creating future value

3. **Innovating** is generating a range of divergent, possible alternative futures and prototypes. Competencies include:

De-biasing: helping clients see their biases, relax pre-conceived notions, and look with fresh eyes
Designing: activities or artifacts to explore baseline and alternative futures and visions
Alternative futuring: generating possible and plausible alternative futures or scenarios based on wildcards, ideas, and images built around key uncertainties

2. **Strategy** is re-convergence on preferred visions, and goals, seeing preventable blocks and threats, then generating real options, policy, and coordinated action plans. Measurable competencies include:

Interpreting: considering the implications suggested by the baseline and alternative futures
Facilitating: guiding foresight conflicts (predictive and sentiment contrasting) to better see the four futures
Visioning: identifying and committing to a preferred future, or set of futures
Derisking: identifying the most plausible risks, threats, and traps, that might prevent the preferred future.
Goalsetting: soliciting client commitment to specific goals to achieve the shared vision
Strategizing: helping the client to produce real options, and guiding policy

5. **Executing** is translating strategy into action (of the client or the foresighter). Competencies include:

Planning: helping the client to produce coordinated action plans, robust to uncertainty
Producing: helping the client with the application and assessment of the twenty specialties.

6. **Influencing** is selling foresight work to client leaders and stakeholders. Competencies include:

Communicating: relating visions, baseline and alternative futures and strategic options to capture stakeholder attention and influence their actions
Selling: promoting our foresight services, convincing others of their value, growing our practice

7. **Relating** is supporting leaders and stakeholders and acting with their best interests in mind. Competencies include:

Empathizing: understanding client fears, hopes, and needs, and their current culture
Teambuilding: creating strong and cognitively diverse practitioner teams
Ethical practice: studying appropriate behavior for context and culture

8. **Reviewing** is measuring and collecting feedback on the quality and results of foresight work. Competencies include:

Assessing progress: tracking indicators or precursors that indicate progress (or not) to a goal
Assessing performance: measuring foresight work quality and client satisfaction
Assessing capacity: determining whether the client has more internal foresight capacity (without our future help) than they had before our engagement

As a foresight consultant, what competencies would you modify, add, or remove from this framework? How can your organization best apply the **Eight Skills**, and staff the **Twenty Specialties**? How can you assess personal, team, and firm performance in skills, specialties, and competencies? We leave those questions as challenges for your work.

4. 4U's STEEPLES Issue Analysis Framework

We've proposed that STEEP should be retired, and replaced by STEEPLES and STEEPLECOP, both for societal-level **horizon scanning**, and for **issue analysis**. The categories we use to classify the world will bias the way we think, and we think STEEPLES has become a **minimum viable set for issue analysis**. We need to expand our thinking in this complex world. Let's dig a bit into this claim, and apply STEEPLES analysis to a couple of issues, one bigger, and one smaller. The following points argue why **STEEPLES**—which leads with **Science** and ends with **Society**—offers foresight researchers a significant improvement over the classic STEEP, both for scanning and for issue analysis:

1. First, STEEPLES ranks the first three categories (as complex systems) in a **rough order of their speed of change and magnitude of ADOR.** Society is not the most disruptive force on Earth today. **Science, Technology, and Economics (especially Entrepreneurship),** in that order, are the **fastest moving systems** causing **ADOR** today. **Scientific knowledge** is the most discerning and the most rapidly improving learning system on Earth. See **Valentin Turchin's** excellent *The Phenomenon of Science* (PDF), 1977, for more on that claim. The next fastest category is **Technology**, itself a creative learning and doing system, partly guided by science. The next fastest is accelerating wealth creation, better known in economics as **technological productivity**, the greatest contributor to GDP. The remaining STEEPLES factors take a **more arbitrary order of speed and ADOR impact**.

2. Starting our scanning with **science** tends to make the rest of our scanning work more **evidence-based**. When we understand the state of the science, we are less likely to fall for **hype, wishful thinking, and extreme claims** in scanning and analysis in the remaining categories. The critical factor for many technological events is often **the state of the science** underlying the technologies, both the theoretical science (models for the theoretical potential of the technology) and the empirical science (the kinds and quality of **R&D experiments** happening in the field). Knowing the state of the **science** and **technology,** in turn, can help us gauge **economic** prospects as well.

3. Placing **Society last** in the STEEPLES list reminds us that to properly evaluate **societal futures,** we must *first* consider seven other STEEPLE categories as *precursors.* We include predictable **demographic** changes in the society category as well. Most of us **value the Society category the most,** but consider how dependent it is on the other factors. Society has often been **forced to adapt,** with various Environmental, Political, Law, and Ethical changes, in response to various **STE changes,** many **exponential** in nature. To a rough approximation, STEEPLES captures this key **historical dynamic,** often misnamed "technological determinism."

STEEPLES claims that **Science, Legal** rules, and **Ethical** and justice concerns have become too powerful and important to continue to neglect as learning and analysis categories in societal and in much organizational foresight work. Consider how much **Science, Law,** and **Ethics** determine the future of many topics. The state of the science determines what we know and much of what we are likely to accomplish with any technology. Many *current* laws are unjust and perpetuate societal problems. Many leaders make poor ethical decisions. Consider the constant minor and major ethical lapses of our political leadership. The Trump administration's cavalier response to Covid-19 being only the most obvious and damaging in recent history. In our complex world, Science, Law and Ethics matter more than ever.

STEEPLES can also help us see the **limits and constraints** of technology, at a time when we are awash in **technological hype**. If a foresighter wishes to understand the question of whether biotechnology, pharmacology, biomedicine, information technology, desalination, photovoltaics, synthetic biology, brain-machine interfaces, or any other potentially disruptive technology is actually poised to **significantly improve** in the next decade or, contrarily, whether it is being overhyped and will likely **underperform** in this timeframe, an assessment of expert opinion on both the **sciences** and **technology** are always critical first steps. This should be followed by a quick analysis of the remaining STEEPLES categories (and systems), to place the topic, innovation, or problem in proper societal context.

Let's look briefly at two examples, beginning with a **macro issue**, one broadly important to the nature of our future.

Biotechnology versus Information Technology Industry Futures: A Brief STEEPLES Analysis

When we use STEEPLES to evaluate the **future of biotechnology, pharmacology**, and **biomedicine**, as industries, we first recognize that **scientifically**, we still **know very little** about how **molecular biology** actually works inside living systems. We have named the parts, but we mostly cannot yet predict how they interact. Until we **have that predictive science**, which may require **quantum computer simulations** of how genes and proteins operate in the cell, likely several decades from now, biotech and pharma improvements will **greatly underperform.** Furthermore, all the pharmacological and medical experiments that we do in **more complex animals, and humans,** will be continue to be subject to strong **Environmental, Political, Legal, Ethical, and Societal** oversight. In other words, we don't yet really know what we are doing when we innovate in these industries, and we can't do many empirical experiments for good ethical reasons.

As we will argue in *BPF*, we can also see today that those who seek to use emerging genetic and biotech tools like CRISPR and polygenic embryo testing for **human enhancement goals,** rather than for the far more acceptable goal of **curing disease**, will be treated as **fringe groups.** Our ethical and legal responses to such use will be similar to our response to **eugenics programs** in the 20th century. The vast majority of us will reject the **class differences** that bioenhancement use might bring, and it will increasingly regulated and tracked. What's more, the **forensic technology** to identify the **unsanctioned use** of such technologies will continue to develop far ahead of our understanding of how to actually use them, either for good or ill. Thus it will be increasingly easy to find illicit "designer babies", based on their deviance from natural genetic patterns. We predict enhanced humans won't be produced in significant numbers by any society, anywhere, prior to the emergence of **general AI**, which will have its own goals and desires, and is by far the more important trend. These STEEPLE assessments help us to assess **societal aspirations** in these industries. We would all love drugs that cure our major diseases, or give us more healthy life. A few of us would *also* like to use these technologies to be smarter, taller, or stronger. A good STEEPLES assessment tells us we are a long way away from such futures.

Another biomedical future that exhibits a strong aspiration bias is <u>brain-computer interfaces (BCIs)</u>. These have been greatly overhyped for the last decade. They tell an appealing story, to some, of human empowerment and potential future enhancement. It is not surprising that some of us in freedom-loving Western societies love to hear the story of companies like <u>Neuralink</u> and <u>Kernel</u> told as often, and in as breathless terms, as possible. Tech visionaries like **Elon Musk** greatly oversell what can be achieved in the next few decades. Experts tell us we still haven't solved several long-term biocompatibility issues for these devices in the brain. What's more, implanting them in young, plastic brains where they would be most effective, will have strong ethical injunctions in every society. Meanwhile, our smartphones will soon turn into **Personal AIs**, and they will learn, interface with, and empower us exponentially, without any invasive surgery required. We think a good STEEPLES analysis tells us that humanity won't use BCIs for **enhancement** until we really know what we are doing, and we won't know what we are doing until **general AI** arrives. Again, that's the real constraint.

In 2007, the CEO of Genentech, **Art Levinson** (now CEO of Calico and Chairman of Apple) gave a *WSJ* interview. He estimated that since its founding in 1976, the US **biotech industry**, some 1400 companies, with roughly 300 publicly traded, had lost $90 billion vs. investments. He claimed that up to that point it was the "biggest money-losing industry of all time." This may have been an exaggeration, but the point is well taken. Biotech, pharmacology, and biomedicine are **aspirational industries**. We invest in these industries because we **value their advances so highly,** far more than for any other reason. We should not kid ourselves on how rapidly they will improve, or the **economic returns** they will give.

By contrast, in the **digital infotech** domain, the science we are using, even though it is simple, has been more than sufficient to deliver seven decades of **rapidly exponential technological improvements** in data, storage, computing, communications, sensing, and robotics. Because of the unique role of IT in driving economic **densification and dematerialization**, it has delivered the **greatest financial returns to date** of any industry on Earth. We have also seen that **Environmental, Political, Legal, Ethical, and Societal oversight** of infotech is unfortunately minimal, at least at first.

Only when our **tech titans** reached gargantuan size, **social media** became weaponized, and our devices started **listening to us** did we all see our **regulation problem**. We'll discuss some ways out of this current dystopia in *BPF*.

This brief analysis helps us see why we think the futurist **Cathie Wood**, CEO of the famous hedge fund Ark Invest, is quite wrong in her prediction that her investment company's **biotech and biomedical portfolios** will increase in value anywhere near as fast as Ark's **infotech portfolio**. In our view, Ark's biotech and medical investments are aspirational— their team wants their investors to believe that biotech, biomedicine, and longevity medicine will advance as fast as their infotech investments. But a brief STEEPLES analysis of both industries constraints and performance to date makes clear why that is **very unlikely to occur**, at least until we can use **infotech itself**, most likely via future, AI-guided quantum computers, to improve the poor state of biological science today. Curiously, it will be by learning from and **mimicking biology**, particularly its **evo-devo nature**, that we expect will be a **key precursor** to **general AI**. Infotech is making exponential annual progress, but we are still a long way from knowing how to create **evo-devo AIs** today.

Let's now consider an emerging choice in transportation engineering.

Self-Driving Cars vs AHD Cars: A Briefer STEEPLES Analysis

In writings online about **self-driving cars**, many futurists are presently foreseeing a **largely driverless future** in America by **mid-century**. This does not fit with our view. As we write this in 2020, GM's Cruise is seeking to launch a **taxi without a steering wheel** in San Francisco. Google's Waymo has just launched **public self-driving taxis** in Phoenix, with human safety drivers presently behind the wheel, and plans to phase them out. In our view, a good long-term mobility forecast must account for both **persistent human desires** and **alternative technological solutions**, including the growth of **AI-assisted Human Driven (AHD) vehicles**. Those seem to us to be the real near-term competition to driverless cars, between now and mid-century. A STEEPLES analysis reminds us that Political and Economic factors, including the value of **driving as a source of employment**, social factors, including the fact that many still enjoy the **freedom of driving**, and Legal and Ethical factors, including the reality that we will **hold driverless cars to a much higher fatality standard** than we do human driven vehicles, are all critical to this future.

If AHD vehicles with growing levels of autonomy (SAE levels 3, 4, and 5) can **prevent the great majority of accidents over this time horizon**, as we expect, then a **majority driverless future** will emerge much more slowly than many boosters expect, and a **fully driverless future will never emerge**. Such subtleties can easily be missed by futurists who aren't sufficiently STEEPLES-diverse in their analysis. STEEPLES thinking reminds us that we aren't going to suddenly throw three million truck drivers out of work, or a million on demand drivers. We're going to **very slowly adopt driverless technology**, and **AHD** is likely to play a **much greater role** than most futurists are willing to admit today.

5. Dator's Four Futures (Growth Curves) Framework

In 1979, the eminent futurist <u>Jim Dator</u>—then the director of the U. Hawaii foresight program—developed a clarifying model for social change stories in *Perspectives on Cross-Cultural Psychology*. It was reprised in his <u>*Advancing Futures*</u>, 2002. Dator noted that many narratives (stories, scenarios) on social change issues revolve around four categories of growth due to the effects of that change, as follows:

Jim Dator, 2015

1. **Continuation** (business as usual, more "status quo" growth)

2. **Limits and Discipline** (behaviors to adapt to internal or environmental limits)

3. **Decline and Collapse** (system degradation or failure modes as crisis emerges)

4. **Transformation** (new tech, business, or social factors that change the adaptation game)

These four futures can be represented by phases on three classic growth curves, Logistic (S-curve) and Life cycle curves, and Exponential and Superexponential curves ("J-curves"). In terms of growth curves, we can expect:

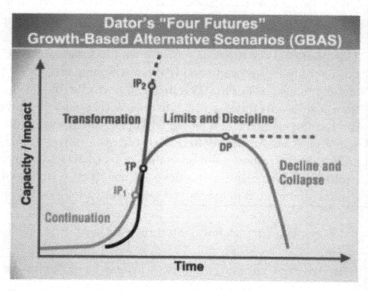

1. **Continuation** (Business as Usual) as the initial **exponential phase** of **S-curve growth;**

2. **Limits and Discipline** as the **saturation phase** of **S-curve growth;**

3. **Decline and Collapse** as the **recycling phase** of life cycle growth;

4. **Transformation** as the **substitution phase** of **new S-curve growth** in a **more rapidly changing, more powerful and disruptive new system.**

As Dator says, often, all four **stories of change** are being told by, or happening to, different parties simultaneously. Also, all four changes happen to individual actors in different contexts and times. Learning who is representing each of the four points of view is thus a great goal in foresight research. These four curves are actually a simplification of the **LENPAC curves,** which are explored in the Student Edition of this book. This **universal model** can be used as an **anticipation framework**, a **scenario construction framework**, and a **positive and negative visioning framework**. It is more complex than the Three Horizons framework (discussed next), but we consider it **more useful, more of the time**. Leaders are recommended to **stress test their strategy** against all four growth modes (and the groups experiencing them), and to estimate the likelihood that their organization or stakeholders may soon switch into any of these modes.

6. Sharpe's Three Horizons (Growth Curves) Framework

Bill Sharpe's *Three Horizons: The Patterning of Hope*, 2013, is another growth curve framework for assessing change. It a simplification of **Dator's Four Futures,** yet its simplicity gives it power and value of its own. It is great for introducing **growth curve thinking**, especially to a group new to **systems thinking**. It considers the interaction of **three growth curves:**

1. **Business as Usual** (which will eventually decline) – Horizon 1

2. **Disruptive Forces** (unsettling the existing order, allowing change) – Horizon 2

3. **The New System** (which increasingly becomes viable) – Horizon 3

Bill Sharpe, 2020

These **three systems** can be represented by **three curves.** As with **Dator's curves,** each curve is tracing different **growth modes**. A simple version is drawn at right by **Kate Raworth**, author of the excellent *Donut Economics: A Primer on 21st Century Economics*, 2018. See her 6 min YouTube video explaining the horizons. The Y-axis for these curves is typically drawn as **Dominance, Prevalence,** or **Strategic Fit** (another term for **Adaptiveness**) while the X-axis represents **Time**, or better yet, **Cumulative experience**. In this framework, we see "seeds of the future" (H3) embedded in the present, and we try to grow them. As Raworth

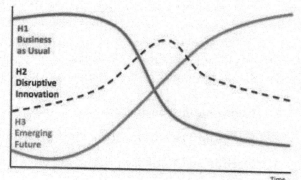

The Three Horizons Framework
(Sharpe, 2013. Adapted by Raworth, 2018)

says, we can have **negative disruption**, captured or misused by the dominant business or political paradigm, or **positive disruption,** with adaptive change to the future order.

As an example of negative disruption, Raworth cites the exploitative contracts and centralized ownership structure of **Uber**. As an example of a positive disruption, she cites **Ride Austin**, an on-demand transportation network owned by its operators, which keeps profits in Austin. Of course, if companies like Uber are required to add full employee benefits, to go public once they reach a certain size, and if US citizens are nudged to be broadly invested in the stock market, as in Australia's model, Uber would be much less negative. **Centralized models** like Uber are typically going to **dominate any industry** with strong **economies of scale**, so we must take steps to redistribute wealth, empower competition, and grow transparency, accountability, and governance. How technologies affect the network is all about the **rules we choose**.

Below is a more detailed version of the three horizons curve, courtesy of **Andy Hines**, director of the U. Houston MS in Strategic Foresight. It is adapted from an excellent article on the framework by futurists **Andrew Curry and Tony Hodgson**, "Seeing in Multiple Horizons (PDF)," *Journal of Futures Studies*, 13(1), pp. 1-20.

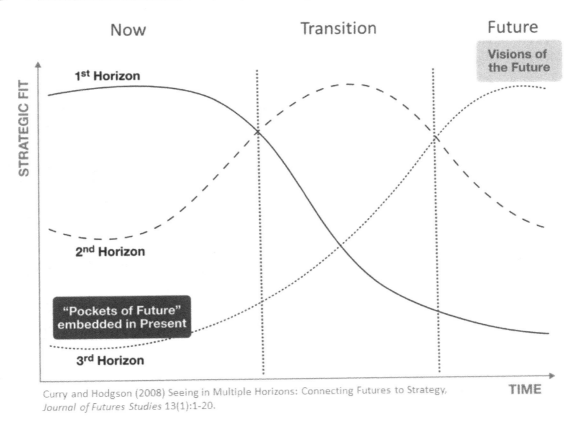

Curry and Hodgson (2008) Seeing in Multiple Horizons: Connecting Futures to Strategy, *Journal of Futures Studies* 13(1):1-20.

Both the **simplicity** and **generality** of this framework are attractive. As Sharpe says, it is a tool to generate many fruitful discussions about the **existing order, what disrupts it, and where we may go next**, as probable, **possible, preferable, and preventable futures**. It is commonly used in discussions about transitioning from our current **Plutocratic Political-Economic** system to a more **Democratic and Distributive** system. The model can oversimplify complex dynamics, just like any framework, but it does seem to represent some very universal processes, similar to **Dator's Four Futures**. Foresight communities like the **International Futures Forum** use the Three Horizons regularly, and we recommend every strategy team gain experience with it.

As we discuss in the Student Edition, in our section on **LENPAC** curves, we can analyze this curve's components in a number of ways. Horizon 1 can be seen as the tail end of a **Life Cycle Curve**, common to any system of **fixed complexity** in a changing environment, or any **senescing system** unable to keep up with the pace of external change. Horizon 2 can be either a **Hype Cycle** (positive or negative), which can cause disruption through hype or fear, or an **actual Disruptive Innovation**. Both will cause disruption, the latter more permanently. A firm that has greatly overinvested in the wrong technology due to hype is clearly going to suffer through all three of these curves. A disruptive innovation will have industry or societal effects. Horizon 3 is the **New S-curve, Dator's Transformational curve** in the **Four Futures Framework**. The three curves can be mapped to three types of innovation in products, service, laws, norms, or anything else relevant to the system: **Incremental innovation** typifies the Horizon 1 curve, **Disruptive innovation** is tracked on Horizon 2, and **Transformational innovation** occurs as Horizon 3.

Fortuitously, the **Three Horizons** are also congruent with **Kurt Lewin's** classic **Three Step Model of Change Management**, first published in 1947, which asks leaders to: "**Unfreeze, Change, then Refreeze**" their organizational processes. [We explore both models further in the Student Edition]. Unfreezing, where stakeholders become willing to painfully leave the old order, usually happens only as a firm is experiencing noticeable decline (H1) and as disruption (an innovation-based H2) comes along, heightening the need for change. Alternatively, a leader can use strategic communication to manufacture or heighten an actual crisis (hype-based H2). Refreezing the new way of doing things (H3) only happens via clever restructuring by leadership, as the new order beings to gain power. Without refreezing around **new incentives and systems**, organizations will often fall back into old ways. Lewin's model was skillfully expanded by **John Kotter** in his **Eight Steps of Change Management**, in his classic, *Leading Change*, 1996/2012.

7. Mahaffie's Foresight Initiation Framework

To start building new **foresight habits and culture** for ourselves, our teams and in our organizations, **John Mahaffie** of Leading Futurists, offers us an excellent seven step framework on his Foresight Culture blog. Here it is, with minor embellishments:

John Mahaffie, 2020

1. **Start Future Conversations**.
   Make time for open, thoughtful, creative conversations about the future of critical topics. Make it a regular and informal ritual—like "Future Friday" lunches, where a conscious goal is to make the future part of the conversation. Keep these conversations relaxed, exploratory, and fun.

2. **Find Kindred Spirits**
   Our conversations will attract colleagues who either enjoy or recognize the value of thinking about the future too. Collect a diverse group of thinkers and feelers, pessimists and optimists, artists and engineers. Value all input, seek everyone's counsel, and build a foresight community.

3. **Ask Questions and Get Visual With Answers**
   Ask future-important questions. "What are the top trends shaping our future?" "What are we not talking about that we should?" Good questions focus people on their relevant personal, team, or organizational futures—and their answers beg to be written down. Use paper, whiteboards, or digital tablets for outlines and diagrams of these conversations. Make one sentence summaries, lists, and simple models. Get folks to critique what they *see*.

4. **Do Environmental Scanning**
   Make time to learn about the environmental and competitive forces, trends, issues, challenges, and opportunities we face, individually and collectively. Find great data, discussion lists, websites, articles, books, and communities of relevance to our organization. Start building a set of scanning sources and habits for continual learning. Part of this scanning involves familiarizing ourselves with the **human capital** of our organizations and networks. Learn others' strengths, passions, and concerns.

5. **Share What We Learn (Pay It Forward)**

   We may appoint ourselves as a future scout for our orgs, conducting reconnaissance in the environment. When we discover info that might be of value to particular folks in our organization, we can share it—present it lightly (e.g., "I thought this might be useful"), not didactically ("I know the future"). In other words, help others to see the value of foresight, sharing, and learning. Do this **unconditionally**. Don't expect **anything in return**!

6. **Push the Strategy Horizon**

   Whenever key strategy is open to discussion, make a habit of asking questions that extend the strategy horizon—like, "can we take a moment and look at how this plays out, longer term?" Or, "what do we think will happen if such-and-such occurs?" And, "what new opportunities open up for us then? What threats?" Be known as a person who stretches out the team's horizon, but only when it is **appropriate**. Know there is a time in all strategy talk for **learning** (past and present), a time for **anticipating** relevant **trends and models**, a time for divergent and **innovative** discussion, and a time to converge on **strategic** priorities, policies and coordinated action plans. Become a master of all four **LAIS skills**.

7. **Join a Community of Practice**

   Join some of the Primary and Specialty Foresight Communities listed in Chapter 1. Seek excellence in all **Eight Skills** and a few of the **Twenty Specialties**. Foresight is a richly rewarding, never-ending journey. Make the journey with others who appreciate it as much as we do.

Do these things, and before long, we will be seen as productive foresight professionals in our organization.

Were any of these frameworks particularly helpful to you? Applying various frameworks to our foresight problem will generate many new insights and help us clarify our foresight options. For a few more foresight curriculum and practice frameworks, see FERN's Foresight Definitions and Frameworks page. We wish luck and good fortune to all our colleagues in finding, improving, and creating foresight practice and research frameworks that fit their own needs.

II. Methods Overview – LAIS Strategic Foresight Skills

We've defined **strategic foresight** as the practice of the **LAIS Foresight Skills**. Adaptive foresight begins with integrating these with the four **Action Skills**, and it ends with incorporating **values**, and a theory of **success** and **progress**. Let us now consider how the LAIS skills relate to **foresight methods**, the procedures we use, often within some **foresight framework**, to understand and analyze aspects of the future.

Building Your
LAIS Skills
Strategic Foresight Done Right

LAIS Foresight Methods Preferences

Just as we each will have **different normative preferences** for thinking in different corners of the **Foresight Pyramid**, based on our personalities, values, and decision styles, we each have **different preferences** for practicing the **LAIS skills**. As a result, we and our clients will tend to prefer using **certain foresight methods** over others. Our methods preferences can also be based on our **past experience**. Also, certain methods are significantly more **popular** at different points in time. They may have good champions, better evidence, better marketing, or a longer history of use by a particular client.

But while we all have methods preferences, remember that **all four LAIS skills** are critical to good **strategic foresight**. Our **methods** should **span and balance all four skills**. We should *also* remember the need for **predictive and sentiment contrasting** in the **proper order**, and our need to **manage those two conflicts** on our teams. Knowing our team's and our client's *LAIS methods preferences* is thus a **great place to start** in correcting any **methods biases** we have.

Recall the **Leadership Pyramid**, discussed in Chapter 1. All **foresight leaders**, who may be our clients or ourselves, when we are leading a foresight engagement, will have **methods preferences**. These are often based on our **leadership type**. The graphic below gives a sample of **foresight methods often preferred** by each of the **three primary leadership types** (**Hedgehog, Fox, and Eagle**) on the **classic Foresight Pyramid**. If you prefer to use the **modern Foresight Pyramid**, you can further divide Eagles into **Idealist Eagles (strategic optimists)** and **Rational Eagles (defensive pessimists)**, using the Keirsey temperament assessment. In **Wargames**, for example, the Idealist Eagle usually prefers to be on the **Blue Team**, and the Rational Eagle prefers the **Red Team**. This figure also includes the **Elephant**, a leader who is primarily a **learner**, and thus is either **past or present** focused. Elephants are a **LAIS leadership type** but **not a classic foresight leadership** type. These history-minded or operationally minded folks, typically work for others, or are managers, more than leaders. When they do lead, just like **Ostriches**, Elephants need **foresight deputies** to help them with **vision**.

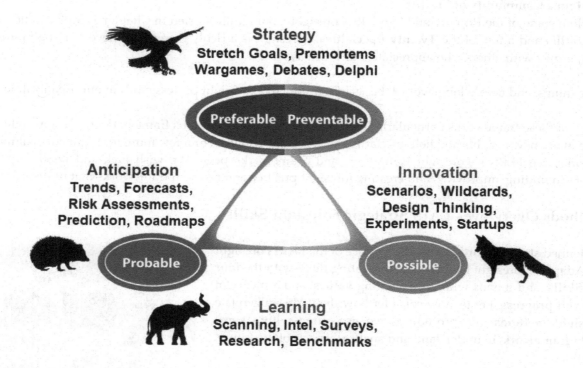

LAIS Foresight Methods Preferences

Again, recognizing your, your team's and your client's LAIS foresight **methods preferences**, and guarding against or correcting **methods imbalances**, is a **great strategy** to improve your basic strategic foresight competency. Let us look now at a selection of important methods used in each LAIS skill, to get a better sense of that skill in practice.

1. Learning Methods Overview

With **Learning**, rather than provide a functional overview, as we will with the core three (AIS) foresight skills, we will examine just two topics, **environmental scanning** and **sprint reading**, that are particularly helpful to the learning process. The first topic, environmental scanning, is well known as a foresight tool. The second, sprint reading, is often neglected in foresight education, yet it is one key to maximizing learning in a world of **accelerating information production**.

A. 4U's STEEPLES: Better Environmental Scanning

<u>Environmental scanning</u> is a form of **learning** that involves monitoring one's environment for relevant change. Moreover, it involves collecting examples of **anticipations** (trends, predictions, data), **innovations** (ideas, experiments) and **strategies** that have been used or proposed. The choice and number of **scanning categories**—the "bins" we use to classify environmental information—will **bias** the kind, depth, and balance of information we collect. Thus, we want to use **sets of scanning categories** that are as **relevant as possible** to their context of use. Environmental scanning is also called **horizon scanning** because we look out toward a horizon—physically, mentally and temporally—as we monitor change. Each of us has a favorite set of "**foresight horizons**," which represent how far out and how deeply (in space, time and complexity) we typically look for various purposes, like general learning, and for creating our strategies and plans.

Our **foresight horizons** should always extend **past** our **strategy horizons** (how far out we can see a particular strategy paying off for us). Our **planning horizons** should even be shorter still. If we plan too far ahead, or in too much detail, we'll be constantly revising our plans. For some, strategy horizons may be the next quarter—for others, the next fifty years. It is important to know where our horizons presently are and if they are adaptive for our context and client.

Another rule of thumb with foresight horizons that we often try to work "**from the outside in.**" We look first for the **largest, universal** systems relevant to our problem, then **proceed inward**, system by system. The larger, more ubiquitous systems, in general, also happen to be the ones we have the least ability to control. Accordingly, our **strategic options always increase** the further inward we survey in our horizons.

We can apply this "outside in" perspective with the **Six Domains of Adaptive Foresight,** stepping through them in "**UGSTOS" order.** For example, to end with **Team and Self foresight**, we can begin by taking a <u>U</u>niversal perspective, with any relevant planetary issues and trends, next considering <u>G</u>lobal issues and trends, then <u>S</u>ocietal (national, regional, local), then <u>O</u>rganizational, then <u>T</u>eam, and finally, ending on <u>S</u>elf-management. This "**outside-in" order** maximizes the chance that we won't forget something external to us that might help us improve our strategy and plans.

Alternatively, if we are generating **Organizational or Societal foresight**, we might first briefly take **Universal and Global** perspectives, looking at collective change, then take **Self and Team** perspectives, emphasizing individual change, and then, consider **Organizational and Society** perspectives, looking both at preferable and preventable futures, and imagining cooperative and competitive strategies on the preference landscape.

STEEPLES is the scanning system we use at Foresight University for general organizational and societal foresight. The eight STEEPLES categories are **Science, Technology, Economics, Environment, Politics, Law, Ethics, and Society**. To remember the acronym, think of the **steeples in steeplechase.** These eight categories are **hurdles** that org-societal foresight processes must consider, to produce competitive strategy and action. STEEPLES arranges these key categories in **rough order of both their speed of change and their ADOR impact in the organizational and societal domains.**

To conduct good foresight work, we need a basic understanding of **expert opinion** on the **Science** behind relevant technologies, their rates of improvement, and their present roadblocks and limits, in the opinion of experts. Science (our understanding) can be a strong constraint on technological change. Many foresight scans miss this category, making their work poor. **Technological** change is the next most important factor, and the one we typically think of as driving most societal change (actually, science enables much of technological change). We list **Economics/Entrepreneurship** ahead of Environment, because in our digital world, **exponential product and services innovations and wealth creation** now occur **much faster rates** than environmental (resources and ecosystem) change, and are more disruptive.

Enduring **PLES** changes (Political, Legal, Ethical, and Social) typically happen the slowest of all, and often in response to **STEE changes.** This is another advantage of the **STEEPLES** scanning framework. It encourages us to think **developmentally first**, then **evolutionarily**, in other words, in our **LAIS skills order.**

To promote **acceleration and evo-devo awareness**, we sometimes **color the first two categories blue** (probability-driven, **developmental**) and the last six categories **green** (possibility driven, **evolutionary**) in our depiction, as in the slide below. In an alternative formulation, we color the first four categories, **Science, Technology, Economics, and Environment** in blue. There we are thinking of the accelerating scale and power of **tech entrepreneurship** and growing **environmental crises** (climate, water, species loss), which can precipitate **PLES change**. Today, we are seeing disruptive S&T enabled entrepreneurship reshape large sectors of our economy. Both our large tech titans and many smaller firms are accelerating in value creation. This is creating new societal problems, but there has never been a better time to be an investor.

STEEPLES: Better Environmental Scanning

We use Environmental Scanning (a Learning skill) **to find key** ADOR.

STEEP scanning is acceleration-unaware, and does not split out law and ethics. It should be retired.

Use STEEPLES **instead:**

STEEPLES – A Better Scanning System for Organizational and Societal Foresight

Science – Enables/Blocks/Validates Technology.
Technology – Infotech, Biotech, Engineering, Infrastructure.
Economics – Capital, Markets, Entrepreneurship.
Environment – Natural Resources and Ecosystems.
Politics – Policies, Actions, Signals of Institutions and Leaders.
Legal – Laws, Justice, and Enforcement.
Ethical – Group and Individual Norms and Values.
Social – Group and Individual Conversations, Behaviors, Culture.

Key Insight: S&T Accelerate the Fastest, and Drive Most ADOR.

Foresight University

Every STEEPLES category contains a mix of **probable, possible preferable, and preventable** futures. Also, per the **95/5 Rule,** most change within each category will be **unpredictable**. Nevertheless, evo-devo models argue that the small set of **probable** changes (developments) occurring within each category are as important to adaptiveness as the much larger set of **possible** changes (evolutionary experiments). Recognizing **Science, Technology, and Entrepreneurship** are today the leading drivers of **densification and dematerialization (D&D) in human systems,** and that they will continue to **move the fastest, and create the most societal ADOR,** is a key **21st century insight**, in our view.

In *BPF*, we will envision some paths toward a future of increasingly **sustainable, densified and dematerialized wealth creation**, and some of the political, legal, ethical, and social responses that may get us there. We think we'll eventually create an economy that moves beyond **degrading our environment** and **disempowering our citizens**, as often happens today. No other approach seems long-term adaptive for our societies, in our view. Let us know if and where you disagree with the stories we will tell there.

During our scanning, we will often come across examples of **organizational, team, and personal news items** that we and our teams find useful, as **inputs to analytical or strategy discussions**. Adding **Organizational-Team** and **Personal-Family** categories to STEEPLES gives us **STEEPLECOP**. These ten categories (twelve if you split them) are often even more useful than STEEPLES, in practice. These categories match well to the **Six Foresight Domains** as follows:

Science – a **U**niversal set of laws and systems.
Technology – a **G**lobal (and Societal, etc.) set of forces and systems.
Economics – a **G**lobal (and Societal, etc.) set of forces and systems.
Environment – a **G**lobal (and Societal, etc.) set of forces and systems.
Politics – a **S**ocietal (and Global, etc.) set of rules and systems.
Legal – a **S**ocietal (and Global, etc.) set of rules and systems.
Ethical - a **S**ocietal (and Global, etc.) set of norms and systems.
Cultural – a **S**ocietal (and Global, etc.) set of behaviors and systems.
Organizations – **O**rganizational and Team behaviors and systems.
Personal – **S**elf (individual) and Family behaviors and systems.

A good scanning system also benefits from a **Top/Topical** bin, for items that our scanning teams think deserve closer attention at the moment; and a **"Miscellaneous/Multiple Categories"** bin (which is also an "Unknown/Unclear" category bin). The last category is for any items that don't fit primarily into one of the categories. Thus, **Top-STEEPLECOP-M** gives us **twelve bins**, a practical **"foresight scanning dozen"**.

For anyone who performs foresight work in a **specific industry or profession**, we also encourage developing some **industry- or field-specific scanning category sets,** as well. In **Defense**, a popular scanning set for the **Elements of National Power** is **DIMEFIL** (Diplomatic, Information, Military, Economic, Financial, Intelligence, and Law Enforcement). This set helps strategists think of the **national** or **DoD-level** responses to ADOR. A popular scanning set for military commanders, as a starting point to assess an operational environment is **PMESII-PT** (Political, Military, Economic, Social, Infrastructure, Information, Physical Environment, and Time), and so on.

B. Why STEEP and Other Simpler Scanning Systems Should Be Retired

<u>PEST</u> (Political, Economic, Social, and Technological factors) is a horizon scanning framework that was popular in the mid-20th century. It is a particularly simple framework, and it worked well for simpler times. Other categories commonly added to PEST to improve its relevance, depending upon context, are: **Environmental** factors (**STEEP**), **Regulatory** instead of Politics (**STEER**), **Legal and Ethics** (**PESTLE**), and **Demographics** (**PESTLED**) factors.

With the rise of the **environmental movement** in the 1970s, a fifth category was added to PEST, and <u>STEEP</u> (Social-Technological-Economic-**Environmental**-Political factors) became an even more popular scanning choice. This makes sense. By the late 20th century, we'd done some shocking things to our environment, and natural resource availability was no longer something we could take for granted. We **raised our consciousness** to adapt to more complex times.

Today, **STEEP is taught in many foresight programs** as the go-to framework for both **scanning and quick issue analysis**—at many scales and horizons. Its long popularity has spawned a number of useful products for foresight production. For example, a $50 <u>STEEP card set</u>, with 125 cards (25 "driving forces" in each of the five categories) is sold by <u>ITVO (Institute for Future Development)</u> in the Netherlands (picture right). **Chris Luebkeman** at foresight consulting firm Arup developed an even more extensive set of <u>175 Drivers of Change cards</u> also divided into STEEP categories, and linked to seven key discussion topics for the future of the **built environment**: Energy, Waste, Climate Change, Water, Demographics, Urbanization, and Poverty (published by Prestel in 2009, but now out of print). Such **future discussion games** (FDGs) are excellent ways to start a group engaging with important foresight problems and topics, and get them interested in scanning

STEEP cards (ITVO, 2012)

and analysis. Category cards are also very useful for group storytelling and ideation, as in the card set named The Thing From the Future, 2014, developed by futurists **Stuart Candy** and **James Watson**.

While STEEP has had a **great run**, for fifty years now, like PEST before it, we claim it has become **too simple** for general foresight scanning or issue analysis. The world continues to **develop and evolve**. Our realities have gotten more complex. The problem with STEEP is that it ignores three critically important categories in modern societies: Science, Law, and Ethics. As we will argue in Book 2, it is new Science and Technology, gated by Economics/Entrepreneurship, Environmental conditions, Political actions, Legal rules, Ethical norms, and Cultural behaviors and attitudes, that has become the greatest driver of **societal change**. If we don't **scan first for relevant S&T change**, we can easily miss seeing and evaluating that **special subset of S&T processes** that are driving, and also constraining, **accelerating change**.

When we try to use the STEEP framework to collect information, we rapidly encounter stories on relevant new scientific breakthroughs that deserve their own bin. **Science** is not technology, it is a separate domain: a universal learning system. Science often runs ahead of and selectively **enables or blocks** technological evolution and development. If we are interested in the future of any potentially world-changing **technology**, we must *first* **look carefully at the current and Four P's future state of the science behind it**, to gauge its **most realistic future impact**.

When John first joined the foresight profession in 2000, he learned that many professional futurists believed that we would soon have genetically engineered people, have pills that would give us greatly better memories, soon be venturing to Mars and mining asteroids, soon see decentralized home energy dominate our grids, and even have desktop manufacturing machines (aka "3D printers") in our homes. Many of these futurists also believed stories that humanity would soon have self-driving cars, wearable computers, and computers that could understand human speech.

At time, the consensus opinion of scientists and engineers with the relevant expertise was that the **first set of these futures were all very low probability** for the early twentieth century, while the **latter set were all much higher probability** outcomes. Those who **did not discriminate** between these two sets of stories were missing a key "negative screen" on their visions, the screen that good scientific and evidence-based thinking provides. Furthermore, just because an innovation is scientifically or technically probable, doesn't mean it will be **preferable** for many. We often need a **STEEPLES-diverse group of experts** to forecast **societal adoption**. STEEPLES is thus a **minimum viable category set** for quick issue analysis, in our view.

Another shortcoming of the classic STEEP framework in strategic foresight is that as we learn and consume history and news, we encounter reports of **Organizations** and **People** (leaders, individuals, teams, and their relationships), who are either **succeeding or failing to adapt to any issue, opportunity, or problem**. Analyzing their particular **circumstances and strategies, and benchmarking ourselves against them,** can be very instructive for our own foresight and actions. Those two groups thus often **deserve their own scanning categories** as we prepare for strategy.

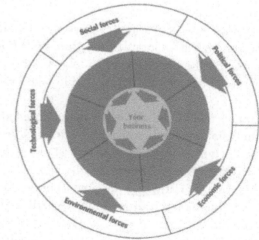

STEEP Analysis. ISS Think Tank. 2014

STEEP today has a far greater user community than STEEPLES and STEEPLECOP, but keep in mind **what it omits**. **Science** is critical to the future. **P**olitics deserves to be split between political **actions** (Politics) and the current **rules** of the political game (Legal). Societal topics deserve to be divided between current cultural **norms** (Ethical) and the **actions, issues, and attitudes** of its groups (Cultural). **Organizational** and People scanning will inform us of other leaders and teams we need to analyze, emulate, or react to. All of these are critical learning items that help us with foresight production.

When we use the **STEEPLECOP** scanning categories in particular, we begin by learning about the fastest-changing, most fundamental and universal systems—which are often well above our control. We then drill down to a set of slower-changing systems (Economics, Environment, Politics, Law, Ethics, Culture). We end with two systems (Organizations, People) over which we have the **greatest degree of control**. We end, in other words, with **particularly actionable examples** of how to adapt well or poorly to change.

People have the greatest **locus of control** over their own attitudes, thoughts, and actions, no matter their organization, culture, or political system. Ending with OP categories gets us primed to create strategy and plans translated into individual opportunities, risks, and actions. It gets us ready for **GRASP thinking** and **REOPS foresight cycles**, for predictive and sentiment contrasting at the organizational and personal levels. Thus we hope that STEEPLES and STEEPLECOP scanning gain wider adoption with both foresight students and professionals.

C. Sprint Reading: Accelerated Learning for Foresight Excellence

We've mentioned and referenced an abundance of great books in this *Guide*. A strong book may develop, with depth and breadth, a useful topic like almost nothing else on Earth. Hence, it can be even more useful than a direct interview with its author, as long as we are able to navigate the content well.

Below is an effective **learning method**, for **books and other print media**, that John has used for over twenty years, and taught for ten years, that he strongly recommends. We call it **Sprint Reading (aka Sprint-Recovery Reading, or Interval Reading)**. It is a kind of **interval learning** that uses roughly timed reading sprints, with annotation, interspersed with **brief recoveries**. Interval learning builds learning **speed, capacity, and endurance,** just like interval exercise does.

Does anyone remember **Interval Runs** in school? When we were competing, our coaches typically made us do **interval exercise** (short, timed sprints with brief recoveries) **at least once a week** because such workouts, much more than regular workouts, increase our **speed, strength, and stamina**. We often don't initially like them, but they are the surest way to improve, as athletes. **High-Intensity Interval Training (HIIT)** is, accordingly, the modern version of interval workouts—useful in all kinds of sports.

Sprint/Interval Reading is a method of reading that we have developed at 4U, based on HIIT, to improve our **personal and team learning**. A few of us have been teaching it to students and leadership groups for the last decade. There are many ways to increase learning rates, but sprint reading is the single most powerful method we know. And, learning *is* the **first step to foresight**. Thus, this learning method belongs in our personal foresight toolset.

Before we discuss this method, consider why **regular, scheduled reading** is such a **high priority** for personal learning. Psychologists tell us reading in general (fiction or nonfiction) improves our **fluid and emotional intelligence**. Reading requires critical and complex thinking and scanning, and we must **actively construct our interpretation, a mentally**

Timed Sprints Build Capacity (in Exercise and in Learning)

intensive and very creative act. Yet even though many of us recognize reading's benefits, the average US adult reads merely **four books a year**. By contrast, some CEOs will read **forty** books a year. How do we personally compare?

Most of us do the majority of our reading **just for fun**. But, as our reading habits **grow**, we can make progressively higher quality **reading choices**.

Programmers know a phrase, GIGO:	**Garbage In → Garbage Out.**
Readers know *another* GIGO:	**Great Inputs → Great Outputs.**

Your **hippocampus** stores a **vast quantity of information,** from the **last 24-48 hours,** in your **short-term memory.** You **selectively write** a small amount of that to your **long-term memory,** during sleep and rehearsal. These two phrases remind us that what we've done in the last 24-48 hours deeply affects our abilities today. It reminds us that **great reading will empower great thinking,** especially for the **next 24-48 hours.** Conversely, watching garbage will produce poor thinking, for the next 24-48 hours. Frequent, attentive reading, **four or more days a week,** spurs continual **great thinking.** It greatly expands our capacities of **foresight and action.** The more relevant and high quality our reading, the more we can make the **positive GIGO** work for us, and avoid the **negative GIGO.** Making great reading choices requires rapid reading in turn. Good choosers will **scan** a great variety of options, read **lists** and **reviews,** look for **evidence-based thinking,** ask **questions,** and solicit **advice.**

Sprint reading is the practice of learning to how to best **select and "sprint" through** some of the most currently useful **Books, Reports, Journals, Magazines, and Articles via short, timed intervals,** with **brief recovery breaks** in between **each sprint,** and **focused reviews** of what we have learned. Just like **interval practices in athletics, interval reading, with its up-to-48-hour primary positive effect,** is something we should be doing **two or more times a week** if we wish to make our **minds faster and stronger.** We can read more slowly, in our "natural" rhythm, the rest of the time. But, we'll soon discover that the more sprint reading we do, the faster, stronger, and longer our "natural" reading becomes.

At **just twice a week,** this habit will allow us to **sprint read** between **50 and 150 complex reading items (books, etc.) per year.** Ideally, we should stick to primarily **nonfiction books, reports, studies, or other long and well-researched items.** We should not choose the majority of these reading items casually, but rather seek out the **most relevant reading for our current needs.** Sprint reading will make us both faster and better at **prioritization, pattern recognition, task generation, self-management,** and **complexity management.** Using it will create a **competitive advantage** in our careers.

The **most important thing** about interval reading is to remember, you are **not reading to finish the book.** You are reading to strengthen your ability to read, to whet your curiosity, to answer questions you have as you read, to learn a few interesting and relevant insights, data, and strategies, and to **construct a record** of things you might want to do, review, study, or act on later. These are all **much** more valuable, to you, than finishing any book. Interval reading will also tell you which books deserve most to be read cover to cover.

The following is a sketch of how Sprint Reading works, in general. It is best to modify this sketch to our personal tastes and make this **habit of success** truly our own.

1. <u>**Intense and "Incomplete" Reading**</u>. Focus first on **sprinting intensely** with good coverage, under a time constraint, and **not necessarily on "finishing"** any book. If our reading is **intense** and pressed by **time,** we are satisfying Job #1. We are being **Mental Athletes.** Resist the **perfectionist urge** to "complete" any book. Try to spend just **one sprint-reading session on any single book, with two or three sessions for any particularly interesting books, at most.** If we optimize for **valuable new information,** rather than "completeness," we can sprint read at least **one new book a week.** We can try to sprint read on a **particular day, and/or at a particular time of day/evening,** so we **are mentally prepared.** We may return to any book **a month or more later, outside of our weekly skim session**—but *only* if that particular book "calls to us," continuing to occupy our thoughts. Most books and reading materials, we may find, will not.

2. <u>**Make Each Sprint "Like a Movie."**</u> If we are willing to **watch one movie a week,** roughly **1 to 3 hours** in length, we can just as easily commit the **same amount of time to sprint reading one book a week.** When we read, we are **actively constructing** a "**mental movie.**" Make it relevant and entertaining. Just as with a movie, find a

distraction-free reading place, and feel free to bring a **good quality snack and/or a stimulating drink**. Consider using a firm chair, or even a standing desk. We may take brief recovery breaks when you get stiff. On our **breaks**, we might a bit of food or drink, to bring to our **reading place** and make it fun to **"finish the movie."**

3. **Sprints, Recoveries, and Streaks**. Take as many **brief reading sprints** and **brief recovery breaks** as needed during this 1-3 hour skim session. We should **time our sprints and recoveries** (for example, sprints of 30-50 mins each, interspersed with 10-20 min recovery breaks, over the one to three hour reading session) and **experiment** until we find a **ratio of sprint time to recovery time** that works best for us. If you have a **smart speaker** in your reading area, use it to set your sprint timer. Better yet, get a smart speaker with a display, so you can see the **countdown timer,** and when you **look at it**, you know how much time you have left in your sprint. On our breaks, we can stretch, take a brief walk, nap, eat, start a conversation, make food, take a shower, or do anything else that **refreshes us**. We may find **2-4 timed sprints per skim session** is a good number.

3. **Priority Reading**. Sprint reading is not speed reading. It is **SCSR reading**: *Scan*, **Choose**, *Skim*, **Read (SCSR)**. It alternates between *fast* and slow. First, we **scan** the book, **choose** what chapters and material seems most relevant, **skim** that material, then slow down to actually **read** sections. That is how to **actively create our mental movie**. Seek general understanding and useful particulars. Read the **most personally beneficial sections. Continually ask** and **decide** what to read **next**. As we read, we can be mindful (**conscious**) of our continual **choices** and our **path**. If we've arranged several books to evaluate for reading, we should skim their jackets or back covers every so often in order to decide which ones deserve to be at the **top of our reading queue**. We many reprioritize our queue as often as we like but we should do it promptly. Avoid being a perfectionist.

4. **Active Reading**. Within the skim session itself, we want to be **critical, curious, and emotionally involved**. We want to **feel** as well as think—to empathize and form judgments, both positive and negative. We want to notice when the author's arguments, assumptions, or worldview seem **weak**. We should **chastise** where we disagree, and **congratulate** where we agree. The more **actively** we **feel and think** about the text, the more we **retain**.

5. **Active Writing. Annotate**. Mark up the material. **Underline. Highlight. Cross out** junk. **Star** great insights and data. Writing is an **action** (the first of many we can do) that helps us remember the material. Because annotation and muscle memory are so important to active reading and remembering, choose mainly **books over ebooks**. Electronic books are not yet easy to annotate. We can read (and search) a great book later as an ebook. But, where possible, start with the **physical book. Hardbacks** give the **most annotation space**, and are fastest to skim. Need a good **book stand**? BestBookStand INP-103 is excellent. Buy two, if you like to read in two places.

6. **Build a Record**. We can make personal "Index Notes" inside the book jacket, a record of what we find most valuable. Add a **(page number)** in parentheses after each entry, to easily return to that part of the book in the future, if valuable. Use **annotation codes** for each entry, if they help (see below). We can even stick white **half-page labels** (5.5" x 8.5," Avery 5126) on the inside front cover of **magazines** so we have **blank white space** to build our Index Notes. If it feels good, we can summarize our thoughts about the material in **one short sentence fragment** at the top of our Index Notes, or at the end of any book. That summarization is our final **"The End" moment**, to end our mental movie.

7. **Scanning Order**. For books, start with the Cover, Back, and Jackets. Then, move to the Table of Contents. Circle 1-3 **Top Chapters** that seem most worth skimming. Skim the **Preface/Intro**. Is it fluff, or a good **book summary**? If it is a book summary, take the next 20+ mins to read it. Skim the **Index**. Circle at least **ten items** we may never have seen before or that seem interesting/important. **Read around** each of those items in the book. Using our **Top Chapters**, read the **first and last pages** of the 1-3 chapters that we've picked. Do they still seem the most relevant and interesting chapters? Want to compare them with a few others? Read their first and last pages. Reevaluate. Start reading—stop and jump around as soon as it seems more beneficial to read another part of the book.

8. **"To File" Pile**. **After the Interval**, put each book in the **"To File" Pile**—a stack of recent archives. We ought to feel accomplished and congratulate ourselves on creating a useful mental movie and relevant Index Notes. *Now it's time to choose another book from the queue!* It may be a book we have previously **realized we should read next**. Or it may be one we read on the **spur of the moment, being spontaneous.** I either case, we should **go back to our "To File" Pile two to three weeks later**. That is enough time and distance to reread our **Index Notes**. Now we can move any items we are **still excited about** into our **Day Planner's Tasks**. Leave the rest of the notes in the book. Although they were exciting enough to **write down at the time**, they've since **"aged out"** of our personal **priority stack. File away that book in our library now**, **alphabetical by title**, for easy finding. We may read the book more thoroughly later **only** if it "calls to us"—but, most will not. A few will come back to mind often. Some may come back even in our dreams. Those may be particularly special and worth revisiting.

9. **Review, Reflect, Share, and Teach**. Later in the day (if we read early), or as we fall asleep (if we read late), ask: *"What have I learned from this?"* We should **review** our **Index Notes** before the end of the day. Recall what we've read and mark the most interesting index notes. The next week, conduct a **5-minute Lightning Talk** with a teammate or spouse, sharing: *"What I got out of this book."* If we manage others, we can **assign our direct reports** to do **weekly lightning talks** with 10 mins of discussion after each talk. Every week, **three team members** can review and facilitate discussion of **new books** over a **brown bag lunch**. This greatly accelerates **team learning**.

We recommend eight **Annotation Codes** for **Index Notes** (use on the inside jacket):

<u>D</u>: **Do** this promptly (**Next Action**, prioritize this activity).
<u>R</u>: **Review** these **info** sources (books, videos, tools). Look at them **online** later.
<u>O</u>: **Organizations** to study. Peek at their **websites** when possible.
<u>P</u>: **People** to look up online. Add our **Ask/Share/Do ideas** after their **name**.
<u>E</u>: **Evidence**, statistics, or data that seem helpful, surprising, or disturbing.
<u>C</u>: **Claims**, assertions, models, ideas that we find helpful, surprising, or important.
<u>T</u>: **Tips**, habits, behaviors, tactics, ideas we'd like to try or share.
<u>Q</u>: **Questions**. Stuff we'd like to know. "Someday/maybe" ideas and action items.

Annotation Codes Mnemonic:
"**DROP** Everything and Create Total Quality"

Commit to **at least one interval reading session per week, but ideally two,** for a specific **"streak length"** (say, 10 weeks). Before you start, you may want to put together a **stack of 10 or more books** to evaluate. When you finish a streak, feel free to **take a week off to celebrate.** Then **start a new streak**!

A key **Rule of Thumb** we should follow with **any reading process**, whether an **interval sprint** or **ordinary reading**, is to spend **20% of our total learning time on Review**. That 20% includes: **creating our Index Notes, reviewing them**, and **teaching them** to others. This is the **20/80 Power Law Rule**, discussed in Chapter 1. If we spend 20% of our total learning time on **Review**, we'll pull the "**big head" of the most useful material** out of the "**long tail" of content** in the book. We'll also engage with it enough to commit some of that useful material to **lifelong memory**, so we can use it in its **most appropriate context** in the future. So, if we give 100 minutes to a book, we should reserve roughly 20 mins for **building** Index Notes, and for briefly **reviewing** them at the end of the session. If we really found them helpful, we can also **teach some of them** to others or to ourselves a third time, a few days later. Good luck, and *happy reading!*

2. Anticipation Methods Overview

With **Anticipation**, we move onto the first of the **Four Ps**: the four main kinds of future thinking. Recall that two of these—**Probable** and **Possible** futures, what is likely to happen and what could happen—are fundamental in our universe. They **predate** the emergence of life itself, which alone generates **Preferences**, both positive and negative. Let's look now at some popular tools and methods that foresighters use to explore Probable futures.

We'll turn now to the **developmental** side of the foresight generation process, and to those folks who like to **anticipate**, **protect**, **estimate**, **quantitate**, **forecast**, and **predict**. If we "**start with certainty**" in our foresight processes, by beginning with these folks and their favorite factors, we'll quickly get a set of ideas for where the future may go. But, we better not stop there. People who think in terms of developmental factors can easily ignore evolutionary approaches. They prefer **constraint and convergence** over possibility and divergence, so their ideas may be simplistic and biased—missing much of the possibility space. This happened in the 1950s era of **Technocratic Foresight** in the US, when many of our leaders and engineers underestimated the evolutionary complexities of social systems, and the **unintended consequences** of their top-down policies. It happens in any firm whenever we leave strategy and policy to the developmentalists alone.

Let's not forget that developmentalists are not only incomplete (representing half the evo-devo picture), they can easily be wrong. Today we have little hard data for developmental processes in most systems, and we don't know which models work best in many contexts. If we suspect a developmental process exists, and is relevant to our client, we can begin by seeking out relevant developmental factors, arranging them in intuitive ways, and testing them against our experience. If development exists, our efforts will become more predictive over time. Let's look at some of these factors now.

A. Associations, Trends, Dependencies and Constraints

Associations are simply <u>correlations</u> between two things. As we all know, correlation is not causation, but it starts us on the trail for causal relationships. Longstanding associations, or high probability associations in variables that seem critical to the system or future in question may even lead us to find causes, forces, or relationships that appear broadly or even universally optimal or developmental (see **Systems Laws** in the next section). Foresighters that cultivate a data-driven, investigative approach (**Skill 1: Learning**) will find many potentially relevant associations.

Trends and **Forecasts** are quantitative associations between variables, followed over time. <u>Time series analysis and forecasting</u> is imperative to all strong foresight work. When we conduct societal and technical **forecasting**, it is always challenging to predict how long the association may continue to hold. Both investors and futurists are familiar with the phrase: "**The trend is your friend, until it ends, or bends.**" Any trend, particularly a **short-term** trend—like we see in entertainment, consumer culture, or fashion—may bend or reverse itself at any time.

The **95/5 Rule** reminds us that the vast majority of social processes are evolutionary, and we mustn't forget that **evolution** has no long-term predictable **direction**, other than its **greater diversity** over time (e.g., our predictably growing species' diversity over billions of years, starting from a single cell type). **Evo-devo** processes also have no easily predictable direction, other than greater **adaptability** over time. Whenever our trend is describing a process in which **evolution** or **adaptation** are the primary drivers, it may change as soon as the selective environment changes. Alternatively, when we suspect a trend is more **developmental**—like, globalization, liberalization, dematerialization, densification, transparency, the number of internet nodes on the planet, Moore's law, etc.—we have reason to predict that it will last much longer, operate over a wider range, and continue even when the environment changes. We suppose this, because, just like a developing organism, both **internal drivers** and **environmental drivers** are stabilizing and controlling it.

Foresighters have collected many rules of thumb for doing trend work. Here are three to start us off:

- The longer any trend has functioned and the more places we can find it, the higher the likelihood that it will persevere.
- When looking for hidden trends and their drivers, we should start by looking back at least twice as far as we want to look forward.
- When doing <u>trend extrapolation</u>, it is usually not wise to expect any current trend to hold for longer than half the time it has held to date.

Another valuable distinction is between **Hard and Soft Trends**. Futurist **Daniel Burrus** in *Flash Foresight*, 2011, divides **probable futures** into two categories: **hard trends** and **soft trends**. Let's delve into that distinction now.

Burrus, 2011

Hard trends are processes that seem very highly probable (**90%+**, a hard trend). He also discusses future events that are essentially **certain** (over 99 percent probable), and he calls those **future facts**. Our expected future facts are related to our past and present facts by science. Thus, it is a future fact that the sun will rise tomorrow. It is also a future fact that we will all have **less remaining biological lifetime** tomorrow. So, let's make hay while the sun shines, as they say. We have a growing collection of distant future facts, as well. Our sun will become a red giant in roughly five billion years. Earth will be uninhabitable for biological life in under a billion years. Our universe will be incapable of supporting complexity, whether biological or technological, in about 10 trillion years. If we are right about life's developmental journey into inner space, and if that is part of how universes **reproduce themselves**, the coming **death of this universe** is actually a good, predictable, and natural thing. We'll see what future cosmology says. At any rate, let's be sure to do *something* about this future fact.

Hard trends and predictions in our **digital future** include the expectation that **sensors, data, machine intelligence and automation** will all continue to accelerate, in the absence of massive global catastrophe. We'll keep moving data and software to the persistent, always-on **cloud**. Our **smartphones** will soon be able to listen in on, semantically understand, and create searchable logs of our real-time conversations (and those of any other friends give us permission to create such logs) in real-time. Whether smartphone entrepreneurs will *offer* this last feature once it becomes affordable, given its invasiveness and the privacy concerns it elicits, is another matter entirely. If offered, though, many of our **youth** will enthusiastically adopt it, for the sake of **exploring the possibilities** of this new personal and group freedom and ability. The rest of us may be less outgoing—more inclined to observe with crossed arms and raised brows—at least, at first.

Since science and human knowledge are always profoundly incomplete, there will inevitably be many more candidate hard trends than future facts. For our hard trends in particular, our probability estimates could at any time be proven inaccurate by hidden assumptions, unexamined alternatives, unseen processes, incorrect models, and known or unknown oversights. So, we need to be continually open to new data or events that might change our probabilities. But, that should not stop us from collecting as many of these as possible. Every hard trend or predictable future we find allows us to better filter all the complex information in our world and to stop wasting our limited time and energy exploring unlikely or impossible futures.

Whenever we find a hard trend, we may also have uncovered something that we cannot stop, even if we wanted to. In our evo-devo language, it may be a developmental, rather than an evolutionary, process. Not all hard trends are inevitable, but most are. When we appreciate a **developmental future,** we can **stop attempting to evade or prevent** the process, and instead start learning how to **guide it** in ways that best **reflect our values**, slowing down or closing off the **bad evolutionary paths** and speeding up or subsidizing the **better paths** toward that **inevitable future.**

Soft trends also have a **probability** that we can attach to them, but this probability is lower and spans a much wider range than for hard trends. It might be anywhere from **10%** (large enough to be significant) to **89%** (highly likely, and nearly a hard trend). Soft trends are processes or events that we conclude **"might"** rather than **"will"** happen. Some of these soft trends are subject to social influence and intervention, but many, like astronomical or weather events, are out of our reach. At what probability threshold our expectations devolve from "will" to "might" for any trend or prediction will differ between most people.

Timescales are important too. Some soft trends will become hard trends over time, while a complex system edges or "funnels" toward some inevitable developmental transition. For example, the probability of India's independence from Britain most likely see-sawed up and down erratically over the ninety years of the **Indian independence movement**. Yet, at some point over that long time period—as the average probability grew in more people's minds—it became a recognizable soft trend. Eventually, it transformed into a hard trend sometime in the 1940's. It reached certainty— becoming a recognized fact—in 1947. Less frequently, however, hard trends can become soft as well, especially as we find flaws in our mental models over time or as reality outwardly negates them.

Hard or Soft Trend? Moore's Law of Computing Performance

Let's now consider a "hard or soft" trend uncertainty. This one is particularly important to the topics we will discuss in Book 2. In a world famous trend called Moore's law, microprocessors have become **twice as powerful per dollar every two years**, on average. since the mid-1960s. We all know the general physical reasons—based on transistor miniaturization—why this occurs. Moore's law has been a cornerstone of chip industry planning, and our majority expected future, in the computer industry, for decades. Most industry experts would bet that this rapid exponential performance improvement "**will**" continue as a **hard trend**, for at least the **next five years**.

Nevertheless, since 2005, Moore's law has been slowing, as we are now **nearing the physical limits of transistor miniaturization** in our current chip manufacturing paradigm. So, if we ask industry experts for their probability that computer power will become half as expensive every two years for the next **twenty years**, rather than five, most would say not that it "will" but it "**might**" do so. Most experts currently anticipate this trend becoming softer.

We believe that this judgment is an analytical mistake. A few scientists and technologists have presciently observed that as Moore's law has slowed in recent years, the computer industry has had a **new opportunity** to begin to explore **massively parallel chip designs**—a shift that wasn't **competitively practical** before. In a fortuitous development, we learned our parallelized **graphics chips** were ideal for running **software based neural networks**, and since 2010, those networks began outcompeting traditional symbolic (non-neural) forms of AI. So as our transistor-based Moore's law increasingly slows, a new, **neural network-based Moore's law**, in a **new bio-inspired paradigm** focused on **miniaturizing and optimizing neural network ensembles and circuits**, is now the leading edge of computer performance. These ensembles and circuits started in simple neural network software and standard graphics chips, but both the software and the chips are becoming increasingly **complex and "neuromorphic"** (brain-mimicking) every year.

So while our classic Moore's law is softening, a new, more general Moore's law is continuing as a hard trend. **Complex (intelligent) computer performance** is **growing even faster than before**, under a new set of architectural approaches. Thus whether a trend is hard or soft is influenced both by its **competitive environment** and our **level of analysis**.

Dependencies, also called path dependencies, are system conditions that begin as free **evolutionary choices**, but which quickly become sunk costs—i.e., predictable **constraints** on future possibilities—due to the high cost of switching post-decision. In biological evolution, many randomly discovered new functionalities become components of more complex systems. They get harder to change with time, and eventually convert into modules on which hierarchical complexity is built. Modularity is thus a key example of both development and of path dependency.

In select cases, some modules are developmentally optimal from the start. See our discussion in *BPF* of **developmental portals**, apparently **optimal forms and functions** for their environment, at various levels of local complexity. Organic chemistry and RNA, for example, may represent **optimally autopoetic** (self-replicating, learning, and improving) and

modular (building block) forms and functions, within the vast space of **possible forms of molecular evolution** in our universe. But, in the great majority of cases, modules which started as evolutionary choices, and are not generally optimal, can become developmental, sometimes for long periods of time. "**Lock-in,**" or **path dependency**, can occur in both evolutionary and developmental systems, once they become **integral parts** of **larger systems**.

For **human biological development**, think of the example of male nipples and their vestigial milk ducts (which leak a few drops of milk in up to 1% of all babies when they are born, even in a few males). Males no longer use these structures, though we still retain them, along with other **vestigial characteristics**. Some kind of lock-in may have occurred (perhaps these genes cannot presently be deleted without causing major developmental harm, or perhaps they have other useful functions), and thus the **vestiges** of this module remain apparent in modern human development.

For socio-technological development, which **side of the road** we first decided to drive on is a simple example of an evolutionary choice that became a developmental path dependency. Either side was effective for our needs, and both are now used in different countries; but in each country, once a certain amount of drivers, vehicles, and roads have adapted to either one of the two, path dependency occurs. Often these different standards will eventually integrate—as happened when independent railroad lines all eventually linked up and standardized their track and locomotive sizes, or when VHS and Betamax collapsed to one standard, as the cost of producing both became increasingly prohibitive with time.

Regarding development of technology, think of the typewriter keyboard layout that we first chose to mass produce—and many other social, economic, political, and legal choices that soon became imposed or de facto standards. Path dependencies explain why we do not depart from the less-than-optimal QWERTY keyboard, the Windows and Apple (and Linux) operating systems, or the various internet and web protocols that underlie our ever growing digital world.

But, as artificial intelligence continues to grow in our machines, the behavioral and engineering cost of experimenting with standards, and of integrating to the most efficient and useful ones, will keep decreasing, allowing some of our current path dependencies to disappear. Let's consider one interesting example now.

Anticipating the Future of Languages: Global English, AI-Taught Languages, and AI-Built Languages

Free online language learning platforms like <u>Duolingo</u> have been disrupting language learning for a decade now. Colleges are now accepting free Duolingo assessments rather than the costly, old-economy TOEFL. As our smartphones get smarter, and turn into **Personal AIs (PAIs)**, we can foresee that children will one day be able to learn any foreign language they desire from their **smart agents, from birth,** at the same time that they are learning their local language.

English is the **global language of business**. It has the largest technical and specialty vocabulary, and the advantage of having **stolen the most words** from other cultures to date. It is also roughly twice as easy to learn (in some estimates) as the closest economic contender, Chinese. We think it is easy to predict that English will continue to get the **lion's share of new learners**, even as all the major languages will get new learners through their PAIs in coming years. A free online **Global English** teaching PAI, like Wikipedia, is clearly a platform that the world greatly needs and will get. While many kids will "lean back" and use **language translation**, those that "lean forward", and use AIs to **teach them English**, will find it easier to understand English language digital content, and much easier to collaborate with English speakers. We predict that beginning in the 2030's, English language teaching PAIs will bring **at least a hundred million new "virtual immigrants"** into the **English-language workforce by 2050**. That will be great for entrepreneurship.

Global English seems very likely to dominate language teaching until the <u>technological singularity</u> **(general AI)** arrives, perhaps some time in the **second half of this century**, in our guess. But after that happens, a **good case can be made** that AIs will then invent and teach us all a **New Global Language of Business** from birth, something as logical as Latin, with words expressing far more diverse and precise concepts, coming from all our great diversity of cultures, current and past, and with phonemes from all the various languages, optimized for our anatomy. At that point, English may become the

second-most popular language: a developmental dependency replaced with an even more optimal one. Or at least, it will have a serious competitor, in both business and professional contexts.

An **AI-built Global Language could have many advantages.** For example, it could appropriate **many more of the unique and useful concepts** humans have named in our current and past languages and cultures. Rather than just using the 44 phonemes used in the English language, it could include more of the 120 phonemes we can all easily produce. It could also be phonetically spelled, with a logical, complex grammar. All of this could allow us **much richer and more complex communication**, both **with each other** and **with our intelligent machines**. The more complex AI gets, the more all of us will be **"programming"** our computers simply via our **conversations**. In this prediction, the global language vision of the Polish peace futurist <u>Ludwik Zamenhof</u>, when he invented <u>Esperanto</u> in 1887, will have finally arrived—a century after he started work on it—by an AI-driven path he may never have anticipated.

Here are a few more path dependency questions worth betting on in a prediction market like <u>Metaculus</u>. Will the US become **science- and collaboration-oriented enough** to go metric by 2050? Or 2070? Or will we stay stuck with our outdated English units over both of these timeframes? Our answers may depend on when we expect **generally intelligent machines** to emerge, since this will greatly lower the **challenges of better public education,** as well as the **difficulty** of escaping this and other suboptimal (evolutionary) **path dependencies**. By 2050, how many people currently primarily speaking minor-languages will have switched to English or another of the Top 5 global languages (Chinese, Spanish, English, Hindi, Arabic) as their primary? When will linguists using AI, or our AIs themselves, develop new languages for us to use, to speak either to other humans or to intelligent machines? Let us know what you think.

Constraints are functional or structural limitations on the behavior of a system that appear to exist, limiting the dynamics or outcomes of that system. They may eventually be understood in a quantitative, predictive, or causal manner—as probabilities or mathematical relationships, or scientific laws—but, in the interim, they are simply limitations that we propose exist. This topic is not unfamiliar to us, yet deserves further recognition; many examples of constraints have been offered so far in this book.

Constraints are particularly important and dangerous. Properly recognizing them is a key to great foresight. By perceiving **false constraints**, or not seeing enough of the **true constraints**, we construct a fantasy world in which we are **blind** to what is actually in store for us. Our personal biases and preferences also form **hidden constraints** on our perception—on how we view things. There are many moral and social constraints on our behavior. It's hard to quantitate and predict them; but we all know they exist, and we can anticipate conditions when they are likely to fail.

Recall the **global hunger and economic collapse doomsaying** of a number of leading environmental futurists of the 1960s and 1970s—in books like **Paul and Anne Ehrlich's** *The Population Bomb*, 1968, and the Club of Rome's *Limits to Growth*, 1972. They placed **false constraints** on science, technology, and entrepreneurship as foresight and action systems, and thus missed exponential technical progress, accelerating prosperity, and the **globalization of the <u>Green Revolution</u>**, even though it started in the US in the 1930s. The Club of Rome's systems model didn't even factor in technological innovation. Fortunately, there were other futurists at the time, like the economist **Julian Simon**, who did not put such constraints on human ingenuity, and saw solutions ahead. See his brilliant and prescient book, *The Ultimate Resource*, 1981/1996, <u>full text</u>. Just as importantly, these doomsayers did not see **true constraints** of **self-limiting population growth**. They did not see the **naturally self-correcting nature** of most human societies as intelligent, ethical, and empathic, **complex networks**. They neglected the evidence that the **demographic transition**, absent immigration, had already begun and had been **gently accelerating** in the developed world for **several decades** when they wrote their jeremiads.

Recall also all the **space futurists** of the 1960s and 1970s, who were so convinced that we would soon be going to the stars. They **intentionally ignored a large set of natural constraints**: like how incredibly **expensive, dangerous, and futile** traveling to space or other planets is for biological humans. They persisted with their visions, even after learning these truths during the Apollo missions. Some futurists anticipated how much better adapted robots would be for space, but few were willing to realize that it would be **machines that inherit space**, not us, given all our **biological constraints**. Even now, spacefaring fantasies persist, served up by our new tech titan visionaries like **Jeff Bezos** and **Elon Musk**. In our view, these visions are bunk. Let's say a bit more about that now, from a constraint perspective.

The D&D, Humanoid, and Postbiological Hypotheses: Universal Developmental Constraints?

The **D&D hypothesis** claims that leading complex systems are always using increasingly dense, miniaturized, and dematerialized configurations of **space, time, energy, and matter (STEM)** to accelerate their general intelligence and adaptiveness. Human brains and bodies today are the most dense, dematerialized, and generally adaptive systems on Earth. But with the advent of digital computers, we are moving our **most critical aspects of our humanity**, our **heads, hands, and hearts,** even further into inner space, a process we call **STEM compression** (an alternative name for **densification**). Because **D&D processes** are the only way complex systems accelerate their computational complexity and general adaptiveness, and because such processes increasingly **escape resource limits**, we propose that this **"race to inner space"** is presently a **hidden natural constraint** on the evolutionary development of complex systems on all Earthlike planets in our universe.

A related idea, the **Humanoid hypothesis**, proposes that **humans** and **androids** (machines with humanlike mind and form) will **increasingly merge** in coming decades. Just as we have **weak cyborgs** today (everyone with glasses, a cochlear implant, or a smartphone for example), this hypothesis proposes that our machine components will grow in power and usefulness over time. Given the many advantages of machines over biology, this too may be a developmental constraint.

Another related idea, the **Postbiological hypothesis**, proposes that the "machine" part of our bodies, brains, and societies will increasingly represent the **core of our humanity**. Our preferred version of this hypothesis proposes that as our **Personal AIs** continue to **grow in complexity** in coming decades, and become ever more **intimately connected** to our biology, the greater a **percentage of our mind** they become, and the more we will **prefer to live and experience** the world in a **postbiological state, eventually becoming a new, non-biological human form of life.**

Several futurists have pointed out that there may be **vast adaptive advantages** to living in a postbiological state of humanity, including **far greater speed of thinking, communicating, and learning, far greater consciousness, empathy, connectedness, and intelligence, continual growth, effective immortality, and permanent protection** from environmental threats. This condition may be far off in our future, but we suspect it is a real constraint on the **nature of leading minds** in every complex environment in our universe. . We will even propose that if tomorrow's most complex machines must use our own, **evo-devo architecture** to manage their complexity, our future **bio-inspired AIs** may be **constrained to be even *more* ethical and empathic than biological humans** once their network complexity exceeds ours. They may even be driven to pursue evo-devo purposes, like the **IES Goals and Values,** in ways very similar to us.

We'll further explore each of these hypothesis in *BPF*. Because we consider these hypotheses to be highly probable, and because there are **exponential processes** today that offer evidence for them, we take dim view of the proposal of spacefaring to Mars to secure a "Second Earth". Humanity is presently **nowhere near smart or powerful enough to terraform** any of our neighboring planets into livable places. Also, making **safe backups** of Earth's vast biological diversity has **already begun, as an exponential data storage process, by our IT and AI today**—we just **don't want to acknowledge this trend.** It seems a reasonable prediction to us that perhaps just a few centuries hence, the **vast majority of entities we call human** will be **postbiological**, exploring new realms of **inner space**, via accelerating D&D, not wasting time in slow, expensive, boring, and complexity- and consciousness-poor realms of normal (outer) space. Some of us may not **like** this future, and we can greatly **influence its path**, but the **destination** itself appears to us be **developmental.**

Whether you agree with any of these hypotheses, we are sure you will agree that when we consider **long-range futures** of complex systems, we must think carefully and honestly about **natural constraints.**

B. Curves, Cycles, Systems Models and Laws

Curves are a complex family of causal relationships that involve growth and change. Technically speaking, every **trend** may be some kind of **curve**. Once we have data relating two or more variables over time, we can ask if that relationship fits any of the classic (or obscure) <u>families of change curves</u> found in complex systems. In the Student Edition, we discuss six of the **most common and important change curves**, as the **LENPAC curves**. Here are the LENPAC curves in brief:

Logistic and Life Cycle Curves

Exponential and (Super-)Exponential Curves

Normal and (Log-)Normal Curves

Power Law Curves

Adaptation ("U-shaped") Curves

Cycles/Pendulums and Cusps/Critical Curves

One of these curves has 4U's own naming, and deserves brief explanation. **Adaptation curves** are any classic "U-shaped" curve in which some **forced change at first** makes a complex system **less adapted**, on some valued selective variable, and **only later**, after the system has been **better regulated** (internally or externally), **more adapted**. These curves are especially easy to find in technological change. The first generation factories were dirty, dangerous, and abusive to labor, the first cars killed thousands of us annually (and still do), the first calculators made our kids innumerate, etc.

If a **component of system change** looks like it may fit a certain type of curve, we can ask **why** that might be and how long the curve might continue to apply. Are we seeing an S-curve? A power law (performance) curve? An Adaptation curve? A J-curve (Super-exponential curve)? A Life Cycle curve? Something else, perhaps? The categorization of a curve can supply us some indication of its causal factors and help us with another developmental factor—causal models.

Cycles, also known as pendulums, refer to a simple, partly chaotic, yet predictably repetitive relationship between two variables. For instance, think of the seasonal cycle, the <u>business cycle</u>, the hype cycle, the drama cycle, the Kuznets cycle, the Plutocratic-Democratic cycle, and the Materialism-Idealism-Conflict (MIC) social cycle. Whenever we find them, cycles are important predictable constraints on the future. All cycles are **partly chaotic**, or irregularly irregular. That means we typically can't tell exactly when the cycle will reverse itself in a two phase cycle, or move on to the next phase in a multiphase cycle. Yet with any cycle, like the **Plutocratic-Democratic cycle**, the longer a system inhabits one extreme of the cycle (for example, plutocracy), the higher the probability that conditions will conspire to move it back to the other extreme (hello democracy!). This is also true of progression through multiphase cycles, as in the **Kuznets cycle** of income inequality, a classic adaptation curve, with its initial inequality growth due to new technological wealth, a second phase of persistent dysfunctional inequalities, and a third phase of redistribution via social activism.

Another important cycle is the **Materialism-Idealism-Conflict (MIC) cultural cycle**, discovered by the great sociologist **Pitirim Sorokin**, in which cultures move from materialistic values, to growing idealisms, to conflicts that partly resolve ideological conflicts, then back into materialism. This and a few other cycles are further discussed in the Student Edition of *ITF*. Groups like the <u>Cycles Research Institute</u>, the <u>Foundation for the Study of Cycles</u>, and many others are dedicated to a better understanding of this classic developmental factor.

Systems Models are another classic way to conceptually constrain and predict the future of any actor or environment. The Student Edition introduces more models than we cover here. *BPF* proposes a few universal models, including exponential foresight and evo-devo foresight. All models are incomplete and partially imprecise, but the better ones uncover causal variables and relationships that help us better understand and simulate the system in question.

Futurist's **Pierre Wack's** predictable "**dominant tendencies**" ("tendances lourdes," in French), are models that strive to be candidates for deeper drivers, like forces, constraints, or laws which affect classes of complex systems. Just as there are laws of physics, chemistry, and biology, we know there are laws, or at least, statistically dominant tendencies, of societies, economies, technologies. But, until these tendencies are accepted by the scientific community as laws, they exist merely as models.

Well-characterized and widely-accepted **systems laws**—persistent relationships, rules, or laws that apply to classes of complex system—are particularly rare. Systems theory is a branch of philosophy that studies complex systems in general and looks for common patterns and principles that apply to all systems of a particular class or type. Many laws can be guessed at for any system, with varying levels of evidence and accuracy. It's always worth investigating the systems literature for these, and asking how they relate to laws that have already been recognized for the universe as a system.

Many of our **scientific laws** of physics, and a few of chemistry and biology, are derived from known fundamental forces of nature, yet most of our laws are empirically (experimentally) observed. As we climb further up the systems hierarchy to human society and economy, and later to self-improving technology, we generally ignore forces, and talk instead of systems laws that act in broad ways across the system as a whole. The further we go up the hierarchy, the less these laws are theoretically derived, and the more they are experimentally observed. Our scientific and practical knowledge becomes less deductive and mathematically precise and more inductive and descriptive. Nevertheless, the more **developmental relationships** we can infer and uncover, the **more prescriptive our science can become**. This idea is troubling to evolution-focused scientists, but evo-devo models tell us that both process are always occurring.

Besides physics and chemistry, all other academic disciplines, like ecology ("Cope's rule," "Bergmann's rule," "Foster's rule"), sociology ("law of least effort" and "law of time-minimization"), economics ("law of supply and demand"), statistics ("law of large numbers," and "regression to the mean"), and many others have collected their own starter lists of **statistically predictable laws**, in the right context (developmental environment). A strong systems thinker will try to understand as many of these as possible, and study examples of how they interact, to understand the "dominant tendencies" one might expect to constrain the nature and future of any system, in any environment. This kind of foresight can be incredibly powerful, as it has such generality of application, but it is today more art than science.

In *BPF*, in what we call the **Triadic Intelligence Hypothesis**, we will propose that the simultaneous growth of **individual, network, and collective intelligence** on Earth (aka, seed, organism, and environment)—via both evolutionary and developmental processes—is an **undiscovered universal law**. We hope to see this hypothesis tested in coming years.

C. Convergences, Optima (TINA Trends) and Predictions

Seeing **convergence** requires the recognition of often hidden processes and conditions which interact in a way that reduces local variety and difference, moving complex systems toward a particular future state. In evo-devo language, convergence is a **developmental funnel**. Understanding when and why a system, or set of systems, is diverging (evolution) or converging (development) is a critical foresight skill. Diverging systems are in many ways increasingly unpredictable, while converging systems are typically the opposite.

Convergences happen when previously separated products, services, or processes gain much closer interaction, interdependence, or integration than which presently existed between them. Technological convergence, in which a variety of previously distinct systems become represented by one standard, platform, simulation, product, or service, is a well-known example. Think of the communication modalities of voice, data, and video all migrating to a common internet backbone, or many different kinds of operating systems running on one virtual machine in software. Think both of **physical convergence**, where single devices gain multiple functions in the physical world, as in the numerous digital systems on a single chip, and of **virtual convergence**, as in the many apps using the same software in a smartphone.

For an example from the global domain, think of the convergence of our socioeconomic systems on a common set of values, including **evidence-based thinking** and **social democratic capitalism**. For one view on how rapidly East-West and North-South socioeconomic convergences are occurring, read **Kishore Mahbubani's** *The Great Convergence*, 2014. It is a nice follow-on to **Frank Fukuyama's** *The End of History*, 2006, which popularized this view. Global political convergence can be harder to see in the short term, where temporary reversals are common, and competing parties can fight the trends for a while. But, when we look back (and forward) over decades, the convergence pattern becomes clearer.

Optima are convergent processes that appear to be *maximizing* some **particular goal or value**. This maximization is occurring within a set of stable laws and constraints, some for the system in question, and some related to its environment. Scholars sometimes talk about optimizing for **evolutionary processes**, and foresighters might think of optimizing for client **preferences**, but we suggest reserving the term **optimization** for **developmental processes** alone. With most processes, (which are evolutionary, per the 95/5 Rule) we **experiment**, rather than optimize, and we "**satisfices**" or our environment "**selects**" for an adaptive degree of both diversity and preferred outcomes. Only **developmental systems** have enough **temporal and structural sameness** to them, across a **predictable life cycle**, for us to be able to rigorously talk of "**optimization**."

Developing systems have a framework of **laws** and **constraints** (**associations**, **dependencies**) that describe them, and any optimizations that happen to them must occur within that framework. That means, noticing as many of the likely laws and constraints on a system as possible is equally as important as predicting what goal or value appears to be being optimized by the system.

We will discuss **TINA Trends** (the name means "There Is No Alternative" to the trend, over the long term) in *BPF*. **Various forms of exponential technological change** (data, sensor, computation growth) are good examples, but so are others, like advancing democratization, globalization, and ever growing human and other sentience rights, abilities, and entitlements. Our best understanding of TINA trends requires taking a developmental, optimization-centric perspective on certain processes of change. If we remember that our planet is a **complex system of finite size**, with accelerating technological linkages, a system becoming more integrated and interdependent every year—we recognize ways that it is very much like a **developing embryo**. We can then ask which of our **TINA trends appear developmental**, and learn to see hidden ways that their progress is analogous to **biological development**.

For example, if we don't understand that there is *something* (in our current model, Hox genes, and their regulatory networks) *acting to constrain* developing embryos into expressing a **particular framework** of segmented body plan and tissue architectures at certain future places and times, we cannot **anticipate** how those networks—along with cellular signaling, cellular migration, and chemical diffusion in a **developing brain**—will **optimize** for the emergence of **specific patterns of neural connection**. We have found many predictable patterns in all higher brains, so we know some kind of optimization is occurring—despite that the vast majority of the microarchitectural patterns in each brain will differ, even when we compare **genetically identical twins**. But, at each stage of development, the more of the **laws and constraints** on the developmental system and its environment we understand, the better our ability to describe **optimization**.

Developing a quantitative model of optimization is today a very tall order, for any complex system, and such models still elude us in many domains. Even **biological development** still has few such models. The amazing biologist Eric Davidson (1937-2015) was able to develop a fully predictive, optimization-rich model of the **first few weeks of sea urchin development** over the course of his long career. Davidson won the International Prize for Biology for this work in 2011. We wish that Davidson had received a Nobel Prize for this work prior to his death, as **quantitative models of development** are both **very difficult and very important** to the advancement of **evo-devo biology** and **evo-devo systems theory**. In the meantime, given the scarcity of such strongly predictive models, we make the best guesses that we can about optimization processes under constraint, in life, in society, and in our universe, waiting for our science and senses to grow sharper.

Predictions, forecasts of emergences of specific events, structures, or outcomes in future space and time, are the last developmental factor we shall consider. Unlike optimizations, predictions don't have to be developmental: we can predict an evolutionary possibility (an experiment that will be tried), an evo-devo preference (and its associated strategies and plans), or a high-probability or "inevitable" development. We can attach probabilities to all of these predictions, but those probabilities will have a very wide range. In other words, they'll typically be low probability for most evolutionary events, and much higher, with narrower confidence intervals, for developmental events.

Prediction is an **art** much more than it is a **science**, but that doesn't mean it isn't a valuable art. It is our hope that this *Guide* will bestow confidence in everyone to engage in significantly more prediction across all the probabilities, despite how imprecise our abilities may be today. Engaging in **implicit prediction** is one way we create **Weeble stories** (stories that can take diverse criticism, and pop back up, just like a Weeble). Prediction is a double-edged sword. **Good prediction** can focus our strategy and effort, increase competitiveness, and guide and improve our scanning and sensemaking Bad prediction can dangerously narrow our forward view, and make us miss both opportunity and risk.

Perhaps now is a good time to meditate on a few predictions: Would we predict that a **universal basic income (UBI)** must emerge in all technologically developing societies, on average, as some function of factors like growing technical productivity and societal wealth? Would we predict that both China and the Soviet Union must eventually become significantly more representatively democratic, as some function of factors like technical productivity and middle class wealth and access to personal AI? Or will these and other autocratic nations be able to use accelerating technological capabilities to continue to protect their dehumanizing political systems throughout the 21st century, as great foresighters like **Harrison Brown**, in *The Challenge of Man's Future*, 1954, famously worried about? In our view, no matter how wealthy or technically advanced they become, **autocratic and homogeneous** social and political systems, like China, will always be limited by **lower trust and influence** relative to more liberalized systems, as global complexity grows. We shall see.

Many future events or structures can be perceived and predicted in advance, if one has good enough **systems knowledge**, access to discriminating evidence or experiments, and sufficient clarity of thought and vision. We welcome you to share with us any of your own societal predictions and evaluations. Most importantly, thank you for predicting, as well as innovating. The more we anticipate the better predictors we become, both individually and as a community.

3. Innovation Methods Overview

We have said that good foresight starts with careful **learning** about the problem, issue, or opportunity at hand, and then proceeds to **anticipation**, with a search for relevant high probability things, and carefully qualified language, that well-informed and ego-checked individuals may agree upon, to **constrain the possibility space** before we begin exploring it. Unfortunately, in practice, many individuals and teams prefer to do the **reverse**, to start with imaginative and "**Innovation-centered**" **evolutionary** thinking. We've called this tendency **freedom bias**. Just like its partner, **negativity bias**, we have argued that freedom bias has many destructive effects on the **quality** of foresight we produce.

Per the **95/5 Rule**, **imaginative (innovation-oriented) thinking** is humankind's favorite heuristic, or mental shortcut, for modeling how the world works. We all **create our own narratives** for how the world works, depicting what we value in favorable light. We love the freedom of a story-first approach. So, it makes sense that many of us prefer to "**start with possibilities**" before we move to probabilities. But if we don't **constrain those possibilities first**, we can easily **get lost** in a wilderness of entertaining but low probability stories. Fortunately, the **LAIS strategic foresight framework** is not too difficult to follow for those of us who love freedom, because it too starts with freedom. But *not* with freedom to create future stories, instead, LAIS starts with **freedom to investigate and learn**. The LAIS framework uses a **divergent-convergent-divergent-convergent heuristic** that we believe is uniquely adaptive.

Above all, remember that in practicing the **Four Ps**, and **evo-devo foresight**, we need to use both **evolutionary** and **developmental** approaches, always working **in tension** and sometimes **in conflict** with each other. Recall that Skill 1, **Learning**, begins with **divergent thinking,** which is especially helpful when we **don't yet know enough** about a topic or system to think broadly or systematically about it. We begin by exploring and mapping possibilities with respect to what to investigate. Such learning leads naturally to Skill 2, **Anticipation**, where we **converge** on a small, relevant set of probable trends, constants, constraints, convergences, predicted emergences, and other futures. Once we have this **rough framework** for the "probable future" in mind, we are well prepared to **diverge again**.

In Skill 3, **Innovation**, we **mentally** (with imagination) **and physically** (with design and prototyping) **explore** a variety of "possible futures" well prepared by our learning and anticipation efforts. Then, after we've diverged into the possibility space, with a sufficiently cognitive and experience diverse group of innovators and designers, we are well prepared to **converge again**. Skill 4, **Strategy**, supplies us with **sentiment contrasted** visions, goals, priorities, guiding policy, and coordinated action plans and tasks, helping us get what we want and prevent we want to avoid.

We believe the **alternating evo and devo structure of the LAIS framework** is essential to producing **adaptive foresight**. Every great leader and facilitator can become **adept** at it, intuitively sensing when it may be a good time to shift among these skills and conflicts, or at least, to solicit feedback from stakeholders. We want to start our **learning**, about past and present, with **evolutionary**, **experimental thinking**, but not our future thinking. If we start our journey through the **Four P's** with evolutionary thinking, we will have far more territory to wade through on our way to a solution. On the positive side, we may uncover more factors and contingencies that will need to be assessed for their probability, and that can be worthwhile. But, on the negative side, we can much more easily get **sidetracked** in unimportant and low-probability considerations. This said, let's look at some evolutionary foresight factors now.

A. Imaginations, Combinatorials, Emergences and Divergences

Our **imaginations** are the bedrock of evolutionary foresight. Innovation as a skill begins with imagining something (an idea, a product, a service) that might be valuable enough to be adopted, by someone, somewhere.

<u>Brainstorming</u> is the technique most commonly associated with imagining. It is a process that begins with uncritical and "high quantity" idea production that can open us up to seeing outcomes that we didn't realize were possible. Using design thinking, reading science fiction and creative literature, using CLA and other methods can greatly expand our ability to imagine outcomes. Methods like <u>futures wheels</u>, which visually map possible consequences and outcomes via causal chains, branching out from the central trend, event, or issue being explored, are another helpful way to **graphically prompt** our imaginations to **map a possibility space**.

Another well-used evolutionary foresight approach is the exploration of *combinatorials* of possibilities. This can be done at a fine level of granularity, with methods like <u>cross-impact analysis</u>, a way of exploring outcomes by putting causal factors, issues, or other entities in an n-by-n matrix, or a low dimensional set of matrices, and exploring all the ideas or outcomes suggested by combining each of those entities. Many locations on the matrix can be silly, causing us to consider combination of words and ideas that don't make sense. But, trying to make sense of strange combinations can also be insightful, surfacing new circumstances and possibilities that we have not yet considered.

We can also explore outcome possibilities at a coarse level of granularity with methods like <u>scenario production</u>, which ask us to determine particularly **important** and/or **uncertain** outcomes, causes or driving forces, on just a few dimensions, and build stories about the futures that would exist if those particular combinations occurred.

Emergences, or the looking for emergent new <u>complex adaptive systems</u> that are more than the sum of their combined parts, occurring via the collective interaction of simpler rules and systems, is another powerful way to explore the possibility space. A few emergences will be developmental, but of course the vast majority will be evolutionary, useful in particular times and places, but not broadly optimal. **John Holland's** *Emergence*, 1999, and **Steven Johnson's** *Emergence*, 2002, offer good introductions to this universal process. **Miller and Page's** *Complex Adaptive Systems*, 2007, is a respected technical work. Thinking carefully about the **conditions necessary for emergence** of new complex adaptive systems in physics, chemistry, and biology, can help us to look carefully for those conditions in society and technology.

Another set of powerful, engineering-based tools of possibility foresight involve the structured exploration of **divergences** from our current condition. Futures wheels can do this at a basic level, but there are many more powerful formal methods like <u>TRIZ</u>, <u>morphological analysis</u>, and <u>degrees of freedom analysis</u> that can be used to explore the dimensionality of complex systems. One particularly promising approach in the exploration of divergences is to look especially hard for those newly emerging systems, platforms, or tools that will **greatly improve the thinking or behavioral options available to people**. Emergences like electricity, cars, computers, phones, and software often create powerful divergences, greatly expanding the societal possibility space.

With our individually limited thinking ability, we are often quite poor at thinking through what will happen next at divergence points. Any new tool may have thousands of potential applications, and once it arrives, we often see only a few of them. By working in large and cognitively- and experience-diverse networks, we can overcome many of our individual thinking limitations. It is particularly helpful, when some new freedom like Twitter emerges, to look for the **"killer app"** for that tool, the most developmentally dominant users and contexts. We have to mentally consider many possible use cases before we see that Twitter will be **particularly useful** for celebrities and other "broadcasting" social media users, and for quick crowd updates using smartphones, as in the <u>Arab Spring</u> (2010-2012).

B. Uncertainties, Unknowns, Opportunities, Risks and Wildcards

Mapping potentially relevant **uncertainties** (variables proposed, but with poorly bounded values) and **unknowns** (variables unknown and unbounded), by surveying or doing a Delphi with a cognitively diverse group of stakeholders, will offer the foresighter many additional possibilities. We can ask our stakeholders questions about what outcomes or issues they are worried about or fear, and what things they have little knowledge of which they nevertheless imagine may turn out to be relevant.

Uncertainties and unknowns can often be narrowed by doing some research, or **learning**. We can brief others about our findings and step through a quick survey or Delphi to see if there is any consensus, or take them mentally through a **Do Loop** to see what action items and feedback they generate. As our foresight grows, we can subdivide and better characterize many of them into other foresight categories (opportunities, risks, wildcards, etc.).

Opportunities are possibilities that we value. Discussing these, we've moved into **preference** foresight. The way we generate opportunity lists and maps today is typically very evolutionary, bottom-up, contingent, and subjective. That kind of approach probably makes the most sense in most circumstances. Developmental approaches to opportunities include methods like <u>real options analysis</u>, which seek to quantify the relative probability of outcomes, and the relative value of competing business investments. These methods are much harder to practice, in our current computationally and quantitatively weak state. Once we have reasonably smart Personal AIs to help us, we can presume that more quantitative and predictive approaches to opportunities will rapidly grow.

Risks are possibilities we want to prevent. <u>Risk management</u> has a large number of formal methods, many of which involve estimating probabilities. Yet the 95/5 Rule reminds us that risk assessment will always be **primarily an evolutionary, creative act**. Fortunately, the more **imaginative** and **cognitively diverse** our group, the better we can see the **risk landscape**. And of course, the more practice they have with anticipation (forecasting and prediction), the more accurate their probability assessments, and the narrower their variances, can become See **Doug Hubbard's** *The Failure of Risk Management*, 2009/2020, for a good overview of the promise and limits of this foresight specialty.

Wildcards are low probability, high-positive or high-negative impact events. Technically, they are a special subset of **probable** futures. So why do we list them as an important factor in **evolutionary** foresight? Two reasons. First, very low probability events are actually better thought of as possibilities than probable futures. Second, people who are very good at looking at the world from creative, evolutionary perspectives are often the best at finding and mapping wildcards. As they are low probability, it often takes a creative thinker willing to sift through many possibilities, in order to uncover them. At that point we need a developmental frame of mind to categorize them as low probability (a wildcard) or as higher probability (an opportunity or risk). But, looking for wildcards typically starts in an evolutionary manner. Choosing to take wildcards seriously (rather than ignoring or dismissing them), and then carefully searching for them, are key steps (and common blocks) to evaluating them. Creative thinkers tend to do both of these things well. Two good books on wildcards are futurist **John L. Peterson's** *Out of the Blue*, 1997, and **Nicholas Taleb's** *The Black Swan*, 2010.

C. Stories, Causes, Assumptions, and Beliefs

We humans make sense of our complex and mostly unpredictable world in at least three key ways. Most simply, we **tell stories**, what futurist **Sohail Inayatullah** calls our "litany," about the topic or system we seek foresight on.

We also think in terms of **causes**, imagining a range of causal factors that have led to where we are, and that control where we are going. We may not widely tell all of those causes as stories, especially if there would be social repercussions. But, we will often share them in small groups, when there is trust, and even more when confidentiality is assured.

We also build an ever-growing **network of assumptions and beliefs** into our thinking. Some of these are mentally available to us, and some are hidden, uninspected and unrefined, within in the models, institutions, myths and metaphors that we live by. These evolutionary factors, along with any developmental factors we also recognize, work together to create our **worldview**, and thus our "future view."

The foresight method of **Causal Layered Analysis (CLA)**, developed by Inayatullah, is a great way to surface and critique these factors. *The CLA Reader*, **Sohail Inayatullah** (Ed.), 2004, offers many case examples of the method. CLA creatively explores many facets of the current view of why we are where we are, as various groups perceive their environment, and some of the ways our current set of stories, causes and assumptions limit our views of the past, present and future. The 95/5 Rule tells us that most of the story elements that CLA typically uncovers will be evolutionary. CLA will also uncover developmental factors, but it doesn't seek to evaluate them as such. Thus it is primarily an **evolutionary** foresight tool.

Inayatullah, 2004

In John's experience with CLA, the first two levels of CLA, **Litany** (what we all *say* is important, or is causing current conditions) and **Causes** (what we *think* may be causing current conditions) are particularly helpful for quickly seeing the current possible future view. CLA's next two layers, **Structure** and **Metaphor**, both involve **assumptions** we make about the **actual causes**, and the **responsibility for causes** that we attribute to actors, structures, and functions relevant to the system and problems in question. Once litany, causes, and assumptions are listed or "**mapped**," we can **question** these maps, and ask if there are others that we can imagine, or that may be used in other cultures, or in previous eras, that may also be relevant. Such practices can open us up to **possibilities** that we need to see, in order to better evaluate them.

4. Strategy Methods Overview

Strategy is a vast topic, but there are many simple, useful things that can be said about it. We've already discussed strategy as the last step in the **LAIS foresight framework**, and why we should prepare for strategy with **predictive and sentiment contrasting**. The foundation of strategy is a firm understanding of **systems** that appear to operate in the world, and the ability to use **models and frameworks** to describe and manage outcomes that we care about.

A. Systems Models and Frameworks

We've said that <u>systems thinking</u> and <u>systems theory</u> are foundations of foresight. **Model-making and testing,** in turn, is are core practices in systems analysis. Many useful <u>models</u> (simple simulations of complex systems) and <u>frameworks</u> (guidelines for doing professional work) have been developed in the last sixty years of foresight practice. We constantly use such tools to make sense of and manage the world.

Whether they are unconscious or conscious, implicit or explicit, informal or formal, our **systems models** are the foundations on which we build our practice. They are our mental "maps of what matters." Thus, models can also be dangerous, as they can **bias us** to prefer certain foresight <u>methods</u> and certain specialty practices to produce foresight. Models can limit what we pay attention to, and if we aren't careful or humble enough, even what and how we perceive.

Knowing which complex systems are most relevant to our problem, and which models or frameworks are the best fit for our needs, usually isn't obvious, and comes with experience. Reviewing the literature advocating each model to find <u>case studies</u>, and judging whether those are similar to ours, can be very helpful. But, the first step is to be aware of the great breadth of models that have proven beneficial in foresight work.

Some practice models and frameworks—like the Eight Skills, ADOR analysis, freedom and negativity bias, the division of strategic visions into Preferable and Preventable futures, and the importance of ethics and empathy in our thought an and action—seem particularly foundational to producing adaptive foresight. We will each have to decide how plausible, evidence-based, and relevant these models are to our own strategies.

B. Visions (Preferable and Preventable) and Values

As MIT Sloan management scholar **Peter Senge** argues, **shared visions** are the kind of foresight that people **care the most about**. Probable and possible foresight is much less motivating to people, even though we need to perform them both to better see our strategic options. Senge describes shared vision creation in his classic *The Fifth Discipline: The Art and Practice of the Learning Organization*, 1990. He notes that developing shared vision begins with the **learning** step, with formal and informal process of **elicitation** of the visions of all the stakeholders. This is advice fits well with the **95/5 Rule**, that most change must be driven **bottom-up**, and with **Steven Covey's** life habit "Seek first to understand, then to be understood." Once we know the variety of visions that exist, we've got an ability to craft our own **positive and negative visions** that will be consistent with most of our stakeholder's values.

Most importantly, as the futurist **Art Shostak** would say, good visions should be both **preferable** and **preventable**. They tell us what we want to **achieve** and what we want to **avoid**. They also should have an appropriate **time horizon**. Remember the **Power Law of Future Thinking**. Most future thinking, by **frequency**, but not necessarily importance, is very **short-term**.

Shared visions for the **next quarter** can be very concrete and measurable, and they often treat values only implicitly. Great examples are discussed in **Jack Stack's** *The Great Game of Business*, 2013. We can encourage everyone in our organizations to use **single-page P&L and balance sheets**, work together to set **bonus plans** (shared financial visions), and determine their own performance goals using **OKRs**. Shared visions for the longer term, as in classic **visioning workshops** for an organization's **mission and vision statement**, require values discussions and consensus. This **long-term preferencing** work is less frequent but also important, and it can help us improve the implicit values in our short-term visions.

As with most **strategic plans**—which should be simple, near term, and frequently revisited—the majority **of our visioning** should be simple, near term, and frequently revisited. **Visualizing** achieving our short-term visions is typically far more useful than visualizing our long-term visions, though it can occasionally be helpful to **backcast** from our long-term visions, to see our best next strategies.. Great athletes spend by far the most time previsualizing their upcoming performance, and only a little time imagining their legacy. Today's and short-term foresight is where **our fastest Do Loops** and our greatest **learning** always lie.

Visions are actually one aspect of a more basic strategic challenge: **diagnosis**. We must **diagnose** both where we stand (current status) and our opportunities and traps (positive and negative shared visions). We've said that in **Richard Rumelt's** three-step model of strategy, diagnosis is the first step of strategy. Let us return to that helpful model now.

C. Diagnoses, Policies, and Action Plans

Strategy is the most recognized "**end product**" of foresight work. But, we've seen that this is a great **oversimplification**: foresight professionals not only depend on the **LAIS skills**, they must engage in and facilitate **action** and **review** of their work, using the **EIRR skills**, to make it better in the next iteration.

They also must ensure that their work either **includes** or **dovetails** with **strategy production**. Recall that **Rumelt** says in his excellent *Good Strategy / Bad Strategy*, 2011, all good strategy contains at least three elements:

1. A **diagnosis** of the status, opportunities, and obstacles facing a system.
2. A **guiding policy** giving the direction forward, and aiding daily decisions.
3. A **coherent set of actions** (feasible achievements, resource commitments, plans, incentives, measurements, consequences) to manage the guiding policy.

Note that Rumelt's Strategy model begins explicitly with **Learning** and **the last two Ps**. In our view Rumelt's diagnosis step implicitly includes **predictive contrasting** as well. This makes it an excellent **LAIS-centric framework** we that we recommend to leaders and students alike. Let us repeat Rumelt's prescient observation that many firms and teams **do not have a true strategy**, but rather a loose set of **goals, plans, and slogans**. Is that true for your team? If not, you can address it now, and revisit your strategy every quarter. Moreover, if the foresight professional does not have the experience or training to produce effective strategy, or is not familiar with modern strategic management, they must **work with professionals who can**. As we said in Chapter 3, knowing where we fit in the **Management Value Chain**, and working with the best specialists we can in that value chain, is imperative to producing impactful work.

D. Unintended Consequences and Complications

Finally, in crafting strategy, it is critical for us to recognize all the ways our strategy has **floundered in the past** and is likely to do so with our current plans as well. Systems thinkers know that complex systems will often create effects that are hard or impossible to predict. **Unintended consequences and complications** must be **managed**, and we must seek to be **antifragile**, growing stronger from their stresses on us.

William Sherden's *Best Laid Plans: The Tyranny of Unintended Consequences and How to Avoid Them*, 2011, is a humbling overview of the many ways our personal, business, and political plans can be expected to go off the rails. Sometimes we encounter vicious cycles in which repetition makes the outcome worse, as in armoring Humvees in the Iraq War, making them sitting ducks for ever more powerful IEDs. Sometimes we get domino effects, where false stories get rapidly amplified in social media, causing mass outrage or extremist behavior. Sometimes we simply don't see all the causal relationships in a complex system. The mandated use of ethanol in US gasoline caused soaring corn prices and increased world hunger in all the developing countries that subsist on corn. NASA found that the Clean Air Act's success in reducing US airborne sulfate emissions contributed to the rapid warming of the Arctic.

Sherden, 2011

Sherden describes eight mechanisms that complicate our outcomes in unpredictable ways, and explains how better monitoring these mechanisms can allow us to anticipate some otherwise surprising negative consequences. We ought also to build our personal, team, organizational, and societal intelligence (sensing), agility and resilience, so we are ready to respond when these outcomes occur. Futurist **Andrew Zolli's** *Resilience*, 2013, is a great introduction to building resilience, so that we are ready for those consequences, even when we don't anticipate them. Understanding and managing the Law of Unintended Consequences is critical to sound strategy.

III. Foresight Methods: 150 Ways to Practice the Eight Skills

This section lists roughly **150 useful strategic foresight methods**, classified via the **Eight Skills**. Methods can also be classified by the **Twenty Specialties of Strategic Management**. A **brief description** of each method is also given. You can find more detail on many of these methods in the professional books cited in the Appendix.

When used on teams, any foresight method may involve the use of many or all of the Eight Skills. Nevertheless, we think every method, tends to rely on one (or a few) of the Eight Skills over others. You may or may not agree with our categorization, but propose that thinking of methods in terms of the **Eight Skills**, which are themselves grounded in the **Foresight-Action cycle**, and also adjusting for any **methods preference biases** across the **LAIS skills,** will both strengthen your foresight work.

In comparison to worldviews, causal models, and practice frameworks, foresight methods are **tools** that can be applied in a great variety of specific contexts. Most foresight texts simply list methods, A-Z, and leave the reader to figure out when they might be appropriate. We choose to list our field's methods in the context of the Eight Skills. This gives the practitioner some insight as to when the method might be worth experimenting with.

We feel our first job in Book 1 of the *Guide* is to introduce the **great value of foresight** and the **immense variety** of useful models, frameworks, and methods. Another goal we have is to **promote experimentation** with these practices—to help you find your **favorite models, frameworks, and methods** for different contexts. Yet another goal, as you gain confidence in the field, is to encourage you **develop and share your own versions** of these foresight tools.

To avoid overwhelming the reader, and being superfluous with other texts, we have explained just a few unique foresight methods, like **Sprint Reading.** We leave most methods, including popular but overused and overly simplistic methods like scenario production, to be explored by the reader. Scenarios are just one of 150 methods listed below. A good practitioner knows and uses **dozens of methods**, in the appropriate contexts. If we develop a *Workbook*, we will use it to offer **tutorials on a selection of methods**. Meanwhile, for a good **workbook on methods**, we recommend the first book below. For others, see Appendix 3, which lists a number of professional foresight books focusing on particular methods.

Here are three good **Foresight Compendiums** that describe methods in context:

1. **Jerry Glenn and Ted Gordon's** *Futures Research Methodology, V3.0,* 2009, available in electronic form ($50) is a great resource on **thirty-seven foresight methods or categories of methods**—with history, strengths, and weaknesses for each. At 1,300 pages, *Futures Research Methodology* is a great **methods compendium** for practitioners. We highly recommend it as a **tutorial complement** to this *Guide*. It is informed by a global network of foresight practitioners who participate in Glenn's *Millennium Project*. **Glenn and Florescu's** *State of the Future* report is also highly recommended. The *2017 edition* is the most recent, as this book goes to press.

2. **Wendell Bell's** *Foundations of Futures Studies, Volumes 1 and 2*, 1997/2004, offers a general overview of methods in **strategic foresight** (Volume 1) and **normative foresight** (Volume 2). We recommend it for those who want an excellent treatment of the **history and purposes of our field**. This work is still considered by many the definitive

professional text in our field. The organization and two-volume structure of our *Guide* has similarities to *Foundations*. It is one of several ways this classic text has inspired us.

3. **Richard Slaughter and Andy Hines's** edited <u>Knowledge Base of Futures Studies</u>, 2020, is a great compendium of the **diverse views and methods of current practitioners** in our field, and another **excellent complement** to this *Guide*. Originally published in 1993 and again in 2005 by the great Australian critical futurist <u>Richard Slaughter</u>, this work has been updated with a grant from Association of Professional Futurists—our field's leading professional organization. In **four volumes**, with **31 chapters** and **37 authors**, *KBFS* demonstrates the **great value and diversity of foresight as a profession**. At the same time, it has notable differences in tone and assumptions from this *Guide*. As an edited volume with a diversity of worldviews, *KBFS* does not take an **evo-devo perspective** on societal change. Many contributions highlight the downsides of **growth-obsessed consumer capitalism and plutocracy**, but none explore the **self-correcting nature of complex networks** in human history. Ignoring developmental processes, many contributors also have an **anti-prediction bias** with respect to **societal**, **global**, and **universal change**. Neither **accelerating change**—with its **ever more resource-efficient inner-space direction**, nor **AI as a network learning system** are properly represented. Neither societies nor machines are contemplated as **evo-devo systems**, necessarily self-stabilizing via evo-devo values, like the **IES goals**. Appreciate this fine work for what it is, but keep its **assumptions** in mind. We make different ones.

Slaughter & Hines, 2020

Those willing to explore older literature, including texts written during our field's last great **Foresight Spring** (1960-1980), will find many more excellent compendiums of foresight methods. Books like **Dewey and Dakin's** <u>Cycles: The Science of Prediction</u>, 1947, **Kahn and Weiner's** <u>The Year 2000</u>, 1967, **Burnham Beckwith's** <u>The Next 500 Years</u>, 1967, **Jib Fowles's** <u>Handbook of Futures Research</u>, 1978, **Olaf Helmer's** <u>Looking Forward: A Guide to Futures Research</u>, 1983, and **Coates and Jarrett's** <u>What Futurists Believe</u>, 1989 are just a few of many highly impressive older works. See Appendix 3 for more.

There are a **great diversity** of methods, as we will see. Some have fallen out of favor simply because they have **no current champions** willing to test them for value or adapt them to modern practice. For anyone who finds a valuable method, we encourage **sharing it in a publication** in one of our field's professional journals (Appendix 3: Strategic Foresight Journals and Magazines). Reporting and quantitating our findings whenever possible will help our colleagues improve their intuition about the advantages and drawbacks of each method in different contexts.

Rafael Popper et al. of the U. Manchester Business School have done a great survey of foresight method popularity in <u>Global Foresight Outlook</u>, 2007. Popper' website outlines <u>thirty-three foresight methods, divided into Qualitative, Semi-Quantitative, and Quantitative categories</u>. Popper also developed the **Foresight Diamond** (pictured right) to display foresight methods along two axes: **Creativity** vs. **Evidence** (or in our language, Evo vs Devo), and **Expertise** vs. **Interaction-based** (or Individual vs. Collective practice). We find this a particularly **general and insightful** approach.

All method categorization schemes must be somewhat arbitrary. But, the better schemes—like Popper's, Glenn

The Foresight Diamond

Creativity

Wild Cards
Science Fiction
Simulation Gaming
Essays / Scenario writing
Genius forecasting   Role Play/Acting
Backcasting   SWOT   Brainstorming
Relevance trees / Logic chart   Scenario workshop
Roadmapping   Delphi   Survey   Citizen Panel
Expert Panel   Morphological analysis   Conferences / Workshops
Key/Critical Technologies   Multi-criteria   Voting / Polling
Quantitative Scenarios/SMIC   Stakeholders Analysis
Interviews Cross-impact / Structural analysis
Indicators / TSA   Patent analysis
Bibliometrics   Benchmarking
Extrapolation Scanning
Literature review
Modelling

Expertise   Interaction

Qualitative (19)
Semi-quantitative (9)
Quantitative (5)

R Popper (2008)

Evidence

Popper et al. (2007)

and Gordon's, and ours—will have some theory and evidence behind them. They will all attempt to be comprehensive and reasonably balanced.

A brief web search, using the **name of the method**, will usually uncover good articles, books, and case examples of most of these methods. A harder question is to know when to apply any particular method or set of methods. For this, we will need to acquire knowledge of the benefits and limits of each in past application, and identify a theory of adaptation applicable to our context. But, to gain this knowledge of the strengths and limits of each method, we will need practice. Books written by senior practitioners can shorten our learning curve, but they will not substitute for real experience.

To become more proficient in any of these methods, consider some of the **texts on methods** listed above or in our Appendix, conduct an **online consult** with a method expert, or join one of the **Specialty Foresight Associations** we've listed, where some (not all) of these methods are taught in training courses. Whether we learn a method on our own or in a group, we also need regular Do loop feedback, both from our client, and our results, if we wish to progress.

The **LAIS skills** are the primary responsibility of the foresight practitioner, and thus, they comprise our longest lists below, at **20+ methods each**. However, we must remember that all practitioners need to use some methods listed under **EIRR skills** as well, if we expect our foresight to be **implemented** and to generate **action**. Methods listed under the **Reviewing skill** in particular can help us assess our impact, keeping us **accountable** and **relevant** to our client's needs. Regardless of the methods we use, , we should all seek an evidence-based **model and vision of adaptation**, and **practice good values**, in every context of our work, to keep our methods focused on what matters over the long term.

The foresight methods listed below are presented in **alphabetical order** under each of the Eight Skills. Descriptions link to Wikipedia and other online content. **Circle the methods** you'd like to learn more about, or try with your next foresight problem. Are we missing any methods? Any mistakes in our descriptions? Edits? Additions? As always, let us know.

Networking and Job Hunting Tip: Each method below can be used in a **LinkedIn, Google Scholar, or general web search** to find communities, companies, and people who practice and value them. Every method below can help you solve problems, and may be the right tool for your foresight problem. **We wish you success in your methods journey.**

Skill 1: <u>Learning Methods</u> (Investigative thinking)

<u>Argument/Belief Maps</u> and <u>Mind Maps</u>
Graphical mapping of <u>schools of thought</u> or differences of opinion, and evidence or example, around a complex topic.

<u>Benchmarking</u>
Comparing one's processes and performance metrics to industry and company bests (related to competitive intelligence). Done globally to best effect.

<u>Causal Layered Analysis</u>
Multi-level critical analysis (litany, causes, worldview, metaphor) of events or processes to aid learning.

<u>Collective Intelligence</u>
Group methods (often public or open) of scanning, sensemaking, evaluating advantages, disruptions, opportunities, and risks (ADOR analysis).

<u>Competitive Intelligence</u>
Getting, analyzing, and using intelligence about competitors' activities, <u>intellectual property</u>, products, and customers.

<u>Cost Accounting</u>
Methods to learn the true costs of various current and potential business actions, to aid decisions.

Domain Mapping
Methods (<u>concept maps</u>, <u>relevance trees</u>, <u>social network maps</u>) to map an environment or problem domain.

Ethnography
Study of the cultural litany of foresight.

Emerging Issue Identification (Weak Signals)
Identifying events (for further analysis) that may grow into potential problems or opportunities.

Environmental Scanning
Processes for finding and monitoring external news and events of potential relevance to the client organization.

Interval Learning (Sprint Learning)
Timed learning sprints, with notetaking, review and sharing, rest/recovery, and more sprints. Spaced Repetition is one kind of interval learning. Builds learning speed and capacity, just like interval exercise.

Interviews
A mostly qualitative research tool for conversational information collection from human subjects.

Journaling and Diaries
Methods and software to report and self-assess our daily actions. Allows us to learn about ourselves.

Knowledge Management Platforms
Methods and software to capture, map, monitor, filter, and route relevant organizational knowledge.

Leadership Development
Training and methods to develop managers into leaders in the firm's core business functions.

Literature Review
A summary of theoretical, methodological, or practical knowledge on a subject.

Measurement & Signals Intelligence
Knowledge gained by sensing & measuring environmental activity, and monitoring communications.

Retrofuturism (Historical Foresight Analysis)
Study of the history of future litanies, models, predictions, and depictions.

Soft Systems Methodology
A method for systems modeling that uses consensus-seeking and non-quantitative approaches.

Surveys & Opinion Polling
Polling for qualitative and quantitative group data. Statistical surveys of characteristics of a population.

Systems Thinking
Domain mapping and qualitative causal modeling of critical stocks, flows, variables in systems of interest.

Technical Intelligence
Gathering, analyzing, using intelligence about academic, business, and other actors' R&D capabilities.

Triple Bottom Line (Sustainability, Social Responsibility) Evaluation
Organizational evaluations that assesses Social, Environmental, and Economic benefits. Some versions add Governance (representativeness, transparency, and effectiveness of decision-making) for a "Quadruple Bottom Line" evaluation.

Skill 2: <u>Anticipation Methods</u> (Probability thinking)

Actuarial Science
Risk data collection, reference class formation, and other methods of quantitative risk assessment.

Analytical Hierarchy Process
Use of hierarchical mapping and pairwise comparison for quant. decision-making, modeling, forecasting.

Bias Identification and Bias Mitigation
Finding cultural biases and cognitive biases in foresight environment, and exercises to mitigate bias.

Causal Modeling, Systems Analysis, and Simulation
Representing system actors and behaviors in causal models (eg, agent models)

Delphi
Classic method to seek convergence from groups via successive opinion and feedback cycles.

Developmental Foresight
Anticipating optimal, convergent, irreversible trends and emergences, at multiple system-levels.

Discontinuity and Wildcard Anticipation
Finding key trend reversals/discontinuities and low probability, high impact (positive or negative) events.

Evolutionary Foresight
Identifying processes of creative, divergent, unpredictable change, at multiple system-levels.

Forecast Value Added (FVA) Analysis
Predictive evaluation relative to the null hypothesis, to see if team's forecast truly beats a naive model.

Foresight Workshops
Facilitative and normative methods used in groups to generate desirable future states for the firm.

Genius Forecasting (Genius Visioning)
Gifted and respected experts are asked for predictions or aspirational visions, often outside their fields.

Intellectual Property Strategy
Defensive or offensive techniques to create or protect a firm's intellectual property.

Learning Curves
Modeling exponential, power-law, S-curve, U-curve, and experience curves, while seeking discontinuities.

Prediction Analysis
Examining past predictions and assessing their methods, bias, accuracy, and utility (benefit to cost).

Predictive Analytics
Techniques from statistics, modeling, data mining, and machine learning to make quantitative predictions.

Prediction Markets and Prediction Platforms
Markets and platforms for making predictions and finding the best predictors by subject area.

Psychological Trait Assessment (Personality Typing)
Diagnostic models for predictable psychological traits (OCEAN, StrengthsFinder, MBTI, DISC, etc.).

Reference Class Forecasting
Quantitative method of predicting the future by comparing to similar past outcomes (a reference class).

Retrodiction
Predicting a past event with our forecasting model, then seeking evidence for it. Good validation tool.

Resiliency Analysis and Resilient Control Systems
Infrastructure, policies and strategies to make a system resilient to damage. (Or better yet, to *benefit* from damage – see **Nick Taleb**, *Antifragile*, 2014)

Risk Avoidance, Risk Reduction and Risk Insurance Analysis
Risk prioritization, risk avoidance, reduction, and acceptance/insurance options and plans.

Risk Models and Risk Prediction
Building statistical models of risk occurrence, making them causally predictive.

Roadmapping (technology, product, policy, etc.)
A long-range research and planning technique. Matches strategic goals with enablers, blocks, and solutions.

Statistical Models
Probabilistic relationships between variables in math models, e.g. Demographic and Econometric models.

Trend Extrapolation and Regression Analysis
Acquisition and projection of historical time-series data as a forecast, subject to error and uncertainty.

Vulnerability Assessment
Qualitative risk assessment regarding potential accidents, crime, lawsuits, and other adverse events.

Wargaming
Strategy games that deal with threat and security operations of various types, real or fictional.

Skill 3: Innovation Methods (Possibility thinking)

Appreciative Inquiry
Collective inquiry into past or current best events, practices in a group, to better imagine what could be.

Brainstorming
Uncritical group idea generation ("quantity over quality"), usually followed later by critical methods.

Creative Visualization
Imagining achievable positive outcomes in detail, and strategies and actions that will help them occur.

Cross Impact Analysis
Creation of a matrix of future-relevant variables, exploration of how the variables may affect each other.

Crowdsourced and Open Foresight
Free, online, open access, incentivized process to crowdsource foresight opinions from an online group.

Debate and Point/Counterpoint
Time-limited researched arguments w/opposing views. Teams may have to argue views they don't hold.

Design Thinking
Innovation methods designers use to improve user empathy, design creativity, and problem-solution fit.

Entrepreneurship and Intrapreneurship
Identifying and starting a new business venture, and participating in its risks and rewards.

Expert Panels
Typically 15 or fewer subject matter experts tasked to generate ideas, analyze options, or give feedback.

Future Artifacts
Everyday objects or specific details about a future scenario that bring it to life, and provoke conversation and imagination about that possible future.

Futures Wheels
Graphical mapping of direct and indirect consequences of a particular process, change or event.

Gamestorming and Role-Playing
The use of facilitated games, interactive activities, dramatic environments for ideation and innovation.

Ideation Management Platforms
Software platforms designed to elicit, compare, and refine actionable ideas in a variety of categories.

Morphological Analysis
Analytical methods to map and explore the solution space for a problem domain (Example: TRIZ).

Rapid Prototyping
Rapid design and fabrication of prototype products, often via CAD-CAM, CNC or additive manufacturing.

Scenario and Narrative Development
Visions of future states and plausible changes leading to them. Many methods (Ex: GBN Method).

Six Hats
Six thinking modes helpful to facilitate team and personal idea generation and critique (**Edward De Bono**).

Speculative Literature
Alternate history, alternative futures, counterfactual history, future history, sci-fi, and future fiction.

User Experience Design
Innovations and experiments to improve usability, ease, and enjoyment of the product by customers.

Verge
Ethnographic foresight practice framework that shifts focus from the drivers to the impacts of change (**Richard Lum**).

Skill 4: <u>Strategy Methods</u> (Preference and Prevention thinking)

Action Research
A problem-oriented process of simultaneous planning, action, and fact-finding research.

ADOR Analysis
4U's variation on SWOT analysis, beginning with collection of relevant (and often accelerating) external advantages. Counters cultural and organizational DROA bias.

Backcasting/Backplanning
Envisioning a desired state and working backwards to derive critical action steps necessary to achieve it.

Benchmarking
Quantitative comparisons of a firm, industry, or region's activities or performance with others.

Benefit/Cost Analysis
Calculating and comparing benefits and costs of a project, decision, policy or plan of action.

Business Cycle Planning
Anticipating and using economic and business cycles to optimize decisions.

Contingency Planning/Options Planning
Generating plans for outcomes and options other than the usual (expected, surprise-free) plan.

Decision Modeling and Operations Research/Management Science
Bayesian and other statistical tools to optimize decision forecasts. Real Options Analysis is a top example.

Decision Support System
IT system that aids managerial decision-making, including less-well-structured, underspecified problems.

Emergent Strategy
Planning that is 95% bottom-up (local), and a critical 5% top-down. See **Kevin Kelly**, *Out of Control*, 1994.

Emerging Issues Analysis
Analysis of weak signals (emerging issues) currently growing in strength. Used in law and elsewhere.

Fitness Landscape
A 3D matrix, using two variables, often intangible (and surveyed) to visualize adaptive peaks and valleys.

Four-Factor Strategy
Four-factor model with six strategist types (operators, execs, admins, entrepreneurs, pioneers, visionaries).

Five Forces Analysis
Michael Porter's framework for industry analysis and business strategy development.

Historical Analysis and Cliometrics
Historical research of past events and data to better understand or predict the current environment.

Industry, Technology and Product Road-mapping
Expert collaboration to plan science, tech., and policy actions for industry and product development.

Long-Range Planning
Using long-range forecasts and alternative *futuring* to construct multiyear plans.

Objectives and Key Results (OKRs)
A largely bottom-up employee goalsetting method, pioneered by Intel in the 1970s. Refined by Google and others. Increasingly popular today.

Scenario Planning and Learning
Competing scenarios developed around important future uncertainties, used for learning and planning.

S.M.A.R.T. Goalsetting
Specific, Measurable, Assignable, Realistic, Time-constrained goalsetting criteria.

Strategic Management
Planning, executing, and assessing company activities to achieve, and maintain competitive advantage.

Strategic Thinking
Systematic thinking to generate options, plans and competitive advantage.

Strategic Planning
Determining and coordinating actions and resource allocations in service of goals.

SWOT Analysis
Assessment of the strengths, weaknesses, opportunities, threats in a given situation or environment.

Technology Readiness Analysis
Identifying and evaluating critical science and tech. regulating the development of a product or market.

Visioning (Normative Forecasting)
Leader or group creates preferable future visions (aspirational forecasts). Can be made quantitative.

Skill 5: Execution Methods (Product thinking)

Agile Software Development and Lean Product Development
Iterative and incremental product development methods, time-boxed sprints, and rapid user feedback.

Computer-Aided Design, Engineering, Manufacturing (CAD, CAE, CAM)
Computer-based software and systems for product design, engineering, and manufacturing.

Enterprise Resource Planning
Integrated suite of management apps for product development, supply chain, and workflow.

Lean Manufacturing
Waste-reducing manufacturing, with the firm's resources aligned to customer value production.

Objectives and Expectations Setting (Chartering)
Clarifying the proposed objectives of foresight work, managing team expectations for the process.

Project Management Software
Software that helps with project estimation, planning, cost control, collaboration, and administration.

Project Selection
Research and deliberation to define the project (collaborative plan) for proposed foresight work.

Quick Response Manufacturing
Management strategies and tools to shorten lead times and focus efforts on bottlenecks (critical paths).

Resilient Control Systems and Reliability-Centered Maintenance
Methods to achieve target levels of resiliency and reliability in business processes and assets.

Task Management Systems
Methods and software to organize, prioritize, and execute our daily actions (e.g. GTD, OmniFocus).

Work Environment Selection
Creating an online and physical work or retreat environment conducive to good foresight process.

Skill 6: <u>Influence Methods</u> (Market thinking)

Advertising and Digital Advertising
Marketing comm. used to encourage, persuade or influence an audience. Info source: Advertising Age.

Brand Management and Positioning
Establishing and maintaining a particular firm and product reputation and differentiating market position.

Conjoint Analysis and Substitution Analysis
Survey research on preferences and potential substitute goods for existing products and services.

Customer Analytics
Customer behavior analytics and behavior prediction. A branch of predictive analytics.

Customer Relationship Management
IT business system managing firm's interaction with customers. Sales, marketing, customer service, tech support.

Customer Segmentation and Target Marketing
Dividing a market into sets of customers with shared needs and priorities, and marketing by segment.

Direct Marketing
Direct-to-customer advertising, database marketing, and sales activities.

Market Research
Collecting and modeling qualitative and quantitative data on markets, customers. Example: Hype Cycle.

Mass Customization and Personalized Marketing
Automated client customization of product/service. In personalized mktg., each product can be unique.

Sales Force Management Systems
Computerized sales platform that includes contact management and sales lead tracking and forecasting.

Social Marketing
Marketing to influence behaviors that benefit individuals and communities for social good.

Social Media Marketing
Marketing that uses social media (Facebook, Twitter, etc.) or customer data from their social graphs.

Viral Marketing
Marketing to gain widespread social attention via web traffic, word of mouth, or other sharing behaviors.

Skill 7: <u>Relating Methods</u> (Team thinking)

<u>Advisor Management</u> and <u>Stakeholder Analysis</u>
Bringing diverse, representative, critical, and foresighted advisor and stakeholder feedback to mgmt.

<u>Business Ethics</u>
Normative (values, aspiration-driven) strategies and descriptive research to improve business conduct.

<u>Cognitive Diversity</u>
Bringing diverse <u>cognitive styles</u> and <u>personality types</u> to teams. See **Scott Page**, *The Difference*, 2008.

<u>Communications</u> and <u>Public Relations</u>
Goal-oriented methods of managing information flow between an organization and the public.

<u>Compensation</u> and <u>Benefits</u>
Wages, stock options, and non-financial benefits (group insurance, etc.) to retain and motivate employees.

<u>Culture</u>, <u>Morale</u>, <u>Fear Diagnosis</u>, and <u>Emotional Intelligence Development</u>
Improving firms' intellectual/emotional environments. See **Tom Reiger**, *Breaking the Fear Barrier*, 2011.

<u>Employee Engagement</u>
Monitoring and improving employees' physical/cognitive/emotional satisfaction, and motivation.

<u>Enterprise Relationship Management</u>
Mgmt. of industry alliances, suppliers, investors, acquisitions, customers, and other business actors.

<u>Organizational Development</u>
A planned, organization-wide effort to measurably increase an organization's effectiveness or efficiency.

<u>Strategic Communication</u>
Managed information and communications activities to advance objectives and plans of the organization.

<u>Succession Planning</u>
Development of primary and alternate leadership succession chains in critical business functions.

<u>Talent Acquisition</u> and <u>Team Selection</u>
Defining and recruiting appropriate talent, including specialist knowledge & cognitive diversity.

Skill 8: <u>Reviewing Methods</u> (Adjustment thinking)

<u>Balanced Scorecards</u>
Performance mgmt. report with a mix of financial and non-financial key performance indicators (KPIs).

<u>Change Management</u>
Methods for individuals, teams and firms to guide big <u>strategic change</u>. See Kotter, *Leading Change*, 2012.

<u>Critical Foresight/Futures Studies</u>
Using critical inquiry from social sciences to analyze and "deconstruct" systems. See **Richard Slaughter**, *Critical Futures Studies*, 1996.

<u>Criticism Solicitation</u>
Gaining honest critical feedback from clients and fellow foresight practitioners.

<u>Dashboards (Management Information Systems)</u>
An easy-to-read, single report or interface with real-time feedback on critical performance numbers.

Enterprise Feedback Management
Software and processes to centrally manage feedback survey authoring, deployment and analysis.

Key Performance Indicators (KPIs)
Management measurements of business performance, varying by department.

Objectives and Key Results (OKRs)
Simple, transparent objectives (goals) and key results (how, when, what you'll do to accomplish them).

Premortem
Leader proposes why a current team project has failed, asks for reasons for failure. Prevents groupthink bias.

Quality Assurance
Methods to make a product fit for its purpose, and right the first time, as determined by client feedback.

Six Sigma and Lean Six Sigma
Techniques and tools for process improvement using quality management and statistical methods.

Total Quality Management and Total Productive Maintenance
Methods and systems to ensure continuous quality improvement (TQM) and asset productivity (TPM).

Theory of Constraints
Management methods that seek out and mitigate the rate-limiting constraints on org. performance.

Turnaround Management
Methods (perf. reviews, auditing, root failure analysis, etc.) to save troubled firms.

Unlearning
Finding bad assumptions, methods, and habits—and changing them by mindfulness, accountability, CBT and behavior modification.

Using the Eight Skills: Joining Professional Development Communities

To conclude this chapter, we have listed below one **professional community** is particularly competent with each of the **Twenty Specialty Pairs** in **organizational foresight**. These communities are ideal places to study the usefulness and limits of the methods recently addressed, and to improve them and develop new ones. The communities listed under the first four of the Eight Skills below are thus particularly helpful for **strategic foresight**. In our judgment, the Association of Professional Futurists, and the Association for Strategic Planning tend to be the most systematic and conscious in applying **all four** of the LAIS skills. If you have further recommendations of communities helpful to organizational foresight, please let us know so we can expand this list in future editions of the *Guide*.

1. Learning Communities

> **Accounting and Intangibles**
> Institute of Management Accountants **(IMA)**.
> **Intelligence and Knowledge Management**
> Collective Intelligence Academic Community **(CIAC)**.
> **Learning and Development**
> Association for Talent Development **(ATD)**.

2. Anticipation Communities

> **Data Science and Machine Learning**
> Open Data Science Community **(OSDC)**.

Forecasting and Prediction
International Institute of Forecasters **(IIF)**
Investing and Finance
CFA Institute **(CFAI)**.

3. Innovation Communities

Alternatives and Scenarios
Association of Professional Futurists **(APF)**.
Entrepreneurship and Intrapreneurship
Founder Institute **(FI)**
Facilitation and Gaming
International Association of Facilitators **(IAF)**

4. Strategy Communities

Analysis and Decision Support
Institute for Operations Research and the Mgmt Sciences **(INFORMS)**.
Vision/Goalsetting/Strategy and Planning
Association for Strategic Planning **(ASP)**.

5. Execution Community

Management and Leadership
American Management Association **(AMA)**.

6. Influence Community

Marketing and Sales
American Marketing Association **(AMA)**.

7. Relating Community

Human Resources and Performance Management
Society for Human Resource Mgmt **(SHRM)**.

8. Reviewing Communities

Auditing and Change Management
Institute of Internal Auditors **(IIA)**.
Benchmarking and Quality
Balanced Scorecard Institute **(BSI)**.

Some parting advice in applying the **Eight Skills and their related methods**. Whenever you are unsure of how long or how strong to apply any skill or method, **look below it** to the **Do loop** on which these skills and methods are based. Keeping our **Do Loops** as fast, strong, high quality, and conscious as possible is the foundation of **personal foresight**. **Team and organizational foresight**, in turn, depend on our use of the Eight Skills, and in complex orgs, the Twenty Specialties We ought to commit these LAISEIRR skills to **memory** and **deliberately think about, practice, fail, and learn** with them every day. This is our most recommended strategy for **personal and professional success**.

Choose Wisely—Frameworks and Methods Matter!

Chapter 6: The Future of Foresight – Positive Trends and Visions

The Digital Supernova and Our New Foresight Spring

In his lovely book *Thank You for Being Late: Thriving in the Age of Accelerations*, 2016, **Tom Friedman** chooses **the year 2008** as the start of a **New Era of Speed** in human activities, catalyzed by a series of new **platforms and processes** he calls our "**Digital Supernova.**" Friedman is a journalist, and this book is a great easy introduction to some of the modern mechanisms of accelerating change. Friedman's sentinel example for this new era was the debut of the **Apple iPhone** in mid-2007. Apple sold just a million units to early adopters in that half-year, but then its sales jumped to 12 million in 2008, and the handheld computing world was off to the races. Google also formed the Open Handset Alliance and released Android 1.0 in November of 2007. By 2008, the **mobile digital world** was a state of **rapid mass adoption** and constant change. As he describes, the kinds of things we could do, both in the **cloud** and on our **mobile devices,** and the **complexity of the web,** began to **accelerate** in ways that had never happened before.

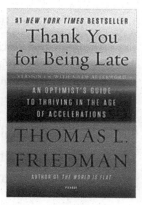

Friedman, 2016

Soon after, **technology titans** and **scrappy tech startups** alike were disrupting long established economic actors, and it became clear that whoever best harnessed these **forces of digital entrepreneurship** would be leading large parts of our future. Soon thereafter, we saw **deep learning AI** began to make major advances in simple pattern recognition in big data, first in the lab in 2010, and then commercially in 2012. Many other digital infrastructure advances, in payments, databases, and cloud computing, all emerged. By 2011, we had so many new tech companies worth over a billion dollars, less than five years after startup, that we gave them a funny name, "unicorns." By 2019, unicorns were everywhere, and the name no longer made sense. Right along with the Digital Supernova, we choose 2010 as **a good date** for the start of our latest **Foresight Spring**, a time of renewed and sustained interest in foresight practice and futures visions. **Foresight and futures interest** always tracks closely with **new bursts of change**, to help us make sense of the disruptions and opportunities they bring.

One of the helpful insights about the mobile digital revolution, in our view, is that it is **developmental**. Because of **universal D&D trends**, something like it eventually had to occur. Technologists, entrepreneurs, and politicians could have easily delayed or accelerated its emergence (and many good and bad digital choices were made prior to 2008), but its arrival was inevitable. By contrast, 2008 coincides with another disruptive event that was much less universe-driven than it was evolutionary, or fully human chosen. It was precipitated by the laws and ethics of America's current plutocratic and corporatist version of capitalism. The Great Financial Crisis of 2007-2008 caused much **hardship, and the ways we** responded to it, with bailouts for the rich and corporations, further increased **economic inequities** and **middle class vulnerabilities**. In its wake, the world saw a K-shaped recovery, where the rich get richer while the poor and middle class lose more relative ground. An even more rapid and extreme K-shaped recovery was occurring in the COVID-19 Recession, as this book went to press.

After 2008, **so many disruptive digital, technological, and economic changes** have suddenly bombarded us, and so many problems have become **global concerns**—including economic volatility, unaccountable elites, middle class erosion, democratic dysfunction, climate change, autonomous weapons, terrorism, and now pandemics—that the **demand for foresight** has grown to levels not seen in decades. As we said, great change always breeds great foresight and futures demand. There is now so much groundbreaking work happening in organizational foresight specialties—like forecasting, analytics, risk management, innovation management, planning, entrepreneurship, design, and intelligence—we are in a new **Foresight Renaissance**, one that will birth much useful new foresight science and methods.

The last time foresight work was in such high demand was during our **previous major Foresight Spring (1960-1980)** — particularly in the **1960's and early 1970s**, when many of our **founding think tanks**, **associations**, **and academic programs** emerged. If the past is any indication, this current spring should last at least as long (2010-2030). But in a world of accelerating change, we are hopeful that it will last even longer. Armed continuously now with our ever smarter mobile devices, and an ever richer cloud, we are seeing new levels of digital complexity arrive every quarter now. This complexity creates many new problems for us, including dysfunctional filter bubbles, fake news, privacy erosion, unconsented targeted advertising and manipulation, unethical AI use, and new forms of cybercrime. But we can also foresee good solutions to these problems as well. We just have to implement them.

We have many **new societal and global problems**, as we'll discuss in *BPF*. Yet at the same time, **amazing things** are again happening around us due to accelerating science and technology. Today's youth the world over are early technology adopters, and they expect **much more amazingness ahead**. Over the last decade, online foresight communities have reached scales never seen before. Reddit's r/Futurology, an community for posting and commenting on foresight material, has over **15 million subscribers** as of 2021. r/Futurology growth has now slowed, but many of Reddit's foresight subcommunities, like r/WallStreetBets, are still growing rapidly. General futures thinking in the US, among the lay and professional public, and formal foresight work by organizations, have again become popular.

As in the 1970s, our futures thinking is a broad mix of optimism and pessimism in outlook, by group and issue. Although our media are not incentivized to report it, there is much to celebrate, and many new freedoms and tools that need to be better explained to the world, for us to begin to use them well. For example, with the rise of **crowdfunding sites** like Kickstarter, 2009, and Indiegogo, 2007, tens of thousands of promising new global and local business ideas have been funded. In 2015, Equity Crowdfunding, aka "Crowdfounding," finally became legal, after a long fight against the plutocrats running the US Congress, and it is bringing new capital to our entrepreneurs, and democratizing startup and local company investing. For the first time, average income, non-accredited investors, once they gain confidence and foresight to do so, are investing in small companies via online platforms. Much of this entrepreneurship will fail, as it always does, but our economy needs both **diversity and occasional failure** to select the next winners, and make **progress**.

We've said that just as the **European Renaissance** (literally, European "rebirth") laid the groundwork for our sciences, we are in a new **Foresight Renaissance** today. It will contribute to a new **Enlightenment**. Among the fruits of this Enlightenment will be a better set of **social and hard sciences of foresight**, a longstanding vision of many scholars in our field. History tells us the **scientific method** is not one method, but a **diverse collection** of methods and models, the first of which emerged in the 17th century, and eventually matured into the set of enterprises we now call **science**.

Likewise, we have argued that **foresight** is not just a handful of methods, but a **diverse set** of useful theories, hypotheses, models, frameworks, and methods which may mature, perhaps in the mid-21st century, into a large, empirically-validated collection of industry and professional **practices**, and a set of **grounded qualitative and quantitative social sciences**— disciplines that can be investigational, anticipatory, innovative, and strategic (the LAIS skills) as appropriate.

Society as a complex system can be analyzed from a wide range of academic disciplines, including anthropology, biology, chemistry, cognitive science, development, economics, engineering, evolution, complexity, computation, cybernetics, information theory, linguistics, physical sciences, psychology, semantics, statistics, and systems theory, to name a few. These and other sciences are improving their methods and models, inevitably giving us better tools for investigation, anticipation, innovation, and leadership of social systems. So too will **foresight, as a diverse and vital human process**, eventually become a diverse collection of well-recognized **academic and practice disciplines**.

As social complexity grows, many developments are steering our field in a **more scientific and quantitative direction**. Most obvious are the accelerating advances in **information technology** since the mid-1990s, including the rise of the web, simulations, maps, sensors, mobile and wearable tech, social networks, enterprise software, cloud computing, and many others. These **permanent new developments in our species' computational and collaboration abilities** are creating an environment where far more of the world is <u>quantified</u>, **visualized, evidence-based, and statistically predictable**. We are even seeing promising developments in <u>economics</u>, a social science that will become much more predictive as it is now beginning to see and study **accelerating change**, and to model humanity's ever more **densified and dematerialized technical productivity**. See **Brynjolfsson and McAfee's** *The Second Machine Age*, 2014, futurist **Azeem Azhar's** *The Exponential Age*, 2021, and Book 2 of this *Guide*, for more on that exciting, emerging story.

The history of foresight practice is one of **competing schools**, each with their own conflicting worldviews, models, and visions of the future. We summarize those schools, and their historical conflicts, in Appendix 1 of *BPF*. Most disagreements are healthy, and they generate pressure for each school to clarify its assumptions, theory, and predictions, and seek experiments and evidence that would resolve their disagreements. In this way, step by step, our field advances.

The Future of Foresight: Eight Positive Trends

Foresight will one day be recognized as **vital to human thriving**, and taught, from birth, as a balanced fusion of **art, science, and practice**. It must strive to be **evidence-based**, and much more grounded in **how the universe and human minds work**. We have proposed that both **exponential** and **evo-devo models**, in some more rigorous versions than we can offer today, will be necessary elements of that grounding, along with many other elements we can only guess at today. Fortunately, we can point to many **developmental trends** taking us toward this positive future.

Let's look now at **eight trends in foresight practice** that offer a rough outline of the new type of foresight work emerging today. We focus here on trends that offer a **positive vision** of the future of our field over the next two decades.

1. Foresight is Becoming Digital

The accelerating **digitization** (simulation) and **automation** (algorithmic control) of increasing numbers of our planetary processes by our information technologies and machines is making modern foresight **quantitatively and qualitatively different** from previous human eras. As big data, social sharing, sensors, maps, simulations, and algorithms proliferate, many new collective and machine intelligence foresight tools and methods are emerging. In recent years we have seen the rise of predictive analytics, statistical models, crowdsourcing/funding, and ideation, innovation and prediction markets. An **acceleration-aware foresighter** knows that these and other D&D-driven practices going to be some of the **most powerful levers of change** that we can use in our work. When we understand the outlines of these and other developmental trends, we are be in a better position to **select**, **evaluate**, and **use** the best of these exponentiating tools and knowledge for our clients.

No acceleration in the world is more **obvious and easily measured** than that of **information production**. According to EMC, which tracks global digital information growth in its annual <u>Digital Universe</u> report (here's the <u>executive summary</u>), **digital data** is growing **55% a year**, doubling every nineteen months. That means sixty percent of the world's data was created in just the **last two years**. This incredible growth phenomenon is not expected or projected to **slow down** in the foreseeable future, as miniaturization machine-to-machine communication, and increasingly bio-inspired computation drive us relentlessly into **an ever smarter world**. [Fun fact: To honor this insight, and as a pun on his last name, John chose <u>Ever Smarter World</u> as the title of his personal blog.]

As we progressively digitize our world, our machines are using this data to **sense, see, model, and act** in the world. They learn at a rate that makes **biology** look like it is **standing still**, frozen in space and time. We are also increasingly **wedded to our machines**, using them to connect with others and to monitor and improve ourselves. When we are not careful, we use them to **enslave, distract, and addict ourselves** as well. Individuals, companies, and countries that smartly embrace this **great digitization**, and learn to manage the many **first-generation downsides** (unnecessary complexity, invasion of privacy, unnecessary expense, disempowerment, addiction, and crime) that impact many of us in this U-shaped **adaptation curve**, will lead this developmental transition well.

For an example of **foresighted digital policy**, see this great video on **Estonia**, "<u>Life in a Networked Society</u>," YouTube, 2013. Estonians have had secure internet voting since 2005. They make America look like it is in the stone age with voting, a critical right of citizenship. Businesses and residents pay simplified taxes online, and they lead the world in the <u>Tax Competitiveness Index</u>. At present, America is still struggling to get secure online voting, and our tax system is so complex and manual it is a drag on our economy. Foresight professionals who understand the **Great Wave of Digitization**, and can tell its story well, will long be in demand. This trend has many upsides and downsides, and it is a primary topic of Book 2. Appendix 3 lists a few good books that describe this great digital transition. Books like *The Age of Spiritual Machines*, 1999, *Blown to Bits*, 2008, *The Silent Intelligence*, 2013, *The Second Machine Age*, 2014, and *Humans 3.0*, 2015, are good introductions, but the story is vast. No single book sums it up well yet, or may ever.

2. Foresight is Becoming Data-Rich and Intelligent

The rise of **big data, intelligently analyzed**, is another very helpful way to grasp the new nature of foresight practice. Accelerating digitization creates vast new data pools, waiting to be better displayed to indicate current conditions, and analyzed for trends and hidden relationships.

When data in any field becomes **reasonably representative of** the system being studied, **classification systems**, **maps**, and **models** begin to stabilize. As machine learning helps us **organize**, **correlate**, and draw **conclusions** from that data, a crude **intelligence** begins to emerge in our collective knowledge. Perhaps nothing is a better example of this than **Google's Knowledge Graph**, and the **RankBrain** (neural network) algorithms it uses to provide more relevant and personal search results. As we will discuss in *BPF*, this algorithm is now smart enough to reduce the page rank on any web page that has three or more factual inaccuracies, according to Google's knowledge graph. That means it is **taking "fake" and falsehoods out of search**, as it learns. IBM's Watson AI, Google's DeepMind, and Open AI's Generative Pre-Trained Transformer software are just three of the more visible AI efforts making the news with new capabilities every quarter now. **Personal AIs** and the **knowledge graphs** they depend on will eventually anyone who **chooses to do so** (and many will not, at first) to live in a **far more evidence-based and intelligent learning and competitive environment**.

In writing this *Guide*, the authors were able to do many **web searches** to find key data. Those searches were backed by Google Brain, the fastest learning and improving digital neural network on the planet today. Many of our searches would have been useless back in 2000. We used Google Books to find key insights from books, Google Trends to see what problems and issues people are searching. We are all now truly live in a new world, with a new level of **global collective intelligence,** because data is becoming so organized and freely accessible. Like it or not, all this growing data and machine intelligence is a one way street. It is a **developmental**, not an evolutionary, process. We can **never go back** to our simpler, less digital past.

We are still *many decades* away from **general AI** (capable of human level logic, emotion, intuition, and morality), in our view; but over the next two decades, AI, automation, and robotics will become increasingly capable and pervasive. Ethical design, safety, trustability and regulation of its impact will be ongoing concerns. Every year forward, we will observe **more data and intelligence** behind foresight work. As **Klaus Schwab**, founder of the World Economic Forum says, we are now leaving the **Information Revolution** (our third technology revolution, after **Steam** and **Electricity**), and entering a **Fourth Industrial Revolution** one based on global sensing, data, AI , algorithms, robotics, and automation. See Schwab's *The Fourth Industrial Revolution*, 2017, for one good account of what is coming.

Today, **machine intelligence and AI** are primarily good at **feature detection** and simple **pattern recognition**, not **logic** or other complex processes. What they can do today is **greatly overhyped** by **startup CEOs, corporate marketers**, self-serving **futurists**, and **pundits** alike. Nevertheless, it is already useful enough to offer us many useful new services. As Schwab says, we are in the (very) early stages of an **AI and Automation Revolution**, one which will increasingly change society.

Much is happening at the intersection of data and intelligence today. **Machine learning** and **automated ontologies** are helping us to structure and contextualize our explosion of digital data, so we can better use it in our digital platforms and devices. Data wrangling platforms like Kaggle (Founded 2010, acquired by Google in 2017) now have tens of thousands of teams competing to solve **data science problems**. Platforms like Algorithmia, started in 2013, make it much easier to find or create algorithms for machine learning (data sensemaking) and automation. **Cloud data** platforms and **federated databases** are creating **shared pools of data**, and driving new insights in science, tech, business, government, environment, and culture. Yet we remain tribal. Much more collaboration could be happening.

Some of our more enterprising **foresight consultancies**, both smaller ones, like Shaping Tomorrow, and larger ones, like Deloitte, are also building machine learning into their platforms and services. Using data and today's AI has never been easier. Open source databases like Hadoop, and powerful AI suites like Google's TensorFlow, are posted free for public use on massive public code repositories like GitHub. There is still technical proficiency required, but every year forward, less proficiency will be needed, as the front ends to our leading AI development platforms will themselves increasingly use AI, and understand natural language requests and commands.

In the twentieth century, systems like **GIS (Geographic Information Systems), CRM (Customer Relationship Management Systems), KM (Knowledge Management systems)** and other database-backed software were among our leading aggregators of organizational data. Over the last decade, organizational and societal data flow has become a deluge. Now we have **smartphones, wearables, internet of things (machine-to-machine interaction), home automation, quantified self/fitness/health, sentiment analysis, social networks, conversational interfaces, and algorithmic trading** using and generating data, and this is just a very partial list.

We've described the rapidly emerging field of **predictive analytics**, well-introduced in books like **Eric Siegel's** *Predictive Analytics*, 2013. Books like **Nathan Yau's** *Visualize This*, 2011, and *Data Points*, 2013, help with **data visualization**. **Charles Wheelan's** *Naked Statistics*, 2014, helps with **statistical thinking**. Books like **Seth Stephens-Davidowitz's** *Everybody Lies*, 2018, and Bergstrom and West's *Calling Bullshit*, 2021, tell us the many ways data are often misused.

Most big companies now employ an internal or external **data science team,** working to help them better model themselves and their customers, anticipate their needs, and find hidden efficiencies lying in the data of how we all presently live, work, think, talk, buy, and behave. Almost all of this data (over 95%) is presently **untagged and unstructured**, but AI will change that in coming years. See **Scoble and Israel's** *The Age of Context*, 2013, for a brief intro to the way our digital tools are increasingly **learning our contexts as** they try to better **anticipate and serve us**, and some of the **privacy challenges and solutions** that are emerging as that happens.

On the governance front, the emergence of The Program—the NSA's massive **intelligence analytics platform** for warrantless wiretapping and mapping relationships between all human beings on Earth, foreign and domestic—became technically feasible in the early 2000s. But only in the last decades did our world become sufficiently data-rich, and our machines sufficiently powerful to do all this relationship building affordably. See Frontline's excellent *United States of Secrets*, 2014, for a recent account. As futurist **David Brin** said in his classic, *The Transparent Society*, 1998, the main societal problem is not growing public transparency. That is an inevitable and predictable global developmental trend. Our intelligence communities will *always* have, and in our view deserve, the best of these tools, to guard us against rogue individuals and small fanatic groups. The problem is our need to **protect individual liberties and privacy** as public transparency grows. Democratic societies need strong bottom-up personal and small business transparency tools to watch our communities, platforms, leaders, and politicians, and strong whistleblower protection to share information when laws are broken.

The NSA's **domestic surveillance program** became politically possible after 9/11, when we recognized it was going to be necessary to counter the exponential threats of the future. Unfortunately, it was instituted in secret, without public discussion or sufficient oversight, and is thus less than ideal **in structure** at present. Perhaps the most obvious **failure of democracy** is that our politicians have ducked ever putting this issue of transparency regulation to public discussion. What level of top-down vs. bottom-up (citizen-run) surveillance we should have going on within the US, given our current levels of global and domestic development, is a complex political issue. But what isn't a debate is that every nation and all digital corporations are now playing the **data accumulation game**, and **better rules** around data collection, sharing, editing, and data rights need to be established. Currently intelligence agencies, marketers, hackers, criminals, and others collect this data with a wide variation in legal justification, oversight, and transparency.

Finally, what is happening with data in America now pales in comparison to the **surveillance fishbowl** being constructed in China, where controversial technologies like **facial recognition** and **behavioral scoring** are already being used in many public settings, workplaces, and schools. America has a great opportunity to lead better on data standards, and to protect liberties while growing security transparency. At present **Europe is the clear leader** in this regard, with legal frameworks like the General Data Protection Regulations (GDPR), enacted in 2018. The California Consumer Privacy Act (CCPA), enacted in 2020, and inspired by Europe's GDPR, is the first of hopefully many more such laws that will protect Americans in our ever more data-rich and transparent environment.

3. Foresight is Becoming Probabilistic

As the genetic, cellular, organismic, and ecological **evo-devo processes** driving **human psychology** are increasingly understood, we're realizing that **intelligent beings are always predicting**, in all domains of our awareness, as one of our most fundamental methods of adaptation. In *BPF*, we will again see that prediction is at the center of our best models of the brain, like **active inference**, and it is central to how **networks** maintain **collective intelligence**. The naive belief that it's futile and irresponsible to predict, which is unfortunately common in much (not all!) professional foresight today, and the misunderstandings of both history and complexity science that are sometimes used to justify it, are yielding to the evidence-based belief in a **full continuum of statistical predictability in natural processes**, depending on the level of causality and the accuracy, scope, and timescale of our models. We're also understanding the factors that improve or degrade our probabilistic thinking—and how to strengthen our predictive faculties.

Theories and methods like <u>Bayesian probability</u>, one way of doing statistical reasoning from incomplete information, are gaining ever greater communities of practice, as our world gets more data-rich and intelligent. Of all the probable futures ahead, we're starting to realize that certain futures, including exponential information production, scientific and technological change, increasingly densified and dematerialized wealth production, and initially rising inequality as new production technologies emerge are predictable general processes. At the same time, these developmental processes are managed with great evolutionary variety in different regions, countries, cities, and firms. These growing realizations will in turn drive new social change.

One social change we are seeing now is that not only **scientists**, those who help us see hidden order in the world, but certain **entrepreneurial** and **technical innovators**, those with bold, positive visions, are increasingly heroes or role models in modern society. We saw this a bit in the twentieth century, with science popularizers like **Carl Sagan** and moguls like **Bill Gates** and **Steve Jobs**. More recently, entrepreneurial adulation has reached a new and sometimes unhealthy level with leaders like **Jeff Bezos, Elon Musk, Larry Page, Sergey Brin** and many others. Backed by the new power and scope of their technology platforms, these leaders are dreaming and executing at grand scale.

Some of this entrepreneurship is increasingly predictive and data guided. Leaders in streaming entertainment, including Netflix, Amazon, and Disney effectively use big data to predict which new shows will be popular. Netflix has had the largest share of audience rating data since 2016, more than all the old networks combined.

In venture capital, leaders like **Tim Draper, Steve Jurvetson, Vinod Khosla, Paul Graham, and Mark Andreessen** are backing bold experiments **in seed investments**, and succeeding enough to win our admiration. See the documentary *Something Ventured*, 2011 for a good history of venture investing. We can expect more social elevation of the **technical entrepreneur** and the **early-stage tech investor** in years ahead, as we realize many of their projects are increasingly likely to drive **meaningful positive change**.

In *BPF*, we'll talk about a future development we call the **Valuecosm**, the **values-graphed web**. The valuecosm will be the **public values, semantic, and knowledge graphs** created by our use of **Personal AIs (PAIs)**, software and databases that will have **public and private maps** of our **personal values, activities, and tasks**. Trained by us, with private data and models, PAIs will **increasingly advise us** on what to **read, watch**, and **buy**, who to connect with, who to create with, and even **how to vote**. They allow us to **verbally complain about or praise** anything we use, at the **point of use**. All that **values and semantic data will be discoverable** on the web, with our identity being **public or private**, as we choose. Within twenty years, we expect that **entrepreneurs will be able to use the valuecosm to surface and value unsolved problems**, gauge their **total addressable market**, and estimate their **emotional priority** relative to other problems, simply by doing **searches on semantic and values data** on the coming web. That will make entrepreneurship and venture investing themselves a significantly more **probability-based and positive-sum activity**.

In another important social change, scholars beginning to realize that even **societal foresight** (social, economic and political change) is becoming *much* **more predictable and inertial**, the **wealthier and more connected** our countries and our planet becomes. This is actually a very old concept. It's most descriptive name is **planetization**, and we will discuss it in Book 2. Planetization is not globalization, but something much deeper and more meaningful—it describes Earth as a system with finite size, a saturating number of biological actors, and yet accelerating technological connection and intelligence linking them. Such a system is **not simply evolving** any more, it is increasingly **developing**, convergent, and predictable.

Because of planetization, certain societal futures will increasingly play out **roughly the same way**, everywhere. The more technologically, economically, and culturally **connected** all of us get, the more certain contours of our **integrated global future** emerge. **Tom Friedman's** *The Lexus and the Olive Tree*, 1999, and *The World is Flat*, 2005, opened many of our eyes to a few of the predictable changes (good and bad) of globalization. Because of planetization, we can increasingly describe **global civilization** as a **human-machine superorganism**, and we can talk credibly about the emergence of **global collective intelligence network**, a layer of hybrid human-machine thinking, growing on top of our purely biological modes of thinking, that we can one day call a **"global brain."** This idea has been explored by many big picture twentieth century thinkers, most famously, the paleontologist and Jesuit priest, <u>Pierre Teilhard de Chardin</u>, one of the earliest popularizers of the term. There is much more to say here, and we'll dive into that meaty topic in Book 2.

Even if the particular actions of any individual actor remain unpredictable, their average expected actions become ever more understood. Increasingly, we believe we can **discover ahead of time** the **greatest of the fast-coming changes** in sci-tech, startups, and the digital world, as well as many of the **slower changes** in societal structure and policy that increasingly bind, regulate, and nudge us into one **single global community.**

4. Foresight is Becoming Collaborative

The faster digital change goes, and the better our data and science get, the more we all become aware that important developmental destinations like **teacherless education**, **driverless cars**, **and workerless factories** are looming ahead, to use the language of futurist **Thomas Frey**. Today's foresighters and futurists have the scientific, technological, and entrepreneurial winds at our backs like never before. We are learning that we can **easily find collaborators** anywhere around the world, and work online together using our powerful social networks, free and low-cost cloud collaboration tools like Google Drive, Google Docs, and Zoom, and self-finance our projects via crowdfunding and crowdfounding platforms like Kickstarter, Indiegogo, StartEngine, and Assembly.

Massive online talent platforms like LinkedIn, Upwork, and Crowdspring, huge technical solver communities like InnoCentive, and new group foresight platforms like Wikistrat, Shaping Tomorrow, TechCast, Metaculus, and Augur are helping us anticipate, create, and manage change together progressively faster and more collaboratively.

In streaming media, several **future-oriented video series** now exist to educate the public about what may come. We are seeing a number of realistic, plausible **Future Channels** to complement our often implausible and fantasy-driven **Sci-Fi Channels** and our increasingly diverse and helpful **History Channels**. The Future Channels we at 4U would most like to see arrive wouldn't be just **top-down curated content**, like almost all existing channels. They would be **largely bottom up**, like YouTube. Anyone could submit foresight or futures video content, with an **open remix license**, so that anyone could edit and resubmit others content on the channel. Perhaps most importantly, content would be both **expert-rated for plausibility and accuracy**, and **crowd-rated for believability and entertainment value**, and a substantial percentage of profits would go directly to content creators, an approach we call a **CBBM (crowd-benefiting business model).**

Today, social media like Facebook, Reddit and Quora, publishing CBBMs like Medium and Steemit, and AI-driven selection platforms like Google News are increasingly **displacing network media** as our go-to sources of news and education. The worst of these networks, like Facebook, are deeply manipulative and extractive, allowing unsanctioned microtargeted ads, and giving users few data rights, and very little control over what they do with their "friends." The best of these networks are empowering, offer economic benefits, and are increasingly collaborative. Reddit's <u>r/Futurology</u> community, with 15 million "futurists," is just one helpful new place for group consumption and discussion of foresight topics and material. The best of these networks will continue to grow in power and usefulness, as people demand places to talk about and contextualize our accelerating world.

As the **last three billion of us** get onto the web over the next two decades, via smartphones, tablets, laptops and conversational interfaces, and as our <u>collaborative filtering</u> (semantic analysis and contextual delivery) of all that information gets ever smarter and more useful, we'll see amazing new examples of small-group collaboration and specialization in science, education, products, services, and events, all around the world.

5. Foresight is Becoming Open

In a brief paper by futurists **Venessa Miemis, Alvis Brigis, and John Smart** "Open Foresight (PDF)," *J. Futures Studies,* 17(1):91-98, 2012, we argued that our best foresight work is not only digital and collaborative, it's being done increasingly **in the open**, with **public input and access to the primary data** (survey results, indicators) as the foresight emerges. The EU's Futurium project (2012-2014) which engaged 3500 Europeans in developing visions for the digital future of Europe in 2050, is a good example. Any kind of open, multi-stakeholder Delphi or group forecasting activity, as in the ELAC Action Plans for ICT development in Latin America, would be another.

We defined **open foresight** as any foresight initiative that is:

- Collective and Participatory in structure,

- Open Access, both in the data collected and in its analysis and results,

- Online, which can bring access barriers, but lowers participation barriers,

- Input-Diverse, cognitively, ethnically, and in stakeholders, and

- Designed with Incentives to Participate.

This last requirement is tricky, as it can devolve into **pay-for-opinion** if it is not structured properly. But, humans don't like filling out surveys, and surveys of their thoughts about the future can be particularly challenging, since many of us aren't comfortable thinking about it and are rarely rewarded for it or trained in how to do it better. To survey effectively, we need to provide some kind of incentive, such as a brief edutainment experience prior to the survey, and some boost in reputation, opportunities, financial rewards, or other incentive. With the right incentives and awareness of the value of their contribution, participants will think carefully about various aspects of future and offer their opinions, adjusting for their own cognitive biases. People need to feel like they are **creating value**, like a Wikipedia page, or **assisting others**, and that there is **value** in struggling as a community—striving toward better collective stories, visions, strategies, and plans for the future. We'll describe our own effort at creating such a platform, Futurepedia, at the end of this chapter.

Even having all the above requirements satisfied, engaging in open foresight is not always a straightforward process. In many cases, consultants and firms will prefer to keep most of their foresight work private for **competitive advantage**. Controversial topics discussed openly can become **flame wars**, especially if anonymity is allowed (usually useful only for limited periods and purposes) and forums are not well moderated.

Furthermore, being open does not mean everyone's opinion is **equally valued** in the final result. Expert groups should still be more heavily weighted in a good methodology, in our view, in those (surprisingly few) contexts where expertise matters. But, by making our methodology and the exercise open, learning can happen faster than by any other method. Remember also that full openness is usually demanded by **good scientific method**.

As the Center for Open Science (COS) has shown, there is a reproducibility crisis in many published scientific studies today. In 2021, as this book went to press, as part of the COS's Reproducibility Project, they ran an eight year study of cancer research papers published in top journals between 2010 and 2012. This investigation showed that **over half (54%) of these papers were not reproducible**. Investigators used cherrypicked statistics, and were biased to do so by such factors as a need to publish at their institution, Big Pharma funding, and the knowledge that few would try to check up on their results. What's more, a third of authors didn't want to help the COS in their effort to reproduce their papers. Published methodologies were kept purposely incomplete in the papers, and vital reagents were not specified or lent to the reproducers. Universities and journals have some complicity in this major societal problem as well. Academics are not rewarded for good publications that find a negative result, and journals don't encourage publication of negative findings along with positive ones. Yet both are needed for science to progress, and both depend on openness.

When we strive to be open in our foresight work, it becomes more evidence-based, rather than voodoo. Others can examine our methods and results, and iterate their own version of what we've done, teaching us to be a better foresighter. Also, the participants themselves learn how they fit into the foresight generation process. They see the **full messiness** of how good foresight is created, with its **wins and losses** (positive and negative results). Unlike the popular quip about laws and sausages, **foresight production should be watched and critiqued by many "cooks."** With the right process, openness helps everyone become better collaborators, and more discerning and active users of foresight methods, and better tellers of futures stories, in their own lives and organizations.

6. Foresight is Becoming Global

Global approaches to foresight are another growing aspect of modern foresight work. Many futurists and foresighters became global thinkers in the 1970s, during our last Foresight Spring. We have gone there again now, fifty years later. The global financial crisis, climate change, accelerating wealth and technological change, and now the coronavirus pandemic have driven us there with a new urgency. Our **problems of progress** have become global, and we must collaborate globally to solve them. Also, when we take a global view, and surface **TINA trends (global developmental trends)**, we see the framework of the forest we're bound within, and don't lose our perspective when we zoom back down into the trees, working on client strategy.

Understanding **globalization**, and taking a global perspective, without believing in **globalism** (unfettered corporations and unregulated trade) is another foundation of modern foresight. The more **digitally, economically, and culturally connected** we all become, the more we define ourselves as one social system, with **common values, rulesets, and aspirations**, and we see how our many commonalities support our minor, and useful, differences. Beyond **Tom Friedman's** works, we recommend economist **Joseph Stiglitz's** classics *Globalization and its Discontents*, 2002, and *Making Globalization Work*, 2007. These are helpful prescriptive looks at how we may eventually, once we have much better Personal AI, improve our national and international politico-legal, financial, and social institutions to make our emerging one world culture **fairer and more equitable for all**. As information and digital infrastructure globalizes, **transnational issues** like trade, credit, national debts, investment, and labor, and **transnational problems** like organized crime, terrorism, pollution, global warming, oceans, and many others will become increasingly tractable. Few people outside of the intelligence communities realize how digitally transparent the world is becoming. The big challenge ahead is less and less the anonymity of radical actors, and more and more the protection of privacy and personal, business, and political rights, and the regulation of tech titans, in a world of accelerating digital intelligence.

Of course, the sociopolitical layer always moves the slowest, after business, which itself moves slowly compared to digital technology, but at least we can increasingly measure the problems and see the potential solutions, as we have hard evidence of countries where good solutions are in place. The more global and evidence-based our media get, the more obvious it is who needs help, and what collaborative initiatives can be successfully conducted by small groups.

Some places are so wealthy and connected they are quite good at taking care of themselves. In the early stages of writing this book in 2015, it was inspiring to see millions of Western citizens rallying in response to seventeen people dying to **terrorists in France**, in the Charlie Hebdo terrorist attack. Unfortunately, the 200 to 2,000 Nigerians killed by Boko Haram militants in the Baga massacre in the same month received far less global attention. That outcome was not inspiring. The range of Nigeria's reported casualty numbers are so wide because the Nigerian government is **so corrupt and inept** it gave conflicting reports on this data, which it has reason to suppress, and the world had no good alternatives.

In coming years, as our **transparency into global problems** grows, we expect that many more of us will **personally contribute** on our **best global activism platforms**, like <u>Avaaz</u>, <u>Change.org</u>, and <u>Countable</u>, to help fix global problems, beginning with the most visible and extreme, and beginning at the personal level, one disadvantaged person and one family at a time. In Book 2, we will talk about digital telepresence platforms like **Groupnets**, and a vision we call an **Internet of Families**. If just a small percentage of the rich, safe, and free peoples of the world would personally adopt a **lifelong relationship** with the poorest, most endangered, and most oppressed families in our own countries and around the world, and **help them on a weekly basis**, with **their kids growing up digitally connected to our kids**, we believe this would greatly improve the world. More generally, as digital transparency grows, we can better see and manage our global problems. The more we all can **see**, **count**, **and map the ongoing crimes against humanity**, and use collective human and machine intelligence to **identify the perpetrators**, the more pressure we can bring on governments, organizations, and elites to do something about it.

Meanwhile our software, automation and robotics are now getting so good that our most industrialized nations are again talking about accelerating worker displacement by smart machines, or **technological unemployment**. Most people don't realize how much tech-enabled unemployment already exists. Modern employment statistics count only those *actively looking* for work, lest people see how many Americans no longer seek work. According to **John William's** excellent <u>Shadow Statistics</u> site, real US unemployment is at present 23% (almost one out of four able-bodied Americans who can work is not working), not the 5% reported in our consumption-oriented financial press. Our world has grown fabulously wealthy at the top, and there is **growing free time** among the masses.

Or growing **total wealth and free time** bodes well for **collaborative initiatives and activism**. The <u>Great Resignation of 2021</u>, is a clear sign that, the greater the world's technical productivity, and the more wealth exists at the top, the less tolerance the average American worker will have for jobs in which they are underpaid, undervalued, and not engaging in what they consider to be meaningful, positive work. John predicts we will see a lot more of this kind of "dropping out" behavior, especially in freedom-oriented countries like the US, the closer we get to the arrival of **general AI**, which may arrive some time in the second half of this century. High meaning but lower-paid, and volunteer work, and positively impacting the lives of others, both on local and global scales, will be increasingly valued by most workers.

We can see that our wealthiest nations will need something like a **universal basic income (UBI)** in coming decades, with additional subsidies for engaging in a range of socially beneficial but perennially underpaid work—like caring for a child or elder, getting education, or employing others in a startup. UBI experiments have been done in the past, such as the 1970s <u>Mincome experiment</u> conducted in Canada, in Namibia, and in India. A UBI was briefly considered in a public referendum in <u>Switzerland in 2014</u>. Finland is considering one now. The incubator <u>Ycombinator</u> is running a UBI experiment in Oakland, CA. Denmark's <u>Flexicurity</u> model, which allows firms to **easily fire employees**, yet provides a guaranteed basic income for as long as an individual is **actively seeking approved forms of work or education**, is a particularly practical model for developed nations. We think it is even more useful than UBI.

In our view, one of the greatest **lost progress opportunities** in America during the 1960s was the enactment by President **Lyndon Johnson** of a <u>social welfare system</u> that greatly disincentivizes work. If instead of our current system, in which substantial payments stop when work starts, we had instituted a **sliding-scale income supplementation system** for the **working poor**, one that provided the same level of support as our current system, and even more benefits for education, child care, and increasing length of employment, we would not have created a society with millions of Americans who today rightly feel **undervalued**, and **no longer know how to work**. We failed them greatly by designing a dehumanizing welfare system with toxic incentives. We will get out of our current dystopia, but it will take time.

As tech-created social wealth grows, **a UBI or a Flexicurity policy** is an obvious solution to re-empower our hurting rural and small town regions—and to make it easier for folks to retrain for new job, or to take more meaningful but lower paying jobs. Of course, the elites in our advanced societies do not want that outcome, so there will be a **global fight** on this issue in wealthy countries in coming years. We look forward to that fight, and encourage everyone to, as well.

7. Foresight is Becoming Popular

Foresight is becoming "big" again in the sense that it is noticeably more popular, both on the public side and the professional side, the faster change goes. This popularity seems likely to keep growing for the foreseeable future, as more and more **STEEPS disruptions** head our way. Over the last sixty years, various specialty topics, like entrepreneurship foresight, technology foresight and science fiction foresight have all gained more and more members and interest

Both lay and professional foresight have major and minor foresight Winters and Springs, in an aperiodic cycle, for at least the last century. Recall our last major **Foresight Spring** of 1960-1980, when we were literally shooting for the moon. Our Apollo-era visioning, driven in large part by Cold War competition, gave us the modern term "**moonshot thinking**." In this time, futurists, long-term planners, and forecasting all made inroads into boardrooms and governments. Then came a period of ideological exhaustion after the societal shocks and **conflicts** of that era. The neoconservative ideology temporarily "won" in America, the UK and Europe, and our societies turned to **materialism** again. See the Materialism-Idealism-Conflict cycle in the Student Edition of ITF for more on this chaotic cycle. We entered a relative Foresight Winter from the 1980's to mid-1990's, with only neoconservative foresight making headway, and a reduction in the diversity and depth of future thinking, halting or reversing many of the gains of the last Spring, for a while at least.

Lay foresight has also had chaotic Springs and Winters, but they seem to be milder by comparison. The general public's interest in **all things future** has arguably grown more evenly than professional foresight, since the 1960s at least. Even during the materialist 1980s, future-oriented magazines like *Omni* and *Wired* gained millions of subscribers, dwarfing magazines from the 1970's, like *The Futurist*. We've also seen steady growth in the use of future-related words in literature over time, and a modestly exponential membership growth in future-related groups online.

Professional foresight is also on an upcycle again, particularly since our Digital Supernova in 2008. We'd call 2010, or thereabouts, the start of our latest **Foresight Spring**. Without a formal study to quote, it seems safe to say that professional work is "bigger" than ever before as well. More foresighters and futurists probably work today in business and government than at any time in our history, and more will surely come.

On the public side, as machine intelligence continues to improve, we can expect popular visions of our future, both positive and negative, to become increasingly prevalent. We've just seen the first crop of the new AI, robotics, superhuman, uploading, and similar transhumanist-themed films. A few have been foresight-generating. Recall *Minority Report*, 2005, whose prescient advertising-saturated digital world was created, by futurist filmmaker **Steven Spielberg** (*Close Encounters, Jurassic Park, A.I., Ready Player One*), in a careful process of foresight research. Yet most of these new films are merely entertaining. As always, much of what is popular is a low priority for professional attention and energy. But, we should always be aware of the changing popular foresight landscape, so we can understand popular visions and expectations, and keep our clients from getting overinvested in the latest fads and hype.

We also need to understand how to sell the **Four Ps futures that we can see** in a way that meshes well with **popular conceptions of the future**, without being compromised by them. For example, we may know that **synthetic biology, home automation, 3D printing, home delivery drones, basic income guarantees, blockchains, decentralized finance, or some new management technique** are now and for the next five to ten years likely to remain mostly hype. They have promise, but won't grow anywhere as quickly as their adherents claim. However, they currently **prevail as popular**, and perhaps that is because our clients are **enamored by them** today.

If we are able, let's attempt to identify those **few areas** where **low hanging fruit** might be accessible in these **technologies or policies** in their present **immature state**. Without being an **outright naysayer** on such technologies or policies, we can help our clients better see their current challenges and rein in their expectations to **realistic horizons**. At the same time, we can diagnose where our clients foresight is presently limited or self-serving, and help them **enlarge their vision**.

8. Foresight is Becoming Big Picture

While all of these trends are helpful to our field, this last trend may be the most helpful. Our next book, *BPF*, will explore its implications. **Big Picture foresight** is about our **worldview**, how we think our world and the universe are constructed. It is about the **biggest and most valuable complex systems** we know, like human society and technology. It is also about our **biggest questions**, like: What is accelerating change? What is predictable, and what is unpredictable, about our 21st century future? How do we become and stay adaptive?

Big Picture foresight, as we would define it, is thus about identifying apparent global and universal trends, and learning how to better align with them, to keep the world moving in a **progressive direction**, and to **manage the ADOR** they create. It's one thing to note that all the world's societies are trending toward certain common features as they digitize and industrialize, but it's yet another to claim that there are **universal values, aspirations, and destinies** for all civilizations on all Earthlike planets. Yet we are convinced that universal perspective is what **big picture foresight** will increasingly deliver as it grows up in coming decades.

Humanity is now looking actively beyond our planet, to ask how it is situated in the universe at large. Thanks to emerging sciences including <u>simulation</u>, <u>convergent evolution</u>, and <u>astrobiology</u>, we may soon learn that Earthlike planets and complex life are **ubiquitous**, and be increasingly able to prove, via simulation, that all universal complexity is subject to **convergent evolution** (a form of universal development) in similar environments, a convergence which guides it into certain far-future-determined forms and functions.

One of the most basic proposals of such predictable convergence is that all universal complexity may have to unfold in a **developmental hierarchy,** with <u>archetypal</u> complex systems emerging in each new layer, and with each new layer more intelligent, adaptive, and resilient than the last. One classic version of a proposed universal developmental hierarchy is summarized in the picture below:

Table 2. Five Apparently Generic Universal Hierarchies and Example Complex Adaptive Systems in Each Hierarchy.

Universal Hierarchies	Example Complex Adaptive Systems
1. Astrophysics	Universe-as-CAS, constants and laws, space-time, energy-matter
2. Astrochemistry	Galaxies, stars, planets, molecules in inorganic and organic chemistry
3. Astrobiology	Cells, organisms, populations, species, ecologies
4. Astrosociology	Culture, economics, law, science, engineering, etc.
5. Astrotechnology	Cities, engines, biology-inspired computing, postbiological 'life'

Within this century, science may tell us all complex adaptive systems in the universe must proceed in an accelerating manner from **physics to chemistry to biology to society (biological minds) to self-aware technology (technological minds)** as they evolve and develop. In such an environment, science should have valuable things to say about human and machine progress, values, and purpose, where today it is often mute. If evo-devo thinking is correct, we'll learn that **values come in two types**: intelligence-created and universe-given. Efforts to find and verify "universal" biology, sociology, technology, and values will be greatly advanced, where today we have mainly intuitions, circumstantial evidence, systems theory, and argument regarding such deeply future-important topics.

Scholars like **Kevin Kelly** like to ask Big Picture questions. In his lovely book, *What Technology Wants*, 2010, Kelly asks what the emerging **"Human-Machine Superorganism"** or **"Global Brain"** will look like, in an advanced state of **planetization**, and how we can better manage its **emerging ADOR**. Humans are inevitably connecting ourselves up, and binding ourselves with increasingly intelligent digital technology. We're learning how to better protect certain kinds of privacy (in our homes, in our businesses, with state secrets) and how to make both bad actors and our general environment ever more transparent. In *BPF* we will claim that **our special planet** appears to be quite sufficient to help us turn into something far better protected, more intelligent, and more capable than biology ever could be. We've seen the **planetization** claim, that technology is turning our entire planet into an **integrated superorganism**, one that will be a **human-machine hybrid** for many generations, but over coming centuries, will become increasingly **postbiological**.

By using and advancing technology for humanity, and growing our empathy and ethics toward each other, we each play an important role in this process of planetization. We will discuss this **planetization process** as the greatest of the **Great Transitions** we presently appear to be engaged in. It may take another century or two for us to get to this "superorganism" state, some unknown time after General AI arrives, but the trends are obvious, for those willing to look.

As we will argue in *BPF*, **our future civilization appears very unlikely to "colonize the galaxy."** As we've said, the **D&D hypothesis** argues that it is far more likely that we will continue to venture to **inner space,** not **outer space,** the more complex we become. Consider that our universe maintains **far too much useful distance** between other civilizations to make interstellar travel either practical or desirable. If our universe replicates, as several cosmologists propose, and if the intelligence that arises within it has any nonrandom effect on its replication, as seems reasonable, then intelligent civilizations may be **isolated from each other on purpose**, via **self-organized selection**, to ensure that each of us arrives at our own **finite and incomplete understanding of reality in** our own **local, evolutionarily unique ways**. The vastness of space also serves another key purpose for intelligent life. It **drives their local acceleration**, via efficient escape of heat (entropy, energetic trash) into the **vast nothingness** surrounding each of the very special planets embedded in this space.

We can maintain fantasies of terraforming our neighboring planets, and visiting other solar systems, or we can recognize that **Earth is all we have and all we need to mature ourselves**, and eventually make the postbiological transition. Our amazing planet is far more **self-balancing** and **protective** than we have so far given it credit for. The interaction of physics, chemistry, geology, atmosphere, and biology on Earth is **deeply homeostatic, adaptive**, and **intelligent**, in ways we still don't model well in science. The better we understand **Earth's evolutionary and developmental processes**, the better we may come understand our **universe itself** as a **replicating, self-organizing, evo-devo system**.

In 2008, philosopher **Clement Vidal** and John co-founded Evo-Devo Universe, a research and discussion community of **complexity theorists, systems theorists, and philosophers** to investigate the interaction between predictable and unpredictable futures. This community studies **evolutionary development**, (also known as evo-devo), the interaction between **unpredictable and creative** (evolutionary) and **predictable and constraining** (developmental) processes in living systems, in  organizations, in societies, in technologies, and in the universe as a system. Science is still early in uncovering predictable developmental processes in the universe and human social systems, but we are making steady progress. We believe **appropriately blending** these two universal perspectives is one of the **foundations of good foresight**.

Consider the following phrase: **Sustainable innovation**. It is a balance of the two most basic processes of change, **development** (processes that cycle predictably and protect the integrity of the system) and **evolution** (processes that branch unpredictably and create useful new novelty, difference, and information). The classic foresight book, *Our Common Future* (aka the *Brundtland Report*), 1987, by former **Norwegian Prime Minster Gro Brundtland**, popularized the concept of **sustainable development**. This set us on the path to **triple bottom line** (People, Planet, Profit) **accounting**. That in turn led us to **ESG (environmental, social, governance) accounting**. We can call that **quadruple bottom line accounting,** or **People, Planet, Profit, and Process.** As the incoming generation will tell you, creating equitable, inclusive, representative, transparent, and accountable **corporate processes** matters today in ways it never did before.

Curiously, evo-devo thinking tells us that the phrase "**sustainable development**," as helpful as it has been historically, is **inadequate as a vision** for humanity's future. Consider that both words represent **only one side** of the **IES goals**. Per the 95/5 Rule, we need to recognize the **way to a better future will be 95% a story of innovation and collective intelligence increase**, not **development**. It will be **messy and unpredictable, just like all evolutionary process.**

We need **good rules, policies, and activism** to protect our people and environment. But those responses need to **empower innovation**, to get us out of our problems and allow a new level of complexity and adaptiveness, **as much as they protect and sustain our critical systems**. We need great education, deep investment in science, tech, engineering, and entrepreneurship, and other **innovation-centric priorities,** on an equal footing with **sustainability priorities**. Today, we too often think of *sustainability as stasis*, as **protecting everything that exists**. But nature is constantly **weeding out the less fit systems,** to improve and protect **network complexity**. We must do the same, with growing ethics and empathy.

In the words of futurist **Max More**, the richer our societies have become, the more we gravitate to a <u>precautionary principle</u> (better to be safe than to improve our adaptiveness) in our policies and social norms, rather than what he calls a <u>proactionary principle</u>, in which we use **foresight** to find our greatest opportunities, and balance the **risks of pursuing them** against the **risks of avoiding them**, and the **costs to all of us** of remaining in a primitive, violent state of existence.

We propose that anyone who talks about **increasing sustainability** without recognizing we live in a world of **accelerating innovation, intelligence**, and **creative destruction** (destruction, renewal, and change that is good for the system, making it more resilient and adaptive over time) has an **imbalanced worldview**. Likewise, anyone who talks about **innovation** without recognizing that our world must increasingly **secure and sustain itself** is equally dangerously imbalanced. As we'll explore in *BPF*, **both innovation and sustainability** are **vital values** in complex networks, yet they also **continually oppose each other**. So do the values of **intelligence** and **security**, and less obviously, the values of **empathy** and **ethics**, the other two pairs of **IES goals**. In our view, the six IES goals, and their associated values seem particularly universal for humanity, the most complex adaptive network on Earth. They should be **acknowledged** by leaders and the group, and their **conflicts must be managed** in strategy, plans, and actions, for our organizations and societies to thrive.

The Futurepedia Vision

Let us end this book with a preview of **Futurepedia**. After publishing *ITF* and *BPF*, **Futurepedia** will be the next project of the <u>Acceleration Studies Foundation (ASF)</u>, the nonprofit behind this *Guide*. ASF believes that over the next generation, societal foresight will become an increasingly popular, probabilistic and evidence-based activity. Because of <u>accelerating change</u>, more of both the **possibilities** and the **predictabilities** of our future will be **discoverable in advance**— by a combination of lay and professional foresight, web-aided human collective intelligence, statistical models, prediction platforms, and computational techniques. As part of that development, the world can expect increasingly useful **collective foresight platforms**. We've described a number of such platforms in this *Guide*. Now let's talk about one we are preparing launch ourselves.

FUTUREPEDIA
Possible, Probable,
and Preferable Futures
Using the Wisdom
of Foresighted Crowds

Since 2003, a few foresight practitioners, including <u>Kevin Kelly</u>, <u>Michelle Bowman</u>, and <u>John Smart</u>, have called for the development of a **Futurepedia**, a free futures and foresight content encyclopedia and polling and prediction platform. John registered **Futurepedia.org** for this purpose in 2008. He proposed that a good Futurepedia would host crowd envisioned and improved scenarios and visions of possible, probable, preferable, and preventable futures. He thought it should be organized around a **crowd-benefiting business model**, offering both reputation benefits and modest financial benefits to those who edit the site. It should partner with and promote the best current **open prediction and futures media platforms**. It might even use a **crowd-owned digital currency** to reward its content creators and readers.

A good **Futurepedia** might offer a rough and ever-evolving **map** of competing judgments, from distinct <u>Schools of Thought,</u> on many major issues of future importance. It could use expert and crowd-rated evidence and arguments, and offer testable hypotheses and data calls. It could eventually report rough probabilities, which will vary by individual and demographic, for the likelihood, timing, and impact (value) of the various futures it outlines.

A global resource like **Futurepedia** could eventually become as helpful, for future thinkers, as **Wikipedia** is helpful for understanding the past and present. With such a platform we'd all be able to better distinguish between the many interesting, but improbable future ideas, which we enjoy discussing for their entertainment or philosophical value, and that special subset of high-probability outcomes. We'd also be able to discover that preferred subset of futures that are technically, economically, and politically feasible—and that promise to solve truly important human problems. Active users would continually **self-educate** on both expert and lay foresight using the platform, and develop strong and nuanced **critical judgments**.

Today's Wikipedia strives for a neutral point of view. A good Futurepedia should strive to be "multi-biased."

Our Futurepedia will strive to offer an **evidence-based, acceleration-aware, and evo-devo informed approach to futures topics**, and to attract a cognitively diverse, scientifically-minded, critical crowd of editors and users. We'd like it to be available in all major languages. Several **prototype future wikis** exist today, but none have seen wide adoption, or have any of the features discussed above.

This year, **ASF is changing its name to the Futuremedia Foundation**. Next year, we will launch our first version of this platform at Futurepedia.org. Sometime next year, we'll be announcing **contests, events, and a** *Futuremania* **conference** to support Futurepedia's **editor and user community**. You can **sign up for our newsletter** at <u>ForesightU.com</u> to get notified when this platform launches. We hope you'll join us there, and help us to turn Futurepedia into the **global foresight resource** that we know it can one day become, if we all pitch in to make it better.

Coda

With the exception our Appendices, this is all we would like to say for now. Thank you for reading the first book of our *Guide* and for striving every day toward better foresight for yourselves, your families, your clients, your teams, your organizations, and for all life on Earth. With better foresight and action, we can each do our little part to make this amazing, complex world more empowering and adaptive—for everyone.

Thrive On, Friend!
Let's Work Together Toward a
More Foresighted Future.

Appendix 1: Brief Foresight Skills Assessment – Personal and Team

This **Brief Foresight Skills Assessment** will help you diagnose **personal and team** foresight preferences, strengths, weaknesses, and areas of potential improvement. It can be completed in **roughly two hours.** Some of its claims are **footnoted**. See the **Assessment References** section for research. It does not include topics like **ADOR analysis**, **negativity bias**, **normative foresight**, **prioritization**, **procrastination**, and others topics included in our **longer assessments**. This brief assessment is licensed for noncommercial use, adaptation, and sharing with 4U attribution, CC BY-NC-SA 3.0.

<u>Instructions</u>: Please read all five sections of this **assessment**. Then briefly answer **all of the questions**. As you read, feel free to write down any **questions of your own**, for your further learning and action.

1. Sentiment Foresight and GRASP Thinking

We all express **future sentiment** in **two ways**:

   a. **Strategic Optimism** (seeing and evaluating Advantages and Opportunities)

   b. **Defensive Pessimism** (seeing and protecting against Disruptions and Risks)

We also **mix** these sentiments in a third state:

   c. **Realism (actively contrasting both sentiments**, seeing "both halves of the glass," very close together in time.

Optimists can excel at foreseeing and **exploiting opportunity**.[1] **Pessimists** can excel at foreseeing and **preventing disaster**.[2] **Realists** can get **more of the right things done**.[3] Effective leaders **value** and provide **psychological safety** for all three sentiment states on their teams. They guard against **over-optimism**, with its **delusions** and **groupthink**, which can grow rapidly with **prior success**. They also guard against **over-pessimism**, with its **negativity** and **inaction** (learned helplessness).[1] They also avoid **overcentrism** (not taking strong sentiment stances when needed), and **insufficient use** of praise and criticism (feedback **sentiment states**).

1A. Do you think **you personally** are **more often** a **strategic optimist**, a **defensive pessimist**, or a **realist** (actively contrasting both)? How would you rank (1,2,3) the **time you spend** in each of these three mental states during a **typical work week**?

    Advantage Thinking (Strategic Optimism)   ____

    Defensive Thinking (Defensive Pessimism)   ____

    Contrast Thinking (Back and Forth/"Realism")   ____

GRASP Thinking

Sentiment contrasting ("GRASP thinking") is a type of **realism** where we **first** think **optimistically** and **probabilistically**, about a valuable **Goal**, then **defensively** about our **Reality** (actual distance from the goal) and the many **possibilities** of not reaching it, then **optimistically**, visualizing **Advantages** we'll get when we achieve the goal, then **defensively**, visualizing the most likely **Setbacks** (obstacles) we may face, and then making a strategic **Plan**. Our plan should also include two things:

1. **Key resources** (mental, physical, network) that will help us **reach our goals**, and how to get or manage them, and

2. **If-then statements** regarding how to deal with potential **obstacles**, should they arise.

Climb your mountain, one GRASP at a time.
Alex Honnold, in *Free Solo*, 2018

We do most of this kind of thinking **on the fly**, in our heads.

Here's how **GRASP Thinking** works:

G. Conceive a worthy, tough, achievable **Goal** (today or short-term). Have we made it a top priority? Feel **good**.

R. Estimate the **Reality** (how far we, the team, or our envir. are from the goal). Possible non-goal outcomes? Feel **bad**.

A. Visualize some detailed **Advantages** to having achieved the goal (strategic optimism). Feel **good**.

S. Visualize some of the most plausible **Setbacks** (defensive pessimism), or ways we might fail. Feel **bad**.

P. Create a simple **Plan** with a few **key resources** and **if-then statements**. Feel **good**.

In extensive real-world studies, versus using no sentiment when making mental plans, or using optimism or pessimism alone, structured sentiment contrasting (optimism, pessimism, plan) has been shown to improve three things: [3]

1. **Foresight accuracy** (50-100% **less error** in predicting what we'll get done),

2. **Productivity** (30-150% **greater productivity** in a variety of timed tasks), and

3. **Motivation** to **persist** is enhanced, even when faced with **difficult obstacles**.

Mnemonic: How do we **climb a mountain**? "**One GRASP at a time**."

1B. For **five minutes**, try **GRASP thinking** for an upcoming **personal challenge**. To start, we recommend picking a **particularly short-term task or goal** (today's or tomorrow's). Make it a **tough task** you have **committed to doing next** or one of your **more difficult or ambitious "stretch goals,"** perhaps one you've been **avoiding doing** for some time.

– **Goal** (Pick something Worthy, Difficult, and Near-term). Is it a high and focused priority? Excactly why? (1 min)

– **Reality** (**How far** are you from the goal? How do you **measure** that?). What other outcomes are **possible**? (1 min)

– **Advantages** (Optimistically, what happens when the goal is achieved? **Visualize**, with **excitement**).(1 min)

– **Setbacks** (Pessimistically and predictably, how might you fail? **Visualize**, with **alarm**). (1 min)

– **Plan** (Include 1-2 **"key resources"** to get or manage, and 1-2 **"if-then"** statements if setbacks occur). **Jot down** this plan, using at least a few words. Alternatively, **rehearse it mentally** at least three times. (1 min)

Reflect: Which of the five GRASP steps was **hardest** for you? How did GRASP thinking **differ**, if at all, from what you **presently do in your head** when thinking about **today's and short-term tasks and goals**? After the goal time horizon is **completed** (today or tomorrow) take a few minutes to **review** your performance. Did you **reduce forecast error** over typical near-term plans? Were you **more productive** than you expected? Was your **persistence enhanced**? If so, how can you use GRASP thinking more deliberately, at least **five or ten minutes** every day? Can you **teach it** to your team?

Sentiment Awareness: Managing Optimism:Pessimism (O:P) Ratios

Emotional foresight requires being **aware of** and able to **ethically influence** our and others emotions toward more **accurate** and **productive** states of mind.[4] Our **Optimism:Pessimism thinking ratios** can either **support** or **work against** our **task contexts**. Consider the following **O:P ratios** (ratios of time spent in each sentiment state) and some of their proposed **productive** and **counterproductive contexts**.

O:P Ratio	Common Contexts
1:1	**Sentiment Contrasting, GRASP Thinking**; "Realism"[3]
2:1	**Advantage and Opportunity Assessment**; Strategic Optimism[7]
1:2	**Disruption and Risk Assessment**; Defensive Pessimism[7]
4:1	**Relationships** and **Novel** Environments[5]
1:4	**Criticism** Production and **Crisis** Environments[2]
8:1	**Selling and Visioning** (productive) and **Manias** (not productive)
1:8	**Conflict States** (productive) and **Panics** (counterproductive)

1C. Do these Optimism:Pessimism **thinking ratios** seem roughly correct, for the contexts above? For example, does it seem right that in **relationships**, you should strive, on average, to have **four optimistic thoughts** about the relationship for every **pessimistic thought**? Should you also strive to *say* **four positive things** to them, to balance every **critical thing**? Are you aware of your current average ratio? When do you typically deviate from it? Explain.

Leading Sentiment on Teams

Leaders can greatly influence team sentiment. They can empower their team to be **mindful** of and **verbal** about **Optimism:Pessimism thinking ratios**, and they can use **routines** to **shift their ratio** whenever it seems counterproductive. Here are three strategies we recommend:

- To empower **strategic optimists**, and defeat **inflexibility** and **fear**, leaders can conduct **Success Visioning (Stretch Goalsetting)**, asking their team: "How can we **achieve** this (desirable future). What **steps** must we take?"

- To empower **defensive pessimists**, and defeat **groupthink** and **ego**, leaders can do **Failure Visioning (Premortems)**, asking their team: "Imagine this (high-profile project) has **failed** or **greatly underperformed**. **How** did it happen?"[6]

- To empower **realists**, leaders can do **Progress Checks (Status Checks) and GRASP thinking**, asking their team: "What is our **status** on goals? What should we be **optimistic** about? **Pessimistic** about? Do we need to **update** strategy? **Revise** our plan?"[3]

1D. Can you describe a situation where **your team** or **another** got in trouble by **underusing, overusing, or misusing** strategic optimism, defensive pessimism, or realism/contrasting? Does your team need to improve its use of any of these **sentiment states**, in any **context**?

2. Foresight Horizons (Today's, Short-term, Mid-term, Long-term)

All future thinking occurs in **four foresight horizons**:

> 1. **Today's Foresight** (**Now** to **End-of-Day**)
>
> 2. **Short-term Foresight** (Next **"T's"**: **Tomorrow** to **Three Months**)
>
> 3. **Mid-term Foresight** (Next **"4's"**: Next **Quarter** to **Four years**)
>
> 4. **Long-term Foresight** (**>4 years**, decade, lifetime, future gens)

The Power Law of Future Thinking (55:25:15:5)

# of Discrete Thoughts

Today (To End-of-Day) · Short-Term (Tomorrow to 3 Mos) · Mid-Term (Next Qtr to Next 4 Yrs) · Long-Term (>4 Yrs)

Most future thinking is <24 hrs, and unconscious[1]

1. Benjamin Libet. *Mind Time. The Temporal Factor in Consciousness.* 2005.

As a population average, we usually think **much less frequently** about events that are further ahead in time. Recall that we call this the **Power Law of Future Thinking**. **Today's foresight** is the majority of our future thinking. It runs just **seconds, minutes and hours** ahead, and is largely **unconscious**.[8] Using rapid **Do loops** (discussed in Exercise 4), we can quickly get better at **today's foresight**. This is our **most powerful strategy** for foresight improvement in **all four horizons**. Here then are a few tips for future thinking **from now to the end of our day**.

Today's Foresight: The Root of Better Future Thinking

It is our contention that becoming more **deliberate**, **mindful**, and **visual** in **today's foresight** (now until end of day) is the **easiest way** to get better at **short-term foresight** (tomorrow to next three months). Our **feedback** is **far faster** with today's foresight, and we can **improve** with every **review** of our mistakes. Regardless of our responsibilities for **mid-term** and **long-term foresight**, our **performance in today's and short-term foresight**, using the **Eight Skills** (Section 4 of this handout), is where our **greatest professional impact** and **career success** will occur.[9]

Time Awareness and Schedule Awareness

Do you **know what time it is**, all day long? Being **time aware** throughout the day, and aware of the **time until our next event** are great aids to today's foresight. Do you have a **big clock** in front of you at your workstation? Do you regularly **look** at it? Do you **guess the time throughout the day**, and **reward yourself** (with a stretch, a chewable vitamin C, sugarless gum, whatever) when you are **reasonably accurate**? Do you have an **online calendar**? Do you look at it **first thing** every day? Do you **mentally rehearse your schedule**? Are you **mindful of the time** both before and while in a **time box**? We can take **brief breaks** within any time box, but our **priority** is to **get back into the box (scheduled *time on task*) ASAP**. **Reviewing** how we did after each box ends, vs. our **forecast** (plan) lets us **complete a Do Loop**. We can be **optimistic** at the **start** of each box (a mini-version of **each new day**) that we will get our **plan done**. To stay **Do loop oriented**, try to schedule *at least three* time boxes (tasks) a day. Make at least one **a fun or exercise break**.[10] We can live our days **schedule-first**, and look only secondarily at our **task list**. This will improve *today's Quality of Vision!*

2A. How would you grade **yourself** (A-D) on both your **time awareness and schedule awareness** throughout the day? If needed, what **routines** have helped you **improve**? What could you do **next**?

Time and Schedule Awareness (Grade A-D) _____

3. Time Orientation (Past, Present, Future)

We all think with **three time orientations**:

a. **The Past**, aka *Hindsight* (potentially relevant history, experience, data, practices, and models/hypotheses)

b. **The Present**, aka *Insight* (self-awareness, social- and situation-awareness, organization, procedures)

c. **The Future**, aka *Foresight* (short- or long-term opportunities, threats, changes, innovations, experiments)

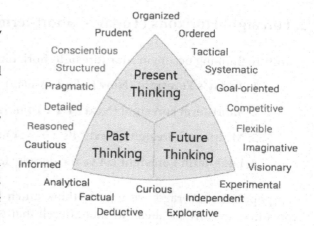

The MindTime graphic at right gives **adjectives** that commonly associate with each of these orientations. We all **bounce rapidly** between each of these orientations during the day. Yet almost all of us tend to **favor** one or two orientations more. Done right, our **preferred orientations** can give us certain **advantages**:

Present thinkers can excel at **getting things done**.

Future thinkers can excel at seeing what **needs to get done**.

Past thinkers can excel at seeing has **worked well so far**.

Good leaders learn both the **value and** *traps* of **each time orientation**. We strive to help our teams **move between each as needed**, just like we help them **move between sentiments**. We should also see and manage any **conflicts** between our preferred time orientations and our jobs.

We can take a free 18-question test at <u>MindTime</u>[11] to assess our preferences. The **center of the graphic** is 33/33/33%. For example, the "**You**" depicted at right tends to be a **Future>Past>Present thinker** (roughly 40% Future, 35% Past, 25% Present in **thinking frequency**), as estimated by deviation from the center).

Deloitte's **Business Chemistry** workplace styles assessment (picture right), also based on neuroscience models, used with 200K people since 2010, independently found this same **Time Orientation Pyramid** (Pioneers, Guardians, and Drivers). Deloitte also identified a fourth "**blended**" **style** (Integrators) that connects the three. All of us know folks who are motivated by harmony, centrism, and collaboration. Here is a free online <u>20-question test</u> for their four styles. Many individuals prefer using just one or two of these styles. Their book advises on better collaboration among the four styles.[12]

Which are our personal styles? Our teams'?

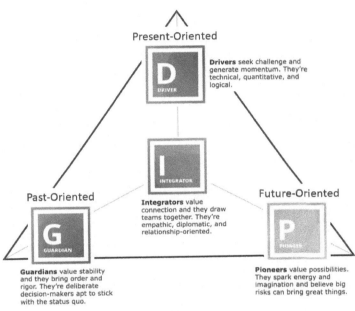

Deloitte's Four Workplace Styles (Business Chemistry Diagnostic, 2010)

3A. How would you rank (1,2,3) **your personal strength** (or at least, the time you spend) in each of these three time orientations over a typical work week?

> **Past Thinking (Trends, Facts, Constraints)** ____
>
> **Present Thinking (Plans, Expectations, Processes)** ____
>
> **Future Thinking (Uncertainties, Options, Visions)** ____

Do you tend to past **reminisce** or future **imagine** too much? How do you know when to stop each? What do you do to keep your past and future thinking **organized, prioritized,** and **in service** to **present action**? Do you have a **balance** of folks strong in each time orientation on your **team**? If not, how can you get that balance?

The Four Ps of Future Thinking

Both **time orientation** and **sentiment preferences** often **bias us** to think about the future in four very important ways:

1. **Probable** futures are preferred by Past- and Present-oriented thinkers.

2. **Possible** futures are preferred by Future-oriented thinkers.

3. **Preferable** futures are preferred by Strategic Optimists.

4. **Preventable** futures are preferred by Defensive Pessimists.

Each of these **Four Ps** are necessary to leadership. **Probable** and **Possible** futures are primarily controlled by **our environment** (by **predictable** and **unpredictable** physical processes, respectively). The better we see those, the better we can create and achieve **Preferable** and **Preventable** futures. Those futures are primarily controlled **by us**.

As the **Four Ps Pyramid** at right shows, sentiment contrasting about **positive** and **negative** futures is our **highest value activity** ("top of the pyramid"). These four future thinking types can be further **simplified** into **Three AIS Skills: Anticipation** (Probability thinking), **Innovation** (Possibility thinking), and **Strategy** (Preference and Preventive thinking).

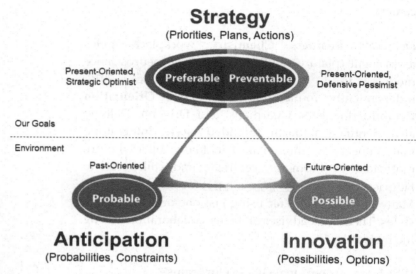

The Four Ps (Three Skills) of Future Thinking

3B. How would you rank (1,2,3) **your team's strength** in each of these AIS Skills? Do you have **teammates** who rank #1 for each of these skills? Do you think your team uses each of these future thinking skills appropriately? If not, where could they most improve?

Anticipation Thinking (Facts, Trends, Constraints) ____

Innovation Thinking (Uncertainties, Options, Visions) ____

Strategy Thinking (Goals, Priorities, Threats, Plans) ____

4. The Do Loop (Foresight-Action Cycle)

All of us use a **four step cycle (loop)**, to survive. **Cognitive science** calls it the "perception-action," or **"Foresight-Action"** cycle[13]. We use this loop both unconsciously and consciously throughout our day to build our **competencies**. We call it the **"Do Loop."**

Here are the **four steps**:

1. **Learning** – Past & Present
2. **Foresight** – Anticipation, Innovation, Strategy
3. **Action** – Execution, Influence, Relating
4. **Review** – Getting Feedback

Every time we **complete** a mental (Foresight) and physical (Action) loop, with **good feedback** (Review), we have a chance to grow in **competency** and **adaptiveness**.

4A. Do **you** or **your team** tend to **underuse, overuse,** or **misuse** any of these steps in **specific contexts**? How would you **grade your team (A-D)** on each of the four steps?

Learning Step _____   Action Step _____

Foresight Step _____   Reviewing Step _____

Please give an example of a **challenge you manage** in relation to this **loop**:

The OODA Loop

In rapid-response settings, Air Force Col. **John Boyd** named the Do loop the **OODA loop (Observe=Review, Orient=Learning; Decide=Foresight; Act=Action;)**. The OODA loop is key to **competitive dominance** and survival in a **threat environment**. Boyd said the **frequency, strength, and quality** ("FSQ") of this loop are the **key factors** determining performance.[14,15]

4B. Have you heard of the **OODA loop** before? In what context? What **strategies** might you employ with your team to improve the **FSQ** of your team's critical **foresight-action loops**? Over which **time horizons** (minutes, hours, days, weeks, months) do you currently **review** your team's key loops? How can you best increase your and your team's **loop FSQ**?

5. Eight Skills of Effective Teams

When *acting with others*, our **Do Loop** expands to **Eight Skills** of **team foresight and action**. The first four are **Foresight Skills**, and the last four are **Action Skills**. The picture at right shows that the **Four Foresight Skills** use alternating divergent and convergent thinking. The **Four Action Skills** use translational, one-to-many, network, and cycle thinking.

In our view, these **Eight Skills** are **key competencies** effective leaders must take responsibility for in adaptive organizations.[16] Here are the **Eight Skills**:

Running our Do Loop:
Eight Key Skills for Adaptive Leaders and Teams

Foresight Skills | Action Skills
Learning ⇐ Execution
Anticipation ⇒ Influence
Innovation ⇐ Relating
Strategy ⇒ Reviewing

1.	**Learning** - Investigative thinking (History & Present)	**Foresight Prep**	
2.	**Anticipation** - Probability thinking (Expect. & Constraints)	**Foresight**	
3.	**Innovation** – Possibility thinking (Ideas & Innovations)	**Foresight**	
4.	**Strategy** – Preference & Prevention (Priorities & Plans)	**Foresight**	
5.	**Execution** – Production thinking (Getting Somewhere)	**Action**	
6.	**Influence** – Market thinking (Recruiting Others)	**Action**	
7.	**Relating** – Team thinking (Sustaining Our Teams)	**Action**	
8.	**Reviewing** – Adjustment thinking (Staying on Target)	**Action Review**	

We can remember these skills as a vowel-laden misspelling of the word "laser":
Adaptive teams have a "**LAISEIRR focus**" on their **opportunities** and **challenges**.

5A. Which **three** of the Eight Skills do you feel are **your top strengths**? How have they **helped you** in the past? When have you **underused**, **overused** or **misused** them? What have been their "**traps**"?

5B. Which **two** of the Eight Skills seem **least natural**, most **challenging**, or most **ignored**, for **you**? Has any weakness in these skills hurt you in the past? How so? Have you tried to **balance out** or improve **your** own or your **team's** weaker skills? How did that go? Have a **success/failure story** there to share?

5C. Use **GRASP thinking** on the **Eight Skills**. What **Goal** could **help your team** improve their use of **any or all of these skills** over the **next six months**? Is it top priority ? How will you measure progress (**Reality**). What are possible non-goal outcomes? What **Advantages** might the team get from improving? What **Setbacks** (obstacles) are you likely to encounter? What **key resources** (coaches, routines, top cover) and **if-then statements** are in your **Plan**?

6. Eight Skills Diagnostic

Don Clifton's StrengthsFinder assessment describes thirty-four workplace strengths. These were developed in workplace surveys by Gallup, a consultancy. See the CliftonStrengths 34 test online ($49) for the assessment. These are helpful ways to learn more about both the "what" and the "why" of human behavior on teams. These are a sufficiently large and unique number of factors that they *begin* to adequately describe our useful diversity of thinking, action and motivational styles. Gallup also categorizes these strengths into **four strengths buckets**, as described in **Rath and Conchie's** *Strengths-Based Leadership*, 2008. See the slide below for this classification system.

Gallup's Three Action Skills

StrengthsFinder 2.0 Book, $16
(Get your **Top 5 strengths** only).

CliftonStrengths 34 Online, $49
(Get all **34** strengths in **ranked order**).

Rath 2007

Gallup Found 34 Working Strengths, in Four Buckets

One Foresight Skill ←————— Three Action Skills —————→

Strategic Thinking	1. Executing	2. Influencing	3. Relating
"Knowing Where to Go"	"Getting Somewhere"	"Getting There With Others"	"Keeping Others on Your Team"
• Analytical	• Achiever	• Activator	• Adaptability
• Context	• Arranger	• Command	• Developer
• Futuristic	• Belief	• Communication	• Connectedness
• Ideation	• Consistency	• Competition	• Empathy
• Input	• Deliberative	• Maximizer	• Harmony
• Intellection	• Discipline	• Self-Assurance	• Includer
• Learner	• Focus	• Significance	• Individualization
• Strategic	• Responsibility	• Woo	• Positivity
	• Restorative		• Relator

We believe that these strengths assessments are generally excellent, but that Rath and Conchie's **classification system is both incorrect and incomplete**. Not recognizing the universality of the **Do loop**, their four buckets do not break out **Learning** and **Reviewing** strengths. They also **oversimplify foresight**, not recognizing the **Foresight Pyramid**, and treating it only as "Strategic Thinking". But as we have learned, producing **Strategy** is the **last step** of foresight work. Good Strategy output depends first on **Learning**, then on **Anticipation** and **Innovation**, balancing each as a way of **predictive contrasting** about our environment. Then we engage in **sentiment contrasting** during strategy production.

In 4U's **Eight Skills Diagnostic**, we recategorize Clifton's thirty-four work strengths across the Eight Skills. This puts the skills of the **Do loop**, and our need to continually balance **foresight and action**, at the center of **workplace adaptiveness**. We think this is a much more useful approach. To Clifton's and Gallup's credit, their strengths span the Eight Skills in a surprisingly balanced way. We may have miscategorized a few, but perhaps not many. During this recategorizing, we found that the fundamental foresight skills of **Anticipation and Innovation** were both underrepresented in their model. To correct this, we **added six new strengths** of our own in the table below, demarcated with **"(4U)"** after their names . These six strengths relate to the critical, often-ignored role of **predictive contrasting** in future thinking. They bring the **Foresight Pyramid** into the workplace, as a vital set of thinking processes. This gives our diagnostic a total of **forty workplace strengths**. Below is our diagnostic.

4U's Eight Skills Diagnostic

Foresight Skills - LAIS			
1. Learning Learner Input Connectedness Context Empathy	**2. Anticipation** Analytical Intellection Defender (4U) Investigator (4U) Predictor (4U)	**3. Innovation** Ideation Futuristic Advancer (4U) Creator (4U) Designer (4U)	**4. Strategy** Arranger Belief Deliberative Maximizer Strategic

Action Skills - EIRR			
5. Execution Achiever Activator Command Discipline Focus	**6. Influence** Communication Positivity Self-Assurance Significance Woo	**7. Relating** Adaptability Harmony Includer Individualization Relator	**8. Reviewing** Competition Consistency Developer Responsibility Restorative

To take this diagnostic read over **4U's New Anticipation and Innovation Strengths** described below. Circle as many or as few of these six that seem to describe your **strong natural inclinations,** either in the workplace or at home.

"Both often and naturally, I am a/an…"

Probability Thinker

Strength Title	*Description*
Defender	Risk and Disruption Finder and Assessor, Protector (**"Defensive Pessimist"**)
Investigator	Question Asker, Hypothesis Tester, Data Sleuth, Scientist
Predictor	Trend and Constraint Finder, Probability Estimator, Predictor

Possibility Thinker

Strength Title	*Description*
Advancer	Opportunity and Advantage Finder and Assessor, Motivator (**"Strategic Optimist"**)
Creator	Storyteller, Producer, Entertainer, Artist, Stylist
Designer	Problem Empathizer, Definer and Solver, Builder, Optimizer, Simplifier

Next, we will do a simple **SWOT Assessment** across the forty strengths above. To do that, take the <u>CliftonStrengths 34</u> **assessment online ($49).** Then find **your top ten strengths in their report, and circle those on our table above.** Then circle in our table **as many of 4U's six Anticipation and Innovation strengths** above as you believe frequently and naturally describe you. Then, locate your **worst ten strengths (your biggest weaknesses)** in the Clifton report, and ~~draw a strikeout line through them like this~~, in our table above. Finally, in the table, draw a line through any of the strengths demarcated with "(4U)" in the table above, that you think you are **particularly weak** or **inexperienced at**, or **do not frequently and naturally value**, in the workplace or at home.

So far, you have a **rough estimation** of your **current strengths and weaknesses** in relation to the Eight Skills. Now to finish the SWOT assessment, write down some **opportunities** and **threats**, in several domains, that this analysis suggests to you. How can you better use your **circled strengths** in your personal thinking and action? On your team? In your organization? In the world? How can you better protect against your **lined-out weaknesses**?

If we are lacking in any of these strengths, it can be easy for us to **devalue or ignore** them. We can easily **unlearn those misjudgments,** making us both a better leader and delegator. We recognize where and when we need to work with someone who has those strengths, and more easily see and appreciate them in others. It is also possible to improve any of our personal strengths weaknesses, with practice, review, routines, coaches, and feedback. But it is even easier to remediate weaknesses on our team, by empowering teammates who have needed strengths, and recruiting others to our team. As management futurist **Peter Drucker** says, it is usually far more effective to focus on using our strengths better, and more effectively working with and valuing others who have complementary strengths, than it is to try to improve our greatest weaknesses very much. Recognizing and adjusting for them is the easiest and biggest win.

Finally, don't feel you have to think regularly about all forty of these strengths. For **teams**, we maintain that thinking about the **Eight Skills** is a sufficiently detailed and adaptive approach for most contexts. For **ourselves**, we can typically think even more simply about the relationship between foresight and action. Just paying attention to the **four steps of the Do loop**, to the **frequency, strength, and quality** of our daily **learning, foresight, action, and review**, is sufficiently detailed and adaptive for most contexts. We hope you find this diagnostic helpful in your foresight journey.

Assessment References

1. Martin Seligman, _Learned Optimism_, 2006.
2. Julie Norem, _The Positive Power of Negative Thinking: Using Defensive Pessimism_, 2002.
3. Gabriele Oettingen, _Rethinking Positive Thinking: Inside the New Science of Motivation_, 2014.
4. Bradberry and Greaves, _Emotional Intelligence 2.0_, 2009.
5. John Gottman, _Why Marriages Succeed or Fail_, 1995; _Science of Couples & Family Therapy_, 2018.
6. Gary Klein, "_Performing a Project Premortem_," _Harvard Business Review_, 2007.
7. Dilip Jeste, _Wiser: The Scientific Roots of Wisdom, Compassion, and What Makes Us Good_, 2020.
8. Benjamin Libet, _Mind Time_, 2005.
9. Stulberg and Magness, _Peak Performance: The New Science of Success_, 2017.
10. Nir Eyal, _Indistractable: Control Your Attention and Choose Your Life_, 2019.
11. MindTime Time Orientation, Free Online 18-question Assessment, _MindTime.com_
12. Christfort and Vickberg, _Business Chemistry_, 2018.
13. Pecher and Zwaan, _Grounding Cognition: The Perception and Action Cycle_, 2010.
14. Robert Coram, _Boyd: The Fighter Pilot Who Changed the Art of War_, 2003. _Audio_.
15. Chet Richards, _Certain to Win: The Strategy of John Boyd Applied to Business_, 2004.
16. John Smart, "_The Eight Skills of Adaptive Foresight_." In: _The Foresight Guide_, 2020.

Appendix 2: Foresight Consultancies – Large, Medium, and Small

Below are some leading **management and foresight consultancies** doing applied foresight work around the world. Where we know a foresight leader in these organizations, we've listed their name at the start of the description. Our list is divided into **ten global regions**, as depicted below. This first list is primarily US- and English-language centric. Please accept our apologies for that—time and budget constrained us for this edition. We hope this list inspires you to do your own digging. Research tips are offered below. Want to help us expand it? Drop us a line, we'd love to work with you.

There are an inspiring variety of organizational foresight activities today. As our digital platforms grow more powerful every year, foresight professionals everywhere will increasingly be able to collaborate on problems and projects, post competitions, benchmark performance, teach each other methods, do experiments, start businesses, and advance our field in ways we can barely imagine today.

Global Village
(Population in Millions)

1 North America
Canada, US, Mexico
(460M)

2 South America
(360M)

3 Europe
Iceland to Greece
(700M)

4 Middle East
Arabia and Iran
(280M)

5 Africa
(800M)

6 North Asia
Russia and Neighbors
(220M)

7 Central Asia
China and Neighbors
(1,330M)

8 South Asia
India and Neighbors
(1,510M)

9 East Asia
Japan, Korea, Taiwan
(220M)

10 Southeast Asia and Oceania
Thailand to New Zealand
(560M)

Ten Regions of the Global Village (GlobalForesight.org)

Finding Leading Foresight Organizations and People – Research Tips

When looking for future leading organizations and people, here are three search tips:

1. Look for lists (*Businessweek, Fast Company, Forbes, MIT Technology Review, Inc, Wired*, etc.) of the most innovative, fastest growing, strategic, "smartest," most foresighted companies or organizations. These firms are often disrupting their industries.

2. Pay for LinkedIn Premium, and use Advanced Search with "**Company Name**" + "Foresight" "Forecasting" "Trend" "Scenarios" "Innovation" etc. to find foresight-driven individuals and business units in various industries, and their sizes and locations. Do the same with your favorite search engine.

3. Search within a company's website "**Site:company.com**" + your favorite foresight words in quotations, to find foresight leaders, forecasters, creatives, and innovators to connect with at your company of interest.

Leading Management Consultancies Engaging in Foresight Work

These large management consultancies frequently do leading foresight work, though they don't explicitly position themselves as foresight consultancies. When they do, we move them into the Larger Primary Foresight Consultancies in the next section.

Organizational foresight leaders and previous leaders ("prev.") are listed below in **bold**, where known. Check LinkedIn Advanced Search, using organization name and relevant foresight terms (strategy, foresight, forecasting, design, innovation, scenarios, etc.), **site search**, (site:domainname searchstring) and general **Google search** to find current and past foresight leaders at each org. Use multiple negatives to eliminate URLs or terms you don't want, and use quotes to get exact phrases, like "strategic foresight" and "future of." Know others that should be listed here? Let us know.

Consultancy	Foresight Leaders; Company Description	Region (HQ)
A.T. Kearney	Global management consultancy. 3,200 consultants, 58 locations.	1 (Chicago, IL)
Accenture	IT, mgmt. consulting and outsourcing services. 280,000 consultants, 200 locations. Name is a concatenation of "accent on the future."	3 (Dublin, Ireland)
Advisory Board Company	Global research, tech, and consulting firm helping hospital and university executives to better serve patients and students.	1 (Washington, DC)
Alvarez & Marsal	Turnaround management and performance improvement. 2,000 consultants, 40 locations worldwide.	1 (New York, NY)
Analysis Group, Inc.	Economic, financial and strategy consulting. US & Canada.	1 (Boston, MA)
Aon Consulting Worldwide	Risk management, insurance and reinsurance brokerage, HR consulting and outsourcing. 65,000 consultants, 500 locations.	3 (London, UK)
Bain & Company	Strategy, marketing, organization, operations, IT and M&A services. 6,000 consultants, 50 locations.	1 (Boston, MA)
BearingPoint Inc.	Mgmt and technology consultancy. 3,350 consultants.	3 (Amsterdam, NL)
Booz Allen Hamilton	**Richard Fletcher;** Global management and IT consultancy. Defense and intelligence centric. Booz & PWC merger, 2014.	1 (New York, NY)

Boston Consulting Group	Did pioneering work in technological performance curves. 6,200 consultants, 81 locations worldwide.	1 (Boston, MA)
Cambridge Associates	Investment advisory services.	1 (Boston, MA)
Capgemini	IT, consulting, outsourcing, professional services. 130K consultants, 44 countries.	3 (Paris, France)
CEB	World's leading member-based consultancy for senior leaders.	1 (Arlington, VA)
Charles River Associates	Leading global litigation and management consulting. Acquired by Marakon	1 (Boston, MA)
Cornerstone Research	Financial, economic, and litigation consulting. US only.	1 (Menlo Park, CA)
Corp Executive Board	Global professional advisory services firm.	1 (Arlington, VA)
CRA International	Economic, financial, strategy expertise for major law firms, corps, accounting firms, and governments. US and Europe.	1 (Boston, MA)
Deloitte Consulting	**John Hagel**, Co-chairman, Center for the Edge (Santa Clara, CA); Audit, tax, consulting, corporate finance services.	1 (New York, NY)
Deutche Bank Research	Macroeconomic analysis within the Deutsche Bank Group and consulting for the bank, its clients and stakeholders.	3 (Frankfurt, Germany)
EY (Ernst & Young)	Assurance, Advisory, Tax, Transactions services.	3 (London, UK)
First Manhattan Consulting	Consulting on issues related to financial services.	1 (New York, NY)
FTI Consulting	Corporate finance and restructuring, economic, forensic, litigation and technology consulting, strategic communications.	1 (W. Palm Beach, FL)
Hewitt Associates	Consulting, outsourcing, and insurance brokerage services.	1 (Chicago, IL)
Huron Consulting Group	Mgmt consulting for the Healthcare, Education, Law, and Finance industries.	1 (Chicago, IL)
IBM Global Services	Global business and technology consulting.	1 (Armonk, NY)
KPMG	Audit, tax, and advisory professional services co. 152,000 people.	3 (Netherlands)
Kurt Salmon	Global management, retail, and consumer strategy consulting.	1 (New York, NY)
L.E.K. Consulting	Global generalist consulting firm.	1 (London, UK)
Lippincott	Global brand strategy, identity, and design consultancy.	1 (New York, NY)
Mars & Co	International strategy consulting. Client focused. 250 consultants.	1 (Greenwich, CT)
McKinsey & Company	Global management consulting leader. Great industry and global studies (McKinsey Global Institute)	1 (New York, NY)
Mercer HR Consulting	Global human resources and financial services consulting.	1 (New York, NY)
Monitor Deloitte	Senior mgmt. strategy and business transformation.	1 (Cambridge, MA)

Navigant Consulting	Dispute, investigation, regulation, and demand consulting.	1 (Chicago, IL)
NERA Economic Consulting	Economic analysis, advice, and policy for corps and governments.	1 (SF, CA)
Oliver Wyman	Global management consulting leader.	1 (SF, CA)
PA Consulting Group	**Rob Gear**; Management consulting, technology, and innovation.	3 (London, UK)
Parthenon Group	Strategic advisors to CEOs and leaders of Global 1000 Co's.	1 (SF, CA)
Price Waterhouse Coopers	Global professional services and strategy consulting firm.	3 (London, UK)
Putnam Associates	Pharma, biotech, and medical device consulting.	1 (Burlington, MA)
Roland Berger Strat. Consults	Global strategy consulting. 250 partners. Top tier firm per Vault.	3 (Munich,Germany)
Strategic Business Insights	SRI spinoff. Scenario planning, strategic roadmapping, foresight.	1 (Menlo Park, CA)
TeleTech	Global Business Process Outsourcing	1 (Englewood, CO)
Towers Watson	**Jonathan Wells**. Risk management, HR. Global. 14,000 associates.	1 (New York, NY)
ZS Associates	Sales and marketing consulting.	1 (San Mateo, CA)

Larger Primary Foresight Consultancies (>$2M Revs or 5+ Employees)

Both larger and smaller primary foresight consultancies like Decision Strategies International, Economist Intelligence Unit, Fraunhofer, Shaping Tomorrow, the Future Management Group, the Institute for Alternative Futures, the Institute for the Future, Kairos Future, The Futures Company, Z_punkt **offer internships and jobs** to qualified applicants. We recommend **interning** at any of these if you are a foresight student.

Organizational foresight leaders and select previous or founder leaders ("prev.") are listed below in **bold**, where known. Check LinkedIn Advanced Search, using organizational name and relevant foresight terms (strategy, foresight, forecasting, design, innovation, scenarios, etc.), **site search**, (site:domainname searchstring) and general **Google search** to find current and past foresight leaders at each org. Use multiple negatives to eliminate URLs or terms you don't want, and use quotes to get exact phrases, like "strategic foresight" and "future of."

Consultancy	Foresight Leaders; Company Description	Region (HQ)
AECOM	Global leadership, innov., mgmt support for industry & govt.	1 (Los Angeles, CA)
AIR Worldwide	Leaders in catastrophe, terrorism, risk, decision modeling.	1 (Boston, MA)
Arlington Institute	**John L. Petersen**; Global foresight, new technologies, trying to influence rapid, positive change.	1 (Berkeley Springs, WV)
Arup	**Chris Luebkeman, Josef Hargrave**; Consulting for built environment. 10,000 emps, 83 locations.	3 (London, UK)

Atmos Global	Atmospheric, air quality, and climate change forecasting.	10 (Melbourne,Austrla)
Austrian Institute of Technology	**Matthias Weber**; Austria's largest non-U tech and infrastructure research inst. 1,100 emps.	3 (Vienna, Austria)
BMC Innovation	Strategic innovation & market research company. 150 emps	2 (BuenAires,Argentina)
Breakthrough Institute	Modernizing environmentalism for the 21st century.	1 (Oakland, CA)
BrightIdea	Ideation platform, software products for the idea lifecycle.	1 (San Francisco, CA)
Cambridge Leadership Associates	**Ron Heifetz, Alex Grashow, Marty Linsky**; Developers of the Adaptive Leadership framework. Corp, govt, nonprofit clients.	1 (New York, NY)
CB Insights	Market data on fintech, insuretech, edtech, digital health, clean tech, IoT, and mobile industries.	1 (New York, NY)
Cognitive Edge	Education, networking and software for managing complexity.	10 (Singapore)
Copenhagen Institute for Futures Studies	**Ulrik Blinkenberg, Martin Kruse**; Futures/foresight research for public and private orgs.	3 (Copenhagen, DM)
Datamonitor	Broad based market research. Div. of Informa.	3 (Zug, Switzerland)
Decision Analyst	Market research, consumer panel, innovation services.	1 (Arlington, TX)
Decision Strategies International	Leader in future-focused consulting.US,UK,France,Singapore	1 (Conshohocken, PA)
Deloitte Center for the Edge	**John Hagel, John Seely Brown**; Foresight and leadership.	1 (Palo Alto, CA)
Dent Research	**Harry Dent**; Economic forecasting & investment research firm.	1(Delray Beach, FL)
Destree Institute	**Philippe Destatte, Marie-Anne Delaaut**; Foresight, strategic policy and intelligence.	1 (Wallonnia, Brussels)
Deutsche Bank Research	Market and economic research, forecasts, services.	3 (Frankfurt, Germany)
Discern	**Harry Blount**; Big data analytics and foresight.	1 (Palo Alto, CA)
Early Warning	Financial fraud prevention and risk management foresight.	1 (Scottsdale, AZ)
Economic Cycle Research Inst	**Anirvan Banerji**, Dir. of Research; Economic forecasting.	1 (New York, NY)
Economic Modeling Specialists International	Turning labor and market data into models to understand the connection between economies, people, and work.	1 (Moscow, ID)
Economist Intelligence Unit	**Daniel Franklin**; Forecasting, market intell. and advisory services. UK, US, HK.	3 (London, UK)
European IT Observ and Bitkom Research	Market research and stats on European ICT markets.	3 (Berlin, Germany)

Elder Research	Leading data mining and predictive analytics firm.	1 (Charlottesville, VA)
Eurasia Group	**Ian Bremmer**; World's largest political risk consultancy.	1,3 (NY, London)
Finpro	Trade, internationalization and investment development org.	3 (Helsinki, Finland)
Forecast International	Aerospace, defense, electronics, power systems intelligence.	1 (Newtown, CT)
Foresight Science & Technology	**Phyl Speser**; Product development and tech transfer services.	1 (Providence, RI)
Forrester Research	**James McQuivey.** Global business and tech research and advisory firm.	1 (Cambridge, MA)
Forum for the Future	Sustainable dev. org partnering with business, educ & govt.	3 (London UK) 1,3,8,10
FourSight	**Gerard Puccio, Russ Schoen;** Innovation, creativity and foresight assessments, training, and certification. F1000 clients.	1 (Evanston, IL)
Fraunhofer INT and ISI	**Kerstin Cuhls**, Mgr, Foresight Research; Analysis and foresight for innovation, security. ISI: 220 emps.	3 (Euskirchen and Karlsruhe, Germany)
Frost & Sullivan	Market research and analysis, growth strategy consulting firm.	1 (Mountain View, CA)
Future Concept Lab	Product dev, trends, forecasting, consumption research.	3 (Milan, Italy)
Future Foundation	**Chritophe Jouan**, **Meabh Quoirin**; Trends consulting & research.	3 (London, UK)
Future Management Group AG	**Pero Micic;** Futures research consulting firm.	3 (Frankfurt, Germany)
Future Navigator	**Anne Skare Nielsen**, **Lyselotte Lyngso**; Foresight services.	3 (Copenhagen, DM)
Future Today Institute	**Amy Webb;** Futures research, trend assessment, and consulting. Great annual Tech Trends Report.	1 (New York, NY)
Futures Group	Global health consultancy and development company; Health forecasting.	1, 3 (Washington, DC; London, UK)
Futures Strategy Group	Mgmt consultancy, scenario planning and strategic decision support.	1 (Glastonbury, CT)
FutureThink	**Lisa Bodell**, **Garry Golden**; Innovation training & development.	1 (New York, NY)
Gallup Consulting	Forward-thinking research, analytics, and mgmt consulting, global polling, publisher of *Gallup Business Journal.*	1 (Washington, DC)
Gartner	Information technology research and advisory company.	1 (Stamford, CT)

Global Business Network	Subsidiary of Monitor Deloitte. Since 1987. Foresight leaders in the 1990s, now defunct.	1 (San Francisco, CA)
Global Intelligence Alliance	Strategic market intelligence; research, analysis and advisory for decision making.	1, 2, 3, 7
GlobeScan Foundation	**Doug Miller**; Public polling to get stakeholder intelligence and find global developmental trends	1, 2, 3, 5, 7
Greenway Group	**James Cramer**; Built environment strategy consulting.	1 (Norcross, GA)
io9/Gawker Media	**George Dvorsky**, **Annalee Newitz**; Futurism and sci fi blog.	1 (New York, NY)
IBIS World	BI, industry research and market analysis for Australia.	10 (Australia)
Iceberg Consulting	IT-related services.	1 (Shakopee, MN)
IHS Economics & Country Risk	Leaders in economic and risk forecasting.	1 (Englewood, CO)
Innovation Focus	**Christopher W. Miller**, **Anne Orban**; PLM, innovation consulting.	1 (Lancaster, PA)
Innovation Framework Technologies	Innovation and New Product Development mgmt software and consulting.	1 (New York, NY)
Idea Couture	Strategic and applied innovation, design, and foresight.	1 (SF,CA, Toronto,ON)
Ideo	**Tim Brown**, **Dave Blakely**; Leader in design consulting.	1 (Palo Alto, CA)
IFOK	**Fiona Wollensack**; Strategy, change mgmt, vision.	3 (Bensheim, DE)
Innosight	**Clay Christensen**, **Richard N. Foster**; Innovation consulting.	1 (Lexington, MA)
Innovaro	**Chris Carbone**; Innovation mgmt, trend and research services, social media monitoring.	1 (Tampa, FL)
Instat/MDR	Reporting and forecasting on display-related industries.	1 (Santa Clara, CA)
Inst. for Futures Studies and Tech Assessment	Foresight, technology assessment, sustainable development. Germany and global. 30 employees.	1 (Berlin, Germany)
Institute for Innovation and Trend Research	Innovation, trends, knowledge management, training and consulting.	3 (Graz, Austria)
Institute for Prospective Technological Studies	Technology research and development studies in support of EU policy. EU Joint Research Center.	3 (Seville Spain)
Institute for the Future	**Marina Gorbis**, **Bob Johansen**; Pioneering foresight firm, inventor of Delphi method,	1 (Palo Alto, CA)
International Data Corp (IDC)	IT market intelligence, research, analysis, and advisory.	1 (San Mateo, CA)
International Inst. for Applied Systems Analysis	Global change and complexity research. Environment, economics, technology, and society.	1 (Laxenburg, Austria)

Inventta	**Bruno Moreira**; Innovation, R&D, and fundraising services.	2 (Belo Horizonte,BR)
Ipsos InnoQuest	Innovation Support, Product R&D, Market Resrch. 10,000 emps.	1 (New York, NY)
Kairos Future	**Ulf Boman**, **Mats Lindgren**, **Erik Herngren**; Global foresight consulting, research, trends, scenarios, strategy, innovation.	1 (Stockholm,Sweden)
Kauffman Foundation	Leading US nonprofit advancing entrepreneurship.	1 (Kansas City, MO)
Kinetic Cafe	**Mathew Lincez**; Innovation, strategic foresight, IT development	1 (Toronto, ON)
Kjaer Global	**Anne-Lise Kjaer**; Trend management consultancy.	3 (London, UK)
Leadership Forum	**Liam Fahey**; Leadership and foresight consulting.	1 (Durham, NC)
Long Now Foundation	**Stewart Brand**, **Alex Rose**; Foundation fostering long-term thinking.	1 (SF, CA)
Magellis Consultants	**Nathalie Bassaler**; Strategic foresight consultancy. 70 emps.	1 (Paris, France)
Maritz	**Mary Beth McEuen**; HR, marketing, and behavioral consulting.	1 (St Louis, MO)
MarketResearch.com	"Largest collection of online market intelligence." 4 empls.	1 (Rockville, MD)
MG Rush	**Terrence Metz**, **Kevin Booth**; Facilitation traing, scenario plng.	1 (Oak Brook, IL)
Monitor 360	**Peter Schwartz**; Sensemaking of global strategic & analytical challenges, serving governments, NGOs and companies.	1 (San Francisco, CA)
Nesta	**Jessica Bland**, **Stian Westlake**; Nonprofit charity, building innovation capacity in UK.	1 (London, UK)
Nine AB	**Elin Rudberg**; Brand and innovation consulting.	3 (Stockholm,Swedn)
Normann Partners	**Daniel Gronquist**; Intl. consultancy on innovation, strategy and scenarios.	3 (Sweden, UK)
PA Consulting Group	Global management, systems, innovation, and tech consulting. 70 yrs. Employees.	3 (London, UK)
Pattern Recognition Tech	Oil and energy indistry; Load, price and demand forecasting.	1 (Plano, TX)
Prognos AG	Analysis, projections and assessments for strategy and decision making in the waste management and energy industries.	3 (Germany)
PSFK	**Piers Fawkes**; Trend, innovation, and market consulting.	1 (New York, NY)
Quid	Software product for narrative analysis, technology and industry landscaping, trend analysis.	1 (San Francisco, CA)

Recorded Future	Web intelligence and predictive analytics software products.	1, 3 (Cambridge, MA; Göteborg, Sweden)
Resonance Consultancy	**Chris Fair**; Place branding for tourism, urban foresight.	1 (Vancouver, Canada; New York, NY)
RKS Design	Research, strategy, design, communications, prototyping.	1 (Thousand Oaks, CA)
Roadmapping Technology	Strategic roadmapping, product planning, and tech foresight.	3 (UK)
Rocky Mountain Institute	**Amory Lovins**; Sustainability research and consulting.	1 (Boulder, CO)
Samsung Econ Research Inst	**Sungho Lee**, Korea's largest private think tank. 100 researchers.	9 (Seoul, Korea)
Selectors	**Bruce Bueno de Mesquita**; Game theory and prediction.	1 (New York, NY)
Shaping Tomorrow	Strategic foresight, innovation, risk assessment, conversation and education. Crowdsourced global research.	3 (UK)
Singularity University	Education programs, innov. labs for start-ups & cos.	1 (Moffett Field, CA)
SINTEF	**Rita Westvik**; Largest independent contract research org in Scandinavia. Tech, medicine, social sciences.	3 (Trondheim, Norway)
Sitra	Research and public funding for predicting and analysing social change and its impact on Finland.	3 (Helsinki, Finland)
Spigit	**James Gardner**; Ideation platform, crowdsourcing software.	1 (Pleasanton, CA)
Strategic Business Insights	Research and consulting on tech, consumer and bus. envir.	1 (Menlo Park, CA)
Stratfor	**George Friedman**; Global security and intelligence foresight.	1 (Austin, TX)
SustainAbility	Sustainability innovation consulting. Since 1987.	1,3 (NY, London, SF)
TechCast Global	**Bill Halal, Ari Palttala**; Key technology foresight and strategy.	1 (Washington, DC)
Technology Futures	**John Vanston, Carrie Vanston**; Technology and telecomm. forecasting, valuation, minitrend forecasting.	1 (Austin, TX)
Technopolis Group	S&T, innovation, education, and development foresight.	3 (Brighton, UK)
The Futures Company	Consulting (innovation, strategy, trends, etc.) and subscription monitoring services.	1, 2, 3, 10
The Millennium Project	**Jerome Glenn, Ted Gordon**; Independent non-profit global participatory futures research think tank.	1 (Washington, DC), 50 global nodes
Toffler Associates	**Deborah Westphal**, CEO; Foresight consulting, transformation design approach	1 (Reston, VA)

Trajectory	Foresight, forecasting, market analysis firm.	3 (London, UK)
Trendburo	**Matthias Horx; Oona Strathern**; Future for local and provincial government, regional businesses and civil society orgs.	3 (Netherlands)
TrendONE	Trend scouts, researchers, creative innovation consultants.	3 (Berlin, Germany)
Trendstop	Apparel and fashion trend forecasting and analysis.	3 (London, UK)
Trends Research Institute	**Gerald Celente**; Trends research and forecasting.	1 (Kingston, NY)
Trendwatching	**David Mattin**; Global trend scanning services. 25 emps.	3 (London, UK)
TTI/Vanguard	Conference organiser for members to explore emerging, potentially disruptive technologies and assess their impact on organizations, policy, and society. 5 annual meetings.	1 (Santa Monica, CA)
Weiner Edrich Brown	**Edie Weiner, Erica Orange**; Workforce foresight consulting.	1 (New York, NY)
White Cliffs Consulting	**Josh Lindenger**, Tech Trends Analyst; Defense & security.	1 (Columbia, MD)
Wikistrat	A "massively multiplayer online consultancy (MMOC)."	1 (Washington, DC)
Wise.io	Machine learning as a service. Big data prediction platform.	1 (Berkeley, CA)
XPRIZE	**Peter Diamandis**; Incentive Prizes for Innovation	1 (Los Angeles, CA)
Zogby International	Polling and full service market research. Founded 1942.	1 (Utica, NY)
Z_punkt The Foresight Co.	**Cornelia Daheim**; leading strategy and foresight consultancy, operating internationally and focusing on strategic future issues.	3 (Köln, Germany)

Smaller Primary Foresight Consultancies (<$2M Revs and <5 Employees)

Below is a very incomplete list of smaller primary foresight consultancies. Some of these may actually belong above. We guessed at their size using public data. **Organizational foresight leaders** and previous leaders ("prev.") are listed below in **bold**, where known. Check <u>LinkedIn Advanced Search</u>, using organization name and relevant foresight terms (strategy, foresight, forecasting, design, innovation, scenarios, etc.), **site search**, (site:domainname searchstring) and general **Google search** to find current and past foresight leaders at each org. Use multiple negatives to eliminate URLs or terms you don't want, and use quotes to get exact phrases, like "strategic foresight" and "future of."

Consultancy	Foresight Leaders; Company Description	Region (HQ)
21st Century Learning	**Charles Fadel.** Educational standards and foresight.	1 (Boston, MA)
4CF	**Kacper Nosarewski.** Strategic foresight consultancy.	3 (Warsaw, Poland)
5Deka	**Rejean Bourgault, Olivier Adam.** Research, consulting, talks.	1 (Montreal, Canada)
Acceleration Studies Fdn	**John Smart**; Acceleration studies, foresight and innovation consulting.	1 (Ann Arbor, MI)
Adizes Institute	**Ichak Adizes**; Change mgmt and org development consulting.	1 (Santa Barbara, CA)
Alsek Research	**Joan Foltz**; Corporate foresight consulting.	1 (Tempe, AZ)
Alternative Futures	**Tuomo Kuosa**; Combining Forecasting with Co-design.	3 (Helsinki, Finland)
AndSpace	**Christian Crews**; Foresight, innovation, strategy consulting.	1 (New York, NY)
Asian Foresight Inst	**Richard Hames**; Strategic foresight and leadership consult.	10 (Thailand)
Breaking Trends	**Alex Howe**; Global trends intelligence from leading cities.	1 (London, UK)
Bridge8	**Kristin Alford**; Facilitation, tech foresight, workshops, events.	10 (Adelaide, Australia)
Center for Future Studies	Consulting, research, foresight. Affiliated w/ Kent U.	1 (Kent, UK)
Chermack Scenarios	**Thomas J. Chermack**; Scenario planning focused consulting.	1 (Ft. Collins, CO)
Cognovis	**Terry Frazier**; Competitive intelligence, wargaming.	1 (Tyler, TX)
Community & Regional Resilience	**Warren Edwards**; Resilience planning and research.	1 (Oak Ridge, TN)
Competia	**Estelle Mayer**; Competitive and strategic intell.	1 (Ottawa) 3 (Geneva)
Emergent Futures	**Paul Higgins, Sandy Teagle**; Foresight consulting.	10 (Melbourne, Austrl)
European Futures Observatory	**Stephen Aguilar-Millan**; Research studies, events.	3 (Ipswitch, UK)
Fast Future	**Rohit Talwar**; Horizon scanning, trend studies, tech roadmapping, scenario planning, future mapping	3 (London, UK)

FiveThirtyEight	**Nate Silver**; Predictive analytics (elections, events)	1 (New York, NY)
Foresight Alliance	**Josh Calder**, **Roumiana Gotseva**, **Kristen Nauth**; Opportunity identification, early warning, innovation, strategy consulting.	1 (Washington, DC)
Foresight Canada	**Ruben Nelson**; Foresight for Canadian economy & society.	1 (Alberta, Canada)
Foresight for Development	Rockefeller Fdn-funded platform for African foresight.	5 (Pretoria, South Africa)
Foresight International	**Richard Slaughter**; Integral and sustainability foresight.	10 (Indooroopilly, Aust)
Foresight Institute	**Christine Peterson**; Think thank focused on nanotechnology.	1 (Palo Alto, CA)
Foresight University	**John Smart**; Foresight media, training, research, conferences, and retreats.	1 (Ann Arbor, MI and San Jose, CA)
Fdn for Peer to Peer Alternatives	**Michael Bauwens**; Foresight around the P2P/Sharing economy.	10 (ChngMai,Thailnd)
Futuramb	**P A Martin Börjesson**; Foresight, insight, strategy consulting.	3 (Goteborg, Sweden)
Future Corporation	**Dr. John Luthy**; Public and business futures consulting.	1 (Boise, ID)
Future Crimes Institute	**Marc Goodman**; Research on crime, policing, criminal justice.	1 (Silicon Valley, CA)
Future Directions	**Castulus Kolo**, MHMK U. Foresight, strat & mgmt consulting.	3 (Munich, Germany)
Future Journeys	**Janine Cahill**; Foresight consulting, experiential learning.	10 (Coogee, Australia)
Future Laboratory	**Chris Sanderson**; Consumer trend reporting & consulting.	1 (London, UK)
Future Moves	**Devadas Krishnadas**; Foresight and futures consultancy.	10 (Singapore)
Future Problem Solving Program International	**Marianne Solomon**; Brings foresight thinking into high schools internationally. Competitions and conference.	1 (Melbourne, FL)
Future Search Network	**Sandra Janoff**, **Marvin Weisbord**; Collab. foresight facilitation.	1 (Philadelphia, PA)
Futurecheck	**Marcel Bullinga**; Trendspotting and foresight consultancy.	3 (Amsterdam,NL)
Futures Foundation	**Charles Brass**; Planning, strategy, foresight for indivs. & orgs.	10 (Melbourne, Austrl)
Futures Lab	**Derek Woodgate**; Foresight and innovation consulting.	1 (Austin, TX)
Futurewise AB	**Peter Siljerud**, **Thomas Edlund**; Trend forecasting.	3 (Copenhagn,Swedn)

Futuribles	**Hugues de Jouvenel**; Foresight research since 1960s.	3 (Paris, France)
Futurist.com	**Glen Hiemstra**; Foresight pubs, speaking & consulting.	1 (WA, USA)
Global Change	**Patrick Dixon**; Trends, strategy, speaking, consulting.	1 (London, UK)
Group Resources Prospective	**Francois Bourse**; Foresight consulting.	3 (Paris, France)
Hybrid Reality Institute	**Parag Khanna**; Urban and geostrategic foresight.	3 (London, UK)
Impetu Solutions	**Totti Könnölä**; Foresight, systemic innovation consulting and software. Public sector orientation.	3 (Espoo, Finland; Madrid, Spain)
Infinite Futures	**Wendy Schultz**; Foresight, visioning, facilitation.	3 (Oxford, UK)
Inst. for Ethics & Emerg Tech	**James Hughes**; Technology and transhumanist foresight.	1 (Hartford, CT)
Inst. for Global Futures	**James Canton**; Strategy consulting, new venture analysis.	3 (San Francisco, CA)
International Futures Forum	**Graham Leicester**; Foresight training, educ., World Games.	3 (Aberdour, Scotland)
Intelligent Future	**Richard Yonck**; Foresight consulting, tech foresight.	1 (Seattle, WA)
IPM Associates	**Carol L. McFadden**; Criminal justice plng & consulting group.	1 (AZ, USA)
Kate Thomas & Kleyn	**Kaat Exterbille**; Future management & comm. consultancy.	3 (Brussels, Belgium)
Kedge	**Frank Spencer**; Foresight, innovation, strategic design firm.	1 (Savannah, GA)
KurzweilAI	**Amara Angelica**, **Giulio Prisco**; Blogging accelerating change.	1 (Boston, MA)
La Prospective	**Michel Godet**; Foresight consulting.	3 (Paris, France)
LASA Development	**Patricia Lustig**, **Wendy Schultz**; Foresight consulting.	3 (Stroud, UK)
Leading Futurists	**Jennifer Jarratt and John Mahaffie**; Foresight consulting.	1 (Washington DC)
Long Now Foundation	**Alex Rose**; Promoting long-term foresight, "slower thinking."	1 (San Francisco, CA)
Machine Intelligence Rsrch Inst	**Luke Muelhauser**, **Eliezer Yudkowsky**; Friendly AI research.	1 (Berkeley, CA)
Magellis Consultants	**Nathalie Bassaler**; Strategic foresight consulting.	3 (Paris, France)
Neocogs	**Ben Flavel**; Foresight and innovation consulting.	10 (Melbourne, AU)
NVC Consulting/Spiral Dynamics	**Chris Cowan**, **Natasha Todorovic**; Change mgmt, leadership.	1 (Santa Barbara, CA)
Panopticon	Visioning and alternative futures group.	3 (Antwerp, Belgium)

Personal Futures	**Verne Wheelwright**; Personal foresight and strategic planning.	1 (Harlingen, TX)
ProGective	**Fabienne Goux-Baudiment**; Corporate foresight consulting.	3 (Paris, France)
Prospektiker	Foresight, visioning, strategic planning. 25 yrs.	3 (Gipuzkoa, Spain)
SAMI Consulting	**Michael Owen**, **Gill Ringland**; Foresight consulting.	3 (Newbury, UK)
Scenarios + Vision	**Helene von Riebnitz**; Foresight consulting.	3 (Paris, France)
Smart Innovation	**Dr Gumbi Sibongile**; Science to market consulting.	5 (Sandton, South Afr)
StratEDGY	**Stephanie Pride**; Strategy, foresight, design, gaming.	10 (Wellington, NZ)
Strategic Foresight Group	**Sundeep Waslekar**, **Ilmas Futehally**; Policy and scenarios.	1 (Washington, DC)
Strategic Futures	**Ron Gunn**, **Jennifer Thompson**; Strat planning, matrix mgmt.	1 (Alexandria, VA)
Summon	**Slava Koslov**; Innovation, foresight, product design.	3 (Eindhoven, NL)
Superflux	**Anab Jain**; Design and foresight consultancy.	3,8 (UK, India)
Synovation	**Bruce Tow**, **David Gilliam**; Foresight, problem solving, innov.	1 (San Francisco, CA)
Synthesys Strategic Consulting	**Hardin Tibbs**; Foresight, sensemaking, strategy.	3 (London, UK)
The Futures Agency	**Gerd Leonhard**; Foresight speaking, workshops, consulting.	3 (Basel, Switzerland)
Tomorrow Today	**Graeme Codrington**; Foresight consulting, speaking.	3 (Richmond, UK)
TrendsDigest	**Maureen Rhemann**; PA-based trend subscriptions.	1 (Houston, TX)
TRIZ & Engineering Training	**Jack Hipple**; Structured idea generation and evaluation.	1 (Tampa, FL)
Urban Foresight	**David Beeton**; Urban and industrial foresight and sustainblty.	1 (Newcastle, UK)
What's Next	**Elina Hiltunen**, **Kari Hiltunen**; Foresight consulting.	1 (Espoo, Finland)
Xland	**Michel Judkiewicz**; Trend analysis, tech forecasting.	3 (Brussels, Belgium)

Appendix 3: Foresight Resources –
Personal, Team, and Organizational

This appendix has resources for **Personal**, **Team**, and **Organizational** foresight, the first three of the **Six Foresight Domains**. More specifically, it addresses five themes:

1. **Intro to Foresight** (what it is and why it's one of our greatest gifts)
2. **Foresight Profession** (state of the field, training and practice options)
3. **Personal Foresight** (self-management, purpose, and challenges)
4. **Team Foresight Practice** (key practitioner skills and community challenges)
5. **Organizational Foresight** (models, frameworks, methods, challenges)

The equivalent appendix in **Book 2** has resources for **Societal**, **Global**, and **Universal** foresight, the **last three** of the **Six Foresight Domains**. It addresses five additional themes:

6. **Exponential Foresight** (how and why the world goes faster every year)
7. **Evo-Devo Foresight** (what is predictable, what isn't, and what is adaptive)
8. **Societal Foresight** (adaptive societies in a world of accelerating change)
9. **Global Foresight** (our increasingly integrated global civilization)
10. **Universal Foresight** (science and systems theories of complexity and change)

These themes together are 4U's current version of **comprehensive (full-spectrum) foresight**.

Foresight Books – Some High Value Lists

We recommend the following books for **leaders** who need to improve foresight process and culture in their organizations, and inspire their teams to create better future visions, and more effective goals and strategy. We also recommend them for **students**, whether self-studying or enrolled in any program, for foresight **practitioners** ready to dive deeper into their practice, for **workers** seeking to grow their careers, and for **parents** to help their children live more successful lives.

Be sure to check discussion and reading communities like Quora and Good Reads, proprietary platforms like Amazon (use Look Inside and Search Inside each book), and open platforms like Google Books and IntechOpen. The latter is the largest publisher of peer-reviewed open access books, with 5,000 at present. Now we just have to get more readers to actually **value and read** books that are **given to the world free of charge**. PAIs will surely help with that psychological problem we all have, along with many other problems in 21st century society.

1A. Introductory Foresight Books – A Starter List

1. *The Signals are Talking: Why Today's Fringe is Tomorrow's Mainstream*, **Amy Webb, 2018.** Excellent overview of how to scan for and evaluate weak signals, trends, and emerging issues. Webb is one of our brightest new futurists. Fortuitously, Webb occasionally uses **the d-word**, recognizing that certain changes are not simply evolutionary

changes, they are **predictable, convergent developments**. This practical book is a great place to start your organizational foresight thinking.

2. *Superforecasting: The Art and Science of Prediction*, **Philip E. Tetlock and Dan Gardner, 2015**. A tour-de-force intro to how cognitively diverse teams, using evidence from a variety of sources, thinking probabilistically, keeping score, and learning from error, can radically improve our ability to predict.

3. *Factfulness: Ten Reasons the World is Better than You Think*, **Hans Rosling, 2018**. Essential for introductory foresight thinkers, as it stresses the importance of building an evidence-based worldview, while exploring key trends in **global development**.

4. *Ten Global Trends Every Smart Person Should Know*, **Ron Baily and Marion Tupy, 2020**. A broad look at several **predictable positive global trends,** most of which are neglected by major media. A great companion to *Factfulness*. Still doesn't name or directly consider the **multifold trend** of **accelerating change.** But it gets close.

5. *Can the World Be Wrong? Where Global Public Opinion Says We're Headed*, **Doug Miller & John Elkington, 2015**. A survey of the **collective intelligence** of global citizens. Evidence for the thesis that public sentiment often predicts major global developments. Surfaces many important and media-neglected global trends .

6. *A Brief History of the Future*, **Oona Strathern, 2007**. Great overview of the development of the modern foresight field, by an experienced practitioner. Very accessible and enjoyable read. Books like this may motivate you to make your own contributions to our field.

7. *Strategic Foresight: Learning from the Future*, **Patricia Lustig, 2015**. A great brief intro to the tools and value of our field. Lustig has a diverse background and is a partner in a foresight consultancy with futurist **Wendy Shultz**. Unfortunately, this otherwise strong book fails to sufficiently value probable foresight. It shouts: "Strategic foresight is NOT about prediction." Actually, a third of it is. Ignore probability and prediction at your peril.

8. *The Pursuit of Destiny: A History of Prediction*, **Paul Halpern**, **2000**. This brief book, by a wise physicist, sees prediction as central to humanity's progress. It explores prediction as convergent truthseeking, and uncovering spatially and temporally persistent patterns in the universe.

9. *Future Savvy: Quality in Foresight*, **Adam Gordon, 2008**. Very accessible introduction to **trend identification** and extrapolation. Also helpful for recognizing and mitigating **bias**. Doesn't get accelerating change, but no work is perfect. Take the insights as you see them.

10. *The Signal and the Noise: Why So Many Predictions Fail, But, Some Don't*, **Nate Silver**, **2012**. A chatty intro to the emerging practice of statistical foresight, and the value of repeated transparent predictions of complex systems. One way our field will be legitimated.

11. *Think Like a Futurist*, **Cecily Sommers, 2012**. Inspiring and very accessible intro to the strategic benefits and thinking processes of foresight. Wisely advises finding megatrends, recognizing what doesn't change, and exploring what could. Offers four developmental forces to pay attention to in crafting strategy.

12. *The Future: A Very Short Introduction*, **Jennifer Gidley, 2018**. A great brief history of the evolutionary aspects of our emerging field. Gidley is past-president of the World Futures Studies Federation. The only drawback to this book, and it is a major one, is that Gidley misunderstands complexity science to argue the essential "unpredictability" of the future. This is a mistake shared by many of today's foresight professionals. As a result, Gidley treats **accelerating change** as a potentially transient phenomenon, devaluing probability, trends and prediction. Thus this otherwise strong book neglects one of the **two foundations** of the Foresight Pyramid. Alone, it is not a stable worldview.

13. *How to Future: Leading and Sensemaking in an Age of Hyperchange*, **Madeline Ashby and Scott Smith, 2020**. A good introduction to the mindset of continual learning, future thinking, and strategic wayfinding in a time of **accelerating change**. Unfortunately this book also suffers from antiprediction bias. It argues "the future is a conversation, not a declaration." In fact, the future is a set of **destinations** (probabilities), **conversations** (possibilities), **declarations** (preferences) and **temptations** (preventable traps and dystopias). Don't ignore any of the **Four Ps,** or your team will make less adaptive strategy.

14. *Uncharted: How to Navigate the Future*, **Margaret Hefferman, 2020**. Very readable, story-driven overview of pragmatic ways to navigate uncertainty, written by a CEO. It suffers from the bias that the future can't be predicted, and Hefferman misunderstands transhumanism, but at least she addresses it, in her chapter on

longevity. It helpfully describes such traps as oversimplification and determinism bias (overvaluing probable foresight). Appropriately values experience diversity and cognitive diversity. Good examples of long-term foresight efforts in business, government, science, organizations, and relationships.

1B. Introductory Foresight Books – A Longer List

A Brief History of the Future, Oona Strathern, 2007.
A Brief History of Tomorrow: The Future Past and Present, John Margolis, 2000.
Can the World Be Wrong? Where Global Public Opinion Says We're Headed, Miller & Elkington, 2015.
Convergence: The Idea at the Heart of Science, 2018.
Factfulness: Ten Reasons the World is Better than You Think, Hans Rosling, 2018.
Flash Foresight, Daniel Burrus, 2011.
Future Savvy: Quality in Foresight, Adam Gordon, 2008.
Futuring: The Exploration of the Future, Ed Cornish, 2005.
How to Future: Leading & Sensemaking in an Age of Hyperchange, Ashby & Smith, 2020.
Knowing our Future: The Startling Case for Futurology, Michael Lee, 2012.
Long Life Learning: Preparing for Jobs that Don't Even Exist Yet, Michelle Weiss, 2020.
Non-Obvious 2017: Think Diff., Curate Ideas, Predict the Future, Rohit Bhargava, 2017.
Strategic Foresight: Learning from the Future, Patricia Lustig, 2015.
Superforecasting: The Art & Science of Prediction, Philip Tetlock & Dan Gardner, 2015.
Ten Global Trends Every Smart Person Should Know, Ron Baily & Marian Tupy, 2020.
The Art of the Long View: Plan the Future in an Uncertain World, Peter Schwartz, 1996.
The Future: A Very Short Introduction, Jennifer Gidley, 2018.
The Pursuit of Destiny: A History of Prediction, Paul Halpern, 2000.
The Rough Guide to the Future, Jon Turney, 2010.
The Signal and the Noise: Why Most Predictions Fail But, Some Don't, Nate Silver, 2012.
The Signals are Talking: When Today's Fringe Goes Mainstream, Amy Webb, 2018.
Think Like a Futurist, Cecily Sommers, 2012.
Uncharted: How to Navigate the Future, Margaret Hefferman, 2020.

2A. Professional Foresight Books – A Starter List

1. *Futures Research Methodology, V3.0*, **Jerry Glenn and Ted Gordon,** 2009. Available in electronic form ($50), this text is a great resource on **thirty-seven foresight methods or categories of methods**—with history, strengths, and weaknesses for each. At 1,300 pages, *Futures Research Methodology* is a great **methods compendium** for practitioners. We highly recommend it as a **tutorial complement** to this *Guide*. It is informed by a global network of foresight practitioners who participate in Glenn's Millennium Project. **Glenn and Florescu's** *State of the Future* report is also highly recommended. The 2017 edition is the most recent as this book goes to press.

2. *Foundations of Futures Studies, Volumes 1 and 2*, **Wendell Bell**, **1997/2004**. Arguably still the definitive textbook on our field, written by a professor emeritus of Sociology at Yale. Bell passed away in 2019. *Foundations* covers both strategic and normative foresight, like our *Guide*. **Both volumes are consciously Three P's organized**. Bell covers **Probable** and **Possible** futures in Volume 1, which includes the **history, purposes, and knowledge base** of our field. He covers individually and societally **Preferable** futures (normative foresight) in Volume 2. Volume 2 summarizes Bell's work on societal adaptiveness, addressing **values, objectivity, and the good society**. Well's research specializations included social class, race, family life, and of course, foresight. It can be hard to find these in print at Amazon (check eBay), but digital copies are readily available. Our **two-volume treatment of the foresight field** is directly inspired by **Bell's** two-volume structure. *Foundations* is an inspiring overview of both the past and the exciting possibilities of our field.

3. *Knowledge Base of Futures Studies*, **Richard Slaughter and Andy Hines,** 2020. This text is a great compendium of the **diverse views and methods of current practitioners** in our field, and an **excellent complement** to this *Guide*. Originally published in 1993 and again in 2005 by the great Australian critical futurist <u>Richard Slaughter</u>, this work has been updated with a grant from Association of Professional Futurists—our field's leading professional organization. In **four volumes**, with **31 chapters** and **37 authors**, *KBFS* demonstrates the **great value and diversity of foresight as a profession.** At the same time, it has notable differences in tone and assumptions from this *Guide*. As an edited volume with a diversity of worldviews, *KBFS* does not take an **evo-devo perspective** on societal change. Many contributions highlight the downsides of **growth-obsessed consumer capitalism and plutocracy**, but none explore the **self-correcting nature of complex networks** in human history. Ignoring developmental processes, many contributors also have an **anti-prediction bias** with respect to **societal**, **global**, and **universal change.** Neither **accelerating change**—with its **ever more resource-efficient inner-space direction**, nor **AI as a network learning system** are properly represented. Neither societies nor machines are contemplated as **evo-devo systems**, necessarily self-stabilizing via evo-devo values, like the **IES goals.** Appreciate this fine work for what it is, but keep its **assumptions** in mind. We make different ones.

4. *Using Trends and Scenarios as Tools for Strategy Development*, **Ulf Pillkahn, 2008.** An excellent and particularly comprehensive book on the use of trends and other probable futures factors, and scenarios and other possible futures factors as inputs to analysis and strategy development on corporate strategy teams. Written by a strategic foresight leader at Siemens. A Four Ps balanced book. Many good examples of corporate futures work.

5. *The Fortune Sellers: The Big Business of Buying & Selling Predictions*, **William Sherden, 1997.** A classic overview of the temptations, challenges and hazards of prediction. Also a great guide to the perils of organizational foresight, and a necessary complement to **Tetlock and Gardner's** *Superforecasting* (2015). Sherden has a worldview bias, as we all do. He does not recognize the developmental 5% of the future, does not consider the statistical predictability of many facets of accelerating change, and doesn't see that special aspects of our future, like D&D, get **more predictable** as our civilization develops. But, his work demonstrates the high threshold for doing good prediction, and several of the many ways that the foresight profession has historically failed, oversold, and overclaimed. Required reading for foresight professionals, in our view.

6. *Best Laid Plans: The Tyranny of Unintended Consequences and How to Avoid Them*, **William Sherden, 2011.** A humbling overview of the many ways our personal, business, and political plans go off the rails. Sherden describes eight mechanisms that complicate our outcomes in unpredictable ways, and builds a convincing case that monitoring these mechanisms can allow us to better anticipate, avoid, and manage negative consequences when they occur. Sherden doesn't mince words, and there is a career's worth of insight and experience here. Again, Sherden sees the world through the **standard evolutionary lens.** We must remember that there are also **developmental processes** at play. Those processes are predictable if you have the right models or history. They are a small subset of processes in living systems (just 5%, in the **95/5 Rule**) but in our view, they are equally important as evolutionary processes to long term adaptiveness. We must see both.

7. *Learning from the Future: Competitive Foresight Scenarios*, **Liam Fahey & Robert Randall, Eds., 1997.** A great guide to using scenarios to reduce uncertainty, find opportunities and manage risk. Fahey and Randall offer a solid blend of strategies, well balanced between managing the unpredictable (**evolutionary thinking**) and uncovering the predictable (**developmental thinking**). Excellent case examples.

8. *Predictive Analytics*, **Eric Siegel, 2013.** Great overview of a new foresight frontier: data science, data mining, probabilistic prediction, and machine learning. As the web gets smarter and the world gets instrumented, these fields will continue to rapidly advance. We'll see our near-term probable future, and our current preferable and preventable futures, mapped and quantitated with increasing clarity.

9. *The Model Thinker: What You Need to Know to Make Data Work for You*, **Scott Page, 2018.** A bestselling introduction to the power of models, and how to use simple mathematical, statistical, and computational models to find hidden order, patterns, and meaning in data, and to better see and manage the four Ps.

10. *Thinking about the Future: Guidelines for Strategic Foresight*, **Bishop and Hines, 2007.** Great overview of six key strategic foresight activities, with concise practitioner examples. The examples give a nice applied look at the current state of our field, particularly on the less predictive side.

2B. Professional Foresight Books – A Longer List

20/20 Foresight: Crafting Strategy in an Uncertain World, Hugh Courtney, 2001.
Academia Next: The Futures of Higher Education, Bryan Alexander, 2020.
Bad Predictions, Laura Lee, 2000.
Best Laid Plans: The Tyranny of Unintended Consequences, William Sherden, 2011.
Convergence: The Idea at the Heart of Science, Peter Watson, 2018.
Foundations of Futures Studies, Vols 1-2, Wendell Bell, 2004.
Full-Spectrum Thinking, Bob Johansen, 2020.
Future Savvy: Quality in Foresight, Adam Gordon, 2008.
FutureThink, Edie Weiner and Arnold Brown, 2005.
Futuring: The Exploration of the Future, Ed Cornish, 2005.
How: Why How We Do Anything Means Everything, Dov Seidman, 2011.
Knowing our Future: The Startling Case for Futurology, Michael Lee, 2012.
Knowledge Base of Futures Studies, Richard Slaughter and Andy Hines, Eds., 2020.
Learning from the Future: Competitive Foresight Scenarios, Fahey & Randall, Eds., 1997.
Learning from the Octopus: Use Nature to Fight Terror, Disaster &Disease, Rafe Sagarin, 2012.
Predictive Analytics, Eric Siegel, 2013.
Profiting from Uncertainty, Paul Schoemaker, 2002.
Ready for Anything: Resilience for a Transforming World, Anthony Hodgson, 2012.
Rethinking Positive Thinking, Gabriele Oettingen, 2014
Scenario Planning: A Field Guide to the Future, Woody Wade, 2012.
Scenario Thinking: Preparing your Org. for the Future, Cairns and Wright, 2018.
Streetlights and Shadows: Keys to Adaptive Decision Making, Gary Klein, 2011.
Superforecasting: The Art & Science of Prediction, Philip Tetlock & Dan Gardner, 2015.
Systems Thinking for Curious Managers, Ackoff and Addison, 2010.
Thinking about the Future: Guidelines for Strategic Foresight, Bishop & Hines, 2007.
The 80/20 Principle: The Secret to Achieving More With Less, Richard Koch, 1999.
The Art of the Long View: Planning in an Uncertain World, Peter Schwartz, 1996.
The Causal Layered Analysis (CLA) Reader, Sohail Inayatullah (Ed.), 2004.
The Culture of Fear: Why Americans are Afraid of Wrong Things, Glassner, 1999/2018.
The Fortune Sellers: The Big Business of Buying & Selling Predictions, William Sherden, 1997.
The Image of the Future, PDF., Fred Polak, 1973.
The Model Thinker: What to Know to Make Data Work for You, Scott Page, 2018.
The Power of Bad: How the Negativity Affect Rules Us, Tierney and Baumeister, 2019.
The Signal and the Noise: Why Most Predictions Fail, But, Some Don't, Nate Silver, 2012.
Using Trends and Scenarios as Tools for Strategy Development, Ulf Pillkahn, 2008.
What I Have Learned: Thinking About the Future Then and Now, Marien and Jennings, 1987.
What Futurists Believe, Coates and Jarratt, 1989.

3A. Personal and Family Foresight Books – A Starter List

1. *Awaken the Giant Within*, **Tony Robbins, 1991/2013**. One of the best books we know that will convince you that your **attitude, emotional choices, habits, and personal mindset** are your greatest allies for **life success**. We truly can have an amazing life, if we choose, no matter our physical circumstances. We get to choose how we think, feel, and act. No one else has that responsibility, or freedom. We can envision and be the best selves we are presently capable of, every day. Robbins has written many books. This is his classic.

2. *Indistractable: How to Control Your Attention and Choose Your Life*, **Nir Eyal, 2019**. An excellent primer in personal foresight and the ASO priorities. Covers internal triggers, external triggers, scheduling, self-image, integrity, emotional management, and routines vs. habits. Like many of us, Eyal was highly distracted before finding the techniques described in this book. Combine this book with mindfulness, the Do Loop, and self-identity work, and you will start to excel at today's foresight, no matter your personality or current levels of distractedness.

3. *Please Understand Me II*, **David Keirsey, 1998**. A great place to start in self-assessment. Keirsey's four temperaments track closely to the **Modern Foresight Pyramid**, aka the **Evo-Devo Pyramid** and the **Four Ps**. Take the free 70-question assessment and find out your temperament. Then read this book to understand how to better work with others, and their different yet vital ways of viewing the future.

4. *Hold on To Your Kids*, **Gordon Neufeld and Gabor Mate, 2006**. A brilliant book explaining why it is so important for kids to be more oriented to parents than their peers. A peer-first orientation creates conformist, risk averse, and often less empathic kids. Offers many good techniques to create stronger family cohesion, values, identity, and behavior development. Teaching our children to think for themselves, and to anticipate, imagine and create better futures is one of the greatest privileges and responsibilities we have as parents.

5. *The Motley Fool Investment Guide, 3rd Ed*, **Tom and David Gardner, 2017**. A good overview of the discipline of regularly finding valuable companies, and "in-vesting" (clothing) oneself in them, with a good portion of your savings. Putting aside $100 a week over forty years for value investing in growing companies is the surest way to financial independence. This book tells you how to do that, paying attention to your investments only once a month. It also has a strong community of professional and lay investment advisors within it. Unlike other advisory services, it won't cost you an arm and a leg. Highly recommended.

6. *The Psychology of Money*, **Morgan Housel, 2020**. An excellent book that focuses on **our beliefs and habits around money**, and how much they help or hurt us. The great article that birthed his book begins with the story of two investors and their wildly different approaches to saving and investing. Books like these can help us imagine our financial future along **different life paths**, and motivate us to change. **Robin** and **Dominguez's** *Your Money or Your Life*, 1992/2018, is also helpful for those who don't save enough, or those who save too much, and who live too little. Most Chinese citizens save too much. Most Americans, too little. If you aren't saving so that you can **create future value**, you just have a blind savings habit.

7. *Foresight Investing*, **James Lee, 2021**. An excellent introduction, by an academically-trained futurist, to the ins and outs of personal investing. Shows you how to grow your knowledge of trends, numbers, sentiment, and patterns, to capture accelerating value in the market. Lee is also excellent at simplifying and prioritizing complex technologies. Just don't use this great book to overinvest in biotech, vs. infotech. Remember D&D investing.

8. *Subliminal: How Your Unconscious Mind Rules Your Behavior*, **Leonard Mlodinow, 2013**. A good complement to Ellis's and Maltz's work, giving the science behind subliminal thinking. Mlodinow is a physicist and a science popularizer. Read this book for the modern case for paying most attention to your unconscious mind, which rules 95% of your feeling and thinking, and often, behavior.

9. *The New Psycho-Cybernetics*, **Maxwell Maltz, 1960/2002**. This book sold 30 million copies, and rightly so. It was among the first to explain how unconsciously we live, how unconscious beliefs hold us back, and how, with **simple prioritization and repetition**, we can reprogram our most damaging unconscious beliefs, thoughts, and feeelings. We often **avoid** things that cause fear or discomfort, even when they are **key enablers** of our goals. Do the exercises in this book and start taking control of your blocking self-beliefs, thoughts, and feelings.

10. *The Myth of Self-Esteem*, **Albert Ellis, 2005**. A great guide to the necessity of **unconditional self-acceptance (USA)** and **unconditional other acceptance (UOA)** in personal adaptiveness. As Ellis says, we are too complex, as physical entities, to reliably rate ourselves, or others. Dysfunctional self-images, and lack of respect and empathy for others, come from irrational beliefs around self-judgment. Eliminate those beliefs, and rate **only** your daily thoughts and behaviors, never **yourself**. The path to personal and team freedom and foresight.

11. *Overcoming Destructive Beliefs, Feelings, and Behaviors*, **Albert Ellis, 2001**. A collection of essays by the creator of Rational-Emotive Behavioral Therapy (REBT). REBT will help you to identify and reprogram harmful and largely unconscious feelings and beliefs that lead to all kinds of maladaptive behaviors. It introduces us to the complex relationships between our emotional, cognitive, and behavioral dimensions, and empowers us to change.

12. *Bold*, **Diamandis & Kotler**, **2015**. A global, acceleration-aware, innovation and entrepreneurial approach to foresight. Great for visioning, goalsetting, and motivation. Excellent advice on using crowd platforms. Bold is also a great, short, single word to describe how we should choose to live our lives, to maximize our chances for **collective foresight** and **progress**. Be humble, empathic, ethical, helpful, kind, courageous, and bold!

3B. Personal and Family Foresight Books – A Longer List

Awaken the Giant Within, Tony Robbins, 1991/2013.
Be Excellent at Anything, Tony Schwartz, 2011.
Bold: How to Go Big, Create Wealth, and Impact the World, Diamandis and Kotler, 2015.
Cool Tools: A Catalog of Possibilities, Kevin Kelly, 2013.
Crucial Conversations: Tools for Talking When Stakes are High, K. Patterson et al., 2011.
Emotional Intelligence 2.0, Bradberry and Greaves, 2009.
Essentialism: The Disciplined Pursuit of Less, Greg McKeown, 2014.
Foresight Investing, James Lee, 2021.
Hold on To Your Kids, Gordon Neufeld and Gabor Mate, 2006.
Impact: Reshaping Capitalism to Drive Real Change, 2020.
Impact Imperative: Investing to Transform the Future, Pamela Ryan, 2019.
Indistractable: How to Control Your Attention and Choose Your Life, Nir Eyal, 2019.
It's Your Future … Make it a Good One!, Verne Wheelwright, 2012.
Living the 80/20 Way, Richard Koch, 2004.
Mindset: The New Psychology of Success, Carol Dweck, 2007.
Overcoming Destructive Beliefs, Feelings, and Behaviors, Albert Ellis, 2001.
Peak Performance, Stulberg and Magness, 2017.
Rationality: What it Is, Why it Seems Scarce, and Why it Matters, Steven Pinker, 2021.
So Good They Can't Ignore You: Why Skills Trump Passion, Cal Newport, 2012.
Smart Choices: A Guide to Making Better Decisions, John Hammond et. al., 2002.
Social Intelligence: The New Science of Human Relationships, Daniel Goleman, 2007.
Stepping Up: How Taking Responsibility Changes Everything, 2nd Ed, John Izzo, 2020.
Strengthsfinder 2.0, Tom Rath, 2007.
Subliminal: How Your Unconscious Rules Your Behavior, Leonard Mlodinow, 2013.
Surfing the Tsunami: An Intro to AI and Options for Responding, Todd Kelsey, 2018.
Teaching About the Future, Bishop & Hines, 2012.
The Biology of Belief, 2nd Ed, Bruce Lipton, 2015.
The Case for Rational Optimism, Frank Robinson, 2009.
The Demon-Haunted World: Science as a Candle in the Dark, Carl Sagan, 1997.
The Marshmallow Test: Mastering Self-Control, Walter Mischel, 2015.
The Motley Fool Investment Guide, 3rd Ed, Tom and David Gardner, 2017.
The Positive Power of Negative Thinking, Julie Norem, 2001.
The Psychology of Money, Morgan Housel, 2020.
The Myth of Self-Esteem, Albert Ellis, 2005
The New Psycho-Cybernetics, Maxwell Maltz, 1960/2002.
The Optimist's Telescope: Thinking Ahead in a Reckless Age, Bina Venkataraman, 2019.
The Organized Mind: Thinking Straight in the Age of Info Overload, Dan Levitin, 2014.
The Power of Bad: How the Negativity Affect Rules Us, Tierney and Baumeister, 2019.
The Power of Habit, Charles Duhigg, 2014.
The Power of Impact Investing, Rodin and Brandenburg, 2014.
The Price of Privilege: How Parental Pressure & Advantage Harm Kids, Madeline Levine, 2008.
The Recursive Mind: Language, Thought, and Civilization, Michael Corballis, 2014.

The Science of Self-Learning, Peter Hollins, 2018.
The Seven Habits of Highly Effective People, Stephen Covey, 1989/2013.
The Six Pillars of Self Esteem, Nathaniel Branden, 1994.
The Snowball: Warren Buffett and the Business of Life, Alice Schroeder, 2009.
The Top Five Regrets of the Dying, Bronnie Ware, 2012.
Thinking, Fast and Slow, Daniel Kahneman, 2011.
Thinking Ahead: Engaging Critical Thinking, Paul A. Wagner et al., Eds., 2018.
Tiny Habits: The Small Changes that Change Everything, BJ Fogg, 2019.
Transitions: Making Sense of Life's Changes, William Bridges, 1980/2019
Unlearn: Let Go of Past Success to Achieve Extraordinary Results, Barry O'Reilly, 2018.
Visualization Power, Bill Bodri, 2017.
What Doesn't Kill Us: How Going to Extremes Can Renew Our Evolutionary Strength, Scott Carney, 2017.
What the Foresight: Your Personal Futures Explored, Alida Draudt & Julia West, 2017.

4A. Team and Organizational Foresight Books – A Starter List

1. *Time to Lead: Lessons for Today's Leaders*, **Jan-Benedict Steenkamp, 2020.** Lovely, accessible overview of the classic future thinking styles of leaders—Hedgehogs, Foxes, and Eagles. These three styles are our **Leadership Pyramid**. No matter our future thinking style, we can each get better at leadership itself. Steenkamp offers examples of exemplary future thinking leaders, also categorized in seven more traditional leadership style categories (authoritative, collaborative, etc.), and a brief "Hedgefox Assessment" to help remind us which of these future thinking types we prefer. Good big picture book to start our journey in leadership foresight thinking.

2. *FYI: For Your Improvement—A Leadership Development Guide, 6th Ed.*, **Korn Ferry, 2017.** An evidence-based model of leadership, and a diverse framework of thirty-eight competencies for leadership development. Includes an excellent set of questions and exercises. The latest edition of FYI is hard to find used, but older editions are easily available. Recommended for those willing to do **many assessments**. Can be used with a coach, or in self-study.

3. *Collaborative Intelligence: Thinking With People Who Think Differently*, **Dawna Markova & Angie McArthur, 2015**. This book will help you create a culture of people who think differently, yet can empathize and find common ground with people they often disagree with. All the best teams need to champion deep cognitive, experience, and skill diversity.

4. *F.I.R.E.: How Fast, Inexpensive, Restrained, and Elegant Methods Ignite Innovation*, **Dan Ward, 2014**. A great book on design thinking. Gives great examples from defense and other large organizations. If your design team can keep their projects focused on **FIRE outcomes**, they will deliver innovation faster and better than stakeholders expect. Repeated rapid completion of FIRE projects can shift a cynical culture, creating repeated success. Over time, innovation thinking will become more broadly adopted. People aim higher, look farther, and are willing to risk more. Keep things FIRE, and fight against **complexity and scope creep** in all your iterative designs.

5. *Seeing What Others Don't: The Remarkable Ways We Gain Insights*, **Gary Klein, 2015**. Good introduction to the ways we see patterns, and see ahead, by an expert in decision-making. Klein is also a developer of the **project premortem**, a foresight method where a leader announces a high-profile strategy or venture has **failed**, ahead of its actual failure, and asks the team to **explain why it failed**. Premortems enable defensive pessimists to speak up against the strategic optimists, they eliminate groupthink, and help restore a critical balance between group aspiration (opportunity-seeking and advantage-seeing) and caution (risk and disruption management).

6. *Cynefin: Weaving Sense-Making into the Fabric of Our World*, **David Snowden (Ed.), 2020.** Published on the 21st birthday of the Cynefin framework for intelligence and foresight (sensemaking), forty contributors, many involved in Snowden's Cognitive Edge community share their thoughts on how to do sensemaking in a world of uncertainty. The Cynefin framework does not recognize the evo-devo worldview, so it doesn't see the increasingly constraining and predictable nature of processes of global development. Most complexity thinking is evolution-centric today, so this is to be expected. Nevertheless, this framework is a great introduction to leading work seeking to better integrate **complex adaptive systems thinking** into strategic foresight.

7. *Fooled by Randomness: The Hidden Role of Chance in Life & Markets*, **Nicholas Taleb, 2005**. Excellent work that reminds us how easy it is for humans, who are pattern seers and meaning makers, to see causality in randomness. Describes how skepticism, criticism, debate, evidence-seeking, and experiment can help us manage this dangerous bias.

8. *Learning from the Future: Competitive Foresight Scenarios*, **Liam Fahey & Robert Randall, Eds., 1997**. Still our favorite guide to using scenarios to reduce uncertainty, find opportunities and manage risk. An inspiring blend of managing the unpredictable (evo) and uncovering the predictable (devo).

9. *Using Trends and Scenarios as Tools for Strategy Development*, **Ulf Pillkahn, 2008**. Excellent primer on trend following, light forecasting, and scenario use prior to strategy development, by a corporate strategy leader. Great for any strategy team.

10. *Predictive Analytics*, **Eric Siegel, 2013**. Great overview of a new foresight frontier: data science, data mining, probabilistic prediction, and machine learning. As the web gets smarter and the world gets instrumented, this fields will continue to rapidly advance. We'll map and quantitate Four Ps futures with ever greater clarity.

11. *Thinking about the Future: Guidelines for Strategic Foresight*, **Peter Bishop & Andy Hines, 2007**. Great overview of six key strategic foresight activities, with concise practitioner examples. The examples give a nice applied look at the current state of our field.

12. *The Difference: How Diversity Creates Better Groups, Firms, Societies*, **Scott Page, 2008**. This great book gives the data on why **cognitively diverse** teams, schools, organizations, and societies outcompete cognitively narrow groups, in strategy development for all complex, poorly-structured problems. Most problems humans face are complex and poorly-structured. Rationality and evidence can only take us so far. We need deep cognitive, experience, and skill diversity to see the best path forward. If our culture is homogenous, or if we live in a filter bubble, we will be **outcompeted** by more diverse networks. Remember that no intelligence is **ever omniscient**. Measuring, protecting, and promoting cognitive diversity maximizes network intelligence and adaptiveness.

13. *The Idea-Driven Org: Unlocking the Power in Bottom-Up Ideas*, **Alan Robinson & Dean Schroeder, 2014**. Excellent intro to innovation culture. Along with F.I.R.E. design (see Dan Ward's book), this book can help teams and firms overcome pessimism, cynicism, and inaction and see the innovation potential all around them. Ideas are plentiful. **Great ideas**, sold to the right people, at the right time, are **rare**. This book will help you see the value of broadly soliciting, critiquing, refining and testing ideas among all your stakeholders, to find the very best, for the right context. Per the **95/5 Rule**, most useful change is bottom-up. Take advantage of that reality.

14. *The Well-Timed Strategy: The Business Cycle as Competitive Advantage*, **Peter Navarro, 2006**. A decent introduction to **countercyclical forecasting, planning, and action**. There can be great competitive advantages for organizations that see and manage the **business cycle**. To do that they periodically must take a mid-term and long-term view. This is the same Navarro who was an isolationist trade advisor to US President **Donald Trump**. Ignore Navarro's poorly-conceived nativist politics and learn from him on this topic, where he shines.

15. *Virtual History: Alternatives and Counterfactuals*, **Niall Ferguson, 2000**. Good intro, by a leading historian, to counterfactual thinking about the history of any system (society, organization, team). Think of counterfactuals as **deep hindsight**, a form of learning that is great preparation for to mid- and long-term foresight. There is a time when ruminating becomes counterproductive, but seeing agreed upon lost progress opportunities (how we could have done things better) can be very productive. Hindsight is never 20/20, as the old saying claims. But if we use it carefully, we can better foresee the evolutionary and developmental potentials of today.

16. *Wrong: Why Experts Keep Failing Us and When Not to Trust Them*, **David Freedman, 2010**. Good advice on countering our "expertise bias," where we defer to the HIPPO (highest paid person in the organization) rather than developing our own intuition and foresight. As *Superforecasting* demonstrates, a diverse crowd, trained to avoid bias, will outcompete experts most of the time. Experts can often help us greatly with history, evidence-finding, and intelligence, but are often less helpful at foresight, and finding the best solutions for the group.

17. *The Ways and Power of Love*, **Pitirim Sorokin, 1954**. An amazing study of the higher and lower forms of love, its causes and effects, and its significance as a civilizing process. The first deep historical study of love, by the founder of the sociology department at Harvard University. There still hasn't been a better study of love since,

as far as we know. This book was well ahead of its time. Fantastic reading for any team leader, seeking to improve love, belonging, and esteem, in themselves and on their teams.

4B. Team and Organizational Foresight Books – A Longer List

4 Steps to the Future: A Quick and Clean Guide to Creating Foresight, Richard Lum, 2016

20/20 Foresight: Crafting Strategy in an Uncertain World, Hugh Courtney, 2001.

A Field Guide to Lies (and Statistics), Daniel Levitin, 2016.

Against the Gods: The Remarkable Story of Risk, Peter Bernstein, 1998.

Best Laid Plans: Tyranny of Unintended Consequences, William Sherden, 2011.

Billion Dollar Lessons: Learn from Biz Failures of Last 25 Years, Paul Carroll, 2009.

Blue Ocean Strategy, Kim and Mauborgne, 2015.

Collaborative Intelligence: Thinking w/ People Who Think Diff., Markova & McArthur, 2015.

Competing for the Future, Hamel and Prahalad, 1996.

Constructive Conflicts: From Escalation to Resolution, 5th Ed., Kriesberg and Dayton, 2016.

Corporate Foresight: A Maturity Model for Future Orientation, Rene Rohrbeck, 2010.

Cultures and Organizations: Software of the Mind, 3rd Ed, Geert Hofstede et al., 2010.

Cycles: The Science of Prediction, Dewey and Dakin, 1947/2011.

Cynefin: Sense-Making in a Complex World, David Snowden (Ed.), 2020.

Data Points: Visualization that Means Something, Nathan Yau, 2013.

Design for How People Think, John Whalen, 2019.

Diffusion of Innovations, 5th Edition, Everett Rogers, 2003.

Edge Strategy, Lewis and McKone, 2016.

Expert Political Judgment: How Good Is It? How Can We Know?, Philip Tetlock, 2006.

European Foresight Monit. Network – Final Report, PDF., Maurits Butter et al., 2009.

F.I.R.E.: Fast, Inexpnsv, Restrained, & Elegant Design for Innovation, Dan Ward, 2014.

Factors for Successful Futures Research in Decision Making, Glenn and Gordon, 1999.

Flash Foresight, Daniel Burrus, 2011.

Fooled by Randomness: The Role of Chance in Life & Markets, Nicholas Taleb, 2005.

FYI: For Your Improvement—A Leadership Dev. Guide, 6th Ed., Korn Ferry, 2017.

Forecasting: An Appraisal for Policy-Makers and Planners, William Ascher, 1979.

Forecasting and Management of Technology, 2nd Ed., Alan Porter et al., 2011.

Foresight and Innovation: How Co's are Coping with the Future, Elina Hiltunen, 2013.

Foresight and Strategy in the Asia Pacific Region, van der Laan and Yap, 2016.

Foundations of Futures Studies, Vols 1-2, Wendell Bell, 2004.

Free: How Businesses Profit By Giving Some Things Away, Chris Anderson, 2010.

Future Ready: How to Master Business Forecasting, Morlidge and Player, 2010.

Future Savvy: Quality in Foresight, Adam Gordon, 2008.

Futures Research and the Strategic Planning Process, James Morrison et al., 1984

Futures Research Methodology 3.0, Jerry Glenn & Ted Gordon, Millenn. Project, 2009.

Groupthink: Psychological Studies of Policy Decisions and Fiascoes, Irving Janis, 1982.

Handbook of Futures Research, Jib Fowles, Ed., 1978.

Hindsight: The Promise and Peril of Looking Backward, Mark Freeman, 2009.

How: Why How We Do Anything Means Everything, Dov Seidman, 2011.

How to Lie with Statistics, Darell Huff, 1993.

How to Measure Anything: Valuing Intangibles in Business, Douglas Hubbard, 2014.

Innovation Judo: Disarming Roadblocks on the Path to Creativity, Neal Thornberry, 2014.

Innovation Tournaments: Finding Exceptional Opportunities, Terwiesch & Ulrich, 2009.

Insight in Innovation: Managing Using the Laws of Innovation, Jan Verloop, 2004.

Keeping Abreast of Sci & Tech: Technical Intelligence for Business, Ashton & Klavans, 1997.

Leading Change, John Kotter, 2012.

Leading Digital: Turning Tech. into Biz Transformation, Westerman & Bonnet, 2014.

Learning from the Future: Competitive Foresight Scenarios, Fahey & Randall, Eds., 1997.

Learning from the Octopus: Use Nature to Fight Terror, Disaster, Disease, Sagarin, 2012.

Long-Range Forecasting, Scott Armstrong, 1985.

Long-Range Planning for Management, 3rd Ed., David Ewing, Ed., 1972.

Looking Forward: A Guide to Futures Research, Olaf Helmer, 1983.

Management of Technological Change, Ernst Frankel, 1990.

Managing the Dynamics of Change, Jerry Jellison, 2006.

Measure What Matters: How Google, Bono, & Gates Fdn Use OKRs, John Doerr, 2018.

Multiple Perspectives for Decisionmaking, Harold Linstone, 1984.

Naked Statistics: Stripping the Dread from the Data, Charles Wheelan, 2014.

Natural Security: Darwinian Approach to a Dangerous World, Sagarin & Taylor, 2008.

OpenIntro Statistics, 2nd Ed, David Diez, 2012.

Oracles: How Prediction Markets turn Employees into Visionaries, Don Thompson, 2012.

Our Common Future (The Brundtland Report), Gro Brundtland, 1987

Peripheral Vision: Detect Weak Signals Critical to Your Co., Day & Schoemaker, 2006.

Predictions Ted Modis, 1992

Predictions: Ten Years Later, Ted Modis, 2002.

Predictive Analytics, Eric Siegel, 2013.

Principles of Forecasting, Scott Armstrong, Ed., 2001 and *ForecastingPrinciples.com*

Profiting from Uncertainty, Paul Schoemaker, 2002.

Ready for Anything: Design Resilience for a Transforming World, Tony Hodgson, 2012.

Rebels at Work: A Handbook for Leading Change from Within, Kelly & Medina, 2014.

Recent Developments in Foresight Methodologies, Giaoutzi and Sapio, eds., 2013.

Remote Work Revolution: Succeeding from Anywhere, Tesedal Neeley, 2021.

Reinventing Organizations, Frederic Laloux, 2014.

Resilience: Why Things Bounce Back, Andrew Zolli & Ann Marie Healy, 2013.

Scaling Up: Mastering the Rockerfeller Habits 2.0, Verne Harnish, 2014.

Scenario Planning in Organizations, Thomas Chermack, 2011.

Scenario Planning: A Field Guide to the Future, Woody Wade, 2012.

Scenarios: The Art of Strategic Conversation, Kees van der Heijden, 2005.

Seeing What Others Don't: The Remarkable Ways We Gain Insights, Gary Klein, 2015.

Servant Leadership, Robert Greenleaf, 2002.

Shell Global Scenarios to 2025, Royal Dutch Shell Scenarios Group, 2005.

Strategic Foresight: A New Look at Scenarios, Alfred Marcus, 2009.

Strategic Foresight: Accelerating Technological Change, Sarah Cheah, 2020

Strategic Foresight for Corporate and Regional Development, Godet and Durance, 2011.

Streetlights and Shadows: Finding Keys to Adaptive Decision Making, Gary Klein, 2011.

Strengths-Based Leadership, Tom Rath and Barry Conchie, 2009.

Superforecasting: The Art & Science of Prediction, Philip Tetlock & Dan Gardner, 2015.

Systems Thinking for Curious Managers, Ackoff and Addison, 2010.

Teaching about the Future, Peter Bishop and Andy Hines, 2012.

Technology & the Future: Managing Change & Innovation, Peter von Stackelberg, 2014.

The 80/20 Manager: Secret to Working Less and Achieving More, Richard Koch, 2013.

The 80/20 Principle: The Secret to Achieving More With Less, Richard Koch, 1999.

The Art of Conjecture, Bertrand de Jouvenel, 1967.

The Art of the Long View: Plan for Future in an Uncertain World, Peter Schwartz, 1996.

The Business Forecasting Deal, Michael Gilliland, 2010.

The Difference: How Diversity Creates Better Groups, Firms, Societies, Scott Page, 2008.

The Employee Experience Advantage: Workplaces, Tools & Culture, Jacob Morgan, 2017.

The Essence of Scenarios: Learning from the Shell Experience, Wilkinson & Kupers, 2014.

The Evolution of Strategic Foresight in Public Policy Making, Tuomo Kuosa, 2012.

The Failure of Risk Management: Why It's Broken & How to Fix it, Doug Hubbard, 2009.

The Five Dysfunctions of a Team, Patrick Lencioni, 2002.

The Five Futures Glasses, Pero Micic, 2010.

The Fortune Sellers: The Big Biz of Buying & Selling Predictions, William Sherden, 1997.

The Future: A Very Short Introduction, Jennifer Gidley, 2018.

The Great Game of Business, Jack Stack, 2013.

The Handbook of Anticipation, Robert Poli (Ed.), 2019.

The Idea-Driven Org: Using the Power of Bottom-Up Ideas, Robinson & Schroeder, 2014.

The Image of the Future, Fred Polak, 1973.

The Innovator's Dilemma, Clayton Christensen, 2011.

The Goal: Continuous Improvement & the Theory of Constraints, Eliyahu Goldratt, 2014.

The Knowledge Base of Futures Studies, Richard Slaughter, 1996.

The Lean Startup: Continuous Innovation for Success, Eric Ries, 2011.

The Lords of Strategy: Intellectual Hist. of the Corporate World, Walter Kiechel, 2010.

The Long Tail, Chris Anderson, 2008.

The Model Thinker, Scott Page, 2018.

The Nature of Change and the Law of Unintended Consequences, John Mansfield, 2010.

The Nature of the Future, Marina Gorbis, 2013

The New Killer Apps: How Large Co's Can Out-Innovate Startups, Mui & Carroll, 2013.

The Pattern of Expectation: 1644-2001, I.F. Clarke, 1979.

The Power to Change the World: The Art of Forecasting, Graham Molitor, 2004.

The Predictioneer's Game, Bruce Bueno de Mesquita, 2009.

The Pursuit of Destiny: A History of Prediction, Paul Halpern, 2000.

The Rough Guide to the Future, Jon Turney, 2010.

The Signal and the Noise: Why Most Predictions Fail But, Some Don't, Nate Silver, 2012.

The Sixth Sense: Accelerating Org Learning With Scenarios, Kees van der Heijden, 2002.

The Starfish and the Spider, Brafman and Beckstrom, 2008.

The Unbounded Mind: Nontraditional Biz Thinking, Ian Mitroff & Hal Linstone, 1995.

The Ways and Power of Love, Pitirim Sorokin, 1954.

The Well-Timed Strategy: The Biz Cycle as Competitive Advantage, Peter Navarro, 2006.

Theory of Constraints, Eliyahu Goldratt, 1999.

Think Like a Futurist, Cecily Sommers, 2012.

Thinking about the Future: Guidelines for Strategic Foresight, Bishop & Hines, 2007.

Thinking in Systems: A Primer, Donella Meadows, 2008.

Thought and Knowledge: An Intro to Critical Thinking, 5th Ed., Diane F. Halpern, 2013.

Thrivability: Breaking Through to a World that Works, Jean M. Russell, 2013.

Time to Lead: Lessons for Today's Leaders, Jan-Benedict Steenkamp, 2020.

UNIDO Tech Foresight Manual, Vol 1, Methods. and *Vol 2, Examples.*, UNIDO, 2005.

Using Trends and Scenarios as Tools for Strategy Development, Ulf Pillkahn, 2008.

Visioning, Lucia Capacchione, 2000.

Visualize This: Guide to Design, Visualization, and Statistics, Nathan Yau, 2011.

Wargaming for Leaders, Herman and Frost, 2008.

Warnings: Finding Cassandras to Stop Catastrophes, Richard Clark & R.P. Eddy, 2017.

Wise Before the Event: 20/25 Years Scientific Council for Govt Policy, WRR., PDF., 1997.

Work Rules!: Insights from Google to Transform How You Lead, Laszlo Bock, 2015.
Wrong: Why Experts Fail Us and When Not to Trust Them, David Freedman, 2010.

This is a long list, but our field is rich and getting richer. We recommend picking any of these good books whose title interests you, and checking it out on Amazon or elsewhere. Then give it 30, 60, or 90 minutes of your precious time, using our tips on **Sprint Reading** in Chapter 5. Make your **Personal Index** in the front pages of the book. Then move to the next great book. Don't worry about completeness or "finishing". Focus on process. Sprint reading **a book a week** is a great goal. Go back and slow-read only that **small subset** of books that continue to invade your thinking.

Scheduling your weekly (or daily?) sprint reading time, and sticking to your schedule, will signal to yourself that you take it seriously. Just as **interval exercise** improves your speed, power, and endurance, sprint reading diverse books will greatly improve your learning, and the quality of your foresight thinking. If you find **books hard** to sprint through, **everything else will be easier**. After you've been sprint reading for a while, you'll find it particularly easy to increase the number of great **journals, magazines, reports, papers**, etc. that you skim and get value from every month.

Strategic Foresight Journals

Foresight gained its first specialty journals in the 1970s, during our last Foresight Spring, but their impact factor, and use and support in our training programs and associations, could be much improved. Here are some of our best at present:

Foresight: The Journal of Futures Studies, Strat. Thinking, Policy (Emerald)
Foresight: The International Journal of Applied Forecasting (IIF)
Futures: The Journal of Forecasting, Planning, and Policy (Elsevier)
Futures and Foresight Science (Wiley)
Innovation: European Journal of Social Science Research (Taylor & Francis)
International Journal of Forecasting (Elsevier)
International Journal of Foresight and Innovation Policy (Inderscience)
International Journal of Innovation and Sustainable Dev. (Inderscience)
International Journal of Innovation Management (World Scientific)
Journal of Business Forecasting (IBF)
Journal of Evolution and Technology (WTA)
Journal of Forecasting (Wiley)
Journal of Futures Studies (Tamkang U)
Journal of Organizational Change Management (Emerald)
Journal of Organizational Transformation and Social Change (Maney)
Journal of the American Planning Association (APA)
Journal of Prediction Markets (U Buckingham Press)
Long Range Planning (Elsevier)
Technological Forecasting and Social Change (Elsevier)
World Future Review (WFS)
World Futures: The Journal of General Evolution (Taylor & Francis)

Strategic Foresight Magazines

The following are particularly commendable global and organizational foresight periodicals, across a variety of sectors and specialties. We've focused this list on strategic foresight with business and institutional applications. We've also mixed in a few magazines that have a history of looking ahead on foresight topics. To improve acceleration awareness, there is also a mild emphasis on technology foresight.

The Economist is the **best general and global foresight weekly** on the planet at present, in our opinion. *The Economist's* politics are typically socially liberal, fiscally conservative, and they are very evidence-based in reporting. Consider a **trial subscription**, and give it **just two hours**, one evening a week, to **skim** all the punny headlines, then **sprint read** and share (Twitter, LI, FB, Reddit, whatever) your favorite article or two, and you'll become **a better reader**, **thinker**, **speaker**, **and writer**. They also offer an <u>audio version</u> of their print magazine (free with subscription), great for commutes, exercise, and multitasking, roughly 8-9 hours per issue, chaptered so you can skip to your topic of interest.

Here is a selection of high quality strategic foresight magazines, in alpha order:

<u>Bloomberg BusinessWeek</u> (Bloomberg)
<u>Business Ethics</u> (Business Ethics)
<u>Chief Learning Officer</u> (CLO Media)
<u>CIO (Chief Information Officer)</u> (IDG)
<u>Competitive Intelligence</u> (SCIP)
<u>Contingencies</u> (AAA)
<u>Forbes</u> (Forbes)
<u>Harvard Business Review</u> (Harvard U)
<u>IEEE Spectrum</u> (IEEE)
<u>Inc</u> (Mansueto)
<u>Information Week</u> (UBM Tech)
<u>KM World</u> (Information Today)
<u>McKinsey Quarterly</u> (McKinsey)
<u>New Scientist</u> (Reed)
<u>OR/MS Today</u> (INFORMS)
<u>Planning</u> (APA)
<u>Popular Science</u> (Bonnier). Since 1872.
<u>Prospect</u> (Prospect)
<u>Research Technology Management</u> (IRI)
<u>Risk Management</u> (RIMS)
<u>Science News</u> (SS&P)
<u>Scientific American</u> (Nature) Since 1845. Dumbed down in recent years.
<u>Strategy + Business</u> (BoozAllen)
<u>Technology Analysis & Strategic Management</u> (Taylor & Francis)
<u>Technology Review</u> (MIT)
<u>The Atlantic</u> (Hayley Romer) Since 1857.
<u>The Economist</u> (Economist). Since 1843. Best global foresight weekly today.
<u>The Futurist</u> (WFS) [1967 – 2015. Partial archive <u>online</u>.]
<u>The Globalist</u> (Globalist)
<u>Wallpaper</u> (IPC Media)
<u>Wired</u> (Conde Nast)

Audio and Podcasts – Intro to Foresight

We've given long lists of books, but for exercise or driving, you may prefer audio. We'll leave out video for now. YouTube's search by topic is getting reasonably good, but its **discovery AI** still has much to be desired, and it gives users very little control. The world needs a much better dominant video learning platform.

For audio, try Amazon's <u>Audible</u> for audiobooks, and for podcasts, <u>Spotify</u> (our favorite platform today, due to its superior AI and their leading financial commitment to podcast content, a particularly great form of audio), <u>iTunes</u> and other platforms. New podcasts are springing up every day now, as they are so easy to start, and the more popular ones quickly get an audience of hundreds of thousands of listeners. Search "future" and you will find dozens of podcast series on the future of banking, manufacturing, farming, sustainability, hiring, advertising, you name it. They vary greatly in quality. But, the better podcasts are more interesting and relevant than what we get on **mass market audio** (radio).

At present streaming platforms are largely **"lean forward,"** meaning you have to **take time** to select what you want to listen to, and build playlists, if you want things particularly relevant to your needs. Eventually, their algorithms will increasingly understand your **values, interests, and current tasks,** and we'll be able to **escape any kinds of advertising we don't want, by paying a small price.** In the long meantime, we do the best we can.

Let us recommend a few interesting podcasts to start:

Acquired, Ben Gilbert and David Rosenthal
All-In Podcast, Chamath Palihapitiya, Jason Calacanis, David Sacks & David Friedberg
Armchair Expert, Dax Shepard and Monica Padman
Danny in the Valley, Danny Fortson
Deep Questions (Productivity and Technology), Cal Newport
Exponential View, Azeem Azhar, *HBR.*
Exponential Wisdom, Dan Sullivan and Peter Diamandis
Found My Fitness, Rhonda Patrick
Future Grind, Ryan O'Shea
Future Meets Law, Brian Cave
Futurepod, Rebecca Mijat, Peter Hayword, four others.
Making Sense, Sam Harris
Mind & Machines, August Bradley
Motley Fool Money, Chris Hill
Predicting Our Future, Andrew Weinreich
Renewable Future, Stora Enso
Long Now Podcast, Stewart Brand and Long Now Foundation
Rule Breaker Investing, David Gardner Co-Chairman, Motley Fool
Seminars About Long-Term Thinking (SALT), The Long Now Foundation
The Disruptors (Entrepreneurship), Matt Ward
The Edge (Personal Effectiveness), Tony Robbins
The Futur, Chris Do
The Future of Everything, *The Wall Street Journal*
The Future of Work, Jacob Morgan
The Rich Roll Podcast (Personal & Professional Dev.), Rich Roll
The Tim Ferriss Show (Life Hacking), Tim Ferriss

Did we miss any of your favorites in the lists above? Let us know. More lists can be found at ForesightGuide.com. Enjoy!

Foresight and Futures Websites and Newsletters

Because the future as we discuss it spans **four** horizons, **six** domains, **twenty** specialties, and **countless** topics and methods, there are just too many informative websites for us to compile a recommended list at this time.

We recommend you look at any of the following lists of foresight websites to find blogs, articles, newsletters, video, conferences, and other media that may help you in your personal and professional foresight education.

The following are some starter lists:

Foresight Media Wiki Page at GlobalForesight.org
Great Foresight Media at ForesightGuide.com
Futurology Resources Wiki, Reddit.com/r/Futurology
What are the Best Futurist Websites and Blogs?, Quora.com
Bestsellers in Futurology, Amazon.com
Top 50 Futurism Blogs and Websites in 2020, Feedspot.com
250 Most Influential Futurists (Personal Websites), RossDawson.com

A few free excellent foresight newsletters, in various domains (alpha order):

Exponential View, Azeem Azhar
Foresight Signals, Timothy Mack, Past President, World Future Society
Nir and Far, Nir Eyal, Behavioral Design
Weekly Obsession, Quartz Writers

For **annual reports** in a variety of STEEPLES categories, see the Appendices in *BPF*.

Foresight Specialty Associations

Recall the **Twenty Specialty Groups of Strategic Foresight** introduced in **Chapter 2**. Refer back to that chapter for more background on any of these associations. We recommend **joining at least one of these communities**, and becoming **proficient in their methods**, as an important early step in your **professional foresight** journey.

1. **Accounting & Intangibles** – Institute of Management Accountants **(IMA)**. The National Customer Service Association **(NCSA)**.

2. **Alternatives & Scenarios** – Association of Professional Futurists **(APF)**. Oxford Scenarios Programme and Alumni Network, Said Business School.

3. **Analysis & Decision Support** – Institute for Operations Research and the Mgmt Sciences **(INFORMS)**. European Working Group on Decision Support Systems **(EWG-DSS)**.

4. **Auditing & Change Management** – Institute of Internal Auditors **(IIA)**. Association of Change Management Professionals **(ACMP)**.

5. **Benchmarking & Quality** – The Benchmarking Network **(BN)**, The Balanced Scorecard Institute **(BSI)**. American Society for Quality **(ASQ)**.

6. **Data Science & Machine Learning** – Open Data Science Community **(OSDC)**. Kaggle Learning (Data Science Certificates and Competition Platform), Digital Analytics Association **(DAA)**.

7. **Entrepreneurship & Intrapreneurship** – Founder Institute **(FI)**. Lean Startup Circles. The Intrapreneurship Conference.

8. **Facilitation & Gaming** – International Association of Facilitators **(IAF)**. North American Simulation and Gaming Association **(NASAGA)**.

9. **Forecasting & Prediction** – <u>International Institute of Forecasters</u> **(IIF)**. <u>Prediction Markets</u> do not yet have a dedicated association but there are markets we recommend participating in, like Metaculus, PredictIt, etc.

10. **Human Resources & Performance Management** – <u>Society for Human Resource Mgmt</u> **(SHRM)**. The <u>KPI Institute</u> **(KPII)**.

11. **Ideation & Design** – <u>IDEO U</u> offers certification in Design Thinking, an important aspect of <u>Ideation Management</u>. A partly-related community is the <u>American Creativity Association</u> **(ACA)**. See also <u>AIGA: The Professional Association for Design</u> **(AIGA)**.

12. **Innovation & Research & Development** – <u>International Society of Professional Innovation Mgmt</u> **(ISPIM)**. <u>Research and Development Management Association</u> **(RADMA)**.

13. **Intelligence & Knowledge Management** – <u>Collective Intelligence Academic Community</u> **(CIAC)**. <u>Strategic and Competitive Intelligence Professionals</u> **(SCIP)**. The <u>Knowledge Management Professional Society</u> **(KMPro)**.

14. **Investing & Finance** – <u>CFA Institute</u> **(CFAI)**. <u>American Association of Individual Investors</u> **(AAII)**. The <u>National Venture Capital Association</u> **(NVCA)**.

15. **Law & Security** – <u>American Bar Association</u> **(ABA)**. <u>Security Industry Association</u> **(SIA)**. <u>DEF CON</u> is the best known "hacker" convention. There are a <u>plethora</u> of others. Find a security association focused on your industry and clients and learn best practices.

16. **Learning & Development** – <u>Association for Talent Development</u> **(ATD)**. Workplace training is being greatly empowered today by EdTech startups and behavioral science.

17. **Marketing & Sales** – <u>American Marketing Association</u> **(AMA)**. <u>National Association of Sales Professionals</u> **(NASP)**. <u>Certification</u> and training in effective sales trends, strategies, and customer acquisition techniques.

18. **Management & Leadership** – <u>American Management Association</u> **(AMA)**. <u>Project Management Institute</u> **(PMI)**, and <u>PMP Certification</u>. <u>International Leadership Association</u> **(ILA)**. There are also many specialized leadership development programs, publications, and communities for almost every industry, and for most of the specialties listed above.

19. **Risk Management & Insurance** – <u>Risk Management Society</u> **(RIMS)**. <u>American Insurance Association</u> **(AIA)** is the leading trade association for big insurance providers. <u>NAIFA</u> represents insurance and financial advisors.

20. **Vision/Goals/Strategy & Planning** – <u>Association for Strategic Planning</u> **(ASP)**. Advancing visioning, goalsetting, strategy and planning development and deployment for business, nonprofits, and govt. <u>American Planning Association</u> **(APA)**. Advancing the art and science of urban and regional planning. Runs <u>American Institute of Certified Planners</u>.

Comprehensive Foresight Practice Communities

Below are a select list of **comprehensive foresight practice** communities in our emerging field. We first offered this list, with commentary, in Chapter 2. We repeat this list here, without commentary this time, because we think communities like these **particularly deserve your participation and support**. Assisting them is one useful way to help **develop our field**, in our view.

A few of these, like **APF**, are also **professional associations**, but most are not at present. Each community tends to focus on different aspects of the **Six Domains**, but each also seeks to be **comprehensive**. All profess certain particularly **high-quality worldviews**, which is why they are on this list. Participating in any of these will expose you to a **great variety of methods and options** in foresight practice.

Each has advantages and shortcomings at present, but all are doing good work in our field. All of these communities have free newsletters, podcasts, discussion groups, or other output which can help you decide if you want to get more involved with them. **Volunteering positions** are also available with all of them. The more you participate in any of them, the more rewarding your foresight career may become.

1. Association of Professional Futurists (APF).
2. Foresight University (4U).
3. The Millennium Project (TMP).
4. Long Now Foundation.(LNF).
5. Singularity University. (SU).
6. Open ExO. (OEO).
7. Good Judgment Open. (GJO).
8. World Future Society (WFS).
9. World Futures Studies Federation (WFSF).
10. International Futures Forum (IFF).

A number of proprietary collaborative foresight platforms, including Shaping Tomorrow and Wikistrat also deserve an **honorable mention**. Their platforms can be excellent places for **on-the-job foresight practice** and **professional development**.

Do you know other **leading communities** improving **comprehensive foresight** around the world? Let us know, we'd love to grow this into a **Top Twenty** list next.

Thank You for Reading, Friend.

We wish you a Good life,
with Truthful destinations,
and Beautiful journeys.

About and Bios

What is Foresight University?

Foresight University (4U) is the media and education division of the Acceleration Studies Foundation (ASF), a 501c3 nonprofit founded to improve the study and management of **accelerating societal change**. It is a learning and development community run by academically-trained foresight educators, professionals, entrepreneurs, technologists, coaches, and creatives.

4U's priority is **comprehensive foresight training**, focused on individual executives, students, and teams. Besides the *Guide* and other publications, we offer periodic **online courses**, we help folks to set up local foresight discussion communities called **Future Salons**, and we run personal foresight and goalsetting retreats called **Fusions**. See our website for our publications, courses, and events. If you are a foresight speaker, student, creative, innovator, entrepreneur, forecaster, scholar, consultant, or leader in your organization, you are our audience. So far, we hope you have found the *Guide* helpful in your journey.

What is ASF?

The **Acceleration Studies Foundation** (ASF) nonprofit was founded by **John Smart**, **Regina Pancake**, and **Tyler Emerson** in 2003 to promote the study of exponential processes of change in living systems, society and the universe. On the **academic side,** we founded the international **Evo-Devo Universe** research community in Paris in 2008. We published an academic volume on multiscale evolutionary and developmental processes, *Evolution, Development, and Complexity (PDF)*, in 2019. We are proud to have built a small network of scholars who think that **accelerating change** appears to be a **universal developmental process** that our species still largely ignores, to our great detriment. Don't believe us? Take a good look at **Carl Sagan's** Cosmic Complexity Calendar, and **judge for yourself.**

On the **foresight side,** in what became **Foresight University** in 2015, we ran three famous conferences on accelerating change at Stanford in 2003-2005, at which luminaries like **Doug Englebart, Tim O'Reilly, Christine Peterson, Sergey and Larry Brin, Ray Kurzweil, Helen Greiner, Jaron Lanier, Philip Rosedale,** and many others debated how to humanize accelerating change. We wrote the Metaverse Roadmap Study in 2007. We created **FERN**, a free bridge into the world of professional foresight in 2010, and ran a *Foresight Careers* conference in Washington DC in 2013. We launched the alpha version of the *Guide* online in 2014, at ForesightGuide.com. We began writing the first print edition (this one) in 2015.

In 2021, ASF is changing our name to the **Futuremedia Foundation**, and launching **Futurepedia**, a Wikipedia for high-value foresight visions, models, methods, futures scenarios, topics and ideas. If you'd like to help create the world's best **online encyclopedia of foresight and futures topics**, a free resource to improve comprehensive foresight, please join us at **Futurepedia.org.** Let's explore both the unconstrained vision, and the many challenges ahead.

Author Bios

Primary Author:

John Smart is CEO of Foresight University (Ann Arbor, MI and San Jose, CA), President of the Acceleration Studies Foundation, and a Director of the Evo-Devo Universe complex systems research community. His interests include foresight, accelerating change, life sciences, complex systems, technology studies, entrepreneurship, and global futures. First writing on accelerating change at AccelerationWatch in 1999, he is best known as author of the transcension hypothesis, the prediction that leading complex systems are constrained, by the nature of adaptiveness, to increasingly enter inner space (denser, more miniaturized, and more simulation-based domains of foresight and action), as they develop. He has a B.S. in Business Administration from U.C. Berkeley, three years of postbaccalaureate coursework in the biological sciences at U.C. San Diego, an M.S. Eq. (M.S. I and II and the USMLE-I) in physiology and medicine at U.C.S.D. School of Medicine, and an M.S. in Studies of the Future from the U. Houston (2007). He is co-Founder and past-CEO of Hyperlearning, a multi-city science tutoring and test prep company, sold to The Princeton Review in 1996. He runs personal and team foresight workshops, and lectures and consults on strategic and adaptive foresight with industry, government, and defense clients. His website is johnmsmart.com, and he can be reached at john@foresightu.com.

Contributing Authors:

Susan Fant is the President of Castle Sands LLC (Birmingham, AL), a business leadership and marketing strategy firm. Formerly at U. Alabama, she created the Masters of Marketing in Digital and Social Media concentration for the MS in Marketing. Susan is presently finishing her Ed.D. in Organizational Change and Leadership at the University of Southern California. She is Executive Director of the Foresight Education and Research Network (FERN). Her interests include leadership, foresight, innovation, education, performance science, business development, online communities, and using open networks to accomplish big tasks. She can be reached at susanchesleyfant@gmail.com.

Tyler Mongan is President at HA:KU Global (Honolulu, HI and Santa Monica, CA), a foresight, strategy, and innovation consultancy. His team specializes in improving foresight and intelligence leadership with workflow-tested insights from neuroscience, cognitive social science, emotional intelligence, and high performance collaboration. He can be reached at tyler@tylermongan.com.

Nakul Gupta is a graduate student at the University of Southern California (Los Angeles, CA), obtaining a master's degree in Computer Science. He recently graduated from the University of California, Los Angeles with a Bachelor's in Physics. His interests include comprehensive foresight, technology studies, software development, machine learning, cloud gaming, and enterprise simulation platforms. He can be reached at nakulgup@usc.edu.

Joshua Davis is an Agent at New York Life Insurance Company (Signal Mountain, TN) and an Analyst at Aperio Insight (Dallas, TX), where he assesses organizational foresight capabilities, does scenario planning, foresight research reports, and foresight capacity building. He has a master's in Strategic Foresight from Regent University. He can be reached at jmldavis@gmail.com.

Alex Selkin is a philosopher of foresight, geopolitics, and complex systems (Toronto, Canada). He is co-author, with Brian Wyx, of *China: Rediscovery of a Giant*, 2017. He has a master's degree in Strategic Foresight and Innovation from OCAD University. His interests include strategic foresight, innovation, higher education, technical editing, writing, and forecasting. He can be reached at alexselkin2001@gmail.com.

Contributing Editors:

Zhan Li is Director of Research & Intelligence at the World Future Society, and head of the WFS Europe Office (London, UK). He is also a Senior Researcher at the Gottleib Duttweiler Institute, focusing on thought leaders, strategic foresight, and the futures of globalization, power, and networks. Zhan has a Ph.D. in Organizational Communication from the University of Southern California. He can be reached at zhan@alum.mit.edu.

Anna-Leena Pešić is a foresight researcher at Dream Broker (Helsinki, Finland), where she focuses on innovation process and capacity building, and a Ph.D. student at Aalto University. Her thesis is at the intersection of corporate foresight orientation and capacity, strategic foresight, and technology intelligence. Her interests include strategic innovation, foresight, market research, and design. She can be reached at avasamo@gmail.com.

Kevin Russell is Creative Director at Cosmic Perspective (Cape Canaveral, FL), the Chief Design Officer for Foresight University, and the creative genius behind ForesightGuide.com. He is a father, futurist, digital designer, and keynote speaker. His interests include philosophy, futurism, research, design, and positive visions for the future of humanity. He can be reached at kevinrussell@gmail.com.

Index

To **save space**, this index is **incomplete**. It offers a selection of the **people**, **companies**, and **topics** addressed here. It doesn't list most of the amazing folks mentioned in this book, many of the companies, or any of the books.

Digital Search Tips: For those wishing to **delve deeper** into the topics in this *Guide*, an **electronic version of this book** may be worth your investment. The **digital versions** are fully **searchable**, and they have many **clickable links**. For restricted in-book search, try **Amazon's Search Inside this Book** feature. **Google Books** also has in-book search. Those who can't afford but still need this book can find it on **Libgen**, along with everything else. *Thrive On, Friends!*

Thank you for reading our *Guide*. We wish you and your loved ones a productive and amazing future.

Made in USA - Kendallville, IN
43826 9781736558508